A
DREAM
OF HOME

Also by Amy Clipston

Acclaim for Amy Clipston

"... will leave readers craving more."
—RT *BOOK REVIEWS*, 4½-STAR REVIEW
OF *A MOTHER'S SECRET*, TOP PICK!

"Clipston's series starter has a compelling drama involving faith, family, and romance."
—RT *BOOK REVIEWS*, 4 1/2-STAR REVIEW
OF *A HOPEFUL HEART*, TOP PICK!

"Authentic characters, delectable recipes, and faith abound in Clipston's second Kauffman Amish Bakery story."
—RT *BOOK REVIEWS*, 4-STAR
REVIEW OF *A PROMISE OF HOPE*

"An entertaining story of Amish life, loss, love, and family."
—RT *BOOK REVIEWS*, 4-STAR
REVIEW OF *A PLACE OF PEACE*

"This fifth and final installment in the 'Kauffman Amish Bakery' series is sure to please fans who have waited for Katie's story."
—*LIBRARY JOURNAL* REVIEW OF
A SEASON OF LOVE

"[The Kauffman Amish Bakery series'] wide popularity is sure to attract readers to this novella, and they won't be disappointed by the excellent writing and the story's wholesome goodness."
—*LIBRARY JOURNAL* REVIEW OF
A PLAIN AND SIMPLE CHRISTMAS

"Inspiring and a perfect fit for the holiday season."
—RT *BOOK REVIEWS*, 4-STAR REVIEW
OF *A PLAIN AND SIMPLE CHRISTMAS*

A
DREAM
OF HOME

Hearts of the Lancaster Grand Hotel

Book Three

Amy Clipston

ZONDERVAN

A Dream of Home
Copyright © 2014 by Amy Clipston

This title is also available as a Zondervan ebook.
Visit www.zondervan.com.

Requests for information should be addressed to:
Zondervan, *Grand Rapids, Michigan 49546*

Library of Congress Cataloging-in-Publication Data

Clipston, Amy.
  A dream of home / Amy Clipston.
    pages cm
  ISBN 978-0-310-33585-6 (trade paper)
  1. Amish—Fiction. 2. Domestic fiction. I. Title.
  PS3603.L58D74 2014
  813'.6—dc23
                                        2014015375

Printed in the United States of America

14 15 16 17 18 19 20 / RRD / 20 19 18 17 16 15 14 13 12 11 10 9 8 7 6 5 4 3 2

*For all the brave women who are serving
or have served in our military*

Glossary

ach: oh
aenti: aunt
appeditlich: delicious
Ausbund: Amish hymnal
bedauerlich: sad
boppli: baby
brot: bread
bruder: brother
bruderskinner: nieces/nephews
bu: boy
buwe: boys
Christenpflicht: Amish prayer book
daadi: granddad
daed: dad
Danki: Thank you
dat: dad
Dietsch: Pennsylvania Dutch, the Amish language (a German dialect)
dochder: daughter
dochdern: daughters
Dummle!: Hurry!
Englisher: a non-Amish person
fraa: wife
Frehlicher Grischtdaag: Merry Christmas
freind: friend
freinden: friends
freindschaft: relative
froh: happy
gegisch: silly
Gern gschehne: You're welcome
grank: sick
grossdaadi: grandfather
grossdochder: granddaughter

grossdochdern: granddaughters
grosskinner: grandchildren
grossmammi: grandmother
Gude mariye: Good morning
gut: good
Gut nacht: Good night
haus: house
Ich liebe dich: I love you
kapp: prayer covering or cap
kichli: cookie
kichlin: cookies
kind: child
kinner: children
kumm: come
liewe: love, a term of endearment
maed: young women, girls
maedel: young woman
mamm: mom
mammi: grandma
mei: my
mutter: mother
naerfich: nervous
narrisch: crazy
onkel: uncle
Ordnung: the oral tradition of practices required and forbidden in the Amish faith
schee: pretty
schtupp: family room
schweschder: sister
Was iss letz?: What's wrong?
Wie geht's: How do you do? or Good day!
willkumm: welcome
wunderbaar: wonderful
ya: yes

Hearts of the Lancaster Grand Hotel Family Trees

Glick Family

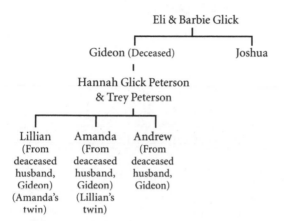

Eli & Barbie Glick

Gideon (Deceased)   Joshua

Hannah Glick Peterson
& Trey Peterson

Lillian	Amanda	Andrew
(From deaceased husband, Gideon) (Amanda's twin)	(From deaceased husband, Gideon) (Lillian's twin)	(From deaceased husband, Gideon)

Lapp Family

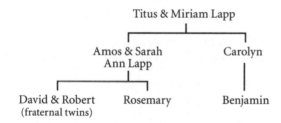

Titus & Miriam Lapp

Amos & Sarah Ann Lapp   Carolyn

David & Robert (fraternal twins)   Rosemary   Benjamin

Ebersol Family

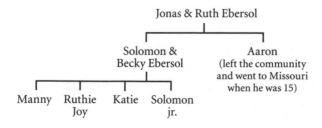

Jonas & Ruth Ebersol

Solomon & Becky Ebersol   Aaron (left the community and went to Missouri when he was 15)

Manny   Ruthie Joy   Katie   Solomon jr.

Beiler Family

Saul Beiler (wife deceased)
|
Emma

Smucker Family

Marcus & Sylvia Smucker
|
Esther

Stolzfus Family

Melvin & Martha Stolzfus
|
Leah McMillan —— Jack McMillan
|
Madeleine Miller

Note to the Reader

While this novel is set against the real backdrop of Lancaster County, Pennsylvania, the characters are fictional. There is no intended resemblance between the characters in this book and any real members of the Amish and Mennonite communities. As with any work of fiction, I've taken license in some areas of research as a means of creating the necessary circumstances for my characters. My research was thorough; however, it would be impossible to be completely accurate in details and description because each and every community differs. Therefore, any inaccuracies in the Amish and Mennonite lifestyles portrayed in this book are completely due to fictional license.

ONE

Madeleine Miller's heart pounded in her ears as she knelt next to the stretcher and held on to its side. "It's going to be all right," she cooed. She was wearing earplugs, but she knew the wounded soldier in front of her, barely clinging to life, couldn't hear her words any more than she could hear his moans. Every other sound was drowned out by the deafening thunder of the C-130's engine.

Suddenly she realized the cargo hold was filled with stretchers bearing soldiers and airmen hooked up to a tangle of oxygen canisters and IVs. Now their groans and pleas for help were nearly drowning out the roar of the aircraft. Madeleine let go of the stretcher, stood, and spun around, searching for her medical crew director, the other flight nurse who was supposed to have flown this mission with her. But Madeleine couldn't find her. The loadmaster, who was responsible for the aircraft's cargo, was also missing. Yet the number of patients on stretchers was still multiplying, and the entire fuselage was closing in on her.

Now, even with earplugs, Madeleine could hear the chorus of agonizing screams, and they overwhelmed her as she stared *helplessly at the scene around her. She had no medicine, no support, no strength.*

She was all alone.

Madeleine took a step backward and bumped into something. Turning, she looked down to see a body bag, and then cupping her hand to her mouth, she gasped as she read the tag: T. ROBINSON.

"Travis! No! No! No!" Madeleine screamed though grief nearly suffocated her. But the sound of her voice was again drowned out by the roar of the engine . . .

Madeleine's eyes flew open. She rolled onto her side and stared at the empty wall.

It was just a dream.

Another nightmare.

Madeleine released a shuddering sigh as she ran her hands down the sweat-drenched T-shirt and boxer shorts that served as pajamas. She kicked off the homemade quilt, sat up, and studied the large bedroom. It was the same room that had been her grandparents' master bedroom. It was still decorated the way they'd left it—with a double bed, two dressers, and four plain white walls.

She looked at the battery-operated clock on the nightstand. The bright green digital numbers indicated it was only 5:15. She sighed and ran her hands through her long, dark hair, which was also sweaty from the dream that had rocked her to her core. Memories of her time as an air force flight nurse haunted her, despite her attempts to leave it all behind. And then there was Travis.

Her gaze moved to a single stream of light that broke through the tiny sliver where the green window shade didn't quite cover the bottom of the window. Madeleine's feet hit the cold floor, and she shivered as she walked to the window. She lifted the shade and stared out at the small, dark field behind the house. She'd spent nearly every summer in this house from the time she was five until she was twelve, while her mother served in the military. She could be with her mother as she was transferred from place to place—with Madeleine moving from school to school—but her happiest childhood memories were created during those summers in this small house in Paradise, Pennsylvania. Therefore, it only made sense when her mother suggested Madeleine move here.

Madeleine studied the two-story farmhouse and line of barns that sat across the field, beyond her single barn and the house she lived in now. She remembered when her grandparents owned both properties and ran a dairy farm. Then nearly ten years ago, they sold the land to an Amish man, who now ran a business on that land.

She turned back toward the bed and gave up on the notion of eight hours of sleep. She hadn't enjoyed a full night of sleep since she'd lost Travis, and it was apparent she wasn't going to enjoy that luxury anytime soon. Instead, she decided to do the one thing most likely to calm her when the nightmares came.

Soon Madeleine pulled her hair into a thick ponytail before changing into a long-sleeved sweatshirt, shorts, and her favorite running shoes. When she stepped out onto the front porch, the chilly September air hit her like a wall of ice. She shivered as she loped down the steps and began jogging toward the paved road at the end of her rock driveway, the one she and her neighbor shared.

Before long, thoughts of the crisp air evaporated as she fell into the zone. All that mattered was the sound of her feet pounding the pavement. She ran a route she had mapped out when she first moved into the house nearly eight months ago. She moved through the community, taking in the patchwork of farms, large homes, and barns. Cows lowed in the fields, and the aroma of a nearby pig farm overpowered her senses. The scenery was peaceful and inviting, just what her soul had craved. She wanted to find a place where she could release all the stress that had built up inside her since joining the military right after earning her nursing degree.

Her faith was shaken after she lost Travis. She'd always felt a close relationship with God, but when Travis died, she was left with nothing but loneliness and doubt. She prayed that coming back to Pennsylvania would help her find her faith again.

She ran until her legs were sore and her mind was free of the images that haunted her—the wounded service members, the body bags, the suffering. Madeleine's route circled through Paradise. The sunrise burst in colorful hues of orange, pink, and yellow as she ran past the Heart of Paradise Bed-and-Breakfast, which was located down the street from her house.

She slowed to a jog and then walked, allowing her breathing to return to normal as she walked up her driveway. She looked past her modest one-story home to the Beiler farm, the land that had once belonged to her grandparents. A large sign down by the street and another next to one of the barns read Beiler's Cabinets, and Madeleine considered walking over to introduce herself. Being an *Englisher*, she'd never thought she should disturb her Amish neighbors. But she longed to take a peek at Mr. Beiler's work. She planned to make a few minor changes to the house, and she had been considering updating the cabinets. She wondered what his prices were, but she assumed he was too expensive for her budget; most Amish-made items were astronomically priced.

Madeleine climbed the steps, to her back porch this time, leaned on the railing, and breathed in the wonderful autumn air. As she stared toward the Beiler farm, she saw a girl walking from one of the barns toward the farmhouse. Madeleine had noticed her before, but they'd never been close enough to make eye contact, not even when they passed her house in their buggy. She guessed she was eleven or twelve. She was wearing a prayer covering and a blue dress with a black apron, and she was carrying a basket.

The girl turned toward Madeleine and then waved vigorously. Surprised, Madeleine smiled as she waved back. She couldn't help but think that the little girl reminded her of herself at that age. Madeleine had spent so much time helping her grandmother in the yard and barn, carrying baskets just like that one.

She walked through her small mudroom into the kitchen and glanced at the clock on the wall. She had less than an hour to shower, eat, and get ready for her part-time job as a housekeeper at the Lancaster Grand Hotel. She'd been glad to find a job where she could earn some money without a lot of stress.

The fog of grief consumed her as she walked through the kitchen and family room toward the bathroom. Moving to Pennsylvania wasn't her original plan. She was supposed to have been married a year ago, but everything abruptly changed when her fiancé, Travis Robinson, died. After losing him, she needed a place to call home, and now she wondered if that place truly was in Amish Country. Had her mother thought so?

As Madeleine stepped into the shower, she pushed away any negative thoughts. Today was a new day, and she wouldn't let nightmares and grief smother the hope that was slowly blooming inside of her.

～∞～

Saul stepped out of one of his workshop buildings and saw Emma holding a basket of eggs in one hand and waving her free arm toward the house adjacent to his farm.

"Emma!" he called as he approached her. "What are you doing?"

Emma continued to flail her arm while a woman standing on the porch across the field waved in return. "I'm waving to the *maedel* who lives in *Mammi's haus.*" She faced him and tilted her head. "Who is she?"

"I don't know, and it's none of our business." He pointed toward their own house. "Are you ready for breakfast? You need to head off to school soon."

"*Ya.*" Emma watched the woman disappear into the house and then started for the back porch. "I'll go make breakfast, and you can finish your chores."

"*Danki.*" Saul's eyes followed his daughter as she climbed the steps and walked into the house. He looked toward the smaller home down the driveway, then finished feeding the horses and cows while questions about the new occupant swirled through his mind. Until she'd come nearly eight months ago, the home had sat empty since Martha Stoltzfus passed away. That was nearly two years ago, and her husband, Mel, had died two years before that.

Though Saul had become well acquainted with Martha and Mel, most of what he knew about the family's history was what older members of the community had told him. Apparently, their only child, the daughter he'd met at Mel's and then Martha's funeral, had left the community, but she frequently brought her own daughter to visit. Early in Saul's marriage, Mel and Martha had sold Saul their farm for a fair price. Soon after, he converted one of the large barns into a shop for his cabinet business, adding two more buildings a couple of years later.

Saul finished feeding the animals and then headed into the house. He shucked his light coat and hat and hung them on a peg in the mudroom before removing his boots. He watched Emma again, this time from the kitchen doorway. She was humming as she fried eggs and bacon on the stove, which was powered by propane.

The early morning sunlight streaming through the kitchen window gave her light brown hair a golden hue, reminding Saul of her mother, Annie. Memories of his marriage assaulted his mind while he watched Emma work. He wasn't Annie's first choice for a husband. Annie had settled for Saul after her boyfriend left the community and moved to a former Amish community in Missouri. He'd known Annie still loved her boyfriend, but Saul had believed he and Annie could somehow build a life together. He'd been blindsided when Annie's boyfriend came back for her and she walked away from both their marriage and their sweet and innocent four-year-old daughter.

He'd told Emma her mother had died to shield her from the painful truth, and somehow the truth had never come out. But the truth continued to haunt him daily because Emma looked like her mother with her sweet smile and pale blue eyes.

Emma turned and gave him a surprised look. "I didn't see you there, *Dat*."

"Everything smells *appeditlich*." He moved to a cabinet and pulled out two glasses.

"*Danki*." Emma slipped the eggs onto a platter. "I'm getting better at making the eggs. They aren't brown at all."

"*Gut, gut*." He put the glasses on the table and then took a pitcher of water from the refrigerator.

Emma brought the platter of eggs to the table and then picked up a basket of rolls and a platter of bacon. "Breakfast is ready."

Saul sat at his usual spot at the head of the table, and Emma sat to his right. After a silent prayer, they began filling their plates.

"The *maedel* in *Mammi's haus* is obviously an *Englisher*. She doesn't dress like us, and she drives a red pickup truck. Who is she?" Emma asked as she buttered a roll.

"I told you I don't know. Why are you asking now when she's been there all these months? You've seen her before." Saul grabbed a roll from the basket.

"I didn't like it at first when someone else moved into *Mammi's haus*. But I'm curious now, I guess. That's why I waved to her when I saw her looking at me. Why would an *Englisher* want that *haus*? Esther told me *Englishers* have houses with electricity. *Mammi's haus* is just like ours, so there isn't any electricity. And, like our *haus*, it's heated with a coal stove. Esther says *Englishers* don't know how to take care of a coal stove. They'll think it's too much work. So why would she want a house with coal heat and no electricity?" She bit into the roll.

"Sometimes people buy houses and then change them."

Her eyes brightened with understanding. "Like when people have you make new cabinets for them?"

"*Ya*, exactly." He wiped his beard with a napkin. "Maybe she's going to make some changes to the *haus* to make it an *English haus*."

Emma's mouth formed a thin line. "She's going to change *mei mammi's haus*?"

Saul forked his eggs. "I told you it's none of our business. We can't tell someone what they can and can't do with their *haus*."

Emma was silent for a moment while she ate, but Saul braced himself for more questions. She'd been asking a lot of questions lately, and he knew soon she'd ask ones he wasn't prepared to answer. Although he'd tried to be both mother and father to his daughter, he could never take the place of a real mother. He'd longed to find Emma a loving mother ever since he'd received word last year that Annie had passed away in an accident.

"Why does that *maedel* put on those shorts and run?" Emma suddenly asked. "Aren't those clothes uncomfortable? Wouldn't she be cold in them this time of year?"

"Some *Englishers* like to run to stay fit. It's exercise to them." Saul lifted a piece of bacon.

"Huh." Emma looked as if she were considering this. "I guess. Farmwork keeps you fit, right?"

"*Ya*, it does." He had seen the mysterious young woman running the other day. She was jogging on the street toward their properties when he returned from picking up supplies in town. Her dark hair bobbed behind her as her legs pounded the pavement, and she had determination in her eyes. She was in her own world, oblivious to his horse and buggy as it moved past her.

"I hope she doesn't change *Mammi's haus*," Emma continued. "I loved visiting her and helping in her garden. I miss her."

"I know you do." Saul had been grateful for Martha's interest in Emma; his daughter didn't have the luxury of knowing his parents or Annie's; they had all passed away. Martha accepted Emma as if she were her own granddaughter, which is why she let Emma call her *Mammi*.

"Do you remember seeing *Mammi's dochder* at her funeral?" Emma asked.

"*Ya*, I do," Saul said as he forked another bite of eggs.

"She dressed liked an *Englisher* too. *Mammi* told me her *dochder* left the community when she was a teenager." Saul kept from looking surprised. He hadn't known Martha told Emma that.

"I imagine that was hard for *Mammi*," Emma went on, "just like it was hard for you when your *bruder* left after your parents died."

"*Ya*." Saul swallowed a sigh as his thoughts turned to Annie once again. He'd never had the heart to tell Emma that her mother had left too; he didn't want her to blame herself for her mother's decision. Someday, he knew, he'd have to tell Emma the truth, but he refused to burden her with it now.

"I want to meet that *maedel*."

"Emma, you should leave her alone. I'm certain she is very busy." He glanced at the clock above the sink. "You need to get ready for school."

They finished their breakfast, and then they had a silent prayer before carrying their dishes to the sink.

"You go on, and I'll make your lunch," Saul said.

"*Danki*." Emma rushed up the stairs.

By the time she returned to the kitchen, Saul had her lunch pail packed. "Have a *gut* day." He handed her the pail, and she smiled up at him.

"You too, *Dat*." He leaned down, and she stood on her tiptoes and kissed his cheek.

Saul followed Emma out to the front porch and then watched

her rush to meet her friends, who were waiting on the corner at the bottom of the driveway. As she passed Martha Stoltzfus's house, the young woman wearing a gray dress stepped onto the back porch. She and Emma exchanged waves again, and then Emma disappeared around the corner with her friends. The woman climbed into her red pickup truck and drove off.

For a brief moment, Saul wondered, too, why the *Englisher* would want to live in Martha Stoltzfus's modest house, but, as he had told Emma, it wasn't any of his business. Yet, like Emma, he was curious, and the question still lingered in the back of his mind: Who was this mysterious woman?

TWO

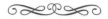

M adeleine steered her pickup truck up the rock driveway leading to Carolyn Lapp's house later that evening. She was excited when Carolyn had invited her to come for supper after work. After working her usual shift at the hotel, she headed toward Gordonville and the farm where Carolyn lived. She drove past the main house and parked in front of the smaller house out back. As Madeleine climbed out of the truck, Carolyn appeared on the porch.

"I'm thrilled you made it," Carolyn, a pretty blonde in her early thirties, said as she rushed over to the truck. "I just put the potpie in the oven."

"Thank you for inviting me." Madeleine glanced around the property. "This is beautiful."

"Thank you." Carolyn nodded. "This is my brother's dairy farm." She pointed toward the large farmhouse. "Amos lives there with his family, and I live here in the *daadi haus* with my parents and my son, Benjamin."

"This is lovely, but you won't be living here much longer." Madeleine grinned. "Your wedding day will be here soon."

Carolyn's smile broadened. "That's true." She motioned for Madeleine to come into the small house.

Madeleine followed Carolyn inside and breathed in the aroma of the potpie. "It all smells delicious. Can I help you with anything?"

"Oh no." Carolyn pointed toward the kitchen table. "Have a seat. We can visit before I need to put the carrots and corn on the stove." As Madeleine sat down, Carolyn poured two glasses of water, then brought them to the table.

"Where are your parents and Benjamin?"

Carolyn sank into a chair across from her. "My mom and my sister-in-law are working on a quilt project. My father is working with my brother, and Ben is working at Joshua's farm in Paradise."

"You must be excited about the wedding. How are preparations coming along?"

"They're coming along well. And I've been thinking about the move to Joshua's house after the wedding. I already have plans to expand his garden in the spring." Carolyn paused before going on. "I'm very thankful for Joshua. I've always dreamed of giving Benjamin a real family. I'll finally be able to do that."

"I bet he's excited too." Madeleine sipped her water. "Does he like working with Joshua?"

"He loves the horse farm. It's all worked out so well for us. I didn't think I deserved a real family because I wasn't married when I had Benjamin. I'm thankful the Lord had other plans for me." Carolyn tilted her head in question. "How are you adjusting to living here? Your grandparents' house must be very different from what you're used to."

"It's very peaceful here. I was tired of living on military bases."

Madeleine thought back to her apartment in California. "The most noise I've heard so far was made by a rooster. It's heaven. I'm certain that's why the town is named Paradise."

"You spent a lot of time with your grandparents when you were little, right?"

"That's right. My mother served in the military, and we moved around a lot. I went to school near the base where she was stationed, and I was in daycare when my mom was working. It wasn't always easy, but my mom did the best she could. We managed. She would bring me to Paradise, especially for summers. I loved it. I would help my *mammi* work in the garden and bake, help my *daadi* care for the animals, and play with the neighborhood children. It was a wonderful break from living on military bases."

Carolyn grinned.

"Why are you smiling like that?"

"You said those words correctly. Do you speak *Dietsch*?"

"I remember a little bit." Madeleine thought back to her childhood. "I loved pretending I was Amish. It was a lot of fun. But it was a difficult transition when I went back home. I remember one year I begged my mother to let me stay and go to school with the neighborhood kids."

"Did you really?" Carolyn looked intrigued. "How did your parents feel about that?"

Madeleine shook her head. "I never knew my father, and I have no idea what he would say. My mother looked sad when I told her."

"Why did she leave the community?"

"She had met my father, and she told me she fell hopelessly in love with him. She hadn't joined the church, so she wasn't shunned. But, at the same time, her parents were devastated.

They never got over it. They were even more upset when she joined the military, but they grew to accept it after I was born." Madeleine ran her fingers over the cool glass of water and thought back to her childhood. "The farm has changed quite a bit since I was little. My grandparents sold most of the land to an Amish cabinetmaker."

"Oh, that's right. Your property backs up to Saul Beiler's land." Carolyn's expression became a little embarrassed. "He's good friends with *mei bruder*. He wanted to date me, but then I got to know Josh."

"I remember you telling me that." Madeleine nodded slowly while wondering what had happened to Saul's wife. "Saul has one child, right?"

"*Ya*. His wife died when his daughter was little. I believe she was four."

"Oh. That's sad." Madeleine shook her head. "That poor little girl. She must've been heartbroken."

"*Ya*," Carolyn said. "Emma is a sweet little girl. I connected with her right away. Saul's a really good father, though."

"That's nice. I haven't met them yet, but Emma always waves to me now."

"She's very friendly." Carolyn nodded. "I hope Saul finds a mother for her someday."

"*Ya*." Madeleine thought about her grandparents. "I was devastated when I got back from overseas and found out my *mammi* had passed away. Apparently I was on my way home when she died, and somehow my mother's messages didn't get to me. I was even too late for the service here."

"I'm sorry to hear that. I'm certain that was a tremendous loss for you."

"It was. My mother was very upset too. She and my grandmother always talked at least once a week."

"Do you think you'll stay in that house?" Carolyn asked.

"Why wouldn't I stay?" Madeleine was confused by the question. "I love that house. It has many wonderful memories in it."

"Well, it's like this one." Carolyn gestured around the kitchen. "No electricity and no modern conveniences like the microwave we have in the break room at the hotel."

"I don't mind. Right now I'm enjoying the quiet."

"You're not going to change the house at all?"

Madeleine shrugged. "I'm not sure yet about modernizing it, but I want to update it a little. The house hasn't been cared for in a while. I'm working at the hotel, and I have some extra money to do a few projects on the house. I want to paint the rooms, replace the cabinets, and maybe replace the bathtub too. I'm going to do a little at a time."

"That sounds nice." Carolyn stood. "I'm going to start making the vegetables."

"Can I help?" Madeleine followed her to the counter.

"Would you like to cut up the fruit for the fruit salad?" Carolyn asked.

"Sure." Madeleine gathered apples, pears, and oranges from the refrigerator and began cutting and slicing.

Carolyn worked on getting corn and carrots into pots. She looked over at Madeleine and frowned. "Josh doesn't want me to keep working at the hotel. He said he wants me at the farm with him."

"Oh." Madeleine wasn't sure what to make of Carolyn's expression. "I guess that makes sense. Most Amish wives don't work away from the home, do they?"

"It depends." Carolyn added water to the pots. "Sometimes they do, but there's also a lot to do at the house. I just can't imagine not working, though. I've done it for so long that it's become part of who I am."

"Are you saying you'll miss the job?"

"*Ya*, I will." Carolyn placed the pot of carrots on the burner and turned it on. "I'll miss seeing my friends too. This is really becoming an issue between Josh and me. We had an argument about it the other night."

"Oh, I'm sorry." Madeleine wasn't quite sure what to say, but she offered some advice that made sense to her. "Maybe you should compromise. Maybe you can cut your hours and only work one day per week or something?"

"No, I'm certain he won't agree with that, even though it's a *gut* idea. He is really adamant that I don't work there."

"Why is he against it?"

"I think he's concerned because of what happened to Hannah."

"Oh, I heard about this. Hannah met Trey at the hotel and they fell in love. Is he afraid you'll decide to become *English* and break off your engagement?"

"I think so." Carolyn put the pot of corn on the burner next to the carrots. "I've tried to tell him I'm not going to leave the community, but he still seems very insecure about it. I'm not sure what I can do to convince him I'm not going to allow the hotel to influence me, but I guess we'll see what God has in store for us."

"That sounds reasonable." Madeleine nodded.

Madeleine and Carolyn continued to talk while they finished preparing the meal. Soon Carolyn's parents came in, and then Benjamin arrived home from working at Joshua Glick's horse farm. Madeleine felt at home while they ate supper. She enjoyed hearing about their day. They talked and laughed while they enjoyed the delicious homemade chicken potpie and vegetables and finished off the meal with fruit salad and apple pie.

After supper and dessert, Madeleine helped Carolyn and her mother clean up the kitchen before heading to the porch with Carolyn. They sat and talked while they sipped hot cups of coffee.

"Everything was delicious," Madeleine said as she moved the porch swing back and forth. "I really had a lovely time. Your family is wonderful."

"I'm glad you could come." Carolyn cradled her mug in her hands. "I could tell my parents really liked you."

"Oh good." Madeleine's thoughts turned to her grandparents. "Sometimes I wonder what it would've been like if I'd grown up here."

"What do you mean?" Carolyn looked curious.

"I used to wonder what it would've been like to have grown up here instead of in a city."

Carolyn studied Madeleine. "Are you saying you wondered what it would be like to grow up Amish?"

"Yeah." Madeleine nodded. "It's peaceful here. Do you ever wonder what it would be like to be *English*?"

"No, not really. This is all I've ever known."

"Do you ever crave more?"

"No, I've always felt like I have all that I need, but I'll finally have a home of my own. Joshua and I will build our own life on his farm."

"I remember that my grandparents hosted church twice a year. Before they sold part of their property, they had a big barn they used for church services. They always had services every other Sunday at someone's farm. My *mammi* loved the off Sundays from church when they went visiting. It was fun to ride around in their buggy and see all their friends. I've visited a few churches around the area, but I haven't felt a real connection to them."

"You should come to an Amish service sometime."

Madeleine couldn't stop her smile. "Really?"

"*Ya*, you should. Everyone would love to see you. I'm sure some of the members of the community would remember you from when you visited as a child. Many of my relatives remember your *daadi* and *mammi*."

"That would be fun. I'd love to come to a service."

"And you'd better come to my wedding."

"I definitely will." Madeleine sipped her coffee and thought about Hannah. "Did you say Hannah is running a bed-and-breakfast now, in Paradise?"

"*Ya*, I think it's called the Heart of Paradise Bed-and-Breakfast."

"That's right near my house," Madeleine said.

Madeleine visited with Carolyn until it started to get dark and then thanked her for the meal and headed home. She parked next to her house and headed up the back porch steps.

When she reached the back door, she stopped and looked out toward Saul Beiler's farm and noticed light spilling out from the largest barn near his house. Her heart ached for this stranger, knowing that he'd lost his wife and was raising his daughter alone. She decided to keep them both in her prayers. She glanced up at the clear evening sky and whispered a prayer right then.

"God, I know you're still there, but I haven't felt your presence since I lost Travis. Help me find my way back to you. Please take away my nightmares and heal the hole in my heart Travis left after he died. I should've been there for Travis when he needed me. I should have protected him, but I failed him. I know I'm not worthy of your love, Lord, but I need you now. Make me feel whole again. In Jesus' holy name, amen."

She walked into her house, hoping she could somehow enjoy a full night's sleep.

∞

Saul continued to sand the cabinet door that was part of an *Englisher's* order for his brand-new house. He was thankful that his business was booming, but he was also starting to feel overwhelmed by so many orders. He desperately needed an assistant. Or possibly even an apprentice who could learn the trade and help him keep up with the volume of requests.

He had always loved the work, and though his father had taught him a lot about woodworking, he was grateful that his uncle, now deceased like Saul's parents, had taken him under his wing at a young age and taught him the craft of fine cabinetmaking. When he'd married Annie, he'd hoped that she'd give him a son who would want to follow in his footsteps. Although he adored Emma, he'd also prayed that she'd one day have a brother, but that wasn't in God's plan for him. At least not with Annie.

He considered his life while he worked. He'd never imagined he'd wind up divorced with a four-year-old, and it was against his beliefs for him to remarry while Annie was still alive. However, that all changed when Saul received the letter from her new husband telling him Annie had died.

The idea of remarrying was frightening because he couldn't even remember how to date. He'd thought he'd gotten the hang of it when he started visiting with Carolyn Lapp, but he'd failed miserably. Yet he wasn't going to give up. Emma deserved a mother, and he'd do his best to find her one—with God's help, of course. And maybe he'd even find a wife who'd want to try to give him a son. At the same time, he wondered if he could trust another woman. Would another wife also abandon him and Emma?

He finished sanding the door and then glanced at the clock on the wall. He had to get Emma into bed and then go to bed himself. The evening was passing too quickly. He'd get busy on his current cabinet project again tomorrow morning.

He flipped off the four battery-powered lanterns he used to light his shop and then picked up another one to guide his journey back to the house. Would the Lord see fit for him to marry again? He didn't know if he'd ever remarry, but he did know one thing for sure—some days he grew weary of being both mother and father to Emma and raising her all alone.

THREE

The following morning, Madeleine awoke with another nightmare. Only this time, with the roar of the C-130 closing in on her, she was giving CPR to a soldier who'd been injured in a land mine blast. And as she often did in these dreams, she wound up trying to revive Travis in the ER. Although the dream had left her shaking, she was grateful she'd slept until nearly seven, which was a new accomplishment. She changed into her running clothes and then set off jogging her usual route around Paradise. Once she hit her stride, she let her mind go, releasing all the stress that plagued her dreams.

As she rounded the bend, the Heart of Paradise Bed-and-Breakfast came into view. She slowed to a brisk walk as she approached the three-story, clapboard house. It had a large wrap-around porch with a swing, and it was peppered with rocking chairs. A wooden sign with old-fashioned letters boasted the name of the establishment.

She remembered hearing Hannah's story. Hannah had left the Amish community and opened the bed-and-breakfast with her new husband. It made Madeleine think of her own mother, who would never discuss why she left her Amish life behind, saying the life just wasn't for her. Madeleine's grandmother also didn't want to discuss losing her daughter to the modern world, but Madeleine always saw tears in her eyes whenever she asked her about it.

Madeleine hoped to meet Hannah soon and find out more about her life and her decision to leave the Amish.

⁓

Madeleine stepped into the break room at the hotel later that day and found her coworkers, Carolyn Lapp, Linda Zook, and Ruth Ebersol, already sitting around the table and unpacking their lunches.

"Hello." Madeleine retrieved her lunch bag from the refrigerator and sat beside Carolyn. "I was running behind on my rooms. Several of them were a real mess. It looked like the guests had thrown a few parties."

"*Ach* no." Linda, a petite brunette in her early thirties, sighed. "That's terrible."

"I heard a sports team checked in a few days ago." Ruth polished a bright red apple with a paper napkin as she spoke. "Gregg mentioned they were loud last night, and a few of the guests complained about the noise."

"That's awful." Carolyn shook her head as she lifted her cup of water. "How could they leave such a mess? You should've called me. I would've come to help you."

"I would've helped you too," Linda offered. "My rooms were fairly easy this morning."

"It's fine, but thank you. I got it all done." Madeleine pulled out her turkey sandwich. "I went for a run this morning and passed Hannah Peterson's house. Do you think she'd want to talk to me sometime?"

As if on cue, Carolyn, Linda, and Ruth all nodded.

"Oh *ya*. Hannah is a sweet person. She'd love to meet you," Ruth replied, her graying hair peeking out from under her prayer covering. "I haven't visited her in a while, but I've been thinking of her."

"I wonder how she's adjusting to her new life." Madeleine tilted her head askance. "She's shunned, right?"

Linda frowned. "*Ya*, she is."

"Are you allowed to be friends with her even though she's shunned?" Madeleine bit into her sandwich while waiting for a response.

"*Ya*, we can still be her friend," Carolyn chimed in. "But we can't eat at the same table with her, and she can't shop at an Amish store."

"She also can't attend worship with us unless she confesses in front of the congregation first." Linda continued to look sad. "I miss seeing her at services, but I'm glad she's happy with her new life. I know it was a difficult decision for her."

"I wonder how her relationship is with her daughter Lillian," Ruth said. "Last I heard their relationship was still strained."

"That's so sad." Madeleine pulled a small bag of baby carrots out of her bag. "I hope she can work things out with her daughter. That has to be heartbreaking."

"I hope so too." Carolyn paused for a moment. "I'd like to invite Hannah to my wedding." She turned to Ruth. "Do you think it would be too painful for her?"

Ruth shrugged. "I don't know. I guess you would need to ask

her. I'm certain Joshua would want his nieces and nephew there. It wouldn't be right to not invite her too."

"*Ya*, that's what I was thinking." Carolyn pushed an errant lock of blonde hair back from her face and back under her prayer covering. "I'll discuss it with Joshua. Hannah never had a good relationship with Joshua's mother, but she's still part of the family."

"My mother left when she was eighteen, but she hadn't joined the church yet," Madeleine said.

"That means she wasn't shunned." Linda finished Madeleine's thought.

"Exactly." Madeleine lifted a carrot from the bag. "But I think it was still difficult for her."

"It's always hard." Ruth's gaze was trained on her sandwich as she spoke. "You never get over it when a child leaves the community behind. It's heartbreaking."

Carolyn's smile faded as she placed a hand on Ruth's arm. "I know you miss Aaron. I'm sorry, Ruth."

"I miss him every day." Ruth cleared her throat. "I always wonder how he is."

"I'm sorry, Ruth. I never meant to bring up a subject so painful for you." Guilt washed over Madeleine.

"Oh no, no." Ruth shook her head. "It's not your fault. I always think of Aaron. It wasn't anything you said."

Madeleine took a bite of her sandwich and thought about how Ruth must feel.

"I hope you hear from Aaron someday soon." Carolyn sliced a piece of homemade bread. "I'm certain God will bring him back to you."

"I don't know. It's been a long time." Ruth met Madeleine's gaze. "Aaron was only fifteen when he went off on his own. He said the Amish life was too restrictive. It's been almost seventeen years now."

"I'm sorry." Madeleine racked her brain for something positive and encouraging to say. "Maybe things will have changed if he has a family. My mother worked things out with my grandparents after I was born."

"*Ya.*" Carolyn's expression brightened. "That's a good point. A baby always changes people."

"Usually it does." Linda continued to scowl. "Sometimes people can't find a way to warm their hearts, no matter what happens."

"Don't give up hope." Madeleine made a mental note to add Ruth and Aaron to her prayer list.

FOUR

Carolyn hugged her cloak to her body as she moved the porch swing back and forth. The early evening air was brisk as she glanced over at Joshua and smiled. "I'm glad you came for supper tonight. I was hoping you would."

"I hadn't seen you in two days. It had been too long." He rubbed her arm.

"I was thinking the same thing." She shivered as a breeze seemed to cut right through her cloak.

"You're cold. Take my coat." He pulled off his coat and draped it over her shoulders. "You need this more than I do."

"*Danki.*" She hugged the coat to her body, breathing in his scent of soap mixed with earth.

"Just think," he said as he covered her hand with his warm fingers, "in less than a month we'll be married. You'll be Carolyn Glick."

"*Ya.*" Carolyn rested her head on his shoulder and smiled. "I'm very thankful."

"That brings up an important issue." Joshua's expression became serious. "You and I will be Glicks, but Ben will still be a Lapp. That may be confusing."

Carolyn's eyes widened as excitement filled her. Was he going to ask what she'd hoped he would?

"How would you feel about me adopting Ben?" Joshua's expression turned hopeful. "I'd like to give him my name, really be his father."

"I would love that." Tears filled Carolyn's eyes. "We should ask Benjamin, but I know he'll say yes."

"*Gut*." Joshua nodded. "I'll ask him before I leave tonight."

"This is more than I could have ever truly hoped for. *Danki*, Josh." She'd finally found someone who would accept both her and her son and love them completely. She gazed up into his blue eyes, and the question that had been haunting her all day surfaced in her mind. "Josh, I have something I want to ask you."

"You can ask me anything." He brushed his fingertip down her cheekbone.

"How would you feel about inviting Hannah to our wedding?" She held her breath in anticipation of his answer.

He hesitated, and she felt the urge to fill the silence.

"Hannah's my friend," she said. "Plus, we want the *kinner* there, and it wouldn't be right to invite the *kinner* and not Hannah. I know she'd want to come. It's only right to invite the whole family."

Joshua rubbed his chin as he stared toward her brother's house. "I don't know how *mei mamm* would take seeing her."

"But how would you feel about seeing Hannah again?"

"I'm fine with seeing her." He looped his arm around her shoulders. "I just don't know how others would react because she's shunned. People are still upset about it."

"Are you thinking of Lillian?" She leaned into his embrace.

"Not only Lillian . . . ," he began. "But if it will make you *froh*, then you should invite Hannah."

"*Ya*?" She smiled up at him. "You mean that?"

"*Ya*." He nodded. "I'll talk to *mei mamm* and ask her to remember to be civil. It's our day, not hers."

"Right."

"Have you started thinking about how you want to decorate the *haus*?"

"Decorate the *haus*?" Carolyn tilted her head in question as she looked up at Joshua. "You want to change it?"

"I want it to feel like a cozy home. After Hannah moved out, when she married Trey and I moved in, there wasn't much of a woman's touch left." He pulled her closer. "My *haus* will be complete when you and Ben move in. It will be more than just the place where I sleep."

"I'll definitely try to think of a few touches to make it ours."

"Have you thought any more about quitting the hotel?" His voice was tentative as if he knew he was treading on uneven ground.

"Josh," she began with impatience radiating in her voice, "we've already discussed this. You know I enjoy my job. I look forward to seeing my friends, and I like contributing to my family financially. I'm going to want to contribute to our family too."

"You will contribute, just in other ways. You can take care of the house and the garden, as well as the books for me. I'll be able to expand the business with your help. We'll grow it together." Joshua angled his body toward her. "We're going to be partners, and that means I need your help running our business."

"I realize that, but you have to understand that this job means a lot to me."

"Does it mean more than our new life together?"

"No." Carolyn shook her head as frustration gripped her. "That's not fair to say. You know I'm looking forward to our life together."

"You want a family, right?" Joshua asked. "You want more *kinner*?"

"Of course I do. I want as many *kinner* as God sees fit to give us."

"*Gut.*" Joshua's expression softened. "Let's not argue."

Carolyn heaved a heavy sigh. "Okay. We won't argue, but we'll discuss this more later."

Benjamin approached them from the barn, holding a lantern in his hand. Although he was quickly approaching sixteen, he was short and thin for his age. "You're still here, Josh. I thought you'd gone home already."

"Your *mamm* and I were just talking." Joshua patted the rocking chair beside the swing. "Have a seat for a minute. There's something I want to discuss with you."

Joshua pulled his arm back to his side, and Carolyn sat up straight.

"What did you want to talk about?" Benjamin lowered his body into the rocking chair.

"Your *mamm* and I were just discussing what's going to happen after our wedding next month. You're both going to move into the house on the farm." Joshua glanced at Carolyn, and she smiled. "Your *mamm* is going to be Carolyn Glick."

"I know." Benjamin gave Carolyn a confused look. "That's pretty standard when someone gets married."

"How would you feel about becoming a Glick too?" Joshua asked.

Benjamin continued to look perplexed. "I don't understand."

"Ben, I'd like your permission to adopt you." Joshua's voice was thick with emotion. "I'd like to be your *dat*."

Benjamin's brown eyes widened. "Really?"

"*Ya*, really." Joshua patted Benjamin's shoulder. "I'd like us to be a family by name too—all of us. What do you think?"

Carolyn's eyes filled with tears as her most fervent prayer came true.

"I think it's a great plan." Benjamin nodded with emphasis. "I'd like that."

"*Gut.*" Joshua turned toward Carolyn. "That's settled."

Carolyn wiped her eyes with the back of her hand.

"Are you okay, *Mamm*?" Benjamin asked.

"*Ya*." Carolyn cleared her throat in an attempt to temper her emotions.

"*Wunderbaar.*" Joshua stood. "I better get home."

"*Gut nacht*," Benjamin said as he stood. "I'll see you tomorrow." He disappeared into the house.

Carolyn followed Joshua down the steps. She handed him his coat when they reached his buggy. "*Danki* for your warm coat."

"*Gern gschehne.*" He pulled the coat on. He opened his arms, and she stepped into his embrace. "*Danki* for supper."

"You know you're always welcome here." Carolyn rested her cheek on his chest. "It means the world to me that you want to adopt Ben."

"I can only pray that I can make you as happy as you and Ben have made me." He kissed the top of her head.

Carolyn looked up at him. "I better let you go. It's getting late."

"*Gut nacht, mei* Carolyn." He kissed her cheek. "Sleep well." He climbed into the buggy.

"Be safe going home." Carolyn waved as his buggy rattled its way down the rock driveway toward the road. She glanced up at the clear night sky and silently thanked God for blessing her and Benjamin by leading them to Joshua Glick.

⌒◇⌒

Saul was sanding a cabinet when he heard the shop door squeak open, allowing a crisp breeze to penetrate the shop.

Emma stepped into the doorway. "*Dat*? Are you coming in? It's getting late."

"Is it?" Saul glanced at the clock on the wall and shook his head. "I didn't realize it was almost seven. I was trying to finish this one cabinet."

"You can finish it tomorrow." She placed her hand on her small hip, and he bit back a smile. At times she seemed like a little wife instead of a daughter.

"You're right, Emma." He placed the sanding block on his long workbench and then turned off the surrounding lanterns.

He followed Emma through the door and was surprised to see a buggy traveling up the driveway. "I wonder who that could be this late in the evening."

"It's Marcus!" she said, announcing the arrival of Saul's best friend. "I wonder if Esther is with him." She started jumping up and down.

"I doubt it, Emma. It's awfully late for visiting. She's probably getting ready for bed, which is what you need to be doing." Saul and Emma approached the buggy as Marcus Smucker brought it to a stop by the barn. "*Wie geht's?*"

"Hi, Marcus!" Emma stood on her tiptoes and craned her neck to see inside the buggy. "Did Esther come too?"

"No, I'm afraid not." Marcus climbed from the buggy. Saul had often thought it interesting that he and his best friend since childhood looked so much alike—dark brown hair and matching beard, about the same height.

"She was getting ready for bed when I left." Saul gave Emma a knowing glance, and Emma nodded her head.

"You'll see her at school tomorrow," Saul said gently.

"I have something for you, though." Marcus held up a basket. "Esther and her *mamm* made a casserole and pie for you and your *dat*."

"Oh." Emma took the basket and sniffed it. "It smells *appeditlich. Danki*."

"*Gern gschehne*." Marcus nodded at Emma.

"Take that inside and get ready for bed now," Saul told Emma.

"Okay." She looked at Marcus. "*Gut nacht*." Emma waved and then headed for the house.

"You can tell Sylvia she doesn't have to keep cooking for us," Saul said after Emma had disappeared through the back door. "Emma and I are doing okay by ourselves."

"Does that mean you're saying you don't like my *fraa's* cooking?" Marcus grinned as he leaned against the buggy.

"You know it's not that." Saul shook his head. "I appreciate everything you and Sylvia do for Emma and me, but we're doing fine. Please tell her thank you for us."

"I will. You know Sylvia feels bad that you're raising Emma alone."

"It's not her fault Annie ran off." Saul leaned back on the fence behind him.

"I know, but she still feels bad." Marcus folded his arms over his coat. "She talks all the time about how the four of us were dating at the same time and then were married within a month of each other. Sylvia and I are still together, and you're all alone. Sylvia still can't comprehend what Annie did to you and Emma."

Saul shrugged as if it didn't bother him, even though Annie's abandonment was still painful. "That was Annie's choice. I guess on some levels it was better for her to go than to stay here and be miserable."

"You don't mean that."

"No, I think I do. Emma would've been able to tell that her *mamm* resented her. I don't believe any *kind* should feel that kind of rejection from a parent."

Marcus frowned. "She still doesn't know the truth about her *mamm*, does she?"

"No, and she doesn't need to know—not yet," Saul insisted. "I'll tell her when the time is right. I don't know when that will be, but not now. She's too young."

Marcus glanced toward the house in front of Saul's property. "I see that *Englisher* is still living in Martha Stoltzfus's old *haus*."

"*Ya*." Saul spotted the woman standing on the back porch while talking on a cellular phone. Her slight body was illuminated by two lanterns.

"Do you know anything about her?" Marcus asked.

"No, she just appeared back in February, so she's been in the *haus* for almost eight months now." Saul rubbed his beard as he spoke. "I guess she's renting the *haus* from Martha's *dochder*. I never saw a For Sale sign go up."

"Is that right?" Marcus looked intrigued. "And you've never met her?"

"No, but I've noticed she likes to go for runs early in the morning." He didn't mention he'd also noticed she was fairly tall, only a couple of inches shorter than his nearly six feet. "She drives that red pickup truck, and she leaves a few times a week and is gone for extended periods of time. It seems like she has a job somewhere. She hasn't had any work done on the *haus*, so she's living without electricity. But she uses that cellular phone frequently."

Marcus raised an eyebrow. "You've been watching her?"

"Watching her?" Saul shook his head. "No, I've just noticed her patterns. Her *haus* is right in front of mine, so it's difficult not to notice things. Emma wants to go meet her, but I keep telling her to mind her own business. We don't need to barge onto her property any more than she needs to barge onto ours."

"Interesting." Marcus motioned toward Saul's biggest shop. "How's business?"

"*Gut, gut.*" Saul rubbed his beard. "I'm trying to keep up with all the orders."

"Do you need some help?"

"Oh no. You're busy enough with your furniture orders."

"You know it's time you hired someone to help you," Marcus said. "Then you can expand and start supplying the local stores with your cabinets. They could take the orders for you, and you could concentrate on the work."

Saul stood up straight. "That's easier said than done, my friend. I'll expand someday, when the time is right."

"I've known you since we were the same age as our girls," Marcus began. "You always go the cautious way. You never try something new. When we all went camping when we were teenagers, you were afraid to jump off that tree branch into the water, even when the rest of us did."

"What does my business have to do with jumping into a lake?" Saul's brow furrowed. "I don't think that's a fair comparison.

You're talking about taking a risk with my *dochder's* livelihood. I can't hire someone and run the risk of going bankrupt when my cabinet sales fall off."

"What makes you think your sales will fall off? You're known for your quality and craftsmanship. That's why your sales are very *gut*." Marcus opened the buggy door and climbed in. "Think about it, Saul. You sell yourself too short. You can expand. Just have faith."

Saul shook his head. "You were always the free spirit."

"I better go." Marcus closed the buggy door. "I'll see you soon."

"*Danki* for the food again. Tell Sylvia we appreciate her meals."

"I will." Marcus paused. "I heard Carolyn Lapp and Joshua Glick are getting married next month."

Saul nodded and rubbed his beard again. "I'm not surprised."

"Don't give up. I'm sure the Lord has plans for you." Marcus grinned. "If not, then you'll just have to start eating supper at my *haus*."

"I told you we're not starving, but we do enjoy the food." Saul waved. "*Gut nacht*."

Marcus returned the wave before guiding the horse back down the lane. Saul saw his neighbor wave as Marcus's buggy passed her house, and he wondered again who the mysterious neighbor was.

FIVE

Hannah scurried around the kitchen, her mind racing with preparations. She was running out of time before her guest was supposed to arrive.

The storm door opened and closed with a bang, and then Trey stood near the kitchen doorway. "Hannah? Are you okay?"

"*Ya.*" She grabbed a bleach wipe and began to swipe it over the counter. "Carolyn called a little while ago. She's coming by to visit."

"Carolyn Lapp?" Trey looked surprised.

"That's right. She asked if she could come to see me. She'll be my first Amish friend to visit the bed-and-breakfast." She opened the china cabinet and studied her best dishes. "I have to make sure everything is perfect."

"Hannah, I'm certain she will be happy just to see you." He crossed the kitchen. "How can I help you?"

"Would you hand me those teacups up top?" She pointed toward her favorite set of teacups, which Trey had bought her as a wedding gift. "I'm going to serve hot tea and the cheesecake I made yesterday." She suddenly stopped as dread settled in. "Oh no. We can't eat together at the same table."

Trey stopped and studied her. "Will she really visit and not share a dessert with you?"

"She's not supposed to." Hannah scowled. "I don't know what to do. How can I not serve her some refreshments?"

"Why don't you set out the cheesecake and then see what she says. She may surprise you. After all, she is coming to see you. She wouldn't come over here and then refuse your food, would she? That would be awfully rude, and I haven't met many rude Amish folks."

Hannah smiled. "You're right."

"Why don't you start the hot water and get the cheesecake out of the refrigerator, and I'll set the table?"

She kissed his cheek. "*Danki*."

The table was ready by the time Hannah heard a car door slam.

"She's here!" Hannah's heart thudded in her chest.

"It will be fine." Trey touched her hand. "Trust me. Go see her. I'll serve the tea."

She rushed to the open front door, pushed open the storm door, and saw Carolyn walking up the front sidewalk with a basket over her arm as a van backed out to the street.

"Carolyn!" Hannah hurried outside and met her in the driveway. "It's wonderful to see you."

Carolyn hugged Hannah with her free arm. "You too." She handed the basket to Hannah. "I brought you some goodies that my *mamm* and I baked. I remember you liked our pretzels and pumpkin muffins."

"Oh, *danki*!" Hannah looped her free arm around Carolyn's waist and led her back toward the house. "Please come in."

"Oh, Hannah." Carolyn caught her breath, cupping her

hand to her mouth. "This *haus* is positively *schee*. You must be *froh* here."

"I am." Hannah dropped her arm from around Carolyn and touched her abdomen. "I'm very happy here. Please come inside, and I'll show you the rest of the *haus*."

Carolyn's eyes moved to Hannah's abdomen, and Hannah saw the flash of a question twinkle in her friend's eyes. She wondered if Carolyn suspected her secret, but Carolyn didn't ask. Instead, she simply smiled.

Carolyn started up the porch steps. "You look *gut*, Hannah."

"You do too."

Carolyn stepped into the front family room and looked delighted. "Hannah, this is lovely."

"*Danki*." Hannah pointed toward a hallway. "Our living quarters are down there. There's a three-bedroom apartment for us and the *kinner*."

Carolyn looked toward the light switch on the wall. "Did it take you awhile to get used to electricity all the time now, instead of only at work?"

Hannah shrugged. "It was a fairly easy adjustment, although I do feel a little spoiled." She gestured toward the stairs. "There are six bedrooms upstairs for the guests."

"It's fabulous." Carolyn nodded. "You must love it."

"We do. Please come into the kitchen." There they found Trey putting finishing touches on the table. "Carolyn, this is my husband, Trey."

"Carolyn." Trey shook her hand. "It's nice to meet you."

"It's nice to meet you too." Carolyn glanced around the kitchen.

Hannah placed the basket on the counter. "Would you like some tea?"

"*Ya*, I'd love that."

"I'll let you two visit," Trey said. "I'll be working out in the barn." He gave Hannah a smile and then disappeared through the mudroom and out the back door.

"He seems very nice," Carolyn said.

"*Danki.*" Hannah gestured toward the table. "Would you like a cup of tea and a piece of cheesecake?"

"That sounds wonderful. You always made the best cheesecake."

Hannah poured two cups of tea and then handed Carolyn a cup. "Did you want to sit here?" She motioned toward the table and hoped her friend would agree to sit with her.

"Well . . ." Carolyn looked at the table and then crossed to a window. "Do you have chairs on your porch?"

Hannah nodded.

"If we sit on the porch together, then we aren't technically eating at the table together, right?" Carolyn asked with a wink.

"I understand." Tension slipped from Hannah's shoulders as she took a serving tray from a cabinet and loaded it up with the teacups, sweetener, and two pieces of cheesecake.

They moved out to the porch, where they sipped the tea and enjoyed the cheesecake.

"It's lovely out here." Carolyn looked out over the large backyard. "I can see why you fell in love with this place."

"*Danki.*" Hannah cradled her teacup in her hands. "Trey likes to go out into the barn and tinker with woodworking. I think he's making a trinket box to give Amanda for Christmas."

"How nice." Carolyn took another sip of her tea and then turned toward Hannah. "I have some news."

"Oh?" Hannah placed her cup on the small table beside her. "What is it?"

"I'm getting married."

"Carolyn!" Hannah clapped her hands together. "That's wonderful news! Who is your fiancé?"

"You know him very well." Carolyn paused. "It's Joshua Glick."

Hannah gaped at her friend.

"That's fantastic!" she finally said. Hannah couldn't stop a smile. She'd prayed that Joshua would find his true love. She'd felt guilty for breaking his heart, but she knew it wasn't in God's plan for her to marry him.

"*Danki.* Joshua is a wonderful man, and he's been *gut* to my son. He wants to adopt Benjamin, and that means a lot to Ben and me."

Carolyn's smile faded, and a look of concern took its place. "I want you to come to the wedding. Please tell me that you will."

Hannah hesitated. "Did you talk to Josh about this?"

"Oh *ya.*" Carolyn nodded. "We talked about it last night, and he agrees that you should come."

"I don't know." Hannah felt stuck. She wanted to see her friend and Joshua get married, but she also knew if she went to the wedding, she'd be in an awkward situation because she was shunned. "Would it be all right if I thought about it?"

"Of course." Carolyn's expression brightened. "You think about it and discuss it with Trey. Of course, Amanda and Andrew are also invited. I'm certain Lily will be there too." She reached over and touched Hannah's hand. "I know you've had a difficult time with Lillian. Josh has told me. We're praying Lillian will forgive you soon."

Hannah studied her teacup as she rubbed her abdomen again. "*Danki*. I pray that every day."

"How are Amanda and Andrew? I bet the *kinner* are getting big, *ya*?" Carolyn asked as she forked the cheesecake.

"They are, and they're doing well," Hannah said. "Amanda is taking college biology classes, and she worries about her grades all the time. She's doing great, though. Andrew is enjoying fifth grade. He has new friends, and he loves the school bus."

"This cake is *appeditlich*." Carolyn wiped her mouth with a paper napkin.

"*Danki*." Hannah sipped the tea. "How's Benjamin?"

"He's doing *gut*. He works on Joshua's farm, and he loves it."

Hannah took a bite of the cheesecake. "How are your parents doing?"

Carolyn talked about her family, and then Hannah asked her how work was going at the hotel. They discussed their friends and acquaintances in the community, paying no attention to the time.

Soon Trey emerged from his workshop and approached the porch. "I'm heading to the hardware store for stain and a few other things. Would you like me to pick up something for lunch?"

"Lunch?" Hannah asked with surprise.

He tapped his wristwatch. "It's almost noon."

"Is it?" Hannah stood. "I didn't realize that. Amanda will be home soon."

Trey pointed toward his car in the driveway. "Do you want me to pick up something from town?"

"No, thank you. We'll make some sandwiches." She turned to Carolyn. "Does that sound *gut* to you?"

"Oh no." Carolyn shook her head. "I don't want to be any trouble. I'll call my driver and have him come to get me. I just need to use your phone."

"Don't be *gegisch*." Hannah waved off the comment. "I insist you stay for lunch, and then we'll take you home later."

Trey headed to his car, and Hannah and Carolyn made sandwiches before returning to the porch with the sandwiches and glasses of iced tea.

"How is business?" Carolyn asked while lifting a chip to her mouth.

"It's *gut*." Hannah nodded. "We've stayed very busy. Right now we have two couples staying until Sunday."

"Are you enjoying it?"

"Oh *ya*." Hannah ate a chip. "I love telling them about the Amish culture and pointing out the best places for them to visit."

"And Trey?" Carolyn asked. "How are things?"

"Things are wonderful between us." Hannah's hand dropped to her belly again before she could stop it. Carolyn's gaze moved down and then back up to Hannah's eyes.

"Hannah . . . ?" Carolyn's question was barely audible.

Hannah nodded, and her cheeks heated.

"Oh, Hannah." Carolyn's eyes filled with tears.

Hannah wiped tears that had formed in her eyes too. "I didn't think God would bless me or Trey again, but he has. I'm praying Lily will find out and realize things have changed, but we'll always be family."

"*Ya*," Carolyn agreed. "I think that is true."

"How's Josh's farm?" Hannah asked. "He's asked me to stop by, but I haven't gone to see it."

"He's been very busy." Carolyn shared stories about Joshua's horses and customers while they finished their lunch.

They were enjoying Carolyn's homemade pretzels when Amanda's blue Ford sedan steered into the driveway.

"Amanda is home!" Hannah said. "I'm glad you'll get to see her."

"Oh *gut*," Carolyn said.

Amanda and her boyfriend, Mike Smithson, climbed from her car and walked to the house.

"Hi, *Mamm*." Amanda climbed the steps and dropped her backpack onto the porch. "Hi, Carolyn. It's great to see you. This is my boyfriend, Mike." She gestured between them. "Mike, this is my friend Carolyn Lapp."

"It's nice to meet you." Carolyn stood and shook his hand. "Would you both like a pretzel? I made them this morning."

"Oh, I'd love one." Amanda took one and passed it to Mike. "These are the best."

"Thanks." The young man smiled as he took a bite. "Oh wow. These are amazing."

"Told you." Amanda grinned and then sat down next to Hannah.

"How was your day?" Hannah asked.

"Oh, it was good." Amanda gestured toward Mike. "Mike is going to help me study for my test tomorrow. We were wondering if we could use the kitchen table for a while."

"Of course you can. Carolyn came over to tell me some news." Hannah smiled at Carolyn. "Would you like to tell Amanda?"

"Oh *ya*." Carolyn wiped her hands on a napkin. "I'm getting married next month."

"Oh!" Amanda's eyes widened. "That's wonderful news! I had no idea you were engaged. Who are you going to marry?"

"You know him very well," Carolyn teased.

"I do?" Amanda pushed her long, thick, blonde braid behind her shoulder while she contemplated the riddle. "I'm not certain who that could be. Tell me."

"Your *onkel* Josh." Carolyn's smile was wide.

"*Onkel* Josh?" Amanda gasped. "That's fantastic!" She turned to Mike. "My *onkel* owns the horse farm where we used to live."

"Oh, right." Mike nodded. "You mentioned that when I walked you home from the deli that one time."

"You need to come by," Carolyn said. "Josh tells me all the time that he wants you all to visit." She turned toward Hannah. "All of you need to visit."

"That would be fun." Amanda pulled the pretzel apart. "I know Andrew would love to see Huckleberry." She looked at Mike. "Huckleberry is Andrew's favorite horse."

"Oh." Mike chewed another piece of pretzel. "I haven't been riding in a long time."

"It would be a blast to show you where I grew up. It's beautiful there. You'd love all the horses."

Amanda shared stories about the farm, and Hannah smiled as happy memories filled her. She'd wanted to visit the farm, but she was afraid the memories might be too emotional for her. Yet now that she was happy with Trey and her new life, the memories of her old life felt more like warm blankets from her past than frozen nightmares. And knowing Joshua was happy with Carolyn made the idea of visiting much easier.

Hannah, Carolyn, Amanda, and Mike visited for about an hour.

"We need to go," Amanda finally said as she tapped Mike's arm. They headed into the kitchen to start studying.

Hannah and Carolyn were still sitting on the front porch when a bright yellow school bus rumbled to a stop in front of the bed-and-breakfast. Hannah and Carolyn walked to the driveway and met Andrew as he hopped down from the bus.

"Hi," Andrew said.

"How was your day?" Hannah took his backpack from his hands.

"It was great. I had pizza for lunch." He smiled up at Carolyn. "Hi. You're Carolyn, right?"

"That's right. How are you, Andrew?" Carolyn asked.

"I'm fine. Are you staying for supper?" he asked as they walked back to the house.

"No, I need to get home and make supper for my family." Carolyn touched his arm. "But I wanted to see you before I went back home. I've spent the day with your *mamm*."

"Oh. Well, it's good to see you." Andrew held the storm door open for them once they reached the porch.

"Carolyn brought homemade pretzels and muffins too," Hannah said as she walked into the family room.

"Oh wow! Thank you!" Andrew beamed. "They're my favorites."

"You're welcome," Carolyn said. "I'll see you next month."

"Next month?" Andrew tilted his head in question. "What's next month?"

"I'm marrying your *onkel* Joshua next month," Carolyn told him. "Will you come to our wedding?"

"Of course I will! That's cool!"

Carolyn laughed. "I'll see you then."

"Where are the pretzels?"

"In the kitchen," Hannah told him. "You can have a quick snack, and then you need to start your homework."

"*Ya, Mamm.*" Andrew ran out of the room.

"He's such a *gut bu.*" Carolyn crossed her arms over her apron. "I'll have to get used to seeing him in *Englisher* clothes and with a short haircut. Amanda looks different, too, but she's still the same sweet *maedel.*"

"*Ya,* they're still my *gut kinner.*" Hannah sighed. "I guess you need to get going."

"*Ya,* I do. I'll call my driver."

"No, you won't." Hannah shook her head. "Amanda can take you home."

"Are you sure it's not any trouble?" Carolyn asked.

"Don't be silly. Amanda loves to drive. She picks up Mike and takes him to their classes most days." Hannah started for the kitchen. "I'll get her for you."

Hannah poked her head into the kitchen and asked Amanda to take Carolyn home. After Amanda agreed, she retrieved Carolyn's basket from the counter and then returned to the family room, where Carolyn was gazing at the family photos lined up on the mantel.

Hannah sidled up to Carolyn and handed her the basket. "She said she'll be ready in a minute."

"*Danki.*" Carolyn pointed to the family portraits. "I like these photos."

"They're Trey's family." Hannah pointed out Trey's parents and also his daughter, who had passed away from carbon monoxide poisoning four years earlier.

"Are you ready?" Amanda walked into the family room, her car keys jingling in her hand. Mike stood beside her with his backpack over his shoulder.

"*Ya*, I am." Carolyn smiled at Hannah. "*Danki* for having me over."

"I'm glad you came." Hannah hugged her friend. "Please come visit me again soon."

"I will, and you need to come to the wedding." Carolyn touched Hannah's arm. "Please consider it. Joshua and I want you and your *kinner* there. You're part of our family."

"*Danki*," Hannah said, her voice thick with emotion. "I appreciate that."

Carolyn started for the door. "I'll see you soon."

"I'm going to drop Mike off at work after I take Carolyn home," Amanda said. "I'll be back soon."

Hannah waved good-bye as they all walked out the door. The need to pray gripped her: *Please, God, let my Lily spend the day at the bed-and-breakfast with me just as Carolyn did. I need Lily back in my life, Lord. Thank you. Amen.*

Hannah sat in the sitting area of her apartment while reading her Bible later that evening. Although her eyes were scanning the book of John, her mind was still stuck on her visit with Carolyn. She was thrilled that Carolyn and Joshua were going to be married, but she wasn't certain if she should go to the wedding. Would it cause more heartache if she went and had an unpleasant discussion with Lillian in front of the whole community? The question churned through her mind while she tried to study the Word.

The door creaked open, and she looked up as Trey entered the room.

"Hi." Trey sat down on the chair across the room from her. "How are you?"

"Fine." She closed the Bible and rested it on her lap. "Andrew is asleep and Amanda is studying for her exam."

"Good." Trey leaned back in the chair. "I was talking to the guests on the front porch. They seem to be enjoying their stay. They appreciated your suggestions for sightseeing, and they said they'd recommend our bed-and-breakfast to their friends."

"That's great news." Hannah knew her voice didn't match the sentiment in her words.

"Is something on your mind, Hannah?" Trey's eyes were full of concern. "You look upset about something."

"I'm not upset." Hannah shook her head. "I'm just confused."

"How do you mean?"

"Carolyn is getting married next month, and she wants us all to come to the wedding."

"That's wonderful." Trey's expression brightened. "We'll go."

"It's not that simple." Hannah sighed. "Carolyn is marrying Josh."

"Oh." Trey nodded slowly.

"I'm very happy for Josh, but I don't know if I belong at his wedding."

"Are you allowed to go even if you're excommunicated?" Trey asked.

"*Ya*, I'm permitted to go, but it may be awkward and painful for my family."

Trey's expression softened. "You mean it may be awkward for you to see Barbie and Lillian." He filled in the blanks.

"*Ya.*" She nodded. "You know me well."

"How would an excommunicated church member be treated at a wedding?"

"I would simply have to sit with the *Englishers* and eat with the *Englishers*. So I could still attend, but it would just be . . . awkward." Hannah ran her fingers over the worn cover of her Bible. "I don't want to cause any more heartache for Lily than I already have."

"But you have a right to be there." Trey crossed the room and sat beside her. "You want to go. I can see it in your eyes. But you don't have to decide tonight. Why don't you pray about it and then make your decision? Talk to Amanda too. I'm happy to go with you and stand by your side. You won't be alone."

"Okay." She smiled up at him. "Thank you."

"You're welcome." He hugged her. "Now let's get some sleep." He patted her belly. "You both had a long day."

She laughed. "*Ya*, we sure did." She looked down and wondered what God had in store for the little person growing inside of her.

SIX

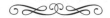

Madeleine leaned against the porch railing while balancing her iPhone between her shoulder and her ear. She listened to the ringing until her mother finally picked up.

"Hello?"

"Hey, Mom. How are you?"

"Maddie! How are *you*?"

"Fine, fine." Madeleine gazed toward the Beiler farm and breathed in the crisp air. "I'm enjoying this gorgeous day. You and Jack need to come out and see me. You can leave sunny California and experience some real fall weather for the first time in a long time."

"Oh, I know." Mom sighed. "I want to visit, but we're both very busy with work."

Madeleine rolled her eyes. She loved her mother, but she had every excuse not to come back to Pennsylvania. "I promise you can stay in a hotel so you'll have electricity."

"You still haven't had it installed in the house?" Her mother's voice was full of surprise. "I thought you would've had electricity put in by now."

"I'm not sure if I want electricity. I sort of enjoy the quiet. I had enough noise when I was working at the hospital." She noticed the little girl on the Beiler farm stepping onto her own porch. The girl waved, and Madeleine returned the gesture. "I wish you could see this adorable girl who lives next door. She and her dad live on the farm that your parents used to own. You know, the property behind *Mammi's* house."

"Oh yes. I remember seeing them at the funeral. Maybe at my dad's funeral too. They seemed nice." Mom paused for a moment. "From what I remember, the father is very reserved and quiet. He's like most of the Amish men I remember from my childhood. But the little girl is outgoing. I think she talked my ear off at the funeral."

"She always waves to me now," Madeleine said. "I should go meet them, but I always seem to have something to do. And I don't want to be an intrusive *Englisher.*"

"How is the hotel working out? Are you still working there part time?"

"It's fine, thanks." Madeleine lowered herself onto the top porch step. "I'm working there three days a week. The other housekeepers are Amish, and I'm enjoying getting to know them."

"Really?" Mom sounded intrigued. "I didn't realize Amish women would work at a nice hotel like that."

"I find it interesting too. They all seem to have a unique story. I'm going to my friend Carolyn's Amish wedding next month."

"Wow. That's nice that they accept you."

"Yeah, I was wondering what would be an appropriate gift. You'll have to coach me on that."

"Oh, I don't know if I can remember what an acceptable wedding gift would be," Mom said. "You might want to ask one of your other friends. It's been a long time since I went to anything like that."

"I'll talk to Ruth—"

Madeleine thought she heard a scream, and she stood up. The shriek sounded again, and she looked over toward the Beiler farm, where the little girl sat on the ground. It looked like she was shaking, probably crying. "Mom, I have to go! Someone is hurt. I'll call you later."

"Maddie?" her mom asked just before Madeleine disconnected the call.

Madeleine took off running toward the farm, shoving her phone in her pocket as she rushed down the rock driveway toward the field where the girl screamed again and was most certainly sobbing now. When she reached her, Madeleine squatted next to her and found her cradling her foot in her hand. The girl looked up in surprise.

"Hey, sweetie," Madeleine said gently. "Are you okay? What happened?"

"I fell," the girl managed to say between sobs.

"Will you let me help you?"

The girl hiccupped and then nodded while tears continued to sprinkle down her pink cheeks. Her eyes were wide as her lower lip trembled.

"My name is Madeleine, and I'm a nurse," she explained. "Would you let me look at your foot?"

"It's my ankle. I think I broke it." The little girl pointed toward a hole in the ground. "I stepped in that hole on my way to the barn."

"Let me have a look." Madeleine hesitated. "Is it okay if I touch your ankle?"

The little girl nodded. "You're a nurse?"

"That's right." Madeleine gently removed the girl's shoe and sock and examined her small ankle. "I normally find out the names of my patients." She glanced up at the girl's pretty pale blue eyes and smiled. "What's your name?"

"Emma Beiler."

"Well, Emma Beiler, it's nice to meet you." She studied the small red spot on her ankle and then moved the girl's ankle slightly. When she looked up again, she saw Emma had jammed her eyes shut.

"You can open your eyes now. I don't think your ankle is broken. I'd say you have a slight sprain. All you probably need is some ice, but if the pain gets worse, then your daddy should take you to the doctor." Madeleine pointed toward her house. "I have a truck, and I can take you to the hospital if your dad wants you to go."

"Okay." Emma tried to stand up and then winced before sitting down on the ground again. "It hurts too much to stand."

"I can carry you." Madeleine turned and pointed to her back. "Climb on."

Emma studied Madeleine. "You want to give me a piggyback ride?"

"Sure." Madeleine shrugged. "Why not?"

"Okay." Emma carefully climbed onto Madeleine's back, wrapping her arms around Madeleine's neck and peeking over her right shoulder. "This will be fun!"

"Where's your dad?" Madeleine asked as she stood up, carefully grasped Emma's legs around her waist, and started to make her way to the farmhouse.

"In his big shop over there," Emma said near Madeleine's ear. "He makes cabinets. That building over there is where he stains the wood, and the other shop is the showroom. This big shop is where he builds the cabinets. He makes the best cabinets in Paradise."

"Really? Who told you that?"

"Marcus did. He's my *dat's* best friend." Emma loosened one arm and pointed. "His big shop used to be a dairy barn, but now it's where he does most of his work."

"I remember when it was a dairy barn."

"You do?" Emma's voice was full of surprise. "How do you know?"

"I know this property really well."

"How?" Emma asked as Madeleine approached the shop.

"I spent a lot of time on this farm when I was little."

"Does that mean you knew my *mammi*?" Emma asked as she craned her neck to look at Madeleine's face.

"Your *mammi*?" Madeleine stopped in front of the shop door and turned her head to look into Emma's eyes.

"*Ya*." Emma nodded with emphasis. "Martha Stoltzfus lived in your *haus*. She was *mei mammi*."

"How was she your *mammi*?" Madeleine studied the girl. "I don't understand."

"She lived in the *haus* where you live now. I used to visit her all the time. We cooked, worked in her garden, and sewed together," Emma said as she tightened her hold. "Why are you living in her *haus*? It's not an *Englisher haus*."

"I inherited the house because she was my *mammi* too."

"She was?" Emma asked, her eyes wide.

"That's right. Now let's get your *dat*." Madeleine pushed open the door and stepped into the large woodworking shop.

The smell of wood dust filled her senses. The soft yellow

light from lanterns perched around the large former barn illuminated the shop. A fairly tall man with dark brown hair and a matching beard stood at a workbench and sanded a cabinet while a diesel generator hummed. An array of tools cluttered a line of surrounding workbenches. A pile of wood sat beside cabinets in various stages of development that were sitting on the benches in the corner.

"*Dat!*" Emma called.

The man stopped working and turned toward Madeleine and Emma. His eyes rounded and his brow furrowed as he stared at them. He turned off the generator.

"What's going on? Who are you? Why are you holding my *dochder*?"

"This is Madeleine." Emma took one arm from around Madeleine's neck and tapped her shoulder. "I fell outside and she came to help me. She says my ankle isn't broken, but it's sprained."

"I'm Madeleine Miller." Madeleine moved a hand out from under Emma's leg and held it out to him. "I live next door."

"I know where you live." Saul wiped his hands on a shop towel and ignored her hand. Madeleine still waited for him to shake it, but he continued to study her with a scowl on his face. "I'm a nurse," she continued in hopes of softening his accusatory stare. "I heard Emma scream, and I immediately ran over to help her. I examined her ankle, and I think she's going to be just fine. It's painful for her to walk on it, so I carried her in here."

Saul remained silent, and she kept talking to fill the awkward space between them. "I believe it's sprained and not fractured. She should elevate it and use ice. The ice will stop the swelling, and a pain reliever would help too. You could give her Tylenol or Motrin if you have it. I have some pain relievers at my house if you need them. If the pain worsens or the swelling continues, then you may want to take her to the hospital and have X-rays done just to be certain her ankle's not broken. I can always drive you if you need help getting to the hospital."

"Fine."

"Do you have an Ace bandage?" she asked.

"*Ya,*" he said. "I believe I do."

"Do you want me to carry her into the house?" Madeleine offered. "I can make up an ice packet and get her settled in a chair or on your sofa so you can keep working."

"No, no. That won't be necessary." Saul took Emma from Madeleine and held her in his arms. "I will handle things from here."

Madeleine studied his stoic face. Why was he being cold to her? After all, she'd helped his injured daughter. She'd never met someone who was that curt or unwelcoming. How had Emma become sweet and friendly with such a quiet and rude father?

"Okay." Madeleine tried to draw him into a conversation. "I can come and check her ankle tomorrow if you'd like me to. I don't mind. I worked in the trauma unit at a military hospital before I came here."

"That won't be necessary." Saul's expression remained stony.

"Madeleine is Martha Stoltzfus's *grossdochder,*" Emma said.

"Oh." Saul started for the door. "Let's get you inside and get some ice on your ankle." He exited, and Madeleine trailed behind him.

Madeleine stepped out into the sunlight and stood by the shop door as Saul carried Emma toward the house.

Emma peeked over his shoulder and waved. "Thank you, Madeleine!"

Madeleine waved. "*Gern gschehne.*"

Emma's face brightened. "You speak *Dietsch*?"

Madeleine nodded. "*Ya,* I do."

Emma looked at her father. "Did you hear that, *Dat*? She speaks *Dietsch*!"

Saul grunted in response.

"Bye!" Emma waved to Madeleine again. "I'll see you soon!"

"I hope so." Madeleine waved again.

Saul and Emma disappeared into the house, and Madeleine shook her head. What had happened to Saul to make him such a cold man? His frosty demeanor most likely had something to do with the death of his wife. Her irritation toward him softened slightly. Still, he had no right to be so rude to her when she was only trying to help his daughter.

Saul stopped just inside the mudroom door and watched Madeleine walk back to her house. His scowl deepened as he studied her tight jeans and snug, long-sleeve shirt. He didn't appreciate that she paraded her inappropriate clothes in front of Emma. She had a lot of nerve marching over to his property and touching his daughter.

"*Dat*?" Emma's voice pulled him from his thoughts. "My ankle is throbbing. Would you please get me the ice? Madeleine said it would stop the swelling and make it feel better."

"*Ya.* I'm sorry." Saul pulled his gaze away from Madeleine and carried Emma into the family room.

He placed her on the sofa and then gathered a bottle of Tylenol, an Ace bandage, and a glass of water. After giving her the painkiller, he wrapped her ankle and then filled a plastic storage bag with ice. She winced when he placed the ice pack on her little ankle. Then he sat in a chair beside her.

"What happened?" he asked.

"I was running to the barn to check on that new litter of kittens, and I stepped in a hole and fell." Emma brushed her hand over her knee.

"Why did that *Englisher* come over? Did you call her?"

"No." Emma shook her head. "I screamed because I was in pain, and she came running."

Saul pushed a stray lock of Emma's hair under her prayer covering. "She just came to check on you?"

"*Ya*," Emma said. "She ran over and asked if she could help me. She told me she was a nurse, and she checked out my ankle. She was very nice. Can you believe she's Martha's *grossdochder*? I wanted to ask her if she's going to change the *haus* at all, but I didn't have a chance. I'll ask her the next time I see her."

"No, you won't. Remember what I told you about staying away from her. You can't go prying into her business, Emma." Saul's tone was gentle but firm. "You need to mind your own business."

"Then I can't go visit her?" Emma frowned. "I want to find out more about her."

"No, that's not a *gut* idea. We need to keep our distance. She's not a member of our community."

"But she's nice." Emma folded her hands as if she were saying a prayer. "I want to be her friend, *Dat*. I think she likes me."

"No." Saul shook his head. "You need to leave her alone."

"Okay." Emma sighed. "I'll stay away."

"*Danki*." He touched her leg. "How's your ankle now?"

"It still hurts."

He grabbed her copy of *Little House on the Prairie* and handed it to her. It was her favorite book. "You stay here and rest. I'll finish what I was doing and then start supper. Sound *gut?*"

"*Ya.*" She opened the book and smiled. "*Danki, Dat.*"

He nodded and then headed back outside. As he descended the porch steps, he looked toward Madeleine's house. Guilt filled him as he considered how rude he'd been to her. He'd reacted in an impolite manner because he was shocked to see that *Englisher* woman standing in his shop holding his daughter.

Saul walked back to his shop. If the opportunity presented itself, he would offer a proper thank you for her help. It was only the right thing to do.

◦∞◦

Saul cleaned up the kitchen after supper and then helped Emma hobble to her room. After she was settled in bed with a new ice pack, he headed outside to take care of the animals. He was exiting the barn when he saw a light on Madeleine's back porch. She was sitting in a chair and talking on her cell phone. Now was the time to go and apologize to her. He took a deep breath and started up the driveway to her house.

Madeleine looked up as he approached the porch steps, and her eyes widened. With her youthful face, he surmised she was in her midtwenties.

"Hey, Mom," she said into the phone. "I need to go. I'll call you soon, okay? All right. Tell Jack I said hello. Good night." She disconnected the call and then stood. "Hi. Please come up."

"Is this a bad time?" he asked as he climbed the steps.

"No, no. Not at all." She pushed her dark hair behind her ears. "Is Emma okay?"

"*Ya, ya.*" He nodded. "She's fine."

"Oh good." Her smile was tentative. "Did you want to have a seat?" She pointed toward a chair. "Would you like a drink or something?" She gestured toward the door. "I have some iced tea and cookies."

"No, thank you. I can't stay long."

"Oh. Okay." She fingered her phone as if she were self-conscious and didn't know what to do with her hands. "What brings you over here tonight?"

He cleared his throat and tried to remember what he'd wanted to say to her. "I didn't thank you properly earlier. I appreciate that you helped my Emma."

"You're welcome." She waved off the comment as if her help were nothing. "I'm just glad I was outside and heard her crying out."

"*Ya.*" Saul fingered his beard. "I didn't hear her over the noises in the shop, and if you hadn't come, she may have been stranded there for a while. So, thank you."

"You're welcome," she said. "Emma is a sweet girl."

"*Ya,* she is." He paused. It was time to apologize, but he wasn't good at expressing his feelings. Annie's abandonment had stolen his ability to express himself. "I had no right to be rude to you earlier. I'm sorry." He held out his hand. "I'm Saul Beiler."

"It's nice to meet you, Saul." She shook his hand. "I'm glad to officially meet my neighbors."

"*Ya.*" He gave her a stiff nod, and because he didn't know what else to say, he thought it was best to just go home. "Good night then." Before she could answer, he turned and started down the steps.

"Saul," she called after him.

He spun and faced her. "*Ya?*"

"Feel free to come and get me if you ever need anything." She pointed toward her red pickup truck sitting in the driveway. "I can always give you a ride somewhere if you have any emergency."

"*Danki.*" Saul quickly started down the driveway toward his house. He felt awkward when meeting new people. Madeleine Miller seemed like a perfectly fine person, but he wasn't comfortable interacting with women, especially *Englishers*. He appreciated her help tonight, but he didn't expect to interact with her again, except for the occasional neighborly wave. They had no business being friends.

As he climbed his porch steps, he looked back toward her house and was surprised to see Madeleine watching him from her own porch. She waved, and he responded with a halfhearted, stiff wave before disappearing into the safety of his house.

Saul Beiler stalked down the rock drive toward his house, and Madeleine shook her head as she stared after him. That was the strangest introduction she'd ever experienced. He'd come over to introduce himself, thank her, apologize to her . . . and then he just hurried away. She'd hoped to draw him into a conversation and possibly have some refreshments too. She'd always enjoyed getting to know her neighbors, but Saul didn't seem to want to get to know her. He just wanted to do the proper thing and then run away.

Saul seemed like a nice man under that crusty exterior. He looked to be in his early thirties, and she also noticed that his deep brown eyes were full of sadness. He must have led a lonely life with Emma, but she knew the Amish took care of their community members too.

When Saul reached his house, he looked back toward Madeleine's place, and she waved. He halfheartedly waved back. Madeleine almost laughed out loud. *When was the last time he laughed?* she wondered. *He looks like he could use loosening up.* But she was certain she would never have the opportunity to get to know him very well.

Still, questions about the man echoed in her mind as she stepped back into the house.

SEVEN

Madeleine sat in the back of the large family room in Joshua Glick's house. She couldn't believe how quickly a month had passed since Carolyn asked her to come to her wedding. Bright sunlight streamed through the window beside her on this Thursday morning. She glanced around the room and estimated about two hundred members of the community had gathered to witness the wedding.

It felt strange to Madeleine that she had to ask for a Thursday off from work. Most non-Amish weddings were held on Saturdays. However, Carolyn explained that Amish weddings were always held on Tuesdays and Thursdays in the fall.

The wedding ceremony reminded Madeleine of the church services she had attended as a child. The benches were set up in the same manner, with the men and women seated separately. The women looked lovely in their best Sunday dresses and prayer coverings. Madeleine was struck by the brightly colored dresses the young ladies wore—a rainbow of teals, blues, purples, and pinks. The men were also in their best Sunday suits with suspenders and crisp white shirts.

Madeleine leaned over toward Ruth, who was seated beside her. "Where are Carolyn and Josh?"

"The bride and groom always meet with the minister before the wedding service," Ruth explained. "We'll sing hymns until they join us."

Ruth handed Madeleine a copy of the *Ausbund* just as the congregation began to sing. Madeleine successfully followed along with most of the hymns, and she was pleased she could still remember some of the Pennsylvania Dutch and German her grandmother had taught her.

After the hymns, Carolyn and Joshua joined the congregation and sat with their attendants. Ruth pointed out Carolyn's sister-in-law, Sarah Ann; her brother, Amos; her niece, Rosemary; and her son, Benjamin. Carolyn, with her attendants by her side, sat facing Joshua, Amos, and Benjamin.

Madeleine studied Carolyn's navy blue dress, which matched Sarah Ann's and Rosemary's. They were the typical Amish dresses Madeleine had seen women wear around the community, and they were nothing like the dresses she had seen in *Englisher* weddings she'd attended when her friends were married.

She leaned over to Ruth again and whispered, "Their dresses are beautiful. I love how simple and elegant they are."

"They made them themselves," Ruth said softly. "Carolyn did the majority of the work with her mother's help, but Rosemary and Sarah Ann helped her finish them up last week. Aren't they lovely?"

"They are." Would her mother's wedding have been like this if she had stayed in the community? Of course, it was a silly thought.

If her mother had remained Amish, then Madeleine wouldn't have been born.

The men in the wedding party wore their traditional Sunday black-and-white clothing. Madeleine studied Benjamin, struck by how his blond hair and cocoa-colored eyes matched Carolyn's. He was truly a handsome young man.

Madeleine sniffed and wiped her eyes as the bride and groom recited their vows, standing before members of their community. She was struck by how no one was taking photographs, but she reminded herself that the Amish didn't allow photographs because they were considered graven images.

Weddings always made her cry, even the *English* weddings she'd attended. She couldn't help but wonder what her wedding would've been like if she and Travis had gotten married. She tried to ignore the sad thought, but it lingered in her mind.

Ruth leaned closer to Madeleine and pointed. "We're going to sing another hymn, and then the minister sitting over there will talk. He'll give a sermon based on the Old Testament stories of marriages."

Madeleine nodded. She did her best to follow along with the hymn but lost her place a few times. Whenever she became confused, she'd glance over at Ruth, who'd point to where they were in the hymn.

Once the hymn was over, the minister began talking. Madeleine occasionally understood German words here and there during the sermon, but she wasn't really listening anyway. She was consumed with thoughts of Travis and her military career. She'd served nearly four years as a flight nurse and then spent the rest of her career working at a medical center on her home air force base in California, where she'd met Travis.

They'd quickly fallen in love, and they were engaged after only a year.

"It's time to kneel for the prayer," Ruth whispered into Madeleine's ear, pulling her back from her memories.

Madeleine followed the rest of the congregation, kneeling for silent prayer and then rising for the minister's reading of Matthew 19:1–12.

"That's our bishop," Ruth explained as an elderly man with a long white beard stood. "His name is Elmer Smucker. He'll preach the main sermon now."

The older man began to speak, and Madeleine tried to concentrate on his words. "He's talking about the book of Genesis," Ruth explained in a soft voice. "He's discussing the story of Abraham and the other patriarchs included in the book."

"*Danki* for explaining it to me," Madeleine said with a smile.

Ruth grinned. "*Gern gschehne.*"

Madeleine scanned the crowd of young, unmarried ladies during the sermon and spotted Linda from work. A modestly dressed *English* woman with deep red hair sat a few rows behind her. She was sitting with people Madeleine thought must be her husband and children.

Madeleine touched Ruth's arm and leaned toward her. "Ruth, is that Hannah?" She nodded toward the woman.

"*Ya*," Ruth said. "And that's her husband, Trey, and her children Amanda and Andrew. I'll introduce you after the service."

Hannah's expression was sad. How did Hannah feel to be back at an Amish service but not a part of the congregation? Was that how her mother felt when she attended *Mammi's* funeral? Hannah met Madeleine's gaze and raised her hand as a greeting. Madeleine nodded in reply.

She looked back toward the soon-to-be newlyweds. Carolyn was radiant in her blue linen dress with her white *kapp*. She beamed at her groom, Josh, whose eyes shone with love for her.

I wonder if I'll ever find such a powerful, all-consuming love again in my lifetime. Does God have a soul mate in mind for me, or did my opportunity to find love die with Travis in that emergency room?

The thought caught Madeleine off guard. She'd resigned herself to enjoying life in Pennsylvania alone, but she hoped God still had a plan for her. She wanted a husband and a family.

She watched the bride and groom as they studied the bishop. She leaned over to Ruth once again. "What is he saying now?"

"He's telling them about the apostle Paul's instructions for marriage included in 1 Corinthians and Ephesians," Ruth whispered. "Now he's instructing Carolyn and Josh on how to run a godly household. Next he'll move on to a forty-five-minute sermon on the story of Sara and Tobias from the intertestamental book of Tobit."

When the sermon was over, the bishop looked at Carolyn and Joshua. "Now here are two in one faith. Carolyn Rose Lapp and Joshua Eli Glick." The bishop then asked the congregation if they knew any scriptural reason for the couple not to be married. Hearing no response, he continued. "If it is your desire to be married, you may in the name of the Lord come forth."

Madeleine was thankful she could understand the bishop and follow along. Next Joshua took Carolyn's hand in his, and they stood before the bishop.

Madeleine sniffed and wiped her eyes again as the bride and groom recited their vows. The bishop read "A Prayer for Those about to Be Married" from an Amish prayer book called the *Christenpflicht*. When the second sermon was over, the congregation knelt while the bishop again read from the *Christenpflicht*. After he recited the Lord's Prayer, the congregation stood, and the three-hour service ended with another hymn.

Once the ceremony was over, the men began rearranging furniture while the women set out to serve the wedding dinner.

"I'll introduce you to Hannah before going to help." Ruth took Madeleine's arm and led her to where Hannah stood with her family.

Hannah's face brightened as they approached. "Ruth, hi. It's so *gut* to see you."

"It's wonderful to see you," Ruth said. "I'd like you to meet my friend Madeleine Miller. She works with me at the hotel. Madeleine, this is Hannah Peterson."

"Hi, Hannah." Madeleine shook Hannah's hand. "We're neighbors, actually. I live a few streets away from your bed-and-breakfast. I inherited my grandparents' house and moved into it back in February."

"How nice." Hannah touched the arm of the man next to her. "This is my husband, Trey. And this is my daughter Amanda and my son, Andrew."

"It's nice to meet you all," Madeleine said as they smiled at her. "I like to run a few mornings a week, and I jog past your bed-and-breakfast a lot. I've thought about stopping in to say hello."

"Oh, you should," Hannah insisted.

"Thank you. I would really like that." Madeleine excused herself before turning back to Ruth.

Women began bringing trays of drinks and food out of the kitchen.

"Should I help with setting out the dinner?" Madeleine asked Ruth.

"No, no." Ruth shook her head. "You're a guest." She pointed toward a corner. "You can sit with the other *Englishers*. I'll join you if you'd like."

"Oh no." Madeleine touched Ruth's arm. "You go and enjoy your family. Thank you for explaining the service to me."

"Did you understand any of it?" Ruth asked.

"I actually did. My *Dietsch* is coming back to me."

"That's *wunderbaar*." Ruth smiled.

Madeleine smoothed her hands over her long blue skirt and hoped her plain blue blouse and skirt were modest enough for the wedding. She wanted to blend in and not offend any members of Carolyn's community. She touched her bun, making sure her thick hair had stayed in place. She'd used nearly half a can of hairspray on it that morning. She also had forgone any makeup, which seemed freeing. She used to worry about choosing the right colors of lipstick and eye shadow, but lately she felt most comfortable without any makeup at all.

"Madeleine!" Emma appeared beside her and grinned. "It's *gut* to see you!"

"It's nice to see you too, Emma." Madeleine touched her arm. "How are you? How's your ankle?"

"It's great!" She danced around. "See? It doesn't hurt at all. The ice and bandage really helped."

"Oh, that's great news." Madeleine touched Ruth's arm as well. "Do you know Ruth? She's my friend from work."

"*Ya*, I know Ruth." Emma smiled up at her.

"It's great to see you, Emma." Ruth nodded at her.

"How do you know Carolyn and Josh?" Emma asked.

"I work with Carolyn and Ruth at the hotel," Madeleine said.

"Oh." Emma nodded slowly. "You need to come by the farm.

One of our barn cats had another litter of kittens, and they are cute. I've been naming them. You can name one too. You can keep a couple of them if you want to. Do you like cats?"

"I do," Madeleine said. "I have cats living in the small barn on my property. In fact, I think there may be a new litter there too. You'll have to come and visit them someday."

"Oh *ya*. I'd love to see your kittens too." Emma glanced across the room. "There's my best friend, Esther. I better go. See you soon."

"How do you know Emma?" Ruth asked as Emma ran off.

"My property backs up to her father's," Madeleine explained. "Actually, my grandparents owned all of her father's property and sold it to him years ago."

"Oh *ya*. I had forgotten that."

Madeleine watched Emma meet up with another girl and walk over to her father.

Ruth's gaze moved across the room. "I see my son and his family over there. Would you like to meet them?"

"Oh, sure." Madeleine smiled. "I'd love to."

"Wonderful." Ruth led Madeleine across the room. "I can't wait for you to meet my family."

❦

Saul was talking with Marcus when he saw Emma and Esther rushing toward them.

"*Dat!*" Emma began, out of breath from running. "You'll never guess who's here!"

"Who?" Saul glanced at Marcus, who shrugged.

"Madeleine! She's here," Emma said.

"That's nice," Saul said.

"She asked how my ankle is, and she told me she was happy to see me," Emma continued. "I told her about the barn cats, and she said she has barn cats too. She wants me to come over and see her new kittens."

"Now, Emma," Saul began. "What did I tell you about leaving Madeleine alone?"

Emma frowned. "I know, *Dat.*"

"What did I say?" he asked again.

"I shouldn't bother her," Emma said, her voice lacking its previous enthusiasm.

"That's right," Saul said.

Emma turned to Esther. "Let's go help them serve the food."

"Okay!" Esther agreed.

The two girls headed to the kitchen.

Marcus sidled up to Saul. "Who's Madeleine?"

"She's the *Englisher* who lives in the *haus* in front of my property." He nodded toward where Madeleine was standing. "She's over there by Ruth Ebersol and her family."

Marcus looked toward the Ebersol family as Saul studied Madeleine. She looked different today. In fact, he almost didn't recognize her. Her dark hair was styled in a tight bun, and she was wearing a plain dark blue blouse and skirt. He was relieved to see her in appropriate clothing. At least she wouldn't give Emma the wrong idea about how a woman should dress.

"I take it that you finally got to meet her then?" Marcus asked.

"*Ya.*" Saul crossed his arms over his chest. "A few weeks ago, Emma fell and Madeleine came over to help her. I was in the shop and didn't hear Emma crying out."

"You never told me this." Marcus's eyes were wide with concern. "Was Emma hurt?"

"She sprained her ankle, but it healed up just fine. Madeleine told me how to care for it. She's a nurse."

"Oh. That's *gut* that Madeleine heard her."

"*Ya*, it was." Saul considered Emma's interest in Madeleine. "But I don't want Emma getting too friendly with this *Englisher*. I don't want her to influence Emma into thinking that it's a *gut* idea to leave the community."

"How would Madeleine do that?" Marcus looked incredulous. "She's just your neighbor."

"Right, but apparently Madeleine is Martha Stoltzfus's *grossdochder*. Martha's *dochder* left the community, and now Madeleine has come back. If Emma gets to know her better, she may influence Emma to leave."

"Just like your *bruder* did." Marcus finished his thought.

Saul sighed. "Exactly."

Marcus leaned over and lowered his voice. "Why don't you just say what you're really thinking? You're afraid she'll leave like Annie did."

Saul gave him a stiff nod. He couldn't admit the words out loud.

"Saul, you can't live in fear of that," Marcus said. "Emma is going to make her own decisions. You just keep doing what you're doing—being a *gut dat* to her. She'll make the right decisions. God has the perfect plan for her."

Saul prayed his best friend was right, but he couldn't stop that nagging fear at the back of his mind.

"Hi, Saul."

Saul turned and found Madeleine standing beside him. "Madeleine," he said with surprise. "Hi."

She stuck her hand out to Marcus. "Hi. I'm Madeleine Miller. I live next to Saul's farm."

"Nice to meet you." Marcus shook her hand. "I'm Marcus Smucker."

"Smucker." Madeleine tilted her head with surprise. "Are you related to the bishop?"

"*Ya*, I am, actually." Marcus nodded. "He's my *daadi*. I mean grandfather."

"I know what *daadi* means," Madeleine said with a smile. "My grandparents were Amish. They were Martha and Melvin Stoltzfus."

"You're living at your grandparents' house?" Marcus asked.

"That's right." Madeleine nodded. "I inherited it."

"I've seen you at Martha's *haus*. It's nice to finally meet you." Marcus turned toward Saul. "I'm going to go find my *fraa*. I'll see you both later." He nodded and then headed toward the other side of the room.

Saul wished his friend had stayed by his side. He had no idea what to say to Madeleine Miller.

"It's good to see you again, Saul," Madeleine began. "I spoke with Emma earlier. She said her ankle has healed nicely."

"*Ya*, she's all better now. *Danki* again for your help." He fingered his suspenders and tried to think of something else to say. "I didn't expect to see you at the wedding. I noticed you were talking to Ruth Ebersol. Do you know her and her family well?"

"I work with her at the Lancaster Grand Hotel." She glanced toward where Carolyn and Joshua were sitting and eating their wedding supper. "Carolyn also works with us."

"That's right," Saul said. "I remember Carolyn worked at the hotel."

Madeleine smiled at him, and her eyes were the color of his morning coffee. "Well, it was nice to see you again, Saul."

"*Ya*, it was nice to see you too," he said, repeating the sentiment.

"Take care." She gave him a little wave and then headed toward a corner where other *Englisher* guests were talking.

Saul studied Madeleine as she approached another guest and began to talk to her. He was surprised she had taken a moment to speak to him. That was friendly of her, but at the same time, he didn't like the idea of Emma getting to know Madeleine. She was much too worldly for his liking, and he needed to shield his precious daughter from the *Englisher* world. After all, Emma was the only family he had left.

EIGHT

Hannah stepped out onto the porch and breathed in the brisk October air. It was surreal to be back at the farm where she'd lived with her first husband, Gideon. This was the same home where Gideon had brought her after their wedding and where she'd had her three children. It was also on this property that Gideon had succumbed to his massive heart attack nearly seven years ago.

Although she'd enjoyed seeing Carolyn and Joshua's wedding, she'd felt a bit claustrophobic surrounded by the members of her former community. No one said anything outright about her excommunication, but the sad expressions people tossed her way, even those who were kind enough to speak to her, were overwhelming. She felt like an outcast in the home that had belonged to her not very long ago.

She descended the porch steps and gazed off toward the barns where Joshua's horses and animals were housed. Her husband's shiny European car seemed out of place inside the sea of buggies clogging the field beside the pasture. It almost seemed like an analogy for her life—she was a lone anachronism when she visited her former community.

"Hannah?"

She glanced up toward the porch to where her former mother-in-law, Barbie Glick, was staring down at her. Her stomach tightened at the sight of the older woman, who had criticized her both while she was married to Gideon and when she decided to leave the community to marry Trey.

"Barbie." Hannah worked to keep her voice even despite her anxiety. "Hello. It was a lovely wedding, wasn't it?"

"*Ya*, it was." Barbie's blue eyes bored into her. "What are you doing here?"

"I was invited." Hannah crossed her arms over her dark blue dress. "Carolyn invited me, Trey, and my children."

Barbie studied her. "Well, I'm glad that your *kinner* came. I like to see my *grosskinner* as often as I can, you know."

"And you also know that you're welcome to see them anytime. I've never kept them from you." Hannah stood her ground, despite her frayed nerves. "All you have to do is call me, and Trey or I will bring them to your house. Amanda drives now, and she can come over on her own as well."

"Fine, then." Barbie nodded and then disappeared into the house.

Hannah blew out a deep sigh when the woman was out of sight. She'd hoped to speak with Lillian, and she'd spotted her across the room a few times after the service. She'd tried to approach her, but each time she started to cross the room, another kind member of the community stopped Hannah to speak with her.

A group of young people was gathered by the horse barn. Amanda smiled and laughed while surrounded by her former school friends. Although Amanda and her boyfriend, Mike, weren't dressed in traditional Amish clothing, she seemed comfortable with her friends. Hannah searched the sea of young faces for Lily's.

"Hannah?" Trey approached her. "I was wondering where you went."

"I'm sorry I left abruptly, but I needed some air." She hugged her coat to her body. "I knew coming here would be difficult, but I didn't imagine just how difficult it would be."

"I'm sorry." Trey rubbed her shoulder. "I'd hoped it would go better. Do you want to leave?"

Hannah sighed. "I don't know. It seems like Andrew and Amanda are having a good time. I hate to pull them away from their friends."

"Mike brought his car, remember?" Trey asked gently. "You can tell them we're leaving and ask Mike to take Amanda and Andrew home. I'm certain it won't be a problem." He continued rubbing her shoulder. "I don't want you to feel like you need to stay here if you're not comfortable. You came and you congratulated Josh and Carolyn. We can go now, okay?"

Hannah hesitated and stared toward the group. *Is Lily over there? If so, will she talk to me? Will today be the day she finally forgives me?* At these thoughts, her hand moved to her abdomen, which had begun to protrude more in the last few weeks.

"You wanted to talk to Lily." Trey said her thoughts aloud. "You were hoping she would want to talk today, right?"

Hannah nodded.

Trey's gaze moved toward the group of young people. "Do you want me to see if she's there?"

"No." Hannah shook her head. "I can't ask you to get involved in this."

"Maybe it's time I get involved," he suggested.

"I think that might make it worse. She might accuse me of trying to bully her into talking with me." Hannah turned back toward the young people, and her eyes quickly found Amanda and Lillian talking off to the side. Lillian was talking while Amanda nodded. Beside them, Mike chatted with Leroy King, the boy Lillian liked.

"I don't know how much longer I can watch you suffer," Trey said. He stopped rubbing her shoulder and turned her toward him. "I worry about you and how it could affect our unborn child."

"I'll be fine." Hannah forced a smile as she looked up at him. "I promise you it will all be fine." She laced her fingers with his. "Let's go home."

"Did you say good-bye to the bride and groom?" he asked.

"I congratulated them earlier." Hannah nodded. "It's all right if we leave."

"Sounds good." Trey led her toward his car, which was parked near the younger people. They stopped close to where Amanda, Lillian, Mike, and Leroy were talking.

"Hi, *Mamm*." Amanda smiled over at them while Lillian's smile faded.

Hannah studied Lillian, who looked down at her shoes.

"We're going to head home," Trey said. "Mike, would you please bring Amanda and Andrew home?"

"Absolutely," Mike said.

Hannah continued to stare at Lillian, who moved her eyes from her shoes to a nearby leaf.

"Do you know where Andrew is?" Trey asked Amanda.

"*Ya.*" Amanda pointed toward the house. "He was with *Daadi* when I last saw him. I'll let him know you left, and I'll keep an eye out for him."

"Thank you," Trey said. "You all have fun, and we'll see you later."

"Lily," Hannah said while watching her daughter's eyes continue to look at anything but her. "Lily, please look at me."

Lillian scowled as she met her gaze. "What?"

"I'd like to speak to you in private before I leave." Hannah held her breath. *Please answer me, Lily. Talk to me!*

Lillian looked at Amanda, who gave her an encouraging expression.

"Fine." Lillian turned to Leroy. "I'll be right back."

Leroy nodded. "Take your time. I'm not going anywhere."

Hannah and Lillian walked past the car and moved behind the large barn that housed most of the horses. "How have you been?" Hannah asked when they stood together.

"I'm fine." Lillian pushed her glasses farther up on her nose and lifted her chin in defiance. "I'm a *gut* teacher, and the school board is very satisfied with my work with the scholars."

"I knew you would be a great teacher." Hannah smiled. "I'm so proud of you."

Lillian continued to scowl.

"I see you're still friends with Leroy King." Hannah attempted to pull Lillian into a conversation.

Lillian shrugged. "We're getting to know each other."

"It looks like Leroy and Mike get along. That's nice, *ya*? The four of you can do things together. Maybe you can all have a buddy day."

"Why are you here?" Lillian narrowed her eyes. "You know you don't belong here anymore."

Hannah winced at her daughter's cruel words. "That's not true. Carolyn asked me to come and bring Trey and your siblings. I have every right to be here. You know that. People who leave the community come back for special celebrations."

"I don't understand why you would want to come back." Lillian spat out the words as if they tasted bad. "Everyone probably feels sorry for you and wonders why you left. It's not good for you to be here. It's hard on everyone—especially me."

"It doesn't have to be hard on you, Lily." Hannah reached for Lillian's hand, but Lillian took a step back, out of her reach. "It doesn't have to be this difficult between us. We can repair what's broken, if you help me."

"No." Lillian shook her head. "That's not possible."

"Does that mean you'll never forgive me?" Hannah's voice was thick while she blinked through her tears.

"I don't think I can." Lillian shook her head. "I need to go. Leroy is waiting for me." She started to walk away.

"Lillian! Please wait. Just give me another minute." Although it wasn't customary for Amish women to discuss something this personal, she had to tell Lillian about her pregnancy. Perhaps this little life growing inside her would be the link they needed to repair their broken relationship. "Lillian, I need to tell you something. It's important."

"What?" Lillian faced her.

Hannah rested her hand on her belly. "I'd like for you to get to know your new sibling."

"You're–you're . . . ?" Lillian stuttered as her eyes widened.

Hannah nodded. "*Ya*, it's a miracle. I'm seeing a doctor who specializes in high-risk cases, and everything is fine so far. This is a tremendous blessing from the Lord. Trey and I are thrilled, and Amanda and Andrew are too."

Lillian's eyes glistened with tears. "I need to go." Her voice broke. She rushed away, leaving Hannah staring after her.

Hannah heaved a heavy sigh and then looked up at the clear blue sky. Tears sprinkled down her hot cheeks as she opened up her heart to God and allowed her most fervent prayer to spill out.

Please, God, help me find a way to prove to my daughter that I love her and need her back in my life. Please help Lillian find a way to accept her new sibling and forgive me. Lord, I miss her, and I love her. Please, God, help us.

⁓

Lillian didn't want to cry in front of her friends, especially Leroy. Things had been going well between them, and she didn't want to scare him away with her family issues. Even though he said he understood how she felt, he could never fathom the pain of her mother leaving the community and abandoning her.

She rushed past her friends, trying her best to avoid their confused stares, and she quickly hurried up the porch steps.

"Lily?" Amanda called after her. "Lillian?"

Lillian headed into the house and up the steps toward her former bedroom, the room she'd shared with her twin until her mother left the community nearly two years ago and she'd moved in with her grandparents. She opened the door and found the room clogged with boxes. A lonely chair sat in the corner by the window. She weaved past the boxes, sank into the chair, and allowed her tears to flow.

"Lily." Amanda appeared in the doorway and closed the door behind her. "What happened?" Her twin pushed a box marked BOOKS over to Lillian and sat on it.

Lillian wiped her eyes. "I'm fine."

"No, you're not." Amanda reached over and touched Lillian's leg. "Talk to me. I'm not leaving until we talk."

"You know what's wrong. I'm the one who was left behind while you, *Mamm*, and Andrew went off and started your new *English* lives." Lillian took a deep breath in an attempt to stop her raging emotions. "If it wasn't for *Mammi* and *Daadi*, I'd be completely on my own."

"You're not alone. You still have us."

"No, it's not the same." Lillian sniffed. "No one could ever possibly understand how I feel. You have no idea how hard it is to watch other families together at every church service." She gestured widely. "I'm always the one people pity. People shake their heads and say they're very sorry that I've lost *mei dat* . . . and *mei mamm*."

"That's not true, Lily. You haven't lost *Mamm*." Amanda frowned. "We've been through this too many times. I've told you over and over again that *Mamm* talks about you all the time. She misses you. We all do. We'd love for you to come by and visit us."

"No." Lillian shook her head. "It's not right for *Mamm* to be with that man."

"You should give Trey a chance. He's a wonderful man, and he's good to *Mamm*. You'd really like him if you got to know him," Amanda continued. "And you'd love the bed-and-breakfast. It's been your choice to stay away from us."

Lillian scowled. "I can't believe you're saying this to me." She pointed toward the mountain of boxes. "This was our room, the one we shared for the first sixteen years of our lives. This is where we belonged. This was our home."

"*Ya*, it was our home, but things change. We have to learn to adapt to the path God chooses for us." Amanda pointed toward her chest. "I've chosen to go to school and become a veterinarian. You've chosen to stay Amish. We can still be sisters and a family. And you need to forgive *Mamm*. She loves you. That will never change."

Lillian glanced out the window and saw Trey's flashy car steering down the rock driveway toward the road. "I can't believe she and Trey are going to . . ." Her words trailed off. She couldn't finish her thought out loud.

"They're having a baby." Amanda tapped Lillian's leg. "Look at me."

Lillian met her twin's gaze. "You're okay with this?"

"*Ya*." Amanda smiled. "We both know *Mamm* had problems with Andrew and almost lost him. She's thrilled this pregnancy seems to be going well. And God is giving Trey another chance to have a child. He lost his first wife and daughter so tragically, but now he can be a *dat* again."

Amanda was right. God did give second chances. And Lillian had been sorry when she'd heard Trey's wife and daughter had died from carbon monoxide poisoning.

"This baby is a gift from God, and we need to embrace it. We're going to have another sibling." Amanda's expression became serious. "You need to be a part of this."

"I don't know if I can." Lillian's voice was thick with emotion again. "I don't know how I can just act like this is okay. This is just so . . . I don't know." She couldn't put her thoughts into words. Her heart was on her sleeve and her emotions were raw. She wanted to cry, scream, and curl up in a ball like one of the cats that lived in her grandparents' barn.

"It will be okay." Amanda gently squeezed Lillian's arm. "Just open your heart and let God lead you. Give him a chance to heal your heartache."

Lillian began to sob, and Amanda hugged her. Lillian rested her head on her sister's shoulder and prayed that God would help her sort through her confusing and painful emotions.

⚬⚭⚬

Trey glanced over at Hannah as they drove home. He couldn't stand to see her cry. He wanted to fix everything. He wanted to make her happy, as happy as she was on their wedding day. He needed God's help to figure out how to make that happen.

"Do you want to talk about it?" He slowed the car to a stop at a red light.

She shook her head and sniffed.

The light changed to green, and he accelerated through the intersection. He racked his mind for something to say to lighten her mood.

"The service was beautiful." He gave her another sideways glance and found her staring out the window. "It was very different from our ceremony. It was strange to not see any flowers or candles."

She nodded but didn't turn toward him.

"I also found it fascinating that all the women in the wedding party were dressed the same, even the bride," he added.

"Carolyn made the dresses," Hannah said. "The bride always chooses the color and makes the dresses." Her voice was raw with emotion, but he was happy to hear her speak.

"Really?" he asked with a smile.

"*Ya.*" Hannah swiped her hand over her pink cheeks. "When I married Gideon, my dresses were blue too."

"Were you married at the same house?" he asked.

"No." She shook her head. "We were married at my parents' house, and then we lived with them for about six months before we moved into that house."

"I never knew that." He steered the car through another intersection. "I also found it interesting to not have any music during the service, but I quickly realized you don't need music. The ceremony was still nice without it." He paused and then considered the food. "And the meal was delicious. That was superb chicken with stuffing. And I really enjoyed the mashed potatoes, gravy, pepper cabbage, cooked cream of celery . . ."

"That's the traditional meal." Hannah cleared her throat and turned back toward the window.

They sat in silence as he drove the rest of the way to the bed-and-breakfast. After parking in the driveway, Trey turned and took her hands in his.

"Hannah," he began, "I know you're hurting. It's apparent in your beautiful green eyes, and it's breaking my heart."

She sniffed as fresh tears filled her eyes. "I thought telling her about the baby would help, but it only made her run away from me. I don't know what else to do, Trey. I've tried everything."

"I know you have. It's time for you to step back and let God work on Lily. Let her come to you."

"What if she doesn't?" Hannah asked, her voice cracking as the tears spilled down her cheeks.

"She will. I know she will." He pulled her into his arms and held her as she cried. The sound of her sobs shattered his heart. He had to do something. He would talk to Lillian. When the moment was right, he'd have a heart-to-heart with her and hopefully make her realize that she needed her mother as much as Hannah needed her.

NINE

Madeleine stood in her bedroom. She held a chip with shades of yellow against the wall and then one with blues. A knock sounded, and she jumped with a start.

With the paint chips still in her hand, she went to the back door and pulled it open.

"Emma." Madeleine smiled at her through the storm door. "What a pleasant surprise."

"Do you like cookies?" Emma held up a plate. "These are chocolate chip. I just made them. Would you like to share them with me?"

"I'd love to. Please come in." Madeleine held the storm door open. "Would you like some milk to go with the cookies?"

"*Ya.*" Emma moved into the kitchen and sat at the table. "That's how I always eat *kichlin*," Emma announced.

"I agree." Grinning, Madeleine nodded her head, placed the paint chips on the table, and gathered a half gallon of milk and two glasses. "Did you just get home from school?" She poured the milk, returned the carton to the refrigerator, and fetched two small plates from a cabinet.

"I got home a couple of hours ago. I took care of my chores

and then made the *kichlin*." Emma pointed toward the paint chips. "What are those?"

"Paint chips." Madeleine placed the glasses and plates on the table and sat down across from Emma. "You use them when you're choosing paint for a room. You decide which shade you like, and then you go back to the store and ask the paint people to mix up the color for you. You have to figure out, of course, how much paint you need." She bit into a cookie and closed her eyes. "These are *appeditlich*, Emma." She opened her eyes and found the little girl staring at her. "What's wrong?"

"You're going to paint *mei mammi's haus*?" Emma frowned. "You shouldn't change her *haus*. That's not right. She wouldn't like that."

Madeleine studied the girl, and her heart warmed. She suddenly lost any interest in painting the walls. "You were close with *mei mammi*, weren't you?"

"I visited her every day. We cooked together and worked in her garden. She taught me how to make a dress." Emma pointed to her green dress. "I made this dress using *Mammi's* instructions."

"You're a great baker and a wonderful seamstress." Madeleine imagined her grandmother standing at the counter teaching Emma how to make cookies and pies, and her eyes filled with tears. She dabbed at her eyes with a finger and took another bite of her cookie.

"Madeleine?" Emma asked. "Are you *bedauerlich*?"

"No, no. I was just thinking of *mei mammi*. She was a special lady." Madeleine smiled and finished the cookie. "You did a wonderful job on these. Did your *dat* help you make them?"

Emma shook her head. "No, he's working in his shop. He's always working. I'm allowed to bake and cook easy things by myself, but he helps me with things that are harder. He lets me make *kichlin* as long as I'm careful." She lifted a cookie and examined it. "I'm always careful."

"I bet you are." Madeleine dunked a second cookie into the milk and then took a bite. Saul was a good father to Emma. She wished her father had been around to do things with her like Saul did with Emma.

"Why weren't you at *Mammi's* funeral?" Emma's words were gentle and not accusatory.

The question was simple, but the words weighed heavily on Madeleine's heart. "I was traveling back from overseas when she passed away, and I missed the service too."

Emma tilted her head. "Where were you?"

"I was in Europe when it was time to come home." Madeleine took another bite of her cookie. "I had to go for work, and I didn't even know *Mammi* was ill. I found out too late."

"Oh." Emma nodded. "Have you traveled a lot?"

"I was in the air force, and I went all around the world."

"You were a nurse in the air force?" Emma asked.

"That's right." Madeleine smiled. "I went to school to become a nurse and then joined the air force."

"Your *mamm* left the church, and that's why you aren't Amish, right?" Emma asked.

"That's true." Madeleine finished her second cookie. They really were good.

"Why did she leave?"

"My *mamm* doesn't talk about it much, but it was because she met my father. He wasn't Amish, and she fell in love with him. She wanted to get married, and so she had to leave the church." Madeleine paused. "My *mamm* was in the military too. That's why

I joined after I became a nurse. I wanted to serve my country like my mother did."

"*Mei mamm* died when I was four. I don't remember her very well."

"I'm sorry to hear that," Madeleine said. "I never knew my father."

"You didn't?" Emma's eyes were wide. "Why not?"

"He left before I was born, and I only had my *mamm* growing up. It's difficult when you have only one parent. But at the same time, I felt blessed that I had a mother who loved me. I know your dad loves you. I could tell by the way he was worried about you when you fell."

"*Ya*, he's a *gut dat*. He just works too hard." Emma bit into her second cookie.

"He has to work hard so he can provide for you." Madeleine took a sip of her milk. "My *mamm* had to work a lot, and I was here with my *mammi* and *daadi* in the summers. I did the same things you did with *Mammi*. We sewed, worked in the garden, baked, cooked, and sang. I also went to church with her."

"Just like I did." Emma smiled as she chewed another bite. "That means you were Amish when you were with *Mammi*."

"Right. I even dressed Amish. I had my own dresses and aprons that I kept in the spare room." Madeleine pointed toward her former bedroom. "I left my *English* clothes in my suitcase, and I wore a prayer covering and apron."

"Do you like to cook?"

"Yes, I do." Madeleine pointed toward a cabinet. "I have all of my *mammi's* cookbooks."

"Oh, you do?" Emma's eyes lit up. "We should cook together sometime. Would you like to do that?"

"I'd love it. You let me know when you want to cook. I usually work at a big hotel Tuesdays, Thursdays, and Fridays, but sometimes I go in for extra hours if my coworkers need to have a day off." Madeleine pointed toward the window. "If you see my truck outside, then you know I'm here. You're welcome to come over here anytime, as long as your *dat* says it's okay."

"Great." Emma ate another bite and then tilted her head again. "My *dat* said you might change *Mammi's haus* to make it like an *Englisher haus*." She frowned. "Are you going to change her *haus*?" Emma picked up the paint chips. "Are you really going to paint the rooms? And add electricity and update the heating system?"

Madeleine shook her head. "The coal stove is enough to heat the little house for now."

"You don't mind having to check the stove twice a day?"

Madeleine shrugged. "Well, I did have to get used to cleaning out the ashes and taking them down to the creek. It's a lot of work, and I had to learn how to adjust it right so that it runs all night long. Once I got that straight, I really started to appreciate the coal heat. It's cozy, and it's economical. I don't think I'm going to add electricity, but I was thinking about painting the rooms."

"I hope you don't paint, unless you paint them white again," Emma said. "The walls should be white."

Madeleine studied the girl. This meant a lot to her. Emma had been close to her grandmother, and Madeleine wanted to respect her wishes. *I can't bear the thought of breaking this sweet little girl's heart.* "Okay. I won't paint if that makes you *froh*."

Emma giggled. "It's funny hearing you speak *Dietsch*."

"Why is that funny?" Madeleine asked with a grin. "I've been told my accent isn't too bad."

"No, it's not bad, but you're wearing jeans and a sweatshirt, and your hair isn't covered."

"Does that mean an *Englisher* shouldn't speak *Dietsch?*" Madeleine asked. "I don't think that's fair."

"You're not a regular *Englisher*, though. You wear *English* clothes and drive a truck, but you don't have electricity."

"I guess I am unusual."

"I saw television once." Emma lowered her voice. "*Mei dat* doesn't know. I was at my friend Rachel's *haus*, and we went to visit her *English* cousins. We actually watched a television show. It was funny."

Madeleine felt like the girl's confidante, and she loved it. "Your secret is safe with me, Emma. I won't tell anyone."

"*Danki.*" Emma picked up one more cookie. "Do you miss electricity? I've heard *Englishers* can't live without it."

"I don't really miss electricity too much. I like using lanterns, and I never watched much television. But I do miss my computer a little."

"Oh." Emma sipped her milk. "And you like your phone, too, right?"

"I do." Madeleine nodded. "But you also use a phone, don't you? The only difference is that I can carry mine with me."

"That's true." Emma lifted her glass. "Do you like to toast? My friend Rachel likes to say a toast. She learned it from her *English* cousins."

Madeleine lifted her glass. "What should we toast?"

"New friends." Emma tapped her glass against Madeleine's.

"Yes, to new and special friends." Madeleine laughed. She was thankful for her special new friend, Emma Beiler.

∽

Saul bowed his head in silent prayer later that evening and then filled his plate with meat loaf and mashed potatoes.

"How was your day?" he asked as he glanced over at Emma.

"It was *gut*." Emma passed the green beans. "I made *kichlin* and took them over to Madeleine's *haus*. We sat and ate them, and we talked about *Mammi*. She would dress Amish and speak *Dietsch* when she stayed with *Mammi*."

Saul studied Emma as he frowned. "You went to see Madeleine?"

Emma nodded. "*Ya*, we had a nice time. She said she was going to paint the rooms, but I talked her out of it."

"Emma, I told you to leave her alone. I know you heard me because you repeated it back to me." How would he ever overcome his daughter's stubborn streak? He opened his mouth to yell at her and then stopped. He didn't want to make her cry tonight. She yearned for a female adult with whom to spend her time, but he preferred her female role model not be an *Englisher*.

Emma's smile evaporated. "I'm sorry, *Dat*. I wanted to bake, and I decided to take some cookies over to Madeleine. She was very *froh*, and we had a very nice visit." She paused for a moment. "We're going to cook and bake together. She has *Mammi's* cookbooks." Emma's face radiated with her excitement. "She served in the air force. She said her *mamm* was in the military too."

Saul gnawed his lower lip, then pointed to the table. "You should stay on this farm, not go spend time with an *Englisher*."

"But you're always working." Emma's eyes suddenly widened as if she realized she'd been disrespectful to him. "I'm sorry, *Dat*. I know you have to work so you can provide for me." She quickly changed the subject to her friends at school and spent the rest of supper telling him about what she learned and all the fun she had on the playground.

After supper Emma took care of cleaning up the dishes, and Saul stepped out onto the back porch. He shivered in the night air while he looked toward Madeleine's place. A single light burned at the back of the house.

It didn't make sense for her to live there. She wouldn't stay.

He knew one thing for certain—he needed to shield his daughter from more heartache. He had to keep Emma away from Madeleine before the *Englisher* put the house on the market and left.

Saul stepped back into the kitchen, where Emma was drying a pot. "Emma, you need to spend your afternoons here at our farm. Do you understand me?"

Emma's pale blue eyes were round as she nodded. "*Ya*, I do, *Dat*."

"*Danki*," Saul said. "I'm going to work for a little bit. I'll be in my shop." He stepped back outside and looked over at Madeleine's house one last time as he walked. He'd talk to her tomorrow and make it clear that she was to stay away from his daughter.

Madeleine stepped out onto her porch the morning after Emma's visit. She hefted her tote bag farther up on her shoulder just before she suddenly remembered her lunch was still on the kitchen counter. After rushing back into the house, she grabbed her lunch bag, shoved it into her tote bag, and glanced at the clock. She gasped. She had to hurry or she was going to be late for work.

As she stepped back outside, she saw Emma hurrying by on

her way to school. "Hi, Emma!" Madeleine called. "Have a great day at school."

"Hi, Madeleine!" Emma waved and kept rushing past toward her friends, who were waiting at the corner.

Madeleine descended the porch steps and headed for her truck.

"Madeleine."

She turned as Saul approached. "Oh. Good morning, Saul. It's nice to see you." She opened the driver's side door and tossed her tote bag into the truck. "I'm late for work, and I have to run. I hope you have a nice day."

"Wait." He held up his hand. "Do you have just a couple of minutes?"

His brown eyes seemed determined, and she couldn't bring herself to say no to him.

"Sure." She closed the truck door and faced him. "What did you want to talk about?"

Saul heaved a heavy sigh. "Emma told me she visited you yesterday."

"She brought over some cookies she'd made, and we shared the cookies and glasses of milk." Madeleine smiled. "We had a wonderful time. Emma's a very special little girl. You should be proud of her."

"I'm not comfortable with her spending time with you." Saul's words were simple, but they sliced through her like carving knives.

"Excuse me?" she asked.

"I'm not comfortable with her spending time with you," he repeated. "I don't want her to come over and cook with you, either."

"I don't understand." Madeleine studied him. "I thought Amish weren't supposed to judge others. You don't even know me."

"Exactly." He pointed toward the house. "I don't know why you're here or how long you'll decide to stay. I don't want her to be upset if you suddenly sell the house and move away."

Madeleine pointed to the house too. "This was my grandparents' home. I'm not planning on moving anytime soon."

"I know how you *Englishers* are. Your plans can change minute to minute, especially because you were in the military. You have no roots." Saul crossed his arms over his wide chest. "Emma doesn't need to get to know you or find out more about your life. I don't want her visiting here, and you don't need to come and visit her at our *haus*. It's best if we keep our distance. *Englishers* and Amish shouldn't mix anyway. The results are never *gut*."

Her spirit deflated as she stared at her neighbor. "I'm sorry to hear you say that. Emma and I have a lot in common."

"Really?" He shook his head. "I find that difficult to believe."

"It's true. Emma and I both loved my *mammi*."

He gave her a stiff nod. "Martha was a *gut* woman."

"Yes, she was." Madeleine held her head high despite her disappointment. "And that's not all. Emma said she lost her mother when she was four. I never knew my *dat*. I know what it's like to have only one parent. Emma and I could learn a lot from each other."

He paused, and for a quick moment, she thought she saw his expression warm. However, he remained stoic.

"I'm her father, and I don't want her to visit you. Please respect my wishes." Saul turned and started back toward his house.

Madeleine stared after him. How could a man who was so warm to his daughter be so frigid to her? She'd never been so insulted in her life. Disappointment and heartache flooded her as she climbed into her truck, started the engine, gripped the wheel, and drove toward the hotel.

TEN

M adeleine rushed into the break room and stowed her tote bag and lunch before pulling on her apron and name tag.

"Madeleine?" Ruth stepped into the room. "I was beginning to worry about you."

"I've been running late all morning." Madeleine shook her head and checked her hair in the mirror next to the lockers. "It's just been one of those mornings when everything goes wrong. My alarm didn't go off, so I got up late, which is unusual for me. I normally wake up before the alarm." She frowned. "And then I had a run-in with my neighbor."

"You had a run-in with your neighbor?" Ruth crossed the room and stood in front of her. "Do you mean Saul Beiler?"

"Yes, I mean Saul Beiler." Madeleine scowled. "He is the most coldhearted, cruel person I've ever met. I always thought all Amish people were tolerant of *Englishers*, but I guess that's not true in his case." She started for the door. "I'm sure Gregg is upset that I'm not cleaning yet."

"Wait," Ruth said. "You have a minute to talk."

Madeleine stopped and faced her. "What is there to talk about?"

"Sit with me for a minute." Ruth pointed toward the table, and they sat down across from each other. "What happened with Saul?"

"Emma came to visit me yesterday," Madeleine said. "She brought me cookies, and we talked for a while. She's a lovely young lady."

Ruth nodded. "*Ya*, she is."

"Emma asked me if we could cook together, and I told her I have my *mammi's* cookbooks. She loved the idea of our using them together." Madeleine ran her finger over the wood grain on the table as she spoke. "I realized Emma was very close to my *mammi*. We have some other things in common too. I really enjoyed talking to her. She's very mature for her age. I assume that's because she lost her mother when she was young."

"I'm certain that's why," Ruth agreed.

"This morning I was leaving for work, and Saul came over just as I was about to get into my truck. He told me he doesn't want Emma spending any time with me."

Ruth's expression was unreadable.

"He basically said that, because I'm an *Englisher*, I could leave anytime, and he doesn't want Emma to get attached to me and then wind up hurt." Madeleine grimaced. "I haven't done anything to make him think I'd hurt her. I don't understand why an Amish person would be so judgmental to assume things about me that aren't true. I would never deliberately hurt anyone, especially a sweet, innocent little girl."

"It's not you." Ruth frowned.

Madeleine studied Ruth's expression. "You know something."

"I do." Ruth rested her hands on the table. "Saul has been hurt."

"I have too." Madeleine folded her arms over her chest. "But I don't treat people the way he does. He really offended me."

"I don't think you understand," Ruth began. "His wife died, but she didn't die seven years ago."

"What? I'm not sure what you're saying, Ruth. You've lost me."

"Annie didn't die seven years ago," Ruth said. "She left Saul and Emma."

Madeleine gaped at Ruth. "She left him? I didn't think Amish divorced."

"Normally, we don't, but sometimes it happens. We just don't talk about it because it's against our beliefs."

"What happened?" Madeleine asked.

"Annie left Saul and moved to the same former Amish community in Missouri where, from what I heard, her boyfriend had gone several years before. He came back to get her once he had settled and established his life there." Ruth shook her head. "Saul was devastated. Emma was only four years old."

"What a minute." Madeleine held her hand up. "Saul's wife had a boyfriend? How does that work?"

"I believe Annie was in love with this other man before she married Saul, but he left the community."

"Does that mean she married Saul simply because he was willing to marry her?" Madeleine asked.

"That's right." Ruth nodded. "And they had Emma together. But then it all fell apart when her boyfriend came back for her. Annie left Saul, divorced him, and I assume she married this other man."

"Oh no." Madeleine gasped. "That's heartbreaking. Emma thinks her mother died. She has no idea what really happened."

"That's right. And because our community doesn't talk about

divorce, Saul has been able to keep the truth from her." Ruth continued to frown. "I heard Saul received a letter last year telling him Annie died in an accident. I assume that's why he started dating again. He was seeing Carolyn for a while, but she married Joshua, as you know."

"Now it all makes sense," Madeleine said. "He doesn't trust me because he thinks I'll leave like Annie did. Like my mother did."

"I can understand his fear, even though I know you would never deliberately hurt Emma."

Madeleine considered this. "I guess he doesn't trust women at all. I don't blame him, but it's sad he feels that way." She paused and thought about Saul and his sweet daughter. "I'll miss Emma, but I can't go against him."

"That's a *gut* plan." Ruth pushed back her chair and stood. "We'd better get to work."

"Thank you, Ruth." Madeleine followed her to the door. "I'm glad I know the truth."

"You're welcome." Ruth touched Madeleine's arm. "Please keep it to yourself. I only know because I'm close friends with Sylvia Smucker's mother. Sylvia is married to Saul's best friend, Marcus. I'm not certain who in the community knows what really happened with Annie. He doesn't talk about her at all, and I don't want word to get back to him."

"I understand. I'll keep it to myself." Madeleine walked to the supply closet. As she filled her cart with fresh towels, she thought about Saul and Emma. She was sorry to hear how hurt Saul had been. She prayed that somehow he would see she'd never hurt him or his daughter.

Saul guided his horse up the driveway leading to Marcus's farm. He stopped the buggy in front of the wood shop where Marcus created the dining room tables and chairs he sold to local stores. After hopping out of the buggy, Saul crossed the driveway to the shop and wrenched open the door. He found his best friend sanding a long table.

Marcus removed his respirator and smiled. "Saul. *Wie geht's?* What brings you here this morning?"

"I was in the area, and I thought I'd stop by." Saul leaned against the workbench and studied the table. "That is a *schee* table. Your work gets more and more impressive. Pretty soon it will be almost as *gut* as mine," he teased, and Marcus chuckled.

Marcus shook his head. "You're avoiding my question. What brings you over here on a Thursday morning? You never stop by during the week unless you need something or something is wrong."

Saul crossed his arms over his middle. "I can't concentrate on my work. I think I made a mistake, and I need to talk to someone. I suppose you'll do."

Marcus laughed again and took two bottles of water from the small cooler under his bench. "Here. Take a sip, and then tell me what's bothering you."

"*Danki.*" Saul took a long gulp and then wiped his mouth. "I told you Emma likes to talk to my *Englisher* neighbor."

"Madeleine Miller." Marcus nodded. "I remember her from the wedding. She seemed pleasant."

Saul explained how Emma had spent the previous afternoon with Madeleine and wanted to cook with her. He also told Marcus about the conversation he'd had with Madeleine earlier in the day. "I told her I don't want Emma over at her *haus*, and I don't want her to come to see Emma at *mei haus*, either."

Marcus grimaced.

"You think that was too much, huh?" Saul asked. "I crossed a line, didn't I?"

"I don't know." Marcus shook his head. "I can't judge you." He paused. "How do you feel about what you said?"

"I think I may have been too abrupt with her." Saul rubbed his temple as he remembered the hurt expression on Madeleine's face. He could tell his words had completely crushed her. Guilt soaked through him. How could he be that cold and cruel to that young lady? "I'm just very confused. Parenting all alone is just too much for me sometimes. I don't know if I'm *gut* at being a *dat*."

"Of course you are."

"I'm worried about Emma. I want her to make the right choices and not leave the community like *mei bruder* did." Saul gripped the bottle of water. "But I don't know if I'm holding her too close or pushing her away. How do I find the right balance, where I'm not pushing her away *or* smothering her?"

"You need to trust God to lead her down the right path. You just raise her the best way you can, the best way you know how, and leave the rest to God." Marcus gulped another drink of water. "You worry too much. You're a *gut* parent, just like your parents were. They are the best examples you can follow."

"But *I* need to lead her down the right path. I have to be actively involved in her life, and I have to make sure she makes the right decisions." Saul shook his head. "I have to do more than my parents. They couldn't convince *mei bruder* to stay."

"His decision to leave wasn't their fault." Marcus leaned forward on the table he was building. "Stop being so hard on yourself.

It's not your fault Annie left, either. Stop punishing yourself for Annie's and your *bruder's* decisions to leave."

Saul nodded, even though he didn't agree with his friend's words. He had to do all the right things to convince Emma to stay Amish. But what exactly were those right things? He needed to pray more and ask God for the right words to say to Emma. He needed answers. He had to know how to be the best parent he could be—for her.

"How are your projects going this week?" Marcus asked. "Are you still drowning in cabinet orders?"

"I'm finally getting caught up." Saul lifted his hat and raked his hand through his thick hair. "I still need to find a way to hire an assistant. I need to find a way to stay more organized with all the orders."

"I know what you mean. I'm considering hiring an apprentice. The furniture stores are calling me every day now." Marcus tapped the table. "After this one, I have three more to make before I'm caught up."

"You do fantastic work. I'm sure an apprentice would be happy to learn from you."

"You too," Marcus countered. "You're the best cabinetmaker in the county."

"No, not really." Saul shook his head. "I've seen better."

"Marcus?" Sylvia appeared in the doorway. "Oh, hi, Saul. How are you?"

"I'm well, Sylvia." Saul nodded. "How are you?"

"Fine, fine. I saw your horse and buggy, and I was wondering who was visiting." Sylvia smoothed her hands over her apron. "Would you like to stay for lunch?"

"Oh no." Saul shook his head. "I don't want to impose."

"Don't be *gegisch*, Saul." Sylvia smiled. "We have plenty. Come and join us. We'd love to have you."

Saul glanced at Marcus, who nodded.

"Absolutely. Have lunch with us." Marcus started for the door. "I'm starved."

As Saul followed Marcus and Sylvia to their house, he prayed God would someday bless him with a wife who would be a good mother to Emma and a loyal helpmate to him.

Madeleine steered her pickup truck into her driveway that afternoon. She'd spent the entire day thinking about Saul and Emma and wondering what she could do to help them. His marriage wasn't any of her business, but she couldn't help thinking of him. She knew what it was like to feel abandoned. And even though she and Travis were never married, after pledging her heart and her future to him and then losing him tragically, failing him, she was afraid she could never love anyone again—or let anyone love her. Was that how Saul felt? Did he also feel unworthy of love?

Madeleine killed the engine and yanked her key from the ignition. She gathered up her tote bag and headed for the back porch. As she climbed the steps, her phone began to ring. She dug it out of her bag and found her mother's number on the screen.

"Hi, Mom," Madeleine said as she held the phone to her ear.

"How was your day?" Mom asked.

"Not that great," Madeleine admitted with a sigh.

"What's wrong? I haven't heard you sound this depressed since you moved to Paradise."

Madeleine shared the story of her visit with Emma, her

heartbreaking encounter with Saul, and then her conversation with Ruth.

"I've never been accused of being a bad person, Mom." Madeleine sank onto the porch swing. "You know I always believe the best in people, and I try to consider others' feelings. It hurts to hear someone say I would deliberately break a child's heart. How could he say that about me?"

"Oh, Maddie." Her mother's voice was warm. "I don't think his anger and disappointment were directed at you. From what you've told me, I think he's hurting because of what his wife did to him and their child. He's afraid his daughter will be hurt again. All you can do is respect his wishes and wait for him to come to you. Maybe he'll realize you're the best neighbor he could hope to have."

"You think so?" Madeleine asked as she ran her fingers over the cold armrest. Her mother's encouraging words gave her a glimmer of hope. Maybe she could convince Saul she was a good person.

"Of course I do," Mom insisted. "You have a wonderful heart. People see that as soon as they get to know you. But you worry about what people think of you. Even in kindergarten, you came home in tears when someone didn't like you. You always wanted everyone to be your friend. Don't give up hope. Saul will see what his daughter sees in you, and you'll wind up good friends."

"Before meeting my friends at the hotel, I did think the Amish tried to stay away from *Englishers*. And for the first eight months I was here, I took that to heart and didn't even introduce myself to Saul." Madeleine stared toward Saul's house as she spoke. "Do you think he'll want to be friends with me, even if he changes his mind about me?"

"My mother had plenty of *English* friends. She used to sew for the *English* neighbors. She had her own seamstress business. I think you helped her with her sewing a few summers, didn't you?"

"That's right. I remember neighbors coming in to see *Mammi* and dropping off their clothes. She taught me how to hem trousers one summer." Madeleine hoped her mother was right. "I don't know why this is bothering me so much. I don't even know him."

"You just want him to know the truth about you—that you're a good person."

Madeleine sighed. "You're absolutely right. Thanks." She stood and unlocked her door. "How's Jack doing?" She stepped inside and started unpacking her tote bag.

"He's fine." Her mother launched into a long discussion of her stepfather's business and how busy they were.

"Well, I should let you go," Madeleine finally said. "Thanks for calling."

"It was good talking to you. Just pray for Saul. Everything will be fine," Mom insisted.

"I will." Madeleine disconnected the call and sent up a prayer for the man she hardly knew.

ELEVEN

Madeleine was flipping through cookbooks the following Monday afternoon when a knock sounded. She went to the back door and found Emma standing on the porch with a basket in her hand.

Regret washed over Madeleine as she studied the little girl's eager smile. She pulled the storm door wide open and leaned against the door frame. "Hi, Emma."

"Hi." Emma lifted the basket, revealing bright red apples. "I thought we could make an apple pie. We can use *Mammi's* recipe. I remember which cookbook it's in."

Madeleine hesitated while she internally debated what to do. She wanted to let the little girl in and spend the rest of her afternoon cooking with her. However, Saul's instructions were explicit—Emma wasn't permitted to spend time with Madeleine either in Madeleine's house or at his house.

"Emma, I would love to cook with you, but your father told me he doesn't want you spending time with me. I'm sorry." Madeleine couldn't stop her frown.

Emma's eyes widened. "He told you that?"

"Yes, he did." Madeleine nodded. "He came to visit me last

Thursday before I left for work. He asked me not to spend time with you. I'm not allowed to come to your house, and he doesn't want you here."

"He told me I shouldn't bother you, but I didn't think he really meant it if we could be friends." The disappointment in Emma's expression caused Madeleine's heart to crumble.

Madeleine recalled her conversation with Saul and tried to think of a way to summarize it without causing Emma more disappointment or hurt. "I think he's afraid that you and I might become close friends and then I might move again."

"You're moving already?" Emma gasped.

"No, no, *no*," Madeleine emphasized the word. "I'm not planning to move, but your *dat* doesn't want you to get close to me and then feel bad if I do move."

"But you're not moving?" she asked.

Madeleine shook her head.

"That means it's okay, right?" Emma's smile was back.

Madeleine paused. "I don't know, Emma. I don't want to upset your *dat*. It might be a good idea if you go home, sweetie."

Emma paused and then smiled again. "I know what would make him *froh*."

"What's that?"

"He would love it if we made him a special supper." She held up the basket. "We could also make apple pie for dessert. If we make him a meal, then he'll see that you're our friend. He'll say that I should visit you more often because we make him *appeditlich* meals. *Mei freind* Esther's *mamm* says the way to a man's heart is through his stomach."

Madeleine laughed and shook her head. "You don't give up, do you?"

"*Mei dat* calls me stubborn for a reason. What do you think?" Madeleine stepped aside to let Emma through. "Come on in."

"Wonderful!" Emma stepped through the mudroom and to the kitchen table, and Madeleine trailed behind her.

"I was thinking you could decide what we make for supper because I picked the dessert." Emma set the basket of apples on the table. "Does that sound like a *gut* idea?"

"That sounds like a perfect idea." Madeleine moved to the counter and pointed to a page in the cookbook she'd just opened before Emma arrived. "I was thinking of making spaghetti and meatballs. What do you think?"

"Oh *ya*. I've never made meatballs. I bet my *dat* will love that." Emma pushed a stool over to the counter and hopped up onto it. "What do we do first?"

"Let's see. I'll get out the ground beef and the spices. We have to mix it all up and then roll the meatballs." Madeleine pointed to the recipe. "You read the ingredients, and I'll pull them out."

Soon they were sitting side by side at the table, rolling out the meatballs and dropping them into a glass pan.

"This is fun." Emma grinned. "I like cooking with you."

"I like cooking with you too." Madeleine hoped Saul would forgive her for breaking his rule. "What's your *dat* doing today?"

"He's installing cabinets at a house over in Bird-in-Hand. He left me a note saying he'd be home by six." Emma hesitated a moment, then asked, "What was it like to grow up without a *dat*?"

"I didn't know any different." Madeleine considered the question. "I guess it's difficult to miss something you never had."

"Do you know what he looked like?"

Madeleine nodded. "My mother has photos of him. I have a

couple of photos from when they eloped and when they moved into their first apartment."

"What does *elope* mean?"

"It's when a couple gets married alone. They don't invite anyone to the wedding. Instead, they go to the city courthouse and get married in front of a judge."

"Oh." Emma considered this. "Do you look like your *dat*?"

"My mom once told me I have his hair and his eyes."

"That's like me with *mei mamm*. I have her hair and eyes too." Emma smiled up at Madeleine. "We have that in common."

Madeleine smiled back. "You're right."

"Where does your *mamm* live now?"

"She's in California," Madeleine said. "I used to live there too."

"I saw a map at school. California is really far away." Emma formed another ball.

"It is, but it's nice there. I liked living there." Madeleine thought about her mom. "My mother remarried when I was about twelve."

"I'm almost twelve, so you were my age," Emma said.

"That's true."

"How did you feel when your *mamm* remarried?"

"It was fine." Madeleine shrugged. "I was in the wedding, which was special. I was my mother's maid of honor."

Emma tilted her head and scrunched her nose. "What does that mean?"

"Oh, it's like being an attendant in the wedding. I was able to stand next to my mom during the service, and I held her bouquet of flowers." Madeleine gathered more of the meatball mixture in her hand. "I like my stepfather. His name is Jack, and he's really nice."

"Did your *mamm* have more *kinner* after she married him?" Emma asked.

"No, she said she was too old, and she was happy to have just me." Madeleine wondered why Emma had so many questions about her mother's second marriage.

"I'm hoping *mei dat* gets married again." Ah, there it was. Emma was thinking about her father.

Emma dropped another ball into the pan. "I'd like to be a big *schweschder.* Remember Carolyn from the wedding?"

"Yes, I do. I work with her at the hotel."

"She and *mei dat* were dating before she met Josh. I was hoping they would get married. She would've been a nice *mamm.*"

"I imagine your *dat* will find someone nice to marry, and you'll have a nice *mamm.*" Madeleine turned to look at Emma. "Don't give up hope yet. Your *dat* is young. He'll find someone nice to marry. I'm certain there are plenty of nice young ladies in the community who would jump at the chance to have a husband like your *dat.*"

"You think so?" Emma looked up at Madeleine.

"Of course I do." Madeleine added two more meatballs to the pan before the stove buzzed, indicating the oven was preheated. "Let's finish up these meatballs and then put them in the oven."

"Okay." Emma seemed to be thinking as she made her last two meatballs and then wiped her hands on a paper towel. "Do you ever wonder what it would've been like if your *dat* had stayed with your *mamm?*"

Madeleine was caught off guard by the question and took a moment to contemplate her response. "No, not really." She paused again. "I suppose I used to wonder why he didn't want to get to know me. But I never really thought about what would've happened if he stayed because I didn't know him. I used to make up stories about him when I was little, though."

"Really?" Emma asked. "What kind of stories?"

"Let's see." Madeleine chuckled to herself. "I used to tell my friends my father was an astronaut or a ship captain or an airplane pilot to make up excuses for why he wasn't around."

Emma laughed. "That's *gegisch*."

"Sometimes I imagined he was a king of a foreign country and that he would come to visit me and bring me lots of expensive presents." Madeleine dropped one more meatball into the pan. "I knew it was all pretend and I would never meet him."

"Have you ever met him or even talked to him on the phone?" Emma asked, her voice full of hopefulness.

"No, I haven't." Madeleine shrugged. "Really, it's okay. Jack has been like a father to me."

Emma was quiet for a moment. "Sometimes I wonder what life would've been like if my *mamm* had lived."

Madeleine reflected on the story Ruth had shared with her, and she tried her best not to frown as she stood, put the pan of meatballs into the oven, and set the timer on the oven. Then she turned back to Emma with a smile. Emma seemed to be thinking.

"I wonder if *mei mamm* and *dat* would've had more *kinner*," Emma finally said, her expression not sad but more curious. "I remember *mei mamm* a little bit."

"Do you?" Madeleine moved to the sink and started filling it with frothy water.

"Oh *ya*. She was *schee*." Emma touched her covering. "Just like *Dat* says, she had light brown hair like mine and light blue eyes like mine. *Dat* says she was the prettiest *maedel* in his youth group."

Madeleine smiled. "I imagine she was."

Madeleine began scrubbing the utensils and dishes they used for making the meatballs. She worked in silence for a minute or two. Emma seemed to be lost in thought again.

"Her name was Annie," Emma finally continued.

"That's a nice name."

"*Ya*, it is. Do you have a middle name?" Emma stood, grabbed a dish towel, and began drying a platter.

"I do." Madeleine placed a bowl in the drain board. "It's Dawn."

"Dawn." Emma repeated the name. "That's *schee*. Some of my friends have nicknames. Do you have a nickname?"

"My mother calls me Maddie."

"Maddie." Emma nodded. "I like that. May I call you Maddie?"

"Sure." Madeleine put the last utensil in the drain board and dried her hands. "Shall we start on the apple pie?"

"*Ya*! I can find the recipe." Emma dried the last spoon and hurried over to the cookbooks.

Madeleine put away the clean dishes and utensils and pulled out the supplies for the apple pie.

"I found the recipe." Emma began to read the ingredients, and Madeleine pulled them from the cabinets.

"I have a couple of premade crusts I was going to use for a pie." Madeleine pulled one of them out of the refrigerator. "It will save us some time."

Emma nodded. "That sounds like a *gut* idea."

"I'm glad you agree." Madeleine smiled.

Soon they were peeling and coring the apples and reminiscing about baking with Madeleine's grandmother. When the meatballs were done, Madeleine put them on top of the stove, and when the apples were ready, Emma had another question.

"Did you like being a nurse?" Emma asked.

"Yes, I did, but I was ready for a change. It's hard work and very stressful." Madeleine mixed their apples with the rest of the filling. After it was all combined and she had poured everything into the piecrust, she slipped the pie pan into the oven and then pulled a tin of cookies from one of her cabinets. "Should we have a snack?"

"*Ya*, let's do that." Emma took the milk from the refrigerator.

They sat down at the kitchen table and ate their cookies and drank milk while the aroma of meatballs and apple pie filled the kitchen.

"Do you want to get married and have a family someday?" Emma asked while they ate.

Madeleine nearly choked on the cookie. "You really get to the point, don't you, Emma?"

"Oh." Emma's eyes were wide. "Am I being too nosy? *Dat* tells me I'm too nosy sometimes."

"No, it's okay. I don't mind answering the question." Madeleine wiped her hands on a napkin. "I would like to get married and have a family someday if that's what God has in store for me."

"Oh," Emma said. "Have you ever had a special friend, someone you might want to marry?"

"Yeah, I have." Madeleine picked up another cookie. "I did have a special friend once, and we were going to get married."

"What happened?" Emma's eyes were full of curiosity.

"He died." Madeleine tried her best to ignore the way her voice thickened when she said the words out loud.

"Oh." Emma grimaced. "I'm sorry."

"*Danki*," Madeleine said, overwhelmed by the sympathy in Emma's expression.

"I bet you get sad and miss him," Emma said.

"I do. Some days are worse than others." Madeleine pointed toward a bag of yarn in the corner of the kitchen. "When I have bad days, I like to crochet. I picked up that yarn at the store the other day. I'm working on an afghan. I have a place to crochet in the spare room."

"Oh." Emma nodded with interest. "*Mammi* taught me how to crochet."

"She taught me too."

"I'm sorry you get sad sometimes." Emma frowned again. "That has to be hard since you're here alone."

"*Danki*, but I'm fine. I'm happy here, and that's what matters." She glanced at the clock. "Let's eat up our snack and then finish making supper. We'll put it all together, and then you can surprise your *dat* with a nice meal. We need to add the tomato sauce to the meatballs. I'll get the jar out of the pantry."

They finished their cookies and milk, and then Madeleine showed Emma how to cook spaghetti to go with the meatballs. By the time all the food was ready, it was close to five o'clock.

"You'd better get going," Madeleine said. "It's almost five."

"Oh no," Emma said. "I can't be late."

"I'll help you carry everything to your house." Madeleine pulled out serving platters and bowls and loaded up the meatballs with tomato sauce, spaghetti, and apple pie, first slicing one piece of pie for herself. "You can take most of the pie. I just want one piece." She pulled a gallon of vanilla ice cream out of the freezer. "Have you ever had apple pie with ice cream?"

"No." Emma's eyes were wide with excitement. "That sounds *appeditlich*."

"It is." Madeleine put a few scoops of ice cream into a refrigerator jar. "You can take some of this too." She put the ice cream and container of spaghetti into Emma's basket. "Let's carry all this over to your house."

When Madeleine and Emma reached the large farmhouse at the end of the driveway, they climbed the back porch steps, entered the house through the mudroom, and stepped into the large kitchen.

Madeleine placed her basket and bowl of meatballs on the counter and glanced around the room. She gasped as she ran her hands over the beautiful walnut cabinets.

"Emma, these are gorgeous." She opened a cabinet door and examined the craftsmanship. "Did your *dat* make these?"

"*Ya*." Emma bobbed her head up and down, causing the ribbons from her prayer covering to dance over her little shoulders. "He made the cabinets and the counters." She pointed toward the long table in the middle of the room. "His best *freind*, Marcus, made the table and chairs a long time ago. It was a wedding gift for my parents. Marcus makes tables and chairs. His *dochder*, Esther, is my best *freind*. We go to school together. I think you met them at Carolyn's wedding."

"Yes, I did. Wow." Madeleine couldn't take her eyes off the cabinets. "I'd love something like this for my kitchen."

"You should talk to my *dat*."

"No." Madeleine shook her head. "I'm certain I couldn't afford his work."

"I'm sure you could," Emma insisted. "He does a lot of work for *Englishers*, and they can afford it."

"I'm certain they have more money than I do." Madeleine

looked at the table. "Your friend Marcus does nice work too." She pointed toward the food on the counter. "Do you need help setting the table or anything?"

"Oh no, *danki*. I can handle it. I do it every day."

Madeleine grinned. "You're a very special little girl."

"I'm not little." Emma shook her head. "I'm eleven."

"Oh, I'm sorry." Madeleine tried to suppress her smile. "You're a young lady, and I'm glad you're my friend." She started for the door. "I better get home. Please tell your *dat* that I hope he enjoys his meal."

"I will." Emma waved. "*Danki*, Maddie!"

Madeleine's smile widened when she heard her nickname. "*Gern gschehne.*"

While she walked home, Madeleine felt the urge to pray. *Lord, I know I went against Saul's wishes today by cooking with Emma, but I couldn't bring myself to break her sweet little heart. Please soften Saul's heart toward me, and let him see that I only have the best intentions in mind. Don't let him be angry with Emma. I hope this meal brings him happiness. I also pray that Saul will allow me to be both his friend and Emma's. In your holy name, amen.*

⁘

Saul stepped into the mudroom and shucked his coat, hat, and boots. "Hello," he called as the aroma of meatballs filled his senses. "What's for supper?"

"It's a surprise." Emma stood in the doorway and grinned. "*Kumm! Dummle!*"

Saul lifted an eyebrow as he followed her into the kitchen. He found the table set with bowls of spaghetti, meatballs, salad, and carrots. He studied his daughter. "You did this by yourself?"

"No." She shook her head. "I had help." She pointed toward the sink. "Wash up and we'll eat. I can't wait to try it."

Saul washed his hands and then sat down at the table. After a silent prayer, he began to fill his plate. "This smells wonderful, Emma. How did you do this?"

"A *freind* helped me." She piled salad on her plate. "I went to visit Maddie, and we cooked together all afternoon." Her expression was tentative.

"Who's Maddie?" he asked.

"Madeleine Miller." Emma's voice was small and unsure.

"You went to visit Madeleine Miller?" Saul snapped. "Emma Kate, I've told you time and again to stay away from her. It's not right for you to barge into her home." He slammed his fist on the table, and Emma jumped.

Emma's lip quivered, and regret coursed through him. He couldn't stand it when Emma cried, but she had to learn to respect him.

"I was home alone, and I decided to go see if I could make an apple pie with Maddie." She sniffed and wiped her eyes with a napkin. "We had all of those *schee* apples, and I remembered that *Mummi* had an *appeditlich* recipe. Maddie had told me she had all of *Mammi's* cookbooks, and I went over to see if she could help me make the pie. We decided to make you a nice meal too." She made a sweeping gesture toward the spaghetti and meatballs. "Spaghetti and meatballs were Maddie's idea."

Saul stared at the food. "Why would she want to make me a meal?"

"Maybe she wants to be our *freind*."

Saul forked a meatball, put a bite in his mouth, and savored the taste.

"Do you like it, *Dat*?" Emma leaned forward, her blue eyes filled with hope.

Saul wiped his mouth and beard with a napkin. "It's very *gut*." Actually, it was outstanding. He'd never had such delicious meatballs before. He ate a few more forkfuls and then wiped his mouth again. "But I told you to stay away from her, and you defied me, Emma. If you don't respect my wishes, then you'll have to spend your afternoons at Esther's *haus*. That would mean you'll have all your chores still to do when you get home later in the day. I need to know I can trust you here alone. You're supposed to do your chores, not visit with neighbors."

"But making supper is one of my chores." She twisted spaghetti around her fork as she spoke. "Maddie said you told her not to spend time with me, but I convinced her to cook with me today. She was helping me out."

"Why do you keep calling her Maddie?" Saul asked before taking a sip of water.

"That's her nickname." Emma was still winding spaghetti around her fork. "Her *mamm* calls her Maddie. Did you know she never knew her *dat*? He left before she was born. Oh, and she has her *dat's* eyes and hair, like I have *Mamm's*." Emma began a long monologue about Madeleine's life, including where she had lived and that she had a stepfather.

Saul continued to eat while he listened. His fear was already coming true—his daughter was becoming attached to this *Englisher*, and he didn't know what to do about it.

"Maddie was wearing pants," Emma continued. "They were lightweight with a stripe down the side. I think I've seen her running in those before. And she also had her hair in a ponytail. I wonder what my hair would look like in a ponytail."

Saul gritted his teeth. Was this Madeleine Miller making his Emma rebellious? "You're not to try on any *English* clothes, Emma. You're not going to change how you look."

"I know." Emma nodded. "I was just saying that Maddie dresses so different from how I dress." She pointed toward the meatballs. "Do you like the food, *Dat*? Did Maddie and I do a *gut* job?"

He nodded. "*Ya. Danki.*"

"Wait until you see dessert." She sat up a little taller. "We have apple pie and vanilla ice cream. I can't wait to try it." She then talked on about Madeleine and how much fun they had together.

When Emma brought out the pie and ice cream, Saul enjoyed them despite his frustration with Emma and Madeleine defying his wishes. He had to admit it was nice to enjoy a delicious meal that was different from what they normally ate.

"What do you think of the pie?" Emma asked.

"It's *appeditlich*. It's the best apple pie I've ever had."

Emma clapped her hands. "I'm glad you like it!"

Saul saw the happiness in his daughter's eyes, and he couldn't bring himself to punish her. He was thankful that Madeleine had made her happy, but he prayed she wouldn't break Emma's heart. Maybe God had brought Madeleine into his daughter's life for a reason, but Saul hoped the reason had nothing to do with stealing his daughter away from the community he loved.

TWELVE

Madeleine couldn't stop thinking about Saul's kitchen as she cleaned hotel rooms. The memory of the beautifully crafted cabinets floated through her mind. Although she adored her grandparents' house, the kitchen had needed attention for quite some time. Her grandmother had loved her little house just as it was and seemed set in her ways, but Madeleine suspected she also wanted to keep the house the way it had been when her mother was growing up and her grandfather was still alive.

Although her grandmother never discussed how heartbreaking it was for her when Madeleine's mother left the Amish community, Madeleine knew she missed the days when her daughter was home. She'd kept all of her clothes, which Madeleine wore when she visited as a little girl.

She was still thinking about her small kitchen when she returned her cart to the supply closet.

"Hi, Madeleine," Linda Zook said while pushing her own cart toward the closet. "How did your morning go?"

"It went fine, thanks. I finished the second floor. How about you?" Madeleine asked.

"I finished my rooms too."

Madeleine thought of her kitchen ideas. "Linda, do you know of an affordable cabinetmaker?"

"A cabinetmaker?" Linda shook her head. "I know of a few around the community, but I don't know them personally. What do you want a cabinetmaker for?"

"I want to do some renovations in my grandparents' house. It's needed some upgrades for a while." Madeleine leaned against a shelf that held paper products. "I want to keep the spirit of my grandparents' house, but the cabinets are falling apart. Last night I was in my neighbor's house, and I was really astounded by the cabinets in his kitchen. He makes cabinets for a living, but I'm certain I can't afford his work."

"What's his name?" Linda asked.

"Saul Beiler."

"Oh." Linda nodded. "He's one of the best in the area, from what I've heard."

Madeleine smiled. "That's all the more reason I can't afford him."

"You don't know that unless you ask."

"But we don't make that much money here. My grandmother left me some money, but I need it to last as long as possible. I'm actually working to earn extra money for home projects."

"That's true. We don't earn a lot here." Linda pointed toward the office. "You might want to talk to Gregg. He can give you some names, or you can look them up on his computer."

"That's a great idea." Madeleine stood up straighter. "Thank you, Linda."

Linda shrugged. "You're welcome. I really didn't do much."

Madeleine headed to her boss's office and found him

squinting at his computer screen. Gregg Larson was a short, plump, balding man in his midfifties, with thick glasses and small, dark eyes.

She knocked on the door frame, and Gregg peered at her over his computer. "Hi, Gregg." She gave him a little wave. "I was wondering if you could give me a recommendation for kitchen remodelers. I want to replace my kitchen cabinets."

"Sure thing." Gregg nodded. "I'll see what I can find. I can also ask my wife to put a list together for you and then get it to you before the end of the day. She knows the contractors in the area because she works at a store in town."

"That would be fantastic. Thank you." Madeleine headed back to the supply closet with a smile on her face.

Later that evening, Madeleine sat on the sofa in the family room and sipped a can of Diet Coke while she examined the list of contractors she'd called. She'd set up times for representatives from three different companies to stop by and give her estimates during the next couple of days.

She finished the soda and then walked into the kitchen. She stared at the cabinets. Two were missing the metal knobs on the doors, which had fallen off before Madeleine came to live in the house. Another was missing a door that had fallen off with a loud clatter just yesterday.

As she made her way to the bedroom, Madeleine imagined how pretty the house could be if she renovated it the way she wanted to. She prayed she could make that a reality in memory of her precious grandparents.

Madeleine stood in the driveway as she watched the last contractor drive away. She stared down at the estimate and shook her head. After meeting with the three contractors, she didn't know which company to choose. She had thought she'd know whom to hire by the end of the week, but she was still as confused as she had been on Tuesday when she'd called the first contractor.

"Maddie!" Emma hurried up the driveway with a piece of paper in her hand. "Do you want to cook? I have *mei mamm's* recipe for chicken and dumplings."

"How did your *dat* like the food we made on Monday?" Madeleine asked, shivering in the cold November air. "I've been wondering if you were in trouble for cooking with me."

"He loved the food. He said it was the best apple pie he'd ever had." Emma held out her paper. "He would love this too."

Madeleine examined the recipe, which looked easy enough. She would have to go to the grocery store for most of the supplies, but she always did her grocery shopping on Fridays, so it wasn't really a problem. Yet, at the same time, she couldn't keep the voice in the back of her mind from warning her not to go against Saul's wishes again. Would cooking with Emma cause more problems between her and her neighbor, who lived in such close proximity?

"How would your *dat* feel about you coming over to my house again?" She studied Emma's pretty face. "Are you certain you're allowed to spend time with me?"

Emma shrugged and then shivered. "I think he'd be happy to have another delicious meal." She smiled, and Madeleine felt her worries evaporate.

"When will your *dat* be home?" Madeleine asked.

"His note said he'd be home around five thirty."

"We'll have to go to the grocery store before we start cooking." She nodded toward the house. "Let me go in and get my purse and keys. Come inside for a minute." Madeleine hoped it would also be acceptable to Saul for her to take Emma along to the store.

"Okay." Emma skipped ahead of Madeleine and opened the back door. "Who was that man in the truck?"

"He gave me an estimate on my cabinets." Madeleine followed Emma into the kitchen and placed the estimate on the counter next to the other two.

"He has a cabinet company?" Emma asked.

"That's right." Madeleine grabbed her purse and keys from the kitchen table. "He told me how much it would cost to replace my cabinets."

"You should talk to *mei dat*." Emma folded her arms over her cloak. "He's the best."

"I might talk to him. Maybe he can give me some guidance." Madeleine jingled the keys in her hands. "Let's head to the store, and then we'll start cooking."

"Yay." Emma clapped her hands. "I love cooking with you."

Madeleine smiled. "I love cooking with you too."

∞

"I think it turned out well." Madeleine closed the lid on the last of the chicken and dumplings after she'd put most of it into a large refrigerator jar. The delicious aroma caused her stomach to growl. "Hopefully your *dat* will enjoy this as much as he enjoyed our creation on Monday."

A knock sounded at the door, and Madeleine glanced at Emma. "Would you please see who that is?"

Emma went through the mudroom and looked out the window. "Oh, it's my *dat*," she called back. "We can ask him what he thinks of the meal."

Madeleine's smile faded as she walked in behind Emma. She hoped he wasn't angry.

Emma wrenched the door open. "Hi, *Dat*! We were finishing up—" She backed up as Saul quickly opened the storm door and stepped inside.

"I have been worried sick about you." Saul wagged a large finger millimeters from Emma's nose while the girl's eyes widened. "I told you to stay home today, but you still came over here. I explicitly told you not to come over here and bother Madeleine."

"But you said you liked the meal we made you on Monday. I thought it would be okay if we made you another one." Emma's voice was tiny, as if she were five instead of eleven.

"You still insist on breaking the rules. I don't know what to do to make you realize that I want you at home, not here with this *maedel*." He looked over at Madeleine and then back at his daughter. "You are supposed to come home from school and take care of your chores."

Madeleine felt like an intruder watching Saul reprimand his daughter. Should she leave? But that was a silly notion. After all, they were in *her* house.

"We made you chicken and dumplings," Emma offered. "It's your favorite recipe."

Saul shook his head. "You're avoiding the issue here. You disobeyed me. It's your job to follow my rules." He pointed to his wide chest. "I'm the *daed*, and you're the *kind*." His voice was gruff, and his face was full of frustration.

Madeleine scowled. He was overreacting. After all, the girl only wanted to cook for her father. What was so wrong about that?

"Let's go!" Saul bellowed as he pointed toward the door.

Emma glanced back at Madeleine and then turned toward her father. "I told Maddie to talk to you about building new cabinets for her kitchen." She pointed toward the counter. "She's gotten some estimates, but I told her that you're the best."

Saul's expression softened a little. "I said it's time to go."

"*Ya, Dat.*" Emma started to leave.

"Emma, wait!" Madeleine said, causing Saul to glare at her. "Your chicken and dumplings are here." She ignored Saul's frown and went back into the kitchen to get the container she'd just filled.

Saul walked into the kitchen behind her and took the container. "*Danki*," he muttered. His eyes moved to the counter, and he stared at the pile of estimates. "Are these the estimates Emma was talking about?"

"Yes."

He looked up at the cabinets and grimaced. "I see. These must be the originals from when this place was built." He touched a door and opened and closed it. "You want to replace them?"

"That's the plan." Madeleine crossed her arms over her hooded sweatshirt.

"Is it all right if I look at the estimates?"

"Sure." She shrugged.

He placed the container on the counter and began studying the paperwork.

"I told Maddie you would give her a better price and do better work for her," Emma said.

"That's true," Saul said before looking up at Madeleine. "Do you know what you want your cabinets to look like?"

"Yeah." Madeleine pointed toward his house. "I want ones like you have in your kitchen. I love walnut, and I really like the simple design."

"My kitchen?" He turned toward Emma. "Madeleine was in our kitchen?"

"She helped me bring the food to our *haus* on Monday." Emma turned to Madeleine. "That reminds me. I need to return your dishes to you."

"There's no rush." Madeleine waved off the comment.

Saul's expression softened, and he seemed embarrassed. "Those were the first kitchen cabinets I made without *mei daadi's* help. I had just gotten married, and I was starting my own business. They aren't my best work."

Madeleine shook her head. "If those aren't your best work, then I can't imagine how amazing your cabinets really are. Those are exactly what I want."

"Really?" he asked. "Those are exactly what you want?"

As he studied her, she took in his bottomless brown eyes. They were warm and comforting, like the hot chocolate she and her grandmother made when she was a child. She pushed the thought away and realized he was awaiting her response.

"Yes," she repeated. "Those are exactly what I want, but I'm certain I can't afford you."

He blanched. "Why would you say that?"

"I know Amish work is the best, and you get what you pay for."

Saul held up the medium price estimate. "I won't charge you much more than this company."

"Really?" Madeleine was intrigued. She moved closer to him

and looked down at the paper. She realized he was only a couple of inches taller than she was, and she estimated him to stand at just under six feet. "You can really keep your price in that range?"

"*Ya*, I can." He gestured toward his property. "Do you want to come over to my shop and talk about the design?"

"Why don't we eat first?" Emma suggested.

Madeleine looked at Saul. "Would you like to eat here, and then we can talk about the cabinets?"

He hesitated and then gave a quick nod. "*Ya*, that sounds *gut*."

"Great." Madeleine looked at Emma. "Would you please set the table? I'll warm up the chicken and dumplings." She glanced at Saul. "You can go clean up if you'd like. The bathroom is down the hallway to the left."

"*Danki*." Saul shucked his heavy coat and hung it on a peg just inside the mudroom before disappearing down the hallway.

Madeleine hoped her taking Emma to the grocery store wouldn't come up.

✌

Saul washed his hands in the bathroom and then stepped back into the hallway. He had visited this home dozens of times when Martha and Mel lived in it. After Mel passed away, Saul frequently stopped by to see if Martha needed any help. He'd taken care of minor household projects, such as fixing her leaking kitchen sink, and also major repairs, including repairing her roof. He was happy to assist her and wouldn't take no for an answer when he asked her if she needed help.

He took a step and stood in the doorway of the master bedroom, which looked nearly identical to how it had looked when

Martha lived in the house. The same quilt was on the bed, and the walls were still bare except for a small mirror and a faded wreath. Why hadn't Madeleine decorated it like the *Englisher* homes he'd visited while installing cabinets? Or was getting new cabinets the beginning of a plan to make the house more *English*?

Then he peered into the spare room, which included a small desk, a chair, a rocking chair, and a pile of boxes with BOOKS written on them in black marker. Beside the rocking chair were a plastic drawer unit filled with yarn and what looked like a half-crocheted, pastel-colored blanket. He was surprised. Crocheting didn't seem to fit with her *English* life.

Saul moved to the kitchen where his daughter and Madeleine were still preparing the meal. Emma was folding napkins while Madeleine carried a pan of chicken and dumplings to the table.

"I hope my *dat* likes this meal," Emma said with her back to Saul. "I made it once before, but I think I cooked it too long."

"I think he'll enjoy it." Madeleine turned toward Saul and gasped. "Oh, I didn't see you there." Her cheeks blushed a light pink. "You can have a seat anywhere you'd like. What would you like to drink, Saul?"

"Water is fine. *Danki.*" Saul sat at the head of the table and folded his hands in his lap.

"I'll get drinks." Emma scurried over to the cabinet for glasses and began preparing the drinks. "Do we have anything for dessert, Maddie?"

"Oh." Madeleine rested her hand on her hip while considering the question. "I believe I have some ice cream." She glanced at Saul. "Do you like vanilla fudge ice cream?"

He nodded. "That would be fine."

"Great." Madeleine examined the table. "I think we're all set. Let me help you with that." She rushed over to Emma and took two glasses of water from her.

She set one next to Saul and smiled at him. He suddenly realized that she had a beautiful smile that caused her dark eyes to sparkle in the natural, late afternoon light flooding the kitchen. He nodded and quickly looked down at the glass.

Madeleine sat to his right and Emma was at his left. After a quick silent prayer, they began to eat.

"What do you think, *Dat*?" Emma asked after Saul had taken his first bite of chicken and dumplings.

He wiped a napkin across his beard and nodded. "It's fantastic."

"Yay!" Emma clapped her hands. "He likes it, Maddie."

Madeleine smiled at Emma, and Saul was stunned by the love in her expression as she looked at his daughter.

"I told you he'd like it. You worry too much, Emma." Madeleine filled her plate. "You're a very good cook. You don't need my help."

"*Ya*, I do," Emma said.

"Why?" Madeleine's expression became facetious. "You need me to buy the groceries, right?"

"No, I need you to reach the spices that are high in the cabinet." Emma giggled.

Madeleine feigned a gasp, and Saul couldn't stop his own chuckle.

"What are we going to make next?" Emma asked. "Have you ever made a ham loaf?" She glanced at Saul. "That's one of my *dat's* favorites."

"No, I haven't made a ham loaf." Madeleine turned toward

Saul. "We'll have to see if your *dat* will allow us to try to make one together." She seemed to be awaiting his approval, and he felt obligated to agree.

"Perhaps we can choose a night for that," he said, and Emma smiled.

Not only was supper delicious, but Saul couldn't get over how Madeleine interacted with Emma. They discussed recipes like old friends. They laughed and talked about everything from barn cats to gardening. His daughter had bonded with the *Englisher,* and it sent conflicting emotions swirling through him. He was amazed at how happy his daughter was, but he also was still concerned about Madeleine's influence.

After supper, Emma and Madeleine cleaned up the kitchen while Saul drank a cup of coffee he'd allowed his hostess to make. He sat at the table, still marveling at how well the two got along.

"Madeleine," he said once most of the dishes were clean, "would you like to look at cabinet samples in my showroom? I have a catalog and some sample cabinets in the smaller shop near my *haus.*"

Madeleine nodded. "Yes, I'd like that."

"All right." He started for the door.

"I'll finish up," Emma offered. "We just have these utensils and pots left. You and *Dat* can go to the shop. I'll probably be home before you will, *Dat.*"

"Are you sure?" Madeleine asked while scrubbing the first pot.

"I can do it," Emma insisted.

"All right." Madeleine dried her hands on a towel. "Just leave everything else in the drain board. I can put them away when I get home." She moved to the mudroom and pulled on her coat, grabbing a flashlight as well. "Thank you, Emma," she called back.

Saul held the door open for Madeleine, and she stepped out onto the porch. "*Danki* for supper," he said as they walked side by side down the porch steps. The setting sun sent bursts of oranges, purples, reds, and yellows across the sky, and the cold air tickled his nose.

"*Gern gschehne*," she said.

He glanced at her. "You really do speak *Dietsch*."

"*Ya*, I do. Is that so difficult to believe?" She gave him a slight smile as they made their way down the rock driveway toward his shop, their shoes crunching against the stones.

"No, it's not difficult to believe," he explained. "It just seems ironic for an *Englisher* to speak *Dietsch* that well."

"I'll take that as a compliment," she teased. "I'm glad you liked supper. I think cooking for you makes Emma happy."

He nodded. "She is eager to please."

"I think she likes to see you smile."

Her comment caught him off guard, and the words hit him square in the heart. Talking about his daughter always touched him deeply. Speechless, he kept walking toward the shop.

"Did I say something wrong?" Madeleine asked.

"No," he said. They approached the showroom, and he wrenched the door open. "It's going to be cold in there."

"I'm not afraid of the cold," she quipped. "I served in Afghanistan with some challenging conditions."

He nodded while studying her young face in the remaining light of the day. How could a sweet young lady like her serve in the military and go to a place where war had been raging for years? She was brave to travel so far without family to protect her. Madeleine was more than she seemed. In fact, she was a mystery. He was certain he had a lot to learn about his neighbor.

"Let me turn the lanterns on." He slipped past her and flipped on the four lanterns located around the shop before picking up a copy of the full-color catalog he'd had designed by a local print shop. He placed it on the workbench closest to the door for her to study. "These are my most popular designs." He pointed toward the wall. "There are more samples there."

Madeleine stood beside him and flipped through the catalog. Her arm brushed his, and he instinctively took a step back. He glanced at her face and was struck by how her hair had a slightly reddish tint in the low light of the lanterns. Her eyes also seemed a lighter shade of brown, resembling milk chocolate.

He quickly looked away. Why would he admire an *Englisher*? Madeleine Miller was only a neighbor, an acquaintance. He was falling into the trap of believing Amish and *Englishers* could be friends. Their lives were too different for that, and he needed to remind Emma to keep her distance. He'd enjoyed their supper, and Emma obviously liked Madeleine, but it was still a mistake to let Emma get so close to this woman.

"I don't know," Madeleine said, wrenching him from his mental tirade. "These are all gorgeous, but I still like the cabinets in your kitchen the best." She closed the catalog. "Would you design something simple for me, like those?"

Saul rubbed his beard. "Are you certain that's what you want? Those are very plain."

"That's what I like, and I think that's what my *mammi* would've liked. She kept her life simple and plain, and I want to do something that would have made her *froh*."

He studied her, fascinated by her love and respect for her grandmother. "All right. I can do something like that. Are you certain you want walnut?"

She shrugged. "Why not?"

"Walnut is dark. Would you rather go with something lighter?" He crossed to the opposite side of the shop and began lifting wood samples. "Would you prefer a light walnut or maybe an oak?"

"Oh wow." She studied the samples. "I don't know." She ran her hand over the boards and then looked up at him. "What do you think? You're the expert."

"It's your kitchen. Whatever you want would be fine with me." She smiled. "I still like your cabinets the best."

"Okay." He pulled out an order form. "What kind of countertop would you like?"

She grinned. "I already told you. I like what you have in your kitchen."

"Fine." He wrote down her name and address on the top of the form. "I can have an estimate to you in a week or so."

"When do you think you can start on my cabinets?"

"A few days after that. I'm finishing up a job now. I'll just have to coordinate with my plumber, but it shouldn't be a problem. Does that sound okay?"

"It's perfect. *Danki*." She shivered.

"You should go back home and get warm." He placed the form on the workbench. "I'll come see you in a few days and take measurements."

"Sounds great." She hugged her arms to her chest. "I'm excited."

He extinguished the lanterns, picked up another to light their way, and followed her out of the shop. After locking the door, he faced her. "I'll see you soon."

"Great." She glanced toward her house and then looked back at Saul. "I had fun tonight. Thank you for sharing Emma with me."

For the second time that evening, her words tugged at his heart. "*Gern gschehne.*"

"*Gut nacht,* Saul," she said.

"*Gut nacht.*" He watched her start down the road with her flashlight shining in front of her, and he suddenly wondered what to call her. "Wait."

She spun and faced him, her pretty face filled with curiosity.

"I don't know what to call you," he said.

"I don't understand." She took a step toward him.

"*Mei dochder* calls you Maddie, but your name is Madeleine," he explained. "What should I call you?"

"My friends call me Maddie," she said. "You can call me Maddie."

"*Gut nacht,* Maddie." He said the words and couldn't help but think that the nickname fit her. She was the most complex *Englisher* he'd ever met.

Madeleine continued down the driveway, turning back once to wave at him. He waved back at her. Would she be a constant in his and Emma's life, or would she stay long enough to get to know them and then leave again? For a split second, he hoped she would stay, but thoughts like that were dangerous. She was only a neighbor who wanted him to design and build new cabinets for her. She would never be any more than an *English* customer. They could not—he could not—get too close.

THIRTEEN

Trey steered his BMW down a winding road. He had finished all the errands he'd planned to run today. At least, he'd crossed everything off his list that he'd told Hannah he'd do today, but he still had one stop he wanted to make. It was an errand he had pondered ever since he'd attended Joshua Glick and Carolyn Lapp's wedding. Something he had to do for his lovely wife.

He drove down another road, passing beautiful Amish farms on either side. The one-room schoolhouse came into view, and he slowed to a stop. Lillian stood by the doorway and waved as a line of children rushed out of the school, talking and laughing as they made their way down the steps and toward their homes. Another young lady, whom he assumed was Lillian's assistant, also waved and smiled as the children left.

Trey had spent two weeks considering what he would say to Lillian if he had a chance to talk to her alone. Now that moment was finally here. He had to find a way to make Lillian understand that Hannah still loved her and wanted—needed—her to be a part of her life.

He waited until it looked like the last child had left the building before climbing from the car and making his way toward the school. Lillian and her assistant had disappeared inside, and as he approached, the other young lady reappeared on the front steps.

When she saw him, her eyes widened with panic. "May I help you?"

"Hi." Trey stopped before he reached the bottom step. "I was looking for Lillian Glick."

"Just a minute." The girl stepped back into the school, and he heard her call Lillian. She then returned to the top step and fiddled with the ties on her prayer covering. "She'll be right here."

"Thanks." Trey cleared his throat and leaned against the railing while he waited for his stepdaughter. The young lady studied him with a suspicious expression.

"Trey?" Lillian asked when she came through the door. "What are you doing here?" Her eyes widened as she looked down at him. "Did something happen to my sister?"

"No." Trey shook his head. "Your sister, your brother, and your mother are fine."

"Oh. Praise God. You scared me." Lillian rested her hand on her chest. "Then why are you here?"

"I'd like to talk to you." Her expression hardened, but he pressed on. "Please, Lily. Let me take you out for a cup of coffee or something."

"No." She pushed her glasses farther up on her nose. "I have things to do. I'm very busy."

The other young lady looked back and forth between them.

"I have things to do as well, but this is important to me." Trey sighed. "Please, Lillian. Just hear me out. Let me take you out for coffee, and we'll talk for a few minutes. Then I'll drive you home. What do you say?"

Lillian's expression remained stoic. "I don't think so."

Trey stood there for a moment. Should he insist she go out for coffee with him, or should he just leave? His heart was torn, but he knew one thing for certain—he was determined to do anything to help Hannah heal her broken heart.

Lillian stepped back into the school, and the young lady stood on the top step watching Trey. Did she think Trey was going to try to hurt Lillian?

His stepdaughter reappeared with a tote bag slung over her shoulder. She locked the school door and then descended the steps with the other young lady close behind her.

"Lily," Trey began, "if you won't go with me, then I'm going to ask you to hear me out right here."

Lillian stopped in front of him and frowned. "I have nothing to say to you."

"That's fine. You don't need to speak, but I need you to listen to me."

The young lady said something to Lillian in Pennsylvania Dutch, and Lillian shook her head.

"It's okay," Lillian responded. "You can go. I'll be fine."

"Are you certain?" the girl asked.

"*Ya.*" Lillian nodded. "I'll see you tomorrow, Anna Mary."

Anna Mary nodded and then started down the street.

"What do you want to say to me, Trey?" Lillian crossed her arms over her apron. "Did *mei mamm* send you here to speak to me?"

"No." Trey shook his head. "She has no idea I'm here. I've wanted to talk to you for some time, but I felt it wasn't my place to get involved. However, things have escalated to a point now that I feel I have to get involved." He took a deep breath. "Lily, I realize this change has been hard on you. What you don't realize is how hard this has been for your mother."

Lillian's frown deepened. "I can't imagine that it's been more difficult for her than it has for me. I lost everything—my home and my family. *Mei mamm* didn't lose anything."

"That's not true." Trey worked to keep his voice calm despite his raging frustration. "Your mom feels that she's lost you. She cries every night. Sometimes she cries during the day. She thinks I can't hear her, but I do. And it's breaking my heart."

"That was her choice." Lillian lifted her chin with defiance, but her green eyes shimmered with tears.

"But it wasn't an easy choice, and it doesn't have to be something that keeps you apart forever." He paused to gather his thoughts. "Lily, your mother loves you. I believe you love her too. I want you to think about giving her a chance. Just come visit us and talk to her. Let her show you how much she loves you."

"I can't do that." Lillian's voice cracked. "I just can't."

"Yes, you can. I can take you over to our house right now. You can stay for supper, and then I'll take you home."

"No." She shook her head. "I just can't."

"Fine. I can't make you want to visit us. When you're ready, you just let me know," Trey said. "I want you to consider something. Your mother is going to have a baby. She wants you to be a part of that baby's life."

Lillian wiped away a tear as it trickled down her pink cheek.

"I don't know if you know my story." Tears stung Trey's eyes. "I lost my first wife and my daughter to carbon monoxide poisoning. I was on a business trip, and they passed away while I was gone. I lost everything, Lily. They were gone, completely gone. I can't see them or talk to them on this earth ever again. But you haven't lost your mother. You've just chosen to ignore her and act like she died."

"It's not that simple," Lillian whispered, her voice thick.

"I think it is," Trey countered. "Your mother brought joy back into my life. And this child she's carrying represents our love. You, Amanda, and Andrew are my family now. I want you to *be* a part of our family. I'd like to bring us all together before this child comes into the world. It would make your mother very happy to have you back in her life. She may have stopped being Amish, but she never stopped loving you or being your mother."

Lily's lip quivered as more tears spilled from her eyes. "I have to go." She turned and walked away before Trey could respond.

"Lillian!" he called after her. "Please think about what I said. We're still a family, Lillian. Let's act like a family again."

Although she kept walking, Trey didn't give up hope that Lillian would consider his words.

∽

Amanda yawned as she climbed the back steps toward the porch. She was exhausted after a day of sitting in classes and then working at a veterinarian's office in Paradise. She yanked open the back door, walked through the mudroom, and found Trey loading the dishwasher.

"How was your day?" she asked before yawning again.

"It was okay." He placed a plate with the others. "How was yours? How's the new job?"

"Exhausting." She let her backpack drop to the floor with a thump and then sat at the kitchen table. "I love working with the animals, but it's tiring. I had to chase one puppy through the office, and then I had to help pacify an angry cat." She pushed her long braid over her shoulder. "Where are *Mamm* and Andrew?"

"Andrew is taking his shower, and your mom is resting." Trey wiped his hands on a dish towel while facing her. "I have your supper in the fridge. I just have to warm it up for you."

"I can do it." She started to stand.

"Don't be silly. I'll get it for you." He pulled a plate from the refrigerator and then stuck it into the microwave. After he pressed a few buttons, the microwave hummed. He brought a glass of iced tea to the table.

"Thank you. Is *Mamm* okay?"

Trey frowned. "She had a rough day."

Amanda stood. "Should I go check on her? Does she need to see her doctor? Is the baby okay?"

Trey held his hand up to calm her. "She's fine now. Her stomach was upset." The microwave beeped, and he retrieved the plate with two slices of turkey roast, noodles, and spinach. He set it on the placemat in front of Amanda and then sat down across from her.

"Thank you." Amanda bowed her head in silent prayer and then began to eat. "I'm sorry *Mamm* isn't feeling well. Is there anything I can do?"

"No." Trey rested his chin on the palm of one hand. "She's also been upset about Lily."

"I know." Amanda ran her fingers over the cool glass of tea while she contemplated her twin. "I've been praying about Lily, and I've even tried talking to her. I don't know what else to say to help her forgive *Mamm*. I hoped she would have come to visit us and talk to *Mamm* by now." She cut up a piece of turkey roast. "I'm at the end of my rope with her."

"I know you've tried," Trey said. "I spoke to her today."

Amanda swallowed a gasp. "You spoke to my sister today?"

He nodded in response.

"How did you manage that?"

"I went to see her at the schoolhouse after I ran errands for your mother." He gave her a little smile. "And she looked about as shocked to see me as you look right now. I tried to convince her to go out for coffee and talk for a while, but she wouldn't go. So I talked to her right outside the schoolhouse."

"What did you say?" Amanda set her fork down beside her plate as her appetite evaporated.

"I told her your mother misses her and she cries for her just about every day. I explained that we want her to be a part of our family and also be a part of our new baby's life." He shrugged. "I said everything you and I have talked about. I told her we miss her and just because your mother is no longer Amish doesn't mean Lillian is no longer part of our family."

Amanda nodded slowly while digesting his words. "That's exactly right."

"I told her we want her to come visit us." Trey shook his head. "I don't know what else to say to her."

"What did she say?"

"Not much." Trey ran his finger over the table. "She cried a little, but she didn't say anything. She just walked off."

"That's my sister. Stubborn and headstrong." Amanda picked up the fork and moved the meat around on her plate. "She seems determined to stay miserable."

"I'm not giving up hope yet," Trey added. "She cried. I could tell this all hurt her deeply. She listened to me, and that was progress."

"Are you going to tell *mei mamm* about it?"

Trey shook his head. "I don't think I should. If Lily said she wanted to visit, then I think it would be beneficial to tell her I had talked to her. But I don't think telling her Lily refused to visit would be a good idea." He tilted his head. "Do you think I should tell her?"

"No, you're right." Amanda frowned. "I keep praying Lily will soften her heart toward *Mamm*. I'm certain God will answer our prayer when he sees fit."

"He will." Trey stood. "Would you like me to get you something else? We have chocolate pie for dessert."

"No, thanks. I'm fine." Amanda smiled at him. "Thanks for talking to my sister today. You're very good to my mother."

"I try to be good to her." Trey started for the door. "I'm going to go check on her."

Trey disappeared toward their family quarters as Amanda picked at her supper. She hoped Lily would come around soon. If only Lillian could see what a good man Trey was. He wasn't Amish, but he was a good Christian man who made their mother happy and provided a good home for them.

While she picked at her supper, she whispered a prayer. "God, please open Lily's heart toward *Mamm*. We need Lily in our family again. Please let her see she needs us as much as we need her. Send her back to us before our new sibling is born. Thanks, God. In Jesus' holy name, amen."

⚮

Carolyn cradled a cup of hot tea in her hands while she sat on the porch. She smiled as Joshua walked from the barn toward the house.

My husband.

She loved the sound of that. They'd been married nearly four weeks now, and she was still basking in the newness of it all. She loved having a husband, a new name, and a home—a *real* home for her and her son.

"Carolyn." Joshua's handsome face glowed in the light of his lantern as he took the steps two at a time. "It's awfully cold for you to be sitting out here. You're going to get sick."

"I'm enjoying the *schee* night on the porch. Our porch."

He smiled, and her heart turned over in her chest. She enjoyed seeing his attractive smile every day. She wondered how different he'd look when his beard grew in.

"I'm thankful you're *froh* here." He sank onto the swing beside her, and his leg brushed against hers. "Do you want me to go get you a blanket?"

"No, *danki*." She rested her head on his shoulder. "The tea is keeping me warm. I was just admiring all those gorgeous stars in the sky. I love this time of year."

"I love every time of year now that you're here." He pushed the swing back and forth. "The animals are set for the night."

"That's *gut*." She closed her eyes and enjoyed the motion of the swing and the comfort of her husband beside her.

"Now that you're settled here, I'd like to have you help me with the books. I've really fallen behind on the paperwork for the recent horse sales. Would you help me with that?"

"Of course I will." She opened her eyes and looked up at him. "I'd be *froh* to help."

"*Gut*." He rested his hand on her leg. "You know that will take a lot of time."

She nodded. "I'm sure it will, but I'll learn it. I know I can do a *gut* job. I'm pretty *gut* with numbers."

"And in the spring, you'll have the garden to care for too."

"I realize that, but Rosemary said she still wants to help with that. She enjoys coming over here and visiting Danny. She likes your assistant a lot, and she also likes spending time with me."

"I'd like to see this farm become your priority." His words were gentle, but she knew where the conversation was leading. "Have you thought any more about quitting the hotel?"

Carolyn sat up. "I don't think I need to quit right now. I'll reduce my hours if I have to, but I want to work there for a while longer."

"Why is working at the hotel so important to you?" His eyes seemed to search her for an answer. "Why don't you want to make this farm your priority?"

"It is my priority," Carolyn insisted. "I just want to keep working there for a while longer. I enjoy my friends, and I like the work."

His expression hardened. "I don't understand, Carolyn. You told me you wanted a home and a family. Now you have a home, and hopefully we'll soon be blessed with *kinner.*"

"I have faith that we'll be blessed with *kinner* soon. Until then, I'd like to keep my job."

He studied her. "I'm trying to understand, Carolyn, but I can't. What is it about the hotel that has you so determined to work there?"

Carolyn paused and contemplated her allegiance to the hotel. "I guess it's because it's something that's mine. I've always contributed to the family by working there, and I want to keep making those contributions."

"But this business is now ours." He gestured toward the barns. "You're my *fraa.* It's our *haus,* our farm, and our business. You have my name. Why isn't that *gut* enough for you?"

"You're misunderstanding me." Carolyn tried to explain how she felt without causing an argument. "I never said this wasn't *gut* enough for me. I just want to keep contributing to the family through my own salary. That's all I'm trying to say."

His frown deepened, stealing his handsome smile. "I need you at home. I need you here to help me with the farm and care for the *haus*." He touched her hand. "And I like having you here with me. I don't want to share you with the *Englishers* at the hotel."

Carolyn studied Joshua's grimace and realized he was still nervous that working at the hotel would cause her to be tempted by the *English* life because Hannah had met Trey while working there. She needed to convince him she wasn't going to leave the community.

"Josh, I'm very *froh* here." She placed her cup on the small table beside her. "Working at the hotel isn't going to change how I feel about you or our life together. I'm just not ready to give up my job yet, and I need you to understand that."

He turned away and stared out toward the farm.

"Can you give me a few months to adjust to the idea of quitting?" she asked. "Just let me ease into it."

Joshua faced her and gave her a quick nod. "I'll give you until spring."

"Okay." She squeezed his hand. "That's fair."

He stood, took her hand, and eased her to her feet. "It's cold. Tea or no, your hand is like a block of ice. Let's go inside."

As she followed him into the house, she tried to accept the notion of giving up her job by spring. She wasn't sure why she wanted to hold on to her former life. What was she afraid of losing? She hoped she could get used to the idea of being a wife without her former independent life.

FOURTEEN

Madeleine was about to carry grocery bags into the house when someone called her name.

"Madeleine." Saul hurried up the driveway toward her pickup truck. "Do you need some help?"

"Hi, Saul." She nodded toward the truck. "There are two more bags in there if you don't mind grabbing them."

He got the bags and followed her up the path to her house. "I was wondering if I could measure for your cabinets."

"Oh, sure. That's fine." Madeleine climbed the porch steps and stood in front of the back door, balanced both bags with one arm, and attempted to dig the house key out of her pocket. "I was wondering when you need to take down the old cabinets so I'll know when to start emptying them." She started to drop one of the bags, and he reached for it.

"Let me take the bags from you," Saul said. "I can manage all four."

"Thanks." She handed him the bags, found her key, pulled open the storm door, unlocked the back door, and pushed it open. "Go ahead." She stepped back, and Saul moved past her.

He placed the grocery bags on the kitchen table and then hung his coat on the peg just inside the mudroom door.

"Thank you." Madeleine placed her coat on the peg beside his and then suddenly felt embarrassed that she hadn't picked up the kitchen. A pile of bills and advertisements was on the counter and a laundry basket filled with dirty clothes was on the floor by the family room doorway. "I'm sorry the house is a mess." She pushed the basket of laundry into the family room. "I was going to go to the Laundromat tomorrow."

"The Laundromat?" Saul raised an eyebrow. "Don't you have a wringer washer out there?" He pointed toward another small room off the kitchen.

"Yes, but I don't remember how to use it. The last time I used a wringer washer I was twelve, and my *mammi* helped me."

"Do you want me to show you how to use it?" he offered.

"Oh no, thank you. I don't want to trouble you." She waved off the question. "I can go to the Laundromat. I just wait until I'm running out of clothes, and then I spend the afternoon there. I take a good book with me."

He studied her and then gave a quick nod. "Fine, then." He pulled a measuring tape and small notepad from his pocket. "I'm going to take some measurements and make some notes. Is that all right?"

"Go right ahead." She began unloading her bags, placing the groceries in the pantry, refrigerator, and freezer while he worked. She tried to think of a way to engage him in conversation. "Did you have a good day?"

He didn't answer. Was he ignoring her, or was he so engrossed in his project that he didn't hear her?

"Saul?" she asked.

"Hmm?" He glanced over his shoulder at her. "I'm sorry. Did you say something?"

"Yes, I did." She laughed, and he gave her a sheepish smile. "I asked you how your day went."

"Oh." He paused as if puzzled by the question. "It went fine. I finished up a small job, so I can start on yours." He shrugged. "The usual—woodworking, sanding, and staining. And how was your day?"

"It was pretty good. I cleaned at the hotel and then, obviously, stopped at the grocery store." She carried a carton of eggs to the refrigerator.

"You know I have chickens, right?" Saul asked.

"You do?" she asked. Now that she thought about it, she realized she had seen Emma out feeding some chickens next to one of their barns.

"I can have Emma bring you some eggs." He pointed toward the carton in her hand. "Just save the boxes, and we'll refill them for you. We have more eggs than we know what to do with. We could eat scrambled eggs three meals a day and still have eggs left over."

"Oh." She was surprised by his thoughtful offer. "*Danki*. I'd love that."

He nodded and turned back toward the cabinets. She put away a few more items—a carton of milk, a package of cheese, and a package of ground beef—while waiting for him to say something else. He was very quiet, but he wasn't rude. *How can I bring him out of his shell? Last week he loved talking about his work while he gave me the tour of his shop. Would asking about his woodworking help him open up to me? Maybe asking about cabinets is the key to becoming his friend.*

"How long have you done woodworking?" she asked.

"I've created things with wood since I was a *bu*. *Mei daadi* taught me in his shop. He mostly tinkered in wood since he was a farmer by trade, but he and my *onkel* taught me almost everything I know." He continued to measure and write. "I became an apprentice to my *onkel* for cabinetmaking when I was fifteen. I opened my own business right before I was married."

"Oh." She silently admired his confidence. He wasn't arrogant, but he was comfortable with his skill. "Do you like working alone?"

Saul shrugged. "I prefer working alone, but I'd like to grow my business. I haven't had the money to do it, but I believe God will give me the means when the time is right. I'd like to be able to take more orders and not have to ask customers to wait too long for their cabinets."

"That makes sense." Madeleine put a bag of chips and a box of noodles in the pantry. "Emma is a great girl. Thank you for allowing her to spend time with me."

"I know she enjoys cooking with you," he said. "It will still be awhile before she gets home from school, but I told her to come here when she does. I thought she could keep me company while I work. It takes me awhile because I always measure everything at least twice, and I take pretty detailed notes. She was surprised but excited too."

"That's great. I'm looking forward to seeing her." Madeleine had finished putting her groceries away. "I'm going to go in the spare room to pay some bills."

Madeleine disappeared into the room she'd made into an office, a storage place for a pile of random boxes she hadn't yet unpacked, and a place for her crocheting supplies. She paid a couple of bills and then moved to the rocking chair to start working on the afghan she'd been crocheting for a couple of months.

But her eyes moved to the unpacked boxes, and she'd moved to sort through some of them when she heard Emma's voice in the kitchen. She longed to go and visit with her, but she thought she should wait for Emma to seek her out just in case the father and daughter wanted to talk privately first.

She'd just opened a box and found it was full of old photo albums and yearbooks when she heard Emma's voice in the hallway.

"Maddie?" Emma called. "Are you back here?"

"I'm in the spare room," Madeleine called. "Come on in."

Emma appeared in the doorway. "Hi. What are you doing?"

"I just started going through a few boxes I hadn't unpacked yet." Madeleine pulled out a stack of yearbooks from her elementary school. "I guess I need to put a bookshelf in here. Does your dad make bookshelves?"

"He can make them. He does special orders." Emma crossed the room and craned her neck to see the books. "Willard School?"

"That's my elementary school." Madeleine held up a yearbook. "I think this was when I was in third grade."

"What is it?" Emma asked.

"It's a yearbook. It has photos of my classmates."

Emma sank to the floor and crossed her legs. "May I look at it?"

"Sure." Madeleine opened the book to her class's page. "Can you find me?"

Emma giggled. "Those are funny clothes."

"That was a long time ago." Madeleine laughed. "Do you see me?"

Emma pointed to a few different girls and laughed each time

Madeleine said she was wrong. Finally Madeleine pointed out where she was in the photo, and they both laughed.

∽

Saul heard his daughter laughing down the hallway and found himself smiling while he worked. He loved the sound of Emma's laughter. It was light and airy—like the song of a little bird. He had decided it was okay for Emma to come to Madeleine's house only because he'd be working there, but he would have to restrict her contact with Madeleine after he finished the cabinet job. Meanwhile, he worked in the kitchen with the sound of Emma's and Madeleine's chatter and laughter as background noise.

"*Dat!*" Emma ran into the kitchen nearly thirty minutes later and shoved a large book into his line of sight. The book was open to a page of small portraits of young people. "Look at this photo! It's from when Maddie was a senior in high school." She pointed to a girl dressed in what appeared to be a formal-looking blouse with her hair down. "Wasn't she beautiful?"

Saul hesitated for a moment, uncomfortable because it was against Amish beliefs to make a graven image of a person. Emma's interest in the photographs reminded him of the risk of Madeleine's *Englisher* influence. But he gave in to his curiosity and studied the photo. Madeleine was beautiful, but he didn't feel comfortable commenting on the photograph. Words agreeing with Emma were stuck in his throat.

"I'm sorry." Madeleine appeared in the doorway and grimaced while her porcelain-colored cheeks flushed a bright hue of pink. "I told her you wouldn't want to see the photo, but she insisted. We've been perusing my yearbooks. Emma likes hearing about my childhood, moving from school to school while my mother was in the air force. That was my life until she married my stepfather when I was twelve."

Madeleine was apparently embarrassed, and he couldn't help thinking she looked adorable with her pink cheeks. He quickly pushed the thought away. She was an *Englisher*, and she was his client. Any thoughts about her otherwise were inappropriate and destructive.

"It's a nice photograph," Saul muttered before returning to his cabinet sketches.

"I'm hungry," Emma announced. "What should we make for supper?"

"Emma, Maddie may not want us to stay for supper," Saul said gently. "We shouldn't invite ourselves."

"It's no problem." Madeleine stepped into the kitchen. "What would you like, Emma?" She opened the freezer. "Let me see what I have in here."

"Pizza!" Emma pointed toward a frozen pizza. "Pepperoni sounds good."

"Frozen pizza?" Madeleine turned toward Saul. "Do you like pizza? It's not a very Amish meal."

He shrugged. "That sounds fine to me. Do you mind sharing your food with us again? It seems like you always get stuck with the cooking."

"We can cook at our house sometime soon too," Emma offered.

"That sounds like a plan." Madeleine read the back of the box and then preheated the oven.

Saul had finished up his measurements, sketches, and notes by the time the pizza was ready. Emma talked about school while they ate, and Saul watched Madeleine's reaction to his daughter's stories. She smiled and listened intently while Emma talked. Madeleine seemed like a genuine woman with a warm heart. He was grateful for her friendship, but she was *English*. Any relationship between them was forbidden.

When supper was over, Emma helped Madeleine clean up the kitchen and Saul sat drinking the cup of coffee Madeleine had insisted on making for him.

"Could I please go see the kittens in your barn?" Emma asked while she dried a dish. "I'll run out there quickly and then come back. I just want to see how big they've gotten since the last time I was here."

Madeleine glanced at Saul as if to ask permission. "It's okay with me if it's okay with your *dat*. I'll finish cleaning up if you want to go now."

Saul nodded. "*Ya*, you can go see the cats, but make it quick. It's getting late."

Madeleine nodded toward the pantry. "I bought a big bag of cat food, and there's a dish in the cabinet by the back door. You can take them some food if you want."

"*Danki!*" Emma filled the dish before pulling on her cloak, grabbing a lantern, and rushing out the storm door.

"I remember being quite excited about the barn cats, too, when I was her age," Madeleine said while scrubbing the pizza pan. "I would sit out in the barn for hours and talk to the kittens. Well, I only was allowed to do that after my chores were done." She glanced back at Saul and smiled.

He admired her smile and realized he needed a distraction. He stood, grabbed a dish towel, and picked up a plate.

"You don't have to help," she said. "I can put the dishes away."

"I don't mind." He busied himself with drying.

"*Danki*," she said. After a moment, she said, "I really love it here in Lancaster County. It feels like home. I moved a lot when I was a child, but I always came back here for the summers. Sometimes my grandparents were the only consistent part of my life."

He nodded and dried another dish.

"I guess that's difficult for you to relate to, right? You probably lived in the same house the whole time you were growing up."

"*Ya*, I did, but I went through some changes too."

"You did?" she asked. "What changes did you have?"

"My parents both passed away before I was married."

"Oh, I'm sorry." Her eyes were sad. "May I ask what happened?"

"*Mei dat* had kidney disease." Saul placed the dishes in a cabinet. "He was on dialysis for a long time. He succumbed to the disease when I was eighteen. *Mei mamm* had cancer. She died when I was twenty."

She reached out as if she were going to touch Saul's arm but then pulled her arm back. "That had to be very difficult for you."

"It was." He took the pizza pan from the drain board and began to dry it.

"Do you have any siblings?"

"I have an older *bruder.*"

"You do? Does he live nearby?"

"No, he left the community when he was eighteen."

"Oh. Why did he leave?"

"He wanted to go to college. He was certain he was meant to be a doctor. He became a pediatrician, and he lives out in Oregon."

"Really?" She faced him. "Do you hear from him at all?"

Saul shrugged. "He sends a Christmas card every year with

a picture of his family. He and his wife have four children. We talked about a year ago, and he mentioned coming out to visit. The plans fell through, though. I don't know what we'd talk about if we ever got together, but I would like for Emma to meet her cousins someday."

"Wow." Madeleine's eyes sparkled. "That's interesting that you have a brother who is a doctor. I had no idea."

"He went after his dream, and he's very *froh*." He held up the dry pan. "Does this go under the oven?"

"Yes." She pointed toward the drawer. "You've lost your parents, and your brother moved away. Do you miss your brother?"

He nodded and avoided her sympathetic eyes by stowing the pan.

"I'm very sorry." Madeleine was silent for a moment while she washed the utensils. "When I decided to leave the air force, I wasn't sure what I wanted to do. My *mammi* had left me a good amount of money and also this property. My mother convinced me to move here."

"She had to convince you?" Saul gave her a sideways glance. "I thought you said you loved it here."

"I do love it here, but it was more complicated than that."

He suddenly felt rude for being nosy. "You don't have to share it with me."

"No, it's okay." She pulled the stopper out of the sink, and the water gurgled and belched as it swirled down the drain. She grabbed a wet rag and began to wipe down the table. "I was supposed to get married, but after my fiancé passed away unexpectedly, my world sort of fell apart."

Saul turned and faced her. "Your fiancé?"

"Yes, I was engaged." She continued to wipe the table, even

though it looked already clean to Saul. "Travis was also in the air force."

"That must've been so difficult for you." Saul suddenly related to Madeleine on a deeper level. She, too, had experienced heartache and loss when her fiancé passed away. Her beautiful dark, sad eyes mesmerized him, and the strong emotion made him nervous. He couldn't allow himself to be attracted to this woman. He didn't want to experience the same temptation that had taken Annie away from the community he cherished.

She finished wiping the table and then tossed the rag into the sink. "I've talked your ear off, haven't I? I'm sorry."

"You don't need to apologize for talking." He dried the utensils and slipped them into a drawer.

"What's next with the cabinets?" she asked. "I assume you still need to design them before making and installing them, right?"

"That's right." He pulled the notepad from his pocket. "I'm going to take these notes and sketches and draw formal designs from them. I'll bring them over to show you once they're done. It will take me a few days. I'll also contact the plumber and get on his schedule."

"Great." She pushed a thick lock of dark hair back behind her shoulder. "I can't wait to see them."

"All done!" Emma burst through the storm door, her cheeks rosy from the cold. "I fed the kittens and talked to them for a few minutes. They're doing well."

"Thank you." Madeleine touched Emma's nose and smiled. "You're cold. You need to get home and take a nice, warm bath."

"That's a *gut* idea." Emma hugged Madeleine. "*Danki* for a fun evening."

The tender moment between his daughter and Madeleine

caused Saul to shift his weight from one foot to the other. The hug affected him deeply, his heart warming at the sight. He walked to the mudroom and pulled on his coat, hoping to make a quick exit.

Emma and Madeleine had followed, and Emma started for the door. "Let's go, *Dat*."

He turned to Madeleine and held out his hand. "*Danki* for supper."

"*Gern gschehne*." She shook his hand. "See you soon."

As Saul followed Emma to their house, he tried to sort through his confusing feelings. Madeleine was only a neighbor and a customer, but he couldn't stop remembering her pretty smile and the way his daughter had hugged her.

FIFTEEN

Madeleine clipped the last pair of jeans to the clothesline with two clothespins and then pushed the line forward. She shivered in the brisk air, and her hands were numb from the cold fabric. She was thankful the laundry was finally done. Now she could go do what she'd been longing to do—crochet.

The nightmare that plagued her last night had been lingering at the back of her mind all day, and she needed to find some peace. When running didn't help clear her mind, she crocheted. It was the only way to escape the pain surging through her soul.

She padded into the spare room, sat in the rocking chair, and began to work on the afghan. She lost herself in the rhythm of the work, hoping to erase the dream that had stolen her satisfying sleep. After a while, she heard the back door bang. She'd seen Saul earlier and told him to just come on in when he came over with the designs he had ready. She knew she'd be in the spare room crocheting, and she didn't want to risk not hearing him knock.

After a moment, she heard him call out for her.

"Maddie? Are you in here?"

"I'm in the spare room," Madeleine called. "Come on back."

The sound of his work boots echoed in the hallway, and he

appeared in the doorway holding a clipboard. He pointed toward the back of the house. "I see you figured out the wringer washer."

"Hi, Saul," Madeleine said. "Yes, I did figure out the wringer washer. My *mammi* would be very disappointed if she knew how much money I was spending at the Laundromat."

Saul smiled as he hugged the clipboard to his chest. "*Ya*, you're probably right."

He had a nice smile, and she hoped to see it more often.

"What are you working on?" He stepped into the room and peered at the afghan.

"It's an afghan." She held it out for him to see. "My *mammi* taught me how to crochet when I was around Emma's age. I've found it's the only activity besides running that helps me when my nightmares get really bad."

"Nightmares?" His handsome face was full of concern. "Why do you have nightmares?"

Madeleine paused and silently debated what to share with her friend.

"I didn't mean to intrude." He stepped backward in the direction of the door. "I have your designs to show you." He held up the clipboard. "I wanted to get your approval and show you the final price before I get started. If this isn't a *gut* time, I can leave them on the kitchen table."

She didn't want him to leave. Instead, she was overwhelmed with the inclination to share her story with him. "Please stay." She pointed toward the desk chair. "Pull up a seat."

Saul paused for a moment and then steered the desk chair toward her and sat beside her. He shucked his coat and set it on the floor next to him before placing the clipboard on top of it.

She took a deep breath and studied the afghan while she

considered her words. "I told you my fiancé, Travis, passed away, but I didn't tell you what happened to him." She started to crochet before going on. "He took his own life."

When Saul gasped, she looked up at his shocked expression.

"I knew he was sick," she continued, "but I thought he was getting better."

"He was sick? Did he have a disease?"

"No." Madeleine's voice thickened, and she cleared her throat. "He was suffering from depression. He told me he was seeing a counselor, but I didn't know it had gotten so bad. If I'd known he was struggling, I would've helped him. I always thought I was a good nurse, but I wasn't good enough to help my own fiancé." She thought back to the night he died. "I was working in the ER at the hospital on base that night. I knew a patient had been brought in with a gunshot wound, but I had no idea it was Travis until I saw him on the stretcher."

"I'm so sorry." Saul started to reach for her hand and then stopped, moving his hand back to his side. Was he going to touch her hand? The gesture was warm and comforting, even though their hands never touched.

"Thank you." Tears stung her eyes. "I'll never forget that image of him. It haunts me. Sometimes I dream I'm trying to revive him. Other times I dream I'm working as a flight nurse and his body is there with me on the aircraft."

"Madeleine." He whispered her name as he studied her. "I can't imagine how difficult it is for you to relive that pain over and over again. Do you know why he took his own life?"

"Yes." She sniffed and wiped her eyes. "He left me a note, taped to my door." She nodded toward the desk where she kept the letter. "I found it when I got home that night. You see, a few months earlier, he had learned he was part of a military unit that accidentally bombed an orphanage while they were fighting in the Middle East. In the letter, he told me he loved me, but he wanted to escape the heartache that had taken over his life. He said he couldn't live with himself knowing he'd accidentally killed innocent children. He said he was certain God wanted him to die because those children couldn't live."

"Did he pray about it? Did he ask God for forgiveness?" Saul asked.

"I told him to, over and over again. We went to church together, and we even prayed together. But I guess he couldn't forgive himself. So he shot himself and left me alone to try to pick up the pieces. At least his parents had already passed away, so they didn't have to suffer."

She paused and collected her thoughts.

"I couldn't work in the hospital after that. I always thought of Travis when I took care of wounded patients. It was too much for me to be around the trauma and the death. My tour with the air force was ending around that time, and I didn't sign up for more time. My mother could see how much I was suffering, and she suggested I come out here to try to find some peace, a place that *is* peaceful. That's why I love it here."

Saul's expression was full of sympathy. "Have your nightmares at least gotten any better now that you're away from the hospital and the military base?"

"I don't have them as frequently, and I've found ways to cope." She held up the afghan. "Sometimes the nightmares get so bad that running doesn't help me. One day I started making this afghan, and I felt better. Lately, I've only had them a couple of nights a week."

He nodded. "I'm glad to hear that. I hope it continues to get better."

The compassion in his expression made her feel secure, and she relished the comfort. She was surprised by how close she felt to him at that moment. They were truly becoming friends.

"You're the first person I've shared that story with, other than my parents," she admitted. "Not even with other women who've been my friends. I don't normally tell people about the letter Travis left me. I'm always afraid they'll judge Travis or that they won't understand."

"*Danki* for trusting me with your story."

The intensity in Saul's eyes caused her heart to skip a beat. Did he feel close to her too? A moment passed between them, and she tried to think of something to say to fill the space. She looked down at the clipboard.

"You put those sketches together quickly."

He shrugged. "It doesn't take me long when I know what I want to do."

"Great." She set the afghan on her lap. "I can't wait to see them."

He handed her the clipboard. "Let me know what you think."

Madeleine flipped through the sketches and nodded. "These are exactly what I want." She tried to imagine the new cabinets in her kitchen. "Should we walk out to the kitchen to talk? I want to compare these sketches to the old cabinets."

"That sounds like a *gut* idea."

He followed her out to the kitchen, and she studied the old cabinets and the sketches. "This is perfect. I think they will look fantastic, don't you?"

He nodded.

"I think my *daadi* built the original cabinets."

"*Ya*, he did. He told me." Saul ran his fingers over the counter. "He did all of the work in the kitchen. He and his *daed* built this *haus*."

"Did you know my grandparents well?" Madeleine asked.

"I did. My best friend, Marcus, told me your grandparents were looking to sell part of their property, and he thought I might want to buy it. I didn't have enough room on the land my parents left me to build a big shop. My *dat* wasn't a farmer, and he didn't have much property at all. I already had a buyer for my land, but I hadn't found anything I liked yet." He leaned against the counter. "I came and met your *daadi*, and we struck a deal. I got to know them well over the years."

Madeleine smiled. "They were really good people. I didn't see them much once my mother remarried and I became a teenager. I got busy with school and college and then my military service. And even when I was here, I only stayed a day or two. Not long enough to meet anyone." Her smile faded. "But mostly, I miss them."

"I do too," Saul said. "After Mel passed away, I used to stop by to see Martha frequently and ask if she needed anything."

"Really?" Madeleine was overwhelmed with appreciation for him. "That's very nice. Thank you for doing that."

"Martha was a very special lady. She had a special relationship with my Emma." Saul looked down at the counter, and Madeleine wondered if it was painful for him to talk about his feelings. "After Annie was gone and Emma got old enough to venture off our property by herself a little, Emma began visiting Martha. Martha became a *mammi* to her. In fact, I'm certain you already know Emma called her '*Mammi*.' I was grateful that God put a mother figure in Emma's life. We didn't have my *mamm* or Annie's *mamm* around."

He rubbed his bearded chin. "Martha taught Emma a lot of things *mamms* are supposed to teach daughters. She taught her how to sew, how to work in the garden, how to cook." He looked at her and smiled. "How to use the wringer washer."

She laughed. "Is that directed at me?"

He grinned, and Madeleine laughed again.

"In all seriousness," he continued, "Martha was a special friend to Emma. It was difficult for us when she passed away."

Tears filled Madeleine's eyes once again. "I hated that I missed the service for her, especially after I had missed my grandfather's funeral too. I was on my way home from overseas when she died, and I didn't get home in time. My mom said it was lovely, though."

"It was." He paused. "Emma was upset for a long time. She cried and cried about Martha. I didn't know how to help her. Your *mammi* meant a lot to her."

"I imagine Emma meant a lot to her too." Madeleine thought back to the time she spent with her grandmother. "Whenever I visited here as a child, my *mammi* let me stay in my mother's room. I wore my mother's Amish clothes, and I went to service with my grandparents. Sometimes my *mammi* would accidentally call me Leah. She would have tears in her eyes, and she would say I looked just like my mother."

Saul nodded slowly. "It had to be difficult for her to see you and think of Leah."

"Did she ever talk to you about my mother?" Madeleine asked.

"Sometimes she'd mention Leah and say that she missed her. I told her I understood because, well—" He paused for a moment, and she wondered if he was thinking of Annie and her abandonment. "My *bruder* had left."

Madeleine longed to ask him about Annie, but she didn't want to say too much. She didn't want to ruin their budding friendship. "It has to be challenging for you to raise Emma alone."

Saul's expression hardened and his shoulders stiffened. He took the clipboard from her and studied the sketches. Madeleine immediately regretted her words. She'd said something that upset him, and she groped for a subject that would make it better.

"You've done a wonderful job with Emma," Madeleine continued. "She's a lovely girl."

"Let me show you the estimate," he said, flipping to the last page on the clipboard. "Does this work for your budget?" He handed the clipboard back to her.

In a flash, his warm, friendly demeanor was gone, and he was all business. Annie was a forbidden subject. Madeleine yearned to take back what she'd said. She longed for the closeness she'd felt with him while they were talking in the spare room.

"Saul." She studied his eyes. "I'm sorry."

"Take a look at the estimate." He tapped the paper. "Does this work for you?"

Madeleine craned her neck and studied the document. "This is fine. How much do you need now to start the job?"

He pointed toward the last line on the document. "There's the deposit. Does that work for you?"

"Yes. I'll write you a check." She headed into the spare room and fished her checkbook out of the desk. She sank into the desk chair and sighed. Why did she have to ruin the nice conversation she was enjoying with Saul? He had a warm heart, and he loved his daughter. She saw glimpses of the kind and gentle man he most likely had been when he was first married. She wanted to get to know him better, but he had built a wall around his heart after his wife abandoned him and Emma. She prayed that she could see beyond that wall and maybe even melt his heart.

∽

Saul stared after Madeleine as she left the kitchen, guilt filling his heart. He knew he'd hurt her feelings when he abruptly changed the subject, but he couldn't bring himself to discuss Annie. The subject was too painful, and opening up that wound made him too vulnerable.

Yet he had immediately felt remorseful when he'd glimpsed the hurt in Madeleine's eyes. She, too, had been hurt by someone, but he wasn't ready to share his feelings about Annie's abandonment with anyone. It was best to keep those feelings close to his shattered heart.

The storm door opened and shut with a bang, and Emma stood in the mudroom doorway with a frown creasing her sweet face.

"*Dat?*" Emma's voice was shaky. "I was looking for you at the shop."

"Emma?" He opened his arms to her. "*Was iss letz, mei liewe?*"

A tear trickled down her cheek.

"*Kumm,*" he said.

She stepped into his hug, and a sob broke from her throat.

"Emma?" Madeleine appeared in the doorway, holding a check in her hand. "What happened?" She turned to Saul. "Is she okay?"

Saul shook his head. "I don't know what's wrong." He looked

down at his daughter and then pulled her next to him as he sat down on a chair. "What's wrong, Emma? Please tell me."

Madeleine pulled a chair up next to them. "Are you okay, Emma?" She touched Emma's arm. "Do you want me to leave so you can talk to your *dat* alone?"

"No, you can stay." Emma wiped her eyes. "It's Jacob. He made fun of me again on the playground."

"Who's Jacob?" Madeleine asked.

"He's a mean *bu* at my school." Emma's face twisted into a scowl. "He makes comments to me every day. Today was worse." Her eyes flooded with tears again. "He laughed when I fell on the playground, and then he called me a wimpy *maedel* when I couldn't hit the softball. He embarrassed me in front of everyone. I yelled at him, and he kept laughing at me."

Saul felt frustration boil inside of him. He knew he couldn't shield her from all the hurt in the world, but he was determined to try.

"You should talk to Teacher Lillian," Saul said. "Tell her how much Jacob hurts your feelings. If that doesn't work, then I'll talk to Jacob's parents."

Madeleine rubbed Emma's arm. "I had a boy tease me when I was about your age."

"You did?" Emma sniffed and wiped her hand over her eyes again. "What did you do?"

"Well, I talked to my teacher, and she said she'd talk to him." Madeleine pushed back a lock of Emma's hair that had fallen from her prayer covering. "But I found something that worked better than that."

"What was it?" Emma asked with curiosity.

"I ignored him," Madeleine explained. "That did more good than talking to my teacher or her talking to his parents."

Emma tilted her head and studied Madeleine. "Why would that work?"

"It would work because he wants to see you get angry. He's saying mean things and making fun of you to get a rise out of you. It's a game, and in his eyes, he wins when you get angry. He wants to see you upset because then he thinks he's the coolest kid in the class. If you ignore him, then he loses and you win the game." While she spoke, Madeleine took a paper napkin from the holder in the center of the table and gently wiped away Emma's tears.

The sweet gesture caused Saul's heart to warm. At that moment, he was overwhelmed with admiration for Madeleine.

"You're saying that I should just ignore him?" Emma asked.

"Right." Madeleine nodded. "That way you don't give him the power to hurt you."

"Should I still tell my teacher how he embarrasses me?" Emma asked.

"*Ya*," Saul chimed in. "I think you need to tell your teacher." He met Madeleine's gaze, and she nodded in agreement.

"You should tell your teacher, but make sure you're in private when you tell her. Don't let Jacob hear you tell her that you're upset. He can't know how much he hurts you because then he wins." Madeleine touched Emma's shoulder. "Do you think you can be strong and not show your emotions?"

"*Ya*, I *can* do it." Emma wrapped her arms around Madeleine's neck and hugged her close. "*Danki*."

"You're welcome." Madeleine smiled. "I'm happy to help."

"Maddie," Emma said, "you're my best grown-up friend."

Saul's shoulders stiffened. He and his daughter were getting too emotionally involved with Madeleine. She was a nice person, someone who had been hurt like him, but she was making her way into their hearts, and this could only lead to trouble. He had to find a way to pull away from her—if it wasn't too late.

"*Danki*, Emma." Madeleine's eyes shimmered, and Saul wondered if she was going to cry. "That's the sweetest thing anyone has ever said to me." She wiped her own eyes and then turned to Saul. "Here's my check." She held out the small piece of paper, and her voice quaked. "Let me know when you need more money."

"*Danki*." He slipped the check onto the clipboard. "I'll get started on the cabinets right away. It should take me about two weeks to build them and the counter, and then I'll need to take these old cabinets down."

"What are we making for supper tonight?" Emma asked.

"Oh." Madeleine glanced at Saul. "I don't know if you have plans . . ."

"How about we make something at our *haus* tonight?" Emma looked at her father. "Would it be okay if Maddie and I cooked at our *haus* tonight?"

Saul hesitated as he turned to Madeleine. Her expression was tentative. Did she feel the tension clenching his jaw?

"Please, *Dat*?" Emma folded her hands as if to pray.

He felt stuck between his eager daughter and his determination not to let Madeleine worm her way any further into their lives.

"We can try for another night," Madeleine said.

"Why not tonight?" Emma frowned. "Do *you* have plans?"

"Tonight is fine." Saul stood. "I have work to do, but you two can figure out a menu. We have plenty of food at our *haus*. I went to the market earlier today."

"*Ya*." Emma clapped. "I know exactly what we can make."

∞

Madeleine dried the last of the dishes and placed them in a cabinet while Emma still prattled on about school and her friends. All during supper she'd wondered how she could make Saul see that she'd never meant to cross the line with him or hurt his feelings by asking about his former wife. She couldn't stand the distance between them. He'd avoided her gaze and studied his plate the whole time they were eating.

"Supper was *appeditlich*," Saul said as he stood by the mudroom door. "I'm going to go out in the shop for a little while."

"Don't stay out too late, *Dat*," Emma said, sounding like his mother instead of his daughter. "You need your rest."

Saul's mouth turned up in a slight smile. "I promise I won't." He turned to Madeleine and gave her a halfhearted nod. "*Gut nacht*, Madeleine."

Madeleine stiffened at the sound of her formal name. She couldn't stand the awkwardness, and she wouldn't sleep until their friendship was back on track.

He disappeared through the door, and Madeleine turned to Emma.

"I think I'm going to head home," she said. "I need to do a few things before I go to bed."

"Okay." Emma smiled up at her. "I'll see you soon."

"Yes, you will," Madeleine agreed. "Now, remember what I

said about the bully. Be sure to stand your ground with him, and don't let him get to you. Let me know what happens."

"Okay." Emma gave her a quick hug. "*Gut nacht.*"

"*Gut nacht.*" Madeleine pulled on her coat and hurried outside. She was going to talk to Saul and set things straight before she headed home.

She found Saul in the shop, rearranging piles of wood.

"Saul."

He turned toward her, and his eyebrows rose toward his hairline.

"Can we talk before I go home?" She shivered and hugged her coat closer to her body.

"*Ya.*" He leaned on the workbench.

She took a deep breath and prayed for the right words. "I'm sorry about earlier."

He shook his head. "I don't understand."

"When you came to see me this afternoon, I know I crossed a line." She hoped his expression would relax. "I was rude, and I didn't mean to be. I would never try to deliberately hurt your feelings or make you uncomfortable."

His expression remained stoic, but she thought she saw a change in his eyes. She needed to continue trying to bring back the warm man she'd glimpsed.

"You know I was hurt too," she said. "I explained it all to you earlier. I never imagined I'd wind up here in Pennsylvania and all alone. I believed I'd be married and have children of my own by now. After losing Travis, I lost my love of nursing. I lost everything." She put one hand on her chest. "Travis left a hole in my heart."

Saul looked toward the workbench, and she knew she'd hit a

nerve. She did a mental head shake. Why had she managed to say the wrong thing again?

"I should go." She jammed her thumb toward the door. "Good night, Saul."

∽

Saul saw the regret in Madeleine's eyes, and he couldn't let her go. She'd bared her soul to him earlier, and then he'd shut her out. She was trying to reach out to him, and he had to tell her the truth. After all, though few talked about divorce, the rumors about Annie when she first left had spread throughout the community like wildfire. Eventually Madeleine could run into someone who would tell her the truth about Annie.

Madeleine reached for the doorknob.

"Wait," Saul said, and her hand fell to her side. "Please don't go."

She faced him, fresh tears shimmering in her eyes.

"Thank you for sharing your story with me. Now I need to tell you the truth about Annie." He heaved a deep breath as he took a step toward her. "Annie left me and Emma."

Madeleine wiped her eyes and studied him.

He paused and stared down at the toes of his work boots. "This isn't easy for me to talk about."

"I'm sorry." Her voice was soft. "You don't have to tell me."

"No, I do." He looked up at her. "You deserve the truth."

She nodded.

"Annie loved someone else, and I knew I was her second choice." He crossed his arms over his chest as if to protect his heart. "She loved my friend Timothy, but he left and went to a former Amish community in Missouri. She was heartbroken, and I tried to console her. When I asked her to marry me, I knew she only said yes because I was her last option. I had saved up money to buy this land and build this shop after also selling my parents' land." He gestured around the room. "I knew she was marrying me out of desperation, but I never imagined she'd leave me."

Saying the words out loud twisted his insides, but he plowed through, moving his gaze back to his boots to avoid her sympathetic expression. "I don't think she expected this, but Timothy came back for her once he was settled and had a home ready for her. It was obvious she still didn't love me the way I'd hoped she someday would, but I prayed she'd make it work between us for Emma's sake." He shook his head. "But she left and never looked back. And then one day I received divorce papers in the mail. I was shattered by that. Our community doesn't believe in divorce. But I signed them because I didn't really have a choice."

A tear trickled down Madeleine's cheek. "I'm sorry."

Saul took in her kind expression and then cleared his throat to avoid showing his own raging emotions. "I told Emma her mother passed away. It was easier to say that than to tell her that her own *mamm* left her for a man. She once asked me how she died, and I said it was pneumonia. I told her Annie had gone into the hospital and never come home, and that satisfied her questions. She never asked me where her mother is buried, never asked if there was a funeral she just didn't remember because she was so young. So it's been possible to keep up the lie. I know lying is a sin, but I would do anything to protect her from the painful truth."

"I understand," Madeleine whispered.

"And that lie is the truth now." Saul leaned back on the

workbench. "Timothy wrote me a little over a year ago and told me Annie died in an accident. He and Annie were spending the day on a friend's boat, and there was a collision with another boat." He shook his head. "She really is gone, and I need to tell Emma the truth someday. I'm waiting for the right time to tell her."

"That makes sense." She fingered the zipper on her coat. "I meant what I said this afternoon when I said you are doing a great job with Emma. She's a lovely young lady."

"*Danki.*" Saul fingered his beard. "Now that Annie is gone, I want to find Emma a proper mother."

"I'm certain you will." Madeleine was silent for a moment, and he felt overwhelmed by the soft expression in her eyes. "You're a good man, Saul, and you deserve to be happy. Annie was blind if she couldn't see that, but don't sell yourself short. You deserve a good woman, one who will appreciate you. You're a wonderful father, a hard worker, and you're thoughtful and kind. You're a good friend."

Saul was speechless. He'd never expected such enormous compliments to come from her lips.

"Thank you for sharing that with me," Madeleine said. "I should go."

He nodded, still not certain what to say.

She started for the door and then faced him again. "Thanksgiving is next week, and I was wondering if you and Emma have plans. I know sometimes there are weddings on Thanksgiving."

"We usually eat at my friend Marcus's *haus.*"

"Oh." She frowned. "I understand. I was thinking about going home to California to see my mom and stepdad, but I'd rather save the money for the cabinets."

"You should come." He extended the invitation before thinking it through.

"What do you mean?"

"Come to Marcus's with us." He stood up straight. "You'll be my guest."

"Oh." She looked surprised. "Are you certain that would be okay?"

"Why not?"

"I don't know if Marcus would want an *Englisher* at his table on Thanksgiving." She gave him a nervous smile.

"It will be fine. I'll let him know."

"What can I bring?" she asked.

"I usually provide dessert. Maybe you can make a pie."

"Great." Madeleine's expression brightened. "I'll make a pumpkin pie. Two of them." She rubbed her hands together. "I have my *mammi's* recipe." She started for the door again. "Good night, Saul."

"*Gut nacht.*" She disappeared from the shop, and Saul hoped he hadn't made a mistake by baring his soul to his new friend.

SIXTEEN

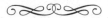

Emma gnawed her lower lip. She had stayed just inside the schoolhouse door as the rest of the students started leaving at the end of the day, and now she was watching Teacher Lillian wave good-bye to them as they filed past. She'd been considering what she'd say to her teacher ever since she'd spoken to Madeleine last week. Today felt like the right time to talk to her.

Teacher Lillian waved to the last student and then turned toward Emma. "Emma? What are you still doing here?" She pushed her glasses farther up her nose and studied her. "Is everything okay?"

Emma fingered the handle on her lunchbox. "Jacob has been bullying me."

"*Ach* no. Let's sit and talk." Lillian made a sweeping gesture toward the desks.

Emma took a seat at her desk and faced her teacher, who pulled a chair up next to her. "He makes fun of me when I miss the ball during softball and he calls me names."

Teacher Lillian shook her head and frowned. "I'm sorry I haven't noticed he was doing that to you."

"I talked to my friend Maddie, and she gave me some *gut*

advice." Emma sat up taller as confidence surged through her. "She told me she had bully problems when she was my age, and she ignored the bully. She said Jacob is just trying to get a reaction out of me, and I'll take away his power if I ignore him."

"That sounds like a *gut* plan."

"*Mei dat* said I should still talk to you about Jacob."

Lillian nodded. "I will talk to Jacob and his parents."

"I don't want him to know he upset me, though." Emma held her hands up as if to stop her teacher. "He can't know I gave him that power. I need him to think it doesn't bother me. Maddie said that's the only way to defeat a bully."

"I'll keep a better watch on the playground and do my best to catch him in the act. After I see what he's doing, I'll talk to him, and I'll also talk to his parents. Would that work?"

"*Ya.*" Emma nodded with enthusiasm. "That would be perfect. *Danki*, Teacher Lillian." She stood and started for the door.

"Wait, Emma," Lillian called after her. "Who is your friend Maddie?"

"She's my neighbor." Emma smiled. "She's *English*. Her *mammi* owned the property where *mei dat* and I live before he bought it. Maddie moved into her *mammi's haus*, and we've become best *freinden*. We cook together, and *mei dat* is replacing her cabinets. We have a lot of fun together."

"Oh." Lillian grimaced. "You know it's best not to get too close to *Englishers*. They aren't like us. They live a different way, and they sometimes offer a temptation to leave our community."

"She wouldn't do that." Emma felt the need to defend her special friend. "She's very nice, and she's my *freind*."

Teacher Lillian paused. "It would be better if you didn't spend too much time with her. Just promise me you'll be careful. You don't want to get too attached to her and then wind up hurt."

"I don't understand. What do you mean by 'hurt'?" Emma contemplated her teacher's caution.

"*Mei mamm* became *English*, and I don't see her anymore. It's been very hard on me," her teacher said. "I know this must be difficult for you to understand, but I miss *mei mamm* very much. She's not Amish anymore, and it's made me *bedauerlich*. I don't want you to be *bedauerlich* if Maddie decides to move away."

"Oh." Emma smiled. "Maddie said *mei dat* has said that same thing, but I don't think she'll move away. Most people stay in their *haus* after they fix it up, right? *Mei dat* says that a lot of times people put new cabinets in so they enjoy their *haus* even more. It's a lot of money to put in new cabinets."

"Right." Teacher Lillian nodded. "You'd better go. I don't want your *dat* to worry about you. Be careful walking home."

"I will. Have a nice Thanksgiving!" Emma waved and then rushed out of the school. As she walked home, she thought about her conversation with Teacher Lillian. Maddie wouldn't leave like Teacher Lillian said. Her teacher had to be wrong. After all, Maddie was her best grown-up friend. She pushed her worries aside as she walked home. Everything was going to be fine. Jacob was going to leave her alone, and Maddie was going to stay.

⌒⌒

Madeleine placed the two pumpkin pies she'd baked into the bottom of a large basket she'd found in the pantry. She hoped the pies tasted as delicious as they smelled and looked. She'd worried all morning about giving Saul's friends a good impression of her, and she'd changed her clothes four times before settling on a matching chocolate-brown blouse and skirt with tights. She'd styled her hair in a French twist and didn't apply any makeup.

A knock sounded, and Madeleine pulled on her coat and carried the basket to the mudroom where she could see Saul and Emma through the window on the door.

"Are you ready?" Saul asked as soon as she swung open the storm door.

"Yes, I am." She held up the basket. "I'm hoping these pies will taste as good as my *mammi's*."

"I'm sure they will." Saul took the basket from her. "I'll carry this for you."

"Let's go." Emma started toward the pickup truck. "I can't wait to see Esther."

Madeleine climbed into the driver's seat, and Emma sat in the middle with her father beside her. Emma spent the short ride to the Smucker farm discussing recipes. Madeleine nodded and agreed with whatever Emma said, but her mind was occupied with thoughts of Saul. She hoped he approved of her outfit, and she prayed she wouldn't say anything that embarrassed him or made him regret inviting her to join them for Thanksgiving dinner.

When they arrived at the farm, Madeleine parked halfway up the rock driveway and killed the engine. She climbed out of the truck and met Saul at the front bumper while Emma ran ahead toward the house. Madeleine studied the farmhouse, and doubt assaulted her mind. Why was she here at this Amish family's house? She didn't have a right to intrude on their holiday. She belonged with her non-Amish family in California.

"Are you all right?" Saul asked.

"Yes." She forced a smile.

He studied her. "I haven't known you long, but I can tell when you're not being truthful."

"Am I that obvious?" she asked.

He nodded. "You are to me."

"I'm nervous about meeting your friends." She smoothed her hands over her coat. "I don't want to embarrass you."

"You won't embarrass me, and they're looking forward to meeting you." He started for the house. "Let's go inside before we freeze out here."

Madeleine followed Saul into the two-story, white clapboard house, and she immediately inhaled the delicious aroma of turkey. They made their way through the spacious family room to the kitchen, where Emma and a little blonde girl were setting the table. She remembered her being with Emma at Carolyn's wedding.

"Hello!" A pretty blonde woman who looked to be in her early thirties smiled at them. "You must be Madeleine. I'm Sylvia."

"It's nice to meet you." Madeleine unbuttoned her coat. "Thank you for having me for supper."

"You're welcome." Sylvia touched Esther's arm. "This is Esther." The girl waved.

"It's nice to meet you," Madeleine told the girl. "I saw you with Emma at Carolyn Glick's wedding, and I've heard a lot about you from Emma."

"*Danki*," Esther said.

Sylvia looked at Saul. "Marcus is in the shop if you want to go see him. I'll send the girls out to get you when supper is ready."

"All right." Saul handed Sylvia the basket. "Maddie made pies."

"Oh!" Sylvia took the basket from him. "That's perfect. *Danki*." She placed the basket on the counter.

Saul held out his hand. "Would you like me to hang up your coat?"

"That would be nice." Madeleine handed her coat to him.

He headed toward the back door, stopping to hang up her coat near the mudroom on his way out.

Madeleine glanced around the kitchen and into the family room and enclosed porch. "You have a lovely home."

"*Danki.*" Sylvia pointed toward a pot on the stove. "Would you please stir the noodles?"

"Oh yes." Madeleine moved to the stove, happy to have a job to keep her mind off how self-conscious she felt.

"Saul told us you work at the Lancaster Grand Hotel." Sylvia pulled a loaf of bread from the bread box on the counter and began to slice it.

"Yes, I work there part-time." Madeleine stirred while she spoke. "Martha Stoltzfus was my *mammi.*"

"I'm sorry for your loss. I remember Martha. She was a lovely lady." Sylvia glanced toward the girls, who were placing utensils by the plates. "Esther, would you please get out the butter and then fill six glasses with water?"

"*Ya, Mamm,*" Esther agreed.

"How long have you known Saul?" Madeleine asked.

"Marcus and I went to school with Saul and—" Sylvia stopped speaking as if to correct herself. "We went to school with Saul and his *bruder.*"

"Oh." Was Sylvia going to say Annie instead of his brother?

Sylvia finished cutting up the bread and placed it in a basket before moving toward the oven. "Excuse me. I'm going to check the turkey."

"Of course." Madeleine stepped away from the stove and

turned toward Esther and Emma, who were discussing friends at school. When Sylvia opened the oven door, the warm smell of the succulent turkey permeated the room.

"I think it's almost ready." Sylvia closed the door and spoke to the girls. "When you finish the table, please go collect your fathers."

Soon the girls pulled on their cloaks and rushed out the door.

"Esther is adorable," Madeleine said. "Emma talks about her all the time."

"*Danki.*" Sylvia nodded toward a cabinet. "Would you please grab some serving bowls from there and put the noodles, vegetables, and mashed potatoes in them?"

"I'd be happy to." Madeleine gathered the bowls and began filling them, and Sylvia pulled the turkey from the oven. "Everything smells delicious."

"*Danki.*" Sylvia placed the turkey onto a platter. "I'll let Marcus carve it." She faced Madeleine. "I want to talk to you quickly before the girls return."

"Oh." Sylvia's serious expression caused Madeleine's stomach to tighten. "What did you want to discuss?"

Sylvia wiped her hands on a dish towel. "I know you care for Emma and Saul. I can tell by the way you look at them."

Madeleine nodded. "I do."

"I have a feeling Saul cares for you." Sylvia's expression was full of worry. "He may seem like a strong man, but he's been hurt."

"I know about Annie," Madeleine said. "He told me what happened, and I realize he's hurting. I only want to be his friend."

"I knew Annie. What she did to Saul practically destroyed him emotionally. He's held it together all these years just for Emma's sake." Sylvia crossed her arms over her apron. "What Annie did hurt us all. She was my best friend, and I never imagined she'd leave her family for another man. I tried to stop her, but she was stubborn. Anyway, Marcus and I have done our best to help Saul. I've tried to be like a *mamm* to Emma. My point is that I don't want to see either one of them hurt."

"I don't want to see them hurt either," Madeleine said. "I care about them, and I would never want to hurt them. It's not my intention to cause problems here."

"You seem like a nice person." Sylvia tossed the dish towel onto the counter. "I just need you to promise me you'll be careful of Saul's heart."

"I will," Madeleine said. "But we're only friends."

Sylvia seemed unconvinced, and she wondered why Sylvia had made the assumption they were more than friends. The question filtered through Madeleine's mind while they continued preparing the table for the Thanksgiving feast.

Saul followed the girls and Marcus into the house, where he hung his coat and hat on the peg by the back door and then stopped just inside the doorway to the kitchen. He watched Madeleine help Sylvia deliver food to the table and noticed she seemed at ease when she instructed the girls to wash up for supper. He was alarmed by his strong emotions for her. Yet simultaneously, he enjoyed having her join him for the holiday. He was conflicted in his feelings, but he pushed the worry aside and decided to enjoy the day.

Marcus turned to Saul and gave him a concerned expression. "Have a seat."

Saul sank into a chair while Marcus moved to the counter and began to carve the turkey.

When Madeleine and Sylvia had finished their preparations, Madeleine sat in a chair across from him. She gave him a tentative smile and then looked down at her plate. Why was she suddenly acting shy toward him?

"Here's the turkey." Marcus brought a platter to the table. "It's time to eat."

Marcus sat at the head of the table to Saul's right, and Sylvia sat at the other end of the table. Emma took the chair beside Madeleine, and Esther sat beside her mother. After the silent prayer, the sound of utensils scraping plates filled the air as arms reached and grabbed for the many platters and bowls.

"How do you celebrate Thanksgiving, Maddie?" Emma asked as she plopped a mound of mashed potatoes onto her plate.

"I celebrate the same way you do." Madeleine spooned some stuffing. "We have turkey and the trimmings."

"Does that mean you do exactly the same thing we do on Thanksgiving?" Esther chimed in. "Do you have any traditions that are different from ours?"

"Well, let's see." Madeleine handed the bowl of stuffing to Marcus. "When I was little, my mom and I would say what we were most thankful for before we started to eat."

"Really?" Esther and Emma exchanged smiles. "Let's do that." Esther turned to her father. "What are you most thankful for?"

Marcus stroked his beard with his free hand as he met Sylvia's gaze. "I guess I am most thankful for my family."

"You guess?" Sylvia raised an eyebrow, and Saul stifled a chuckle.

"No, I don't guess," Marcus quickly added. "I am most thankful for my family."

"That's better." Sylvia smiled. "I'm most thankful for my family and our health."

"*Ya*, that's a *gut* one." Marcus picked up the meat platter, selected a piece of turkey, and dropped it onto his plate. He passed the platter to Saul. "Who's next?"

"I am!" Esther raised her hand as if she were in school. "I'm most thankful for our home. I've heard of people who don't have a place to sleep at night, and they must be cold." She pointed toward Emma. "How about you, Emma?"

"I'm thankful for my *freinden*." Emma smiled up at Madeleine. "God has given me wonderful *freinden*."

Madeleine returned the smile, and Saul felt his heart turn over in his chest. The love between his daughter and Madeleine was overwhelming. He tried to look unaffected, however, when in his peripheral vision he saw Marcus was studying him.

"What are you most thankful for, Maddie?" Emma asked.

Madeleine glanced down at her plate and then looked over at Emma again. "I'm thankful for my new home and my new life here in Lancaster County." She then looked across the table at Saul. "What are you most thankful for, Saul?"

Saul looked into her beautiful orbs and then at Emma, who smiled over at him. "I'm most thankful for my family and my *freinden*."

Emma smiled, and he returned the gesture.

∽

Saul thought he might burst after enjoying the scrumptious Thanksgiving meal and then delicious pumpkin pie. After dessert,

Emma and Esther cleaned off the table, and Madeleine and Sylvia began washing the dishes.

Marcus touched Saul's arm. "Let's go outside and check on the animals."

Saul followed him to the back, where they pulled on their coats and then stepped out into the crisp evening air.

"What are you doing?" Marcus asked as they made their way to the barn.

"What do you mean?" Saul asked.

"I see how you look at her." Marcus shook his head. "I know you're lonely, but you know how this is going to end for you."

Saul stopped walking and stared at his best friend. "Are you accusing me of having a relationship with Maddie? We're only *freinden*. Emma enjoys visiting her, and I'm replacing the cabinets in her *haus*."

Marcus snorted with sarcasm. "Please, Saul. I'm not blind, and I'm not stupid. You call her Maddie. You only use nicknames for people you're close to. I thought it was strange when you asked if you could bring her over for supper today, but I never expected you to be this attached. I thought maybe you'd taken pity on her because she's alone. It looks to me like it's more than just pity."

Saul heaved a heavy sigh and leaned against a fence. He'd been caught with his feelings exposed.

"Saul, I've known you since we were *kinner*. I don't want you to wind up hurt. You need to take a step back before she breaks your heart. You've been through enough." Marcus stood beside him. "I'd rather see you meet someone in our community or even someone from another church district. Emma is attached to her, too, and you don't want her to experience another loss, do you?"

"No." Saul shook his head while he stared at Madeleine's truck. "You're right."

"You know I am." Marcus started for the barn.

Marcus disappeared into the barn as his words soaked through Saul. Marcus was right, but Saul didn't know how to let go of the strong and overwhelming emotions that were swelling within him.

∞

Later that evening, Madeleine kicked off her shoes before she went to her bedroom. She was full both physically and spiritually after the day she had spent at the Smuckers' farm. The food was delicious and the company was delightful. She only wished she could get Sylvia's warning to cease echoing through her mind. Why had Sylvia felt the need to warn her? Why would Sylvia assume Madeleine would hurt Saul? They were only friends!

She was just starting to pull off her tights when her iPhone began to buzz. She reached over to her dresser and picked it up.

"Happy Thanksgiving, Maddie!" Mom's voice sounded in her ear.

"Hey, Mom." Madeleine smiled. "How was your day?"

"It was good, but we missed you. I've been trying to call you all day. Did you get my messages?"

"Oh, I'm sorry. I went out, and I left my phone here at home." Madeleine balanced the phone between her neck and shoulder while she pulled off her tights and skirt. "I just got home, and I haven't had a chance to check my voice mail."

"Where were you all day?" Now she started pulling on yoga pants and slippers.

"I had Thanksgiving with friends."

"Which friends? Someone from work?"

"No. Saul, Emma, and their friends," Madeleine said. "I had an Amish Thanksgiving."

"What?" Her mother gasped. "I thought you were convinced Saul didn't like you."

"Oh, he's been much nicer recently. He's going to replace my kitchen cabinets." She tried to pull off her blouse but wound up tangled in it. "Hang on a minute." She placed the phone on the dresser and changed into a long-sleeve shirt. "Okay. I'm back."

"Madeleine Dawn!" her mother snapped. "Tell me about Saul and Emma."

"I will. Just calm down." Madeleine sank onto the edge of the bed. "We've been spending time together lately, and I asked them if they had Thanksgiving plans. Saul invited me to go with them to have Thanksgiving dinner with his best friend, Marcus, and his family. We had a really nice time."

"And he's replacing your cabinets?"

"Right," Madeleine said. "He's a cabinetmaker, and the kitchen cabinets are almost falling off the walls. You had to have noticed that when you were here for *Mammi's* service."

"*Ya,* I did." Her mother's voice was softer. "My *daadi* helped my *dat* build those cabinets a very long time ago."

Alarm seeped through Madeleine. She'd never heard her mother use *Dietsch* words before. "Do you want me to leave them? I can ask him to fix them instead of replacing them."

"No, no," her mother said. "It's your house now. You do what you want with it."

"No, Mom." Madeleine shook her head. "Don't be like that. I don't want to upset you."

"It's fine, really. Tell me about your day with Saul and his friends."

Madeleine shared what they ate and how much fun they had talking. "It was a great day. I'm enjoying my new Amish friends. I really feel like I belong here. I mean, I don't even miss electricity or television. I only use my phone to talk to you. And Saul is very sweet. I'm enjoying getting to know him and Emma. Emma told me I'm her best grown-up friend. I helped her figure out how to handle a bully the other day." She paused, but her mother remained quiet. "Hello? Are you there, Mom? Did we get disconnected?"

"I'm still here. I was just listening. I know you like spending time with Saul and Emma, but you need to remember that they're Amish."

"How could I forget that, Mom?" Madeleine asked while rolling onto her side and facing the wall. "I know we're from different worlds. I'm just enjoying their company."

"Well, you sound like you're really close to them."

"They are sort of like my family, even though we're not related." Madeleine shook her head. "I'm not making sense. I'm enjoying being here and being a part of their community. I think I want to go to a church service. *Mammi* used to take me to them. I might call Carolyn and see if I can go to a service with her again."

"That sounds nice," Mom said. "I remember you enjoyed going to services with your grandmother. Just be careful, okay? I don't want you to get hurt. You have to remember that Saul lives by certain rules, and those rules are strict."

"Is that why you left?" Madeleine asked.

"Yes, that's part of the reason."

"And my father was the other reason."

"Yes, I met your father, and we wanted to see the world together."

"Was it easy to leave?"

"No." Mom paused. "It was a difficult decision to leave the only life I'd ever known. I had to say good-bye to my friends and my family. But I was certain I was in love. I was too young and immature to realize the mistakes I was making. I had tunnel vision, and I only wanted to get married to your father. I was anxious to feel grown up even though I was pushing myself too hard."

"I'm sorry. I'm sure it was hard on *Mammi*. I know she missed you."

"Yes, I know it was." Mom sighed. "But your father and I were certain we'd conquer the world. We both wanted to join the military and travel, and the Amish community wouldn't allow me to do that."

"Did you ever regret leaving?" Madeleine asked.

"I missed my parents and my friends, and I often felt alone. It's a big world outside the tight-knit Amish community. I didn't appreciate how the community took care of its members until I was out on my own. It wasn't easy after your father left me, but I never regretted my choices. After all, I had you."

Madeleine smiled. "You should come and visit me. Maybe we could find some of your old friends."

"I might someday," Mom said. "I'm not sure if I'm ready yet."

"Well, you'll have to come and see my new cabinets."

Mom laughed. "That's a deal."

Madeleine sat up. "Tell me about your day."

While her mother talked about her Thanksgiving, Madeleine couldn't help smiling. Her mother was happy in California, but Madeleine had experienced a perfect day in Lancaster County. She was thankful for her new life.

SEVENTEEN

Madeleine called Carolyn Saturday morning. The phone rang several times before someone answered.

"Hello," a feminine voice said. "This is Glick's Belgian and Dutch Harness Horses. How may I help you?"

"Carolyn? This is Madeleine Miller."

"Madeleine!" Carolyn sounded surprised. "How are you?"

"I'm well, thanks. How are you doing?"

"Just great. I'm surprised to hear from you. Is everything all right?"

"Everything is fine," Madeleine said. "I was wondering if I could go to church with you tomorrow if there's a service in the district."

"Actually there is a service, and I'd love for you to come," Carolyn said. "It's going to be held at Ruth Ebersol's *haus*."

"Wonderful," Madeleine said. "I'll meet you there. What's the address?"

"Hang on one moment. Let me check my address book . . . Oh, here it is." Carolyn rattled off the address and directions. "I'll see you tomorrow."

"Great!" Madeleine disconnected the phone and smiled. She

felt such a strong connection to the Amish community, and she wanted to experience more of it. She looked through her closet to find the most appropriate outfit to wear. She couldn't wait to experience another Amish church service and meet more members of the community. She was certain her grandparents would be happy to see her immersing herself in the culture again.

⤸

Madeleine parked her pickup truck on the road beside Ruth's house Sunday morning and then slipped her keys into her skirt pocket as she walked up the driveway. Her eyes moved to the sea of buggies parked by the barn. Would Saul and Emma be at the service today?

She smoothed her hands over her skirt as she entered the kitchen where the women were gathered before the service. She hoped she looked presentable. She'd found her grandmother's cloak and pulled that over her skirt and blouse. She'd also found a Mennonite lace prayer doily and attached it to the back of her head over a tight bun.

"Madeleine!" Carolyn emerged from the circle of women and hugged her. Her eyes took in Madeleine's long black skirt and navy blue blouse. "You look *schee*." Carolyn reached around and touched the lace prayer covering Madeleine had put on her head. "Where did you find that *schee* covering? I love it."

"*Danki*," Madeleine said as she pulled off her cloak and hung it over her arm. "I found it in my *mammi's* sewing closet. I think she used to make these and sell them to the local Mennonites."

"That's wonderful!" Carolyn pulled her toward the circle of women. "Come meet my family and *freinden*."

Madeleine smiled and shook hands as Carolyn introduced her to the circle of women. She felt a part of the community, and she was thankful for Carolyn's help. After she met everyone in the room, Carolyn led Madeleine over to a quiet corner.

"How have you been?" Carolyn asked. "I haven't had time to talk to you at work."

"I've been fine," Madeleine said. "How was your Thanksgiving in your new home?"

"It was *gut.*" Carolyn pushed the ribbons from her prayer covering behind her shoulders. "We had Joshua's parents over, and my family stopped by for dessert. We had a *gut* time. How was yours?"

"It was very nice. Saul and Emma Beiler invited me to eat with them at Marcus Smucker's *haus.* I really had a lovely time. I took two homemade pumpkin pies."

"How fun!" Carolyn smiled. "Did you enjoy your first Amish Thanksgiving?"

"I really enjoyed spending the day with Saul, Emma, and their friends. They made me feel comfortable and welcome. It was perfect." Madeleine considered telling Carolyn what Sylvia had said to her, but she decided not to. She didn't want to give Carolyn the wrong impression about her friendship with Saul.

"I'm glad you're getting to know Saul and Emma." Carolyn's smile suddenly faded. "I want to tell you something, but I don't want anyone else to hear." She moved closer to Madeleine and lowered her voice. "Josh still wants me to quit the hotel, no later than spring. I really don't want to quit yet. I want to keep working there, maybe even longer than spring. But he's insistent."

"Oh." Madeleine studied her friend. "Why do you want to keep working there? Doesn't he need your help with the horse business?"

"He does, but the job at the hotel was all I had for a long time. It doesn't feel right to give it up. Not yet."

"But you're his wife now. Aren't you expected to be home and helping him?" Madeleine asked. "Aren't you supposed to be his helpmate?"

Carolyn sighed. "I know you're right. I want to be his helpmate, but I also want to help our family by bringing in my own little salary. I can save that money for Benjamin. I can help him buy his own *haus* when he's old enough."

"I'm certain Joshua will help him buy a *haus*. Isn't Joshua going to adopt him?" Madeleine asked.

Carolyn smiled. "*Ya*, he is. Benjamin will be a Glick soon."

"You don't need to worry about Benjamin as much now." Madeleine touched Carolyn's arm. "Josh is going to take care of you both. You know he will."

The kitchen clock started to chime nine.

"It's time to head into the barn." Carolyn pointed toward Madeleine's cloak. "You're going to need that."

"Madeleine!" Ruth approached them with a wide smile and hugged Madeleine. "What a nice surprise."

"It's great to see you too," Madeleine said. "I called Carolyn yesterday and asked if there was a service today."

"I'm glad you came. Would you like to sit in the back with me?" Ruth asked.

"I'd love that." Madeleine followed Ruth and Carolyn as they made their way toward the large barn where the backless benches were set up.

Carolyn touched Madeleine's hand. "I'm going to go sit with my sister-in-law. I'll see you after the service."

"Okay," Madeleine said. As soon as she was sitting in the

back beside Ruth, she scanned the congregation and spotted Emma with the other young girls, sitting beside Esther. Emma met her gaze and waved. Madeleine smiled as she waved in response.

She looked over to the area where the married men—and obviously men who had been married—sat. Saul was leaning over and talking to Marcus beside him. Saul was handsome in his Sunday best. The thought took her by surprise. Was she attracted to Saul? Did she have a crush on him? She thought of Sylvia's warning, and suddenly it made sense. Had Sylvia noticed an attraction between Madeleine and Saul? She swallowed a groan. Any relationship between Saul and her would be forbidden. She couldn't tempt him to break the rules, which was what her mother had been trying to tell her on the phone Thursday night.

Madeleine had to dismiss any romantic feelings she may have for Saul. Besides, after losing Travis, she didn't need another broken heart. She was better off alone.

Soon the congregation began singing, and Madeleine followed along in the *Ausbund*. She lost herself in the beauty of the Amish service and thought of her grandparents. She would have loved to worship with them in her adult years.

Saul followed along with the opening hymn. But soon the sound of the congregation singing was only background noise to his churning thoughts. He'd spent the past couple of days working on Madeleine's cabinets and thinking of her. Marcus's warning echoed in his mind constantly. He needed to find a way to get her out of his thoughts, but it seemed impossible.

His eyes scanned the congregation, and when he spotted her in the back row, he froze.

"Saul?" Marcus whispered. "*Was iss letz?*"

"Nothing," Saul muttered.

"Something is wrong. You look upset," Marcus prodded.

"No, no." Saul looked down at the *Ausbund*. He tried to join in the singing, but his gaze was drawn to Madeleine as if she were a magnet pulling him to her without his consent or control. She was beautiful with her cloak over a navy blue blouse, and her hair was pulled back in a bun. His heart thumped in his chest. She followed along with the hymn, and her mouth moved in time with the rest of the congregation. She could actually read and understand the words to *Lob Lied*? This left him stunned.

Saul tried to imagine Madeleine as a member of the church, but the idea was preposterous. How could someone who'd grown up *English* and had even served in the military make the ultimate sacrifice of giving up all her worldly possessions and joining an Amish church district? She could never settle for the plain life after seeing the world. Conversions rarely happened, and he didn't expect her to be the first *Englisher* to join his church district.

But if she were to join, then we could be together.

He shook his head. Madeleine wasn't going to join the church, and he had to stop taunting himself with the idea. He needed to stay loyal to his church and his beliefs and also be the best example possible for his daughter. He would finish Madeleine's cabinets and then go back to being only a neighbor to her. They would wave if they saw each other outside and leave it at that.

Saul trained his eyes on the *Ausbund*, but he couldn't bring himself to sing. Instead, his thoughts were stuck on Madeleine and the temptation he felt when he was near her. The women he allowed in Emma's life had to be proper influences. Perhaps Marcus and Sylvia would help him find a widow or unmarried woman who would consider dating him.

Throughout the service, Saul didn't hear the minister's or the bishop's words; instead, he was thinking of his daughter.

His thoughts were interrupted when the minister recited a verse from the book of James. "'Therefore confess your sins to each other and pray for each other so that you may be healed,'" he said. "'The prayer of a righteous person is powerful and effective.'"

The verse felt like a punch to Saul's chest. *I need God to lead my life in the right direction.* When he thought about Madeleine and her beauty, he was allowing himself to be just as sinful as Annie. *I have to stop this before it's too late. It's my job to lead Emma toward the plain life, and I need God's help.*

Saul closed his eyes and prayed for God to cleanse his thoughts and his prayers.

∞

Madeleine helped Ruth and Carolyn deliver food to the tables after the service before moving around the long tables to fill coffee cups and greet the members of the congregation. She smiled at everyone.

She was filling the last cup when she noticed Saul sitting with the other men at one of the tables. She had tried to catch his eye during the service, but he was so engrossed in the service that he never looked her way. When he finally met her gaze, she smiled at him. He returned the gesture with a tentative smile and then turned back to Marcus. Why wasn't he as friendly as he'd been on Thursday? She hoped to talk to him privately later.

"Maddie!" Emma appeared behind her. "It's *gut* to see you here at church."

"Hi, Emma." Madeleine held up the empty coffeepot. "I'm heading back to the kitchen. Would you like to walk with me?"

"*Ya!*" Emma fell into step beside her. "I can help you fill cups if you'd like."

"We'll see what Ruth needs us to do," Madeleine said. "It was a nice service."

"Could you understand it?" Emma asked.

"I understood most of it," Madeleine said as they stepped into the kitchen.

Madeleine and Emma helped deliver more food for the men and then ate lunch with the women. Afterward, they assisted with cleaning up the kitchen.

Once the kitchen was clean, Madeleine found her cloak and pulled it on as she moved to where Carolyn and Ruth were talking. "*Danki* for including me in the service today. I had a really nice time."

"We loved having you," Carolyn said. "I'm *froh* you could come."

"Absolutely," Ruth agreed. "I'll see you at work on Tuesday."

"Have a nice afternoon," Madeleine said before stepping out to the driveway.

She was almost to her truck when she saw Saul standing outside with Marcus, Sylvia, and the girls. She waved, and she was certain that Saul and Marcus exchanged concerned expressions. What did those expressions mean? Certainly they had nothing to do with her.

Saul said something to Emma, and they began walking toward her.

"Maddie!" Emma ran over with Saul following closely behind.

"Hi, Emma!" Madeleine hugged her and looked to where Saul stood. "Hi, Saul. I didn't get to talk to you much today."

"I was surprised to see you here." His expression was devoid of the usual warmth. He glanced down at Emma. "Go to the buggy. I'll be there in a moment."

Emma gave him a curious expression and then turned to Madeleine. "I'll see you later."

"I look forward to it," Madeleine told her before she headed off. She looked back at Saul. "I was hoping you and Emma could join me for supper tonight. I was going to make something special."

Saul cupped his hand to the back of his neck and frowned. "I'm sorry, Madeleine, but I don't think that's a *gut* idea."

"Oh?" Her stomach twisted with worry. "Why not?"

"Look, I like you, Madeleine. I like you a lot, but I don't think you're the best influence for Emma. It's better to keep our relationship neighborly."

"Neighborly?" She shook her head. "I don't understand."

His expression was cold, as if they'd just met, but his eyes seemed sad again. "I'm going to have your cabinets ready for installation in a couple of weeks. Until then, I don't think we should see each other."

"But we had such a nice time on Thanksgiving." Madeleine groped for an explanation to his sudden coldness. "What's changed?" She glanced past him to where Marcus was watching them. "Is it Marcus? Does he disapprove of our friendship?"

"I'm sorry, Madeleine. It's better this way. I can't risk losing my *dochder* to the outside world. She's all I have left."

"I don't want to take your daughter or tempt her to leave the

Amish church." Madeleine's voice was thick with disappointment and hurt.

"I'm sorry," he repeated.

They stared at each other, and tears stung her eyes.

Without uttering another word, Saul turned and started for his buggy.

She wiped the tears that splattered her cheeks.

What have I done to make him reject me as if I were a total stranger? I'm not even worthy of Saul's and Emma's friendship. I've failed again, just like I failed with Travis. I'm not worthy of the Amish community.

c∞ɔ

Lillian saw Ruth across the kitchen talking to her aunt Carolyn and an *Englisher* woman. She'd longed to talk to Ruth all day, but she wanted to get her alone to keep their conversation private. She waited until Carolyn and the *Englisher* left, and then she crossed the kitchen and stopped next to Ruth.

"Ruth," Lillian said. "I was hoping to talk to you."

"Lily!" Ruth smiled at her. "How are you?"

"I'm fine, *danki*." Lillian looked around the kitchen at all the women talking and laughing. "Could we please speak privately?"

"Of course, dear." Ruth pointed toward a doorway. "Let's go into my sewing room."

"That would be perfect." Lillian followed the older woman into a small room containing a treadle sewing machine, two chairs, and a table cluttered with piles of material.

"You look troubled." Ruth sank into a chair and motioned for Lillian to sit beside her. "What's on your mind?"

"I've been struggling with something." Lillian's voice was thick with her emotion. "I tried talking to *mei mammi*, but she doesn't understand. I thought you might be able to help me sort through my feelings."

"Of course, *mei liewe*. What is it?"

"I used to believe I was supposed to completely shun *mei mamm* and not have anything to do with her." Lillian's eyes filled with tears. "I thought I should punish her for leaving me. But now I don't know what I'm supposed to do." She stared down at her lap, plucking some fuzz off her apron. "I found out that *mei mamm* is going to have a *boppli*."

"She is?" Ruth gasped. "What a blessing!"

Lillian looked up and Ruth smiled with tears glistening in her eyes. "I know," she whispered. "A *boppli* is always a blessing, and I want to be a part of my new sibling's life."

"Of course you do." Ruth touched Lillian's hand. "That *boppli* is your family, just as your *mamm*, Amanda, Andrew, and even Trey are your family."

"But I don't know how to forgive *mei mamm*." Tears trickled down her hot cheeks, splattering her glasses. "I don't know how to let go of the anger I have about her leaving me. Like I said, I tried to talk to *mei mammi* about this, but she doesn't understand how I feel stuck in the middle. She says *mei mamm* doesn't deserve to be forgiven for taking my siblings away from her and also for leaving the church. I want to have my family, but I also want to stay Amish."

Ruth nodded. "I understand how you feel."

"You do?" Lillian asked. "How can you understand?"

"My son left Paradise," Ruth said. "He moved to a former Amish community in Missouri."

"I had no idea." Lillian removed her glasses and wiped her sleeve over her face before rubbing a corner of her apron over the lenses. "When did he leave?"

"It's been about seventeen years ago now." Ruth had a faraway look in her eyes. "I miss him every day, but I'm also angry and hurt that he left."

Lillian nodded slowly. "That's exactly how I feel. I still love *mei mamm*, and I miss her. But I'm angry and hurt that she left me."

"But we have to remember what the Lord says in the book of Matthew. 'If you do not forgive others their sins, your Father will not forgive your sins.'"

Lillian contemplated the Scripture verse. "You're saying I need to forgive her."

Ruth nodded. "Yes. It's not easy, but you need to forgive her. I've forgiven my son, even though it's been hard." She patted Lillian's hand. "Think about it, and pray about it, Lily. Let the Lord guide your heart."

"*Danki*." Lillian stood and hugged her friend.

"*Gern gschehne*." Ruth patted Lillian's back. "You can talk to me anytime you need to."

EIGHTEEN

G uilt rained down on Saul as he guided his horse toward his house after the church service. He hadn't been able to stand the sadness and disappointment in Madeleine's eyes when he told her they couldn't be friends anymore. He still couldn't. He had to sever their close relationship, but saying the words out loud to her cut deeply into his soul. He hadn't experienced such a deep attachment to a woman since he was a young man. Yet he had to suppress those feelings and concentrate on raising his daughter the right way, teaching her to live within the confines of the *Ordnung*.

"Emma," he said while keeping his eyes trained on the road ahead, "we need to discuss something serious."

"What's that, *Dat*?" Emma asked while sitting beside him.

"I need you to stop spending time with Madeleine."

"But you said I could go to her *haus* while you were working on her cabinets."

"I made a mistake. I should've stuck with my original decision to keep our distance," Saul said. "I was wrong. You need to be with other Amish."

"But she was Amish at one time."

"No, she wasn't. Her grandparents were Amish. She was raised *English*, and you know that, Emma."

"But she's my best *freind*," Emma said, her voice raising an octave.

"No, she's not your best *freind*. Esther Smucker is your best *freind*. It's not right for you to spend all your free time with an *Englisher* adult."

"But, *Dat!*" Her voice pitched even higher. "She's my best grown-up *freind*. I like being with Maddie."

"Please don't whine, Emma. You know I can't stand it when you whine." He stared at the road ahead. "I was wrong to allow you to spend so much time with Madeleine. I need you to remain at home."

"I don't understand." Emma crossed her arms over her cloak in defiance. "We had a lot of fun with her. You like being with her too. If you didn't like her, then you wouldn't have invited her for Thanksgiving at Marcus's *haus*."

Saul knew he'd been caught, but he was the parent. He had to lay down the law. "I was wrong, and now we need to stop breaking the rules. We need to stay with the Amish."

"I'm going to miss her." Emma sniffed. "She was going to teach me how to make more of *Mammi's* recipes."

"You can learn to cook from Sylvia. Maybe you should go and spend more time at their *haus*."

"It won't be the same," Emma muttered while staring out the window with her back to Saul.

His daughter's disappointment was breaking his heart, but he had to stand firm. "I need you to respect my rules, Emma. If I catch you over at Madeleine's *haus*, then you will be in trouble."

"*Ya, Dat.*"

Saul guided the horse into the driveway just as Madeleine walked out to the small barn behind her house. He quickly moved his gaze toward his house and tried to pretend Madeleine wasn't there, even though he already felt himself missing her friendship.

❧

Madeleine tried to concentrate on dusting a hotel room, but her mind kept wandering back to the painful conversation she'd had with Saul on Sunday. She'd tried to erase it from her mind and ignore how much he'd hurt her, but there was no avoiding it.

Her nightmares had also returned in full force. When she closed her eyes both Sunday and Monday night, she found herself back on the C-130, trying to keep wounded military personnel alive while working alone without enough medical supplies. Travis was there too—dying in her arms as she begged him to stay and tried to revive him. She thought being in Amish Country had finally healed both her broken heart and her nightmares, but losing Saul and Emma's friendship had brought them back.

"Madeleine?" Ruth's voice rang into the room.

She turned to see Ruth standing in the doorway with a concerned expression. "Hi, Ruth." Madeleine pushed her long ponytail behind her shoulder. "I didn't see you there."

"Do you realize it's after one?" Ruth pointed toward the digital clock on the nightstand. "You missed lunch."

"Oh." Madeleine shrugged and tried to smile. "I was very busy and didn't realize what time it was."

"You need to eat." Ruth stepped into the room. "You can finish your work later."

"I'm not hungry." It wasn't a lie. Her painful encounter with Saul on Sunday had stolen her ability to sleep and eat.

"What's going on?" Ruth sank onto a corner of the king-size bed. "You seemed *froh* on Sunday. What happened to you to change your mood during the past two days? Talk to me, Madeleine."

Madeleine pulled out the desk chair and sat across from Ruth. "I don't know how to explain it because I don't really understand it." She placed the duster cloth on the dresser behind her. "I'd been spending a lot of time with Saul and Emma. We were sharing meals, and he even invited me to Thanksgiving dinner at Marcus Smucker's house."

Ruth nodded. "What happened?"

"He seemed to be avoiding me on Sunday, and I finally had a chance to talk to him after the service was over and right before I left." Madeleine slumped back in the chair. "He basically told me I am a bad influence for Emma, and I can no longer be friends with him or his daughter."

"And this hurts you." Ruth filled in the blanks.

"I'm crushed," Madeleine said. "Saul and I were becoming close. I had told him about my fiancé committing suicide, and he had shared with me what happened with Annie."

Ruth cupped her hand to her mouth. "I had no idea your fiancé had committed suicide. I'm very sorry."

"Thank you." Madeleine cleared her throat as a lump swelled. "That's why I moved here. I needed to start over and try to find a way to cope with the loss."

"I can't imagine the pain you've felt after losing him."

"I was finally feeling better, but then . . . I never imagined Saul would cut me off like this." Madeleine pointed toward the clock. "That's why I missed lunch. I feel like my heart has been punched.

Saul and Emma have come to mean a lot to me. They were like my surrogate family. I shared things with Saul that I had never told anyone. In fact, in some ways, I've felt closer to Saul than I did to Travis. When I talked to Saul, I knew he was truly listening to me. Travis was distant, especially after he returned from serving overseas. I think I connected with Saul on a deeper level because we both had experienced a great loss. Saul's friendship meant so much to me, but now it's gone."

Ruth frowned. "I'm sorry, Madeleine. I don't know what to say."

"Why would he do this?" Madeleine asked. "We had such a nice time on Thanksgiving. I was wondering if they would consider having Christmas dinner with me, but I guess I'll be alone on Christmas."

"You don't need to be alone. I would be happy to invite you over for Christmas."

Madeleine shook her head. "You don't need to do that. I might look into a flight home to see my mom and stepdad." She paused. "How can he go from inviting me to spend a holiday with him and his daughter to telling me he doesn't want his daughter to visit me because he's afraid I'll tempt Emma to leave the community?"

"I think he's scared of getting too close to you," Ruth explained. "He lost Annie, and that made him leery of getting too close to any woman. And he's afraid Emma will want to learn more about your *English* background and then consider leaving the church."

"I'm a good person, Ruth." Madeleine shook her head. "I adore Emma. We had a lot of fun cooking together. I thought maybe she'd help me plant a garden in the spring." She considered her home. "I'm almost living like an Amish person. I don't have any electricity, and I went to a service on Sunday. How can I be a bad influence?"

Madeleine stared toward the large, sliding-glass door that led out to the balcony a moment before turning back to her friend. "My mother told me to be careful, and Sylvia Smucker asked me to be careful with Saul's heart. I didn't understand then why they warned me, but now I do. I care for Saul too much."

"I'm sorry, Madeleine." Ruth shook her head and frowned. "He can't be with you unless one of you makes a sacrifice."

"I know. Thanks for listening. I'll just have to learn to live without them in my life." Madeleine stood. "I'd better get back to cleaning."

"Madeleine," Ruth began. "Give him time. Maybe he'll realize you can be friends without crossing a line into dangerous territory."

Madeleine nodded. "I think I need to just go about my business and let him come to me. Maybe it will get easier."

"It will." Ruth touched her arm. "Pray for him."

"I will," Madeleine promised. "I always do."

The two weeks since Saul had told Madeleine they could no longer be friends had passed at a painful snail's pace for him. Not only had Saul hammered his fingers more than once while building her cabinets, but the project had also kept Madeleine in the forefront of his mind. The mental picture of her dressed plainly at the church service stayed in his head almost constantly.

Truth be told, he'd wanted to get the cabinets finished as quickly as possible because he looked forward to working in her kitchen again. But now on this Monday afternoon, he'd finally completed his work and told himself he needed to get the installation over and done with. He had to keep his resolve to sever the ties they'd built over the last couple of months.

Saul stepped outside his shop, spotted Madeleine's truck in the driveway, and started toward her house. He hoped to work on installing the cabinets even while she was at work so he could keep their contact to a minimum. He prayed he could install them in a couple of weeks' time at the most.

Saul climbed the steps to Madeleine's back porch and knocked on the door. When she appeared, clad in jeans and a long-sleeved shirt, he couldn't help but notice how beautiful she was. Her thick, dark hair cascaded past her shoulders, and he couldn't take his eyes off of it for a moment. He longed to feel the texture of her hair. Was it as soft as it looked? What did it smell like?

"Saul," she said, her eyes open wide. "Hi."

"Uh, I have your cabinets ready to install," he said. "I was wondering if I could get a key so I could work even when you're at the hotel."

"That would be fine. My days at the hotel are usually Tuesdays, Thursdays, and Fridays, so I work tomorrow." Madeleine opened the storm door and motioned for him to step into the house. "Come on into the kitchen. I'll find the spare key."

She went on through to the hallway, and he stood in the kitchen, glancing around and remembering the meals they had shared there. He missed those times, but he needed to forget them. It was better that way.

She reappeared a few minutes later and handed him a single key on a round key chain with an *M* hanging from it. Her fingers brushed his, and he felt a spark ignite between them. He quickly jammed the key into his pocket.

"*Danki.*" Saul cleared his throat. "I'll start by removing your old cabinets tomorrow. Would you please empty them out tonight?"

"Sure," Madeleine said, her determined eyes boring into his. "How's Emma?"

"She's *gut.*" He gave her a stiff nod. "I'll get started first thing tomorrow. What time do you leave for work?"

"I normally leave around seven, but you can come over anytime. It's not a problem."

"I'll be here after seven." He started for the door.

"Saul," she called after him.

He faced her, anxious about what she wanted. Would she say something that would melt his heart and cause him to be tempted again?

"How long do you think the installation will take?" she asked.

He shrugged. "Approximately two weeks. I'll do it as quickly as I can, and I'll see when the plumber can come in and take care of your sink. I also wondered if you wanted me to paint before I put up the new cabinets. I can go by the home improvement store and pick up some white to match what you currently have on your kitchen walls."

"That sounds fine. I'm okay with any shade of white." She looked down at the table where a stack of papers sat. "Whenever I'm here, I'll do my best to stay out of your way so you can finish without any interference from me."

"Oh." He wasn't sure how to take her comment. "That will be fine. But I'll do my best to finish quickly and before you return home on the days you work."

"Fine. Have a good night. Tell Emma I said hi." Madeleine stayed at the far end of the kitchen while he headed out through the mudroom.

Saul fingered the key in his pocket as he walked home. He was glad she'd given him the spare key. Now he had a way to avoid Madeleine, at least on the days she was at work. The intensity in her eyes was almost too much to bear. He missed her friendship. He longed for their special talks. Every day he thought of something he wanted to share with her, but he knew he couldn't dare take the chance. His feelings for her went much deeper than what he ever felt for Annie. He could never open his heart to her.

He gripped the key in his pocket. With that key he would lock his heart away from Madeleine. He didn't want to work on the cabinets with her in the house. He was better off working alone whenever he could, when she wasn't there to remind him of how much he longed to be with her.

The following afternoon, Madeleine returned home from work and was surprised to find Saul still there in her kitchen. His back was to her as he pulled another of the old cabinets down. His shoulders were broad, and his back was muscular as he moved. She stood in the doorway of the mudroom in awe.

When he turned to face her, she quickly looked away and pulled off her coat.

"I didn't hear you come in," Saul said. "I got a late start, but I'm almost done."

"Take your time. I'll stay out of your way."

Madeleine put her keys in her coat pocket, hung up her coat, dropped her tote bag on the floor, and started for the hallway. She quickly moved past him, careful not to trip over the broken cabinets or the pile of tools.

She hurried to her bedroom, forcefully closing and locking the door behind her. She quickly changed into running pants and a long-sleeve workout shirt, hung up her work clothes, and grabbed her phone. As she sat down on the bed, she punched in her mother's number. She had made a decision about the holidays today, and it was time to tell her parents the news.

After four rings, her call went to voice mail, and she heard her mother's voice. "You've reached Leah McMillan. I can't come to the phone right now. Please leave me a message. Thanks!"

"Hey, Mom." Madeleine flopped onto her back, allowing her head to hit the pillow. "I'm coming home for Christmas. I hope that's okay. I really miss you and Jack, and I thought it was the best time to come." She paused, gathering her confused thoughts. "I know this is really last minute, but I hope it's okay. I'll fly home on the 23rd and then come back on the 29th. Give me a call when you get this message. Bye, Mom."

Madeleine disconnected the call and dropped her phone onto the bed. She closed her eyes and rubbed her forehead. She missed her parents, but truthfully she just couldn't bear to spend Christmas alone. Going home to her family made the most sense, even though she was going home with her tail between her legs. Even though she'd told her mother she was certain she belonged here in Amish Country, now she knew she'd failed. Still, she wasn't giving up. She'd regroup and make this place her home. After the holidays.

Madeleine rolled onto her side and stared at the wall. She couldn't go back out to the kitchen with Saul there. Seeing him was torture. Instead, she would hide in her room until he left. It was childish, but hiding was easier than looking into the face of the person who had caused her such heartache.

❦

Madeleine disappeared down the hallway. After getting a late start because of some new orders that came in that morning, Saul had been so engrossed in his work that he hadn't heard the door open, and she'd surprised him. But then she was gone in a flash. Her bedroom door slammed, and then the lock clicked.

After several minutes, her voice sounded through the door. He didn't mean to listen to her conversation, but the small house made it difficult not to overhear.

His mouth dropped open when she said she was going home to California for Christmas. The news was like a knife slicing into his heart. Why would she go there after she said she had to save her money for the cabinets? Why had she decided to go at the last minute? The questions continued to echo through his mind while he took down the last of the old cabinets before preparing the walls for painting.

What was she was doing back there? Was she upset? Did she need someone to talk to?

Why did he care? He couldn't be her friend. He needed to do his job and not worry about her. This was strictly business. He had been hired to do a job, and he was going to do it.

❦

Madeleine stared at the ceiling while she listened to Saul working in the kitchen. After several minutes, she pulled her Bible from her nightstand and began to read it. Reading her Bible always provided her comfort and strength when she was serving overseas. She found her way to the second book of Thessalonians, and two verses in the second chapter seemed to speak to her. She read them out loud.

"'May our Lord Jesus Christ himself and God our Father, who loved us and by his grace gave us eternal encouragement and good hope, encourage your hearts and strengthen you in every good deed and word.'"

The Scripture verses rang through her. She needed to keep Jesus in the forefront of her thoughts and not worry about her friendship with Saul. Jesus would take care of her and lead her down the correct path.

She closed her eyes. *Lord, please help me. I thought my heartache after losing Travis had healed, but now I have a brand-new one. I miss Saul and Emma more than I ever imagined I would. It hurts to see them. Please help me navigate through this heartache. Only you can give me the strength I need to find happiness. I thought you had led me to Amish Country to start over again, but now I'm lost and hurting once again. Where do I belong, God? Will I ever find anyone who will love me? Am I even worthy of love? Help me, Lord. Amen.*

After she prayed, she continued reading. Soon the noise in the kitchen subsided, and she assumed Saul was gone. She needed to go figure out what to make for supper.

When she entered the kitchen, she saw that all the old cabinets had been removed from the wall, but only a couple of them were on the floor. Where were the others? Why was it so cold in there?

She found the storm door propped open and saw Saul positioning the old cabinets outside. He had taken them out on the porch, seemed to be making room for the last one, and was sure to come right back in. Madeleine went back to the kitchen and examined the last two cabinets. She lifted one in an attempt to take it out to the porch for him. She was prepared to do anything to get him out of her house for the day.

She hefted the cabinet into her arms, and her eyes widened. It was much heavier than she had imagined. She wasn't certain how she was going to get to the door without injuring her back.

"Stop." Saul came up behind her. "I'll take that."

"I've got it," she muttered.

"Don't be stubborn," he snapped. "I'll carry it. I'm taking all of them out to the porch so I can get out of your way. I need to hurry. It's cold with the storm door propped open."

Saul reached around her and took the cabinet. As he grabbed it, his arm rubbed up against hers, and she felt his body heat radiate through her sleeve. His sinewy arm moved down hers, and she shivered at the contact, not at the cold air coming in from outside. She quickly stepped aside and averted her eyes, trying to recover from the thrill of his touch. Why was she attracted to someone she couldn't have? It was pure torture.

He carried the cabinet out to the porch and then walked back into the kitchen, his expression full of determination.

"Where are you taking the old cabinets?" she asked, rubbing her arms against the cold air.

"To my shop, if that's okay with you. I can make something out of them."

"That's fine. Why don't you load them into the bed of my truck, and I'll drive them down to your shop?" she offered.

He shook his head. "I was going to go get a wagon and a horse."

"Don't be silly." She pointed toward the door. "I'll back my truck up to the porch, and we can load up the cabinets. It's no trouble at all. Then I'll come hold the storm door open for you while you take out the last cabinet."

He gave her a quick nod. "Fine."

His curt response and stoic expression cut her to the bone. How could he have gone from being her good friend to treating her like a stranger in only a few days? He could turn his emotions on and off like a light switch. How could he be so unfeeling? She could never turn her emotions off the way he did. She'd never understand Saul, and she was only hurting herself by trying to analyze him.

"I'll get my truck," she said as she moved past him before grabbing her coat and closing the storm door behind her.

Madeleine backed her truck up to the porch and then climbed the steps to the row of cabinets, shelves, and doors. She opened the storm door for Saul to bring out the last cabinet.

"Do you want me to start loading them into the truck bed?" she asked as she closed the door behind him.

"You can't lift them." He set the cabinet down. "I'll load them."

"I'm a nurse. I used to lift patients and equipment." She pointed toward the cabinet doors. "I'll load the doors and shelves."

"Fine," he said.

Madeleine placed the doors and shelves into the bed of the truck while Saul loaded the cabinets. She tried her best to avoid touching him, but they brushed past each other a couple of times. Once all the cabinets were loaded, she climbed into the driver's seat, and Saul got in beside her.

They drove the short distance in silence. When they reached the shop, Madeleine unloaded the shelves and doors and placed them on a workbench while Saul carried in the cabinets and set them at the far end of the large room. After everything was unloaded, she went outside, slammed the truck's tailgate, and glanced across the property. Was Emma home? If so, then was she instructed to avoid all contact with Madeleine?

"I'll start painting tomorrow, and once it's dry, I'll start installing the new cabinets."

Madeleine glanced over her shoulder to where Saul stood in the shop doorway. "Sounds great." She started for the driver's side door and then faced him. "Tell Emma I said hi."

He nodded and then disappeared into the shop.

NINETEEN

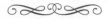

Saul's shoes crunched the rock driveway, and the crisp morning air tickled his nose as he headed toward Madeleine's house. His gaze fell on her pickup truck, and he scowled. Although he knew she didn't work on Wednesdays, he'd hoped she would be out running errands this morning, maybe even for the whole day. He gripped the cold metal handle of his toolbox in one hand and a can of paint in the other as he climbed the steps leading to her back door. After opening the storm door and knocking, he waited for her to come.

Through the door's windowpane, he could see Madeleine enter the mudroom. She was clad in tight black running pants that stopped at just above her ankles and a snug-fitting pink, long-sleeve, athletic-looking shirt that accentuated her thin but healthy body.

"Good morning," she said after she wrenched the door open.

Her lips formed a smile, but the sentiment didn't reach her sad eyes. He hesitated just a moment as she quickly slipped on a matching windbreaker and zipped it, and he noticed her hair was pulled back in a thick ponytail that flittered around her shoulder as she moved. As his eyes took in her beautiful face and fit body, he felt his resolve crumbling. He needed a distraction before he broke his vow to stay away from her.

"Hello." Saul moved past her and placed the toolbox on the floor of the kitchen. "I'm going to get started installing the cabinets tomorrow." He kept his back to her and began pulling out tools. "Today I'll paint and then let it dry overnight. Tomorrow I'll work on getting the walls ready for the installation, and then I'll load up the cabinets and bring them over."

"That's fine. I have a bag of new paintbrushes and other painting supplies in the spare room. I'm going for a run. There are drinks in the refrigerator if you get thirsty." Madeleine stepped back to the still-open back door. "See you later."

"*Ya,*" he said, turning toward her. "See you."

She headed out, closing the door hard and letting the storm door slam shut behind her with a loud bang.

Saul shook his head. Why was it this difficult for him to maintain his composure when she was around? But looking into her dark eyes nearly melted his restraint. She was beautiful, more beautiful than any woman he'd ever met. If he was reading her expressions correctly, she felt an attraction too.

Saul had spent more than an hour last night lying in bed, staring at the ceiling, and contemplating Madeleine. He remembered the spark of electricity when they'd accidentally brushed against each other yesterday. He analyzed the emotion in her eyes when they'd said good-bye last night. He mulled over the phone call he'd overheard. Was she going to California for the sole purpose of getting away from him? He couldn't stand the thought of her leaving. He wanted to be with her, but it was impossible. He longed to be her friend. *At least* her friend.

I'm a mess. I need help, and only God can provide the help I need, he thought. He needed to pray more and listen for God's responses.

As he headed to the spare room to find the painting supplies, he sent up a silent prayer to God, begging him to help keep his emotions in check and guide him. He needed God to help him stay true to his beliefs.

⌒∞⌒

Madeleine's feet pounded the pavement as she pushed her body to run, run as fast as she could away from her house. She'd hoped to be gone from the house before he'd arrived this morning, but things didn't work out the way she'd planned. Instead, she'd had to be civil and then exit as quickly as she could.

She followed her usual path through Paradise, jogging past the beautiful farms that were a part of the place she considered home. As she rounded a corner, she saw the sign for the Heart of Paradise Bed-and-Breakfast. Madeleine had run into Hannah a few times at the market, and she had promised to visit her. She wondered if Hannah was busy or if she could take some time to talk with her this morning.

Madeleine picked up speed and headed toward the bed-and-breakfast. A black sedan sat in the driveway. Hopefully Hannah was home. She climbed the front steps and rang the doorbell. A few moments later, the door opened, and Trey greeted her as he swung open the storm door.

"Hi, Madeleine."

"Hi, Trey. I wasn't sure if you'd remember me."

"Oh, of course I do. How are you doing?"

"I'm fine, thanks." Madeleine worked to catch her breath. "I was wondering if Hannah is home."

"She is. Come on in. Hannah will be happy to see you."

"Thank you." Madeleine followed him through a small sitting area decorated with poinsettias, holly, ivy garland, and red-and-green candles. A porcelain nativity scene sat on a bookshelf.

"Hannah," Trey called. "You have a visitor."

Hannah hurried in from the hallway. "Madeleine! It's good to see you. I've been thinking of you. I'm so glad you came by."

"Hi, Hannah." Madeleine gave her a little wave.

Trey turned toward Madeleine. "It was nice seeing you. I'm going to head into town." He grinned at Hannah. "I need to do some Christmas shopping."

Hannah wagged a finger at him as she gave him a facetious smile. "Don't spend too much money."

"I can't make any promises." He kissed her cheek. "I'll be back soon. Enjoy your visit," he called back as he headed out through the kitchen.

"I hope this isn't an inconvenient time," Madeleine said. "I'm sorry to just stop in, but I was literally jogging by." She glanced down at her outfit. "You must think I don't own any presentable clothing."

"Don't be silly." Hannah motioned toward the kitchen. "Would you like a cup of tea?"

"That would be wonderful." Madeleine pointed toward the nativity scene. "I love your Christmas decorations. They're lovely."

"Thank you." Hannah glanced around the room. "Trey wants me to put up a tree, but I'm not sure about it. We never put up Christmas trees in the Amish tradition, and I have mixed feelings. We're still learning how to best blend our cultures."

Madeleine considered that observation as she followed Hannah into the kitchen. "Blending your cultures must be a challenge."

"We've hit a few snags, but we're both willing to compromise." Hannah filled a measuring cup with water, added two tea bags, and then put the measuring cup in the microwave. "Christmas shopping is a good example. I'm used to being thrifty and only buying small, practical gifts, while Trey wants to spoil me with jewelry, expensive clothes, and what I think are unnecessary appliances. Neither one of us is right or wrong. It's just a different way of thinking and living." She pulled a box of donuts out of a cabinet. "Would you like one?"

"Yes, please," Madeleine said. "Thank you. I didn't expect you to feed me."

"Oh, I don't mind." Hannah brought the box to the table. "I always have food around for our guests. We had two couples leave this morning, so it's nice to have a little break. Another couple is arriving Saturday."

"It's wonderful that you're staying busy. May I grab some mugs or cups for you?"

"Yes, please." Hannah pointed toward a cabinet. "You can find mugs in that cabinet next to the sink."

Madeleine took out two mugs and then found spoons in a nearby drawer. She placed the mugs and spoons on the table and sat down.

"How have you been?" Hannah asked as she brought sweetener and creamer to the table. "It was nice to see you when we were at the market at the same time last week."

"Well, I want to talk to you about something." Madeleine tugged a paper napkin from the holder at the center of the table and began to fray the edges. "It's interesting that you brought up the differences between the Amish and *English* cultures." Her voice became thick. "An issue has come up with my Amish neighbor."

Hannah studied Madeleine. "Are you okay? You look upset about something."

"I don't know if you know that my house is located by Saul Beiler's property. He's a widower, and he has a daughter," Madeleine said. "His daughter used to come to see me frequently, and we cooked together."

"That's nice. I know who Saul and Emma are from church services, when I was still a part of the community. I'm sure she appreciated that with her mother being gone." The microwave beeped, and Hannah brought the tea to the table. She filled the mugs and then placed the measuring cup on the counter. "How old is his daughter again?" she asked as she sat across from Madeleine.

"She's eleven." Madeleine mixed in sweetener and cream as she talked. "She's a really special young girl. I got to know Saul and Emma very well, and they even invited me to join them for Thanksgiving at his best friend's house."

"Oh." Hannah looked surprised. "That's very nice."

"But then everything changed after Thanksgiving." Madeleine shared Sylvia's warning on Thanksgiving and then how cold Saul had been at the church service. "He told me not to spend time with Emma, and he's been standoffish while working on my kitchen cabinets. It's as if he changed overnight."

Hannah frowned as she chose a donut from the box in the middle of the table. "I think I understand how he feels."

"You do? Could you please explain it to me?" Madeleine asked before sipping her tea.

"Madeleine, do you have feelings for Saul? You can be honest with me. I won't judge you or tell you how wrong you are to feel something for an Amish man."

Madeleine nodded as her eyes filled with tears. "They were like my surrogate family."

Hannah touched Madeleine's hand. "You know the position he's in, right?"

"That's why he's pushing me away." Madeleine plucked a cream-filled donut from the box, even though her appetite had disappeared when Saul told her he couldn't be her friend. She thought she might have even lost some weight.

"Absolutely." Hannah's expression was serious. "He knows if he crosses the line, he'll be excommunicated until he confesses his sins and repents."

Madeleine stared down at the donut. "I've been doing my best to avoid him ever since he told me he can't be my friend. But he's at my house right now working on installing new cabinets, which is why I made a point of going for a run this morning. Yesterday I came home from work and found him in the kitchen, and I hid in my room until I thought he'd left. Everything is so awkward now."

"I'm sorry." Hannah broke her glazed donut in half.

"I actually asked for unpaid time off work and made a flight reservation to go home to California for Christmas. I'm running away to avoid sitting in my house alone on Christmas Day, staring across the field toward his house. I left my mother a message yesterday and told her I'm coming. She called me back last night, and she was almost in tears because she was so delighted. I couldn't bear to tell her the truth—that I'm really spending Christmas with her and my stepdad just to avoid feeling sorry for myself here."

Madeleine cradled the warm mug in her hands. "You were talking about being thrifty at Christmastime. Well, booking a trip to avoid seeing someone is probably the biggest waste of money you've ever heard of."

Hannah shook her head. "I'm not judging you. At least you'll be with your family, right?"

"Yes, that's true." Madeleine sipped her tea again and then took a bite of her donut. Although it was filled with sweet, smooth cream, the taste did little to brighten her sour mood.

"Saul probably received a warning from a friend. You mentioned that you had Thanksgiving at his best friend, Marcus's, house. Maybe Marcus said something to him?" Hannah lifted her mug. "If his wife said something to you, then she must have discussed it with Marcus before you visited them."

"I'm sure that's it." Madeleine wiped her mouth with a napkin. "Saul has to obey certain rules, but I had hoped we could be friends. I moved around most of my life, but this place represents the best parts of my childhood. After I met Saul and Emma, I felt as if this was going to be my permanent home. That's why I'm investing in the cabinets. Now that I've lost their friendship, I don't want to give up, but I don't feel secure."

"Why don't you feel secure?" Hannah asked.

Madeleine explained about her nightmares and how she lost Travis. "Now that Saul has pulled away from me, my nightmares and sleeplessness have returned. I'm back to grieving for Travis constantly. It's as if I've lost Travis all over again. I feel like I'm losing what I've loved about this place—that feeling of home."

"Oh dear." Hannah shook her head. "Please don't give up on Paradise. You love other things here, right? You have other friends. You have Carolyn, Linda, Ruth, and me. And you have the house you love. I'm sure memories of your grandparents give you comfort."

"Yes, that's very true." Madeleine considered Saul and his sad eyes. "I just don't know how to get over this pain I feel when

Saul is around." She heaved a sigh. "I hope he's done with the cabinets by the time I get back from California. After that I won't have to see him much—unless I go to church service with Carolyn and Ruth again." Tears trickled down her cheeks. "My emotions are a mess."

"I know that feeling well," Hannah said. "That's how it was when I met Trey. I wanted to see him, but I also prayed for God to remove that longing out of my heart because I knew it was going to put me in such a difficult position with my community. Falling in love with Trey was both the most wonderful and the most challenging emotion I ever had to sort through."

Madeleine sniffed and wiped her eyes with a tissue from the pocket in her windbreaker. "I wonder if that's how Saul feels. He shields his emotions behind his stony expression. But I also see sadness in his eyes."

"He probably knows how to hide his sadness after losing his wife." Hannah broke another piece off the donut. "I did the same thing after I lost my first husband."

"How did you decide to leave the community for Trey?"

"It wasn't easy, and it's still not easy. I left everything I'd ever known, but I believe that's the path God wanted me to choose. I prayed a lot, and I'm still praying my daughter Lillian will forgive me and become a part of my new family." Hannah patted her abdomen. "I'm going to have a new family member in the spring."

"Oh, Hannah." Madeleine smiled. "That's a beautiful blessing from God."

"You're right." Hannah's green eyes glistened with tears. "God has wonderful days in store for you too. Just pray and be patient."

"I will," Madeleine promised.

Hannah's advice rang through Madeleine's mind while she jogged back to her house. When she came in the back door, Saul was painting the walls, and the aroma of paint filled her nose. She stood in the kitchen doorway while he worked, enjoying the view of both the crisp white wall and the self-assured way he worked.

He looked over his shoulder at her, and his expression softened slightly.

"It looks nice," she said as she pulled off her windbreaker. "The kitchen really needed a new coat of paint."

"*Danki.*" Saul raked his hand through his dark brown hair. "How was your run?"

The thoughtful question caught her off guard for a brief moment. "It was fine." She moved to the table and picked up her shopping list, the one she'd made as an excuse to leave the house again. "I'm going to the store now. Did you and Emma need anything?"

"No, *danki.*" His eyes lingered on her for a moment, and then he moved back to painting the wall.

"Oh, by the way, I'm going to California for Christmas. Do you want me to give you a check for the remaining balance before I leave?"

"That won't be necessary," he said without looking back at her. "You can pay me when you get back."

"Okay. You can keep working while I'm gone. Would you mind bringing in the mail for me?"

"That won't be a problem." He kept his back to her. "I'll watch out for your *haus* and leave your mail on the kitchen table."

The sight of his back caused her frustration to flare. Why couldn't he look at her? Did he find her that revolting? Or was sidestepping her stare another coping mechanism to avoid facing the feelings he had for her?

"Would you ask Emma to look after the cats in my barn too?" she asked.

"*Ya.*" He nodded.

"Thank you." She folded up the shopping list and shoved it into her purse. "I'm flying back to Pennsylvania on December 29. Do you think you'll be done by then?"

"*Ya*," he repeated. "I should be finishing up by then. I'll be sure my mess is all cleaned up too."

"Great." She moved past him and stepped into the hallway. "I'm going to get changed and then head to the market."

He grunted a response as she moved down the hallway. After a stop to wash up in the bathroom, she moved into her bedroom, closed the door, and leaned against it.

"Lord, give me strength," she whispered.

As she stripped off her running clothes, Madeleine considered how she could show Saul that he and Emma still meant a lot to her. An idea popped into her head while she pulled on her jeans. She would leave special Christmas presents on the table the day she headed out to California. In keeping with the Amish tradition, she would find something meaningful but not extravagant. She pulled on her shirt while pondering what the gifts would be. She'd find something special, and maybe then Saul would be convinced to be her friend.

The idea was superb! Now she just had to find the perfect gifts.

TWENTY

Saul shivered as he and Emma headed to Madeleine's house the following Monday morning. Flurries danced through the air, and Emma lunged and laughed while trying to catch them in her mouth. He shook his head and suppressed a smile. His mother's favorite winter saying echoed through his mind: *"God created snow for the* kinner."

"You need to stop playing around, Emma," he warned her. "You're going to be late for school."

"I have to feed the cats, and I want to come into Maddie's *haus* with you and see the cabinets." She raced ahead of him and up Madeleine's porch steps. "You said I could come and see them after she left for her trip." She frowned. "I still don't understand why I can't watch you work when she's home. I promised I wouldn't cook with her anymore, even though I miss it."

"We've been through this nearly a hundred times." He pulled the house key from his pocket. "It's inappropriate for you to spend time with her—"

"Because she's *English*," Emma finished the statement while scowling. "Jesus told us to love one another and love our neighbors as ourselves. She's our neighbor, and I love her."

Saul pushed the door open. "You can see the cabinets, and then you need to quickly take care of the cats. Understand?"

Once inside and through the mudroom, Emma gasped, dropped her school bag on the floor, and rushed past him to the kitchen table. "*Dat*! Look! Presents!" She jumped up and down while holding a gift bag that was a swirl of red, green, and gold. "Maddie left us presents!"

"Calm down." He held his hand up. "Why would she leave us presents?"

"Because it's Christmas." Emma studied him as if he were an imbecile.

"Let me see that." He reached for the colorful bag, and she turned it for him to see. EMMA was written across it with a black marker.

"It's for me." Emma pointed at the table. "That one has to be yours." She began sifting through the knot of red tissue paper in her bag.

Saul looked at the large box wrapped in red paper. An envelope taped to the top displayed his name written across it. He swallowed a lump in his throat as raw emotion slammed through him.

Emma squealed. "Look, *Dat*!" She held up a tattered cookbook. "Maddie gave me one of *Mammi's* cookbooks! Listen to this note: 'Dear Emma. I know how much *Mammi* meant to you, and I want you to have her special cookbook. *Frehlicher Grischtdaag!* Love always, Maddie.'"

Tears stung Saul's eyes as he watched his daughter flip through the book. His words were stuck in the lump swelling in his throat. Emma looked up at him.

"What are you waiting for, *Dat*?" She pointed to the box. "Open yours!"

He nodded and removed the card from the box.

"Open the card!" Emma picked it up. "Want me to read it to you?"

He nodded again.

"Let's see." Emma pulled out a card with a photograph of a poinsettia on the front. "'Dear Saul, I know my grandparents meant a lot to you and Emma, and I thought you'd enjoy something that belonged to my *daadi*. *Frehlicher Grischtdaag!* Fondly, Maddie.'" She clapped her hands. "I can't wait to see what it is! Open it, *Dat*! Open it!"

Saul ripped off the paper and found a plain cardboard box. He opened the flaps and spotted a set of screwdrivers he remembered Mel using on many occasions when they worked on home improvement projects together.

"Wow." Emma touched one of the screwdrivers. "These belonged to her *daadi*?"

"*Ya*." He fought to hold back his threatening emotions by clearing his throat. "I remember them."

"How nice." Emma gnawed her lower lip. "I need to think of something to give Maddie."

"That won't be necessary." Saul closed up the box. "We don't need to give her anything."

"That isn't right. If Maddie gave us something, then the proper thing to do is to give her something. I'll think about it at school."

"You need to feed the cats before you go to school."

"I know." She grabbed a scoop of dry cat food from the pantry and then glanced past him. "The cabinets are *schee*. Maddie will love them. I'll be right back." She rushed outside.

Saul studied the card while trying to comprehend why

Madeleine had left gifts for Emma and him. Why would she want to give something to them after he'd shunned her friendship?

Because she cares about you and Emma.

The response came from deep in his soul, and he tried to suppress the sentiment attached to it. Tears pricked his eyes.

Emma hurried into the kitchen again and dropped the scoop in the pantry before picking up her school bag. "I'm heading off to school. Bye, *Dat!*" She waved as she rushed out again.

"Have a *gut* day." After she was gone, he moved to the counter and surveyed the remaining cabinets he had to install. But then he turned toward the refrigerator and found an envelope with his name on it stuck to the door with a magnet.

He opened the envelope and pulled out a check along with a note from Madeleine that said, "Saul—Here is the remaining balance for the cabinets. Thank you for your hard work. I'm certain that my kitchen will look brand-new. Fondly, Maddie."

He studied the note and leaned against the refrigerator. Pretending only to be her acquaintance was much more difficult than he'd ever imagined. Even her handwriting conjured up strong feelings within him. How could he continue to be aloof when she returned from California? He already missed her, even though he'd seen her in passing a few times before she'd left for her trip. He needed strength to continue to maintain this facade.

Saul placed the check on the table beside the Christmas gifts and then started on his installation. And while he worked, he prayed, begging God over and over again to renew his heart and set his spirit right.

On Christmas Eve, Madeleine sipped a mug of eggnog while sitting beside her mother in front of her parents' tree. She'd arrived late yesterday and spent most of the afternoon shopping with her mother, right up until the shops closed to let their employees go home to be with their families. Although she was keeping a smile plastered on her face, she couldn't get Saul and Emma off her mind. What were they doing? Were they visiting Marcus and his family today? Had they found her gifts? If so, did they like them? And, most important, did her gifts change Saul's feelings about her?

"Are we going to the midnight service?" Mom's voice broke through her mental tirade.

"Yes," Madeleine said quickly. "It's been a long time since I've gone to a Christmas Eve service."

Mom studied her. "You don't seem to be too excited to be home. What's going on, Maddie?"

"Nothing." Madeleine forced a yawn. "I think I'm just suffering from a severe case of jet lag."

"Hmm." Mom continued to study Madeleine while looking unconvinced. "Well, we should get ready for church then. Let me go and see what Jack is doing."

"Sounds good." Madeleine finished the eggnog and then headed to the guest room to change into a dress and fix her hair.

Madeleine sat in the backseat of her stepfather's SUV and took in the colorful lights and inflatable Christmas decorations during the drive through town.

Once they arrived at the church, Mom looped her arm around Madeleine's waist as they walked through the parking lot. "Are you certain you're okay?"

"I'm fine, Mom." Madeleine smiled at her. "It's great to be home with you and Jack at Christmas."

Mom squeezed Madeleine to her. "We're glad you're here too."

Madeleine enjoyed singing the traditional Christmas carols during the service. She had tears in her eyes when the congregation lit candles and sang "Silent Night" at midnight. Although this was the kind of church she'd been accustomed to since she was a child, she couldn't help but think of her Amish friends. She missed the Amish service—the plain and simple way of worshiping God without the flowers, candles, and musical instruments.

When they returned home, it was close to one in the morning, but Madeleine and her parents gathered around the tree once again.

"Are we going to keep with tradition and open one gift?" Jack asked as he picked up a small box from under the tree.

"What do you think, Maddie?" her mother asked. "Do you want to open one gift for old time's sake?"

"Sure." Madeleine yawned as the time difference and lack of sleep drowned her. She longed to curl up in the guest room bed, but she didn't want to disappoint her parents. Opening one gift on Christmas Eve was a tradition going back to her early childhood when Madeleine and Mom lived alone.

"This is for you, sweetheart." Jack handed her mother a small box. "Merry Christmas, Leah."

"Oh, Jack." Mom took the box and then handed him a small box as well as he sat down beside her. "This is for you. Merry Christmas, honey."

Madeleine hugged a sofa pillow to her chest while she watched her parents open their gifts. Her mother gasped as she opened the jewelry box, revealing a sparkling diamond solitaire necklace. "It's gorgeous. Thank you." She leaned over and kissed Jack.

He opened his package and held up an expensive-looking watch. "I love it, Leah. Thank you."

Madeleine yawned again and imagined how warm and comfortable the bed would be when she finally crawled into it.

"This is for you, Maddie." Her mother handed her an envelope. "We thought you could use this right now."

"Thank you." Madeleine opened the envelope containing a $200 gift card to a home improvement store. "Jack. Mom. This is too much."

"We know you're working on your house, and we want to help," Jack chimed in. "You can buy whatever you need."

"Thank you." Madeleine stood and hugged each of them. "You really didn't need to spend that much money. It's extravagant."

Mom raised an eyebrow in disbelief. "We want to help you out. We're happy to do it."

"I really appreciate it." Madeleine yawned again. "I need to go to bed."

"Good night, dear," Mom said. "Merry Christmas."

Madeleine walked to the guest room and changed into her pajamas. As she snuggled down in the bed, she closed her eyes and then fell asleep wondering how Saul and Emma were.

⁂

Madeleine poured herself a cup of coffee in her mother's kitchen. She'd spent nearly an hour opening gifts with her parents. Her mother had showered her with new clothes, more gift cards, and jewelry. Madeleine was overwhelmed by her parents' generosity. Was the Amish way of being thrifty but thoughtful already rubbing off on her? Why did she even bother thinking the way the

Amish did? After all, she wasn't worthy of their community. She would never be accepted as one of them.

Mom stepped into the kitchen and smiled. "May I have a cup of coffee with you, Maddie?"

"That would be nice." Madeleine poured a cup for her mother and handed it to her. "Merry Christmas." She sat down at the table.

"Yes, Merry Christmas." Mom sat across from her. "Thank you for the gift card and the sweater."

"You're welcome." Madeleine sipped her coffee. "I feel bad for not giving you and Jack as much as you gave me."

Mom waved off the comment. "Don't be silly. You spent all of that money coming out here to see us. Besides, it's the thought that counts. We're just happy you're here."

A news anchor on the television sounded from the family room where her stepfather sat on the sofa.

"I'm happy I'm here too." Madeleine said the words, but she felt as if she'd left her heart in Pennsylvania.

"Tell me the truth. Why did you really come out here?" Mom asked.

Madeleine studied her mother. "What do you mean?"

"Maddie, I know you. You're not quite as impulsive as you pretend to be. Normally, when you make up your mind about something, you follow through. You told me more than a month ago that you wanted to spend your first Christmas in your new house. You even said you didn't care that the house didn't have central heat and you had to deal with that coal stove." Mom studied her. "Why did you change your mind?"

"I just wanted to be here." Madeleine pushed her hair back from her shoulder. "I wanted to have another Christmas in California."

Mom frowned. "Something is bothering you. What is it?"

"I'm fine." Madeleine sipped her coffee. "Everything is great."

"Does it have something to do with your neighbors?"

Madeleine knew she was caught. She nodded and sighed. "Yes, it does. It has everything to do with them." She told her mother the whole story, starting with the church service after Thanksgiving and ending with the gifts she'd left on her kitchen table for Emma and Saul. She'd managed to share her feelings without getting emotional, but the heartache swelled within her.

Mom listened with sympathy in her eyes, and Madeleine was thankful for her mother's patient silence.

"But honestly, I didn't come out here just to get away from Saul and Emma. I also didn't want to be alone on Christmas. It only made sense to come and see my family." She gestured dramatically. "That's it. That's my messed-up life in Amish Country. You told me to be careful, but I wound up getting hurt." She held her breath while waiting for her mother's response.

"I know how Saul feels," Mom finally said.

"You do?"

"I don't know if I ever told you, but I had been participating in baptism classes before I met your father. I wasn't in the exact same position Saul is in. However, I was preparing to give my heart to the church when I met someone who wasn't a part of the church. Your father had no intention of becoming Amish." She gave a wry grin. "He had no intention of being true to me or to any church. I was too young and naive to realize the kind of man he was."

Madeleine nodded. She'd heard the stories before about her father's lack of loyalty to anyone but himself.

"Saul is confused, and he doesn't know what to do. He feels caught between his loyalty to the church and his feelings for you."

Mom's expression was sad. "He has a child to think of, and I doubt he's going to choose you. I'm sorry, Maddie. I think you need to try to forget him."

Madeleine gripped the cup in her hands. "I thought we were close, and then he rejected me. I never expected this to hurt that much."

"You grew attached to him and his daughter." Mom touched her hand. "I understand. Maybe it would be better if you sold the house and came back here. Maybe Amish Country isn't right for you."

"No, that's not true." Madeleine shook her head.

"I worry about you being out there alone. You've been through a lot, losing Travis the way you did." Mom's eyes glistened with tears. "I hate that you're all alone."

"I'll be fine, Mom. I promise," Madeleine insisted. "I love it there. It feels like home. I just need to find a way to let go of these feelings for Saul and Emma."

"You have to forgive Saul, and then yes, let it go." Mom squeezed her hand. "Leaving the community was the most difficult decision I've ever made. I knew I was breaking my parents' hearts, and I felt guilty for leaving my friends. At the same time, however, I believed God was leading me on a new path."

"Did you think you misread God's plans for you after my father left?" Madeleine asked.

"No." Mom shook her head, and her hazel eyes still glistened with tears. "You are the greatest blessing in my life. I believe I was supposed to have you. You're my blessing, and you were a blessing to your grandparents."

Madeleine smiled as tears filled her eyes too. "Thank you, Mom."

"I mean that, but you have to appreciate Saul's position in the community. You told me his wife left him, right?"

Madeleine nodded. "His wife left him for another man and divorced him."

"See, that's even more devastating for him because he's Amish. When she left, she broke her vow to him and to the church. And to make matters worse, she divorced him, which the Amish believe is a sin. He can't possibly consider leaving the church to be with you after his wife abandoned him and their child—even though she's dead now."

"I understand that." Madeleine nodded. "I'm not asking him to leave the church for me."

"I know you're not asking him to do it, but he may feel tempted by you. Your giving him space is a good plan."

"That's one of the reasons I'm here." Madeleine lifted her cup. "I'm giving him a chance to finish the cabinets. Once he's done, we won't have to see each other except in passing."

"It will be fine," Mom insisted. "Just give him time. Maybe he'll find a way to be your friend after he sorts through his feelings." She stood. "How about some coffee cake? I'll put a fresh pot of coffee on too."

"That sounds good." Madeleine sent up a silent prayer for Saul and Emma. She prayed they were enjoying a nice Christmas and that God would find a way to heal her broken heart.

Later that evening, Emma rushed into the family room and ran over to the small pile of gifts Saul had given her that morning. Christmas Day had been exciting for her.

"I love my new ice skates!" Emma pulled off her shoes and straightened her socks. "I can't wait to use them. Do you think the pond will be frozen by the weekend? Maybe Esther and I can skate together."

"It might be." Saul sat down in a chair across from her and watched her pull on one of the skates. All the way home, he'd been thinking about how thankful he was that Marcus and Sylvia invited them over on Christmas every year to make sure they weren't home alone.

"I wonder if Maddie is having a nice Christmas," Emma said as she pulled on her second new skate. "I miss her, *Dat.*"

I do too. I miss her smile. I miss her sense of humor and the way she likes to tease me. I miss her laugh. I miss everything about her.

The mental response caught Saul off guard, and he frowned.

"She's with her family, which is where she belongs," he said, even though he didn't truly believe the words. He'd eventually move past the feeling of loss that haunted him. After all, he'd gotten used to being without his parents and his brother. He still missed them, but the pain wasn't as bad. The loss eventually transformed into a dull ache that loomed in the back of his mind. Surely losing Madeleine would get easier as the years wore on.

"I made her a card." Emma laced up the skates while she spoke. "It's on my dresser in my room."

"You did?" he asked. "I told you not to give her anything."

"It's just a thank-you card." Emma examined her white skates. "It's only proper to give her a thank-you note after receiving a gift from her. That's what Sylvia says."

He nodded. "Fine, but I'll leave it at her *haus.* I'm going to finish installing the cabinets and countertop and try to get the plumber there before she gets home."

"I'll put my note in the kitchen when I feed the cats tomorrow. You know I love spending time with them. Her kittens are just as cute as the ones in our barn." Emma moved her feet back and forth and studied her skates. "These are very *schee. Danki, Dat. Frehlicher Grischtdaag.*"

"*Frehlicher Grischtdaag.*" He looked at the clock on the wall. "We need to go to bed. It's late, Emma."

"I know." She started unlacing the skates. "I can't wait to try these out."

"I'm certain you'll have plenty of opportunities to skate this winter."

"I wonder if Maddie likes to ice-skate." Emma looked up at her father. "I'm just wondering. I'm not going to ask her to skate with me."

"It's bedtime, Emma." Saul stood and watched her remove the skates. How could he convince Emma to stop thinking about Madeleine when he couldn't stop himself from thinking about her?

TWENTY-ONE

Madeleine pulled her wheeled suitcase up the back porch steps, and before unlocking the back door, she glanced back toward Saul's house. She saw a dim light flicker in his kitchen window. Saul and Emma were probably getting ready for bed. Although she'd only been gone for six days, it felt more like a lifetime.

She pulled open the door, closed it behind her, and stepped through to her kitchen, which greeted her with the sweet smell of new wood and stain. She flipped on the two lanterns on the table and looked at the beautiful new countertop and cabinets lining the far wall. She blew out an excited gasp. Saul's creations were more beautiful than she'd ever imagined!

After letting go of her suitcase and setting her bag on the table, she rushed over to the cabinets. She ran her hands over the smooth wood and opened a door, then another. She was stunned to find all her dishes, cups, and bowls lined up perfectly.

Madeleine shook her head. Even though he was acting cold and aloof, Saul had taken the extra time to arrange things for her. She studied the cabinets and countertop for several minutes, taking in the beautiful artistry of Saul's work.

She stepped over to the table to sift through the stack of mail, sorting out bills and advertisements. She thumbed through an advertisement for the home improvement store where her parents had bought her gift card before placing it back on the table. Then she spotted an envelope with her name handwritten on it, and her heart thumped in her chest. She picked up the envelope, wondering if Saul had written her a note. Had he been touched by her gift and felt compelled to write her a letter?

She opened the envelope and found a letter inside that said:

Dear Maddie,

Thank you for the cookbook. You were very generous to give it to me. I'm excited to try *Mammi's* favorite recipes. I'll let you know how the oatmeal cookies and chocolate cake come out. Maybe I can sneak over and give you some. *Mei dat* appreciates the screwdriver set. I saw him using them in his shop yesterday. I think it means a lot to him that you gave him those special tools. He loved *Mammi* and your *daadi* too. I wanted to make you something as a gift, but *mei dat* said it was best if I kept my distance.

Even though I'm not supposed to be your friend, I want you to know that I miss you. *Mei dat* does too, but he won't admit it. I hope you had a nice Christmas with your family. We miss you.

Love,

Emma (and Saul too!)

Madeleine read the letter over and over until she practically had it memorized. She was touched to hear the gifts had meant something special to Emma and Saul. Maybe she could find a way to prove to Saul that she had no intention of threatening his world, that she just wanted to be a part of his and Emma's life. She couldn't just let them go and act as if they were only strangers who lived on the adjacent property. She had to show him how much she cared.

◦∞◦

Emma hummed to herself as she made her way out to her father's shop. She was excited to tell him what she'd made for supper. All by herself, she'd followed *Mammi's* recipe for crepes! They were actually easy to make—easier than she'd thought they would be. Now she had to convince *Dat* to come in from working. She couldn't wait for them to enjoy her delicious creation!

She picked up her pace as she approached the shop door and then stepped into the showroom where her father was sanding a long piece of wood. "*Dat!*" she yelled. "Supper is ready. I made crepes." She stood up a little taller and hugged her cloak to her body to try to shield herself from the early January cold. "It's ready."

"Emma." *Dat* looked over at her, frowning. "Would you do me a quick favor?"

"*Ya.*" She nodded.

"I think I left my favorite work gloves on my dresser." He pointed toward the house. "I need them so I can finish up this one piece of wood."

"But supper is ready." She jammed her hand on her small hip. "Can't you look for them after we eat? I worked hard on this meal for you. I want to show you how much I've learned about cooking."

"I know you did, *mei liewe*, and I appreciate it. You're a *gut* cook. I just want to finish this one piece of wood. I promise I won't take long."

"All right. I'll be right back." Emma rushed into the house and upstairs to her father's bedroom.

She searched his dresser and didn't find the gloves. She sank to her knees and looked under the bed in case he had dropped them and they'd fallen underneath it. She spotted something under the middle of the bed, and she crawled under and grabbed what turned out to be a metal box. She gripped its handle and yanked it out from under the bed.

She crossed her legs under her and examined the small, cold box. She'd never seen it before. Why would *Dat* keep it under the bed? Had he forgotten about the mysterious box? Or had he accidentally pushed it under there and been searching for it?

After turning the box over in her hands, she clicked open the latch. She lifted the lid and found a stack of papers. While pulling them out, her eyes focused on a tattered envelope at the bottom of the stack. The envelope, which had already been ripped open, was addressed to her father and contained a letter. She pulled out the handwritten letter, and even though it was wrong to snoop in her father's things, she had to read it.

Dear Saul,

I hope this letter finds you well. I know you never expected to hear from me, but I thought it was only right for me to inform you of the sad news. Annie has passed away. She died tragically in a boating accident almost two months ago. I've spent the past two months grieving, and I felt you had a right to know about it.

She and I liked to spend our weekends during the summer months boating with friends. We had been out for the day when our boat was involved in a collision. Annie fell and hit her head, and she died from massive head trauma after two weeks in a coma.

I know there is a lot of bad blood between us, and I'm sorry. I was wrong to come back for Annie and steal her away from you and Emma. At the time, my focus was only on my own needs, and I never considered that I had broken up a family. Now that she's gone, I know what it's like to experience real loss. I never thought about how much I had hurt you and your daughter until now. I guess I'm also writing to say I'm sorry. I've been selfish and hurtful.

I know I can't fix the past, but I wanted to at least tell you I'm sorry. I've lost Annie now, but you and Emma lost her years ago. Please forgive me.

Sincerely,

Timothy

Emma read through the letter two more times, trying to comprehend it. Who was Timothy? And what did he mean that Annie had died? Annie . . . Was this letter about her *mamm*? And didn't her *dat* say she had pneumonia and died in a hospital? If her *mamm* was the Annie mentioned in this letter, then why was she in a boat? It didn't make sense.

She read the letter for a fourth time and then examined the envelope. According to the postmark, it had been mailed more than a year ago from Missouri. If Annie was her *mamm* and she was in Missouri, then . . .

Emma gasped. *My* mamm *was alive?*

Then it hit her like a thousand bales of hay falling from the loft in the barn: Mamm *didn't die more than seven years ago. She abandoned Dat and me!*

"No, no, no!" Emma yelled. "This can't be true! It can't be!"

Tears gushed from her eyes like powerful waterfalls. Emma needed answers. She needed to hear the truth from her father, and she needed to hear it *now*.

Emma jumped up and ran down the stairs, gripping the letter in her hand.

By the time she'd reached her father's shop, she was sobbing and the letter was crumpled in her fist.

"Emma? What happened?" *Dat's* eyes were wide. "Emma, *was iss letz?*"

"What is this?" She shook the letter in front of his face. "What does this mean? Who is Timothy? Why did he write this to you?" And then she found the courage to ask the question that was burning through her. "Did *mei mamm* leave me? Did she leave us?"

Dat took the letter from her, and his expression hardened. "Where did you find this?"

"Answer my questions!" Her voice croaked on her sobs. "Tell me the truth, *Dat*. Did *Mamm* leave us?"

He gave her a quick nod. "She left the Amish."

"Why?" Emma's question came out in a wail. "Why?"

He stared at her. "She just . . . left."

"Why did she leave?" Emma demanded. "Where did she go? Who's Timothy?"

Dat blew out a heavy sigh and shook his head.

"Tell me, *Dat*. I need to know why she left." She wiped at her tears with the back of her hand. "Why didn't she come and see me? Why didn't she call me?" Her questions thundered through her like a midsummer storm. "Why didn't she write to me? Didn't she love me at all?"

"We're not going to talk about this now. You need to calm down. Let's go eat supper."

Dat reached for her, but Emma stepped away. "I can't eat." Emma shuddered as more tears filled her eyes. "I need to know why *mei mamm* left me."

"Just go in the *haus* and wash up. I'll be right there." He patted her arm. "I'll be right behind you in a minute."

Emma stepped out into the cold evening air and shivered as confusion and frustration nearly overcame her. Large, fluffy snowflakes danced down from the sky and wet her cloak. She wiped away the snowflakes that pelted her cheeks while considering the news that had just shattered her heart. She needed to know the truth, and she wanted to hear it from her father.

Why wouldn't he answer her questions? How could her mother leave her and never contact her again? None of this made any sense! Everything her father had told her since she was four had been a lie. How could he lie to her? He was the one person she'd always trusted the most, and he'd lied to her!

She looked at her house and couldn't bear the thought of sitting down to supper as if nothing had happened. She needed time alone. She had to have some quiet time to think and try to figure everything out. Instead of following her father's instructions, she began to run.

Emma rushed out of his shop, and Saul blew out a deep, shuddering breath. He knew he'd have to tell her the truth about her mother someday, and he'd always been afraid someone else would tell her. But he'd never expected her to find out on her own. Several times he'd considered burning Timothy's letter, but instead he'd kept it in case she wanted proof that her mother had left of her own accord. He was certain his hiding place had been sufficient, but it had only proven to be a painful way for Emma to find out the truth without his guidance and support.

He studied the crumpled letter and shook his head. Did Annie have any idea how much pain she'd caused when she'd walked away from their daughter? It was one thing for her to hurt Saul; he was an adult and he'd found a way to recover. But the pain in Emma's eyes was enough to crush his heart and his spirit. Now he had to pick up the pieces and try to console her. He'd needed a few minutes alone to collect himself before he could help her.

He folded up the letter, shoved it into his pocket, put his tools away, and set the wood aside. After extinguishing the lanterns, he left the shop. Large, wet snowflakes peppered his coat and hat as he strode toward the house in the dark.

"Emma?" Saul stepped into the mudroom. "Emma? Where are you? Let's sit down and have supper. We'll talk after you've calmed down." He moved into the kitchen and found the table set with a platter of crepes and trimmings in the middle. "Emma Kate?" He walked through the kitchen to the family room. "Emma Kate? Where are you?"

He stood outside the bathroom door and gently knocked. "Are you in there?" He knocked again. "Emma, please answer me."

The house remained deathly silent. He stuck his head into the laundry room and still didn't see her. With a lantern in his hand, he climbed the stairs to the second floor and stepped into her bedroom, hoping to find her sitting on her bed, maybe reading her Bible for comfort.

"Emma Kate, where are you?" He stalked down the hallway,

glancing into the sewing room and spare room on his way to his bedroom. "Emma! Where are you?"

When he found his bedroom also empty, Saul's mind began to race. He rushed down the stairs and outside with a lantern. He held the lantern out in front of him and moved through the now blinding snow toward his barns and shops. He searched the horse barn and the area by the chicken coops while calling out her name. He walked behind the house and yelled into the field.

"Emma!" he screamed. "Emma, come out now! Where are you?"

As the curtain of snow falling down from the heavens intensified, terrifying visions flashed through Saul's mind. Had Emma run off toward Marcus's house and gotten hit by a car? Had she fallen into a ditch by the side of the road? Did a passerby kidnap her?

The worries slammed through him, and his heart pounded against his rib cage as he rushed toward his largest shop, where he kept a phone. He needed to call his friends and neighbors and ask them to help him find his precious daughter.

While dialing Marcus's number, he prayed someone would hear the phone ringing in their barn.

"Please answer, please answer," he muttered. After nearly two dozen rings, someone finally did.

"Hello?" Marcus's voice sounded through the receiver.

"Marcus!" Saul almost yelled. "I need help. Emma is missing. I can't find her anywhere. I've searched my *haus*, my barns, and my shops, and now it's getting dark. And the snow is falling heavily, and I—"

"Whoa," Marcus said. "Slow down. How long has she been missing? Where was the last place you saw her?"

"It's been about twenty minutes," Saul said. "I sent her to look for something in my room, and she found the letter from Timothy. She read it, Marcus." His voice quavered. "She knows the truth now about Annie. She brought the letter out to me in the shop. She was really upset, and she asked me several questions I wasn't prepared to answer. I told her to go back into the *haus* and that we'd talk after supper. I went in to find her, and she was gone. She may be on the way to your *haus*."

"All right. I'll ask Sylvia to look around our property, and I'll head your way in a horse and buggy. I'll also tell Esther to call a few neighbors," Marcus said. "You call neighbors too. We'll organize a search party."

"*Danki.*" Saul nodded. He was grateful his best friend had taken control of the situation, because he didn't seem to have the presence of mind to do it.

"I'll be there soon. We'll find her." Marcus hung up.

Saul called two of his surrounding neighbors and asked them to help him search for his daughter. While he waited for his neighbors to arrive, Saul gazed across the field and spotted a light shining at Madeleine's house. He jogged down the driveway and hurried up her back porch steps.

Her door opened before he even had a chance to knock. She must have been looking out the window and seen his lantern.

"Saul?" Madeleine asked, her eyes round as she swung open the storm door. "Is everything all right?"

"I'm looking for Emma. Is she here?"

"No." She shook her head. "I haven't seen her since I got back from California. What's going on?"

"I can't find her," Saul said while working to catch his breath. "I think she ran away."

"Oh no." Madeleine started to reach for him and then stopped. "Why would she run away?"

"She found the letter telling me about her mother's death. She knows the truth now, and she was so upset . . ." Madeleine gasped again. Saul couldn't go on.

"Let me get my boots, and I'll help you. Just give me a minute." She opened the storm door wider. "Step inside. It's freezing out there." Madeleine hurried down the hallway toward her bedroom.

He waited in the kitchen, his mind racing with worry. Madeleine reappeared a few minutes later clad in a heavy coat, scarf, and boots.

She held a large flashlight toward him. "Would you like to use this? I have two of them."

"*Danki*." Saul took the flashlight, and their hands brushed. "I've called a few friends and neighbors, and they are going to help."

"Do you want me to call the police?" Madeleine pulled out her phone. "I can dial nine-one-one right now."

"*Ya*," he said. "You call them, and I'll go organize the neighbors."

"I'll be out as soon as I can and find you."

"*Danki*." Saul headed out the door and prayed he'd find his daughter soon—before it was too late.

Madeleine's heart raced with panic after she disconnected her call to the police. The emergency dispatcher promised to send out an Amber Alert and send police officers to Saul's farm. The worry and panic in Saul's eyes had cut right through Madeleine's soul. She couldn't bear the thought of something happening to his sweet little girl.

Armed with her large flashlight, Madeleine hurried outside and up the driveway toward Saul's house, where she found him standing with a group of Amish men.

"The police are coming," she said as she approached. She recognized Marcus. "How can I help?"

"We're going to knock on doors and search the fields," Marcus said. "We need someone to stay at the *haus* in case she comes back."

"I want to help you search for her," Saul said, his eyes shining with worry. "Someone else can stay here and talk to the police."

"I'll stay," an older man said. "I'll sit on the porch and wait for the police. I'll also call for Emma."

"*Danki*," Saul told him.

"I'll help you go door-to-door," Madeleine said.

"No, you should drive your truck around and shine your headlights into the fields," Marcus said. "We'll go door-to-door."

Madeleine glanced at Saul, who nodded in agreement. "I'll do it," she said.

"Let's go. It's getting colder, and the snow isn't letting up at all." Marcus gestured for the group of men to follow him toward the road.

She stepped over to Saul and took his cold hands in hers. She wished they both had gloves, but that didn't matter as much as finding Emma.

"We'll find her, Saul. I promise you."

"*Danki*." His eyes filled with tears.

Unable to speak, Madeleine nodded and then hurried toward her truck.

For more than two hours, Madeleine drove around the surrounding area in search of Emma. The hum of the windshield wipers was the only sound she heard as she combed the dark roads, struggling to see past the glare of her headlights reflecting off the snow. She prayed constantly, begging God to bring Emma home safely. She prayed for him to give Saul strength and to help Emma accept her mother's actions without allowing them to break her heart.

After Madeleine had driven through Paradise three times, she turned around and steered her truck toward her house. She parked in the driveway and then jogged up the driveway toward Saul's house. She found two Amish men standing on the porch and talking to a police officer.

"Did she come home?" Madeleine clasped her hands together.

The same older Amish man shook his head. "We haven't seen her."

Madeleine's heart sank. "Where's Saul?"

"He's still out searching," the older man said.

"What can I do to help?" Madeleine asked. "I've driven through Paradise three times."

"Miss, I think you've done all you can do," the officer said. "We're handling things now."

Madeleine frowned. "Please let me know when you've found her." She pointed toward her house. "I live right there."

"We will," the officer promised.

Madeleine walked through the raging snow toward her house. She put a kettle of water on the stove, wrapped herself in a blanket, and stared out her window toward Saul's house while she continued to silently pray for Emma.

After drinking a cup of tea, she read her Bible and then

climbed into bed fully clothed, the best way to keep warm on a night like this. Her thoughts were still with Emma and Saul as, despite her efforts not to do so, she was drifting off to sleep.

A thought hit her, and Madeleine bolted up.

"The kittens in my barn!" She leaped out of bed.

TWENTY-TWO

Madeleine hurriedly pulled on her coat, scarf, and boots and then grabbed her flashlight before rushing outside to her barn. When she got there, she climbed up into the loft and found Emma asleep and curled up on the quilt Maddie had left next to the mother cat and kittens. Her heart melted at the sight of the little girl snuggled next to the animals.

She slowly sank into the hay and brushed Emma's hair back from her face. Emma sighed and rolled over onto her back, and Madeleine could see tearstains on her pink cheeks.

"Emma," Madeleine whispered. "Emma, wake up. Emma?"

Her eyes fluttered open. "Maddie?" She rubbed her eyes.

"Everyone is looking for you. The whole community and the police are searching." Madeleine continued to run her fingers through the hair that had fallen out from underneath Emma's prayer covering. "You've scared us all to death."

Emma sat up, and her lip quivered. "I had to come here to be alone. I found out *mei mamm* didn't die when I was four. She left me." Tears flooded her pale blue eyes, and Madeleine pulled her into her arms.

"It's okay to cry," Madeleine murmured against Emma's prayer covering. "Let it all out, sweetie."

"I always thought *mei mamm* died because she was sick. Now I know she left because she hated me, and she wanted a better life without me."

"No, no," Madeleine said while rocking her. "That's not true. She didn't hate you."

"*Ya,* she did." Emma sniffed. "If she didn't hate me, then she wouldn't have left. Instead of staying and being *mei mamm,* she moved away and went on boat rides with a man named Timothy. That's all she cared about. She never cared about me."

"Now, I need you to listen to me, and then we have to go tell everyone you're safe." Madeleine rubbed Emma's back. "Your mother didn't hate you. But some people in this world don't know how to be parents. Your mom was one of those people. My father was like that too. My mother told me a long time ago that my father didn't know how to be a daddy, and that's why he left. I used to think he hated me, but my mother told me he didn't. He just was too selfish to be a father. It takes a very special person to be a good parent."

Emma sniffed again.

Madeleine looked down at Emma. "Your father is a very good *dat.* He loves you with all of his heart. I can tell by the way he talks to you and by the way he takes care of you. Has your *dat* given you everything you needed?" She lifted Emma to her feet as she spoke.

Emma nodded. "*Ya,* he always has taken care of me."

"He gives you food, and he provides your clothes. He keeps you safe, right?" Now Madeleine was preparing to take steps toward the ladder, ready to lead Emma with her arms still around the little girl's shoulders. She had to let Saul know his daughter was safe.

Emma wiped her eyes with her fingertips. "*Ya*, he's always been there for me."

"Exactly. Your *dat* loves you enough for a *mamm* and a *dat*." Madeleine pointed to the mother cat. "It's sort of like a *mamm* cat. She makes sure her babies are fed and warm. We give them some food, but they're really getting all they need from their mama. The food we give them is keeping their mama healthy so they can nurse from her. She's keeping them safe up here, away from other animals and the cold snow."

Emma reached down and stroked one of the kittens. "I just don't understand why *mei mamm* would leave me. Why didn't she ever call me or write me? Did she wonder how I was? Did she want to know what I look like?" Fresh tears glistened in her eyes. "Did she even care that I have her eyes and her hair?"

Madeleine's heart splintered at the sadness in Emma's eyes. Keeping her arms tight around the little girl's shoulders, she gently steered her toward the ladder. "I don't know the answer to that. I used to wonder why my father didn't want to get to know me too. I used to think that someday he'd come back to see me, and he'd be a part of my wedding or spend time with my children. I eventually gave up that dream because he never reached out to me. He paid child support to my mother until I turned eighteen, but we never heard from him. He would just mail the checks."

She rubbed Emma's arm and then guided her down the ladder as she continued. "I know it hurts, sweetie, but you have to listen to me. Many, many people love you. Sylvia and Esther love you.

I'm certain Marcus loves you too. My grandparents loved you, and the rest of the community loves you. They love you to the moon and back, as my mother used to say."

When they'd both landed on the barn floor, Emma smiled at Madeleine and wiped her eyes.

"And I love you too, Emma," Madeleine went on as she pushed another lock of hair away from Emma's face. "I love you very much."

"I love you too, Maddie. But you're not Amish." Emma frowned. "*Mei dat* doesn't want me to get too attached to you. He's probably afraid that you'll leave me just like *mei mamm* did. My teacher even told me not to get too close to you because you might leave."

Madeleine shook her head. "No, they're both wrong about me, Emma. I promise you with my heart that I won't leave you."

"Prove to me that you won't leave." Emma's expression was serious.

"All right." Madeleine nodded slowly. "I'll find a way to prove to you that I won't ever leave you."

"*Danki*." Emma hugged her again, and she shivered as Madeleine wrapped her in her arms and walked them to the barn door.

"We need to get you home. Your dad is so scared." Madeleine took Emma's hand and led her out into the snow.

They hurried across the field toward Saul's house. She could see the same group of Amish men standing with the police officer. Even with little light, she could see that Saul was there too.

"Saul!" Madeleine yelled. "Saul! I found her!"

"*Dat!*" Emma yelled. "*Dat!*"

Saul broke into a run and met them halfway through the

field. He lifted Emma into his arms and spun her around. "I've been worried sick about you. Where were you?"

"In Maddie's barn." Emma pointed to Madeleine. "She found me."

"She was asleep with the kittens." Madeleine hugged her coat to her body. "I was falling asleep when I realized we hadn't checked the barn."

"*Danki*." Saul's voice was thin and shaky. "I can't thank you enough."

"You're welcome." Madeleine studied his eyes, wishing they were friends again. She longed to hug him and console him. It was going to be hard for him to answer all Emma's questions.

The Amish men and police officer hurried over and surrounded Saul and Emma. Madeleine slowly backed away from the group and walked home.

As she put on pajamas and climbed back into her bed, she contemplated her conversation with Emma. She wanted to prove to the girl that she would be a part of her life, but she also wanted to finally have roots in a place she could call home. She closed her eyes and prayed, asking God to lead her to the right decision in her life. How could she become a part of Emma's community?

And then the answer appeared in her mind—she could become Amish.

Madeleine loved everything about the Amish culture—the simplicity, the focus on God and family, the community. The answer was right there before her, clear as a cloudless blue sky. It was as if God was speaking to her and directing her thoughts. For the first time since she'd lost Travis, she felt God's presence holding her and comforting her. This was the answer she'd been searching for. This was where God had been leading her all along, but she couldn't see past her own insecurities to see the answer that was right before her eyes. She was supposed to come to Amish Country and start again. She was finally home.

The thought settled comfortably in Madeleine's mind, and she fell asleep with a content and warm feeling in her heart. She slept soundly without any nightmares. And she dreamed of her baptism.

⌒⊗⌒

After everyone else had left, Saul tucked Emma into bed. Although he was now furious that she had run away, he was thankful she was home and safe again.

"I'm sorry for running away." Emma pulled the quilt up to her chin. "And I'm sorry for scaring you."

"I forgive you, but you can't ever do that again." Saul touched her pink cheek. "The whole community was worried about you."

"I know." Emma nodded. "Maddie told me everyone was scared. Especially you."

Saul's heart turned over in his chest at the mention of Madeleine's name. "I'm grateful she thought to look in the barn. I was so frantic that I never thought to check with the kittens."

"I went there to think. I like going to see the kittens and thinking by myself." Emma frowned. "I told Maddie I was upset and that I thought *mei mamm* hated me. Maddie explained that *Mamm* didn't hate me. She said that some people aren't *gut* at being parents. She said her *dat* was the same way. He left before she was born, but he didn't hate her. He just didn't know how to be her *dat*."

Saul nodded slowly, overwhelmed by Madeleine's wisdom.

"Maddie said you love me enough for two parents, and the community loves me too," Emma continued. "And Maddie said she loves me, and she'll never leave me."

Tears filled Saul's eyes, and he couldn't speak. Instead, he leaned down and hugged her.

"*Ich liebe dich, Dat,*" Emma said. "Thank you for being my *dat* and taking such good care of me."

Tears flowed from Saul's eyes as he held on to her.

"Are you okay, *Dat?*" Emma asked.

"*Ya.*" He sat up and wiped his eyes. "We're both tired. I think we need to get some rest. We'll talk in the morning." He kissed her forehead. "*Ich liebe dich. Gut nacht.*"

"*Gut nacht.*" Emma rolled over onto her side and extinguished the lantern on her nightstand.

Saul sauntered to his bedroom and sank onto the edge of the bed. He placed his lantern on the nightstand and then stared up at the ceiling. How had the evening taken such an emotional turn? Not only had Emma learned the truth, but Madeleine had helped her sort through it so quickly. It was all so surreal.

His feelings for Madeleine were stronger than ever, and he didn't know how to stop them from growing. He needed God's help to sort through all the confusing emotions surging through him.

He closed his eyes and prayed. *God, thank you for delivering my dochder back to me safely. Thank you for the wonderful members of my community who surrounded me and helped me search for her. Thank you also for Madeleine, who found Emma and brought her home.*

Lord, I'm confused. I know I need to stay true to my baptism vows, but I can't stop how I feel about Madeleine. She was there for Emma and me in our time of need, and she even helped Emma cope with the truth about her mother. How do I stop feeling close to some-one who has done so much for my dochder and me? I've asked you repeatedly to help me sort through all of these confusing feelings, and I'm not hearing your answers.

Are you listening to me, God? I know I need to wait for your per-fect timing, but these feelings are getting stronger by the day. I need your help now, Lord. Are you hearing me? Why aren't you answer-ing? Please help me stay true to my beliefs. Please lead me to your perfect path. I can't do this alone.

Saul stripped off his clothes and pulled on his pajamas before climbing into bed. As he fell asleep, his thoughts turned to Madeleine and how thankful he was that she saved Emma—in more ways than one.

∽

Madeleine awoke refreshed the following morning. Now her deci-sion to become Amish had settled not just in her mind but in her heart, and she couldn't wait to talk to a friend about it. She was thankful she had already scheduled a personal day from work.

She ate a quick breakfast and then dialed Carolyn's number, hoping Carolyn would be somewhere near where they kept their phone so she wouldn't have to leave a message. After several rings, Carolyn answered her phone.

"Carolyn," Madeleine gushed into the phone. "It's Madeleine. Would it be all right if I came to visit you today?"

"*Ya,* that would be fine." Carolyn's voice was tentative. "It's Tuesday, though. Don't you have to go to work?"

"I took the day off."

"Oh. I'd love to see you. Come by anytime."

"Wonderful," Madeleine said. "I'll be right over."

Thirty minutes later, Madeleine was sitting in Carolyn's kitchen and sipping coffee with her.

"I heard what happened with Emma Beiler last night." Carolyn shook her head. "That is scary. I'm thankful she's okay."

"Yes, it was scary." Madeleine shivered as she remembered how worried she'd been. "I drove around searching for her for more than two hours. It didn't occur to me until I climbed into bed that Emma might be in my barn because she likes to visit the cats there. I don't know why I didn't think of that earlier."

"I think sometimes when we're panicking the most obvious solutions don't occur to us." Carolyn lifted her mug. "How have you been?"

"I'm doing well." Madeleine took a deep breath. "I've made a decision, and I want you to be the first person I share it with."

"Oh?" Carolyn raised her eyebrows. "What is it?"

"I want to become Amish." At saying the words aloud for the first time, she smiled. The decision felt so right that it warmed her soul. She no longer felt alone, and the tight grip of grief that had strangled her heart was slowly letting go. The Lord had spoken to her, and she heard his words loud and clear. This decision was certainly divine.

Carolyn's eyes widened. "Are you certain?"

"I'm positively certain. I've wanted to find a home, and I believe God has been leading me here all along. What do I need to do?"

"Well, you'll need to meet with the bishop. He's a very kind man, and I know he'll be more than willing to talk to you." Carolyn smiled. "And you'll need a proper dress, apron, and prayer covering. I can help you make those."

"When can we get started sewing?" Madeleine asked.

"How about right now?" Carolyn stood. "I have plenty of fabric in my sewing room. We can start on a dress and apron this afternoon."

"Thank you very much. I'll pay you for it." Madeleine clapped her hands together. "I can't wait to get started."

By the time Madeleine left later that afternoon, she had a dress and apron half made. That evening she searched through her grandmother's sewing room and found fabric to make more dresses and aprons. She also found two of her grandmother's prayer coverings.

Madeleine worked late into the night, finishing the dress and the apron and then starting on another dress. She spent the next day sewing and finished the second dress too. While she sewed, she thought about her grandparents and her happy memories of being with them. She wondered what they would think if they were alive and knew about her decision to become Amish. The thought warmed her heart. She knew her grandparents would be happy for her. She wondered how her friends at work would take the news.

ᜒᜒ

Madeleine found Ruth and Linda eating in the break room at lunchtime on Thursday. She sat down at the table and unpacked her bag.

"How's your day going?" Ruth asked Madeleine.

"It's going fine, thank you." Madeleine pulled out her sandwich and bottle of water. "How about yours?"

"The usual." Ruth turned to Linda. "And yours?"

Linda shrugged. "Dirty rooms and unmade beds."

Madeleine smiled. "I wanted to tell you something. I've made a decision."

Ruth raised an eyebrow. "What decision is this?"

"I'm going to become Amish." Madeleine waited for their reaction.

Linda nodded slowly, and Ruth studied Madeleine.

Then Linda frowned. "Do you realize what you have to give up? You can't use your cell phone or drive your truck."

"I know." Madeleine nodded. "I'm comfortable with that."

"Why do you want to be Amish?" Ruth asked. "Does it have to do with your neighbors?"

Madeleine nodded. "Partly it does. When I say I want to be a part of the community, I *am* thinking of Emma Beiler. I made a promise to her, and I intend to keep it. But I also want to be Amish for myself. I want to feel closer to God, and I think being a part of this community of faith will help me do that."

"What promise did you make to Emma?" Ruth asked.

"Does this have something to do with when she went missing the other night?" Linda asked. "I heard about that when I stopped at the market yesterday."

"Yes, it does." Madeleine opened her bottle of water. "Emma was upset, and I promised her I would never leave her."

"Have you spoken to the bishop?" Linda asked. "You'll need to talk to him about joining a baptism class and living as an Amish person for a certain amount of time."

"I'm planning to go see him this weekend." Madeleine sipped her water.

"Do you want me to go with you?" Ruth offered.

"No, but thank you." Madeleine smiled at Ruth. "I need to do

AMY CLIPSTON

this myself." She looked at Ruth and then Linda. "Do I have your blessing?"

"Of course you do." Linda touched her hand. "You have my blessing. And if you change your mind, I'll still support you. Becoming baptized is a big decision, and you might change your mind after you start the classes."

"I don't think I'll change my mind." Madeleine turned to Ruth. "How do you feel about this, Ruth? I really value your opinion."

"If you feel God is leading you to this, then I support it." Ruth smiled. "I have a feeling he *is* leading you, and I'm glad to hear it. If you feel this is your home, then you belong here."

"Thank you." Madeleine hoped the bishop would feel the same way.

TWENTY-THREE

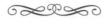

S aul was staining a cabinet when he heard a knock on the door frame behind him. He looked over his shoulder and saw Marcus standing in the doorway. He stepped back from the workbench and pulled off his respirator.

"Marcus," Saul said. "*Wie geht's?*"

"I was in the neighborhood, and I thought I'd stop by." Marcus stepped into the shop, closed the door behind him, and craned his neck to look at the cabinets. "Nice work."

"*Danki.*" Saul pointed toward two stools across from the workbench. "Would you like to have a seat?"

"*Ya.*" Marcus hopped up on a stool. "Sylvia and I have been worried about Emma. How is she doing?"

"She's fine." Saul grabbed two bottles of water from the cooler by his workbench and handed one to Marcus. "She's actually taken the news a lot better than I thought she would. I feel bad for keeping it from her for this long, but I was afraid of how much it would hurt her."

Marcus sipped the water and shook his head. "I don't think you did anything wrong by waiting to tell her. She's just a little girl."

"But she had a right to know." Saul sat on the bench across from Marcus. "I guess I need to give the credit for how well Emma is doing to Maddie. She's the one who helped Emma understand that her mother left because she couldn't handle being a mother. That's what matters, not that Annie left me—though I'm sure questions about her mother choosing another man will eventually come up."

"Why was Madeleine the one talking to her?" Marcus asked.

"Maddie comforted Emma as soon as she found her and told Emma that although Annie left her, she has plenty of people who love her. She told Emma that I'm the only parent she needs because I can love her as much as two parents would." Saul sighed. "Maddie knew how to say all the right things because her father left her before she was born. She knows how it feels to be abandoned by a parent. She was there when Emma needed her most. I feel God put Maddie in Emma's life because he knew Emma was going to need her."

Marcus eyed Saul with suspicion. "You still have feelings for that *English maedel.*"

"I just appreciate what she did for Emma. She's the one who found Emma. And she talked to her and calmed her down too. I don't know if I could've done that."

"*Ya,* you could've. You're her *dat.*" Marcus scowled. "You know her best. I'm grateful that Madeleine found Emma before it got any later or colder, but don't give her all the credit. You're doing the best you can with Emma, and you're doing a fantastic job as *mamm* and *dat.*"

Saul took a long drink of water. "I don't know. I still feel Maddie was helpful. Emma seems much more content knowing the truth than I thought possible."

"You're treading on dangerous territory." Marcus's eyes were full of concern. "You really do have feelings for her, don't you?"

"No, I don't." Saul knew he was lying to his best friend, but he couldn't admit the truth out loud. He wouldn't dare confess that he'd been thinking of Madeleine nonstop ever since she'd found Emma. He couldn't tell Marcus he was starting to wonder if he should take another chance with Madeleine and invite her over for supper.

"You need to be careful," Marcus warned. "You don't want to risk losing Emma to the outside world. If Emma thinks that much of Madeleine, then she may start asking questions. She might want to know what it's like to join the military or drive a car. You don't want to lose her like you lost your *bruder*."

"I know. I know." Saul shrugged. "I'm not going to lose Emma. I'm just thankful Maddie is our neighbor. That's all I meant."

"You have to be careful. Emma is at a very impressionable age." Marcus stood. "I need to get home. Tell Emma hello for us."

"I will." Saul waved to his friend. "*Danki* for stopping by."

❧

"I saw Maddie outside earlier," Emma said while washing dishes later that evening. "I waved to her, and she waved back."

"What was she doing?" Saul brought a bowl to the counter.

"She was carrying grocery bags into her *haus*." Emma scrubbed a pot while she spoke. "I was going to go and help her carry in her bags, but I didn't want you to be upset with me."

Saul nodded as Marcus's warning rang through his mind. "That was a *gut* choice. It's best that you leave her alone."

"I miss her." Emma frowned up at him.

"I know." Saul touched her arm. *I do too.* "We appreciate all she did when she found you, but we need to give her some privacy."

"But she said she'll always be here for me." Emma's eyes were determined. "Why can't I be her friend?"

Saul sighed. He felt torn between the Amish community and the outside world. "I know it doesn't make much sense, but I'm only trying to do what's best for you. Right now I need you to follow my rules. You'll understand why when you're older." He paused, waiting for her to argue with him. Instead, she simply nodded.

"Okay, *Dat*," she said before turning her attention back to the dishes.

He breathed a sigh of relief. For now, the argument was settled, but he knew she would keep asking him why she couldn't be friends with Madeleine. And soon he would run out of explanations.

Madeleine parked her truck in front of Bishop Elmer Smucker's house the following afternoon. She climbed out and then smoothed her hands down her cloak. She'd dressed in her new purple dress and apron that she'd completed with Carolyn's help. Her hair was styled in a traditional Amish tight bun and covered with a prayer *kapp* she'd found in her grandmother's closet. Wearing the prayer covering made her feel closer to both God and her grandmother. She only hoped the bishop would see that her intentions were pure.

She walked up the front path leading to the bishop's white, two-story house and knocked on the door. She folded her hands in front of her cloak and shivered in the cold breeze.

The front door opened, and Elmer Smucker stood inside the storm door with a confused look on his face. Madeleine estimated he was in his late seventies. He was short and stocky with a long, graying beard. After a moment, he held open the storm door. "Hello. May I help you?"

"Good afternoon," Madeleine said. "I'm Madeleine Miller. I'm Martha Stoltzfus's granddaughter."

"Oh, Madeleine. How are you?" He opened the storm door wider. "What can I do for you?"

"I'm well, thank you. I was hoping I could talk to you. Is now a good time?" She paused while gathering her thoughts. "It's a personal matter."

"Of course." Elmer made a sweeping gesture. "Please come in. Would you like to have a seat?"

"Thank you." Madeleine followed him into a large family room. She removed her cloak and folded it in half. She sat on a sofa and placed the cloak beside her while Elmer sat across from her in a wing chair. "I guess I should've called first."

"It's no problem," Elmer said. "What can I do for you, Madeleine?"

Madeleine paused for a moment and then decided to plow forward with the full truth. "I've been doing a lot of thinking and praying, and I want to know what I need to do to become Amish."

"*Ach.*" The bishop's eyes flew open as if he were startled by an unexpected noise. "You want to be Amish?" He asked the question slowly, as if trying to comprehend the words.

"Yes," Madeleine said. "I inherited my grandparents' house, and I spent a lot of time with them when I was a child."

"They were *gut* people." He suddenly smiled. "Now that you

say it, I recall seeing you with them. Martha was always *froh* when you were here."

Madeleine nodded. "I was *froh* too. I cherish those times. Becoming Amish and a part of this community would give me the chance to have a real home."

The bishop studied her while fingering his beard. "This is something you've been considering for a while?"

"Yes," she said. "I've spent the past several months in prayer about my life, and the other night I realized I belong here. I believe God has told me to become a part of the Amish church."

"But your mother left before you were born." The bishop's expression was pointed. "It's rare an *Englisher* joins our community. What are your true intentions?"

"I work with the Amish at the hotel, and my closest friends are Amish." She paused and considered what else was in her heart. "I learned *Dietsch* from my grandparents, and I understood the language when I went to Carolyn Glick's wedding and when I went to church with Carolyn." She cupped her hand to her chest. "My heart belongs in this community, and I'm ready to start living like a true member."

The bishop's expression softened. "Are you certain your reasons are pure?"

Madeleine paused, thought of Emma, and knew she needed to be honest with the bishop. "I'm sure you heard about Emma Beiler running away. The truth is, I made a promise to her that night when I found her. I told her I love her, and she asked me to prove that I'll never leave her. By becoming Amish, I will not only join your community, but I will prove to Emma that I'll never leave her."

Elmer studied Madeleine. "You're saying you want to convert

to keep a promise to Emma Beiler?" He raised one of his bushy gray eyebrows. "It's not my place to judge, but I'm not certain that's a strong enough reason to become Amish."

"My reasons are pure because it was God who brought me to this decision after months of praying. This wasn't a hasty decision," Madeleine said. "I've searched my heart and soul, and I know I need to convert to feel whole again. When I'm at home in *mei mammi's haus*, I feel as if I belong here." She folded her hands as if to pray as her thoughts turned to Travis. "I lost my fiancé tragically, and that caused me to refocus my life toward God. I believe *mei mammi* left me her *haus* because she knew how much I loved this community, and it's as if she's calling me back home."

The bishop rubbed his beard and was silent for a moment. "You truly believe God put this decision in your heart?"

"Absolutely," she said, emphasizing the word. "I could never have decided this without his guidance."

Elmer paused. "I believe you. Now, back to your request to join the church. What would your family say about your decision to convert?"

"My parents will understand." Madeleine fingered her apron. "I plan to call my mother tonight and tell her."

Elmer fingered his beard. "And your *mamm* left the faith before you were born, right?"

"That's right. She hadn't joined the church before she left, but she told me that she always felt as if she were shunned." Madeleine sat erect, hoping to look serious and respectful. "Her relationship was strained with her parents until I was born, after my father left her. I have a great love and respect for the Amish faith. Now it seems God is leading me to the faith more than ever."

Elmer nodded while contemplating her words.

"I know this seems sudden, but I truly have thought this through." She nodded emphatically.

"You realize you can't simply decide to be Amish and then quickly convert," Elmer said. "You'll need to live as we do without any of your modern conveniences. And you must complete baptism classes."

"I understand," Madeleine explained. "My house is already an Amish home. I'll stop my cellular phone service, and I'll sell my truck. I'll find a ride to work. I'll have the phone in the barn hooked up and use that to make calls. I've already been worshiping in your district, and I've made some Amish clothes." She glanced down at her dress and apron. "Carolyn Glick helped me make this dress and apron, and I found prayer coverings in my *mammi's* closet. I'm ready to make a full commitment to this community and to my new life right away, and I'll be ready for my instruction."

"Wonderful." Elmer stood and crossed the room, coming to a stop in front of her. "I'd like to welcome you to the Amish community." He shook her hand "You're invited to join the baptism class in the spring."

"Oh, thank you!" Madeleine clapped her hands together. "I mean, *danki*! This is wonderful. I'm so grateful. I appreciate your time."

Elmer chuckled. "*Gern gschehne.* I'll see you at church."

"Yes, you will." Madeleine pulled on her cloak. "Have a good afternoon."

⁂

Madeleine finished her supper at the kitchen table that evening before pulling out her cellular phone and dialing her mother's number. Anxiety coursed through her while she awaited her mother's voice on the other end of the line.

"Hi, Maddie," Mom said. "How are you doing today?"

"I'm doing great, Mom. How are you and Jack?"

"We're fine. I was just trying to figure out what to make for supper. What did you eat?"

"I had veggie burger and corn." Madeleine chuckled. "It was a gourmet meal."

"Yes, it was." Mom laughed. "What's new with you?"

"Well, I met with Elmer Smucker today." Madeleine gathered up her dirty dishes while she spoke, her phone between her shoulder and neck. "He's the bishop for this church district."

"Why did you meet with the bishop?"

"I've decided that I want to convert." She placed her dishes in the sink. "I want to become Amish."

"What did you say?"

"You heard me." Madeleine leaned against the sink. "I want to be Amish. I love this community, and I want to be a part of it."

"Are you certain?" Mom asked.

"I'm positive."

"You realize what you have to give up, right?" Mom continued. "You need to get rid of your truck, and you love that truck. And what about your phone? And the Internet, music, and movies."

Madeleine smiled. "Mom, I can live without the truck. I'll have to pay for rides, but I'll eventually get a horse and buggy. I already have a barn and a fenced pasture for a horse. There's a phone in the barn, and I'll just have to have it hooked up again. I'm living without music, movies, and the Internet now. I've thought this through. I know what I'm doing."

Mom was silent for a few moments. "Are you doing this for that man next door? For Saul?"

Madeleine shook her head. "No, I'm doing this for me."

"Are you sure, Maddie?"

"I am doing this in part for his daughter. But deep in my heart, I've always felt as if I belonged here." Madeleine paused to gather her thoughts. "I hope you support my decision, Mom. This is very important to me."

"If this is really what you want, then I will support you. But I hope you're not doing this to win a man's heart. You need to do what's right for you, not someone else."

"I know that, Mom." Madeleine began to fill the sink with hot water. "I feel closer to God when I'm in this community. This is what I want to do."

"When will you be baptized?" her mother asked.

"I'm going to join a baptism class in the spring. I'm going to shut my cell phone off soon. I'll have the outside phone hooked up next week, and then I'll call you and give you the number."

"Okay." Mom sniffed. "I never expected this. I'm really surprised. My mother would be so proud of you, Maddie. She really would. And I'm proud of you too."

"Thank you, Mom. That means a lot."

"Well, I'll let you go. Call me next week."

"I will." Madeleine disconnected the call and smiled. She was thankful for her mother's support.

TWENTY-FOUR

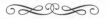

M adeleine was sweeping her kitchen floor when she heard squealing tires and a crash. She dropped the broom and ran to the front window, where she spotted a buggy twisted at the side of the road, at the end of the driveway and near a sedan with a smashed front end.

"Oh no!" Madeleine grabbed her first aid kit from under the bathroom sink and her phone before rushing out the door with her coat thrown over her shoulders. She ran to the buggy and pried the door open. She found Marcus slumped over the seat and moaning. His head was bleeding profusely.

"Oh, Marcus." Her hands trembled as she gently held his head to protect his neck and spine from injury. She snapped into trauma nurse mode, mentally clicking through the list of procedures she'd learned while serving in the military. "Talk to me, Marcus. Stay with me."

Marcus continued to moan.

"Miss?" A man walked up behind her. His face was pasty white and his hands were shaking. "I didn't mean to hit him. I didn't see him at first, and when I did, I couldn't stop. The roads are icy from the snow we got yesterday." His voice quavered. "I didn't mean to hit him. I really didn't. Is he okay? Is he alive?"

"He's alive, but he needs help." Madeleine pulled out her iPhone, unlocked it, and handed it to the man. "Call nine-one-one right now." She used one hand to open the first aid kit and fish out gauze pads. "Marcus? Stay with me, buddy. Marcus? Can you hear me? Answer me if you can hear me."

"*Ya.*" Marcus's voice croaked, but his eyes remained closed while blood poured from his forehead.

She pushed the pads up against his head while silently saying a prayer for him.

"Where are we?" The driver stuck his head back in the buggy. "I have the paramedics on the phone, but I have no idea where I am."

Madeleine rattled off the address. "Tell them to hurry."

The driver moved away with her phone still against his ear.

"Marcus?" Madeleine pressed the gauze against his head, and it was immediately soaked with blood. She applied pressure to the wound while continuing to stabilize his neck. "Stay calm, Marcus. I'm here with you." Sirens blared in the distance, and she swallowed a sigh.

"My leg." Marcus breathed the words. "It hurts."

"The paramedics are on their way. They'll take good care of you. I promise you."

"What's happened?" Saul's voice boomed nearby. "Oh no. Marcus?"

"He'll be okay," Madeleine called. "We've called for help." She looked over her shoulder as Saul approached.

"How is he?" Saul's eyes were full of worry.

"He's hanging in there," she said. "He has a head wound. I think his leg is injured, and the paramedics will have to put it in a splint when they arrive."

"What can I do?" Saul asked.

"You might want to take care of his horse. He looks awfully scared over there. And the driver of the car could use a kind word. He doesn't look hurt, but he's shaken up." She turned back to Marcus. "Just breathe and relax, Marcus. Everything will be okay."

∽

After Saul made sure the driver of the car was all right, Saul moved back by the buggy and lingered behind Madeleine for a moment, marveling at how she was caring for his best friend. She was gentle but confident as she tended to Marcus's wounded head and assured him that help was on the way. He was overwhelmed by the Christian love in her eyes and her nurturing heart. For the second time in less than a week, Madeleine was taking care of someone he loved.

Sirens sounded as an ambulance barreled down the road, shaking him from his thoughts.

Neighbors from nearby farms began to gather in their shared driveway.

"Saul?" A young man from a neighboring farm appeared behind him. "Who's in the buggy?"

"It's Marcus Smucker," Saul said. "He was on his way to see me. He must have just been turning into the driveway when the car hit him."

"Is he going to be all right?" the young man asked.

"*Ya.*" Saul nodded. "It looks like he will."

"Can I do anything to help?" the young man asked.

"*Ya.*" Saul pointed toward the horse. "Would you take his horse to my pasture?"

"*Ya.*" The young man walked over to the horse. "I'll make sure he's okay."

"*Danki,*" Saul said as a crowd gathered around him.

"Is that Marcus Smucker?" a neighbor asked.

"Who's caring for him?" a second asked.

"What happened?" someone else yelled.

"My neighbor, Maddie, is taking care of him," Saul said. "She's a nurse."

The ambulance stopped in front of the buggy, and two paramedics jumped out. Saul stood with his neighbors while the paramedics talked to Madeleine. A fire engine blared its sirens and horns as it roared down the street and stopped near the ambulance. Soon a group of firefighters and emergency medical technicians were caring for Marcus and the driver of the car, and a police car arrived as well.

Madeleine finished talking to the emergency responders and then joined Saul. His eyes moved down her gray blouse and blue skirt, which were both stained with blood.

"How is he?" Saul asked her.

"Marcus has a gash on his head, and I suspect his leg or ankle may be broken." Madeleine crossed her arms over her blouse. "He was talking when the paramedics came. They're going to take him out of the buggy on a board just to make sure he doesn't have any back or neck fractures."

"Oh." Saul studied her, taking in her beautiful face and eyes.

He was thankful for her and for her caring heart. *"Danki* for taking care of him."

She gave him a strange expression as if she were shocked by his words. "You're welcome."

One of the police officers asked if anyone in the crowd had seen the accident happen, but no one had. Then a woman with an EMT uniform came over as well.

"Does someone know this man's name?"

"Ya, he's Marcus Smucker. He was on his way to my farm." Saul pointed behind him. *"Mei haus* is back there. He was going to help me with a project."

"Would you mind helping with some paperwork?" the woman asked. "Would you also inform his family?"

"Ya." Saul turned to Madeleine. "Then would you give me a ride to get Sylvia and take us both to the hospital?"

"Of course." She glanced down at her blouse. "Let me just get changed. I'm a bit of a mess."

The EMT touched Madeleine's arm. "Miss, you did a wonderful job keeping Mr. Smucker stable before we arrived."

"Thanks." Madeleine gave her a shy smile. "I've had a lot of experience with trauma patients, and I'm glad I was here to help."

"I am too," Saul told her.

She turned toward him, and her gaze locked with his. It was as if they were the only two people in the world. His heart turned over in his chest. He longed for her friendship. *I miss you, Maddie. I miss you so much I ache.*

"I'll go get changed." Madeleine's voice wrenched him back to reality. She walked over to the EMT vehicle, retrieved her phone from the driver of the car, and then picked up her first aid kit. After jogging to her house, she disappeared through the front door.

⌒∞⌒

Madeleine changed into a black skirt and plain blue blouse before pulling on her coat. She checked her hair in the mirror to make sure her hair was still secure in the tight bun she'd fixed earlier in the day. When she returned to the scene of the accident, she found Saul still talking to the EMT who was filling out paperwork on a clipboard. She stood back by the crowd of neighbors and waited until he was done.

Saul walked over to her as the ambulance pulled away with the lights flashing. She had been surprised by the tenderness in his eyes earlier when she was helping Marcus. Had he felt a spark between them? Or was he only worried about his friend? She had to have misread the heat in his eyes. Certainly he was only concerned about Marcus.

"You don't need to worry," she assured him as he stood next to her. "He was lucid when the EMTs arrived."

He nodded. "The woman told me the same thing. She thinks he'll be okay. I pray she's right."

"Do you want to go get Sylvia now?" Madeleine pointed toward her truck.

"*Ya*, please." He looked up the driveway. "Why is there a For Sale sign in your truck?"

"I've decided to get rid of it." She pulled the keys from her coat pocket.

"Why?" he asked as they walked side by side toward the vehicle.

"I need a change." She opened the door and hopped into the driver's seat. Although she knew he'd find out soon that she was going to become Amish, she didn't want to tell him just yet. She was more concerned about Marcus and his family.

"Oh." Saul climbed in next to her in the passenger seat.

They drove to the Smucker farm in silence. What was going through Saul's mind? Although he was stoic, there was something different about him. The cold vibe she'd felt from him before she went to California was gone. Was the way he felt about being her friend changing? Was he ready to be her friend? The questions echoed through her mind while they steered through Paradise toward Marcus's home.

When they pulled into the Smucker driveway, Madeleine hopped out of the truck and followed Saul to the front door.

Sylvia opened her inside door, then the storm door, and stepped out onto the porch before they even knocked. "*Was iss letz?*" She looked at each of them. "Where's Marcus?"

Madeleine touched Sylvia's arm. "Marcus was in an accident, but he's going to be fine. I just need to take you to the hospital."

"An accident?" Tears filled Sylvia's eyes. "What happened?"

Madeleine looked at Saul. "Tell her what happened, and I'll go get her things. Where are your coat and purse, Sylvia?"

"By the back door in the mudroom," Sylvia said before turning to Saul. "Is Marcus okay?"

Madeleine rushed into the house and grabbed Sylvia's things. When she returned to the porch, Sylvia was sniffing and wiping her eyes with the back of her hand.

"Madeleine took *gut* care of Marcus until the paramedics arrived," Saul said. "He will be fine. I promise you."

"*Danki.*" Sylvia hugged Madeleine. "You're a blessing, Madeleine. *Danki* for taking *gut* care of my husband."

"You're welcome." Madeleine met Saul's gaze, and her pulse skittered. "Let's get you to the hospital."

Sylvia sat between Madeleine and Saul in the truck. When they arrived, Madeleine steered up to the emergency entrance.

"Do you want me to stay with you?" Madeleine asked.

"That won't be necessary," Saul said as he climbed out.

"I'll call my driver when Marcus is ready to go home," Sylvia said. "*Danki*, Madeleine, for all you've done."

"You're welcome. Do you want me to call anyone?" Madeleine offered. "Do you need me to take care of the girls?"

"I'll call my mother-in-law," Sylvia said. "She'll meet the girls at the school and take them home."

"Okay." Madeleine nodded. "Saul, you have my number if you need anything. I'll be home today."

"*Danki*," Saul said.

"That's what neighbors are for," Madeleine said.

<hr />

Later that evening, Madeleine noticed headlights reflecting off her family room wall while she was reading her Bible. She rushed to a window and saw a van parked by Saul's house. She pulled on her coat and hurried up the rock driveway, then waved at the van as it steered back down the driveway toward the road.

Madeleine climbed Saul's back porch steps and knocked on the storm door.

Emma pulled open the inside door and then smiled as she swung open the storm door. "Maddie! How are you?"

"I'm fine," Madeleine said. "How are you?"

"I'm *gut*." Emma looked over her shoulder. "*Dat*! It's Maddie!"

Saul came to the door. His eyes were tired. "Maddie. We just got home."

"I saw the van, and I came right over," Madeleine said. "I don't mean to intrude, but I want to know how Marcus is doing."

"He's fine." Saul unbuttoned his coat. "He has a sprained ankle, and he has stitches in his head. They ran all sorts of tests to make sure his injuries weren't any worse than they appeared. He'll be as *gut* as new in a few weeks."

"Good." Madeleine breathed a deep sigh. "I'm relieved to hear that. Are Sylvia and Esther okay?"

"*Ya*, they're fine. Sylvia and I stayed at the hospital with him, and her mother-in-law took care of the girls." Saul gestured toward the kitchen behind him. "Do you want to come in?"

"Oh no, thank you." Madeleine backed away from the door. "I'm letting the cold into your house, and I'm certain you're tired and hungry."

"Come in," Emma insisted. "I made some *brot* that you have to try. Esther and I baked with her *mammi*. We had a lot of fun."

"Oh no, thank you. Maybe I can try it some other time." Madeleine shook her head. "It's late."

"*Danki* for the cookbook," Emma said. "I love it."

"You're welcome." Madeleine looked at Saul. "I never got a chance to tell you that the cabinets and countertop are gorgeous. Thank you."

"I'm glad you like them." His expression softened. "And thank you for the screwdrivers."

"You're welcome." Madeleine jammed her thumb toward her house. "I'd better go. I'll see you soon."

"Good night!" Emma called after her.

Madeleine hurried down the driveway and sent a prayer up

to God, thanking him for protecting Marcus. She then asked him to give her strength as she prepared her heart to begin living as a member of the community.

∽

"How are you feeling?" Saul stood with Marcus after the worship service the following Sunday.

Marcus shrugged while leaning on crutches. "I'm all right. I'm just very sore. I feel like I've been thrown from a horse."

"I know that feeling," Joshua Glick chimed in. "I've been thrown a few times, and it's rough. I hope you feel better soon."

"*Danki*, Josh." Marcus frowned. "It's not easy to work when I have to stay off my ankle."

Saul glanced across the barn to where a pretty young woman was talking to Emma while they delivered platters of food for lunch. The young woman had dark hair peeking out from under her prayer covering, and she was dressed in a traditional purple dress and black apron. While the woman seemed vaguely familiar, he couldn't put his finger on how he knew her.

"Josh." Saul leaned toward the other man. "Who is the *maedel* talking with Emma?"

Joshua glanced over at the woman and then turned to Saul. "That's Madeleine Miller. You don't recognize her?"

"That's Maddie?" Saul asked, surprised. "But she's dressed Amish."

"Are you sure that's Madeleine?" Marcus asked. "I was trying to figure out who she was too."

"I'm certain it's Madeleine. She was talking to Carolyn before the service started," Joshua said. "I guess she's converting?" He looked across the room to where Carolyn was waving at him. "*Mei fraa* is calling for me. I'd better see what she wants."

Saul's mouth gaped open as Madeleine smiled and talked to Emma and Esther. Madeleine was a vision of beauty in her traditional Amish clothes. Although he'd always found her beautiful, this was different. Seeing her in the raiment of his community made her more appealing than ever. It was as if his heart opened up and he could finally allow himself to feel close to her. She was no longer forbidden. His heart and soul warmed at the thought of her becoming Amish.

He loved her. Truly loved her. He was ready to trust another woman, and Madeleine was the one who had shown him how to let someone into his heart again. He'd seen glimpses of Madeleine's heart when she talked to Emma after she'd run away and also when she helped Marcus after the accident. She was the woman he wanted to marry; she was the woman who would be a proper mother to Emma. But Madeleine would also be a wonderful wife, someone with whom he'd want to share his life.

Instead of being selfish and cold like Annie had been, Madeleine was warm and caring. This love was different and deeper than anything he'd ever felt for Annie. He had never felt secure with Annie because he wasn't her first choice. But when he was with Madeleine, he was certain he was her first choice. She made him whole; she made him feel loved. Madeleine would be his partner, his helpmate.

The realizations settled in his soul, and the wall he'd built around his heart finally shattered.

Emma grabbed Madeleine's hand and pulled her toward Saul. "*Dat!*" she called. "*Dat!*"

Madeleine smiled and laughed as they weaved through the

knot of people and headed toward Saul. His gaze was glued to Madeleine's beautiful face.

"*Dat,*" Emma said as she brought Madeleine to a stop in front of him. "Look at Maddie! She's decided to become Amish."

"Hi, Saul." Madeleine gave him a shy smile. "*Wie geht's?*"

"Maddie." He shook his head, unable to express the words in his heart. "You look *schee.*"

"You think so?" Madeleine smoothed her hands over her apron. "I'm still getting the hang of sewing, but I'm practicing."

"Maddie is keeping her promise to me." Emma looked up at Madeleine. "She promised she wouldn't leave me, and she's going to be Amish like us. She'll be a member of our church district."

"That's right." Madeleine looked down at Emma with love shimmering in her eyes. "I made a promise to you, and I will keep it."

"Maddie," Saul said. "Can we talk somewhere alone?"

"*Ya,* of course." Madeleine touched Emma's arm. "I'm going to go talk to your *dat* for a few minutes. Would you please help Carolyn fill coffee cups?"

"*Ya.*" Emma rushed off toward the women who were serving the meal.

Saul and Madeleine headed toward the barn door. She picked up her cloak from the back of a chair, and he pulled on his coat before they walked out into the cold air. They walked together toward a pond at the back of the property.

"You're surprised," Madeleine finally said.

"*Ya.*" Saul nodded. "I'm shocked, but I'm *froh.*" He stopped walking by the icy pond, which glistened in the afternoon sun. "When did you decide to convert?"

She looked out over the pond. "I spoke to the bishop last week."

"That's why you put a For Sale sign in your truck."

She nodded. "*Ya.* I actually sold it yesterday and got a ride here today. I'm going to turn off my cell phone at the end of the month, and I'm having the phone in the barn hooked up. I'm going to join the next baptism class in the spring. I'll be baptized in the fall after I complete the classes."

"Why didn't you tell me?"

Madeleine's expression became unsure. "I guess I was afraid."

"Why would you be afraid to tell me?" He searched her eyes.

"I didn't want you to think I was converting for the wrong reason. I want to be Amish because I love this community. After dreaming of a place I could call my home, I've finally found it. I also want to keep my promise to Emma. She's very important to me."

"You're very important to both of us." He took her hands in his. "Maddie, I'm sorry I've been cold to you. When Annie left, I built a wall around my heart. I didn't know how to let someone past that wall because I was afraid of being hurt again. I also was overprotective of Emma because she was all I had left." He paused and stared deep into her eyes. "You've changed me. You've taught me how to love again. You've awakened feelings in me that I haven't felt in years."

Madeleine sniffed as tears filled her eyes.

"Marcus once said I was too scared to take risks, and he was right. But I'm not scared anymore." He took a deep breath and mustered all of his strength. "Maddie, seeing you today has made me realize that I'm ready to give my heart away again. God has given me a second chance to love someone by bringing you into my life. I'm thankful for you."

Madeleine wiped her eyes with one hand.

"I want you to be a part of my life, Maddie. I also want you to be in Emma's life. Would you give me a chance to show you how much you mean to us?" He squeezed her hands. "I'd like to get to know you, and then we can officially start dating after you're baptized. Does that sound *gut* to you?"

"*Ya*." She sniffed, and a tear trickled down her cheek. "That would make me so *froh*. I thought I would never love again after losing Travis the way I did. My heart was ripped out of my chest when he killed himself. I felt guilty for not seeing the signs that he needed more help than he was getting. After he died, I felt all alone, but you and Emma have become my family. God gave me another chance at love too. I'm so blessed to be here with you and Emma."

"*Ich liebe dich*," he whispered as he wiped away her tear with the tip of his finger.

"*Ich liebe dich*." She repeated the words, and they were like a sweet melody to his ears.

⚬⚬

Madeleine couldn't stop smiling as she and Saul walked together back to the barn. She knew that joining the church was the right decision and that God had put that decision in her heart. She not only had found a home, but she'd also found a family with Saul and Emma Beiler.

"Madeleine!" Linda Zook rushed over to Madeleine and Saul as they approached the barn. "Ruth is in the hospital."

"What?" Madeleine gasped. "I was wondering why she wasn't here this morning. What happened?"

"Her husband just called to say she's had a stroke. She told me on Friday that she wasn't feeling well and she was going to go home and rest. I never imagined it was this serious." Linda's eyes were wide. "We have to get to the hospital."

Madeleine looked up at Saul. "Could we call your driver?"

"*Ya.*" Saul nodded. "I'll call right away."

∽

Madeleine, Saul, Carolyn, Josh, and Linda walked into the hospital that afternoon. Madeleine rushed to the front desk and asked where she could find Ruth, and they hurried to Ruth's room.

"Do you think we should take turns going in?" Linda asked. "We might overwhelm her if we all go in at once."

"*Ya*, that's a *gut* point." Carolyn looked at Madeleine. "You go first. We'll wait in the sitting room down the hall."

Madeleine turned toward Saul, who nodded in agreement. Madeleine knocked on the door and then opened it. Ruth's husband, Jonas, sat beside Ruth's bed with his hands folded in his lap. His gaze was frozen on Ruth, who had an oxygen tube in her nose. Machines next to her beeped and hummed.

"Jonas," Madeleine whispered as tears filled her eyes. "How is she?"

The older man shook his head and frowned. The sadness and worry in his eyes caused the tears to sprinkle down Madeleine's cheeks.

Ruth stirred, turned toward Madeleine, and reached out her hand. "M–Madeleine. *K–kumm.*"

"Ruth," Madeleine took her hand. "How are you?"

Ruth's eyes were wide as she weakly pulled Madeleine toward

her. "I n–need to s–see A–Aron. You h–have to g–get h–him. You have to t–tell him to c–come."

Tears streamed down Jonas's cheeks as he rushed out of the room.

The machines hummed and clicked while Madeleine gnawed her lower lip. *What should I do? How can I find Aaron? What should I tell Ruth?*

"M–Mad–eleine," Ruth said again, her words slow and garbled. "I n–need to s–see Aa–ron. He l–left a l–long t–time ago, and I n–need h–him to c–come b–back to m–me. I have to t–talk to h–him."

Madeleine nodded. "*Ya*, I understand, Ruth. I will try to find him."

Ruth squeezed Madeleine's hand. "I h–have to s–see h–him r–right a–away." Her voice rose. "*D–dummle!*"

"Okay." Madeleine felt her heart breaking as she studied Ruth. She looked different. She wasn't the same strong and steady Ruth who had been a pillar of wisdom and patience. This woman was agitated and excitable. The stroke had changed Ruth, and it was difficult to accept.

The door opened, and Jonas reappeared with a man in a white coat.

"I'll give her something to calm her down," the doctor said. "We'll take care of her, Mr. Ebersol." The doctor approached Ruth. "Mrs. Ebersol, I need you to rest now."

"I n–need to s–see Aaron! He h–has to c–come b–back."

"Miss," the doctor said, addressing Madeleine. "We need to restrict Mrs. Ebersol's visitors for now. You can come back and see her later on when she has calmed down."

"I understand." Madeleine cleared her throat. "Good-bye,

Ruth." More tears rolled down her cheeks. "I'll pray for you." She glanced at Jonas, and he gave her a solemn nod.

Madeleine hurried out of the room and down the hallway to where Saul, Josh, Carolyn, and Linda were waiting. She tried to calm her frayed nerves and stop her tears, but they continued to flow.

When she reached her friends, Saul stood and reached for her. "What happened?"

"Ruth isn't herself." Madeleine sat down beside Saul. "She's weak, and her speech has been affected by the stroke. She's also upset and agitated. She's asking for Aaron. She begged me to find him and make him come home to see her. She was insistent."

"*Ach*, no," Carolyn gasped, and Joshua rubbed her arm.

"That's *bedauerlich*," Linda said.

"*Ya*," Carolyn agreed. "We need to do something for her."

"We do. She was very upset. She told me to hurry, that she needed to see him right away." Madeleine looked at Saul. "Can we help her? Can we find a way to contact Aaron?"

"I'll have to look into it," Saul said. "I'll do my best to find him."

"The doctor has restricted her visitors, which means we can't go in to see her right now." Madeleine sighed. "I'm very upset to see her this way."

"It will get better." Saul touched her arm. "The doctors will take *gut* care of her."

"I hope so." Although her heart was breaking for her friend Ruth, Madeleine felt comforted with Saul by her side.

∽

Later that evening, Saul tucked Emma into bed and then went into his room and sat on the edge of his bed. He'd told Madeleine he would do his best to find Aaron, and he intended to keep that promise. All afternoon he'd tried to think where Aaron could possibly be and how he could find him. He'd heard Aaron had gone to a former Amish community in Missouri, but he had no idea how to find him there. His thoughts kept going back to the letter he'd received from Timothy.

He retrieved the metal box that was now in a drawer in his nightstand, sifted past the legal documents Annie had sent him, and found the postmarked envelope that had held Timothy's letter. He studied the crumpled envelope, and then the solution hit him like a ton of bricks—the embossed return address on the envelope said Paradise Builders. He suddenly remembered a conversation he'd had with Aaron when they were fifteen.

They were spending time with friends at a youth gathering and discussing their dreams for the future. Aaron told Saul that someday he hoped to open his own construction business and call it Paradise Builders. Could this company be the one Aaron Ebersol had dreamed of when he was a child? Had Aaron moved to Missouri and started his own company? If so, did Timothy work for Aaron?

Saul's pulse accelerated while he stared at the Paradise Builders logo. Now he had to figure out a way to contact the company and confirm that his hunch was right. The best way to confirm it was to call the company, but how would he find the phone number? He'd heard that the Internet was the best place to find information quickly. Perhaps Madeleine still had Internet access on her fancy cell phone.

Saul stuffed the envelope into his pocket and headed down

the hallway to Emma's room. After knocking, he opened the door and stepped through the doorway.

"*Ya, Dat*?" Emma sat up in bed. "Is something wrong?"

"No, no, *mei liewe*. Everything is fine. I just need to step outside for a few minutes. Will you be okay here alone?"

"I'll be fine. Be sure to wear your coat. It's cold out there."

Saul smiled. "I promise to wear my coat. I'll be back soon. You get to sleep." He rushed downstairs, pulled on his coat, and hurried down the driveway to Madeleine's house. He was glad to see a light glowing in her kitchen. He knocked on her storm door, and she quickly opened both doors when she saw him through her inside door's windowpane.

"Saul?" She tilted her head. "Are you okay?"

"*Ya*, I just need to talk to you."

"Come in." They sat down at the kitchen table. "What's going on?"

"Do you still have Internet on your phone?"

"Yes. I just charged my phone at work the other day." She took the phone from her purse. "What do you need?"

"Can you find an address for a company in Missouri?" He fished the envelope from his pocket and smoothed it out on the table. "I think I found Aaron Ebersol."

Madeleine glanced at the envelope and then looked up at Saul. "You think he works there?"

"No, I think he owns that company." He tapped the envelope. "This is the envelope Timothy's letter came in. I was trying to figure out how to find Aaron earlier, and intuition told me to look at that letter. When I saw the envelope, I felt like this was the sign we needed. When we were kids, Aaron told me he wanted to open up his own construction business and call it Paradise Builders."

"Oh, Saul!" Madeleine grinned. "You're a genius!"

"No, I just have a really *gut* memory." He pointed to the phone. "So can you find a phone number?"

"I can try." She typed with her fingertips, and soon she smiled and turned the phone around so he could see. "Look at what I found."

The company name, address, and phone number were displayed on the screen.

He smiled. "Now you're the genius."

Her cheeks flushed bright pink, and she was adorable.

"Would you please dial the number?" he asked. "I'll do the talking if you'd like. I'm the one who knew Aaron."

"Let's hope the phone number is current." She pushed on the screen and then handed him the phone. "Hopefully it will ring."

Saul took the phone and nodded. "It's ringing."

After the third ring, a recording began. "You've reached Paradise Builders. We're not in the office right now, but if you leave a message, we will return your call as soon as possible."

After a beep, Saul said, "This message is for Aaron Ebersol. This is Saul Beiler in Paradise, Pennsylvania. Your mother needs you now. Please call me." He left his phone number and handed the phone back to Madeleine. "Now we'll have to pray that he calls me back."

Madeleine looked determined as she turned off the phone. "He will call you back. I can feel it."

"I hope so." Saul stood. "It's late, so I'd best let you get to bed. *Danki* for your help."

Madeleine touched his arm. "Ruth will be thrilled that you found Aaron."

"That's only if I found him. We won't know unless he calls

me back." Saul sighed. "Let's keep this to ourselves until we hear something."

"I agree. Good night, Saul." She smiled. "I'll see you and Emma tomorrow."

As he headed back toward the house, Saul lifted up a prayer to God, asking him to soften Aaron's heart toward his mother. He prayed Aaron would call back before it was too late. But no matter what was going to happen, he knew in his heart that God was and would always be in control.

Discussion Questions

1. Toward the end of the book, Madeleine realizes she longs to convert to the Amish way of life. Have you ever longed to make a huge change in your life? If so, did you follow through with that change? How did your family and friends react? What Bible verses helped you with your choice? Share your experience with the group.

2. Saul feels God is giving him a second chance when he falls in love with Madeleine. Have you ever experienced a second chance?

3. Ruth quotes Matthew 6:15: "If you do not forgive others their sins, your Father will not forgive your sins." What does this verse mean to you?

4. Saul has been nursing a broken heart since his wife left and divorced him, leaving him to raise Emma alone. At the beginning of the book, he wants to find someone who'll simply be a good mother for Emma because he doesn't believe he will ever love again. Think of a time when you felt lost and alone. Where did you find your strength? What Bible verses helped during this time? Share with the group.

5. Saul believes he's shielding Emma from hurt when he keeps the truth about her mother from her. In the end, it's still painful when Emma finds out the truth. Do you think Saul's decision to withhold the truth was justified? Have you ever found yourself in a similar situation? If so, how did it turn out? Share with the group.

6. Carolyn is happy that she finally has her dream—her own home, a husband, and a father for Benjamin. Although she's content with her new life, she still feels the pull of two worlds—working on the farm for her husband and keeping her job at the hotel. She wants to be a good, dutiful wife, but she also wants to contribute to the family by making money on her own. If you were in her situation, would you give in to Joshua's request and quit the part-time job at the hotel?

7. In *A Hopeful Heart* and *A Mother's Secret*, Lillian is convinced her mother is selfish and betrayed her by leaving the Amish community. In this book, we see Lillian still struggling to forgive her mother, but she's also beginning to accept her mother's decision to leave. Do you think it's time for Lillian to forgive her mother and move on? Share what you think with the group.

8. Which character can you identify with the most? Which character seems to carry the most emotional stake in the story? Is it Madeleine, Emma, Saul, or someone else?

9. Saul grows as a character throughout the book. What do you think caused him to change throughout the story?

10. What did you know about the Amish before reading this book? What did you learn?

Acknowledgments

As always, I'm thankful for my loving family, including my mother, Lola Goebelbecker; my husband, Joe; and my sons, Zac and Matt. I'm blessed to have such an awesome and amazing family.

I'm more grateful than words can express for my patient friends who critique for me, including Margaret Halpin, Janet Pecorella, Lauran Rodriguez, and, of course, my mother. I truly appreciate the time you take out of your busy lives to help me polish my books.

I'm thankful for the people who helped me with research, especially Ginger Annas, Stacey Barbalace, Jason Clipston, Mark and Rebecca Hefner, Kimberly Moity, and Janet Pecorella.

Special thanks to my special Amish friends who patiently answer my endless stream of questions. You're a blessing in my life.

Thank you, my wonderful church family at Morning Star Lutheran in Matthews, North Carolina, for your encouragement, prayers, love, and friendship. You all mean so much to my family and me.

To my agent, Sue Brower—you are a blessing to me. I'm

thankful that our paths have crossed and our partnership will continue long into the future.

Thank you, Becky Philpott, my amazing editor, for your friendship and guidance. I'm grateful to Julee Schwarzburg and Jean Bloom, who helped me polish and refine the story. Julee and Jean, I hope we can work together again in the future.

I also would like to thank Laura Dickerson for tirelessly working to promote my books. I'm grateful to each and every person at HarperCollins Christian Publishing who helped make this book a reality.

To my readers—thank you for choosing my novels. My books are a blessing in my life for many reasons, including the special friendships I've formed with my readers. Thank you for your e-mail messages, Facebook notes, and letters.

Thank you most of all to God—thank you for giving me the inspiration and the words to glorify you. I'm grateful and humbled you've chosen this path for me.

HERE BURNS
MY CANDLE

This Large Print Book carries the
Seal of Approval of N.A.V.H.

HERE BURNS
MY CANDLE

LIZ CURTIS HIGGS

CHRISTIAN LARGE PRINT
A part of Gale, Cengage Learning

GALE
CENGAGE Learning·

Detroit • New York • San Francisco • New Haven, Conn • Waterville, Maine • London

GALE
CENGAGE Learning

LIBRARY OF CONGRESS CATALOGING-IN-PUBLICATION DATA

Higgs, Liz Curtis.
   Here burns my candle / by Liz Curtis Higgs.
      p. cm. — (Christian Large Print originals)
   ISBN-13: 978-1-59415-275-7 (softcover : alk. paper)
   ISBN-10: 1-59415-275-6 (softcover : alk. paper)
   1. Nobility—Scotland—Fiction. 2. Family secrets—Fiction.
3. Scandals—Fiction. 4. Scotland—Social life and customs—18th
century—Fiction. 5. Large type books. I. Title. II. Series.
PS3558.I36235H47 2010
813'.54—dc22   2010001002

Published in 2010 by arrangement with WaterBrook Press, an imprint
of the Crown Publishing Group, a division of Random House, Inc.

Printed in the United States of America
   1 2 3 4 5   14 13 12 11 10
ED097

For two treasured Elizabeths in my life:
Elizabeth Crawford Potts,
my beloved mother,
who left this world too soon,
and
Elizabeth Sullivan McLain Higgs,
my precious daughter-in-law,
who brings our family such joy.

And for Bill,
always and forever.

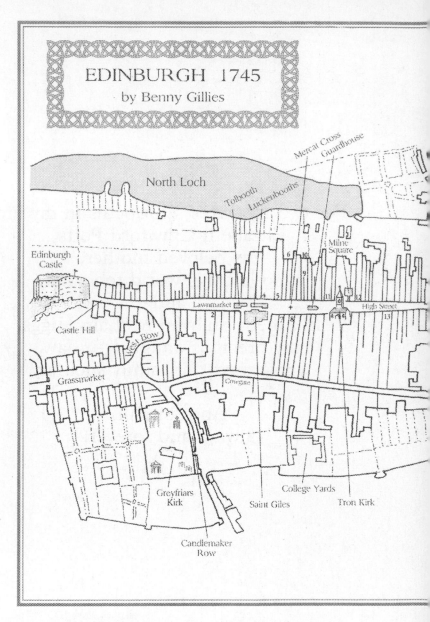

EDINBURGH 1745
by Benny Gillies

North Loch

Mercat Cross
Guardhouse
Tolbooth
Luckenbooths
Milne Square
Edinburgh Castle
Lawnmarket
Castle Hill
West Bow
High Street
Grassmarket
Cowgate
College Yards
Greyfriars Kirk
Saint Giles
Tron Kirk
Candlemaker Row

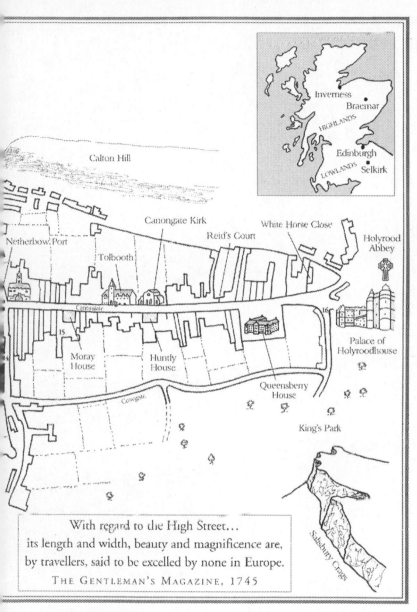

With regard to the High Street…
its length and width, beauty and magnificence are,
by travellers, said to be excelled by none in Europe.

THE GENTLEMAN'S MAGAZINE, 1745

All the darkness in the world cannot
extinguish the light of a single candle.
SAINT FRANCIS OF ASSISI

ONE

Night's black mantle
covers all alike.
GUILLAUME DE SALLUSTE DU BARTAS

Milne Square, Edinburgh
14 September 1745
Lady Marjory Kerr heard a frantic tapping at the bedchamber door, then her name, spoken with marked urgency.

"News from the Royal Bank, *mem.*"

At this hour? Marjory lifted her head from the pillow, her gaze drawn to the wooden shutters, closed for the night. The coals in the fireplace had faded to a dull glow. She squinted but could not read the clock on the mantelpiece. Had she slept at all?

"What is it, Peg?" Marjory called out.

Her maidservant answered in a breathless rush of words, "They're moving the bank's effects to the castle."

The hair on the back of Marjory's neck rose. Transporting money and documents

11

from the foot of New Bank Close to Edinburgh Castle involved a long climb up a winding street where brigands and thieves lurked in the shadows. The Royal Bank would never embark on so risky a venture. Not unless the day's alarming reports had proven true.

" 'Tis the *Hielanders*," Peg whispered through the crack in the door as if the word itself might bring a hoard of savages thundering up the stair, brandishing their swords. "Folk say the rebel army will reach Linlithgow by morn."

At that, Marjory flung off her bedcovers, any notion of sleep forgotten. Linlithgow Palace was less than twenty miles west. The army was too near her door. And far too near her sons, one of whom stood ready to bear arms at the slightest provocation. Was there nothing she could say to dissuade him?

She hurried across the carpet barefooted, too distraught to hunt for her brocade slippers. All of Edinburgh had followed the ominous approach of the Highland rebels led by their bonny Prince Charlie. Determined to reclaim the British throne for his exiled father, James — *Jacobus* in Latin — the young prince and his loyal Jacobites were marching toward Scotland's capital, intent on capturing the city.

"May it not be so," Marjory said under her breath, then swept open the bedchamber door to find her maidservant perched on the threshold, her linen cap askew, her brown eyes filled with fear.

"What are we to do, *Leddy* Kerr?"

"Bolt the door at once." Marjory tightened the ribbons on her sleeping jacket, warding off the night air that seeped in, however fast the shutters. Her trembling had nothing to do with the fearsome Highlanders, she told herself. Nae, not for a moment. "Make haste, lass."

She watched Peg scurry through the darkened drawing room into the entrance hall, holding aloft her candle stub, which cast a pale circle of light on her tattered nightgown. Small for her seventeen years, with hair the color of a dull copper ha'penny, Peg Cargill was hardly a beauty. Her eyes were set unbecomingly close together, and her small nose disappeared amid a sea of freckles.

By the fire's glow Marjory caught a glimpse of herself in the silvery looking glass by her side. She quickly turned away but not before her thoughts came round to taunt her. *Hardly a beauty.* She touched her thinning crown of hair and her sagging chin, then sighed, wishing the glass offered better news. Had it not always been thus?

In her youth few gentlemen had taken note of her until they learned she was the daughter of Sir Eldon Nesbitt. Even then their gazes had fallen on her father's impressive property rather than on her unremarkable face or figure. Time had not improved matters.

Peg reappeared, bobbing a curtsy. " 'Tis done, milady."

Marjory gestured toward the adjoining chambers, where her sons and their wives had retired for the night. "Have you told the others the news?"

"Nae." A faint blush tinted Peg's cheek. "I heard them . . . that is . . . Mr. Kerr . . ."

"See they're not disturbed," Marjory said firmly, wanting no details. "And keep the stair door bolted." She dismissed the girl with a nod, then locked the chamber door behind her. Let the Highlanders storm the crumbling walls of Edinburgh. They would not gain entrance to the Kerrs' apartments. Mr. Baillie, the merchant who owned her residence, would see to that.

Alone once more Marjory lit a candle at the fireplace, then drew a steadying breath and knelt beside the canopied bed, as if preparing to offer her nightly prayers. Instead, she reached down and loosened one of the boards along the edge of the thick, woven carpet. Her servants, even her family members, believed the Kerr fortune rested safely among the Royal Bank's effects, now bound for the castle. She alone knew the truth. Lord John Kerr had never trusted banks.

The board gave way, revealing a musty repository between the joists. Marjory bent

14

closer, her nose wrinkling at the dank smell, her eyes seeking a cluster of leather purses in the flickering candlelight. *There.* The mere sight of them put her mind at ease. Nearly two dozen purses lay hidden beneath her chamber floor — a tribute to God's provision and her late husband's prudence.

She chose the nearest one, taking pleasure in its weight before slowly emptying the purse onto her bedding. One hundred gold guineas poured out, each coin stamped with the profile of her sovereign, King George. Marjory counted the lot, then set aside a few guineas for the coming week's expenses and returned the bulging purse to its nesting place.

Greengrocers and fishmongers expected payment upon purchase. But mantua makers gladly extended credit if the Kerr women might display their gowns at the next public ball. Although a nervous town council might demand its citizens remain withindoors, ending their festive Thursday evenings at Assembly Close . . .

Nae, surely not!

Marjory sank onto the edge of her bed with a soft groan. What a dreary social season lay ahead with the rebel army afoot! No weekly visits to Lady Woodhall's drawing room to share cups of tea and savory tidbits of gossip. No rainy afternoons spent with Lady Falconer, listening to country airs sung by a

15

daughter of the gentry. No rounds of whist in the affable company of Lord Dun. Nothing but royalist dragoons patrolling the High Street, bayonets at the ready.

A sharp knock at the adjoining bedchamber door made her jump, nearly spilling the handful of guineas from the bed onto the carpet. "Who is it?" she asked, unhappy with herself for sounding frightened.

"Donald," came the low reply.

Lightheaded with relief and grateful for his company, Marjory deposited the money on her dressing table and ushered her older son within, then closed the door as quickly as she'd opened it. With no central hallway in their apartments, each room had adjoining doors, one chamber leading to the next. Even among Edinburgh's wealthiest residents, privacy was rare.

"Forgive the intrusion, Mother." He looked down at her, candle in hand, his smooth brow gleaming. The cambric loosely tied at his neck could not hide the sharp lines of his collarbones. Ten years of dining on Edinburgh's finest mutton and beef, and still his frame remained as slender as a youth's. " 'Tis late, I know," he apologized.

"The hour matters not." Marjory touched his cheek affectionately, struck afresh by the family resemblance. Donald had the same long nose Lord John once had, the same thin-lipped smile. "Look how the father's face lives

16

in his issue," she quoted, testing him. It was a favorite pastime between mother and son.

"Ben Jonson," he answered, naming the playwright without hesitation.

Few gentlemen in Edinburgh were better read than Lord Donald. She'd made certain of it. Heir to the Kerr title and lands, he'd proven himself an attentive son and a faithful husband. If he was not yet a doting father, that was no fault of his.

"Still in your boots," Marjory observed. "I thought you'd be off to bed by now."

The corners of his mouth twitched. "I will be shortly." He scanned the chamber, his gaze finally landing on the pile of coins glimmering in the candlelight. "Do you think it wise to leave your gold where anyone might find it?"

Donald not only looked like his father; he sounded like him. Marjory swept the coins into her silk-fringed reticule and pulled the drawstrings taut. "We have far greater worries this night. The rebel army is nearing Linlithgow."

"*Aye,* Gibson told me." The stoic Neil Gibson, manservant to the household, took pride in keeping Donald and his younger brother well groomed and well informed. "I've come to put your mind at ease, Mother."

"I see." She chose her next words with care, keeping her tone light. "Does that mean

17

you'll not be joining the Gentlemen Volunteers?" She watched his blue eyes for a flicker of interest. Hundreds of young men had enlisted in support of the royalist troops, many from Edinburgh's finest families. Lord willing, her sons would not be numbered among the recruits.

"I've no such plans," Donald confessed, "though I cannot speak for Andrew. You know his penchant for flintlock muskets."

She did know, much as it grieved her. Lord John had urged their second son to pursue a career in the military, despite her motherly protests. Pistols, swords, and a dozen French muskets decorated Andrew's bedchamber walls. Even walking past his many weapons unnerved her. Monsieur Picard, their fencing master, had trained the lads well. But he'd done so for sport, not for battle.

That very afternoon Andrew had observed the Volunteers drilling in the College Yards. Marjory had counted the hours until he returned home for supper, then listened with a heavy heart as he regaled the family with stories of grizzled sergeants marching the lads through their paces. "Have no fear," Andrew had said soothingly at table. "The Lord Provost took no notice of me, Mother."

She was unconvinced then and even less so now, with his older brother paying a late-night visit. "I have your word?" she prompted Donald. "You'll not encourage Andrew to

18

take up arms against the Highland rebels?"

He brushed aside her concerns. "Whatever you say."

Donald began circling her chamber, with its oil paintings and Chinese porcelain, its silk bed hangings and red lacquer commode. Piece by piece she'd had her favorite *plenishings* delivered from Tweedsford, their estate in the Borderland, until their rented Edinburgh rooms were filled to bursting.

When Donald paused at one of her windows and unfastened the painted shutter, Marjory's breath caught. Might a Jacobite spy be abroad at this hour? Pale and fair-haired, Donald would be easily spotted from the High Street below.

"No moon in sight," he observed, resting his forehead lightly on the glass. "No Highlanders either."

"They'll arrive soon enough." Marjory extinguished the candle by her bed, shrouding the room in darkness. "Sleep while you can, Donald. And keep that bonny wife of yours close at hand."

"Aye." The smile in his voice was unmistakable. "So I shall."

He left by way of the drawing room door rather than the one leading to his bedchamber. Bound for the kitchen, no doubt. He'd eaten very little at supper. Mrs. Edgar, their housekeeper, would not let him retire on an empty stomach.

Marjory closed the shutters, then returned to bed, determined to sleep however dire the news. Her beloved sons were safe beneath her roof. Nothing else mattered.

Two

For Donald was the brawest man,
And Donald he was mine.
          ROBERT BURNS

Lady Elisabeth Kerr pushed her sewing needle through the thick wool, straining to hear the conversation next door. She could not fault Donald for visiting his mother's chamber. Even the Dowager Lady Kerr needed reassuring on so unsettling a night. Alas, little sound traveled through the thick blanket of books that lined their bedchamber walls. Whatever Donald and his mother were discussing was lost to her.

Nor could she hear Andrew and Janet in the other adjoining chamber, for which Elisabeth was exceedingly grateful. The couple, married only six months earlier, was determined to present the dowager with her first grandchild. "You've had two years to produce an heir," Janet had chided Elisabeth on the eve of her March wedding. "Now 'tis our turn."

What response could Elisabeth offer when her empty womb spoke on her behalf?

Nae. She pressed her silver thimble more firmly in place, refusing to dwell on the subject. A healthy woman of four-and-twenty had little cause for alarm. Surely a child would come in due season: a wee son to match her *braw* Lowlander with his high forehead and intelligent eyes.

Elisabeth drew the thread taut, pulling the button shank against the fabric. Not for Lord Kerr the new fashion of ending a gentleman's coat buttons at his waist. Instead, he insisted on an unbroken line of pewter buttons, neck to hem. Reaching for her scissors, she breathed in the night air, moist with the promise of rain. A fire burned low in the grate, barely dispelling the autumn chill. Peg would appear at dawn with fresh coals. Until then, Elisabeth counted on her husband to warm her hands and feet. "And your bonny nose," Donald often teased, capturing the soft tip between his slender knuckles.

Though she considered her nose overlong, Donald deemed it patrician. "You've the finest profile of any lady in Scotland," he'd told her only that morning. "To prove it, I shall have a cameo engraved in Paris, carved from the largest queen conch shell my guineas can buy." Her husband enjoyed making extravagant promises. Sometimes he even kept them.

Elisabeth looked up at her new lavender

satin gown, pressed and waiting for the Sabbath and hanging from an ornate hook. It was a belated gift from Donald, meant for her May birthday but not delivered until Wednesday last. The sleeves were generously trimmed with two layers of the finest lace, the pleated embellishments on the bodice were made of silk gauze, and the ivory-trimmed stomacher was richly decorated with tiny buttons.

" 'Tis a rare beauty," Donald had commented. "Like you, my love."

He'd beguiled her from the first, strolling into Angus MacPherson's tailoring shop one bright September day, seeking a new velvet coat. She was there by chance, delivering a customer's waistcoat she'd embroidered to earn a bit of silver. In Donald came, with his regal height and polished manners, a long queue of powdered hair curling down his back. Unwittingly, he'd praised her handiwork. "No man embellishes a buttonhole more cleverly than you do, MacPherson."

Angus had quickly confessed, " 'Tis not my *ain* skill with a needle that produced those fine stitches. Rather, Miss Ferguson here is to be commended."

Elisabeth still remembered Donald's frank appraisal. Some men found her height daunting. Lord Kerr's reaction was quite the opposite, his approval evident when his level gaze met hers. "You've the bearing of a

23

queen, milady. Did I not see you at the Tron Kirk on the Sabbath last, seated with Mrs. Effie Sinclair of Blackfriars Wynd?" When she inclined her head, his smile broadened. "Ah, just as I thought. You are under her tutelage, then. A more respectable lady cannot be found in all of Edinburgh."

In a few short months Donald had won her heart. Not with his considerable wealth, his impressive title, or his handsome face. Rather, he treated her as an equal, discussing books, music, and society as if Elisabeth had grown up in a gentleman's household and could manage her end of the conversation. Somehow, she did.

That Yuletide Donald had ignored his mother's wishes and married her, Elisabeth Ferguson, a humble weaver's daughter. "Not to spite the Dowager Lady Kerr," he'd insisted, though he'd certainly done so. "I want you by my side, my bonny Highland Bess. To have and to hold, a wife good and true."

His tender words had burrowed deep inside her, crowding out the murmured warnings, the whispered concerns voiced by others. *Lord Kerr has a mistress. Two, some say. Guard your heart, for he'll not honor his vows.*

Elisabeth's hands stilled, the pewter button cold beneath her thumb. Doubt crept in once more, pervasive as the evening fog, clouding her thoughts. Donald had changed since then, had he not? This husband she loved and trusted with all her heart?

Season after season she'd pushed aside her fears, ignoring the faint rumors that ebbed and swelled in the street and on the stair, hinting at red-headed widows and comely maids. She'd had no reason to believe them, not when Donald was so attentive. He'd never come home bearing another woman's scent or tasting of another woman's kisses. Nor had she found a lady's handkerchief tucked in his pocket or a suspicious strand of hair caught in the fibers of his waistcoat.

But on Thursday last at Assembly Close when he'd danced the allemande with the Widow Montgomerie, a ripple had moved through the room. Heads turned. Eyebrows lifted. Voices whispered. Elisabeth had feigned indifference, keeping her smile firmly in place from first note to last and reclaiming her husband when the music ended.

She'd said nothing to him, certain the gossips were wrong. Though dalliances were common among the peerage, Lord Donald was cut from a different cloth. If he admired a woman in passing, Elisabeth praised her too, rather than give envy a toehold. When others fluttered their fans at Donald, she drew him closer, reminding herself that, come day's end, she alone would have the pleasure of his company.

However improper Donald's behavior might have been before their wedding, he did his duty by her now, did he not? Her skin warmed at the thought. *Aye, you certainly do, my love.*

While her diminishing candle measured the time, Elisabeth worked at a steady pace and waited for Donald to return. Clearly the dowager needed more attention that evening than Elisabeth had imagined. Or perhaps Donald had wandered off to the kitchen, hungry for a slice of cold mutton.

Finished at last, she draped the damask coat across Donald's desk chair, hoping he might notice and be pleased. Her bedside candle flickered as the night wind found its way round the shutters. The hour was late indeed. Shivering, Elisabeth slipped beneath the covers and fixed her gaze on the adjoining chamber door, certain Donald would not tarry much longer.

At long last the bedchamber door creaked open. Donald stepped within, the amber light from the hearth gilding his features. Her husband wore his seven-and-twenty years well, with a noble air and a rakish grin.

"Come to bed," she beckoned him, stretching out her hand as he crossed the room. "The Sabbath dawn is almost upon us."

" 'Tis five hours hence," he protested, sitting long enough to pull off his boots, then abandoning his clothes on the floor in a heap. He wet his thumb and forefinger and snuffed the candle with a deft touch. "I had in mind

26

how we might spend one of those hours."

She smiled into the darkness. "Oh?"

In an instant he lay by her side, enveloping her in his warmth. " 'Tis all your fault, dear Bess." His voice was low and as tender as a caress. "I have a weakness for beautiful women."

"Is that so?" She smoothed her hand across his wheat-colored hair, cropped short to accommodate his wig, and discovered the fine strands were damp and cool, as if he'd been out of doors. Impossible, of course. He'd gone no farther than the kitchen. The familiar scent of him, the welcome sensation of his rough cheek against her skin dismissed any niggling concerns.

"I thought you might never come to bed," she scolded him lightly. "Did you satisfy her?"

He hesitated. "Beg pardon?"

"Your mother. Did you allay her concerns?"

"Oh, aye." Donald relaxed at once. "She seems to think Andrew is in danger of taking up arms."

Elisabeth met his gaze, a handbreadth away. "You've no desire to fight the Highlanders?"

"Nae," he murmured, pulling her closer still, "for I've a Highland wife."

Her eyes drifted shut as he brushed a kiss across her cheek. "No regrets?"

His lips touched the curve of her ear. "Banish any doubt on that score," he whispered just before his mouth met hers.

THREE

No man does anything from a single
  motive.
SAMUEL TAYLOR COLERIDGE

Would he never sleep? Donald stared at the
silk bed curtains draped above him, feeling
utterly spent yet maddeningly frustrated. Two
hours of solid rest would do him. One, if it
came to it. Yet his eyes remained open.

O Sleep, why dost thou leave me?

He grimaced, knowing his mother would
recognize the line from *Semele* at once. William Congreve, a loyal patriot and a middling
poet, was one of her favorites. Why the
Dowager Lady Kerr took delight in testing
him on such things, Donald could not say. A
childhood game better left in the nursery.
Still, he indulged her.

O Sleep, again deceive me.

Donald exhaled into the darkened room. If
he was indeed deceived, 'twas a fair turnabout. Earlier that night after quitting his
mother's room, he'd paid a brief visit to

young Lucy Spence, the fisherman's widow in nearby Halkerston's Wynd. A dangerous practice, so close to home. But wasn't an element of risk part of the pleasure?

Guilt inevitably followed. Never at the start and seldom in the moment, but afterward his conscience always prodded him. Now, for instance.

When a moment later his stomach growled, Donald slowly sat up, taking care not to wake his wife. He'd had little appetite at supper, even with the first oysters of the season on his plate. If he could not sleep, then he would eat. Their cold Sabbath breakfast was already prepared and waiting in the kitchen. A boiled egg would do nicely. Or a slice of bread. Even tea would suffice.

He stood, then pulled on a silk robe and tied it loosely round his waist. Best to go through Andrew's room since his brother was a sound sleeper. It was also a more direct route to the kitchen than traveling through his mother's bedchamber, the drawing room, and then the entrance hall, where Gibson lay sleeping. Whoever designed Baillie's Land had given little thought to nighttime forays.

Donald navigated his bedchamber with caution, avoiding the tottery pile of books stacked by his reading chair. In truth, he'd claimed every flat surface in the room for his growing library. Atlases and almanacs from London covered the writing surface of his mahogany secretary, and parchment maps lay neatly rolled and tucked in its many pigeon-holes. He had his mother to thank for such bounty. Whenever a bill arrived from Mr. Creech, his favorite bookseller in the Luckenbooths, she paid the balance without protest.

Donald paused before entering Andrew's bedchamber, listening for his brother's labored breathing. He opened and closed the door without making a sound, a useful skill in the wee hours of the morning. Treading softly, he passed by Andrew's bed and stole a quick glance. The couple was fast asleep, Janet's arm draped across his brother's chest. Andrew, always more interested in weapons than in women, had let their mother choose a wife for him. However brief and business-like their courtship, the two were managing well enough.

Another door to slip through, and he would reach the kitchen. The hinges creaked a bit. Nothing to be done there. In any case Mrs. Edgar would no doubt stir the moment he set foot in her domain. But she did not. Curled up on a long shelf beneath the wooden dresser, the housekeeper lay perfectly still, clearly lost in her dreams. He envied her that.

Only then did he notice Peg, their new maidservant, standing in the corner nearest the hearth. How small she was! "I beg your pardon," he murmured, easing toward her. "I did not mean to wake you."

"Nae, nae, milord. I wasna sleeping." She tried to curtsy and instead fell forward a step, her pale legs showing beneath her nightgown. "Oh!"

In the shadowy corner he could almost feel her blushing, so acute was her embarrassment. "Not to worry," he said softly, meaning to put her at ease. "I could not sleep either."

"Oh," she said again, bobbing her head.

Donald took a step closer. "I confess, I came looking for a bite to eat. Anything you might suggest?"

"W-we've fresh cheese, if ye like." She hurriedly put several slices on a plate, then poured a small glass of ale and gingerly placed them both in his hands. "Will there be anything else, milord?"

A dangerous question, lass.

She stood before him, trembling, her hands clasped behind her back. The light from the hearth burnished her freckled skin and lit her coppery hair until it glowed. Such a pretty little thing. He could not remember how old Peg was. Sixteen, perhaps, yet she had the body of a woman. Her thin cotton nightgown made that fact all too evident.

He looked down at her, unable to resist. "What else might you have to offer me, Peg?"

This time he was certain she was blushing. Her gaze flitted about the room, looking for somewhere to land. His gaze moved as well,

31

slowly tracing every curve and line from her tousled head to her delectable little toes. His hands were occupied, or he might have measured her in a more satisfactory manner.

Or perhaps not. She seemed most uncomfortable.

Donald stepped back. "This will be quite enough," he assured her, lifting his plate and glass.

"Aye, milord." She curtsied once more, inching away from him as she did.

Turning toward the door, he realized he could never manage with both hands full. He tossed the ale down his throat, nearly choking on it in the process, then retraced his steps, gripping the plate of cheese, any appetite lost.

Whatever had he been thinking? Making overtures to his own maid in his own kitchen. True, he'd not harmed the lass. Had not laid a finger on her, in fact. But that did not make him innocent. Nae, it did not.

To his great relief, Elisabeth was still sleeping when he reentered their bedchamber. He quietly deposited his plate on the nearest table, then shrugged off his robe, and slipped into bed beside her. Even deep in slumber, Elisabeth Kerr was the most beautiful woman he'd ever clapped eyes on. And far better than he deserved. Far, far better.

Out of habit or necessity, he lightly touched her unbound hair and rubbed the silky strands between his fingers. *Forgive me, Bess.* A daily request. Sometimes hourly.

At the first faint glow of dawn he rose from their bed and took refuge in the closet. Peg would soon be along with hot water and fresh coals. The lass would never breathe a word about their brief encounter — not to him or to anyone else. Peg had her reputation to consider. And his.

He quietly shut the closet door, not caring that he had no candle. Not caring that the room was as dark as night.

FOUR

Gently on tiptoe Sunday creeps.

JOHN PETER HEBEL

Morning sunlight filtered through the wooden shutters, drawing pale lines on the carpet. Except for the soft blur of voices rising from the street, Milne Square remained blessedly quiet. It seemed even the rebel army feared disturbing the Sabbath.

Elisabeth eyed the empty pillow next to hers and smiled. *My sweet Donald.*

The rest of the house was stirring as well. Yawning, she stretched her arms and legs, then sat on the edge of the bed, rubbing the sleep from her eyes and contemplating the hours ahead.

The night had been too short, and the day would surely be long. At least she would have Donald by her side, at kirk and at home, to ease her mind and heart. Sundays were always difficult. How could they not be when her childhood faith was sorely tested Sabbath after Sabbath?

She touched the broad wedding band on her left hand, a constant reminder of their spoken vows. *They twain shall be one flesh.* She and Donald shared a home, shared a bed, shared a life, but they did not share the same beliefs. He didn't know that. But she did.

Then she touched the ring on her right hand: a heavy circle of silver engraved with words hidden against her skin. *So long as the moon endureth.* Great-grandmother Nessa had worn the ring first. Then her grandmother Jean. And then her mother, Fiona, who'd slipped the sacred ring on Elisabeth's finger one midsummer night, her eyes glistening with tears.

"Dinna forget the *auld* ways," her mother had whispered.

Elisabeth lifted her gaze to the High Street window where she often stood on the sixth day of the moon, hand pressed to the glass, besecching the Nameless One. *Thou moon of moons.* Aye, she still recalled the simple rituals and sacred words her mother had taught her. What Elisabeth no longer remembered was why they mattered.

"We worship a heavenly body we can see," her mother had once said, "rather than a faraway God we canna see."

With the innocence of a child, she'd responded, "I see the moon, Mother. But does the moon see me?"

The question haunted her still. Not only on the sixth day of the moon but every Sabbath day, when she walked through the doors of the Tron Kirk with her Lowland family. Elisabeth did her best to follow their rituals and repeat their sacred words, yet all the while she was seeking answers. Did their God see her when she took her seat each Sunday? Did he hear her when she sang the gathering psalm or read the words in the *Buik*?

Above all, did this Almighty God, this Holy One, reach down to his people when they reached up to him? Elisabeth feared the Nameless One did not. Lately she had little sense of being heard and even less hope of being answered.

Her husband knew nothing of the lunar calendar she followed or the engraving inside her silver ring or the monthly entreaties made in secret. She could only imagine the look of horror on his face if he learned the truth. However great his love for her, it would not stretch far enough to embrace the auld ways.

And the dowager would be terrified. Would no doubt banish Elisabeth from the house and report her to the kirk session. Pointed questions would be asked, and accusations might be made. 'Twas a very real danger in this land of repentance stools in the kirk and wooden gallows in the marketplace. In decades past women were burned at the stake for such beliefs . . .

Nae. Elisabeth stood, shaking off her fears. In three years no one in the Kerr household had uncovered her secret. Nor would they do so this Sunday.

Breathe, Bess. Just breathe.

While Donald tarried in the water closet that morning, she had the chamber to herself. Better to quickly bathe alone rather than ring for Peg. The water pitcher was freshly filled, was it not? A bar of Castile soap sat by the washbowl, and the fireplace, newly replenished, would keep her warm.

She filled the porcelain bowl with steaming water, then soaked a fresh cloth before rubbing it with soap. Made of pure olive oil, the white soap was fragrant but slippery and splashed into the bowl more than once. Peg handled things more efficiently, but expecting a maidservant to scrub her long, bare limbs each morning seemed vain and self-centered.

Like Janet.

Elisabeth splashed her face with water but could not douse her unkind thoughts. What a spoiled ninny her sister-in-law was! Morning after morning Janet dithered over which gown to wear, tossing freshly pressed clothes onto her bedchamber floor, forcing Mrs. Edgar to iron them again. At mealtime her sister-in-law sat at table, hands folded in her lap, waiting for Gibson to fill her glass when the claret

37

was easily within reach. And how many times had Janet dispatched Andrew on some petty errand, fully aware of how taxing it was for him to climb the stair?

Enough, Bess.

Ashamed of herself, she dried her cheeks more vigorously than necessary, letting her irritation run its course. However demanding her sister-in-law might be, at least Janet never forgot her place in society. She, on the other hand, seldom thought of herself as Lady Elisabeth Kerr. Who could ever live up to such a title? Despite her years at Mrs. Sinclair's Boarding School for Young Ladies, Elisabeth had spent too many childhood mornings in her mother's kitchen, too many afternoons round her father's loom, learning to use her hands, learning to be helpful. 'Twas ill preparation for the idle life she now led. A life which Janet Kerr had mastered and she had not.

"Good morning, my love," Donald said, rejoining her. "Managing your toilette alone, I see."

"I'm perfectly capable of bathing myself," she chided him, then wished she had not. The poor man looked as if he'd not slept a wink.

"I meant only to compliment you," he murmured, then bent to kiss the oval birthmark above her heart. No bigger than a thumbprint, the color of café au lait, her faint

38

blemish was easily covered by a judicious use of lace round the neckline of her gowns. The simple linen chemise, however, hid very little.

Donald lingered over the spot for a moment, then straightened, affection shining in his bleary eyes. "The auld wives would insist your mother must have touched her heart while she carried you, overcome by some strong emotion. Fear or desire, do you imagine?"

Elisabeth smoothed her fingertips over the mark. "She told me it was love."

Voices in the adjoining room drew near. They'd not be alone much longer.

Her husband sighed. "I shall see to my newspaper before Gibson appears, periwig in hand." Dressed in a silk nightgown, Donald draped himself across an upholstered settee and unfolded the four-page broadsheet, holding it higher than necessary.

She knew his actions were a ruse. He'd already scoured every word of Thursday's *Edinburgh Evening Courant.* Her husband was merely giving her a moment's privacy since Janet had absconded with her dressing screen soon after her wedding.

"I'm newly married," Janet had said, "and therefore more . . . ah, modest." With a toss of her auburn hair, Janet had ordered Gibson to move the tapestry-covered screen to her adjacent bedchamber. There it remained, with their mother-in-law's blessing.

Elisabeth told herself it mattered not. As a child she'd dressed behind a linen bedsheet thrown over a wooden beam and slept at the foot of her parents' bed. Privacy in a Highland cottage? Her mother would laugh at the very notion.

While Donald pretended to read, Elisabeth reached for her brush. Her dark, elbow-length hair required patient hands and gentle strokes, or the bristles became hopelessly tangled.

"What news of Prince Charlie?" she asked between brush strokes. From Perth to Stirling to Falkirk, she'd followed Charles Edward Stuart on his journey south. Many Highland folk, her family among them, supported the Stuart cause — a treasonous admission, particularly in the Lowlands. Elisabeth had not revealed her Jacobite loyalties to a soul except her husband, who'd held his index finger to his lips. *Shhh.*

Donald had not discovered all her secrets, but he knew that one.

"According to the *Evening Courant,*" he said, "we've no reason to fear Prince Charlie and his men, however barbaric their reputation. Listen to this." Donald cleared his throat and held the newsprint closer. "Not one half of them have tolerable arms and as such are a pitiful, ignorant crew." He lowered the paper long enough to catch her gaze. "Perhaps Andrew should hide his muskets in the same way Mother hides her gold."

Elisabeth paused, her brush in midstroke. "Is her money not safely in the bank?"

"Nae." He tapped his bare foot on the carpet. " 'Tis under the floor of her bedchamber. Have you not heard her in the wee hours of the morn, tiptoeing about, prying up boards, and counting guineas?"

"You know how soundly I sleep." Elisabeth gazed at the adjoining door, thinking of the many times she'd walked through her mother-in-law's room, unaware of the fortune beneath her feet. "Donald, what if the servants learn of it?"

He chuckled. " 'Twas Gibson who first alerted me." Her husband returned to his broadsheet, clearly unconcerned. "You've seen how the staff jumps to do Mother's bidding. Rest assured, they'll not breathe a word of her secret to anyone. Nor, my pet, shall we, for 'tis our fortune as well."

Hearing a light tapping at the door, Elisabeth straightened the neckline of her thin chemise. " 'Tis Peg, come to dress me."

"Ah." Donald lifted his newspaper a bit higher, concealing his face. "I can assure you, I'll not look."

FIVE

The Sabbath-day is the
savings-bank of humanity.

FREDERICK SAUNDERS

Janet Kerr plucked at the Brussels lace on
Elisabeth's new gown while the family gathered in the entrance hall. "This color was
quite fashionable last season."

"So it was," Elisabeth agreed, dodging the
pointed barb. "How fortunate Lord Kerr
enjoys lavender whatever the season."

Janet said no more, busily smoothing back
a few stray wisps of hair. Small in stature, her
sister-in-law piled her auburn locks high on
her head, adding a light dusting of powder.
People of quality called Janet handsome, and
rightly so. Her style and manner were impec-
cable, her wit sharp. But they did not call
Janet beautiful.

"The first bell has tolled," Marjory announced, then started down the turnpike
stair.

Elisabeth touched her corseted waist, grateful she'd had only tea and a pinch of bannock to break her fast. She could hardly breathe, so tightly had Peg laced her stays. "We must show your new gown to best advantage," her mother-in-law had insisted earlier. "And your waist is uncommonly small."

A rare compliment, Elisabeth wondered, or yet another reminder of her childless state? "Let us away," she said, pulling on her gloves. "The dowager does not like to be kept waiting."

"Indeed she does not," Janet murmured.

Donald, poised on the threshold to the stair, glanced over his shoulder. "Mere months in the family and already our sister-in-law knows the way of things."

"Oh, my husband has divulged all your secrets," Janet remarked coyly, taking Andrew's arm. "And doesn't he look handsome this morning in his peacock blue waistcoat?"

Slender and fair like his brother, though not so tall, Andrew thrust out his chin as if striving to appear worthy of the woman on his arm. "After you, Lady Kerr."

Elisabeth turned sideways, navigating her whalebone hoops through the narrow doorway. By fashion's decree, oval panniers had grown more slender from front to back yet broader on each side. Sitting gracefully required an entire sofa.

When she joined her husband on the stair,

Donald eyed her gown with obvious pleasure. "Just as I'd imagined, the color flatters your skin."

"So you always say," Elisabeth reminded him, smiling. Donald had complimented every gown in her clothes press with precisely the same words. "But they cannot *all* flatter my skin," she'd once protested. To which he'd replied, "My dear, 'tis your lovely skin that flatters the fabric."

No wonder every woman in Edinburgh found Lord Kerr appealing. No wonder every gossip whispered his name. They were jealous, Elisabeth decided. Wasn't she the fortunate one to call him her own?

The couple began the steep descent down the enclosed turnpike stair, following Helen Edgar, a widow of forty-odd years and housekeeper to the Kerrs since their arrival in Edinburgh. Peg led the way, dutifully sweeping aside the worst of the debris, including a litter of mice. "*Aff* with ye!" the maidservant scolded, shaking her straw broom before tucking it out of sight, lest she be caught laboring on the Sabbath. The Kerrs were not always diligent about honoring the Lord's Day behind closed doors, but in public the dowager insisted on pious behavior. "No work or recreation, only prayer and meditation," Donald often grumbled.

Moments later the Kerr party emerged into Milne Square, where the air was fresher but no warmer. Tall lodging houses, or *lands,* rose on three sides — Allan's Land, Baillie's Land, Oliphant's Land — topped with a milky blue rectangle of sky, smudged with soot. Men stood about the square, heatedly discussing the approaching Jacobite rebels, while children skipped across the flat paving stones, and women waved dainty handkerchiefs like flags, calling out greetings.

As Donald stepped aside to speak with a gentleman acquaintance, Lady Woodhall, a venerable member of Edinburgh society, descended a nearby *forestair.* Her silver hair was fashionably curled and powdered, and her silken plaid matched her russet gown. When the Kerr women turned as one, Lady Woodhall pinned them in place with her small, sharp eyes. "Good morning, Lady Kerr," she said, her voice strong despite her advanced years.

Elisabeth curtsied at once. "And a fine Sabbath to you, madam." When no response came, she realized Lady Woodhall had addressed the dowager, not her. Before Elisabeth could make amends, both women strolled off with Janet sandwiched between them and Andrew on their heels, abandoning Elisabeth in their wake.

Dismayed, she stared at their departing backs, hoping none in the square had taken notice. Would society — nae, her own family — never draw her into their circle?

At once Donald appeared by her side. "Now then, Lady Kerr. Allow me to escort you to kirk." He offered his arm, his eyes filled with compassion. "Unless you prefer commiserating with Lady Woodhall over low-born rebels and the high cost of tea."

"I do not," Elisabeth said firmly, curling her hand round the crook of his elbow. The scent of his wig powder tickled her nose. Mixed with finely ground starch, orrisroot was redolent of warm meadows and dark woods. And Donald.

She drank in the heady fragrance as they crossed the square, listening to the clamorous bell of the Tron Kirk toll the half hour. "Tell me, Lord Kerr, do you suppose Mr. Hogg will expound this morning on the folly of supporting the Highland rebels?"

"Aye, though some will resist his lecturing, I daresay." Donald leaned closer to wink at her. "The ladies of Edinburgh seem rather taken with bonny Prince Charlie."

Elisabeth pretended to look shocked. "Surely not, milord!" She knew Donald had little interest in politics and even less in the divine right of kings. Her support of the Jacobite cause did not concern him in the least.

The square was especially crowded that morning. Countesses and dancing masters, advocates and wigmakers, judges and cobblers all shared the same buildings and, hence, the same stairs, spilling out onto the *plainstanes* of Edinburgh like buttons from a sewing box — carved horn, enameled brass, ornate silver, and unadorned wood, all jumbled together.

Out of the corner of her eye, Elisabeth watched a young woman approach them. Miss Hart was a silk merchant's daughter, though Elisabeth could not recall her Christian name. Emma, was it? Nae, Anna. The diminutive lass wore her flaxen hair gathered into a becoming knot. Her jade green gown, a perfect match for her eyes, swayed rather provocatively for a Sabbath morning.

Miss Hart slowed as she drew near. Propriety would not allow her to address the Kerrs first. Ever the gentleman, Donald bowed and greeted the young woman, then seemed at a loss for what to say next. "So . . . Miss Hart," he began after an awkward silence, "shall you embrace Prince Charlie when he arrives?"

"Why, Lord Kerr," the lass trilled, curtsying in such a way that her bosom was amply displayed. "I choose carefully whom I embrace and never tell a soul."

"Very wise of you," Donald murmured. "Of course, you know my wife, Lady Kerr."

Anna Hart barely glanced at her. "Indeed." A second curtsy, more perfunctory. "Yet I confess, Lord Kerr, I know you better."

Elisabeth stiffened. She'd grown accustomed to women of all ages flirting with her husband, but *this* was inexcusable.

47

Donald dismissed the young woman's brazen comment with a curt nod. "Come, Lady Kerr. The bell tolls for us all."

He abruptly veered away, taking Elisabeth with him, while the silk merchant's daughter laughed behind a brightly painted fan.

Elisabeth walked beside her husband in silence, nettled by the exchange. 'Twould seem Donald was well acquainted with Miss Hart. Had they been introduced at Maitland Hart's shop? Danced together at a ball? Shared a game of whist? As they neared the High Street, Elisabeth could bear it no longer. "How is it you know Anna Hart?"

Before Donald could answer, they were rudely pushed aside by two young caddies eager to reach the main thoroughfare. All of Edinburgh, it seemed, had quit their lodging places and were pouring into the busy High Street. Beggars to barbers to booksellers pressed against one another while gentlefolk, dressed in their Sabbath finery, struggled to make their way round sedan chairs and carriages.

As they moved through the unruly crowd, Elisabeth tightened her grip on Donald's arm. "The Highland army must be drawing closer."

"Aye," he said grimly, "so 'twould seem."

An uneasy murmur filled the air like a piper's drone as neighbors and strangers alike exchanged words that reeked of fear.

"The city *wa'* shan't hold, I tell ye."

" 'Tis no higher than a garden wall —"

"And falling *doon* at that!"

"*Whaur* stands the Edinburgh Regiment?"

"*Och!* Nae *mair* than two hundred men."

Elisabeth lifted her voice above the din. "Is the city's defense so poor as that?"

"The government is ill-prepared," her husband admitted. "Gibson remained at home to guard our effects, should the rebels breach the walls." Donald surveyed the chaotic scene a moment longer, then tugged her forward. "Come, we'll find no safer haven than the kirk."

Across the High Street rose the square tower of Christ's Kirk at the Tron, its spire piercing the cloudless sky. Elisabeth held on tight as the Kerrs made for the wooden door. The paved street was more than seventy feet wide, as broad as any marketplace and twice as crowded. Crossing it proved hazardous as careless elbows and knees found their unintentional mark.

Lady Marjory was shaking and teary-eyed by the time they reached the kirk door. "Mother?" Donald took hold of her shoulders, for she appeared ready to faint. "Shall I deliver you to Lady Glassie in Niddry's Wynd? She lodges but a few steps hence."

"Certainly not." Marjory stiffened noticeably, and her color returned at once. "Rebel army or no, we're expected at service."

49

Elisabeth paused while the servants quickly brushed off hems and sleeves, then she followed the others withindoors, skirting long rows of seats until they found their own and settled in. When Donald produced a handkerchief, Elisabeth whispered her thanks, touching the white linen to her brow, then her cheek, then her throat, willing her heart to cease its frantic pace. She'd not forgotten the troubling encounter with Miss Hart. But this was not the time or place for such questions.

Their gazes drifted upward as the enormous kirk bell rang once more, calling the parishioners to worship. Dozens of nobles lined the galleries above. From her boarding school days in Blackfriars Wynd, Elisabeth had dutifully learned their many names and titles, never dreaming she would one day be counted among them.

She'd departed the Highlands at eighteen, telling anyone who asked that she meant only to improve her mind and expand her horizons in Edinburgh. " 'Tis whaur ye belong," her mother had agreed, pressing a worn leather purse into her hands. Elisabeth still kept the purse hidden in her jewelry box, a ha'penny tucked in its rough folds. The truth was less sanguine: she'd fled from home for her mother's sake and her own. Who could have imagined she would marry a worthy husband, far above her station?

She glanced at Donald, pale but proud, and

50

swallowed the lump rising in her throat. If only she might give him just one son, a fair-haired lad with bonny blue eyes. All the Miss Harts of the world could not compete with such a prize.

When the precentor stood to lead the gathering psalm, the chattering ceased, and hundreds of voices sang in unison without benefit of a pipe organ. "The LORD is my light and my salvation; whom shall I fear?" By the look on their faces, Elisabeth knew exactly whom the parishioners feared that morning: the bonny prince and his rebel army.

Women lifted their chins, and men squared their shoulders, daring the enemy to come forth, as they sang more loudly than ever. "Though an host should encamp against me, my heart shall not fear." Elisabeth envisioned the Highland encampments drawing nigh to the gates and remembered Gibson's candid description of thieving, naked ruffians. She knew better. The Highland folk of her acquaintance were generous and kind and honest in their dealings — at least with one another if not always with the English.

As the psalm drew to a close, the parishioners sang with even more conviction. "Wait on the LORD: be of good courage, and he shall strengthen thine heart." Elisabeth closed her eyes briefly, letting the words sink in. A strong heart — aye, she would need that.

In the hallowed silence Reverend Dr. George Wishart, a humble man in his middle years, ascended the steps into the pulpit for his opening prayer. He carried a sword at his waist, prepared to defend his flock if necessary. The minister's earnest prayer rolled down the center aisle, followed by Mr. Hogg's half-hour lecture loosely drawn from the book of Isaiah. Later that morning Reverend Wishart's sermon would be twice as long and half as vitriolic. Until then, James Hogg commanded their attention.

As Elisabeth had anticipated, Mr. Hogg spoke vehemently against the Jacobites. "For it is a day of trouble," the lecturer intoned, "and of treading down." His hearers nodded or shrugged, depending on their political persuasion, but none interrupted the man's discourse.

Another psalm followed, longer than the gathering psalm. Only when the last note faded into the air did Elisabeth hear the clang of a distant bell.

Not a kirk bell, a fire bell.

"Nae!" Mrs. Millar, a midwife in the parish, leaped to her feet, clutching her reticule to her breast. "My *hoose* is wood, *a'* wood!"

Pandemonium broke out as young and old, rich and poor abandoned their seats. In a city replete with thatched roofs and oak beams, fire was a constant danger. Who could forget the great fire in the Lawnmarket that had consumed everything it touched?

Donald gripped Elisabeth's hand so tightly she feared her bones might break. "Stay with me," he told her, though she needed no prompting. His mother and Janet remained close on their heels as they fled down the aisle with Andrew not far behind them.

When the door of the kirk flew open, Elisabeth watched in horror as the first parishioners who'd reached the street were knocked to the ground by the human tide. Folk surged past, heading uphill toward the Lawnmarket, shouting and pushing, any sense of decorum forgotten. Was Parliament Close ablaze? The Luckenbooths? Saint Giles?

A grimy-faced chimney sweep appeared, leaping up and down to be heard. " 'Tis not a fire!" the lad cried, his voice hoarse from shouting. " 'Tis the Hielanders!"

Six

While throng'd the citizens with terror
  dumb,
Or whispering with white lips —
"The foe! they come! they come!"
GEORGE GORDON, LORD BYRON

"Lord, preserve us!" Marjory cried out as her legs crumpled beneath her.

Andrew leaped forward and caught her in his arms. "I'm here, Mother," he reassured her, supporting her until she could stand on her own.

The sweep's report, shouted in the street, fueled the mob's frenzy even as the fire bell continued to clang. Instead of flames leaping from their rooftops, a deadlier prospect loomed: Highland rebels charging through their doors.

Sheltered against the rough stone wall, Marjory felt every one of her eight-and-forty years — nae, twice that. Her body ached, and her mouth was as dry as ground oats. "Mr. Kerr," she said between coughs, "you must

54

see to your wife."

Janet slowly walked toward them, leaning on Peg's arm, her neatly dressed hair coming undone, her countenance ashen.

"My dear girl." When Marjory stretched out her hand, Janet was soon beside her: a loyal daughter-in-law whose aristocratic family brought honor to the Kerr name. Hadn't Marjory chosen Janet herself? Written to Lord and Lady Murray in Dunkeld? Made all the necessary arrangements? Andrew seemed well satisfied. Without question, *she* was.

"There, there," Marjory said, lightly stroking the young woman's gloved hand. "Even if the rebels have reached our gates, the Lord Provost will not let them enter." Despite her brave speech, Marjory cast a wary glance downhill toward Netherbow Port, which was not a harbor for ships but one of six fortified gates in the ancient city wall — guarded, she prayed, by a vigilant porter.

"Lord Kerr is away to the Lawnmarket," Janet said, drying her eyes.

Marjory nodded, having seen Donald strike out on foot, a determined expression on his face. "He shan't rest until he knows how things stand. In the meantime, Mr. Kerr, your place is here."

Andrew gazed toward the Lawnmarket and sighed. "Aye."

Marjory pretended not to see the wistful

look in his blue eyes. Her son was but five-and-twenty, young enough to still be foolhardy. Would that she'd sent his pistols and muskets home to Tweedsford, lest he be tempted to use them. The British army had already refused him a commission, citing insufficient vigor and poor health. But she feared the Gentlemen Volunteers might not be so selective.

Waiting in the shadow of the Tron Kirk, Marjory took in the distressing scene before her. Some were weeping, others called out for news, while many ran to and fro as if activity alone might calm their fears. Across the broad expanse of the High Street stood Milne Square. Though deceptively close, the Kerrs had little hope of reaching their house without getting bruised, if not trampled.

Her housekeeper, Mrs. Edgar, was nowhere in sight. "And wherever is Elisabeth?" Marjory wondered aloud, scanning the faces of those nearest the kirk. She caught sight of her daughter-in-law bent over a tearful maidservant, dabbing at the girl's cheeks with her handkerchief. "Lady Kerr!" Marjory said, more sharply than she intended.

Elisabeth looked up, then paused to tie the apron strings of a flustered mother with a wriggling *bairn* as Marjory watched her daughter-in-law in dismay. Did Elisabeth not know her first duty was to her family? Furthermore, she'd ruined her new gown, dragging her lacy sleeves through the muck and staining the satin hem. To what end? Helping some poor, ungrateful souls?

A line from a psalm, memorized long ago, flitted through Marjory's mind, unbidden and unwelcome. *Do justice to the afflicted and needy.* She bristled at the reminder, feeling only a twinge of guilt. Hadn't she been kind to Elisabeth, allowing her into the Kerr family despite her lowly upbringing? *He giveth grace unto the lowly.* Marjory turned her head as if she might dislodge the voice nagging at her conscience.

But she'd learned the words too well. Bound them to her heart. Listened to the holy teachings at her mother's knee. Held the psalm book in the old preaching house at Selkirk . . .

"Mother?" Andrew touched her shoulder.

Marjory looked up in time to see Elisabeth wrap her best handkerchief round a man's bleeding hand, knotting the ends with the skill of a surgeon. A moment later she deftly skirted an empty sedan chair, smiling as she drew near. "I beg your pardon, milady. Have you need of me?"

"Naturally." Marjory sniffed. Shouldn't both her daughters-in-law attend her?

Two spots of color dotted Elisabeth's cheeks, yet she did not lower her gaze. "I meant only to be helpful."

57

Marjory started to chastise her, then thought better of it. *She reacheth forth her hands to the needy.* Wasn't a charitable heart the mark of a gentlewoman? Softening her tone, Marjory conceded, "Mrs. Edgar may know some means of restoring your gown. In the meantime we shall wait for your husband to return and escort us to Milne Square."

"Might I carry ye *hame,* Leddy Kerr?" An able-bodied chairman, dressed in a tartan uniform, presented himself with a deep bow. "Mr. Henry Schaw at yer bidding."

Marjory eyed the worn leather covering his sedan chair. "I suppose you'll charge the usual sixpence, even for so short a distance?"

"Nae, mem, I'll not take a penny." He held up his hand, bandaged with Elisabeth's lace handkerchief. "Kindness comes o' will," he said with a crooked smile. "It canna be bought."

"Very well," Marjory told him, "if you'll not require payment." She glanced at his partner, who stood behind the black sedan chair, holding his end of the carrying poles. "Might you return for my daughters-in-law as well?" she asked.

"Aye, aye." Mr. Schaw nodded vigorously. "We'll be glad to take them. 'Tis an *unchancie* day for fine leddies to be about." He reached inside and dusted off the cushioned seat meant for one. "If ye please, mem."

"I'll follow close behind," Peg assured her, then bent to gather the sweeping hem of her mistress's gown.

Marjory climbed inside the sedan chair with its pivoting seat, designed to remain horizontal even on Edinburgh's steepest inclines. The movable seat made her feel queasy, though the men lifted her with care and proceeded slowly to avoid bouncing her about on the pliant poles.

She leaned back and took a deep breath, trying to calm her nerves if not her stomach. The interior smelled of boot leather, hair powder, and stale perfume. Inquisitive eyes stared at her through the glass windows as the crowd parted slightly to make room. When they reached the northeast corner of Milne Square, she exhaled in relief.

Home.

Located midway between garret and cellar, the Kerrs' fifth-floor lodgings were the most prestigious in Baillie's Land. Above and below them resided cobblers, bookbinders, lint merchants, wigmakers, and the unfortunate Mr. Hill, a junior clerk forced to climb all ten stories each evening to reach his inexpensive garret lodging.

If any souls were in residence that morn, they hid behind their curtains, for the whole of Baillie's Land appeared deserted. The courtyard, however, teemed with people carrying their household goods on their backs as if preparing to quit the city. The sight made Marjory shudder. Was that her family's only recourse? To flee for their lives?

"Aye, and here we are." The chairman handed her out at the foot of her stair, where Peg waited, no worse for wear after crossing the High Street on her own.

Preoccupied with her thoughts, Marjory reached for the coins tucked in her hanging pocket, then remembered the chairman's generous offer.

Mr. Schaw already had the carrying poles in hand. "*Guid* day to ye, Leddy Kerr," he said with a bob of his head. The two men set off at a trot, weaving their way through the noisy, milling crowd.

"Come, Peg." Marjory took her maidservant's arm. "I've need of hot tea and a warm fire."

After their long, slow climb, the two were met at the door by Mrs. Edgar in an agitated state. Stray wisps of hair escaped the confines of her white cap, and her gaze darted about the low-ceilinged entrance hall like a bird seeking a safe perch. "*Whan* the bell started ringing," she said, "I flew *oot* the kirk and across the High Street, certain I spied yer brown silk from afar. Then I reached Milne Square and found 'twas not ye . . ." She rubbed her brow, clearly unhappy with herself. "Begging yer pardon, mem, but I couldna return."

Marjory held her tongue. How could she berate the woman when her plea was so earnest? "I was trapped as well," she finally admitted, slipping off her cape. "If a chairman hadn't rescued me, I would be there still." She gestured toward the stair. "My daughters-in-law and Mr. Kerr will be along soon. I trust you'll have tea waiting for them. It's been a very difficult morning."

"Oo aye." Mrs. Edgar dropped a curtsy. "Peg will bring a tray to yer chamber at once."

Marjory pulled off her kidskin gloves. Beneath the single, high window in the entrance hall stood her late husband's mahogany desk, polished to a gleaming finish. She lightly touched the wood in passing. A small vase of fragrant damask roses freshened the stale air with their perfume. On the opposite wall hung Gibson's folding bed, fastened shut during the day and much of the night. Serving the household as both valet and butler, Gibson was the first to rise and the last to retire.

She found him in the drawing room, counting the plates for dinner. His livery was neatly pressed, and the silvery fringe of hair circling his balding head was trimmed and combed. He looked up, the relief on his wrinkled face apparent. "Guid to have ye hame, Leddy Kerr."

"I feel quite the same," she told him, then hastened to her bedchamber, thinking only

61

of her porcelain washbowl and a pot of tea.

Minutes later Marjory lifted a steaming cup to her lips, relishing the fragrant aroma and the strong, sugary taste. Her tea table, dressed in white linen, stood in a well-lit corner facing Milne Square on one side and the High Street on the other. In the capital a family's wealth was measured in windows, and the Kerrs claimed a sizable number, with six rooms rented for a goodly sum. From this vantage point she could look down on the world through glazed windows and pretend all was well.

But all was *not* well. Doors banged above and below, and hurried footsteps sounded on the stair. Voices from the street rose on the autumn breeze — angry, frightened, and confused. Other folk sounded jubilant, wearing their Jacobite sentiments on their sleeves. People with no loyalty to King George. People with nothing to lose.

When she glimpsed a familiar sedan chair entering the square, Marjory leaned toward the glass for a closer look, then sighed. *Elisabeth.* The chairmen wasted little time at the stair and were soon moving again, the empty chair bouncing between them.

Her younger daughter-in-law crossed the threshold moments later, then tarried in the adjacent drawing room chatting with the servants before she finally paused at Marjory's bedchamber door. "Might I join you,

Lady Marjory? Or do you prefer solitude?"

After a slight hesitation, Marjory caught the housekeeper's eye. "A second cup, Mrs. Edgar."

"I'll only be a moment," Elisabeth promised, then proceeded through Marjory's bedchamber to reach her own.

As she sipped her tea, Marjory pictured Tweedsford in Selkirkshire with its commodious chambers, high ceilings, and fine view of the countryside. An agreeable place, to be sure, and a generous reward for Lord John's loyalty to the crown. Yet the dreary social life of the Borderland couldn't compare to Edinburgh's heady mix of culture, commerce, and political intrigue. Who wouldn't trade the boredom of the country for the pleasures of the capital? *Lord John, for one.* Marjory pushed away the reminder before it nagged at her without ceasing.

"I'm grateful for your patience," Elisabeth said warmly, gliding back into the room. She'd changed into a pale green silk gown, one of Donald's favorites. After claiming a seat at the small table, she arranged her skirts about her and reached for her teacup. "You must be quite concerned about Lord Kerr."

Marjory made a slight noise of assent, distracted by her daughter-in-law's graceful gestures. However common her upbringing, Elisabeth had the manners of a gentlewoman. She held her china teacup, which had no handle, with four fingertips lightly touching the rim, her hands poised like birds in flight. Of course, Donald had married Elisabeth for her exceptional beauty alone. No one pretended otherwise.

"Naturally I am worried about my son," Marjory finally said, craning her head to see out the window overlooking the square.

"So am I," Elisabeth admitted.

The steady tick of the clock in the nearby drawing room filled the long silence that stretched between them. Marjory did not dislike Elisabeth. For a Highland lass, she was well read and well spoken. But she'd not been to London or Paris, had in fact never been farther south than Edinburgh. And however boundless her love for Donald, she'd failed to conceive the next Lord Kerr.

"The chairmen have returned with Janet," Elisabeth said, looking down at the square five floors below. "I'm afraid my brother-in-law appears quite winded."

Marjory put aside her empty teacup with a sharp clink, unhappy at any mention of Andrew's condition. "Can you not see anything else?" She rose from her chair, for once envying Mr. Hill his garret view across the rooftops. In the square below she saw little more than gentlemen in wigs and coats, scurrying about like the mice in her wainscoting.

The instant she heard Andrew and Janet walk through the stair door, Marjory abandoned Elisabeth to her tea and hurried toward the entrance hall, hands outstretched. "Come, what news?"

His brow damp with exertion, Andrew delivered his hat and gloves into Peg's waiting hands. "No news, I'm afraid. And no sign of my brother."

SEVEN

And he that does one fault at first,
And lies to hide it makes it two.

ISAAC WATTS

Donald traveled along the crowded High Street, weaving in and out of the coarse fabric of Edinburgh without getting tangled in its threads. 'Twas not social discourse he sought nor the company of an obliging woman. He simply wanted answers. Who'd rung the fire bell, and why?

As he made his way uphill, folk surrounded him on every side. A decrepit man, reeking of brandy, stumbled across his path before righting himself. The sharp scent of lye clung to the skirts of a laundress, her teeth badly stained, her muslin cap more so. Men shouted in Gaelic, in English, in Scots, all demanding to be heard, while high above the paved street, mothers and sisters leaned through open tenement windows, waving their arms, pleading for news.

"Lord Kerr!" a woman called, close behind

him. "Will you not wait for me?"

Donald paused, recognizing her voice. Susan McGill of Warriston's Close. A widow of surpassing beauty. A woman not easily forgotten. He turned and reached for her gloved hands, if only to steady her. "Whatever is the matter, Mrs. McGill?"

Susan looked up at him, her green eyes fraught with worry, and her face pinched with fear. "The Gentlemen Volunteers are mustering in the Lawnmarket, summoned by the clang of the fire bell. They're to join the dragoons. My son . . ." She gripped his hands. "Oh, Lord Kerr, my dear son marches with them."

Donald recalled a bowlegged boy of ten playing with wooden soldiers. "Can the lad be old enough to bear arms?" he asked, incredulous.

"Aye." Tears filled her eyes. "Jamie is seventeen now."

Seventeen? Donald could not mask his surprise. Had it been so long as that?

"You and I . . ." Susan bowed her head and began again, her voice strained. "That is, we've not . . . shared each other's company . . . in some time."

Donald merely nodded. They both remembered what had transpired between them during the dark winter months after his father's death. Susan McGill had been his first lover but hardly his last. From one season to the next, eager young widows had welcomed him into their beds. Jane Montgomerie of Geddes Close, with her azure eyes and graceful step. Red-haired Barbara Inglis of Libberton's Wynd, whose late husband had worked in the *tolbooth.* And clever Maggie Hunter of Brown's Land, who never failed to amuse him.

None of them was a gentlewoman, of course, yet all were exceedingly discreet, with reputations of their own to protect. Susan in particular had a winsome air about her, as well as a charming face and figure. Even at five-and-thirty she was a bonny sight that morning in her watered silk gown.

" 'Tis good to see you again," Donald finally said. He gently lifted her chin, relieved to find her tears had subsided. "If you intend to find the lad, you'll need an escort." When he offered his arm, she took it willingly. "Jamie, is it?"

"Aye, after his father." Susan pressed against Donald's side, slowing the pace of their steady climb with her pattens and hoops.

Even through his twilled woolen coat he felt the warmth of her body, the softness of her form. A whiff of lavender greeted him, stirring to life a vivid image of her, wrapped in his embrace . . .

Nae. He forced himself to think of something else, anything else. Why did the fairer sex affect him so? No matter how firm his resolve, the women of Edinburgh proved impossible to resist. Only that morning he'd traded innuendos with Anna Hart in Milne Square. Nor was he above seeking a brief interlude with an accommodating maidservant.

Peg Cargill had not been accommodating, though. Nae, she had not.

His skin warmed, remembering the frightened look on her face. She'd avoided him all morning, and he'd done the same, consoling himself that he'd not said or done anything improper. Still, his intentions were clear enough.

My sin is ever before me. Aye, so it was — morning, noontide, and night.

Donald inched away from the beautiful widow on his arm and vowed to concentrate on delivering Susan to her son. "Tell me," he said as they passed the Luckenbooths, where jewelers, mercers, and clothiers sold their wares. "How might I recognize the lad now that he's grown?"

"Jamie is tall and broad like his father but with my coloring." Her shrug was dismissive. "Common as poppies in June."

There is nothing common about you, madam. He dared not confess his thoughts, but they prodded at him nonetheless. Her hair was the color of honey, her eyes like spring grass, and her generous mouth . . .

Nae! Desperate to curb his imagination, he

shifted their discussion to politics, a decidedly unromantic subject. "Mrs. McGill, it seems you are still a confirmed royalist."

"Oo aye," she said emphatically. "You'll find nary a Jacobite in my household." She looked at him from beneath her long lashes, then continued with equal fervor. "If my brave son is willing to lay down his life for King George, so should every nobleman."

Donald wondered if her challenge was innocently spoken or a pointed barb. He had no interest in fighting the rebels, but Andrew would gladly bear arms for any worthy cause. Mother would not hear of it, of course, nor would their physician. Andrew had yet to resign himself to that sad truth.

"Every nobleman who is able," Donald amended firmly, then sought a fresh topic of conversation, though he was finding it difficult to be heard above the crowd.

The throng grew louder when they reached the Lawnmarket, an expanse as wide as the High Street. Tall lands towered six stories above them, with wooden booths in the first-floor arcades, shuttered for the Sabbath. Seeing an array of muskets poking their steel noses above the crowd, Donald guided Susan toward the head of the West Bow. A precipitous street, shaped like the letter Z, the West Bow was lined with quaint, gabled houses and connected the high, broad Lawnmarket to the broader Grassmarket below.

70

The youthful Volunteers stood about in haphazard fashion, weapons in hand, while mothers, wives, sisters, and friends hung on their coat sleeves, begging the lads to reconsider. "Willie, ye canna go!" one older woman pleaded, while a young lass wept copious tears. "*Brither,* if the Hielanders take ye, ye're a *deid* man."

With similar laments filling the air like chimney smoke, Donald leaned down to ask Susan, "Are you here to convince Jamie not to march?"

"On the contrary." Her eyes narrowed. "I am here to wish him Godspeed. No son of mine will dishonor his father's name with a show of cowardice."

Again Donald felt the sting of her words.

"Look!" she cried, surging forward, dragging him with her. " 'Tis my Jamie."

Donald spotted her son, just as she'd described him. Handsome as his mother was beautiful, Jamie McGill stood apart from the other recruits, with their sagging shoulders and frightened expressions. Jamie's posture was straight, his jaw line firm, his weapon properly held. He was a fine-looking son, whom any father would gladly call his heir.

Father. Donald pulled Susan back, grinding his heels into the muck. "Tarry a moment, madam."

She spun round, irritation sharpening her features. "What is it, Lord Kerr? Are you

71

afraid Captain Drummond will strap a musket to your shoulder and force you to defend your country?"

Now Donald had his answer. She'd meant to wound him. Since he was the one who'd ended their weekly trysts, this was her subtle revenge, however unplanned.

"I have no fear of George Drummond," he assured her evenly. "But I'd prefer to avoid an awkward encounter with your son. If by chance he —"

"Jamie was ten." Susan released her grip on his arm. "I am the only one in my household who remembers your visits."

By the look on her face, she intended to forget them. Forever.

" 'Tis best if you leave me here," she said, edging away from him. "I'd prefer not to introduce you to my son."

"Then I bid you farewell." Donald offered her a deep bow and turned on his heel lest she notice his heated countenance. No woman had ever trampled his pride so thoroughly. Nor so deservedly.

EIGHT

How slow the tardy moments seem to roll!
What spectres rise of inconsistent fear!
                                        MARY TIGHE

Elisabeth could not ignore the mounting
clamor from the street below. Fear lodged
itself in her throat like a pinch of stale cake.
No matter how firmly she swallowed, 'twould
not move. Instinctively she clasped her wedding ring, slowly spinning it round her finger.
Come home, Donald. 'Tis not safe in the street.

The Kerrs sat in a crescent near the glowing fire. A cold Sabbath dinner, prepared the
past evening, awaited them on the dining
table. Thin slices of mutton, hard cheese,
smoked haddocks, a finely ground wheaten
bread, and lemon tarts were all covered with
linen until one o' the clock.

When Janet drew her chair closer to Marjory's, Elisabeth was reminded again of their
uncanny resemblance, as if the two were
mother and daughter, related by blood rather
than by marriage. Except for a few touches

73

of gray in Marjory's auburn hair, the women mirrored each other in appearance, style, and manner. Wide-set hazel eyes. Pronounced noses and chins, both drawn to a point. Small mouths, gathered in a bow. And all the social graces of their class. No wonder Marjory favored her older daughter-in-law. In Janet, the dowager saw a younger version of herself.

"I've learned this much," Andrew began, shifting forward in his chair. "While we gathered at the Tron Kirk for service, the Gentlemen Volunteers convened in the College Yards and were summarily marched to the Lawnmarket."

"By whom?" Marjory wanted to know.

"George Drummond."

"I see."

Elisabeth wasn't surprised at Marjory's sharp tone. One spring Drummond had pursued the dowager with marked interest. Flattered at first, Marjory had welcomed Drummond's advances until she learned how many other wealthy, available widows he'd courted over the years.

Marjory was frowning now. "Captain Drummond found it necessary to muster his troops on the Sabbath?"

"So he did," Andrew told her. "Our Volunteer forces are to engage the rebels before they reach Edinburgh."

Elisabeth's heart sank. The Volunteers were young, untried, and poorly trained. "How near are the Highlanders?"

"Eight miles hence in Kirkliston. The Lord Provost rang the fire bell to summon reinforcements."

Janet arched her brows. "And sent us all running into the street."

"An unfortunate choice for a signal," her husband agreed. "By now the whole of Edinburgh is at sixes and sevens."

Elisabeth could bear it no longer. "But what's become of Lord Kerr?"

Andrew's features softened. "Forgive me, milady. Truly, I've nothing else to report." He rose and began slowly pacing before the fire. "As you well know, my brother is not easily dissuaded. He won't return home until he's certain of the situation. I could, of course, go in search of him —"

"What?" Marjory protested. "And leave the three of us here alone and unguarded?"

" 'Tis not so bad as that, Mother." Andrew paused to consult his watch. "Gibson is here. And the city will be well defended. Hamilton's dragoons are expected from Leith within the hour."

Elisabeth pictured Donald's carefully rendered map of Edinburgh and its environs: the village of Kirkliston to the west, the seaport of Leith to the north. He'd commissioned maps of Berwickshire, of Roxburghshire, of Selkirkshire. But nowhere in the house could be found a map of Aberdeenshire, her own county to the north. Nor a painting of the grass-covered glens she'd loved as a child. Nor a sketch of the lofty hills surrounding Castleton of Braemar, the Highland *clachan* she'd once called home.

She'd left in haste, and for good reason. Now that all was resolved, she longed to visit her mother's heather-thatched cottage with its tidy kitchen garden by the door. To clasp the hand of her younger brother, Simon, and climb the steep slopes of Morrone. To meander among the ancient pines and share secrets, as they once had.

Yet each time Elisabeth mentioned the possibility of a journey north, her mother-in-law found some reason to object. The considerable distance. The unpredictable weather. The miserable condition of the roads.

Any suggestion that her family travel south to Edinburgh was met with further resistance — their cramped lodging being the chief impediment. "Wherever would your mother sleep?" Marjory fretted when the subject came up again last month. "I would be the worst of hostesses with only a drawing room to offer her."

In spite of Elisabeth's assurances that a pile of blankets near the hearth would suit Fiona and Simon Ferguson very well, Marjory would not hear of it. "Perhaps next summer," her mother-in-law had said. As she always said. And so Elisabeth dreamed of the hills and glens of home and woke with tears in her eyes, then brushed them away before anyone noticed.

She was dry-eyed at the moment, though her thoughts were far from easy. Rather than hear Hamilton's dragoons march through the city, she longed to hear Donald's footsteps on the stair. She gazed at the coals nestled in the grate, willing her husband home. *Please, Donald. Soon.*

Janet was still complaining about the morning's disruptions when the bells of Saint Giles began to ring. And those of the Tron Kirk. And the parish kirk in the Canongate to the east. Elisabeth and the others were on their feet at once, headed for the dowager's chamber and her windows facing the High Street.

Andrew lifted one sash, then another. "Listen!" Not only bells resounded through the *wynds* and *closes,* the winding streets and narrow passageways that branched off the main thoroughfare. Now they also heard the distinctive staccato of drums. "Dragoons!" Andrew breathed, not bothering to hide his excitement.

Elisabeth leaned out as far as she dared, tightly gripping the windowsill. The other Kerrs joined her as all along the street sashes flew up and startled faces appeared. Though she couldn't see them, Elisabeth heard the clatter of hoofs on the paving stones and the sound of raucous cheers. "Huzzah! Huzzah!"

She peered down the High Street, lined twenty deep with citizens. The staccato drums grew louder, the military rhythm more marked. At long last she caught a glimpse of red, a flash of white.

"Aren't they splendid in their uniforms?" Janet clutched the generous cuffs of Andrew's coat as she hung out farther still.

"Have a care," Marjory cautioned, withdrawing into the safer confines of her bedchamber. "They'll march below our windows shortly."

Elisabeth lowered her heels and eased her shoulders inside. Without Donald to anchor her, it was perilous to lean out so far. She dropped to her knees, propped her elbows on the low sill, and settled her chin in her hands. Even from a distance she could see the soldiers' bright red coats, brass buttons parading down the front. Close-fitting white breeches were tucked into polished black boots, cuffed at the knee. And on their heads sat black military hats, proudly cocked, the wavy edges trimmed in gold.

In years past she'd mended her share of officers' uniforms at Angus's shop, replacing lost buttons or repairing torn seams. "Just as *weel* their coats are red," Angus had observed dryly. "The *bluid* from a Highlander's dirk willna show."

A friend of her late father's and a fierce Jacobite, Angus MacPherson had guarded her welfare from the first hour Elisabeth had arrived in the capital. The tailor was no doubt roaming the town that afternoon, shadowed by his taciturn son of eight-and-twenty. She still remembered the way dark and brooding Rob MacPherson had watched her whenever she visited his father's shop, the young man's eyes like bits of coal, black and hard. Born with a club foot, Rob still had a marked limp, though he managed it well. The lads of Castleton had teased him unmercifully. Perhaps if they saw Rob now, with his broad shoulders and thick arms, they might not be so quick to taunt him.

"Look at that, will you!" Andrew cried, exultant.

Elisabeth looked down in time to see the mounted dragoons clash their swords as if engaged in battle. Each mock skirmish was met with roars of approval from the throng. Louder than the drums or swords were the voices of women, old and young, gentle and common, calling out from their window perches — some with buoyant good wishes, others with unbridled scorn. "Ye're nae match for the Hielanders!" shouted one.

Picturing a broadsword in the hands of a rugged clansman, Elisabeth feared their sharp-tongued neighbor might be right. When the dragoons passed by, her consternation grew. They, too, were young, and their mounts seemed skittish and unaccustomed to crowds.

However fine the soldiers' uniforms, their beardless faces and slender limbs told a truer tale.

"Mr. Kerr, where are they headed?" she asked.

"Corstorphine," Andrew told her, "to join Gardiner's regiment. All told, less than six hundred men."

So few. Elisabeth gazed toward the Lawnmarket. "Will the Gentlemen Volunteers march out with them?"

He paused before answering. "Aye."

Elisabeth frowned. Surely Donald would not join their campaign, however great the need. Though his sword dutifully hung by his side, he'd had no military training, nor was he a skilled horseman. Still, with Andrew itching to enlist, might Donald be persuaded?

Or was someone else persuading Lord Kerr that afternoon and in quite another direction? Miss Anna Hart, perhaps, with eyes the color of jade. The young woman's words jabbed her like a saber, the sharp tip bared. *I choose carefully whom I embrace.* Had the lass dared to embrace Lord Kerr, on this day or any other? Surely a merchant's daughter would not be so careless with her virtue nor a husband so thoughtless with his favor.

Only then did Elisabeth recall his whispered endearment. *I have a weakness for beautiful women.* A compliment, as she'd imagined?

Or was it a confession?

Elisabeth slowly rose, brushing the wrinkles from her skirts. *Nae, Donald. I'll not believe it. Not until you tell me so.* With a leaden heart, she stood waiting for the others as the dragoons disappeared from sight.

"Beg pardon, Leddy Kerr." Gibson stood at the bedchamber door, his posture ramrod straight despite his sixty years. " 'Tis one o' the clock."

"Pour the claret," Marjory told him, sweeping past the others. "Rebellion or not, dinner is served."

NINE

Nature's loving proxy,
the watchful mother.
EDWARD ROBERT BULWER, LORD LYTTON

"Any moment Lord Kerr will breeze through the door like an autumn leaf," Marjory declared soon after they sat down to their Sabbath dinner. "We've no need for concern." She felt the heat of false bravado rise to her cheeks. Or was it the claret warming her from the inside out?

She hid behind her glass, hoping no one noticed she'd hardly touched her food. What mother could have an appetite with an army approaching and her son amid the fray? For the others' benefit, she treated Donald's absence as a trifling matter. For her, it was yet another reason to worry.

Their first winter in Edinburgh both her sons had been weakened by a bout with consumption. Donald had regained his strength, albeit slowly, while his brother still struggled to breathe. Whatever their late father's wishes, Andrew could never hope to serve in the military, and his older brother had never expressed any desire to do so. But if Donald saw his friends bearing arms and heard the cadence of the dragoons, might he not be tempted? Might he not join the Volunteers?

Holding the glass to her lips, Marjory sent a brief prayer heavenward, then drank deeply, as if sealing a bargain. *Bring my son home, Lord, and do not tarry.* She waited for the familiar sense of peace that had once followed her prayers. But such assurance did not come; only an empty silence.

As the others dined on lemon tarts and tea, Marjory's gaze kept returning to the tall case clock in the corner of the drawing room, its brass pendulum counting the seconds. Nearly two o' the clock and still no word from Donald. When Gibson finished his serving duties at table, Marjory quietly dispatched him to the Lawnmarket, knowing he would return with her son or with news of him.

The afternoon sky was gray but not threatening when the four of them put aside their linen napkins. "Shall we read beside the hearth?" Marjory suggested. Much as she longed to soothe her troubled mind with a game of whist, the Sabbath afternoon was better spent in spiritual pursuits. She sent Elisabeth to collect Reverend Boston's book from her bedchamber and made herself comfortable by the fireplace.

Her daughter-in-law soon reappeared, the thick volume in hand. "Shall I begin?" Elisabeth offered, opening to the page marked from their last Sabbath reading.

Marjory pursed her lips. 'Twas Andrew's voice she wished to hear, with the familiar cadence of home. Or Janet's well-bred accent, honed from her years in Edinburgh society. Elisabeth's speech, still tainted with a Gaelic air, grated on the ear. Too musical by half and too lively. *Human Nature in its Fourfold State* deserved a more sober reading.

But Elisabeth had already settled into an upholstered chair, her long feet balanced on a velvet-covered footstool. "Man's life is a stream," she read aloud, "running into death's devouring deeps. They who now live in palaces must quit them . . ."

Marjory let the words wash over her, keeping only those sentiments that pleased her. "This world is like a great fair or market." Aye, the High Street especially. "Youth is a flower that soon withers." Her looking glass proved that. "Christ has taken away the sting of death." A reassuring thought.

But the vanity of man's life, the sinfulness of man's nature, the certainty of man's demise — Marjory did not dwell on those subjects. The tragic loss of Lord John had taught her all she needed to know of death and more than she wanted to know of guilt.

His portrait hung above the marble mantelpiece, a tacit reminder of a marriage ended too soon.

Marjory sank back against the chair, closing her eyes so she might listen without distraction. Elisabeth's voice played on, like a music box, the sound growing fainter and fainter . . .

"Mother?"

Marjory slowly lifted her head and blinked, trying to make sense of things. The drawing room bathed in shadows. The warmth of the fire. Flickering candles on the mantelpiece. Donald touching her shoulder.

"You sent the right man," he said, smiling down at her. "When Gibson found me in the Lawnmarket, he insisted I come home and refused to hear otherwise."

"The Lord bless him for it." Marjory studied Donald's face. He was paler than usual with a fine sheen on his brow and upper lip and a bruised look to his eyes. *Poor lad.* He'd had a difficult afternoon. Though Donald no longer suffered as Andrew did, she'd sent Gibson none too soon.

Relieved to have them both home, Marjory sat up and patted her hair in place, knowing she must look frightful. How had she slept so soundly? When she glanced at the clock, her eyes widened. "Is it past six?"

"Aye." Donald nodded toward the window.

"The light has long faded."

"Now black and deep the night begins to fall." Marjory paused, waiting to see if he recognized the line of poetry.

"Much too easy," he chided her, "or have you forgotten I acquired a new edition of Thomson's *The Seasons*?"

She sniffed. "I know better than to test you after I've been napping."

Elisabeth spoke from across the room. "Do forgive us for not waking you." She sat before a tambour frame, embroidering one of Donald's silk waistcoats, the scarlet thread in constant motion, a bank of candles lighting her tiny stitches. "Lord Kerr mentioned you did not sleep well last night."

"On the contrary." Marjory abruptly stood, ignoring a slight twinge of pain. "I slept very well." She took a turn round the room, hoping to ease the stiffness in her knees. "What news from the Lawnmarket, Lord Kerr? You've no doubt informed the others." When she paused at one of the windows overlooking Milne Square, Donald joined her, briefly touching her hand, a thoughtful son comforting his mother.

"I reached the Lawnmarket not far ahead of Hamilton's dragoons," he began. "An hour later the Gentlemen Volunteers marched down the West Bow. You know what a winding, zigzag of a street it is, giving men with second thoughts a chance to slip off unnoticed through open doorways or narrow wynds. By the time the Volunteers reached the Grassmarket, only forty soldiers remained."

"Forty?" Marjory looked up at him, aghast. "I thought they numbered four hundred."

Donald looked out into the deepening twilight. "Family members pulled many aside, convincing them to stay behind. Other men couldn't find the courage to go on. Then the parish ministers arrived, pleading for the youth of Edinburgh and the hope of the next generation." He shook his head. "When Reverend Wishart spoke of the lads being made prisoners and maltreated, there was no hope for it. Captain Drummond marched what was left of his company back to the College Yards and dismissed them."

Marjory envisioned George Drummond — his long bob wig and short neck, his bushy eyebrows and florid cheeks — and thanked heaven she'd refused his suit. He'd made a fine mess of things this day. "So the dragoons are all that stand between us and the Highlanders?"

"Aye," Donald sighed. "Folk say 'twill be decided on the morrow."

Despondent, Marjory turned away from the window. If only she'd left Edinburgh with her household that morning — nae, a week ago, a month ago! Now the roads would be unsafe and every horse and carriage spoken for.

When her gaze landed on Elisabeth, quietly embroidering, a tinderbox inside Marjory ignited. "How can you ply a needle," she demanded, "when our very lives are at stake?"

Elisabeth looked up, her hands poised over her work. "The steady rhythm calms me. Perhaps you have something I might embellish —"

"I have nothing for you," she retorted.

"Mother," Donald said firmly, "Elisabeth meant only to please you."

Ashamed of her outburst, Marjory said no more. An uneasy silence fell over the room. The servants' chatter in the kitchen, barely audible a moment ago, seemed to fill the air while the nearby clock ticked like musketry.

Marjory took a step backward, regaining her composure. "Sabbath or not, I'm of a mind to play hazard." Gibson had whittled her a fine pair of dice, so light they danced when she rolled them. "Kindly send Andrew to my chamber."

"My brother's away," Donald said, glancing at the clock. "He left for Mrs. Turnbull's an hour ago." The tavern across the High Street was a favorite haunt.

Exasperated, Marjory threw up her hands. "Now I must watch for Andrew?"

"The more stalwart of the Volunteers are convening there," Donald explained. "A good number plan to offer their services to Johnnie Cope the moment he sails into port."

"*Sir* John Cope," Marjory amended. As commander of the government forces in Scotland, the gentleman was worthy of his title. "Donald, you don't think . . . that is, Andrew has no intention of *joining* these young men?"

"I hardly think so." He stifled a yawn. "When the town guard beats the drum at ten o' the clock, you can be sure Andrew will appear at our door, damp with fog and reeking of smoke from Turnbull's fire."

Marjory took solace in his words. Donald was nothing if not trustworthy. As for his brother, Gibson would see to the lad's needs when he returned.

Within the hour Marjory bid her family good night and repaired to her bedchamber. Peg relieved her of gown and corset, then dressed her in a fine linen nightgown trimmed with a swath of lace.

"How quiet you are this evening," Marjory told her. The maidservant usually prattled on while she worked, sharing the latest gossip from the square. "Are you well?"

"*Verra* weel, mem." But she looked down when she spoke.

Marjory didn't press her. Who knew what concerns a servant might have? Peg quit the room a short time later, extinguishing the last candle and taking her troubles with her.

Silence weighed on Marjory like a woolen blanket as she pulled the bedsheet to her chin and stared into the darkened room. Sleep would be hard to come by, especially with her afternoon nap and all the commotion from the street assaulting her ears. Would folk never seek their beds? Elsewhere in the house voices were muted and footsteps muffled. The faint glow from the dying coals cast an eerie orange light about the chamber, making Marjory shiver, though the night air was mild.

When she turned away from the fireplace, thinking to find a more comfortable position, her gaze landed on the empty pillow next to hers. She smoothed her hand across the linen and sighed. Had he truly been gone seven years? Despite the nightly cups of foxglove tea Lord John drank to ease his chest pain, he'd succumbed on a cold winter's morning, the first of January 1738. It was as if he could not bear another year in the city, another year apart from his beloved Tweedsford.

Marjory pulled his pillow to her heart, fighting the unexpected wave of loneliness that swept over her. *Would that you were beside me this night, John.*

She squeezed her eyes shut, but the painful images persisted: an aging husband, who'd indulged his headstrong bride and reluctantly moved his family to Edinburgh; two pale sons lying in their feather beds, struggling to breathe; and a widow who'd knelt by her husband's grave in Greyfriars Kirkyard and wept for all she'd lost and the little she'd gained.

No wonder the Almighty had turned his back on her. Or had she turned her back on him? Marjory was no longer certain. In the morning she would lift her head and face another day, leaving behind such melancholy thoughts. For now, she could only endure them.

TEN

But be faithful, that is all.
                    ARTHUR HUGH CLOUGH

Elisabeth gazed across the room at her husband, his body relaxed, his head buried in a goose-down pillow. Donald had not stirred when she rose from their bed nor when she lit a candle at the fireplace. But he would not sleep much longer. Not with dawn creeping across the windowsills.

After quietly moving the perfumes and powders on her dressing table, she reached for her *Ladies' Diary,* a slender almanac no bigger than her hand. Each month had its own page, with the phases of the moon across the top, then below them a descending calendar of days. She'd already circled the most important one that month: *20 September.* The sixth day of the moon.

The rest of the almanac was filled with enigmas, rebuses, and charades meant to sharpen a woman's intellect. Elisabeth turned the pages in search of an engaging query or some clever rhyme, but the lettering was too small and the candlelight too faint to read at that hour.

In truth, 'twas not her mind but her heart that needed tending.

She'd waited all evening to claim Donald for herself. But he'd retired earlier than usual, then fell asleep before she could broach the subject that pressed down on her like a millstone. *Are you truly mine, Donald, and mine alone?*

The mere thought tied her stomach in knots. *Are you mine?* How could she say those words aloud? How could she look into her husband's eyes and repeat the ugly bits of gossip she'd heard over the years? Or ask how intimately acquainted he was with Anna Hart?

Elisabeth had her own secrets, to be sure. But nothing like this. Much as she dreaded his response, she needed to know the truth, else how could she go on?

Resolved to seek what help she could find, she pressed open her almanac to the last page, dipped a sharpened quill into the ink pot, and added yet another item to her long list of entreaties for the sixth day of the moon. Unless she wrote them down, she couldn't hope to remember them all when the time came. She chose her notations with care, lest anyone discover her almanac. *A. H.*

would suffice for the young woman in question.

Much as she longed to plead with the Nameless One at that very moment, her request would have to wait. "Thou moon of moons," Elisabeth whispered in Gaelic, glancing at the windows, still veiled in gray. Better a faith riddled with doubt than no faith at all.

When her husband awakened at cock's crow, she would ask him straight away before she lost her nerve. *Please, Donald.* She sprinkled sand across the ink, silently pleading with him. *Please tell me the truth.*

A male voice floated across the room. "Writing in your diary, I see."

"Oh!" Elisabeth turned in haste, scattering sand across table and floor. "I didn't hear you rise."

"Nor I you." Seated at the edge of their bed, Donald slowly yawned, dragging a hand over his face.

She stood, brushing the sand from her lap, summoning every ounce of courage she possessed. "Donald, I wonder if we might discuss something?"

A sly grin stole across his features. "At this early hour we might do a great many things."

"Then let us speak." She crossed the room and sat beside him on the woolen mattress. Close, but not too close. "Donald . . ." She swallowed and began again. "Yesterday morning when we stood in Milne Square, a young woman . . ."

His smile quickly faded. "You mean Miss Hart."

"Aye," Elisabeth sighed, relieved he'd offered the name first. "She seemed . . . that is, her comments implied . . ."

"Och!" Donald pounded his fist into the mattress. "Anna Hart is a brazen lass who delights in making mischief. Were I her father, I would wrap the girl in a bolt of inferior silk and keep her in the store 'til she acquired some manners."

Convincing as his speech was, Elisabeth had to be certain. "But she claimed she . . . knew you."

"Only as a customer of her father's. I purchased the satin for your lavender gown from Maitland Hart." Donald clasped her hands, imploring her with his eyes. "Believe me, Bess. We were barely introduced. Miss Hart means nothing to me. Less than nothing."

After a long pause Elisabeth said, "I do believe you." And she did. Anyone would mark the silk merchant's daughter a coquette.

But what of the unseemly rumors that swirled round the closes and wynds of Edinburgh from time to time, clinging to her skirts like dust on a warm August day. Could he explain those away so easily?

Elisabeth gently pulled her hands from his

grasp. "Donald, I've also heard . . ." She looked down at the toes of her brocade slippers, searching her heart for the right words. "There have been . . . reports," she finally confessed. "Of young widows . . ." Flushed with embarrassment, she could say no more.

"My bonny Bess." He smoothed his hand across her hair, unkempt from a troubled night's sleep, then lifted her chin until their gazes met. "Why would I seek out another man's widow when I'm married to the most beautiful woman in Edinburgh? Nae, in all of Scotland."

Elisabeth heard the sincerity in his words and saw it shining in his blue eyes. She wanted to believe him. Truly, she did.

" 'Tis idle gossip," Donald continued, lightly tracing the line of her cheek, then the curve of her neck, then the ruffled edge of her chemise. "Auld women spreading auld news."

"But at Assembly Close on Thursday last —"

He kissed her before she could say more, drawing her into his embrace. "I'll not lie to you, Bess." His voice was soft against her ear. "Before we married, I made the acquaintance of many women." When her breath caught, he pressed his rough cheek against hers. "I am sorry, my love. 'Tis best you know the truth."

She closed her eyes but could not stop her

ears. *Many women.* The truth was harder to hear than she'd imagined. Was Jane Montgomerie one of those women? What of the Widow Inglis, who'd smiled coyly at Donald in passing when they visited the Luckenbooths a fortnight ago? Or the Widow Forbes of Trunk Close, who often exchanged glances with him at kirk? *Nae!* The woman was nigh to his mother's age.

"Donald, how could you?" Elisabeth whispered, turning her head away, sickened at the thought of her husband in another woman's embrace.

"But don't you see, my love?" His persuasive words poured over her like honey. "These . . . ah, events happened long ago. Before we met. Now I have only to stand near a woman, and a new tale is told. Folk who deal in gossip seldom forget. And never forgive." He kissed her forehead, then her cheek. "My darling wife, I hope you might find it in your heart to both forgive *and* forget."

"Please, Donald." She pulled away, needing to breathe, needing to think. "This is very . . ." Unexpected? *Nae.* On their wedding night Elisabeth had realized she was not the first woman to share her husband's bed. But had his affairs truly ended? Were the rumors no more than crumbs of stale bread, fed to ravenous birds?

She rose and started toward the washstand,

unsure of what to think, what to feel now that she knew the truth. Should she pretend his past indiscretions did not matter? Forgive the man and be done with it? Among the gentry of Edinburgh, 'twas mere sport, it seemed.

The morning light cast a gray pallor across the room. Beyond their bedchamber door the household was stirring. Peg would soon come knocking, bearing fresh coals and hot water. Life would go on, whether Donald was faithful or not. *Oh, but let him be faithful!* A faint mist of tears clouded Elisabeth's vision. *Please let him belong to me and no other.*

"Bess?" He was standing behind her now, his voice low, his words gentle. "You alone have my heart."

She bowed her head, undone by his tenderness. "I want to believe you, Donald."

"Then do." He gently brushed aside her hair and kissed the back of her neck. "Please?"

She slowly exhaled. Could she trust this husband of hers? And believe his philandering days were over? With no evidence beyond hearsay, 'twas unfair to condemn the man she loved. And she did love him, abundantly so. However many women he'd bedded in the past, Donald had but one woman now.

Elisabeth closed her eyes and offered a brief entreaty. *Strengthen me, thou moon of moons.* She knew her plea was in vain. Only on the sixth day of the moon might she be heard. And perhaps not even then.

A light tapping at the door announced Peg's arrival. While her maidservant quietly attended to her duties, Elisabeth took her husband's arm and drew him toward a window overlooking the High Street, hoping to put behind them the last hour and all its painful revelations.

A cloudless sky hung over the town. Across the square, shutters were thrown open, ushering in the morning air. Elisabeth wondered aloud, "Whatever shall this Monday bring? Highlanders in the street?"

"If so, you can be sure all of Edinburgh will be bound for the *mercat* cross," Donald told her, then cocked his head. "Shall we share a leisurely breakfast, then join them?"

Elisabeth kept her voice even. "Just the two of us?"

"Aye, milady." His smile was still the devil's own. "Two is quite enough."

ELEVEN

In no city in the world do so many people
live in so little room as at Edinburgh.

DANIEL DEFOE

Donald had never seen such a crowd, far
worse than yesterday morning. Every tinker,
baker, and candle maker in town stood cheek
by jowl round the mercat cross. Tall as he
was, he couldn't make out the octagonal
building. Only the slender pillar itself, bearing the Scottish unicorn, rose high above the
masses. So did an unholy aroma.

"The flowers of Edinburgh are in full
bloom," he grumbled, sorry he'd recom-
mended they venture out of doors. After three
days of chamber pots being emptied into the
street and no scavengers appearing at dawn
with wheelbarrows to carry off the refuse, the
High Street was even more malodorous than
usual.

The incessant clang of the fire bell made
discourse nigh to impossible. But he'd promised to bring his wife to the mercat cross, and

this was not a day for breaking faith. By some miracle Elisabeth had accepted his glib answer for the never-ending gossip about him. It seemed she'd all but forgiven him, though who could understand the workings of a woman's heart?

Discretion was his new by word. No more dancing with former paramours at Assembly Close. No more flirting with unmarried daughters in the street. *Losh!* Whatever had possessed him? He should have snubbed Anna Hart rather than addressed her. And no more midnight trysts with Lucy Spence, whose door in Halkerston's Wynd stood tantalizingly close to his own . . .

"Lord Kerr?"

With a guilty start, he turned to find Elisabeth facing him, her elegant features shadowed beneath a straw-brimmed hat. He cleared his throat, wishing he might banish his wayward thoughts so easily. "Have you had enough, milady?"

"No indeed." Her blue eyes gleamed above a sachet of rose petals pressed to her nose. "Not with the bonny prince almost at our gates."

"Aye," Donald admitted begrudgingly. "It seems the dragoons failed to stop him."

They'd already heard the story numerous times since arriving in the marketplace. An advance party of Highlanders had startled the mounted dragoons near Colt Bridge and fired their pistols — in sport or in defiance, none could say. Panic-stricken, the dragoons turned round and headed for Leith, abandoning their baggage and arms. The citizens of Edinburgh had watched in dismay as both Hamilton's and Gardiner's men fled on horseback across the Lang Dykes north of town, leaving the capital undefended.

On the High Street tradesmen deserted their shops and stood about, bareheaded and empty handed, armed with only their indignation. Two regiments of royalist dragoons unmanned by a handful of Highlanders? The shame was not to be borne.

Donald was of the same opinion. Were there no true soldiers among them? Andrew would be livid when he heard of the dragoons' humiliating retreat.

A nearby poultryman, wrapped in a bloodied apron, bellowed in protest. "Ne'er mind the dragoons. We'll fight the rebels ourselves!"

"Aye," growled a sawyer, "*wha* better?"

But there were other voices, stronger ones, begging for surrender. A saddler cried out, "Ye're a' daft if ye're thinking o' defending the *toun* now."

Beside him, a pressman waved his ink-stained hands. "If we dinna surrender, we'll be cut doon in our beds!"

All the while, a bold contingent of Jacobites sang so loudly they almost drowned out their detractors.

Oh, set me ance on Scottish land,
With my guid broadsword in my hand!
To see King James at Edinburgh Cross,
With fifty thousand foot and horse!

Donald snorted when he heard the exaggerated figure. "Not so many as that, I'll wager. Five thousand men at best."

"I'm glad the young dragoons were spared," Elisabeth said. "If Prince Charlie and his men take the city peaceably, so much the better."

Donald rolled his eyes in mock disdain. "Spoken like a true Jacobite."

"Nae, spoken like a woman," she countered. "Peace is always preferable to war."

"Unless war is needed to restore the peace." Donald looked up at the ancient cross of Edinburgh. "If anything's to be announced, 'twill happen here." The mercat cross not only marked a place of commerce. Proclamations were also made there. And executions.

Elisabeth touched his arm. "Angus MacPherson and his son are coming this way. May we speak with them?"

He could hardly refuse. The tailor was a family friend, who'd departed Elisabeth's Highland clachan some years past, then welcomed her when she'd arrived in Edinburgh. Donald owed the tradesman a cordial greeting if naught else. "MacPherson," he said with a brief nod.

"Lord Kerr." Angus bowed as best he could

in the crowded street. "And Leddy Kerr, 'tis *aye* a pleasure."

"For me as well," Elisabeth said warmly, clasping the tailor's hands. "You are in good health?"

"A' the better, seeing ye here," Angus said, a twinkle in his gray eyes.

The man was well in his fifties, Donald supposed, since his black hair and trimmed beard were shot through with silver. Angus MacPherson was a head shorter than he and a good deal rounder, yet the tailor was surprisingly fit, with the bearing of a man nearer the age of his son, who shared his solid, muscular build.

Elisabeth turned to smile at the younger man. "Mr. MacPherson, you're looking well."

"As are ye, milady," he responded, offering her a deep bow. Despite being the size of a small mountain, Rob was as soft spoken as his father was gruff, his deep voice barely audible amid the hubbub. Black hair sprang from his head like thick winter wool, and his coat was neatly brushed, as befitted a tailor. But it was his eyes Donald noted: dark as night, even on a fair day.

"Have you news of the prince?" Donald inquired, suspecting the MacPhersons were loyal Jacobites.

Angus eyed him warily. "Why would a tailor from the Luckenbooths *ken* His Royal Highness's whereabouts?"

Ever the peacemaker, Elisabeth stepped between them. "Lord Kerr is aware of our sympathies, Mr. MacPherson." She gave Donald a sideways glance. "You'll find my husband quite trustworthy."

"Is that *richt,* sir?" Angus asked, his brow creased with doubt.

Donald grunted his assent, though his gaze was fixed on Elisabeth. *Trustworthy.* Was she toying with him? Testing him? Had she seen through his duplicity after all?

"As it happens, I do have news," Angus continued. "Come the morrow Edinburgh will have a new sovereign."

His bold pronouncement caught Donald's ear, drawing him back to the issue at hand. "Have you nothing more to tell us than that, MacPherson? 'Tis common knowledge no army stands between the rebels and the capital."

Angus wagged his index finger. "Aye, but how and whan they'll arrive is not so widely *kenned* —"

A shout sliced through the air like gunfire, ending any discussion. All at once folk began moving en masse toward Parliament Close, bumping against one another like sheep being herded into the fold.

Elisabeth reached for Donald's hand as Angus and Rob were swept away by a different current. If the snippets of conversation flying about could be trusted, the Lord Provost had convened a public meeting. Donald fought to keep Elisabeth close by his side, while she gripped the brim of her hat, lest it be knocked to the ground and she along with it.

Twelve-story buildings lined the narrow confines of Parliament Close, shutting out much of the late afternoon sunlight. The shoving, jostling, elbowing crowd made their way toward the High Kirk of Saint Giles, their voices at a fever pitch. Donald guided Elisabeth up the low steps leading to the massive arched entranceway. Both wooden doors had been thrown open to receive the human flood.

He found a seat for his wife at once and stood behind her, hands resting on her shoulders. The aisle quickly filled with an anxious citizenry, subdued for the moment by the cool, dank interior of the old kirk with its Gothic arches sweeping high overhead.

" 'Tis easy to feel insignificant in such a place," Elisabeth said, her head tipped back to take it all in.

Donald was about to respond when he spotted the lithe figure of Lucy Spence. The fair-haired widow, still young at two-and-twenty, stood amid a knot of women huddled against one of the broad stone pillars. Had Lucy seen him? Would she turn those cool green eyes his way?

Aye.

However difficult, he averted his gaze. It

was perilous even to look at Lucy with his wife so near.

The crowd began to stir, drawing Donald's eyes toward the front of the church. "Ah, there's the Lord Provost," he told Elisabeth, lightly squeezing her shoulders. "Now we shall see what's to be done."

Almost immediately the shouting resumed. "Surrender!" rang out the loudest. When the Lord Provost asked if the dragoons should be brought within the town walls, the assembled cried, "Nae dragoons!" When he pressed further, demanding to know whether or not Edinburgh should mount a defense, the answer was clearly, "Nae defense!"

No sooner had the Lord Provost finished than a commotion at the door captured the crowd's attention. Heads craned and young lads stood on tiptoe as a plainly dressed messenger made his way toward the front. "A letter for the town council," he called out, waving his offering.

Mr. Orrock, the dean of shoemakers, broke the seal and unfolded the letter with a flourish, then began to read.

"Cease!" the Lord Provost demanded, bearing down on the man. "I will know the signature before I'll allow this letter to be made public."

With noticeably less confidence, Mr. Orrock read aloud, "Charles P. R."

Elisabeth stifled a gasp. "Prince Regent,"

she whispered, looking up at Donald.

He nodded grimly. Charles Edward Stuart was asserting his right to wrest the throne from King George's grasp. Could the prince and his army manage such a feat?

"Enough!" The Lord Provost snatched the letter from the shoemaker's hand. "The town assessor will rule on the reading of this." He stamped out of the kirk, a stream of people trailing in his wake.

Donald helped Elisabeth to her feet. "Suppose we find my brother. I would know his view of the day's events."

"Andrew will have much to say," she agreed, taking Donald's arm as they merged with the crowd flowing back into Parliament Close.

The conversations round them were more heated than ever. "Ye dare not sleep in yer beds," one older fellow warned, stabbing the air with his walking stick to punctuate his words. "They'll run ye through with their swords!"

"Och, they'll do nae such thing," shouted a fishmonger with a basket of oysters strapped to his back. "They're Hielanders, not savages."

" 'Tis a' the same," a red-faced woman complained, her frown a permanent fixture.

Donald and Elisabeth had not moved ten steps when Rob MacPherson reappeared, his skin flushed, his eyes like pierced tin lanterns, dark but glowing. "A moment if I may, Leddy Kerr." Rob leaned closer to Elisabeth, his voice too low to be overheard. Did the man never speak up?

Donald watched the two of them, heads bent together, surprised at the spark of jealousy that shot through him. Rob MacPherson was a tailor's son, unworthy of Elisabeth's regard. She was merely being polite. Yet whatever Rob was saying, her eyes had widened considerably. News from home, perhaps?

All at once Donald felt a woman's hand brush the small of his back. *Lucy?* He'd almost forgotten she was there. Almost, but not quite.

Elisabeth seemed rather engaged. Could he risk a quick glance? Fighting a losing battle, Donald looked over his shoulder in time to see the fisherman's widow pass by, hiding a knowing smile behind her handkerchief.

TWELVE

Vexations may be petty,
but they are vexations still.
                    MICHEL DE MONTAIGNE

Lady Woodhall's clock chimed half past six. The brief, muted sound drew no one's attention, save Marjory's. She'd purposely sat facing the mantel, her back to the window, preferring not to see Edinburgh in a state of misery and chaos.

A trio of like-minded friends shared the round tea table. Lady Falconer dabbed at her mouth with a linen napkin while Lady Ruthven stirred yet another spoonful of honey into her cup. Plates of lemon cake dotted with orange peel had come and gone, as had several hands of whist. Only tea and lukewarm conversation remained.

The sterling spoons were numbered so when the maidservant whisked away the china cups to be refilled, they were returned to the proper guest. A spoon resting on the saucer was an unspoken request for another cup of tea. Marjory had lost track of how many she'd enjoyed. Four? Five? But they were such *small* cups. Despite the exorbitant price demanded by smugglers and merchants alike, surely Lady Woodhall would not begrudge a thirsty friend.

Marjory lifted her spoon, wondering if she dared place it on the saucer again.

"Have another," Lady Woodhall insisted, crooking her finger to summon her maidservant. "Fresh cups all round, Jenny, before the Highlanders abscond with my silver."

A moment later Marjory's hands shook as she lifted her cup. Would Prince Charlie allow his men such liberties? Entering a widow's home? Stealing her valuables? When a fleeting image of her hidden leather purses came to mind, Marjory gulped her tea, hoping to drown her fears.

Lady Joanna Falconer was the eldest among them. Her white hair no longer needed powder, and she'd given up rouging her papery cheeks some years past. Marjory found herself particularly drawn to the woman, if only because she shared her late mother's first name and her birth year as well. "What think you of Mr. Hogg's lecture yesterday morning?" Lady Falconer asked the group.

"Rather strident," Lady Ruthven replied, still eying the pot of honey. The youngest among them, Charlotte Ruthven proudly wore her black hair in a dramatic sweep of curls, without hat or powder to diminish its raven beauty. One hardly noticed her pudgy features or sallow complexion. "I have little sympathy for the Jacobite cause," she added, "but if we're forced to endure another diatribe like that one, I may shift my allegiance."

"You'll do no such thing," Lady Woodhall scolded her. "Not while your title and wealth are wholly dependent on King George's favor."

"Speaking of the peerage . . ." Lady Ruthven fixed her gaze on Marjory, then leaned forward. "On Sunday afternoon Trotter and I ventured up to the Lawnmarket, where I spotted Lord Kerr. He was not alone."

"I shan't wonder. 'Tis a very crowded place," Marjory replied, nettled by the impudent smile tugging at the corners of the woman's mouth. Charlotte Ruthven was little more than a gossip, albeit a titled one, dragging her manservant about town in search of the latest scandal.

Before anything more could be said, the butler of the house made an abrupt appearance. "News from Saint Giles, mem."

"Let us hear it." Lady Woodhall put aside her teacup and sat up straighter. "Go on, Stevenson."

"A letter was delivered to the Lord Provost from the enemy camp." He paused, seeming reluctant to continue. "Signed by Charles, Prince Regent."

"Such presumption!" Lady Woodhall fumed. "What did this traitorous letter say?"

"If *onie* opposition be made," Stevenson reported, "the prince willna answer for the consequences."

Dread washed over Marjory like a chilling autumn rain. Surrender was certain now.

"What else?" Lady Woodhall prompted him.

Stevenson shifted his weight. "If onie in the toun are found in arms against the prince, they'll not be treated as prisoners o' war."

"Meaning . . . what?" Lady Ruthven sputtered.

His face was stony. "Meaning the prince's army will cut doon onie man caught with a *wappen* in his hands. 'Tis why the Gentlemen Volunteers returned their muskets to the castle."

The four women exchanged nervous glances before Lady Ruthven broke the silence. "If the prince takes the throne on behalf of his father, what then?"

"Why, we'll stitch white cockades and pin them to our gowns," Lady Woodhall answered coolly, arching her silvery brows. "It seems the Jacobites have claimed the little white rose of Scotland as their badge. No doubt your daughters-in-law could fashion a bit of silk into rosettes for us all, Lady Kerr."

"No doubt." Marjory heard the disdain in her friend's voice. Highlanders were barely tolerated in her social circle and Jacobites not at all.

A moment later a solemn Gibson was ushered into the drawing room. "Sorry to be early, mem. Ye're wanted at hame."

Marjory felt a slight constriction in her chest. Having turned her back on the world beyond the window, now she had to face it squarely and sooner than she'd hoped.

Gibson offered his free arm, holding aloft the lantern with the other. "This way, mem."

The wavering candlelight cast ghostly patterns on the walls of the turnpike stair as the two made their descent, hastened by the chilly night air. Gibson, seldom forthcoming, was even quieter than usual, leaving Marjory to imagine the worst. *Wanted at home.* Was one of her sons ill or injured? Had distressing news arrived from Tweedsford? Would she find Highlanders ransacking her bedchamber?

"Come, Gibson." She tugged his arm midway across the darkened courtyard, where men huddled in groups of two or three, backs to the wind, conversing in low voices. Some bore firearms, and the smell of fear hung round them. "You must give me some inkling of what's afoot."

He looked down at her, his gray eyebrows nearly touching, so fierce was his scowl. " 'Tis best if Peg tells ye herself."

Peg? Marjory leaned on Gibson's arm as

114

they started up the stair toward the fifth floor. Had her maid broken a treasured goblet? Lost a favorite brooch? In a month of service, Peg Cargill had done little to annoy her. In fact the lass had proven quite useful. Elisabeth's copious hair looked more presentable, thanks to Peg's agile comb, and the table silver didn't have a speck of tarnish.

The moment they stepped withindoors, Marjory called out the maidservant's name, then tarried in the entrance hall, cape unbuttoned, waiting to hear Peg's leather shoes scuffle across the kitchen floor. "Peg?" she tried again. The stillness in the house was unnerving.

Only one candle burned in the vacant drawing room. Had her family retired at so early an hour? "Donald?" She pretended not to notice the tension creeping into her voice. "Andrew?"

Gibson lifted the cape from her shoulders. "Beg pardon, mem, but Lord and Leddy Kerr have yet to return from the mercat cross."

"Mrs. Edgar, then. She'll know something."

He gestured toward the empty kitchen. " 'Tis Mrs. Edgar's day aff. She'll not be hame for a wee bit."

Marjory almost stamped her foot so great was her frustration. "Then where is Peg, or has she quit the place as well?"

A small voice behind her said, "Here I am,

115

Leddy Kerr."

Marjory turned to find her maidservant dressed in the same brown rags she'd worn the day she entered into service. "Have you ruined your blue gown? 'Tis but a fortnight old."

"Nae, mem. I left it hanging in the kitchen with my apron."

"I see." Marjory did not bother to hide her displeasure. "Am I to assume you, too, have elected to make this your day off?"

"In a manner o' speaking, mem." Peg lowered her gaze, her freckled cheeks scarlet. "I'm bound for Coldingham, whaur my sister lives. And I'll not be coming back."

"What?" Marjory cried. *The ungrateful chit!* "You've been here only a month."

"Aye," Peg said softly, then lifted her chin. "Forgive me, Leddy Kerr, but I canna stay. Not with . . ." Her voice faltered. "Not with the Hielanders at *oor* door."

A handful of arguments rose to Marjory's lips and fell just as quickly. Hadn't one of Lady Falconer's servants abruptly left that morning? Like rats leaping from a sinking ship, peasantry and gentry alike.

"I'll not provide a written character," Marjory cautioned. Her only weapon, yet one with a dull blade. Any servant could account for an idle month between positions. With some reluctance she pulled a silver coin from her hanging pocket. "As to your wages, I'll

116

give you the one shilling you're due and not a penny more."

"I canna blame ye, mem." Peg curtsied longer than necessary, then stood, clutching the single coin and a small bundle of goods to her chest. " 'Tis *thankrif* I am, Leddy Kerr. Ye were kind to take me into yer hame."

The maid's meek demeanor pricked Marjory's conscience, softening her tongue. "Away with you, then, since I cannot force you to stay."

Peg nodded, already inching toward the door. " 'Tis a *lang* road to the sea."

"Aye, it is." Marjory turned, hiding her disappointment. "Gibson will send you with supper."

Marjory waited until the two servants slipped into the kitchen, then sought her bedchamber. A dull, relentless pain throbbed beneath her temples. Too much tea and far too much gossip. And now this.

She paused by the window and stared into the inky expanse below. Torches and lanterns danced about as if borne on the wind. *Wars and rumours of wars.* How long until she heard the cadence of rebel soldiers marching down the High Street? The sound alone might stir Andrew's patriotic fervor beyond recanting. Was he enlisting even now, signing his life away and dragging Donald into battle with him?

As she massaged her aching brow with her

fingertips, Marjory glanced at the door to the adjoining bedchamber. Might she find some hint of their whereabouts? Curiosity drew her over the threshold, candle in hand. She was greeted by the distinctive scent of musty paper mingled with the richness of leather. Even shrouded in darkness, Donald's room revealed his bookish nature. He was a scholar, not a soldier. His place was here, surrounded by great minds and lofty thoughts.

From the corner of her eye, she spied a small volume on Elisabeth's dressing table. *The Ladies' Diary: For the Year of our Lord 1745.* One of Donald's many gifts to his wife. Marjory opened the cover and was surprised to find the almanac well used. Notations in Elisabeth's hand filled the narrow margins.

Marjory squinted, holding her candle closer. On each page the new moon was marked and another date circled: *27 January. 26 April. 24 July.* Keeping track of her courses, perhaps? The next one fell four days hence: *20 September.* Marjory would say nothing, merely be mindful of Elisabeth's changing moods come Friday.

She'd almost closed the book when she found a line of verse handwritten inside the front cover. *Ye moon and stars, bear witness to the truth!* Milton? Or was it Dryden? Marjory gazed at the poet's words, wondering what they signified for her dark-haired

118

daughter-in-law. *The moon. The truth.* A keeper of secrets, that one.

Marjory's attention drifted toward the entrance hall. Were those footsteps on the stair? And familiar voices? She abruptly shut the book and quit the room, her headache forgotten. Gibson had already thrown open the door by the time she reached his side. In a trice the hall was filled with people, all talking at once.

"We were almost home," Andrew began, "when the Deputy of Magistracy sent out a coach."

"Bound for Gray's Mill." Donald handed his cape and gloves to Gibson. "The deputies are meeting with Prince Charlie."

Marjory's breath caught. Gray's Mill was but two miles away. Were the rebels so near?

" 'Tis not all we've learned." Andrew's eyes shone, and his skin was flush with excitement. "Sir John Cope and his troops have been spotted off the coast of Dunbar. In a day or two they'll be marching toward Edinburgh."

"Isn't it thrilling?" Janet slipped her arm round Marjory's waist. "Oh, the things we've seen and heard today! However shall I sleep?"

"Come, you must tell me everything," Marjory insisted. "And I've news to share as well. Our Peg Cargill has deserted us. Frightened off by the Highlanders."

Donald's eyebrows lifted. "Truly? She said that?"

"What a shame," Elisabeth commented, the only one among them who seemed genuinely saddened by Peg's departure.

"A maidservant is easily replaced," Marjory assured her. "A monarch, however, is not. With a rebel prince at our gates, none of us may sleep tonight."

THIRTEEN

'Tis morn. Behold the kingly day now leaps
The eastern wall of earth with sword in
  hand.
JOAQUIN MILLER

Slowly, quietly Elisabeth eased her legs over the edge of the bed. Something had awakened her, like the sharp cry of a wounded animal. Or had she dreamed that? All was silent now. Beside her, Donald slept undisturbed. She could only guess the hour. Four o' the clock perhaps. Their bedchamber was bathed in darkness, the coals having long since turned to ash.

She'd tossed to and fro most of the night, troubled by Rob MacPherson's whispered news at Parliament Close. "Yer brither has come oot for Prince Charlie."

"Simon?" Her heart had leaped to her throat. "Are you certain?"

"Make nae mistake, Leddy Kerr. He declared his *lealty* and stands ready to fight, *whatsomever* patch o' God's green grass lies beneath his feet."

Simon was barely eighteen, yet a more loyal Jacobite could not be found in Castleton of Braemar nor in the hills and glens round it. All through his youth he'd recited the failings of the foreign Hanoverians and sung the praises of the royal Stuarts — sentiments learned at their father's table. When James Ferguson died, his son's zeal only grew stronger.

Elisabeth knew this day would come, when Simon would fight for the Stuarts. She was proud of him, aye. But she was frightened for him as well.

Rob had also whispered, "Come to the shop afore daybreak, and dinna tell a soul."

She glanced at the inky windows facing the High Street. Did the MacPhersons know her brother's whereabouts? Was that why they'd summoned her to their shop? If so, she might be reunited with Simon that very hour, before the sun gilded the rooftops.

Hurry, lass!

Elisabeth found her way across the darkened bedchamber all the while listening for Donald's steady breathing. Guilt tightened her stomach. But had she told him of her errand, her husband might have forbidden her to go and that would never do.

Still, if the town guards stopped her en route, if they thrust out their long wooden poles and snapped the metal hasp round her neck . . .

Nae. Elisabeth yanked hard on her stays, refusing to consider such a dire turn of events. She would come and go with the utmost haste, speak to no one except the MacPhersons, and return home before the household lifted their sleepy heads.

A simple costume was in order. She donned a plain drugget gown, the sort a servant might wear, without hoops or excessive petticoats to encumber her. Her low-heeled shoes were leather, not brocade, and a hooded cape in heathery gray wool concealed her unbound hair and much of her face.

Having properly disguised herself, she faced another challenge: walking through a slumbering household undetected. Janet and Andrew's bedchamber came first. Elisabeth tiptoed past the sleeping couple, averting her gaze, grateful for the thick carpet.

In the kitchen the lingering aroma of lamb stew hung in the air. Mrs. Edgar did not stir when Elisabeth passed by the housekeeper's makeshift bed beneath the wooden dresser nor when she took a lighted candle from the mantel over the hearth.

Nor did she wake Gibson, snoring in his folding bed in the gloomy entrance hall. Elisabeth waited until he drew a loud, rumbling breath before she moved the heavy bolt. When he snored again, she pulled open the door and slipped out, then started down the stair, feeling rather than seeing each step.

The morning damp crept through the folds of her wool cape. She shivered, though not from the cold. Every noise round her was magnified. When a door creaked somewhere below, she nearly lost her footing, so loudly did the hinges complain. A dog barking in the distance sounded near enough to bite her ankles. When at last she reached the deserted square, she cupped the flickering candle with her hand and hastened across the plainstanes.

Daybreak would not be long in coming. Already the rectangle of sky above her was changing from deepest blue to dark, smoky gray. Gulls sailed over the sleeping town, their cries muted by the moist air. Few folk were abroad at that early hour, and none met her gaze. Such solitude would not last. In another hour merchants would throw open their shutters, taverns would welcome their first patrons, and Edinburgh would greet the day with fear and trembling.

But not yet.

Just beyond the Tron Kirk stood the town guardhouse, a low, shabby building erected in the middle of the High Street. The "black hole," some called it, a disreputable place for all its civic importance. Elisabeth always gave it a wide berth. Several decaying guards usually hung round the door in threadbare uniforms and rumpled tricorne hats, sharing a pint of ale.

But not this morning.

Elisabeth's steps slowed, and her eyes widened. *'Tis not possible.*

A company of soldiers surrounded the guardhouse: armed, silent, and alert. Even in the murky light, she recognized their belted plaids and short coats, their broadswords and targes, their blue bonnets and white cockades. *Highlanders.*

Her heart began to thud.

The prince's men are here. In Edinburgh.

Elisabeth could not move, could hardly breathe. For weeks all had waited for the rebels to come charging through the West Port. Now they stood before her on a dark Tuesday morning, having quietly overtaken the town.

Tears stung her eyes as an ancient pride welled inside her. Think of it! Highland clansmen guarding the capital and a Stuart king returning to the throne. How many Jacobite Risings had there been in years past, with no success? Two? Three? Now it seemed as if there might be a chance.

Emboldened, she drew close enough to hear the soldiers' voices, rich with Gaelic. To a man they were built for warfare, with broad shoulders and sturdy legs. No wonder the dragoons had galloped off at the sight of them.

Her candle, exposed to the capricious morning breeze, was quickly snuffed out.

Still, she could see the men well enough. And they could see her. A gruff voice demanded in English, "State yer business, lass."

She spoke as boldly as she dared. "I am bound for the tailoring shop of Angus Mac-Pherson." If they knew of his Jacobite ties, his name alone might keep her safe.

The men consulted one another, eying her as they did. She heard Angus's name repeated several times along with that of Lochiel, chief of Clan Cameron. These were his men, it seemed, from the western Highlands.

Elisabeth studied their ruddy faces, weathered by years on the mountains and moors. Strong, square jaws set off their prominent features. Untamed hair poked from beneath flat bonnets. And a fierce glower darkened each gaze.

Their spokesman appeared to be an officer, with his greatcoat and tartan trews. When he addressed her again, his voice had lost its rough edge. "Aye, we ken the name Mac-Pherson but canna tell ye whaur to find him."

Only then did the thought strike her: Simon might be a stone's throw away. 'Twas unlikely he was part of Lochiel's contingent. But if he was. Oh, if he was . . .

She braved a second question. "What of my brother, Simon Ferguson, from Castleton of Braemar. Does he stand with you?"

The officer looked to his men. All were shaking their heads. "Beg pardon, lass. We

126

dinna ken yer brither."

Disappointment seeped into her soul, chilling as the morning mist. "I'm sorry to have troubled you."

"Och! A bonny lass is the best sort o' trouble," one of the soldiers called out. The others round him laughed.

Elisabeth lifted her chin, a retort on the tip of her tongue. She'd not been addressed in so coarse a manner in many seasons. Her title, however, would not serve her well this morn, nor would her pride. She slipped the cooled candle stub and holder in the hanging pocket round her waist and turned to go.

"Bess!"

Startled, she spun round to find Rob Mac-Pherson heading toward her, a looming mass in dark brown serge with a broadsword strapped to his side. His club foot altered his gait but did not slow his steps.

Elisabeth hurried to meet him. "Mr. Mac-Pherson, did you know —"

"Aye," he admitted, taking her arm and steering her away from the guardhouse. "An hour ago my *faither* waited on this side o' the Netherbow Port for a detachment o' the prince's army approaching from the east. The porter, as daft as they come, opened the gate to let a carriage through." Rob grinned. "Nae Hielander worthy o' his plaid would've missed such a chance."

"How many men?" she asked.

"Two dozen at the gate with nine hundred on their heels. Captain Macgregor led them through the port with drawn swords and a *frichtsome* shout."

Elisabeth nodded as the pieces fell together. "Their battle cry woke me."

Rob looked up at the rows of shuttered windows. "Still the toun slumbers."

"But you've not slept."

He shrugged, his eyes bleary, the shadow of a beard darkening his cheek. "Wha could on such a *nicht?*"

As they started downhill together, Elisabeth asked, "Have you any news of Simon?" When he shook his head, she explained, "I thought that might be why your father summoned me to the shop."

"Aye . . . weel . . ." Rob cleared his throat, his face turning ruddy. " 'Twas not my faither's idea."

"But —"

"I meant to be waiting at the foot o' yer stair," Rob said in a rush of words. "To escort ye to Netherbow Port so ye might watch the Hielanders enter the toun and *mebbe* catch sight o' yer brither. But the army slipped through the gate sooner than we *thocht . . .*" He shrugged, clearly embarrassed. "Forgive me, Leddy Kerr. I didna mean for ye to be alone on a murky street with Lochiel's men."

"I was not alone for long," Elisabeth reminded him.

Rob glanced back over his shoulder. "Keppoch, Ardshiel, and their clansmen are gathering at Parliament Close. 'Twill be a rude awakening for the magistrates."

And for the Kerrs. Elisabeth gathered her cape about her. "I must away, sir."

"So ye must." He glanced up at the sky, growing lighter by the second, then turned his dark gaze on her. "Make haste, milady, or ye'll be missed."

FOURTEEN

All is to be feared
where all is to be lost.
GEORGE GORDON, LORD BYRON

Home. Home. Home.

The words pounded in Elisabeth's heart as she fairly flew down the High Street toward Milne Square. She could not delay, or the household might wake to find her gone.

Nae, a hundred times nae!

Only now did the gravity of her situation sink in. A married woman of quality always traveled with a chaperone, not only for her own safety, but also to guard her husband's good name. Yet she'd dashed into the street without giving either concern a passing thought. Elisabeth weighed those things now, hastening across the empty courtyard. However would she explain her absence?

Mr. MacPherson sent an urgent summons. No need to mention which MacPherson. *With the rebel army upon us, our visit could not wait for dawn.* That sounded plausible, did it not? *I thought it might concern my Highland family.* Surely the Kerrs would be sympathetic, unless the dowager demanded to know where her daughter-in-law's loyalties rested.

The first light of day followed Elisabeth up the forestair: a pale wash of gray lapping at her skirts. She turned at the landing and tarried beside Mr. Baillie's doorway, letting her eyes adjust to the darker steps ahead, wishing her candle still burned.

All at once the merchant flung open his door, startling Elisabeth out of her wits.

"Leddy Kerr," he cried, "I thocht ye a bluidy rebel!" Mr. Baillie sank against the doorjamb, knocking his nightcap askew. His gray hair stuck out like pins in a cushion, and his chin bore two days' worth of stubble. "Pardon my appearance, mem. I feared the Hieland army had slipped into toun like *reivers* in the nicht."

"So they did," she confessed. "A small company took the guardhouse."

Mr. Baillie groaned. "Here at last, then. But are there not thousands o' men?"

Rob MacPherson's tally came to mind, but she thought better of sharing it. Instead, she repeated Donald's words. "Not so many as that."

"Whatever the number, we've an unchancie day afore us." The merchant wagged his head. " 'Twas kind o' ye to bring yer auld landlord the news."

Elisabeth fell back a step. Mr. Baillie thought she was abroad for his benefit! How else to account for her appearance at his door? She held her tongue, rather than speak a lie into the cool morning air.

"*Awa* with ye now, Leddy Kerr." He glanced up the stair with a weary smile. "Ye'll be wanted at hame."

Elisabeth lifted her skirts and dashed up the stone steps, her heart pounding like a brass clapper, as the bells of Saint Giles tolled the hour of six. *Too late, too late.* Why had she tarried in the street and on the stair? Gibson and Mrs. Edgar were surely awake by now, though without Peg's assistance, they might be slower in attending to their morning duties.

When at last she eased open the front door, Elisabeth held her breath. *Let the house be dark. Let the Kerrs be sleeping.*

But her silent pleas were not answered.

Candles blazed in every corner, and voices echoed in the adjoining rooms. Gibson met her in the entrance hall, his voice as thin as watery porridge. "Leddy Kerr," was all he said as he gave a timid bow. Nearer the kitchen Mrs. Edgar curtsied, her face pallid.

Elisabeth slowly closed the door behind her. "Is Lord Kerr —"

"He is." The dowager stood at the threshold of the drawing room. Her hands were by her side, clenching her skirts.

Elisabeth waited for her mother-in-law to say more. To chastise or scold or belittle. Finally Elisabeth could bear the silence no longer. "I had business with Mr. MacPherson that could not wait." Her rehearsed words sounded like nonsense to her now. "Do forgive me —"

"It is not my forgiveness you need." Marjory's features were stony. "Your husband is the one who discovered you'd abandoned his bed without a word of explanation. What were we to think? That you'd run off to Gray's Mill to conspire with the enemy?"

"Nothing of the sort," Elisabeth protested even as a measure of guilt rose inside her. She *had* spoken with the prince's men, and much closer to home.

Marjory moved forward, her eyes narrowing. "Or was your nighttime outing more personal in nature?"

Elisabeth gasped. "Nae!"

"That's quite enough." Donald entered the room, stepping round his mother as if she were a statue. "My wife is home now. 'Tis all that matters."

Elisabeth felt the hardness of his gaze, the coolness of his touch as he clasped her hand and drew her to his side. "Forgive me, Donald," she murmured, not caring who overheard her informal address. "I meant to return long before this."

Marjory made a *st-st* sound against her teeth and showed the couple her back, marching into the drawing room with a single command. "Breakfast."

While the servants hurried to do their mistress's bidding, Elisabeth remained in the quiet entrance hall with a husband who had every right to be furious with her. She turned to face him, searching for the right words. "Donald, I —"

He kissed her, his mouth hard against hers, muting her apology. When he finally eased away from her, his eyes bore a faint sheen of tears.

"Please, Donald —"

"Listen to me." His voice was rough with emotion and dangerously low. He pulled her into a corner where the household could not see them. "I know you're a grown woman, capable of fending for yourself. But when I woke . . . when you were gone . . ." He gripped her shoulders as if he might shake her. "Elisabeth, you cannot imagine . . . you cannot fathom what I thought."

"Oh, Donald!" she cried softly. "I never meant —"

"Don't you see? I thought I'd lost you."

Her mouth fell open. "Lost me?"

"To the Jacobites. To the Town Guard. To some . . . lothario, some seducer of women." Donald released her, his expression one of pure agony. "You do not know what men are

134

capable of, Bess. You do not understand."

"But I do." *Oh, dear husband, I do.* "I am truly sorry I left without telling you. Foolishness on my part, nothing more."

"You are many things, Bess, but foolish is not one of them." After a moment he brushed a kiss across the crown of her head, then lifted the wool cape from her shoulders. "So, what was this vital errand that coaxed you from my bed?"

Elisabeth hesitated, not wanting to anger him afresh. "You'll remember Rob Mac-Pherson approached me in Parliament Close yesterday. He asked me to come to the shop before dawn. And to tell no one."

Donald frowned. "You were most obedient on that count, milady."

"I thought it might be news from home," she hastened to explain. "Simon is eighteen now. Old enough to follow his convictions." Would Donald grasp her meaning? Perhaps she'd best speak plainly. "Simon came out for Prince Charlie."

Donald arched his brows. "Your brother intends to fight?"

"He does. I thought the MacPhersons might know Simon's whereabouts, might take me to him." She touched his arm. "Donald, I *had* to go, don't you see?"

"Not entirely." His scowl seemed mostly for effect. "Why didn't you let me escort you to MacPherson's door?"

"Because you are Lord Kerr," she said simply. "I thought it best not to involve you in Jacobite matters."

"Guarding my reputation, were you?"

"As it happened, Rob met me near the town guardhouse." Elisabeth paused, certain he'd not heard the news. "I discovered the prince's men there, standing at attention."

Donald's scowl faded into a look of disbelief. "You saw the rebel army?"

"I did." Elisabeth took his arm and nodded toward the drawing room, glad to be back in her husband's good graces. "Suppose we have breakfast, and I'll tell you what's transpired while Edinburgh slept. Auld Scotland is about to have a new king."

FIFTEEN

But who the pretender is, or who is King —
God bless us all — that's quite another
thing.

JOHN BYROM

Standing in the forecourt of the palace, Marjory longed to cover her ears, so deafening was the drone of the bagpipes. But she could not risk letting go of Donald for fear of being trampled. The music, the shouting, the constant huzzahs made conversation difficult. They could only nod at one another or raise their voices like common folk.

She'd come because her loved ones had insisted. "Royalist or Jacobite, all of Edinburgh will be bound for Holyroodhouse," Donald had assured her over a hasty breakfast. Unwilling to be left behind, Marjory had reluctantly agreed to join them, though she made certain her family knew this outing was not to her liking.

The Kerrs stood amid the throng awaiting the arrival of the young pretender to the

137

throne. Marjory refused to give him any other title. Charles Edward Stuart was by no means *her* Prince Regent. Thousands filled the grounds. Nae, tens of thousands. The heath-covered Salisbury Crags loomed over the scene, silent and brooding, while all eyes were trained on the masonry palace with its matching pairs of round towers north and south topped with conical roofs.

At least the weather was tolerable. A scattering of thin clouds hung in the forenoon sky, posing no threat of rain, and a light breeze stirred the air. Unkempt heads and tartan-covered shoulders impeded her view, but if she stood just so, she could spy the old king's tower, where the Stuart heir would soon hold court.

Nae, it cannot be. Marjory swallowed hard, trying to grasp the awful truth of it: Jacobites had commandeered the Palace of Holyroodhouse.

The Highlanders crowding the streets hadn't brandished their swords or fired their pistols, but they carried them just the same, reminding the citizenry which side had won the day. Though cannon shots were fired by the royalist forces defending Edinburgh Castle, little else was done to dissuade the rebels who'd overrun their city.

Meanwhile, Marjory's neighbors had spent the morning plying the enemy soldiers with food and drink in an effort to placate them.

She'd not followed suit. Meat and ale were too dear. Let the bonny prince fill their bellies. "Where *is* His Royal Highness?" she fumed, loath to see him, yet impatient as well.

Janet turned round to address her. "You must admit, madam, 'tis a worthy occasion. We've not had a royal visitor in Scotland for sixty years. Not since his grandfather James climbed the great stair at Holyroodhouse."

Marjory surveyed the battered stonework, the grimy windows and could only imagine the neglected palace interior. "Does he know the sorry state of his lodgings?"

"If the prince succeeds in reclaiming the throne," Andrew observed, "he'll likely reside in London."

But he cannot succeed. Must not succeed.

Marjory held her tongue, mindful of all the Jacobites within earshot. Surely Elisabeth was not sympathetic to their cause, despite that wretched business this morning. Whatever was her daughter-in-law thinking, stepping out of doors before sunrise with an invading army afoot? Naturally, Donald had defended her. Never was a lad so blinded by beauty.

From the moment they'd departed Baillie's Land, heading downhill through the Canongate, Marjory had watched her daughter-in-law survey the rebels pouring into town as if she were looking for a familiar face.

She studied Elisabeth now, resplendent in her damask gown, and hoped her daughter-in-law hadn't intentionally dressed to match the Highlanders' blue bonnets. Her cheeks were pinker than usual, and her eyes glowed with uncommon zeal. Elisabeth lacked only a white silk cockade pinned to her bodice to be counted among the rebels. *Most imprudent, lass.* Marjory would caution Elisabeth to store her blue gown in aromatic wormwood, at least until Sir John Cope and his troops resolved the Jacobite problem once and for all.

"He comes!" someone cried, diverting her thoughts. A fresh wave of anticipation rippled through the forecourt. More bagpipes stuttered to life, and the shouting grew louder. "The prince! The prince!"

Marjory stood on tiptoe, trying to see what she could. When the crowd shifted, she finally spotted the young pretender, mounted on a fine bay gelding, with some seventy or eighty Highland officers following in attendance.

Her first impression was of a tall, slender man in the prime of youth, wearing Highland dress from his tartan short coat to his red velvet breeches. He conducted himself — she could not deny — in a most princely way, generously offering his hand to the many Lowland lassies who ran forward to touch his garments or to bestow him with kisses and handkerchiefs.

But it was his light-colored periwig and fair skin, his elongated face and small mouth that gave Marjory pause. Who could have guessed that Charles Stuart would bear a striking resemblance to Lord Donald Kerr?

"Madam," Janet exclaimed over her shoulder, "I did not realize you had a third son."

"Nor did I," Marjory answered, surprised to find her poor opinion of the prince somewhat altered. It was hard to despise a young man who favored her cherished offspring.

"Lord Kerr is the better looking," Elisabeth insisted, "though the likeness is remarkable."

"One braw lad in the family will do," Donald said, poking his brother's shoulder. "The gentleman on the prince's left is his aide-de-camp, Lord Elcho."

Before Marjory could respond, one of her Monday tea-table companions appeared at her elbow. "A noble family," Lady Ruthven declared, nodding toward the handsome Elcho heir. "He's a year younger than your Andrew."

Marjory eyed the woman, curious to find her mingling so freely among the prince's admirers. Perhaps Charlotte *had* shifted her allegiance, just as she'd hinted she might at tea. "What brings you to Holyroodhouse?" Marjory asked, keeping her tone nonchalant.

The younger widow inclined her head, her dark hair swept into a loose knot, her plump mouth curled upward. "I might ask the same of you, madam."

A filthy lad in tattered clothes held up a

fistful of white muslin rosettes. "Cockades for ye, leddies?"

"Certainly not." Marjory brushed away his offering as one might a cloud of midges.

"The prince's faither will be king afore lang," the boy mumbled, trudging away. "Then ye'll change yer tune."

Charlotte glanced at Lord Kerr, then leaned closer to Marjory, an odd light in her eyes. Her voice was low, conspiratorial. "Tell me, dear friend, is all quite well with Lord and Lady Kerr?"

Marjory bristled. "Whatever do you mean?"

"Only that —"

"Leddy Ruthven?" Her manservant had arrived to collect her. Hard of hearing, Trotter could be depended upon to interrupt his mistress at the worst possible moment.

"Coming, coming," she told him, patting her hair. "Well, Lady Kerr, I am bound for the mercat cross, where a host of Highland folk are busy making grand proclamations." She winked at her. " 'Tis quite entertaining, I'm told. Care to join me?"

"I've seen enough." Marjory was beginning to wish she'd never come. Mrs. Edgar had done a poor job lacing her stays, and her new brocade shoes pinched her toes until they were numb. And now this strange business of Charlotte Ruthven worrying about Donald's marriage. "Dinner and a comfortable chair sound more to my liking," Marjory told her.

Charlotte tugged her gloves back in place. "Our paths will soon cross again. I trust your family will see you home."

The moment the widow took her leave, Elisabeth stepped round to Marjory's side, an eager expression on her face. "Could we tarry a bit longer? The prince may show himself at the tower window, perhaps even speak to his people."

"We are not his people," Marjory said evenly. "Remain here with Lord Kerr if you're determined to do so. The others can escort me to Milne Square."

" 'Tis a long walk," Andrew advised, "and all uphill. Suppose I hire a sedan chair for each of us."

"There's a good lad," she said, taking his arm. "Escort me to the foot of the Canongate. We'll find chairmen eager for our sixpence."

All at once a tradesman's voice rang out from the crowd. "If it isna Lord Kerr!"

Marjory looked round to find Donald's tailor approaching their party, his son close behind, impeded by a slight limp. The two were dressed in the manner of their trade, without wigs or hats to distinguish their appearance.

"I've a *wird* for Leddy Kerr," the tailor said. "A private wird, if I may."

Marjory bit her tongue, lest she lash out at the man. *Private? The very idea!*

"If you insist," Donald said, stepping aside. "Milady, I shall be a stone's throw away if you need me."

Marjory watched Elisabeth swiftly turn and greet the men in a too familiar manner. Why, their bowed heads were nearly touching! "Lord Kerr," Marjory fretted, "an intimate conversation between a gentlewoman and two tradesmen is not at all appropriate."

"Angus MacPherson has known Elisabeth since childhood," Donald reminded her. "Let the man speak his piece. 'Twould seem to be good news."

Marjory glanced over her shoulder. Whatever the tailor was saying, her daughter-in-law's face beneath her straw hat shone like a candle. Nae, like a chandelier.

Sixteen

Do not think that years leave us
And find us the same!
Edward Robert Bulwer, Lord Lytton

"My brother is here?" Elisabeth looked from father to son. "You are certain?"

Angus smoothed back the hair from his brow. "We've yet to speak with the lad, but 'twas Simon Ferguson we saw and none *ither.*"

Her heart felt ready to burst. "Please, tell me whatever you can."

Rob leaned closer, his broad shoulders casting a shadow across her. "We saw the lad enter the King's Park through a breach in the wa' this forenoon."

She gazed toward the expanse of land south of Holyroodhouse. "Did he look well?"

"I suppose," Angus said after a lengthy pause.

She frowned, uncertain of his meaning. "Has he been wounded, then?"

"Yer brither was limping a bit," Rob admit-

145

ted, "but 'twas the change in his face we noticed. Something to do with the *leuk* in his *e'e*."

Elisabeth pictured Simon as she last saw him: a lad of twelve, green as the pastures in May. He was standing at their cottage door, watching her ride off to Edinburgh. Chocolate brown hair, like hers. Mischievous eyes. Coltish legs. And a wistful smile.

Alas, that Simon was grown and gone.

Angus clapped a hand on Rob's shoulder. "Come, Son. 'Tis cruel to keep Leddy Kerr waiting, with Simon *sae* near the palace. Let us awa."

Rob looked toward Donald, his features hardening. "What o' Lord Kerr?"

"I shall ask him to join us," Elisabeth said, thinking to make amends for her predawn outing. She wove through the milling crowd, her eye on her husband.

"News of Simon?" Donald asked the moment she reached him.

"Aye. He's been seen." She studied his face, trying to gauge his reaction. "Will you escort me to him?"

Donald offered his arm without hesitation. " 'Twould be an honor, milady."

The martial cadence of a pibroch brayed through the air as the foursome crossed the palace grounds. Elisabeth ignored the knot in her stomach and concentrated on putting one foot in front of the other. Soon she would hold Simon's hands in hers. Soon she would know what Rob had seen in her brother's eyes.

The MacPhersons led the way through the crowd, gesturing toward a battalion gathered in the shadow of Holyrood Abbey, adjoining the palace. "Simon wore a belted plaid," Angus said. "Ye'll nae doubt ken the weave."

Aye, she would. For many years Braemar parish had but one weaver — their father, James Ferguson — who dyed his fleeces with lichen and berries, then fastened the color with sorrel. Didn't she keep a length of plaid from home hidden in her clothes press? When she saw the same hues kilted round a young Highlander, she'd recognize her brother, no matter how much he'd changed.

Donald slowed his pace as they neared the company of soldiers. "You've no need to worry," Elisabeth assured him in a low voice. "Once he sees I'm being well cared for, Simon will gladly call you his brother."

"We shall see what he calls me," Donald muttered.

She examined the men round her, looking for a familiar thatch of brown hair beneath a blue wool bonnet her mother might have stitched. A weaver like his father before him, Simon Ferguson would be well garbed. But for how long? Winter came early to Scotland,

and the windswept, barren hills made a cruel bed.

Angus and Rob were deep in conversation when her gaze settled upon a young man wrapped in a Braemar plaid. He was sitting on the ground with his back against the abbey wall, his head bent over a long-branched bayonet stretched across his lap. He had the graceful hands of a fiddler. Or a tailor.

Or a weaver. Like our father.

"Simon?" she whispered, too uncertain to address him.

He looked up. Whether he'd heard her or not, she couldn't say. Nor was she certain it was her brother. The lad sitting before her hadn't shaved that week. Nae, nor any day since Lammas. Though she couldn't make out the shape of his mouth, his long nose resembled the one she saw in her looking glass.

Then his gaze met hers. And she knew.

"Simon!" She started across the trampled grass, clutching her skirts.

He leaped to his feet, his weapon forgotten. "Bess? Nae, it canna be!"

"Aye!" With a soft cry, Elisabeth threw herself into his waiting embrace. *My dear brother.* She buried her face in his shoulder and soaked his wool coat with her tears. Soldiers stood round them on every side — shouting, arguing, cursing — the rank odor of their bodies unavoidable. Yet Elisabeth heard but one soldier, one whose plaid smelled of heather and of home.

"Six years, Bess." He held her tight against his chest. "I feared I'd *niver* see ye again."

"And I, you," Elisabeth whispered, her mind flooded with childhood memories. Clambering o'er the ruins of Kindrochaide Castle. Fishing for brown trout in the Clunie Water. Weeping at their father's grave. Laughing round their mother's table. *Simon, dear Simon!*

Finally she eased away from him, then straightened her straw hat and dried her cheeks with the back of her hand. "Forgive me," she murmured, certain she'd embarrassed him.

"Nae, my sister," he said gruffly. "Ye'll not apologize to me."

She looked at his unkempt hair. His dark, scruffy beard. His features carved from stone. He was the Simon she'd always known and yet he was not. "You're taller than I remembered," she finally said, keeping the rest to herself. "And broader."

He dragged a hand over his beard, his brown eyes studying her. "Ye've changed as weel, Bess."

She smiled at his gentle taunting. "I hope those changes are for the better."

"If ye mean yer fine gown, 'tis naught but cloth. And ye're a guid deal older."

"Now, Simon," she chided him. "No

149

woman enjoys having her attire so easily dismissed. And I'll thank you not to mention my advancing years."

"Four-and-twenty," he reminded her. "Like blackbirds in a pie."

"Simon!" she scolded him. He'd proclaimed her age loudly enough anyone might hear. No gentleman would do such a thing. But her brother wasn't a gentleman. He was a weaver's son. *And you, Bess, are a weaver's daughter.* Her years of education fell away like scales, and she saw herself as Simon did: a simple Highland lass in borrowed splendor. Older but no wiser.

Angus cleared his throat. "Leddy Kerr, ye'll be wanting to introduce yer husband, aye?"

Composing herself, Elisabeth stepped back to take Donald's arm. "Lord Kerr, may I present my brother, Simon Ferguson."

Neither man moved nor spoke, taking measure of each other.

Elisabeth implored Simon with her eyes. *Please, dear brother.* He'd yet to acknowledge the introduction. *Do something, say something.* Simon had indeed changed. A look of insolence had replaced his boyish mischief. She hadn't noticed it earlier through her tears. Now the change was unmistakable.

Finally Simon tugged at his forelock, an ill-mannered excuse for a bow. "Lord Kerr."

Elisabeth sensed the tautness in Donald's body, though he offered a slight nod in

150

response. Relieved, she reached for a safe question to ask her brother. Anything to prompt a civil conversation. "We've been following the prince's movements," she began. "Reports in the broadsheets, news in the street. Do tell us what it was like to march with him from Perth."

" 'Twas a grand adventure," Simon admitted, "fording the River Forth and marching in a lang column, three abreast." He leaned back against the abbey wall, wincing as he shifted his weight. "I twisted my leg in a ditch while tramping round Stirling Castle."

Elisabeth glanced down at his right leg, propped at an uncomfortable-looking angle. However great his pain, Simon would not welcome her sympathy. "Yet here you are, still on your feet," she said, hoping to bolster his spirits.

"I was little use at Corstorphine," he confessed, "though my strength grows by the hour." He took a few halting steps to prove it. "Whan the time comes to rout Johnnie Cope, I'll not be left behind."

"Weel said, lad." Angus beamed at him. "The prince is fortunate to have ye. Cope's men canna hope to match yer *smeddum*."

"I'm curious." Donald rested his hand on the hilt of his sword. "Was any man here ever loyal to King George?"

SEVENTEEN

All truths are not to be told.

GEORGE HERBERT

Elisabeth held her breath. *Donald, remember where you are.* Angus, Rob, and Simon turned as one to face him. Hundreds more might have done the same, had they heard Donald's question. As it was, several men nearby regarded the Kerr party with marked interest, ears cocked and gazes narrowed.

"We're a' *leal* to the king," Simon answered evenly, his brown eyes reduced to pinpoints. "The *rightfu'* one across the water. Divinely appointed."

Elisabeth looked to her husband. *Please, Donald.*

To her great relief, he slowly lowered his hands to his side. "I've no quarrel with you, lad. If God has chosen James Stuart to rule the country, and Charles Stuart after him, then rule they will."

Elisabeth rested her hands on each of their

sleeves. "We'll know soon enough. For now, I hope you'll behave as brothers-in-law since that is what you are."

The men nodded at each other, a silent truce.

"Begging yer pardon, Leddy Kerr." Rob MacPherson shifted from one foot to the other, either from discomfort or impatience. "My faither and I are to be at the mercat cross by one o' the clock."

Elisabeth nodded, knowing the MacPhersons were busy with Jacobite matters now that the prince and his men occupied the capital. She clasped Angus's hand with affection. "You've done my family a great service this day. We shall see you both in the High Street, I'm sure of it."

"And I shall see you at the Luckenbooths," Donald told them, "since I've need of a new frock coat."

Angus regarded him with thinly veiled surprise. "Ye'll not object to a Jacobite stitching yer seams?"

"Expect my custom before Michaelmas."

"Verra guid, milord," Angus replied. After exchanging courtesies, the tailors took their leave, soon disappearing amid a sea of clansmen.

"I must attend to my duties as weel," Simon told her. "But afore ye go . . ." He began patting round his wool coat. "I've a letter from hame." He dug in several pockets before

153

producing a tattered square of paper. The creases were filthy, but the seal unopened. "I've not read it," he hastened to say. "*Mither* bade me give it to ye, should we meet. And that we have." When a smile flitted across his mouth, Simon became the younger brother she remembered.

Elisabeth looked to her husband. "If I might have a moment alone to read her letter?"

"Your brother and I can manage without you" — he glanced at Simon — "provided we speak of the weather."

Stepping round a tottery stack of provisions, Elisabeth moved a few feet away. She'd received no more than a handful of letters from home in the six years she'd been gone. No matter how often she wrote her mother, a response seldom came. Bits of wax fell to the ground as the seal crumbled in her hands. Her throat tightened when she saw the familiar handwriting scrawled across the page. The Gaelic was ill formed and the lines uneven. But Elisabeth had only to read the words to hear her mother's lilting voice.

To Lady Elisabeth Kerr
Monday, 2 September 1745

My Daughter,

If this letter has found you, then so has your brother. I trust he arrived unharmed and in good health. I know you will write to me as soon as ever you can and let me know of his welfare and yours.

Elisabeth looked up to find Simon engaged in spirited discourse with her husband, his hands in constant motion. *Aye, he is well, Mother.*

When a passing soldier fell against her with a mumbled apology, nearly knocking her over, Elisabeth planted her shoes more firmly in the soft ground and tightened her grip on the paper as she read on.

No one in Castleton of Braemar was surprised when Simon came out for the prince. Yet how can a mother bid her only son farewell with gladness?

Elisabeth swallowed. She could not fathom sending a loved one off to battle, even for the most worthy of causes. Not a father, nor a husband, nor a son. Nae, nor a brother.

Now to the point of this letter, Bess. It seems I am soon to be married. You may remember Mr. Cromar.

Elisabeth stared at the page, certain she'd misunderstood. *Mother, you cannot mean this. Not Ben Cromar.*

I fear your brother will not be pleased at the

news. He does not care for the man.

Nor do I. Elisabeth swallowed the bile rising in her throat. She had never told her mother. Nae, she had never told anyone what she thought of Mr. Cromar. The bullish, red-haired blacksmith, with his callused hands and his gruff speech, first appeared not long after their father died. Mr. Cromar made himself useful for an hour or two each day, chopping wood or replacing the thatch on their roof. But even as he'd feigned interest in their mother, he'd fixed his dull but predatory gaze on her.

Elisabeth had done everything to avoid him, and still she discovered him lurking about the garden when she hung linens to dry or watching intently as she washed dishes by the hearth. Mr. Cromar never touched her, never spoke amiss to her. But each day his gaze grew bolder. She knew the time would come when he would find her alone in the cottage . . .

The thought sickened her still.

Oh, Mother, 'tis why I left. To spare us both.

When she looked down at the letter, she could not see the words for the tears in her eyes. She'd run away, thinking to protect her mother, hoping Mr. Cromar would lose interest. When her mother never mentioned his name, Elisabeth had assumed he'd stopped coming round their cottage. But he had not.

156

Please, Mother. You cannot marry him.

Alas, the letter made her mother's intentions clear.

> We plan to wed at Michaelmas. I should have told Simon before he left home. But once the prince arrived in Perth, your brother was gone almost before I could kiss his cheek. Might you tell him for me, Bess?

She looked at Simon and imagined herself reporting the dreadful news. *Mother intends to marry Ben Cromar.* How could she say those words, knowing what she knew?

> I realize it is a great deal to ask of you, and so I am grateful.
>
> Your mother

Elisabeth slowly folded the letter, wishing her brother had lost it on the march south. Aye, she would tell Simon their mother's news. She would also share her own grave misgivings.

"Bess?" Simon appeared at her side. "Is something wrong?"

She slipped the letter inside her hanging pocket. "Brother, we must speak. Alone."

"That may prove difficult, lass." Her brother sketched an arc round them, encompassing a thousand soldiers or more. "I've nae roof o'er my head nor a bed to call my ain. We'll find

157

nae privacy here."

Elisabeth nodded, her mind turning over the possibilities. Perhaps a public room, some distance from Milne Square . . .

"The inn at White Horse Close," she said at last, relieved to have thought of it. "Not far from here, at the foot of the Canongate. A crowded place, full of strangers. We'll not be noticed."

His brow darkened. "I dinna like the sound o' this."

"Naught but a bit of family news." Elisabeth hoped that would appease him for the moment. "When can we meet, lad?"

Simon rubbed his hand on the back of his neck for a moment. "I canna say. On the morrow, mebbe the day after. I'll send a caddie with a note." He looked up as a bank of clouds moved across the sun, casting a shadow over the palace. "Mark my wirds, Bess. We'll be loading oor muskets by week's end."

EIGHTEEN

Where's the coward that would not dare
To fight for such a land?
SIR WALTER SCOTT

Donald eyed the older man at his elbow. "This isn't your first rebellion, Mr. Barrie."

"Nae." He laughed, revealing several missing teeth. " 'Tis not."

While Elisabeth spoke with her brother, Donald had made the acquaintance of a veteran soldier in Simon's company. Judging by the slump of the man's shoulders and the loose skin round his neck, Tom Barrie was seventy years of age or more. But the Highlander's mind was sharp, and his valor could not be discounted.

"I fought at Sheriffmuir in the '15," Mr. Barrie said, the hair beneath his bonnet gray and thin. "A bitter *cauld* morn with frost on the marshes —"

"And now here you are," Donald smoothly interjected, "prepared to fight again." He'd already listened to a lengthy description of the Earl of Mar raising the standard for James Stuart in 1715. Donald couldn't help admiring the Highlander, with his chin scraped clean and his worn clothing neatly mended.

Mr. Barrie focused his rheumy eyes on Simon. "He learned his faither's trade, then cared for his widowed mither after Bess flitted to Edinburgh. A fine lad, that one."

"Aye." Donald watched Simon walk toward them with Elisabeth on his arm, his head held high, despite his limp. At Simon's age could *he* have taken on Cope's army? And with an injured leg? Donald well knew the answer. *Nae.*

His wife's countenance seemed troubled, yet she brightened at seeing Tom Barrie. "Look who's come to Edinburgh!" she cried, hastening to the man's side.

" 'Tis only richt I march oot with the prince," he told her, "though I fear I'm too auld for the task."

"Not at all," Elisabeth protested. "Simon will see you have food to eat and a warm plaid at night. Won't you, lad?"

Simon threw his arm round the man's shoulders. "And ye, Mr. Barrie, are charged with keeping me oot o' ditches." To which Tom, fifty years his senior, responded in kind, clamping his arm round Simon.

Donald felt an unexpected twinge of envy. Was it their easy camaraderie he envied? Their courage in the face of daunting odds?

Their willingness to die for what they believed? He'd never been part of something larger than himself — a noble cause, a glorious sacrifice. Was this what it looked like?

Maybe the warmth of the crowded park was to blame or the dust from so many footfalls, but the skin beneath his periwig began to itch. The prince's men wore naught on their heads but flat wool bonnets. Donald found himself longing to return home, toss his wig at Gibson, and go about the house scratching his scalp at will.

Elisabeth looked at him quizzically. "Is something wrong?"

"Nothing of consequence," he said, despite his prickly skin and his nagging conscience. "Milady, we've kept these men from their duties long enough."

Elisabeth gazed at her brother and sighed. "As always, Lord Kerr, you are right."

He was not always right — was often terribly wrong, in fact — but his wife's praise was a balm to his soul nonetheless. If she believed him to be a good man, perhaps he might yet become one.

They bade the men farewell and started for home. As Donald guided his wife round the north side of the palace, every soldier in the prince's army appeared ready to cut him in twain and claim Elisabeth for himself. "You've caused quite a stir," Donald observed, glaring at each man who dared catch her eye. "If you intend to visit Simon while the men are camped here, you'll not do so alone."

She paused, as if considering something, then said, "We're to meet at White Horse Close. I'll have Gibson escort me. No need to trouble you with such a task when you've more important duties."

Donald could think of no duty more pleasurable than spending time with his wife. Had he told her so of late? Or was he too busy leering at innocent maidservants and slipping through a widow's door in Halkerston's Wynd?

A jolt of pain moved through him. Not a physical ache, though it felt real enough.

Elisabeth looked at him askance. "Lord Kerr, are you quite all right?"

He banished the lie that rose to his lips and spoke the truth instead. "Nae, madam. But I am improving."

Not all battles are waged on grassy fields, he reminded himself, and not every skirmish requires bloodshed. To overcome his base desires, to do away with guilt and shame would be a worthy victory.

They made their way across the uneven cobblestones, navigating through a steady stream of townsfolk heading downhill toward the palace: pie sellers advertising the day's aromatic offerings; fishwives with baskets strapped to their backs and colorful handkerchiefs tied round their heads; lodging-house keepers wearing dingy aprons full of jangling keys. And everywhere they turned, Highlanders in kilted plaids, looking very pleased with themselves.

Donald nodded toward the sign painted on the wall. "Have we time for coffee at the Netherbow?"

"Aye," she quickly agreed. "I could do with a cup."

He ducked his head beneath the crooked lintel of the Netherbow coffeehouse, ushering Elisabeth withindoors. Low ceilinged and dimly lit, the crowded room smelled of strong coffee, bitter ale, and savory meat pies.

The affable Mr. Smeiton led the couple to a small table, where they were served almost before they settled onto wooden benches. "I've been here a' the morn lang," the proprietor told them while they stirred their hot drinks. His snug waistcoat was tailored with a thinner man's figure in mind, and his shirt sleeve bore evidence of the rich gravy in his pies. "What news from Holyroodhouse, Lord Kerr?"

While Donald described all they'd seen, Mr. Smeiton listened intently, punctuating each sentence with a nod. "Aye," he finally said, "Charlie's a braw lad. *Meikle* ado at the mercat cross this noontide as weel. Did ye hear the pipers?" He laughed and flapped his hand. "Och, how could ye not? They say

Mistress Murray o' Broughton is sitting on her horse handing oot white cockades." The proprietor winked. "In case ye need such a thing for yer bonnet."

Donald merely lifted his coffee cup, a prudent response on a day when political sympathies were shifting like the September breeze, blowing one direction, then the other. As Mr. Smeiton quit their table to welcome the next patron, Donald met Elisabeth's gaze across her steaming cup. "Your brother's a bright lad. Unwavering in his opinions."

She smiled at that. "Simon has always known what he believed and why. Tom Barrie as well. Such men can be very persuasive."

"Indeed they can." When Donald laid his hand on the table, palm up, she responded to his unspoken invitation and placed her hand in his. "Bess, I would know your thoughts on this Jacobite business."

His wife's blue eyes shone with conviction. "If you're asking do I believe James Stuart has a rightful claim to the throne, then I do."

Her answer did not surprise him, only her fervor. Did she fully grasp what a change in monarchy would cost them? Titles, lands, wealth? Those things had never mattered to Elisabeth in the way they mattered to his mother.

Before he could respond, Elisabeth pushed aside her saucer. "What of *your* heart, Lord Kerr? Have you any sympathy for our cause?"

Her question took him aback. *Well, man? Do you?* He'd seldom given much thought to politics. But he could not discount what he had seen in Simon and Tom. Their honor, their bravery struck a chord inside him, one he'd not heard before.

Donald clasped her hand more firmly. "I am" — he searched for the right word — "intrigued. More than that I cannot promise. But if you've noble arguments to offer, I'm obliged to consider them."

She leaned toward him, her countenance glowing. "No cause could be nobler than supporting the descendants of Mary, Queen of Scots. If James Stuart is restored to his rightful throne, he'll let his people worship whom and how they please." She squeezed his hand. " 'Twill be a happy day for Scotland when our king comes o'er the water."

Her ardor was undeniable — nae, irresistible.

By the time they left the coffeehouse and started uphill toward home, she'd filled his head with brave tales from past Jacobite Risings and the heroes who'd championed the cause. Caught up in the moment, Donald squared his shoulders, imagining he marched beside Simon and Tom, a plaid kilted round his legs and one of his brother's French muskets in hand.

Elisabeth matched her gait to his. "Methinks you hear the drums, Lord Kerr."

"Ah . . . well . . ." He varied his steps at once, embarrassed. "Bagpipes at least."

Was Elisabeth laughing at him? A quick glance put that concern to rest. It was not amusement he saw on her face but pride. Clearly his support of the Jacobites would please Elisabeth more than any lace-trimmed gown or conch-shell cameo.

The dowager, of course, would be inconsolable.

As they walked up the High Street, the skirl of the pipes grew louder. So did the crowd. The formal ceremonies at the mercat cross apparently had ended, with King James VIII of Scotland, England, and Ireland duly proclaimed. As the bells of Saint Giles rang out, many in the crowd sported white cockades or streamers over their shoulders.

Not every face was jubilant. Donald saw fear, anger, even hatred reflected in the eyes of some who trudged past. Prince Charlie occupied the town, but he'd not yet conquered all her people.

Elisabeth lifted her straw brim to see ahead. "Ah! Margaret Murray of Broughton. Come, Lord Kerr, for I hear she's a sight to behold."

At the mouth of Carruber's Close, they met up with the renowned Jacobite woman, surrounded by admirers. Tall in stature, with milky skin and a dark mass of hair, the wife to the prince's secretary cut an elegant figure on horseback. She wore a fur-trimmed coat and a blue bonnet with a long feather. Her drawn sword was longer still. White ribbon cockades fluttered from her bridle: a bold invitation to all willing to support the cause.

"Would you have a cockade?" Donald inquired, certain of Elisabeth's answer. He led the way, weaving through the crowd until the couple reached the woman's side.

Though the two were strangers, Mistress Murray gazed down at Elisabeth like an old friend. "I know a Jacobite rose when I see one," the gentlewoman said, her voice as regal as her posture.

Elisabeth accepted the offered cockade, expressing her thanks, then stepped aside to give others room. Only when the Kerrs reached the edge of the crowd did she open her hands to reveal not one cockade, but two.

"For Janet?" Donald guessed.

"You know better than that," Elisabeth admonished him. "My sister-in-law may be a Highlander, but she's no Jacobite. Nae, I had someone else in mind."

As she gazed at him, Donald saw the truth in her eyes. " 'Tis for me."

She tucked the silk flower deep inside his waistcoat pocket. "When the time is right."

"*If* 'tis right," he said sternly. His faint protest was unconvincing, even to himself.

Elisabeth used a hairpin to fasten the silk flower inside her sleeve, which belled from her elbow. "I fear your mother would ne'er recover if I strolled through the door with a Jacobite rose pinned to my bodice."

He tugged on the lace edging. "So you're wearing your heart on your sleeve instead?"

Elisabeth's smile was bittersweet. "Aye." She slipped her hand through the crook of his elbow and pointed him in the direction of Milne Square, stealing an occasional glance at the silken folds of the little white rose of Scotland brushing against her forearm.

By the time they crossed the threshold of the Kerr apartments, his mother was already seated at table, a look of impatience on her face. "We were about to start dinner without you."

"And now we're home," Donald informed her, feeling more headstrong than usual. He *was* Lord Kerr, was he not? He repaired with Elisabeth to their bedchamber long enough to visit the washbowl, then they joined his brother and mother at table.

Janet slipped into the drawing room a moment later, her hair in place, her gown freshly brushed. "I am here," she said, as if giving the household permission to begin.

Smoked salmon, veal collops, and roasted grouse — fish, flesh, fowl, in true Scots fashion — appeared on Donald's plate and was consumed just as swiftly. The last course, a generous serving of flummery, hot from the fire and aromatic with rose water and nutmeg, arrived in tandem with a loud and

168

untimely knock at the stair door.

Gibson nodded at the dowager, then hurried to answer the summons.

While they waited round the table, a spark flew out of the candle nearest Elisabeth and landed beside her plate.

"Expecting a letter, are you?" Donald asked, eying the black speck. According to the old custom, such a spark meant news on the wing.

Gibson reappeared, bearing a sealed note. "For ye, Leddy Kerr," the manservant said with a bow, giving it to Elisabeth. When the last plate was cleared, she slipped away to their bedchamber, breaking the wax seal as she went.

Donald tarried by the fire, reading Monday's edition of the *Evening Courant,* while the others congregated beside a window, discussing the activities below. When Elisabeth did not emerge after several minutes, he could bear the suspense no longer. Donald tossed aside the newspaper and tapped on their chamber door. "Lady Kerr?"

Elisabeth pulled him into the room, her eyes bright with concern. " 'Tis well I did not open this at table." She held up the letter. "Angus MacPherson has invited me to meet the prince this very night at Holyroodhouse. It seems they've arranged a reception."

Donald shook his head in disbelief. Hadn't the Highlanders stormed the Netherbow Port only that morning? "They waste no time, these Jacobites." Though he spoke begrudgingly, he could not deny being impressed. After the government's bumbling efforts to defend the town, it was heartening to see what men of action could accomplish.

"The prince is determined to win every heart in Edinburgh," Elisabeth said.

He grimaced. "Aye, and every purse." Rebel armies seldom had full coffers. "Who else is on the guestlist?"

"According to Angus, relatives of those bearing arms for the prince. Mothers, wives, daughters. And in particular the prince wishes to include" — Elisabeth consulted the letter, then read aloud — "a great many ladies of fashion."

None were more fashionable than his bonny wife. Donald studied her, uncertain of her intentions. "Do you wish to attend?"

"I would dearly love to, but . . ." Her lengthy sigh was laden with regret. "Donald, I cannot go without you."

"Nae, you cannot," he said firmly. The mere notion tied his stomach in a knot.

"But if you escort me, your family will think I've poisoned you, turned you against them." She stepped closer, imploring him with her eyes. "Have I done so, my love?"

He breathed in her potent scent and drew her into his embrace. "Bess, you've done nothing more than honor your family's convictions."

"But *you* are my family."

He swallowed, caught off guard by her tender words. Had he ever thought of her as his family, equal to his mother and brother? *Nae.* The bald truth shamed him to the core.

" 'Tis you who matter most to me," he said at last, for his benefit as well as hers. "If the Jacobite cause is dear to your heart, then I suppose it must become so to mine."

Her eyes glistened like stars. "Donald, are you certain?"

He kissed her, hoping his ardor might suffice for an answer. "We've others to persuade as well," he reminded her. "To that end, tonight's reception must come and go without us."

"There'll be another," Elisabeth assured him.

Donald glanced at the letter in her hand. "For now, 'tis our secret, aye?"

"Aye." She smiled, touching the silk cockade hidden within her sleeve.

Nineteen

The secret known to two
is no longer a secret.

ANNE L'ENCLOS

" 'Tis a' folk can *blether* about." Mrs. Edgar laced Elisabeth's stays as if she were trussing a partridge for roasting. "They say the candles at the palace blazed *bricht* on Tuesday eve. And *ilka* leddy curtsied to the prince in turn." The housekeeper lowered her voice, meeting Elisabeth's gaze in the looking glass. "Not a' the lords and leddies o' the toun were invited, o' course. Only the Jacobites."

Elisabeth glanced at the jewelry box where she'd hidden her white cockade. Donald's remained tucked in his waistcoat safely out of view, yet there nonetheless. The thought of it made her heart leap with joy. Her Lowland husband sympathetic to the cause!

Mrs. Edgar stepped back, assessing her handiwork. With Peg gone and three Kerr women to dress, the housekeeper's skills were

172

sorely tested. Elisabeth's coppery silk gown was poorly ironed and her hair swept into a lopsided knot loosely fastened at the crown. "Och! 'Twill have to do," Mrs. Edgar said, throwing up her hands.

"And it *will* do," Elisabeth assured her. Simon would neither notice nor care. Fine gowns were naught but cloth, he'd said.

A moment later Elisabeth found Janet in the drawing room. Lady Marjory and her sons had already had breakfast and gone abroad on various errands, leaving just the two of them. Too restless to eat, Elisabeth joined her sister-in-law at table and sat before an empty plate.

A caddie had brought round a note from Simon last evening. She would meet him in less than an hour.

"Think of it!" Janet said, carving the air with her butter knife. "A reception on the prince's first night at the palace. All the rebel ladies you might expect were there: Lady Balmerino, Miss Blair — you know, the bonny one — Lady Kilmarnock, and that wealthy Miss Christie."

Elisabeth could have named another dozen but simply nodded. "Quite a showing of support."

"*I* might have been invited," Janet said with a sniff. "Lord James Murray, one of the prince's joint commanders, *is,* after all, a distant relation of mine."

Very distant, Elisabeth knew. Still, if Janet might be won to the prince's cause, Andrew would surely follow. And if all the Kerrs came round, lending their name and their fortune to the Jacobite effort, imagine what good might be accomplished!

"If your smile grows any wider, Lady Elisabeth, your face will suffer for it." Janet was glaring at her. " 'Twould appear my family connections amuse you."

"Not at all," Elisabeth hastened to say. "Lord James Murray is vital to the cause and would surely welcome your support." *There.* She'd planted the seed and would water it often. "Janet, I confess my mind is elsewhere this morn. I'm to meet with my brother at ten."

"Oh. I'd forgotten." Janet's voice lost its sharpness. "Simon, isn't it?"

She nodded. "He was twelve when I left Braemar."

"Both my brothers are older," Janet said, not quite looking at her. "I've not seen them since I married."

Elisabeth treaded lightly, so mercurial were her sister-in-law's moods. "They've both settled in Dunkeld?"

"Aye. For good, I imagine." Janet sighed. "And here's Gibson to escort you to White Horse Close."

He stood at the drawing room door. "Whenever ye say, Leddy Kerr."

■ ■ ■ ■

Elisabeth eyed a vacant table. Even from some distance she heard the great bell of the Canongate Kirk chime ten o' the clock. "When my brother arrives," she told the innkeeper, "I shall be waiting for him there."

"Will ye, now?" The middle-aged woman squinted, her eyes disappearing in grayish brown folds of skin. "And ye'll both have a plate o' green kale, ye say?"

"Aye, mem," Gibson told her, then guided Elisabeth to the table she'd chosen, well away from the entrance in a nook all its own.

Thick, soot-blackened beams hung low across the room, and worn flagstones covered the floor. A few small windows cast enough light to see the rising dust motes. Wooden benches, rather than chairs, were drawn up to a dozen or so tables occupied by travelers, soldiers, tradesmen, and merchants. Not many women among them, Elisabeth realized, and too many male gazes pinned on her.

She perched on a bench facing the door and hoped Simon would soon appear. When her kale arrived first, she abandoned the watery, flavorless dish after the first spoonful. The round, plate-sized bannock, baked from coarse meal, had more to recommend it. She pinched off one bite, then two, until at last she spied her brother walking toward her, his limp somewhat diminished.

When Simon reached the table, Gibson said with a parting bow, "I'll be at the door, Leddy Kerr, if ye need me."

Simon dropped onto the bench without ceremony and sniffed at her plate. "I need mair than green kale if I'm to march to Musselburgh come the morn." His voice was rough as gravel. Although he'd not changed clothes since she'd seen him on Tuesday, his face was scrubbed and his unruly hair combed.

When the innkeeper appeared with a second plate of kale, Elisabeth waved it away and ordered a serving of barley broth with mutton instead. " 'Twill put meat on your bones," she promised her brother. She waited until the innkeeper lumbered away before giving Simon her full attention. "What can you tell me of Prince Charlie's plans?"

"Verra little," he confessed. "We're to quit the toun and spend the nicht in Duddingston, east o' the crags."

She well knew the Salisbury Crags, rising like a fortress overlooking the city. On the morrow she would stand atop those steep, whinstone cliffs and hail the moon, just as their mother had taught her. *Number the days and measure the moon. Circle the silver and speak the truth.* Simon and their father had always known about their monthly ritual but

176

never joined them. 'Twas a woman's art.

When her brother's rich meat broth appeared, he said nothing for several minutes, his spoon constantly moving from dish to mouth. Fistfuls of bannock followed until the plate was clean and a single gulp of ale remained to wash down the crumbs. A moment later he banged down the cup with a satisfied groan. "What's on yer mind, Bess? I canna stay lang."

She studied the table, uncertain where to begin. "Tell me about home."

"Castleton's the same as ever." He stretched out his bad leg, wincing as he did. "Hills and glens, cottages and sheep."

She lifted her gaze to meet his. "I meant, how is Mother?"

A cloud moved across his features. "She's weel enough. In guid health and guid spirits." He lowered his voice. "She and Ben Cromar are behaving like married folk, if ye ken my meaning."

Her heart sank. The mother she remembered would never have brought such shame to her door. "No wonder she bade me share her news."

"Do they mean to wed?" Simon asked her bluntly. "Is that what this is about?"

"Aye," Elisabeth confessed. " 'Tis why she wrote me."

Simon shook his head, clearly disgusted. "The woman made me carry her letter for a fortnight whan she might have told me herself? Och!"

Elisabeth could hardly defend their mother's actions, but she did try to soften the blow. "Whatever her faults, she loves you, Simon. And she knows you don't approve of Mr. Cromar."

"Aye, ye could say that," he muttered. "I'd gladly toss Ben Cromar in the River Dee and watch him drown."

Her brother's words frightened her. His expression even more so. *Something to do with the leuk in his e'e.* Aye, she saw it too. A wound that refused to heal. A memory he could not erase.

Elisabeth felt a tightening in her chest. "Simon, did this man . . . did he hurt you?"

He looked down. A long silence followed.

When he spoke, his voice was low, his words broken. "If Prince Charlie hadna come . . . I'd have left on my ain."

"Oh, Simon." She clasped his hands, not letting go when he tried to pull them away. "Will you not tell me what happened?"

" 'Twas a lang time ago. Best forgotten."

"Surely Mother —"

"She niver kenned. He's a sly one, that Cromar."

"Aye, he is." Elisabeth waited, giving Simon time, thinking he might explain. Instead, he slowly dropped his chin to his chest, revealing an ugly red scar along the nape of his neck. A burn mark, long and flat, shaped like a blacksmith's iron bar . . .

"Nae!" She squeezed his hands, fighting tears. "When did this happen? Simon, why did you not write to me?"

He slowly lifted his head. "I was four-and-ten, Bess. How was I to send a letter whan ye were far awa at boarding school?"

She closed her eyes, feeling sick. "This is my fault. I should have stayed in Braemar. I should have protected you —"

"Dinna blame yerself, Bess." He sat up, easing his hands free. "I'm sure ye left hame for a guid reason."

Ben Cromar. She made herself open her eyes. Made herself look at the brother she'd abandoned. "Mr. Cromar was the reason I left, Simon."

A spark of anger shot through his brown eyes. "Did the man hurt ye as weel? He'll not live if he did —"

"Nae, nae, Simon." She was embarrassed to confess it now. "Ben Cromar only looked at me. Nothing more, only looked."

"Oh, aye," he growled, "I ken the leuk ye mean. Had ye stayed, lass, he'd have done mair than leuk."

She nodded, grateful he understood. "Still, I should have taken you with me —"

"Nae, Bess." He gently dried her tears with the back of his hand. "Ye didna ken. Anyway, 'tis done."

There was little else to say.

He pushed back the short bench and stood. "I fear I must leave ye, Bess. I've been gone too lang as it is."

"Can you not tarry a few more minutes?" she pleaded.

"I'm sorry." He offered her his arm. "Walk with me?"

Gibson was waiting for them at the entrance. She nodded, hoping he would know to follow them. At the moment words escaped her.

Simon led her out of doors and down the stair into White Horse Close, a broad courtyard paved in stone and crowded with horses, stablers, and wheeled conveyances. Elisabeth held on to his arm with both hands, slowing her steps as they walked through the vaulted *pend* that led to the Canongate.

When they reached the main thoroughfare, Simon glanced toward the King's Park, then turned and took her hands in his. "I *luve* ye, Bess," he said gruffly.

She kissed his cheek, though her mouth was trembling. "And I love you, Simon."

He regarded her at length, as if memorizing every feature of her face. "I canna say whan we'll meet again." For an instant, she saw the young boy she'd left behind in Braemar, standing at the door with his heart in his eyes. "Hail the moon for me, Bess?"

"I will." She could not bear to let him go.

Could not bear to say good-bye. "Tomorrow, Simon. I'll not forget."

TWENTY

Early and provident fear
is the mother of safety.

EDMUND BURKE

Marjory flattened her palm against her stomach, willing her dinner to cease its arguing. Mrs. Edgar insisted she'd flavored the spiced salmon with a light hand, yet Marjory could still taste the sharp black pepper and pungent cinnamon. At least she had the house to herself. Unusual for a Friday afternoon.

Seated at the mahogany desk in the entrance hall, Marjory drew the candle nearer, peering at the latest entries in her cashbook.

Mrs. Gow, for six bottles of port: one pound, three shillings.

Mr. Noble, for two bob wigs: two pounds, one shilling.

Mr. Chapman, for ten *bolls* of meal: five pounds, seven shillings.

After Lord John's death such bookkeeping

duties had fallen to her, since Donald was more interested in words than numbers. The rental income from their Tweedsford tenants, who lived on their estate and worked the land, had to be managed each quarter. And Donald's inheritance needed careful tending.

"All gold and silver rather turn to dirt," he'd quoted the last time he'd found her squinting over the cashbook.

"Shakespeare," she'd answered after a moment's reflection. "But when that soil surrounds Tweedsford, it is rich dirt indeed."

Donald had merely smiled, as though their Lowland property was of little concern to him. He was not his father's son on that score. Lord John spent all his daylight hours walking the estate, dreaming of the gardens and trees he might plant, finding satisfaction in the fertile land and its bounty.

But then he married you, Marjory. A woman who is seldom satisfied.

Stung by the reminder, she scratched at the paper with her quill, nearly tearing the page. Hadn't she done what she could to make her husband happy? And to please her father as well? Lord John was already forty and graying when her father declared him a suitable match for a baronet's daughter with a plain face and few prospects. Their betrothal was toasted with glasses of port, a wedding was arranged in haste, and the new Lady Kerr was delivered to Tweedsford near the end of her eighteenth year.

Eight-and-ten. Had she ever been so young?

Marjory held her pen over the ink pot rather than mar the lined page swimming before her eyes. Aye, she'd been young. And impetuous too, insisting her aging husband spend his guineas showing her the world. Paris, London, Amsterdam, Brussels. Each time they'd returned to rural Selkirkshire, she'd complained of their dull life at Tweedsford.

Tedious, she'd called it. Uneventful in the extreme.

After endless cajoling on her part, the Kerrs had finally moved to Edinburgh. One season became two, then three. And then Lord John died.

Because of you.

Marjory gripped her quill. She'd learned, had she not, and so had put her sons' happiness before her own? She could not undo the past. But if she protected the Kerr inheritance, she might yet honor her husband's name. She dipped her pen in fresh ink, determined to finish before her sons returned home.

Donald and Andrew had adjourned to Mrs. Turnbull's tavern across the High Street. They'd left behind their swords but undoubtedly not their talk of the rebellion. Donald had spoken of little else since the prince's unwelcome appearance.

184

At least she'd heard one bit of good news on the stair. The Jacobite soldiers had departed from Duddingston early that morning, marching east to engage Sir John Cope and his men in battle. Donald believed their numbers were evenly matched, but she was certain Sir John would trample the rustic Highlanders beneath his well-polished boots and arrive in Edinburgh by the Sabbath, standard held high.

With the streets a bit quieter, Janet had slipped down to Carruber's Close in search of doeskin gloves for winter. Elisabeth had seemed on edge all through dinner, eying the clock, leaving her salmon untouched. Close on the heels of Donald and Andrew, she'd flown out the door at the strike of two, her gray cape swirling round her, a ready excuse on her lips. "With the army gone, I can safely visit Mrs. Sinclair in Blackfriars Wynd," she'd said. "I've not seen her in ever so long."

Something about her swift departure bothered Marjory. Though she wouldn't alert Donald until she had proof, she felt certain Elisabeth was a rabid Jacobite. A traitor in her own household! Marjory shut her cashbook, not caring whether or not the ink was dry. She swept through the house, her mind fixed on another book, one she'd discovered earlier that week: Elisabeth's almanac. Might she find an answer there?

The moment her gaze landed on the *Ladies'*

Diary, Marjory snatched it from the dressing table. With the midafternoon light pouring through the open shutters, she examined each page. Again she found the monthly record of the sixth day of the moon, including, oddly, *this* day. But there was nothing else of use. Only some marginal notations in Gaelic, which she could not begin to decipher. And a strange list of letters and abbreviations inked on the final page. The first entry made no more sense than the last: *A. H.*

Vexed at not uncovering a more telling snippet of information, Marjory circled round to her first notion: that the calendar was marked for Elisabeth's courses. After nearly three years without a child, her daughter-in-law's concern was understandable. No gentlewoman discussed such things, of course, but servants were often more informed and less discreet.

"Leddy Kerr?" Mrs. Edgar stood in the doorway, a market basket on her arm.

"Goodness, woman!" Marjory closed the book with a snap.

"Beg pardon, mem. I didna mean to startle ye." The housekeeper eyed the almanac. "Isna that Leddy Kerr's buik?"

Marjory lifted her chin. "I am merely trying to ascertain if my daughter-in-law . . . that is . . . if I'm to be . . . a grandmother."

Mrs. Edgar's brow knitted for a moment. "Oh, I ken what ye're saying now. I dinna

186

think sae, mem. Not this month." Mrs. Edgar dug in her apron pockets until she came up with a letter. "Mebbe this will cheer ye. Leddy Ruthven's man bade me deliver it to ye. We met in Fleshmarket Close just now."

Marjory took the letter with some misgivings. She'd not spoken to Charlotte Ruthven since their paths crossed in the forecourt of Holyroodhouse, but she remembered the woman's pointed inquiry: "Is all quite well with Lord and Lady Kerr?" Naturally they were well. What a thing to ask!

The woman was an incurable gossip who saw things that weren't there and revealed more than she knew. But since Lady Ruthven traveled in the highest circles, Marjory could not ignore her. Not completely.

"We'll have supper at eight," she told Mrs. Edgar. Surely her family would return well before then. Ordering one pair of gloves could not take Janet all afternoon, and her sons would eventually tire of the noise and smoke at Mrs. Turnbull's. Effie Sinclair was known to tarry round her tea table longer than most, but she would send Elisabeth home well before sunset. Even with the Highland rebels gone from town, the High Street was no place for an unescorted woman after dark.

Marjory retreated to her bedchamber to read Charlotte's letter. The seal opened easily, and the lines were few.

Friday, 20 September

My dear Lady K —

It is imperative that we speak. Your son's honor is at stake. Call at my door as soon as ever you can.

Lady R —

Marjory stared at the words. *Your son's honor.* Whatever was Charlotte suggesting? No son could be more honorable, more faithful than Donald Kerr. Or was it Andrew she meant? Just because he could not serve in the military did not mean her son's honor was at stake. What kind of woman made such accusations?

Marjory read the letter once more, then thrust it into the nearest candle flame and watched Lady Ruthven's words turn to smoke.

Twenty-One

How like a queen comes forth the lonely
  Moon
From the slow opening curtains of the
  clouds.

George Croly

Elisabeth stood atop the Salisbury Crags and swept her hands across the eastern sky, wishing she might part the layer of clouds that threatened to obscure her view. She had work to do and little time to spare. Without gloves, her hands were growing cold, and her unbound hair fluttered round her face whenever the capricious winds blew up the mountainside, carrying the briny tang of the sea.

Her ascent that afternoon was easily managed. The grassy slope rose gradually, leading to a rocky path near the summit. To the west lay the city in medieval splendor, the tall lands wreathed in chimney smoke. Due east was Duddingston, the small village where the Highland army was encamped. And far to the north stretched the Highlands, though with so many clouds, she could only imagine those faraway hills.

But she'd not come for the view. She'd come to worship. Nae, she'd come to do her duty.

If she knelt at the proper times, if she repeated the sacred words, might that be enough? She was certain the Nameless One could not see inside her heart. If she no longer trusted, if she no longer believed, would the waxing crescent moon be the wiser?

A chill skipped down her spine. *Be careful, lass.*

Prodded by her conscience, Elisabeth lifted her eyes, intent on her task once more. On the sixth day the moon trailed across the daytime sky in a low arc. She had yet to catch sight of it. But she knew the moon was there, so she dutifully beckoned it forth, certain her mother was performing the same rituals on the summit of Creag Choinnich, a mossy crag not far beyond their cottage door.

May the moon of moons
Keep coming through thick clouds,
On me and on every woman.

Elisabeth tried her best to sound expectant. Instead, she sounded desperate. So many concerns pressed on her heart. Her brother, her husband, her mother. Aye, and her prince as well. She'd carelessly left her almanac at home and would have to rely on her memory for the long list of entreaties.

But she required no prompting to recall the sacred words Fiona Ferguson had taught her. Elisabeth only needed the courage to say them now that they tasted like dust in her mouth.

Hail to thee, thou new moon
Beauteous guidant of the sky.

The moon was beautiful, aye. But a trust-worthy guide?

Come, Bess. She clasped her grandmother's ring. *Do not entertain such doubts. Not here. Not now. Not if you want to help Simon.*

The moon would reach its highest point near sunset, but she dared not linger. An hour was needed to pick her way down the grassy slope and reach Blackfriars Wynd. Once there, she would share a cup of tea with her former schoolmistress, just as she'd told Lady Marjory she would. "You always have a place at my table," Effie Sinclair once said.

But first Elisabeth had a promise to keep. *Hail the moon for me, Bess?* Aye, she would. Anything for Simon. Anything to make amends.

As she watched, a faint crescent, like a freshly trimmed fingernail, appeared at the edge of the sky. The time had come. *Now,*

Bess. She drew a breath and stretched her hands above her head, palms open. Like a hymn without notes, she lifted up the sacred words.

> When I see the moon,
> It becomes me to lift mine eye,
> It becomes me to bend my knee,
> It becomes me to bow my head.

With each line in turn, Elisabeth did what she knew she must. She raised her eyes, just as she'd raised her hands. Then dropped to her knees on the grassy hilltop. Then bowed her head low before the moon, not once but three times.

Now came what truly mattered: her requests, many of them pent up inside her for a full month.

She spoke them aloud. She spoke them to the Nameless One.

Simon came first. Then her beloved Donald. Then her mother, though she hardly knew what to ask for. Yet, after each heartfelt entreaty, she felt nothing from without or within. Not a whisper. Not even a faint stirring.

When her words were all spent, she waited as the minutes crawled by and her knees grew sore and any hope of being heard was lost.

She cried out to the translucent moon, "But what about my dear brother? Will you not help him? Will you not guard him and keep him safe?" Distraught, Elisabeth leaped to her feet and shook her skirts, scattering blades of grass. "Please take care of him. I promised him you would. Please!"

Nothing, nothing, nothing was there.

Elisabeth stumbled down the steep hillside, not caring if she fell, thinking only of Simon. *Please do not abandon my brother! Not like I did. Not like I did.*

Twenty-Two

On such a theme it were impious to be
  calm;
passion is reason, transport, temper, here!
                                EDWARD YOUNG

" 'Tis his crown by divine right!" Donald pounded his fist on Mrs. Turnbull's wooden table with such force that their tappit-hens jumped, sending the hinged lids clanking and ale sloshing over the side.

Andrew regarded him through narrowed eyes. " 'Twould seem Prince Charlie has won a new adherent to the cause."

Donald looked round the smoke-filled tavern, his hand gripping the pewter tankard. "Mind what you say, Andrew, and where you say it." He drank another swig of ale, bolstering his resolve. Had he truly admitted his growing affinity for the Jacobites? Aye, he had, on a Friday afternoon with half of Milne Square convened at Mrs. Turnbull's.

"The tongue that needs guarding this day is yours." Andrew held up his tankard toward

194

the boisterous crowd. "Lord Mark is in Berwick at the moment, but our cousin has many a friend in the castle. And who knows how many in the town?"

Donald nodded, swallowing the bitter truth as surely as he'd swallowed too many tappit-hens of ale. Lord Mark Kerr, a distant cousin, was a military man of high rank and no small repute. Though his quick temper had led to several duels, the flamboyant soldier held himself and others to a high standard. And as Honorary Governor of Edinburgh Castle, his loyalty to King George was unswerving.

"Aye, but what can the man do to us?"

"Do?" Andrew sputtered. "He's lethal with a blade, for one thing, and his father is the Marquis of Lothian."

"And our father is dead." Donald sank back in his chair. "Cousin or not, Lord Mark holds no sway over us."

Andrew frowned. "You underestimate him, Brother."

"He hardly knows of our existence," Donald grumbled, "considering what a trifling mark we've made in the world."

He stared into his glass of ale. Was there a man in Edinburgh who truly respected them? He and his brother were indeed gentlemen, but did they roll up their sleeves at cockfights, ready to spar with the man who'd bested their gamecock? They did not. Nor did they challenge Patrick Manderson or David Lyon to an impromptu horse race across the Lang Dykes lest Andrew tumble from his mount, unable to breathe, or either of them make a poor showing of it.

Gentlemen, aye, but not truly men.

Susan McGill's words gnawed at him. *If my brave son is willing to lay down his life for King George, so should every nobleman.* Even now, this very day, young Jamie McGill was sharpening his bayonet on the moors east of Edinburgh, while Lord Donald Kerr was sending down roots at Mrs. Turnbull's tavern, exercising only his elbow.

Disgusted with himself, Donald leaned across the table, the sleeves of his coat dragging through the spilled ale. "Do you never grow weary of caution, Andrew?"

"You know I do." His brother's sullen expression said more than his words.

"Choose a side, then, and throw yourself into the fray." He poked his index finger into Andrew's chest. "Your bedchamber wall is covered with weapons, polished and waiting. Yet what good are they?" Donald flapped his hand in the general direction of Duddingston. "Give the lot to Charlie's men. They'll see your French muskets put to proper use."

Andrew bristled. "I know very well how to handle my weapons."

"Well, then?" Donald pushed aside his ale, sorry he'd not done so sooner. "Are you strong enough to march uphill with a regi-

196

ment? Can you match your steel to another man's as soundly as you match your wits?"

Andrew worked his jaw back and forth, grinding out an answer. "Aye," he finally said, "with practice, I might make a respectable soldier."

"You would, Brother." Donald nodded emphatically. "And so would I. What satisfaction can be found in living an untested life?"

Andrew shook his head, a wry smile on his face. "Brother, I never imagined you, of all people, urging me to take up arms."

Is that what I'm doing? Goading him into battle? Donald sighed, massaging his forehead, where a headache was brewing. "Perhaps 'tis the ale talking, eh?" He consulted his pocket watch. "Past five o' the clock. What say we walk for a bit —"

"And clear our heads," Andrew finished for him, already standing. They left sufficient silver for their ale and ventured into the street, blinking at the late afternoon light.

"Up to the West Bow and back?" Donald challenged him, striking out with more energy than he'd felt in months. Nae, in years. The air was neither fresh nor fragrant, but he filled his lungs and lengthened his stride. "Whether we choose to fight or not, Andrew, I would have you at my side."

"And I, you."

The incline of the High Street robbed Andrew of any spare breath for speech. But his pace did not flag nor did his spirits. By the time they reached their goal, his brother was red-faced and breathing hard but still grinning.

"Well done, lad," Donald said, only a small lie.

Andrew turned to face Milne Square. "Downhill will be easier."

"Aye." They struck out in tandem, retracing their steps. "What think you of the prince?" Donald asked, testing the waters.

His brother shrugged. "He's about my age and favors you in appearance."

"Commendable from the start, then. And by all accounts an able soldier."

"He did have a fine seat on that gelding," Andrew agreed. "We'll know soon enough whether he's battleworthy."

"Very soon," Donald agreed and said no more.

Twilight had begun settling over Edinburgh, bathing their surroundings in shadows and mist. Men and women of every station crowded the High Street in no hurry to find their doors, while fresh gossip continued pouring into town. According to reports, the two armies were prepared to spend the night in view of each other.

The brothers passed the town guardhouse, now firmly in Jacobite hands, and were nearing Milne Square when Donald spotted a familiar figure wrapped in a gray cape. *Elisa-*

198

beth. He hastened to greet her, curiosity and concern lengthening his stride. *Where have you been, lass? Out alone, I see.*

When she looked up, mere steps away, a host of emotions crossed his wife's face. Alarm, then surprise, then pleasure. "Lord Kerr! How thoughtful of you to come looking for me."

Donald closed the gap between them. "I confess I did nothing of the kind, though I'm glad I found you." He captured her hand and tucked it round the crook of his elbow. "Andrew and I —"

"Have been sampling Mrs. Turnbull's ale," she finished for him, "while I've been drinking tea with Effie Sinclair."

He guided his wife toward home. "I trust you had a good visit with the old . . . ah, the . . ."

"We had a lovely time," she said quickly, offering no details.

Andrew stood waiting at the entrance to the square, his neck cloth untied and his wig listing slightly. "If it isn't Lady Kerr come to see these wayward lads home."

She surveyed the two of them, her dark brows arched. "I'd suggest a few minutes with Gibson before the dowager sees you."

"Och! What a clever lass you married." Andrew claimed Elisabeth's other arm and struck out across Milne Square, pulling the couple along. "You, madam, have made a Jacobite of my brother."

"Not altogether," Donald protested, though his complaint had no teeth. "In any case, history favors the Stuarts."

Andrew snorted. "So you keep insisting."

"Can it be true, Lord Kerr?" Elisabeth turned to look at him, hope shining on her face. "Are you prepared to side with the Jacobites?"

Aye, man. Say it. Donald tried to form the word but could not. Not with his brother undecided and his own conviction wavering. "At the very least," he finally said, "the time has come to tell our household of Simon's allegiance to the prince."

"You are brave indeed," Elisabeth murmured, turning her head, though not before he saw the disappointment in her eyes.

Andrew halted in midstep. "Do you think that wise, Brother?"

"I do." Donald threw back his shoulders, all at once as sober as a reverend mounting the pulpit stair. "If Simon is not already fighting, he will be come sunrise. I say we lift our glasses at table and toast his safe return."

"We've lifted our glasses quite enough this afternoon," Andrew reminded him. "But, aye, the lad deserves our support. Besides, 'tis better Mother hear this unwelcome news at home rather than at Lady Woodhall's tea table."

"Far better," Donald agreed, tipping his

head back to gaze at their fifth-floor windows, where the dowager's silhouette darkened the glass.

Twenty-Three

It is as easy to draw back a stone
thrown with force from the hand,
as to recall a word once spoken.

Menander

Candles shone up and down the supper table as Elisabeth sat unmoving, from one course to the next, certain Donald would mention her brother at any moment. How could she possibly eat with her heart firmly lodged in her throat? Her glass of claret remained untouched, the napkin in her lap pristine. Seated at the head of the table, Donald watched her closely, almost as if he could sense her inner workings.

Please speak your heart, Donald. Please speak the truth.

"Kindly eat something," her sister-in-law prodded her, "or Mrs. Edgar will think you do not like her cooking." Janet lowered her voice to add, "She's a mediocre lady's maid, but we must at least applaud her culinary skills or risk losing her completely."

Elisabeth dutifully sampled a forkful of duck breast while Donald and Andrew consumed everything in sight. Full platters of stewed oysters, kidney collops, and roasted duck were reduced to scraps. A loaf of wheaten bread, slathered in butter, utterly vanished, and a dish of potatoes and turnips followed close behind.

As for Marjory, she ate in silence, meticulously cutting and chewing each bite of food, clearly vexed about something, yet unwilling to voice her displeasure. Did the dowager suspect what Donald intended to share? Or was she merely unhappy about being left to entertain herself all afternoon? Lady Marjory Kerr was not an easy woman to read. Nor was she easy to love. However deep the waters inside her stirred, on the surface her mother-in-law remained as hard as a Highland pond in January.

Janet filled the awkward gaps in conversation with neighborhood gossip gleaned from a fruitful hour at the glover's. "Mr. Colquhoun's daughters have fled to their country estate in Lanarkshire," she announced. Her hazel eyes shone with excitement, the long curls draped along her neck fairly bouncing with each breathless revelation. "Our friend, Lady Boghall, fainted in the street when they fired the guns from the castle rampart. Can you imagine it? And Mrs. Scott, the minister's widow, is bound for Dalmeny parish, taking

Mary Dundas with her."

"What a shame," Elisabeth murmured, recalling Mary and Peg meeting on the stair, happily exchanging the day's blether. Now both lasses were gone. How many other residents had left Milne Square for safer quarters? The steady stream of leather trunks and wooden *kists* flowing down the outer stair at all hours gave evidence enough.

When their polite exchanges dwindled to sighs, Donald finally spoke up. "My brother and I have news as well, gleaned at Mrs. Turnbull's. As of a few hours ago, Sir John Cope had yet to engage his men in battle. Apparently he's waiting for the Highlanders to attack."

"True to form," Andrew grumbled. "A fussy little man, by all accounts. Neither brave nor bold in his actions."

"Aye, but there *are* courageous men on the field well prepared to fight." Donald caught Elisabeth's eye, then leaned toward his mother, his voice softening. "You may not be aware, Mother, that Lady Kerr's brother is of an age to bear arms."

Marjory swallowed the last bite of her food, apparently in no hurry to respond. Finally she said, "What has this young man to do with our family?"

"He is a member of our family." Donald emphasized each word, his irritation showing. "Simon Ferguson is my wife's only

204

sibling. His welfare should be of interest to everyone at this table."

"His welfare?" Marjory carefully placed her dinner knife across her empty plate, then waited for Gibson to remove it. "Have we cause for concern?"

"We do," Donald said firmly. "Simon marched east from Edinburgh this very morning."

Her face slowly hardened to stone. "This brother of yours . . . is a Jacobite?"

Elisabeth cleared her throat. "Aye, madam. He is."

Marjory looked away as if she could not bear the sight of her. "How has such treachery found its way to our doorstep?"

" 'Tis not treachery," Elisabeth countered without apology. " 'Tis loyalty to the rightful king."

"Rightful?" Marjory turned back to face her. "Will you now confess you are a Jacobite rebel as well?"

Elisabeth weighed her answer with care. Her family had been loyal to the Stuarts since Mary, Queen of Scots, gave birth to James VI at Edinburgh Castle. She would not deny her sovereign king. Yet her mother-in-law might never look at her in the same light. Their relationship, tenuous at best, would be strained to the breaking point.

Finally Elisabeth said what she must. "Aye, Lady Marjory. I am, as you say, a rebel."

205

Her mother-in-law turned to Donald at once. "How long have you known the truth?"

"From the first," he admitted. "Elisabeth has never concealed her support of the Jacobite cause."

"Not from you perhaps," Marjory said coolly.

" 'Twas not of any import when we married." He nodded toward Elisabeth, doing his best to include her in the conversation. "We seldom discussed the subject, lest it divide us."

"Well advised for a marriage. But you've an entire household to consider, Lord Kerr. And your title and property to protect."

Elisabeth sensed the tension in his posture as she saw his countenance darken.

"Not for one moment, Mother, have I neglected my duties."

"Son, I was not suggesting —"

"And what if Prince Charlie and his men are victorious? Have you considered that? If the Stuarts are restored, my title will be worthless and Tweedsford lost."

" 'Tis not likely," Marjory said with a sniff.

"Do not be too sure." Andrew folded his napkin haphazardly and dropped it beside his plate. "The prince has already taken Edinburgh. Who knows what the hours ahead may hold?"

Elisabeth glanced at the time. Almost nine o' the clock. "Gibson?" She beckoned him closer. "I wonder if you might make a brief visit to Mrs. Turnbull's."

"For ale, Leddy Kerr?"

"Nae," she said softly, "for news."

The manservant bowed and was gone in a trice, the door closing soundlessly behind him.

Janet stifled a yawn, then gazed meaningfully at her husband. "Sir, 'tis time we retired. I did not sleep well last night."

"Nor did I." Andrew was on his feet at once, bidding the others a good night before taking Janet's arm and disappearing with her into their bedchamber.

Elisabeth stared across the room at the dying fire, more ash than coal. Sitting with her back to the windows, she felt the cold night air seeping through the shutters. Autumn was upon them in earnest with winter not far behind.

Had she not felt a keen bite in the wind atop the Salisbury Crags? Colder still was the silence. Effie Sinclair's tea had warmed her and the lady's company more so, but Elisabeth would never forget the frozen stillness that followed her down that hill. She had done all she knew to do and said all she knew to say. Would it be enough?

Come home to me, Simon. Come home to us all.

Only her husband and mother-in-law remained with her at table. Neither appeared inclined to leave, though the air between them was as chilly as that out of doors. At least Marjory had not asked Donald where *his* sympathies lay.

Mrs. Edgar cleared the table in haste, perhaps sensing her mistress's mood. "Guid nicht to ye, Leddy Kerr," the housekeeper said and took her leave.

"Will you have a glass of port by the fire?" Donald asked his mother.

"What I will have is the truth." Marjory pressed her back into the chair as if settling in for a long evening. "You have informed me that Simon Ferguson is a Jacobite. I'd already suspected as much. And your wife has confessed that she, too, is a traitor —"

"Mother!" he said sharply.

She held up her hand. "When a Kerr opposes the reigning king, no other word will suffice. Her misplaced loyalty is no surprise to me. I feared such all along."

Elisabeth tamped down her anger but could not still her tongue. "Because I am a Highlander?" she asked, wishing her words did not sound so sharp.

"Nae," Marjory insisted, "because you hide things. Even from your husband."

"You go too far," Donald warned her. "My wife does not keep secrets."

Marjory stood, throwing down her napkin like a gauntlet. "We shall see." She practically marched into her bedchamber and left the door ajar as she continued into the next room.

Donald frowned. "Whatever is she after?"

"I cannot imagine." Elisabeth couldn't see past the corner of Marjory's bed nor through the open door beyond it. Her great-grandmother's ring was safely on her right hand. All else she carried in her heart.

A moment later the dowager reappeared in the drawing room, concealing something among the folds of her skirt. "You'll recognize this, I'm sure." She held out a small book with a look of triumph.

Heat crawled up Elisabeth's neck. "My *Ladies' Diary.*" She accepted it gingerly, as one would a scalding hot cup of tea. Had the dowager read her scribbled notes? Could she possibly have understood them?

Marjory eyed her son. "This almanac belongs to your wife, does it not?"

" 'Twas a Yuletide present," Donald said evenly, "from me."

"Lady Kerr, kindly explain the meaning of your many notations."

Elisabeth drew a long, steadying breath. "I follow with great interest the phases of the moon." She opened the book with care, intending to show Donald only the monthly calendars. "Farmers and gardeners do the same, of course. In my case the moon has a more . . . ah, personal meaning."

She stopped short. *Personal meaning?* However would she explain that? When her husband plucked the book from her hands, she nearly gasped. *Nae, Donald!* She cared little what her mother-in-law thought of her, but her husband's opinion was another matter.

"Personal, you say?" He opened to the first page and looked down at the line of poetry written in her hand. "John Dryden's translation of Virgil," he said, smiling. "A favorite of mine as well." He pointed at another line, written on the second page. "But this, I'm afraid, I cannot unravel."

Elisabeth translated the Gaelic, hoping the phrase would signify nothing to the Kerrs. "Comes the night before the day."

He nodded as if the phrase was not wholly unfamiliar. "Day unto day uttereth speech," he said, "and night unto night showeth knowledge."

She did not recognize the words, but she liked them. "A poet from your bookshelf?"

The dowager pounced on her words. "Do you not know the psalms, Lady Kerr?"

"Oh! I . . . that is . . ." *Foolish, foolish Bess.*

Donald rescued her at once. "King David was indeed a poet. And the Bible holds a place of honor on our shelf." He slowly paged through the monthly calendars. "I see you chart the moon's journey very closely, milady. Month in and month out."

"I do," Elisabeth admitted, searching for a simple explanation to give her husband.

Stargazers, fortunetellers, and mariners followed the moon's phases. But she was none of those.

Donald closed the small volume and placed it in her hands. "We'll speak of it no more, dear wife, for I know the truth."

Twenty-Four

Stay a little
and news will find you.

George Herbert

Elisabeth woke with a start, still clinging to the wispy fragments of a dream. Mist rising from the ground on a cold autumn night. The skirl of a bagpipe. And Donald, looking into her eyes, smiling as he spoke. *I know the truth.*

When he'd uttered those words last eve at table, her heart had nearly thudded to a stop. *I know the truth.* She'd feared her husband had discovered her worship of the Nameless One, now that she was uncertain she even believed in the auld ways. What a cruel irony that would have been!

As it happened, Donald had meant something else entirely. When she found the courage to ask him in the privacy of their bedchamber, Donald had kissed her brow, then explained, " 'Tis obvious you follow the waxing and waning of the moon each month as a means of reckoning . . . ah . . ."

"My courses?" When he'd nodded, relief had poured over her like a *plumpshower* on a spring day. She could never lie to her husband. But if he came to a wrong conclusion, sparing them both, what benefit could be found in correcting him?

Donald slept beside her now, his body curled toward the fireplace. She envied him his restful pose. Constantly worried about Simon, she'd tossed and turned most of the night, chilly one moment, overheated the next. Gibson had returned from Mrs. Turnbull's with little to report. In the anxious hours ahead they were sure to have news from the battlefield.

Guard him and keep him safe. She'd shouted those words to the pale moon. *Will you not help him?* Soon she would have her answer. No wonder she could not sleep.

The room was as black as newly mined coal except for the flickering seam of light along the door to Marjory's bedchamber. Was her mother-in-law awake, or had she left a candle burning through the night? Elisabeth eased from the bed, tiptoed to her door, and listened until she heard Marjory's slow, even breathing.

They'd not ended their day together well. Marjory had quit the drawing room in a huff, her parting words as sharp as any bayonet. "Would you be loyal to this family, Lady Kerr? Or to the relatives you left in Castleton

213

of Braemar?"

"I hope I may be true to *both* my families," she'd said. Wasn't that a daughter-in-law's duty?

But now in the dark of night, Elisabeth realized she'd spoken amiss. She was not loyal to either family. She'd fled from her mother's cottage, abandoned her only brother, and never found her way back home. As for the Kerrs, she lived with them, yet honored another king, worshiped with them, yet entreated another god.

Elisabeth stared into the remains of the fire, numb with a kind of grief. She had always thought herself faithful. But clearly she was not. Not to anyone.

Nae, lass. You are faithful to Donald.

Her heart lifted at the thought. Aye, she *was* a faithful wife who loved her husband completely.

Elisabeth hastened across the room, needing to be near him, needing to know that Donald was truly hers and that she'd not failed him too. She quietly slid beneath the bedcovers and fitted her body against the warm curve of his back. A deep sense of relief washed over her. *Donald, my husband, my own.*

Taking care not to wake him, she slipped her arm round his waist and let her eyes drift shut. Time would answer some of her questions. Another hour of rest might calm her fears. But the man who shared her bed offered her the deepest solace of all.

"Peace to you, my love," she whispered and drifted off to sleep.

Elisabeth's spoon clattered onto the rim of her china plate, her porridge forgotten, the morning's peace shattered. "What is it, Gibson? Good tidings or ill?"

"Dragoons, milady, charging up the High Street!" Red-faced and panting, Gibson stood at the end of their breakfast table. "Four royal lads riding hard from Gladsmuir."

"Are they bound for the castle?" Andrew cried, nearly standing.

"Come, Gibson!" Donald urged him. "You must know something."

"Let the man catch his breath," Elisabeth said, resting her hand on Donald's. "Just tell us what you can, Gibson. Has the fighting begun?"

"Aye, milady." He hastily straightened his livery, then offered a belated bow. "And ended."

Janet gasped. "Ended?"

"I ken verra little," Gibson said apologetically, "but the dragoons are seeking sanctuary up at Edinburgh Castle."

A look of horror filled Marjory's face. "Do you mean to say . . . the Highland rebels . . . have . . . won the battle?"

"I canna be sure, mem." Gibson looked

down at the floor as if ashamed to be the bearer of bad news. "But, aye, 'twould seem they did."

Elisabeth's hand flew to her mouth, stifling her cry of joy. *Victory! Oh, Simon.*

Donald was already on his feet. "Come, Andrew. We'll make for Mrs. Turnbull's and see what other news can be had."

Without thinking, Elisabeth grasped the sleeve of his coat. "Might I join you?"

"Lady Kerr!" Marjory admonished her. " 'Tis no place for a gentlewoman —"

"On the contrary." In one graceful motion Donald drew Elisabeth from her chair to his side. "My wife's place is here. With me."

Andrew glanced at Janet, seated next to him, but her only response was a petulant sniff. He stood as well, nodding at Donald, his expression stoic. "The three of us, then."

They hastened down the stair and into the gray morning light. News had spread quickly, and the square was crowded with folk seeking answers. How had a ragged army of rebels bested King George's men? Women wept into their aprons while men with unkempt hair and bannock crumbs in their beards stumbled about the square. Boisterous lads chased after one another with wooden sticks, pretending to be soldiers, making their younger sisters shriek with terror and delight.

Elisabeth took each brother's arm as they traveled across the High Street toward the tavern next to the Tron Kirk. " 'Twill be more crowded withindoors," Donald warned her, raising his voice lest his words be lost amid the noisy throng. He steered them round the muck and refuse, then quickened their pace at the sound of hooves thundering up the street.

A small company of dragoons galloped by — their uniforms torn, their faces haggard — and shouted to all who would listen.

"The rebels cut us down!"

"Hundreds are dead!"

"All is lost!"

However glad she was for a Highland victory, Elisabeth remembered the Sabbath last when the same lads had trotted through the city, polished and proud, engaging in swordplay for sport. "They were so young," she murmured, imagining the wives and mothers who would see their loved ones no more.

"Aye," Donald said grimly, then guided the threesome through the tavern door.

Crowded as it was, heads turned when the Kerrs entered. Far more men than women filled the long, narrow room with its dearth of windows and abundance of wooden chairs and tables, all spoken for.

An older fellow with copious whiskers but few teeth bobbed his head in their direction. "Lord Kerr, yer leddy is *walcome* to my chair." He brushed off the seat with his bonnet, then bowed and fitted the wool cap back on his head.

Murmuring her thanks, Elisabeth sat at a well-scrubbed oak table. Two of his friends gallantly sacrificed their places as well so Donald and Andrew could join her.

Her husband pulled the tallow candle closer, the wax nearly spent, the flame guttering. "You'd be the talk of Mrs. Turnbull's this morning, Lady Kerr, if 'twere not for more pressing matters." He ordered a small glass of sack for each of them, then called out to John Elder, a shoemaker from Marlin's Wynd and a proud Jacobite, seated at the next table. "Mr. Elder, what news have you to share?"

The shoemaker grunted as he turned in his chair, his posture bent from years of stretching leather over a wooden last. Yet his blue eyes sparkled, and his mind was as sharp as the point of his awl. "I'll tell ye whatsomever I can, Lord Kerr. A story o' woe for some, blithe tidings for ithers."

Donald gripped him on the shoulder. "None can spin a tale like you, John."

He folded his hands, the creases lined with dye, and leaned closer. "The stars still shone bricht in the nicht sky whan the prince's men made their way o'er a bog to face the royal army. Their brogues are made o' soft leather, ye ken, and they had nae horses, so the Hielanders couldna be heard."

At that moment Mrs. Turnbull appeared

218

with wine and a fresh candle. "Here ye be, Lord Kerr." The red-headed proprietor plunked down three glasses without spilling a drop, lit the new candle from the old, fitted it into the candleholder with its puddle of soft wax, then took her leave — all done in the blink of an eye.

"A model of efficiency, that woman," Andrew observed, then raised his glass. "To victory."

"To victory," the others responded, though no sides were taken. It was a very public place.

"The mist was starting to lift," the shoemaker continued, waving his hands about as he spoke. "The Hielanders *pu'd* aff their bonnets and prayed to God. Then they sounded their battle cry, and the pipes pierced the morn air."

Elisabeth swallowed hard. *The rising mist. The skirl of a bagpipe.* Had such a scene not awakened her before dawn?

"The prince's men discharged their arms, then cast them aff and drew their broadswords and scythes. Och, 'twas a bluidy rout." He took a long drink of ale, then shook his head. "I canna describe it with a leddy present. It didna take mair than a quarter hour. The dragoons fled, the infantry fell, and the rest o' Cope's men surrendered. O' course, 'tis nae surprise whaur they fought." John leaned forward, his eyes as bright as buttons. "On Gladsmuir shall the battle be."

Elisabeth's breath caught. What Highlander didn't recognize the words of Thomas the Rhymer? Here was another medieval prophecy fulfilled. "Between Seton and the sea," she recited from memory, "many a man shall die that day."

"Weel done, Leddy Kerr," the shoemaker said, offering her a gap-toothed smile. "Gladsmuir sits a bit east o' the battleground but close enough for the Hielanders to claim 'twas a victory foretold."

Elisabeth turned toward the open door, her thoughts ever drawn back to Simon. "What of the prince's men?"

"Not *monie* Hielanders were lost." John leaned back in his chair. "As for the rest, ye'll see a few this day, mair on the morrow. Those Hielanders wha think their duty is done will take their bounty hame." He inclined his head toward the High Street. "Ye'll not find a surgeon in Edinburgh this morn, for the prince bid the lot o' them come and leuk after the wounded."

If Simon lay among the injured, Elisabeth would insist on tending his wounds at Milne Square. Her mother-in-law could not refuse her brother a clean bed and a warm hearth. Nae, she could not.

Elisabeth abruptly stood, brimming with conviction. "Lord Kerr, if you will, kindly escort me home. I want everything in readiness for my brother's return."

Twenty-Five

Uncertainty!
Fell demon of our fears!

David Malloch

Donald had never felt so restless — nae, so useless — in all his seven-and-twenty years. Having delivered Elisabeth to their drawing room, he'd begged her indulgence, then retraced his steps down the stair, no clear destination in mind. Now, on this cool, cloudy morning, he stood in the heart of Milne Square surrounded by neighbors yet longing for solitude.

"I need a good, bracing walk," he'd told Elisabeth. He needed far more than that — time to reflect upon his past, time to consider his future — but dared not burden his wife, who had worries of her own. "I'll not be away more than an hour or two," he promised. After saying a word to Gibson, Donald had left the house before the dowager could fill his ear with woe or with guilt. She was very good at both.

He strode toward the High Street, uncertain which direction to turn, so conflicted were his emotions. Out of habit he bore west, heading uphill toward the castle. He'd left Andrew at Mrs. Turnbull's, drinking sack. Donald paused in the midst of the crowded street, giving thought to rejoining him, when a familiar voice called above the din. "Lord Kerr?"

He looked up to see his oldest friend in Edinburgh, Patrick Manderson, striding toward him. Heir to a prosperous Milne Square merchant, Patrick resided in nearby Oliphant's Land. The two had closed many a tavern in their youth and stumbled home at the beating of the ten o' the clock drum.

"You're especially well turned out this morn," Donald told him, admiring his brown velvet coat with its wide satin cuffs embroidered in gold. "Shall I compliment Angus MacPherson the next time I see him?"

Patrick made a sour face. "That Jacobite? Nae, 'twas William Reid who took my coin."

"Your father's coin," Donald corrected him, an old ploy between them.

Patrick rolled his eyes on cue. "I thought *you* were the one who freely spent his father's silver."

"You have me confused with my mother," Donald said, glad for any excuse to smile.

The two men walked side by side, their light banter giving way to the sense of gloom that hung over the city like a chilling sea fog in winter. "Tell me what you've heard from Gladsmuir," Donald said, "then I'll do the same."

" 'Twas a grim business," Patrick said. "A sharpened scythe in the hands of a Macgregor is a deadly proposition." He shuddered, pointing toward a knot of women gathered at the mouth of Mary King's Close. "Please God, those wives and mothers will ne'er be told how their loved ones died."

Donald glanced in their direction, then looked away, undone by the abject sorrow on the women's faces and the tears that flowed unabated. Jacobite or royalist, any loss was tragic. For Elisabeth's sake he was glad Simon had fought for the prince. Her brother would return to Edinburgh a victor instead of a prisoner.

Patrick's steps slowed as they neared Writer's Court. "I am to meet David Lyon at the Star and Garter. Join us for a wee pint?"

Donald eyed the busy tavern, tempted not by the ale but by the amiable company and the fresh news he might glean. He would pay a price for it, though: the inescapable noise, the crush of people, the fetid air.

"Another time, sir." Donald touched the brim of his hat, bidding his friend farewell before he pressed on. It seemed the solitary walk he'd hoped for could not be had in Edinburgh that day.

When he found himself at Warriston's Close, he ignored his nagging conscience and paused at the arched entrance, remembering how many times he'd slipped through the narrow passageway to seek the company of a certain widow. He thought of Susan McGill now for an entirely different reason. Her grown son, Jamie, was all Susan had in this world. Was he among the hundreds who'd fallen beneath a Highlander's blade?

Donald gazed down the shadowy close, wondering if he might spy a familiar face. Perhaps a friend or neighbor who knew the McGills. He could not possibly call on Susan, but he might inquire about her son.

A woman's voice interrupted his thoughts. "Looking for someone, Lord Kerr?"

With a guilty start, he turned away from the close. "Ah. Lady Ruthven." He offered the widow a hasty bow. Charlotte Ruthven was not a person to be taken lightly. She traded in gossip, scandal, and innuendo like Maitland Hart traded in silk.

She peered round him, her plump face aglow with curiosity. "Imagine finding you here."

Donald cleared his throat and stepped farther into the High Street. "I planned to visit the Luckenbooths." He gestured toward the buildings behind her. Anything to draw her attention away from Warriston's Close. "I've a book in mind to order from Mr.

Creech."

"My dear Lord Kerr, has no one told you?" The widow rested her hand on his coat sleeve, then tipped her dark head of curls so near she briefly unseated his hat. "The Luckenbooths are indeed locked on this unfortunate day." She swept round him so the two were facing in the same direction. "Might you escort me to my lodgings in Swan's Close?"

" 'Twould be an honor." He did his best to sound sincere for the dowager's sake. This was one widow whose charms did not tempt him in the least.

Donald headed downhill at a sprightly pace, pretending not to notice Charlotte's proprietary grip on his arm. Rumors flowed from her lips in an endless stream. Mrs. Rattray this and Lord Semple that and Mr. Noble something else. Did she speak disparagingly of him too? *Lord Kerr thus and so.* His mother knew nothing of his indiscretions. Donald prayed the same could be said for Charlotte Ruthven.

When they reached Swan's Close, Trotter was waiting for his ladyship inside her stair door, a look of concern on his face. "Beg pardon, Leddy Ruthven, but I didna hear ye leave."

"I traveled no farther than the Luckenbooths," she assured her manservant, "and I had a fine escort bring me home." She squeezed Donald's arm before he could untangle himself from her grasp.

"Good day to you, madam." Donald strode off in such haste he almost collided with a burly cooper rolling a wooden barrel toward the High Street. Then he dodged a barber's boy toting a freshly styled wig. Was there nowhere he might go for a moment's peace?

When Donald reached the thoroughfare only to be met by a sea of troubled faces, he plunged headlong down the street, bent on reaching Milne Square without further delay. A quiet afternoon spent with his maps in the privacy of his bedchamber suddenly held great appeal.

He lengthened his stride, like a horse nearing a stable, until he nearly trampled Rob MacPherson coming out of the town guardhouse. Donald stepped back and tipped his hat. "Apologies, sir."

The tailor's son regarded him evenly, his dark eyes unblinking. " 'Tis guid we've met, Lord Kerr. Might I have a wee bit o' yer time?"

Donald stifled a groan. Would he never reach home? "The Duke's Head Tavern is not far," he suggested.

"Nae, a short walk will do." Rob continued downhill with his lopsided gait. "My faither will be leuking for me at the palace afore lang."

Donald matched his voice to Rob's low

pitch. "Is the prince expected?"

Rob shook his head. "His Royal Highness willna leave the field o' battle 'til a' the deid are buried. 'Twill likely be the morrow afore we see him in Edinburgh."

An image of Jamie McGill flitted through Donald's mind. "And the prisoners?"

"Headed for the tolbooth," Rob answered bluntly.

At least Jamie's mother could visit him there. "Lady Kerr is most eager to see Simon," Donald told him. "Should he cross your path, please assure my brother-in-law he is welcome at any hour."

"Ye'd shelter a Jacobite?" Rob eyed him closely. "I thocht the Kerrs were the staunchest o' royalists. On Tuesday last ye stood in the midst o' the Jacobite army, asking if onie present had once been leal to King Geordie."

Donald grunted. "You've a keen memory."

"It has served me weel." A hint of a smile crossed Rob's features, then disappeared. "I've reason to believe ye've had a change o' heart." He glanced up at the Kerr apartments, then fixed his gaze on Donald. " 'Tis why I wanted to speak with ye, Lord Kerr."

He swallowed, doing his best to sound nonchalant. "Oh?"

Rob did not mince words. "Have ye and yer brither come round to the cause? Certain men have informed me o' such, and they're seldom wrong."

"Spies, you mean."

Rob shrugged. "If ye like."

Plagued with uncertainty, Donald stared at the dirty plainstanes beneath his feet. It was risky to support the prince. Perhaps riskier still not to. "I would speak with my brother first," he said finally. "When you ask me again, Mr. MacPherson, you shall have your answer."

TWENTY-SIX

And when the hour strikes, as it must . . .
I beg you very gently break the news.
                    THOMAS BAILEY ALDRICH

Elisabeth could not recall a Sabbath when
the pews of the Tron Kirk groaned from the
weight of so many parishioners. Some folk
sought a respite from the noisy street,
crowded with returning soldiers bearing
whatever spoils they'd claimed from the field,
mostly weapons and supplies. Others longed
for solace after a crushing defeat at the hands
of the Highlanders. Many despaired for their
lives and their families. A few came only for
the gossip.

Since yesterday Elisabeth had waited impa-
tiently for Simon's safe return. A tear-stained
list of fallen and injured Jacobites had traveled round the taverns. Gibson assured her
Simon's name was not among those tallied.
"I leuked up and doon the list," he promised,
"and there was nae Simon and nae Ferguson." Elisabeth wished she'd seen the list

herself, just to be certain. Simon would laugh at her for worrying so.

Hundreds of soldiers, both royalist and Jacobite, had already streamed into the capital. The tolbooth was swollen with prisoners. Englishmen, mostly. Duddingston was once again an army encampment. The last of the prince's men, including her beloved Simon, were expected in town by day's end.

Elisabeth cast her gaze about the sanctuary. The Jacobites in the congregation were easy to spot. They were the ones sporting the brightest colors and the broadest smiles. Her royal blue gown well suited the day, with its open robe in polished satin displaying a quilted petticoat. Peacock feathers sprang from the knot of hair on her crown, and over her heart she'd pinned her white cockade. "Be proud, but not prideful," her mother would say. Elisabeth hoped she'd struck the proper balance, though she might have overdone things a bit. *For you, Simon.*

Marjory and Janet wore solid gray gowns, their unsmiling faces turned toward the pulpit. Both women had shunned Elisabeth since she'd confessed her allegiance to the prince. Over time she hoped to regain their trust. At the moment Donald's mother seemed unwilling to look in her direction, let alone speak to her. Would the dowager truly welcome Simon at their door as Donald had promised?

The kirk bells had already tolled the hour, and the precentor had finished lining out the gathering psalm. Elisabeth folded her gloved hands and waited for Reverend Wishart to climb into the pulpit and offer his opening prayer.

She waited a bit longer. Then longer still.

Up and down the pews, anxious words took flight. "Is the reverend not coming?" "Has he taken ill?" "Is he burying the fallen at Gladsmuir?"

Amid the clamor Mr. Hogg rose and slowly walked toward the front. By the time the lecturer climbed into the pulpit and closed the small door behind him, a solemn hush had fallen over the congregation. Without prayer or preamble, he commenced his morning lecture, drawn from Psalms. "Some trust in chariots, and some in horses," he intoned. "But we will remember the name of the LORD our God."

When he spoke against the Jacobites, murmurs of disapproval swept round the sanctuary. But when he spoke in favor of King George, the crowd remained strangely silent. Elisabeth touched her white cockade and noticed how many others had bloomed on her neighbors' waistcoats and gowns since the Sabbath last. Could the tide of opinion be turning? Donald had not objected when she appeared at breakfast wearing hers. He had, in fact, winked at her, when no one was paying attention.

Mr. Hogg's lecture was followed, not by a prayer or a benediction, but with the briefest of announcements. "Reverend Wishart is not present. There will be no sermon."

The congregation looked at one another, aghast. Would no one shepherd them?

Within the hour the members of Tron Kirk discovered theirs was not the only empty pulpit. Most of Edinburgh's parish ministers, faithful to King George and fearing for their safety, had retired to the country, refusing to preach while the Highlanders occupied the city.

Of the Kerrs, Marjory was the most upset, dabbing at her eyes with a handkerchief while her Sabbath meal sat untouched. "I thought Prince Charlie sent all the ministers a letter last night, urging them to carry on as usual?" When all seated round the table assured her they'd heard the same report, she wailed, "Then how could Reverend Wishart abandon us?" Her color high, she quit the dinner table with Janet close on her heels. A moment later the dowager's bedchamber door closed firmly behind them.

In the wake of silence, Andrew stood. "Well, then," he said, brushing the crumbs from his waistcoat, "the coffeehouses should have their doors open by now. Join me, Donald?"

Elisabeth gazed at her husband, longing to

keep him by her side yet not wanting to encumber him. "Do as you wish," she said, smiling lest he doubt her sincerity.

Donald reached across the table and took her hand. "I prefer to remain at home. We're expecting Lady Elisabeth's brother to appear at our door. In truth, he could knock at any moment."

Andrew pushed in his chair. "Should I hear any news of import —"

"Aye, aye." Donald waved him off. "We'll send Gibson for you the instant Simon arrives. You'll be pleased to meet my brother-in-law, though he cannot hold a candle to his sister."

Andrew smiled at her. "I know that's so, Lady Kerr. I'll return before nightfall."

Elisabeth enjoyed a companionable hour with her husband at table while he finished his plate of cold Sabbath fare. She sipped her claret, keeping an eye on the clock.

"Shall we read?" Donald asked her, putting his napkin aside. They both kept books by the fireplace so they would be close at hand whenever the mood struck.

But when Elisabeth looked down, the page before her was a sea of ink, demanding more attention than she could spare. Her thoughts belonged only to Simon. Had Rob Mac-Pherson relayed their message? Would her brother indeed come to Milne Square, or did he have duties that might keep him in Duddingston? How could she be certain he was safely home?

When the clock struck five, she could bear it no longer. "Donald . . . might you . . . Is there some way we could . . ."

He closed his book at once, not bothering to mark the page. "If it will put your mind at ease, Elisabeth, I will gladly send Gibson to Duddingston. Or if you prefer, I will go myself."

"Oh, Donald, *would* you?"

"Aye —"

A knock at the stair door brought them both to their feet. "Simon!" she cried, hastening toward the entrance hall, her concerns forgotten. Marjory and Janet emerged from their bedchambers to see who'd come to call even as Gibson, ever dutiful, was already greeting their visitor.

But it was not Simon after all.

Elisabeth stepped back in surprise when Tom Barrie crossed the threshold. "Lord Kerr, look who's come to see us! Our friend Mr. Barrie, returned from Gladsmuir." She ushered the veteran soldier into the dim entrance hall with its single window. His exhaustion was evident in the slump of his shoulders. "Simon will be along shortly, aye?"

When Tom raised his head to meet her gaze, his skin was ashen, and his eyes were wet with tears.

A knot of fear tightened round her throat.

"Whatever is the matter, Mr. Barrie?" Then she saw the folded cloth in his arms.

A Braemar plaid. Stained with blood.

Twenty-Seven

Tears are the silent language of grief.
Voltaire

Elisabeth could hardly form the words. "Is Simon . . . Is he . . . dead?"

Tom's lower lip began to tremble.

" 'Tis not possible," she whispered even as she received her brother's plaid.

Donald quietly slipped his arm round her shoulders. "Elisabeth . . ."

"Nae!" she moaned, clutching the plaid to her heart. " 'Tis not possible, don't you see?" *Nae Simon and nae Ferguson.* "Gibson said . . . His name . . ." She tried to breathe, tried to speak. "His name . . . was not . . ." She pushed against Donald's firm embrace. *Nae, nae, nae!* "Simon cannot be dead. He cannot!"

"Come, dearest." With some effort her husband guided her to an upholstered chair in the drawing room while the household watched, shocked expressions on their faces.

Elisabeth sank into the cushions, holding

Simon's plaid on her lap. Tears streamed down her cheeks. *Not my Simon. Not my dear brother.*

"Forgive me, Bess." Tom Barrie pulled off his tattered bonnet and knelt beside her, his wrinkled hands capturing hers. "I tried, but I couldna save the lad . . ."

Elisabeth bowed her head, not quite listening as she carefully traced the pattern woven by their father. When she finally looked into the older man's eyes, she found a sorrow to match her own. "Tell me about Simon."

"The charge was sounded just afore dawn. Yer brither was one o' the first to fire his musket. Och, he was sae brave! But then I . . ." Tom bowed his gray head, and his hands dropped to his side.

"Please, Mr. Barrie." She withdrew her handkerchief from her sleeve and pressed it to her eyes. "Please, I must know."

He began again, barely above a whisper. "The field was newly harvested, covered with stubble. And I . . ." He choked on the word. "I . . . fell."

Elisabeth touched his shoulder with an unsteady hand. " 'Twas not your fault."

"Aye, but it was. When Simon reached doon to help me, an Englishman shot him." He touched his ribs, showing her where. "Not a fatal wound, ye ken. Not at first."

Elisabeth closed her eyes, imagining the hot, sharp pain of a musket ball piercing his side. *My dear brother!* "Did no one attend him?"

"Oo, aye. Whan the surgeons came from Edinburgh in the forenoon, a Mr. Eccles dressed his wound. But Simon insisted on burying the deid. Not monie soldiers were willing, ye ken."

Donald frowned. "Why not?"

"Some Hielanders thocht it beneath them to bury the English," Tom admitted, his shame apparent. "And the country folk ran aff in fear. Simon dug graves for the fallen men 'til the gloaming. But his bleeding wouldna stop . . ."

Elisabeth looked away, trying to banish the painful image. *Simon, dear Simon. Why did you not rest?*

Tom sat back on his haunches with a weary sigh. "By the time we started home on foot this morn, yer brither was burning with fever. And by the time we reached Mussel-burgh . . ."

She moaned. "Simon was gone."

"Aye, Bess. He didna suffer lang."

" 'Tis some consolation," Donald said, pulling her closer.

Elisabeth curled over Simon's plaid as a low keening sound rose from deep inside her. "Where . . . where is my brother?"

"I buried Simon in a wee corner of a plowed field." Tom struggled to his feet, brushing his hands as if dirt still clung to his palms. "And I built a cairn on his grave sae the farmer would ken 'twas not to be disturbed."

His grave. Elisabeth shuddered at the thought of Simon's body cold and lifeless in the damp ground, buried beneath a pile of stones. *Nae, it cannot be!* She pressed into the plaid, the wool scratchy against her skin. The coppery scent of blood mingled with the faint aroma of heather that still clung to the fabric.

Donald stood, offering Tom Barrie his hand in thanks. "Such sorrowful news is better heard from a friend than from a stranger."

"She'll be wanting this as weel." He gave Donald a folded square of paper. "A lock o' the lad's hair."

Elisabeth lifted her head so Tom might see the gratitude in her eyes, though she did not trust herself to speak.

Tom nodded, understanding all she could not say. "I kenned Simon Ferguson whan he was a bairn. 'Twas an honor to serve with him." He sighed, then brushed his bonnet against his knee and pulled it over his brow. "Forgive me, Bess. They'll be leuking for me at Duddingston."

The men moved toward the entrance hall, leaving her with Marjory and Janet, who'd not said a word since Tom's arrival. The two women stood side by side near the fireplace, still dressed in their gray gowns.

Her sister-in-law spoke first, her voice soft

and low. "Lady Elisabeth, I am truly sorry for your loss."

The uncommon tenderness of Janet's words brought fresh tears to Elisabeth's eyes. "Have you a handkerchief?" she asked a moment later, holding up the limp remains of her own.

Marjory produced a clean square of linen at once, a hint of lavender wafting through the air as she pressed it into Elisabeth's hands. " 'Tis the least I can do, my dear." Her eyes were moist, and her concern, however unexpected, seemed genuine. "I know what it means to lose someone you love. You have my deepest sympathy. You and your mother."

Elisabeth's heart sank. *Mother.* How could she tell Fiona Ferguson that her beloved son was dead?

"Donald, she cannot learn this from a letter." Elisabeth adjusted her head on the pillows, hoping she might see his expression more clearly in the firelight. The hour was late. A chilling westerly wind blew against the windowpanes and forced its way into their bedchamber, making her shiver.

" 'Tis not wise to tarry with this news," Donald reminded her, "or your mother is sure to hear it from another." He lay beside her with one hand resting on her hip and the other tucked beneath her cheek. The sympathy in his gaze, the downward curve of his mouth mirrored the compassion she'd heard in his voice all evening. *'Tis a tragedy, sweet Bess. He was so young, so brave. If there is anything I might do, I stand ready.*

She turned to kiss his palm. " 'Twould be best if my mother were told in person by someone who cares for her. Annie Coutts was a dear friend, and Rose MacKindlay, the parish midwife. But I'm not certain they still live in the area."

"Tom Barrie is the man for it," Donald said, "but it may be many weeks, even months, before the Rising ends and he returns to Castleton."

If he returns. Elisabeth heard the words, though Donald did not say them.

She looked into his eyes. "Please, let me go home, Donald. Let me tell her myself."

"I cannot, Bess. 'Tis far too dangerous —"

"But Murray of Broughton's wife travels about," she protested, starting to pull away from him.

"Aye, with the entire Jacobite army as her guardsmen." Donald drew her close once more. "Even if Andrew and I both escorted you north, 'tis a long, lonely road with perils at every turn. Not at all safe for my bonny Bess." He kissed her brow, then her cheek, then her lips, lingering at the last.

"Please?" she whispered, his mouth still near hers.

"Nae, beloved." He kissed her once more,

rather firmly, putting an end to the subject. "We must find another way to inform your mother. I'll not have my wife riding o'er the countryside while men are engaged in battle." When she did not respond, Donald asked more gently, "You do understand?"

Elisabeth turned her head, hiding the tears that pooled in her eyes. She'd wept off and on through the evening, soaking every handkerchief in Mrs. Edgar's linen closet. "Good night, then," she told her husband, too weary for more words. In the morning she would find some way to relay the tragic news. *Forgive me, Mother. I would come to you if I could.*

Shifting beneath the bedcovers until she found a comfortable position, Elisabeth heard Donald do the same and so closed her eyes, seeking the gentle embrace of sleep.

But sleep did not come.

After the firelight faded and Donald had drifted off, Elisabeth still lay wide awake, gazing into a room filled with shadows. Memories of Simon filled her mind. Sitting beside the turbulent waters of the Linn of Dee on a late summer's day. Watching the salmon ascend the waterfalls on their way upstream. Climbing the high road south of Castleton on a wintry November afternoon. Listening for the eerie mating call of the red deer echoing round the frosty hills.

Simon, dear Simon. Nothing will be the same. Each time the linen beneath her cheek grew damp, she turned the pillow, until it seemed she'd soaked every inch. *I water my couch with my tears.* Familiar words, though she could not place them. Donald would know the poet.

Pressed down by an aching, unrelenting grief, she exhaled into the still night air. How could Simon be gone from her life forever? They'd been together just three days earlier. She'd seen her brother, spoken with him, held his hands in hers. They'd shared their secrets and their tears and their mutual loathing of Ben Cromar.

Oh, Mother, you cannot marry him. You cannot.

They'd planned to wed on Michaelmas, one week hence. Could a letter be delivered by then?

Elisabeth pressed her face into the pillow, exhausted. So much to think about. So many questions. If ever she needed to reach beyond herself for strength, it was now. She touched her sleeping husband, drawing comfort from his presence. If only seeking assurance from a god were so simple!

Her entreaties for Simon atop the Salisbury Crags came to mind. *Guard him and keep him safe.* However heartfelt her pleas, they'd not been answered. She touched the silver ring on her right hand, fresh doubts stirring. *Are you listening? Can I trust you?* She remained motionless yet sensed nothing. Not in the room nor in her heart. The silence bore down on her until nothing remained but sorrow and an unanswered question. If the Nameless One was not real, who would watch over her and those she loved?

The faint ticking of the clock, two rooms away, began to lull her to sleep. Grateful for any respite from her pain, Elisabeth sank deeper into her pillows and closed her eyes.

Incline your ear, and come unto me.

She slowly raised her head, her heart quickening.

Hear, and your soul shall live.

The words were distinct, as if spoken aloud, yet she knew they were not. Had the Nameless One come after all? A response followed, swift and sure.

My people shall know my name.

Not the Nameless One, then, but another One.

Elisabeth sought refuge beneath her bedding as the phrases rose and fell inside her. *Come unto me. Know my name.* Not demanding, not insistent. Simply inviting her. Tenderly wooing her. Easing her into sleep.

TWENTY-EIGHT

The early gray
Taps at the slumberer's window pane.

RALPH HOYT

"Leddy Kerr?" Mrs. Edgar stood at her bedside, laden with towels. "Will ye be wanting yer bath?"

Elisabeth blinked at the housekeeper. The gray light of morning filled every corner of the room. "What . . . what time is it?"

"Eleven o' the clock, milady."

"Eleven?" Elisabeth threw aside her bedcovers in dismay. She'd never slept so late in all her life. Nor so soundly.

" 'Tis a' my fault." Mrs. Edgar helped her down from the high bed. "I didna *wauken* ye, thinking ye needed yer sleep." She lowered her eyes. "I'm verra sorry about yer brither."

Elisabeth acknowledged her kindness as realization dawned and sorrow returned. *Simon is gone. And Mother must be told.*

"Yer water is *het,* milady." Mrs. Edgar

246

poured the steaming contents of the pitcher into the porcelain bowl, then laid the soap and towels where Elisabeth could easily reach them. "I've pressed yer dark gray satin. Yer mither-in-law sent a note to Miss Callander this morn, asking her to come round and fit ye for a black gown."

Elisabeth murmured her thanks as she moved to the washbowl, still rubbing the sleep from her eyes. The last time she'd worn mourning clothes was after her father's death. She'd stitched a plain gown from her father's own finely woven wool, dyed in fresh sorrel and birch ashes. This time her gown would be fashioned of black silk with very little lace, no ribbons or bows, and no embroidery. She would gladly wear such dreary attire for six months to honor Simon's memory. Nae, she would wear it the whole of her life if it might somehow bring him back to her.

Elisabeth bathed in silence, mingling the soapy water with her tears.

Across the room Mrs. Edgar fussed over the dark gray satin Elisabeth would wear until her mourning gown was ready. With obvious reluctance, the housekeeper snipped off the elegant bow that decorated the bodice. "Och! It doesna leuk the same without it," she fretted. "Ye can wear only pearls. Naught with a shine to it. Still, best to do what's proper."

"Aye." Elisabeth slipped on a clean chemise, then donned the gray gown. Standing before her looking glass, she knew her husband would find it difficult to say the color flattered her skin. Marjory and Janet, with their auburn hair and peach complexions, both wore gray well. But against her pale skin and dark brown hair, the dull hue robbed her of any vibrancy. It mattered not. "For Simon," Elisabeth said, reaching for a clean lace handkerchief to tuck in her sleeve.

Mrs. Edgar fastened the last of her buttons, glancing toward the window as she did. " 'Tis a *dreich* day. As lead colored as yer gown." She touched a comb to Elisabeth's hair, poking at it with more determination than skill. "A fitting day for mourning," she observed, then lowered her voice. "I put oot bread and water should yer brither's spirit come leuking for it."

Elisabeth nodded, thinking of the auld Scottish customs that would not be observed because Simon had died on a lonely country road rather than beneath their roof. The tall case clock would continue to measure the hours, and her looking glass would not be draped in black. But her heart would. Aye, and her body.

Marjory's bedchamber was vacant as Elisabeth passed through to the drawing room with Mrs. Edgar in her wake. "Whilst ye were sleeping, Lord Kerr and the ithers slipped aff to see to their errands," the housekeeper explained, "but they'll not be lang. I'll bring yer tea, milady."

Elisabeth circled the drawing room while she waited, feeling unsettled. *Incline your ear.* She'd drifted to sleep with those words ringing inside her. Not like a deid bell in the hands of a beadle, clanging out mournful news, but like the gill bells of Saint Giles, sweetly playing at noontide. *Come unto me.* How gently the voice had resounded within her. Was she willing to listen?

Mrs. Edgar served her tea with a slice of seedcake. " 'Tis the custom," she said, sympathy in her eyes.

Elisabeth bit into the sweet cake and pronounced it delicious, sending Mrs. Edgar back to her kitchen a happy woman. Alone once more, Elisabeth edged the rich food aside and sipped her tea in silence.

Her brother's plaid, left in her chair by the fireside, stirred another memory of Simon, seated beside his father at the loom, learning to throw the shuttle back and forth across the stretched wool. *How can you be gone, Simon? How can you be dead?* She reached for her linen handkerchief to catch the first tear before it fell.

A knock at the door drew her attention, then familiar voices echoed in the hall: Angus MacPherson and Rob as well, come to pay their respects.

"Visitors to see ye, Leddy Kerr." Gibson stood aside as the two tailors entered the drawing room.

She stood to greet them, her knees shaking. The moment their eyes met, Elisabeth could not hold back her tears. Angus looked stricken as well. Only Rob remained dry-eyed, though his Adam's apple bobbed up and down as if it was an effort to keep his composure.

"I canna say how sorry I am, Bess." Angus patted her hand while she dabbed at her swollen eyes. "Victory for our cause came at a great expense. None greater than the loss o' young Simon."

She nodded, her throat tight. Would every soul who paid her a visit affect her so? *Nae.* Beyond these walls few in Edinburgh meant more to her than Angus MacPherson.

"Yer brither was a hero," Angus assured her, "and I've proof of it." He drew from his coat pocket two letters on thick stationery, sealed in black wax, the color of mourning. "One for ye and one for yer mither. From the hand o' Charles Edward Stuart."

Elisabeth caressed the seal with her thumb before she gingerly broke it loose and unfolded the letter with care. She held the paper at arm's length lest a stray tear mar the ink. The prince's words swirled across the page in elegant loops. Evidently he'd not written in haste nor on the field of battle but seated at a desk with a newly sharpened quill and plentiful ink.

"The prince returned to the Palace of Holyroodhouse *yestreen*," Angus said. "Whan the final list o' casualties was presented to him this morn, he sat doon at ance to write the families."

She absently rubbed a corner of the paper between her fingers, imagining other grieving parents and siblings who would hold such letters. "How many were lost?"

"Less than forty," Rob answered, "yet ilka man will be greatly missed."

My brother most of all. The words swam before her as she began to read.

To Lady Elisabeth Kerr, Milne Square
Monday, 23 September 1745

My Dear Madam,

I pray you will accept my deepest condolences and most sincere appreciation for the life your brother sacrificed on behalf of our cause.

Lord George Murray informed me that Mr. Ferguson demonstrated particular bravery at the initial charge and, despite his injury, continued to engage the enemy with valor.

In the aftermath, when many were unwilling to bury the dead, your brother again proved his loyalty, which I witnessed firsthand.

May these few words convey the gratitude

of all who fought beside him at Gladsmuir.

Charles P. R.

She lightly touched the prince's signature: a bold, slanted script with the *l* leaping upward from the *r* like a raised standard. However zealous her father had been for the Stuarts, would he have freely given his only son? And what of her mother? Would she consider Simon's young life well spent? *Nae, nae!* No earthly cause was worth so great a sacrifice.

Elisabeth quietly folded her letter, eying the other one. "I must deliver the prince's letter to my mother. However much his words meant to me, they will signify even more to her."

Deep furrows lined Angus's brow. "Ye canna mean to do it in person." When she did not respond immediately, Angus wagged his finger inches from her nose. "Dinna entertain the notion o' making such a journey yerself, Bess. 'Tis too dangerous."

"But who will go on my behalf?"

Angus sighed heavily. "I would gladly ride to Castleton o' Braemar. Truly, I would. But my duties o' late claim ilka waking hour. Might Lord Kerr do ye this service?"

"I have not asked him," Elisabeth admitted. She didn't voice what she knew to be true: Donald's mother would never allow it.

Rob MacPherson stepped forward. "Then I'll go. My faither can spare me and sae can the prince." He rushed on before Angus could object. "Dinna worry about my foot."

"You are certain?" Her spirits lifted for the first time since Tom Barrie had crossed their threshold. "The stores in our larder are yours, and we've silver for your journey. But . . ." She paused, needing to be very sure. "You'd be gone a fortnight. Are you truly willing?"

"Mair than willing." His dark eyes searched hers. "If yer husband canna go, I'll gladly serve in his place." He held up the prince's letter. "Yer mither will want to hear from ye as weel, aye?"

Her mother. The wedding. In her grief Elisabeth had all but forgotten.

"I shall pen a letter at once," she promised, her hands growing cold at the mere thought of it. "Might you arrive in Castleton by Michaelmas?"

"Six days from now?" Rob frowned. "I canna promise, but . . ."

" 'Tis a great deal to ask," she admitted, "but if you might reach her before Sunday, 'twill make all the difference." *More than you can imagine, Rob. More than I can tell you.*

He nodded thoughtfully. "Mebbe if I depart this noontide . . ."

"Could you?" She leaped at the idea before he changed his mind. "Gibson can arrange for a carriage at once, and Mrs. Edgar will gladly pack food for your journey." When Elisabeth caught their eyes, both servants nodded and hurried off.

Come Marjory's return, Elisabeth would have much to explain after ordering her servants about and spending her money. But surely her mother-in-law would understand. If not, Donald would. Had he not agreed they must find a way to inform her mother? She had found a way: Rob MacPherson.

Angus piped up, "If ye mean to leave at ance, lad, I'll pack yer kist and have it delivered to White Horse Close. Save ye time, aye?"

"That would be wonderful," Elisabeth told him. She bussed his rough cheek before he departed down the stair. A moment later only Rob remained, still standing in their drawing room. "You'll not mind waiting while I write my mother?"

"Go on," Rob assured her. "I'll be here whan ye're done."

Elisabeth offered him a grateful nod and repaired to her bedchamber, already composing her letter. When she had pen and ink in hand, she began at once, lest she lose her train of thought. Or lose her nerve.

To Mistress Ferguson, Castleton of Braemar
Monday, 23 September 1745

254

Dear Mother,

I know Rob will have told you our tragic news. He is a good friend to do our family this kindness. Still, I wish I could be there in his stead and mourn with you.

Her heart tightened at the image of her mother hearing the sad news thrice — from Rob, from the prince, and from her daughter — yet with no one there to hold her, to weep with her, or to dry her tears.

No one except Ben Cromar.

Sickened by the thought, Elisabeth pressed on.

Perhaps you and Mr. Cromar have already wed. But if my letter reaches you before Michaelmas . . .

She paused, uncertain of her course. Dared she add to her mother's sorrow the same hour she learned of Simon's death? Or would it be unthinkable to let her marry Ben Cromar without telling her how violent the man could be? Unless her mother already knew . . .

Elisabeth squeezed her pen so hard the quill dented her fingers. Where could she turn for wise counsel? None of her family knew the situation. Only Simon knew, and he was gone. *My dear brother.*

For a fleeting moment she wished the

Nameless One were real. That she could cry out for help and know help would come. Not just on the sixth day but every day. But the moon cared nothing for her heartache. She would have to decide for herself.

Aye, Bess. Just tell her.

. . . I beg you, Mother, do not yoke yourself to Ben Cromar. I left Castleton because he frightened me, and Simon left because of his cruelty. I cannot bear to think of you suffering at his hand.

Elisabeth closed her eyes, remembering the red scar on Simon's neck. *Please, Mother. Don't let him hurt you.*

Or was it too late? Elisabeth sighed, then wrote what she must.

If you have already taken him as your husband, I will ask your forgiveness and entreat the One we know to keep you safe.

She signed the letter in haste, wishing she could say more. Much more. But time was short, and Rob was waiting.

A moment later her sanded and sealed letter was in Rob's hands. "Before Michaelmas?" she pleaded.

"Dinna fear, milady. I'll do my best."

Twenty-Nine

To grief there is a limit;
not so to fear.

FRANCIS BACON

Marjory held out one of her son's cherished volumes. "I know of no better remedy for heartache than poetry."

Dressed in their gray gowns, the Kerr women had gathered round the fireplace after the midday meal, Donald and Andrew having escaped to the Netherbow coffeehouse.

Janet took *The Seasons* from her hand. "Have you some passage in mind?"

"Any will do," Marjory told her, glancing out the window, surprised to see the sun still shining.

Three days of fine weather had not brightened the melancholy atmosphere of a household in mourning. Elisabeth's grief was understandable, losing her only brother at the cusp of manhood. Marjory understood. Her one sibling, Henry Nesbitt, was Donald's age, seven-and-twenty, when he was killed while hunting in the Ettrick Forest. She well remembered the heartache, which time had eased but never erased. She intended to support Elisabeth, despite her Jacobite convictions. Who could say if such a tragedy might not cool her daughter-in-law's fervor?

After a morning filled with sympathetic callers, Marjory had decided a brief respite from so much sadness was in order. Janet was showing signs of restlessness, yet they could not rightly pass the time playing whist, hazard, or cribbage. Poetry would have to do.

"Here's something from *Autumn*." Janet held the book in one hand and pressed open the pages with the other, pretending not to squint as she read aloud.

Oft let me wander o'er the russet mead,
And through the saddened grove, where
    scarce is heard
One dying strain —

Marjory cut her short. "Something more cheerful," she insisted, barely concealing her irritation. Compassion was not Janet's strong suit. Nor was her older daughter-in-law particularly fond of Elisabeth. But today of all days an effort was called for.

Janet turned to another page. "Ah, here we are," she said smoothly.

Meanwhile, the moon
Full-orbed and breaking through the
   scattered clouds,
Shows her broad visage in the crimsoned
   east.

When Elisabeth raised her head at the word *moon,* Marjory narrowed her gaze. Was the passage an arbitrary choice on Janet's part? Or was she baiting her sister-in-law? A strand of guilt wound through Marjory's conscience. Perhaps telling Janet about the *Ladies' Diary* notations had been unwise.

A new arrival in the entrance hall captured everyone's attention, as Gibson announced Mrs. Effie Sinclair.

Elisabeth was on her feet at once, welcoming her boarding school mistress. She had to bend down to do so. No taller than a girl of twelve, Mrs. Sinclair had a wasplike waist and tiny features. "Like a fairy," Lady Ruthven had once observed. If so, a well-bred one, Marjory thought, watching the woman's elegant manners, suited to the granddaughter of Sir Robert.

Effie Sinclair's voice was high and sweet, like birdsong. Her small eyes glistened with tears. "On behalf of all my scholars, Lady Kerr, you have our utmost sympathy."

A chair was quickly produced, and small glasses of claret served. Marjory had sipped one glassful since breakfast, trying to be frugal. The hospitality surrounding Sir John's funeral had cost more than two hundred guineas in ale, wine, and meat. She could not afford to drain the family coffers for a Jacobite, however beloved by his sister. Elisabeth abstained completely, but Janet drank to Simon's memory with every guest in turn though she'd never met the young Highlander.

Effie trained her eyes on Elisabeth. "Lady Kerr, I did not have the pleasure of knowing your late brother. Might you tell me something about Mr. Ferguson?"

Marjory listened as Elisabeth described Simon's childhood in Castleton, his skill at the loom, his passion for the Jacobite cause, and his brave deeds at Gladsmuir, all the while dabbing her eyes. Marjory found her words quite affecting. Had she ever spoken of her late brother, Henry, so tenderly?

Elisabeth recited the prince's letter by memory, then confided, "Rob MacPherson, the tailor's son, is delivering the sad news to my mother in Castleton. How I wish I might have done so myself."

"Your mother will understand," Mrs. Sinclair assured her. " 'Tis not safe to travel. Mr. MacPherson is to be commended for his service to your family."

Elisabeth agreed. "He is a true friend."

Marjory hid her slight irritation. *A true Jacobite, you mean. And a tradesman.* But his willingness to carry her daughter-in-law's sad news was commendable.

Mrs. Sinclair put aside her empty glass, then looked about the room. "Your needle has been busy, I see. This embroidery bears your fine stamp." She plucked a pillow from a nearby armchair and traced the intricate pattern with her fingertips, praising Elisabeth's tiny stitches and her bold use of color. "You are a credit to my school," Mrs. Sinclair told her, "though you arrived at my door with more skills than any young woman I've ever taught."

Elisabeth blushed at her praise, the first color Marjory had seen in her wan cheeks in several days.

"You also have a talent for costume," Mrs. Sinclair said, replacing the pillow. "I trust you are still sewing."

"On occasion," Elisabeth said, though she did not elaborate.

Marjory hastened to add, "Miss Callander in Lady Stair's Close usually fashions our gowns."

"Miss Callander?" Mrs. Sinclair's voice lifted another half octave. "What a pity when you have such a gifted seamstress beneath your own roof."

Marjory opened her mouth and, having no proper answer, closed it again. She could not deny her daughter-in-law's talents. But Marjory shuddered to think of anyone outside the household knowing that Elisabeth stitched many of her own gowns, let alone that she'd once earned silver with her needle. Heaven forbid!

"I fear I have overstayed my welcome." Mrs. Sinclair was already standing. "Might I ask one favor, my dear Lady Kerr? Several of my scholars have written poetry in honor of His Royal Highness." She produced a narrow roll of writing papers. "You are far more likely than I to have an audience at Holyroodhouse. The young ladies would be most grateful if you delivered their poems to the prince."

After sitting in a glassy-eyed stupor through most of the conversation, Janet came to life. "Oh! Might I read them?"

Mrs. Sinclair hesitated only a moment before placing them in Janet's eager hands. "If you wish."

Elisabeth promised to see them delivered posthaste, even as Marjory shot her older daughter-in-law a pointed look. Whatever had possessed Janet, behaving so rudely? Too much claret, perhaps.

Farewells were said and curtsies exchanged before Gibson escorted Mrs. Sinclair to the door. Marjory and Elisabeth both sank into their upholstered chairs, their energy spent from endless rounds of well-meaning visitors.

"A nap is in order." Janet exited the drawing room without further comment, Effie Sinclair's poems in hand.

262

When she was well out of earshot, Marjory leaned toward an exhausted Elisabeth. "Do forgive your sister-in-law. She is not accustomed to offering sympathy."

Elisabeth nodded slowly. "You, however, have been a great comfort."

The compliment took her aback. "I am glad," Marjory finally said. "I keep thinking of your poor mother. 'Twould be the saddest hour of a woman's life, losing a son."

"Or losing a husband." Elisabeth's tender voice struck a chord. "You must have suffered greatly when Lord John —"

"Aye." Marjory pressed her lips together, hoping to put an end to the matter. She could speak of many things but not of Lord John.

Gibson appeared at the door to announce a new visitor. "Leddy Ruthven."

Marjory inwardly groaned. *Charlotte, of all people.* She was in no mood for the woman's gossip. And Charlotte would not be pleased that she'd ignored her letter. Nae, she would not. Whatever friendship they'd once enjoyed had faded into mere tolerance for the sake of society. Few hostesses genuinely welcomed Charlotte's company.

Even Elisabeth was standing near her bedchamber door, poised to make her escape. "Ladies, I hope you will excuse me —"

"Very well." Lady Ruthven sailed across the drawing room, waving her gloved hand. " 'Tis your mother-in-law I've come to see, though you have my deepest sympathy. A Jacobite brother. Such a terrible loss."

Elisabeth murmured her thanks and quit the room as Lady Ruthven deposited her scarlet cape in Gibson's hands and smoothed her billowing skirts, festooned with an alarming number of ribbons and bows.

Marjory eyed the clock. "Perhaps you've already had your tea?"

"I have not. Will it be seedcake, then?" Charlotte made herself at home by the fire while Marjory dispatched Mrs. Edgar to prepare a tray. "We missed you at Lady Woodhall's on Monday," Charlotte began, "but of course your place was here."

"It was," Marjory said firmly. "I'm sure the three of you had much to discuss."

"Naturally." Charlotte eased back against the chair cushions as if settling in for a long afternoon. When the tea tray appeared, Charlotte added a generous dollop of honey to her cup, then let Mrs. Edgar put three slices of seedcake on her plate before feigning her dismay. "Please, 'tis too much."

Marjory took a small bite and chewed it at length. Anything to avoid further conversation. The sweet cake was flavored with nutmeg and laced with brandy. Too rich for Marjory's taste but well suited to Charlotte's.

When they had the drawing room to themselves, Lady Ruthven quickly got to the point of her visit. "I've been expecting to see you at my door. Did you not receive my note?"

Your summons, you mean? Marjory kept her voice even. "Your note was received and read at once. But my family has needed me every hour since." Not *every* hour perhaps but most of them.

"So you say." Charlotte looked down her none-too-attractive nose. "If Lord Kerr's reputation does not concern you, I'll not bother you with details."

"Come, come," Marjory scolded her lightly. "Naturally I'm concerned."

"You should be." Charlotte lowered her voice, eying the adjoining doors before she continued. "On the Sabbath before last, I saw Lord Kerr stroll through the Lawnmarket with Mrs. Susan McGill, a widow of dubious repute."

Marjory had heard such tiresome stories before. Invariably a young widow was involved. On the High Street. At Assembly Close. In Mr. Creech's bookshop. Nothing untoward ever occurred. Donald was merely seen in the vicinity of a woman who was not his wife.

"Did he kiss this widow?" Marjory asked her guest bluntly. "Escort her into a tavern? Press her against the tolbooth wall?"

Charlotte's mouth dropped open. "Marjory, really! I never —"

"Indeed." Marjory stood so quickly she surprised herself. "I am weary of lies being tattled about by small-minded folk who have nothing but time in their pockets."

"But I —"

Marjory held up her hand, unwilling to hear more. "Lord Kerr is handsome, wealthy, charming, and titled. Naturally women flock to him, whatever their station. Nonetheless, he is faithful to his wife and a devoted son to me." Hot tears stung her eyes. "If you have finished your tea, Charlotte, I have a grieving daughter-in-law to console. Gibson will see you out."

What have I done?

Marjory leaned against her bedchamber door, her heart in her throat. Lady Ruthven had departed in a state, wool cape swinging, eyes blazing with indignation. Marjory had meant to silence the woman. Instead, she'd likely spurred Charlotte to take her revenge, spreading rumors like marmalade on toast — juicy and thick.

"Mother?" Donald's voice, following a light tap on her door.

Marjory quickly washed her hands, still sticky from the seedcake, then shook the crumbs from her skirts and bid him enter. Her words burst forth before she could contain them. "Donald, I'm afraid Lady Ruthven —"

"I know." A broad grin stretched across his face. "Andrew and I passed her on the stair.

That is to say, she nearly ran us down. Whatever did you put in the woman's tea?"

Marjory huffed. "She came here not to offer condolences to your wife but to peddle a barrow full of rubbish about you and the Widow McGill."

His eyes widened ever so slightly. "And you sent her packing?"

"I suppose I did." Marjory fell back a step, touching her brow. "I . . . spoke rather plainly, Donald."

"Well done," he said, though something in his tone suggested otherwise.

Shame warmed her cheeks. "I am not certain what came over me. 'Twill be difficult to show my face at Lady Woodhall's come Monday."

"Perhaps the time has come to expand your social circle." He paused before adding, "The Traquair ladies would gladly make you welcome at Holyroodhouse."

"Those . . . Jacobites?" Marjory said, appalled at the thought. Only then did she see the *Caledonian Mercury* tucked under his arm.

Donald held up the broadsheet with a flourish. "Come, let me read to you." Before she could protest, he led her into the drawing room, where Andrew stood by the fire, sipping tea. "Brother, 'tis time our mother heard from the prince himself."

Andrew saluted them with his teacup. "See to it, then."

Stunned, Marjory watched Donald unfold the traitorous newspaper. How had it come to this? Her sons turning their backs on all she held dear?

He read the prince's words with due solemnity, "Gentlemen, I have flung away the scabbard. With God's assistance I don't doubt of making you a free and happy people."

"But we're already free and happy," Marjory cried, feeling her sons pulling away from her like ships no longer anchored to port. "Do we or do we not honor King George in this household?"

"We should honor the *rightful* king," Andrew said with certainty.

"Aye." Donald slapped the folded paper against his leg. "I, for one, intend to support the king chosen by God. With my sword, if necessary."

Marjory stared at him in horror. "Son, you cannot . . . nae, you *must* not fight."

"We can, Mother," Andrew insisted. "And if our bonny prince will have us, we shall."

THIRTY

Come Donald, come a' thegither
And crown your rightfu', lawfu' king!
    CAROLINA OLIPHANT, LADY NAIRNE

The crowd eddied round Donald in the Lawnmarket as he studied the enlistment notice, thrust into his hand by a Jacobite soldier. A fortnight ago he would have crumpled the paper and tossed it into the nearest fire. Now every word seemed written for his benefit.

Abbey of Holyroodhouse, 26 September 1745 . . .

Dated that very day. The printer's ink might yet smear under his thumb.

All those who are willing to take arms . . .

Staring blankly at the wooden facades lining the street, he searched his heart and mind. Was he willing to take up arms? Andrew certainly was. Donald had left his brother at Milne Square cleaning his French muskets.

To the deliverance of their country . . .

This phrase gave him pause. Did he mean to fight for Scotland? For Prince Charlie? Or to prove he was a gentleman worthy of his title? Donald hadn't yet sorted out his many reasons, but he wanted — nae, *needed* — to enlist, of that he was certain.

Repair this day at two in the afternoon . . .

Three hours hence. Sufficient time to enjoy his last dinner at home, polish his steel, and march with Andrew to Holyroodhouse to begin their new life. A soldier's life.

Donald slid the notice inside his waistcoat, taking care not to bend the corners. Elisabeth might be glad to have the paper. Women sometimes kept such things. A lock of Simon's hair wrapped in paper rested in a corner of her jewelry box. She'd unfolded it many times that week and gingerly traced the brown curl, her eyes moist with tears.

Donald started for Milne Square, more determined than ever. He would brook no further arguments from the Dowager Lady Kerr. Were he and his brother not grown men, able to decide their own futures? Their mother had wept on and off for two days, twisting her handkerchief into a soggy knot and growing more hysterical by the hour. Donald had fled for the Lawnmarket that morning, seeking a moment's peace, while Andrew had retreated to his bedchamber, polishing cloth in hand.

Now that his mind was thoroughly fixed on a course of action, Donald could face the dowager again, if only to assure her. With one decisive battle the Jacobites already held sway over Scotland. England would succumb in short order, and the Kerr brothers would return home victors, their lands and title well protected. Wasn't security what their mother desired? They would see to it, then.

He crossed the street at Old Bank Close, with its handsome row of houses and turreted stairs. The air was mild for late September and decidedly fresher since the scavengers had returned with their wheelbarrows. Thin clouds, like muslin, stretched above the chimney tops. A large flock of swallows with their distinctive, two-pronged tails flew southward, as if pointing the way for the prince's army.

Donald lengthened his stride past the mouth of Libberton's Wynd, where Barbara Inglis lodged. He'd not seen the red-haired widow in a twelvemonth. They'd traded glances in a crowded oyster cellar, nothing more. Yet, to hear Lady Ruthven tell it, he was slipping into some widow's bedchamber thrice weekly and twice on Sundays. The nerve of the woman!

At least Charlotte Ruthven had not convinced his mother of his many transgressions. Was there ever a more stalwart mother? For Lady Marjory Kerr to concede her son a profligate, two dozen young widows would have to appear at her door bearing blue-eyed, fair-haired bairns and naming him as the father. In seven years of scattering his seed to the four corners of Edinburgh, no such misfortune had occurred. Some men might be concerned. For his part, Donald was relieved.

That afternoon when he passed through the Netherbow Port, he would leave his sordid history behind him — yet another benefit of enlistment.

Approaching the Luckenbooths, he eyed the ground-floor shop where the MacPhersons labored at their tailoring. He'd promised Angus his custom. What better time than the present when he needed a uniform in Jacobite blue?

Donald opened the shop door, a tinkling bell announcing his arrival. The Highlander kept an orderly establishment, though the low ceiling and small front windows made for a dim interior. Thick candles, placed a safe distance from fabric, patterns, and thread, illuminated the smooth-edged wooden cutting table and a tidy sewing cabinet with its many small drawers. Waistcoats and breeches hung from the walls in various stages of repair.

A long looking glass was given pride of place near the front, though the surface was marred with dark patches where the silvering had worn thin. Donald paused to straighten the stock at his neck, more from habit than necessity.

Angus MacPherson appeared a moment later, emerging from his lodgings behind the shop. A band of linen covered with pins lay draped round his neck, and a wide grin split his broad face. "Lord Kerr," he called out jovially, "have ye come for that new frock coat?"

"Another time, perhaps," Donald said, matching the tailor's grin. "At the moment 'tis an officer's uniform that's needed."

Angus's expression slowly changed, his eyes widening and his chin dropping until his round face resembled a turnip carved for Hallowmas Eve. When he found his voice, it was filled with a breathless sort of incredulity. "D'ye mean . . . ye've decided for the prince?"

"I have." He offered a gallant bow. "Lord Donald Kerr, at your service."

"Hoot!" Angus crowed, clapping his hands together. "*Anither* fine Lowlander won to the cause." He danced an impromptu jig, stirring the dust round his feet until he was forced to stop and catch his breath. "Won't Rob be surprised?" he said, wheezing a bit. " 'Twill

be the first news my son hears whan he returns from Castleton."

The reminder didn't sit well with Donald. He should have been the one to travel north on his wife's behalf rather than sending a lowly tailor's son. No remedy for it except to swallow his pride. "I daresay Rob will not be convinced of my fealty until he sees me in uniform, bearing arms."

"Aye, weel." Angus reached for his paper measuring tape. "Ye've already been to Holyroodhouse, then?"

Donald shook his head, a bit discomfited. Had he erred in stopping here first? "My brother and I are to present ourselves at the Great Hall come two o' the clock. Perhaps we should wait —"

"*Wheesht!*" Angus flapped his hand through the air, the measuring tape trailing behind. "The prince will gladly walcome ye both. Come and let me fit ye properly."

Angus took his time, jotting numbers on a slate with a bit of chalk, all the while filling Donald's ear with news from the prince's camp. "The city has delivered one thousand tents to Duddingston, and none too soon," the tailor reported, pulling the tape snugly round Donald's waist. "A' the while the prince has men traveling up and doon the country in search o' mounts and arms."

"We've no horses," Donald admitted, "but if he'll part with them, my brother has a fair collection of pistols and muskets."

"They'll be needed," Angus said bluntly, continuing to scribble Donald's measurements onto the slate. "I'm sure ye heard the cannons discharge yestreen round ten o' the clock." The tailor snorted. "Naught but some wee goats scrambling uphill to Edinburgh Castle. But the garrison lost their wits and fired into the toun."

Donald had already heard the rest. "At least one house in the West Port was damaged and a woman and child wounded."

"Cowards, the lot o' them," Angus muttered, clearly disgusted.

Donald merely nodded, overwhelmed at the thought of fighting against the British forces, cowards or not. He squared his shoulders, mentally preparing himself.

"Aye, that'll make yer coat a better fit," Angus said gruffly, patting his shoulder blades. "The Lord *bliss* ye, Lord Kerr. Ye'll send yer brither to see me?"

"Within the hour," Donald promised.

The gill bells of Saint Giles were ringing as he strode into the street. 'Twas half past eleven, when merchants and tradesmen closed their doors and headed for their favorite taverns to take their *meridian,* a gill of brandy or a pint of ale. Donald had time for neither.

When he reached Baillie's Land, his brother met him at the foot of the stair, descending at a clip. "Och, there you are!" Andrew slapped him on the back. "I feared you'd enlisted without me."

"You know better than that."

His brother's cheeks were ruddy with excitement. "I've stripped the weaponry from my bedchamber walls," he boasted, "and hired two lads with a wheeled cart to follow us to Holyroodhouse this afternoon."

Donald wished he had something of value to offer the prince. "Do you suppose my Lowland maps might be of some use in the campaign?"

"Aye, and why not?" Andrew made way for an unruly knot of young men, pushing and shoving their way across Milne Square.

Donald showed him the enlistment notice, then pointed his brother in the direction of the Luckenbooths. "I stopped by Angus Mac-Pherson's shop. He's expecting you next," he informed him. "See that you're home at one o' the clock for dinner."

Andrew pretended to raise a glass. "Here's to the king, sir." He winked, finishing the rebel's rhyme. "Ye ken wha I mean, sir." With that, he was gone, whistling as he strolled across the plainstanes.

Minutes later Donald pushed open the door to their apartments intent on finding Elisabeth. If his mother would not support him, surely his wife would. In passing he noted Andrew's polished weapons stacked in a wooden crate by the stair door, and his pulse quickened. No turning back now.

"Ah, there you are, Elisabeth." Donald reached the drawing room at the same time she entered through the opposite door. Her complexion was wan, the skin beneath her eyes bruised from lack of sleep. Donald searched for some way to cheer her. "A new gown, is it?"

"So it is." Elisabeth curtsied, the black silk rustling round her. "Miss Callander, the mantua maker, left a wee bit ago."

" 'Tis . . . well made." What else could be said about a mourning gown with its severe lines and utter lack of adornment? The color did not flatter her skin in the least. But the plain gown was meant to honor her brother's memory, not catch a gentleman's eye.

"Only six months, Donald." She'd read his expression, it seemed. "Then I'll be free to wear something more to your taste."

"You look as beautiful as ever," he quickly assured her, pulling off his gloves before he reached for her hands. "Come, milady, for we've much to discuss."

They sat together by one of the windows facing the square, the noontide sun illuminating the faint lines creasing her brow. Elisabeth had not smiled in days. Not even that morning when he and Andrew had discussed their plans at breakfast. Now that they had the drawing room to themselves, Donald did not hesitate to sit closer than propriety allowed, cradling her face in his hands, lightly rubbing his thumb across her sweet mouth.

"Bess," he began, keeping his voice low, "what say you of my enlistment in the prince's army?" He pulled the printed notice from his waistcoat and laid it on the table beside her, feeling a bit daft for saving it. "You were so quiet at table this morning, I could not be certain."

"Oh, Donald." She drew a long, even breath, then released it with a sigh. "I am proud you've chosen to support Prince Charlie. But to give up your freedom . . . to risk your life . . ." Elisabeth bowed her head, though she could not hide the tears in her eyes.

After a moment he reminded her gently, "Simon thought the sacrifice worthwhile."

She looked up. "How can you be sure? In his last hours my brother may have rued the day he came out for the prince."

"Bess, you know he did not." Donald brushed back the loose strands of hair that touched her cheek. "Simon fought willingly. And died bravely." He swallowed hard, watching her eyes fill with fresh tears. "Now, 'tis my turn to take up arms."

"For Scotland?"

"Nae, my love." He brushed a kiss against her brow. "For you."

THIRTY-ONE

Hope, folding her wings,
looked backward and became regret.

GEORGE ELIOT

Elisabeth lowered her gaze. "Serve the prince because you believe in his cause. But not for me, Donald. Never for me."

"Why not, Bess? I thought 'twould please you."

The yearning in his voice made her look up. She saw it in his eyes too: some urgent need, some longing far deeper than desire. "You've . . . nothing to prove," she began, searching for the right word. "Nothing to atone for."

"You are wrong, dear wife." He stood abruptly, showing her his back. "I've much to atone for, as you well know."

Elisabeth studied his posture, wishing he'd spoken more plainly. Did he mean his affairs before they married? Or something else altogether, something more recent? "Whatever you may be seeking," she finally told him, "you'll find naught on a battlefield but death. Simon is proof of that."

"On the contrary." Donald turned to face her, sunlight gilding his hair. "Your brother is proof there are valiant souls in this world. Men who put honor before self." His voice softened. "Simon laid down his life for what he believed. Will you not let me do the same?"

"Nae, I will not." Marjory closed her bedchamber door with a firm bang, startling them both. As she drew near, her gaze narrowed. " 'Tis quite as I feared," she said evenly. "You, Lady Kerr, have corrupted both my sons. And I intend to put a stop to it."

Elisabeth rose to defend herself even as Donald protested, "Mother, you cannot —"

"I can," the dowager said, "and I will. Within the hour I shall write a letter to this prince of yours and inform him of a certain weakness of your brother's —"

"Nae!" Donald balled his fists at his side, his face like flint.

Elisabeth touched her husband's arm, hoping to calm him. "Are you speaking of Andrew's bout with consumption?"

Donald ground out the words, "We are."

His mother jerked her chin at him, as angry as Elisabeth had ever seen her. "You may not remember how your brother suffered, but I do. His fevers, his flushed cheeks, his violent coughing. I feared Andrew would not live to see the spring."

"Mother, I —"

"Listen to me, Donald. You have recovered completely, but your brother has not. The lad cannot even climb the stair without stopping to catch his breath." His mother sighed, her fury beginning to abate. "Whatever Andrew's reckless Jacobite convictions, his health will not permit it."

Donald growled, " 'Tis *you* who'll not permit it. You cannot do this to Andrew, Mother. Nae, you *will* not."

When the dowager shrank back at his harsh tone, Elisabeth quickly intervened. "Dearest, your mother means only to protect him."

He glared at her. "You would side with her, then, and not with your own husband?"

Elisabeth turned from mother to son, struck anew by their similar natures. Obstinate. Unbending. "Lord Kerr, I *am* on your side," she finally said, "and so is your mother. We both want you and your brother alive and well, safely residing with us in Milne Square."

Her mother-in-law gaped at her. "Aye, that's precisely what we want."

"Then I must disappoint you both," Donald said flatly, motioning Gibson to his side. "Pack a small trunk for me at once," he ordered, "and bring me a whetstone."

Elisabeth's heart skipped a beat. *Nae, Donald. You cannot do this. Not for me.* When he moved toward the fireplace to claim his sword, she stepped in his way. "If you truly

281

want to please me, Lord Kerr, you'll not act in haste."

He maneuvered round her as neatly as if they were dancing a minuet, then plucked his mounted sword from the wall. "I've given the matter a good deal of thought, Lady Kerr. So has my brother. We'll not stand by and let other men fight in our stead. The Stuarts are sure to reclaim the throne. We'd be wise to support them."

When his mother opened her mouth to protest, Donald stemmed her words with a raised hand. " 'Tis my decision alone, Mother. See that you do not blame my wife or her family. The consequences are mine alone to bear."

"I shall bear them too," the dowager reminded him. "So will Elisabeth."

At the sound of her Christian name, Elisabeth paused. Seldom did the dowager address her so informally. Or so personally. "Lord Kerr, will you not reconsider?" she pleaded. "There are other ways to support Prince Charlie. Fill his coffers with gold. Sing his praises in the street."

"Or march out with his men," Donald said, more gently this time.

Gibson reappeared with the whetstone and placed it by the window. "I'll have yer kist ready afore lang," he promised, then hastened toward the bedchamber.

Elisabeth exchanged glances with her

mother-in-law. Was there nothing else to be done? A shared sense of helplessness hung in the air. Standing side by side, they watched Donald oil the whetstone, then polish the blade across the surface with slow, measured strokes. Elisabeth knew they dared not speak. Even a momentary distraction might cost him a fingertip.

When he finished, Donald wiped the blade clean with great care, then hung the sword from a broad leather belt stretched from shoulder to hip. Not a gentleman's method of wearing a sword, but a soldier's.

He already looked the part of a Jacobite officer, Elisabeth realized. His dark blue coat and red waistcoat would suffice until a uniform could be stitched for him, and his buff-colored breeches and boots would serve him well on cold autumn nights.

"I am proud of what you're doing," she confessed in a low voice, not looking at his mother. "Yet I cannot bear to lose you."

"Indeed, you've sacrificed enough." He touched her cheek. " 'Twill all be resolved by Yuletide. And then I'll come home to you."

Her vision blurred as she smoothed a hand along his sleeve. *Please, Donald. Please don't leave me.* No one in the household loved her but Donald. No one cared if she lived or breathed, if she ate or slept. Such selfish thoughts! Yet she could not deny them.

"Forgive me," she whispered, unsure whose

pardon she sought. Donald's? Her mother-in-law's? Whom else had she wronged by urging her husband to support the prince, then begging him to stay?

"There's nothing to forgive," Donald assured her. "Charles Edward Stuart won my allegiance with his victory at Gladsmuir. Despite my mother's charge, you did not corrupt me."

She knew better, remembering all too clearly her words meant to persuade. *No cause could be nobler.* Donald might not hold her accountable for his decision, but guilt pressed down on her all the same.

A moment later Gibson deposited a heavy leather trunk at Donald's feet, then held out a dark blue tricorne. "Yer hat, milord."

When Donald pulled a white cockade from the recesses of his waistcoat, his mother let out a soft cry. "Nae!" She clutched his forearm as if to shake the Jacobite symbol from his hand.

He gripped the silk rosette, pinning it firmly to the upturned brim.

"You cannot fight for Charlie!" his mother pleaded.

His gaze bore down on her. "Would you have me fight for Johnnie Cope?"

"Nae! I would not have you fight at all." Marjory collapsed onto the nearest chair like a canvas sail bereft of wind.

Elisabeth knelt beside her mother-in-law,

lightly resting her hand on the small of her back. There was nothing she could say or do to comfort her. But she could stand by her.

The next two hours were a blur of activity as Andrew returned home from Angus's shop, boasting of the handsome uniforms they would wear and the fine weapons they would carry. If he had any concerns about being fit to enlist, Andrew did not voice them. His mother's anguished pleas did nothing to dampen his enthusiasm.

When dinner was served at one o' the clock, Elisabeth dutifully moved a small amount of food from fork to mouth but did not taste it. Instead she sat close to her husband, thinking of excuses to brush her hand against his, capturing his gaze whenever possible. They would have very little time together before his departure. A few quiet words, a lengthy embrace, and Donald would be gone from her side.

At half past the hour, Donald and Andrew were at the stair door, depositing muskets into the arms of two lads dressed in rags, both eager for the coins they would earn that afternoon. The men had already bid farewell to their mother, who'd retired to her bedchamber, a handkerchief pressed to her eyes.

Mrs. Edgar and Gibson slipped into the kitchen, allowing the couples a moment of privacy. Andrew drew his wife aside, and Donald did the same, wrapping Elisabeth in his embrace and cradling her against his chest.

After a long moment Donald said softly, "I'm sorry, Bess . . ." His voice broke. "Sorry for all the ways I've failed you as a husband."

She stood on tiptoe to press her cheek to his. "You have not failed me, Donald. Not if you love me."

With a low groan he pulled her closer still. "I do love you. God help me, I do." His mouth found hers, and nothing more was said.

THIRTY-TWO

Words are women, deeds are men.
GEORGE HERBERT

Holding the book of sonnets in her hand, Marjory carefully guided Donald's paper knife along the folded edge, letting the curved blade do its work, freeing the page to reveal the printed text. Odd that Donald had not finished opening the leaves himself.

She'd borrowed his whetstone to sharpen the narrow blade, trying not to let her thoughts dwell on the swords her sons carried. Sharp enough to wound. Sharp enough to kill.

She quickly laid down the paper knife. *Think of something else, Marjory.*

September had ended, and October had begun. In the week since her sons' enlistment, she'd done nothing but worry. Were they eating well? Were their tents dry and their plaids warm? Were they safe from harm? She'd not slept well since their departure.

How could she when her sons lay beneath a moonless sky without wives or servants to attend them?

Marjory put aside the book of sonnets, too tired to read and too restless to sleep, even at that late hour.

Janet fled their quiet house each forenoon, seeking the companionship of her young friends. She remained abroad, feasting on teacakes and gossip until the supper hour, then chattered all through the meal and retired early, exhausted from her daily ventures into society. If she pined for Andrew, Janet kept that sentiment entirely to herself.

Elisabeth was still in deep mourning for her brother. She'd heard nothing from home, and the tailor's son had yet to return. A sad business, delivering such news. Most days Elisabeth remained withindoors, stationed by the drawing room window, embroidering or sewing from dawn until dusk. Such dreary, solitary work! To her credit, Elisabeth quickly put aside her needle whenever Marjory required attention: to brush the tangles from her hair, to read poetry to her, or to engage in a round of piquet. Elisabeth, an expert player, had far more patience with the French card game than Janet, who grew bored long before they reached the obligatory hundred points.

Marjory reached for her playing cards whenever she pleased now that public worship on the Sabbath was no longer permitted. Instead, the sanctuaries were filled with soldiers — some wounded, some prisoners. How very strange on Sunday last to drink tea well into the morning, looking out at a deserted square, listening for a kirk bell that never rang.

As for afternoon tea at Lady Woodhall's, Marjory couldn't possibly join them again after her unfortunate exchange with Charlotte Ruthven. Nae, not an exchange. A diatribe and one-sided at that. Marjory felt certain she was the sole topic of conversation on Monday last, served up like shortbread, flavored with scandalous tidbits about her beloved Donald. Just as well she did not attend, though Mondays would never be the same.

Wrapping her sleeping jacket round her shoulders, Marjory quit her bedchamber and picked up a single burning taper to light her way. When she reached the drawing room, she glanced at Janet's chamber door in passing and saw no light along the threshold. Sound asleep, then. Gibson, too, was curled up in his folding bed in the entrance hall, snoring too loudly to notice his mistress tiptoe past him.

When she pushed open the door to the kitchen, Marjory found Mrs. Edgar perched on a stool beside the wooden dresser, a long table used for dressing meat. Scrubbed clean, it doubled as the housekeeper's desk. She was huddled over the day's broadsheet, squinting at the small print, holding a candle as close to the paper as she dared.

"Mrs. Edgar?"

"Och!" She stood so quickly her tall stool threatened to topple over. "How may I serve ye, mem?"

Marjory scanned the dimly lit kitchen for some reasonable excuse to offer. Finding none, she spoke the truth. "I couldn't sleep and thought, if you were awake, you might not object to company."

"Weel, then." Mrs. Edgar curtsied and patted the lone stool, a tacit invitation to sit. "Is it tea ye'll be wanting? I've coriander biscuits, if ye like. And a wee slice o' hard cheese, if ye're feeling peckish."

A late-night repast was quickly prepared. Mrs. Edgar held up the tray, tipping her head as she asked, "Would ye prefer to sit at yer tea table?"

Marjory hesitated. She *would* be more comfortable. But she would also be alone. "Add a second cup and join me," she finally said, surprising even herself.

"Aye, mem." Her housekeeper's eyes were as round as the dishes on her tray.

A moment later the two women were sipping tea in her bedchamber. Marjory noticed that Helen sat on the edge of the chair as if she were uncertain of her place. "Mrs. Edgar,

I've not read the *Evening Courant.* What news might you share?" Reading was a source of great pride for Helen. Such a discussion might put her at ease.

"Weel, mem, *syne* ye asked." The housekeeper folded her hands in her lap as neatly as any lady. "Monie folk are flitting to the countryside, taking a' their effects."

Marjory had seen the exodus firsthand. "We could do the same," she admitted, gazing at the dark windows facing the High Street. "Return home to Selkirkshire until the rebellion ends. You've not been to Tweedsford, but it's a fine estate."

She'd mentioned the possibility to Donald and Andrew before their departure, but they'd been adamant: Edinburgh was their home now. Under no circumstances was she to think of moving forty miles away, especially not when a brief visit from their wives could sometimes be arranged.

Their stubbornness chafed at Marjory. When had her sons become so headstrong?

"I've niver seen the Borderland," Mrs. Edgar admitted.

"You'll find the counties to the south far greener than Edinburgh," Marjory told her. "The hills are lush and rolling, the rivers and *burns* are lined with trees, and the gardens rival any in Scotland."

Mrs. Edgar gave her a timorous smile. "How *loosome* ye make it a' sound, mem."

Marjory nodded absently. "I was born there. So was my late husband, and so were our sons."

"Hame is kindlier than onie place else," Mrs. Edgar said, then drained her teacup.

Home. Marjory seldom thought of it kindly. Too rural, too quiet, too isolated. But with her sons risking the family's claim on Tweedsford, more drastic measures might be required to guard their estate. She eyed her writing desk across the room. Come the morning she would see what could be done.

"I'll leave ye to yer bed, mem." Mrs. Edgar curtsied, tea tray in hand. "Thank ye for . . . weel, thank ye." She curtsied again and left at once, the dainty china cups dancing in their saucers.

Marjory woke to a sharp autumn chill in her bedchamber. She bathed in haste, grateful for the steaming pitcher of water by her washbowl. Mrs. Edgar had come and gone without waking her. By the sound of it, the housekeeper was busy next door, dressing Elisabeth in her mourning gown.

Remembering the dreadful twelvemonth that followed Sir John's passing, Marjory hoped never to wear black again. Even the latest fashion — black silk embroidered with crimson flowers — held little appeal.

She tapped on the adjoining door, summoning her housekeeper.

"I'll not be a moment," Mrs. Edgar promised, then was as good as her word, slipping through the door before Marjory had finished cleaning her teeth, using a frayed bit of licorice root daubed in cream of tartar. She rinsed the bitter taste from her mouth, then submitted to Mrs. Edgar's ministrations, donning a simple cranberry-colored gown with only a touch of lace edging the square neckline.

No need for ribbons and bows when her vital task of the day was to pen a letter. She'd promised her sons she would not write Holyroodhouse informing the prince of Andrew's health concerns. But she'd made no such vow regarding Lord Mark Kerr, the Honorary Governor of Edinburgh Castle.

Having risen to the rank of general, Lord Mark surely understood the appeal of military life. He would know how to speak to her sons and convince them of the very real danger they faced if this Jacobite rebellion failed as others had before it. The Kerr lands and title would be forfeit, if not her sons' lives. Wasn't Viscount Kenmure summarily tried, found guilty, and beheaded for supporting the Stuart cause in 1715? And could the same not happen to Donald and Andrew?

Her stomach clenched at the mere thought. *Not my sons. Never my sons!*

"Will ye want a cooked breakfast, Leddy Kerr?"

"Nae." Marjory pressed a hand to her waist. "Something lighter. Oatcakes, if they're fresh. But I've a letter that needs writing first. Tell the others I'll join them in a bit."

Alone for the moment, Marjory carried her wooden writing desk across the room and placed it on her tea table, hoping to capture what morning light she could. Once seated, she inked and blotted her sharpened quill, then composed her thoughts, praying for the right words to persuade this man she barely knew but whose assistance she desperately needed.

To General Lord Mark Kerr, Governor of Edinburgh Castle
Thursday, 3 October 1745

My Dear Lord Mark,

I would never presume to take advantage of the distant relations between your noble family and that of my late husband, Lord John Kerr of Selkirk.

No doubt Lord Mark would see through her artifice, knowing she fully intended to exploit the family ties that bound them, however thin. She'd met him on a handful of occasions, all of them formal, with little chance for discourse. He would remember her, though; she was certain of it.

I come to you as an anxious mother of two sons, Lord Donald and Andrew Kerr, whose recent behavior may well dishonor the family name and bring into question our long allegiance to King George.

She could hardly put things more plainly. Even if Lord Mark did not give a fig what happened to her sons, he would care very much if they soiled the name *Kerr.*

Both my sons have imprudently aligned themselves with the Young Pretender. They have enlisted in his service and reside within his camp at Duddingston, where rebellion against the crown is their daily portion.

Marjory nodded at the paper, pleased with her wording. Identifying Charles Edward Stuart as pretender rather than prince would sit well with Lord Mark. But the news of her sons' deep involvement would not. She was counting on a heated response that would stir Lord Mark to action.

A brief letter from your hand impressing upon my sons the gravity of their decision might put a swift and welcome end to things. My own pleas have been ignored, yet I am confident they will heed your advice above all others'.

Honesty was always the wisest course. Flattery helped too. She closed with a reminder of their familial bond in the meekest words she could think of.

I will be ever grateful for any courtesy you might extend to these, your relatives and my beloved sons.

Your faithful, humble servant,
The Dowager Lady Marjory Kerr
Milne Square, Edinburgh

Marjory signed her name with a flourish of ink, then wondered if her sweeping script might negate any claim to humility. She cast a sprinkling of sand across the page and let the ink thoroughly dry before shaking the loose grains into the fireplace.

"Leddy Kerr?" Mrs. Edgar was at her door. "Ye've a caddie here w' a letter from Duddingston."

Marjory quickly sealed her outgoing letter, then hurried to the entrance hall. A young lad in shabby clothes waited for her, as did the rest of the household, eager for news. The caddie held out a folded letter and an open palm, then grinned, his teeth surprisingly white.

"You'll wait while I read it?" she asked, depositing a coin in his hand.

"Oh, aye, mem." He slipped the ha'penny into his pocket. "I've a letter for Leddy Kerr as weel."

Elisabeth stepped forward to receive it, offering the caddie a second copper. No letter for Janet, it seemed. She pouted most unbecomingly.

Marjory moved to the window for more light, praying as she broke the seal. Perhaps Donald had come to his senses. If so, she would not need to beg Lord Mark for assistance. Her son's familiar hand brought a lump to her throat. *God be with you, Donald.* She skimmed the lines, looking for some hint of regret, some change of heart. The letter contained no such admission. Instead it was filled with praise for Prince Charlie and the Highlanders in his charge, with many assurances that their meals and sleeping arrangements were satisfactory.

Cold porridge and watery broth, Marjory feared. And hard, unforgiving ground.

"Shall I take that for ye?" the caddie asked, nodding at her sealed letter.

"Aye," she said, wishing it were not so. "Tell the guard at Edinburgh Castle to see this is delivered to Lord Mark Kerr with haste." She pressed an extra coin in the caddie's hand, rather than trouble Lord Mark with the expense. Caddies were remarkably trustworthy. In crowded Edinburgh, where news scurried up and down the closes like mice, messengers could not afford to cheat their customers.

The lad turned to Elisabeth, a look of expectation on his dirt-streaked face. "Milord said to wait for an answer."

As Elisabeth gazed at Donald's letter, Marjory noted a faint sheen in her daughter-in-law's eyes. Was the news ill or favorable?

"Tell my husband I shall not disappointment him," Elisabeth said at last. "I cannot join in the dancing, but I will proudly stand by his side."

"Dancing?" Janet all but snatched the letter from Elisabeth's hands, then quickly scanned the contents. "Ah! There's to be a ball at Holyroodhouse. On Friday next."

To Marjory's dismay, Janet waved the letter about as if the handwritten missive was no more personal than the *Evening Courant*.

"Kindly inform my husband as well," Janet sang out. "Tell Mr. Andrew Kerr his wife will gladly attend!"

THIRTY-THREE

Women, like princes, find few real friends.
        LORD GEORGE LYTTLETON

The night of the ball was as black as Elisabeth's gown. All the stars were in hiding, and so was the waxing moon. Iron lanterns with scraped horn windows bobbed up and down the High Street, toted by servants doing their masters' bidding, and coal fires belched smoke into the foggy air.

Elisabeth tightly clasped her silk reticule and the poems from Effie Sinclair's students as her sedan chair bounced and swayed through the Netherbow Port, headed for the Palace of Holyroodhouse. At the dowager's insistence, Elisabeth had taken the first chair they'd hailed. "You are the one Lord Kerr will be watching for," her mother-in-law had said. "We'll not be far behind." The chairmen momentarily gave way to a noisy contingent bound for Mr. Smeiton's coffeehouse, then started off again at a trot, eager to deliver their passenger and earn another fare.

Elisabeth steadied herself, pressing the toes of her kid shoes against the door. Was Rob MacPherson being jostled about in a carriage bound for Edinburgh that night? She expected a visit from him any day, bearing news from home, perhaps even a letter from her mother. Dared she let herself hope?

Touching her hair, Elisabeth was relieved to find the dowager's string of pearls still neatly entwined in her topknot of curls. Mrs. Edgar had taken great pains with Elisabeth's toilette, brushing her dark eyebrows into smooth arcs, powdering her face, neck, and arms, then dabbing her cheeks with rouge. "Ye must leuk yer best for the sake o' yer brither's memory."

Simon. If only he were waiting for her at the palace. Standing proudly at the entrance. Wearing his Braemar plaid kilted and belted round his waist. Holding out his hand, inviting her to dance. *Come, my sister.*

Elisabeth sighed into the narrow confines of the sedan chair. *Hail the moon for me, Bess.* His last words to her. Though she'd pleaded with the Nameless One, her brother was gone. Now her husband had followed in Simon's brave footsteps and thrown in his lot with the prince. *But not to the same end, beloved.* As an officer, Lord Donald could simply give orders while others took to the field. For that small blessing Elisabeth was most grateful.

"Yer husband will be pleased to see ye," Mrs. Edgar had said earlier as she added a faint spray of rose water across her shoulders. "I *jalouse* ye're keen to see him as weel."

"I am indeed," Elisabeth had confessed. *Very keen.*

Not much longer now.

Lady Marjory and Janet had dressed for royalty, wearing feathery plumes, rich brocades, and damask slippers. Elisabeth had dressed for Donald. The couple had not seen each other in a fortnight, the longest they'd ever been apart. She missed his company, his literate discourse, his clever smile. Aye, and his touch.

Her husband's letters had been rather short and not as descriptive as she'd hoped, but at least he wrote to her. Janet had received only one letter from Andrew, and that a list of forgotten items to be sent to him at the Duddingston camp. Donald's comments were a bit guarded, as if he feared his letters might be intercepted. King George's spies lurked everywhere, but there were Jacobite informants too.

All of Edinburgh followed the prince's daily rounds with rapt attention. After meeting with his morning council, he enjoyed a midday meal with his principal officers in a public place where any citizen might stand about and admire him. Then he rode out to review his army, attended by his Life Guards and a host of elegant spectators in coaches and on horseback. The most fashionable ladies of the town were waiting to be received in his drawing room when the prince returned. A public supper followed, often with music and, as on this night, a ball.

Elisabeth's sedan chair bounced to an abrupt stop. "Here ye be, milady," the chairman announced as he opened the narrow door. She placed her feet carefully on the muddy ground, glad for her pattens. The moment she deposited a sixpence in his open palm, he and his stout-armed partner went on their way, hailed by a gentleman wearing a pronounced scowl beneath his full-bottomed wig.

Elisabeth looked over the milling crowd adorned in brightly colored silks and satins, their breaths forming small clouds as they called out to one another. Gaiety and conviviality were the order of the evening. Torches blazed across the grounds, casting bright pools of light, illuminating some faces and shadowing others. However would she find Donald at the appointed hour?

"Leddy Kerr?"

Not Donald's voice, yet one she'd been waiting to hear.

She whirled round to find Rob MacPherson standing behind her, his broad frame encased in blue wool and a length of tartan fastened over one shoulder with a round silver brooch.

"You're home," she breathed.

"Aye, milady." He stepped closer. "Only just now."

Rob's soft voice belied the size of him. Everything about him was sturdy and thick: head, neck, arms, chest. If not for his foot, Rob MacPherson would be a man to be reckoned with in the pitch of battle.

"Tell me about Castleton," she urged him. "How fares my mother?"

His dark eyes spoke before his words. "She took the news verra hard."

Elisabeth looked away, awash with guilt. Her poor mother, learning of Simon's death from a friend rather than from her own daughter. "I should have made the journey myself, Mr. MacPherson, rather than burden you."

"Nae," he quickly assured her, "for 'twas nae burden." Unlike some men who looked round when they spoke, Rob kept his gaze fixed on her. "Yer mither was pleased to have the prince's letter. 'Twas a meikle comfort to her."

"What of *my* letter?" she gently pressed.

Rob shifted his stance. "She read it."

Even in the torchlight Elisabeth could see his cheeks turning ruddy.

"Ye'll not be pleased to hear it, Bess. Yer mither tore yer letter in two. Tossed it in the fire. Said 'twas too late."

"Oh." Her face warmed as well. "I didn't

realize you arrived after Michaelmas —"

"Nae, milady," Rob hastened to say. " 'Twas Saturday morn whan I reached Castleton, the day afore the wedding."

Elisabeth stared at him, hoping she'd misunderstood. "Even after she read my letter she married Ben Cromar?"

"Aye, she did, by the banks o' the River Dee. Not monie folk came. 'Twas a rainy afternoon and the Sabbath besides."

Elisabeth stared at the ground, her emotions reeling. She was hurt, aye, but she was angry too. Did a daughter's opinion count for so little? Was Simon's ugly scar of no consequence? She twisted the silken strings of her reticule, waiting for the threat of tears to subside.

"Ye're not happy with her choice."

"Nae, I am not." At least she'd kept her voice even.

After a moment Rob said gently, "Whatsomever ye think o' Mr. Cromar, the man's not afraid o' hard work. Her cottage is in guid repair. And yer mither seemed blithe to take him as her husband."

Elisabeth swallowed her pride. " 'Tis done, then."

He nodded but said nothing more.

In the silence she found the strength to apologize. "Please forgive me for entangling you in family matters."

He lifted her chin, his ungloved hand

surprisingly warm in the cool night air. "I've kenned ye a' my life, Bess. And yer family." He withdrew his touch but not his steady gaze. "If ye'll not mind me asking, why have ye not visited yer mither a' these years? Will yer husband not let ye leave his side?" Before she could answer, he added, "Not that I blame his lordship. I'd feel the verra same, were ye mine."

Elisabeth looked away, embarrassed by a question that had no proper answer. "Lord Kerr is a busy man —"

"Aye, sae I've heard." He glanced down at the roll of papers she kept turning round in her hands. "What have ye there?"

"A gift of poetry for His Royal Highness." She held up the offering tied with a royal blue ribbon. "Written by Mrs. Sinclair's young ladies. Perhaps there is someone I might trust to present them to the prince?"

"Ye might trust me," he chided her. "But the prince will gladly take them from the hand of a loosome leddy like yerself." Rob leaned forward, his breath on her cheek. " 'Twill be an honor to introduce ye to him, Bess."

She eased back, suddenly aware of the solid warmth of his body and the undeniable heat of his gaze. "I am . . . ever in your debt, Mr. MacPherson."

"Och, lass." His voice was low, his tone persuasive. "Can ye not call me Rob as ye once did?"

"Nae, I cannot." Elisabeth sank into a low curtsy, bringing their conversation to a swift and necessary end. "Thank you for your service to my family." She waited, head down, until he responded with a curt bow.

"The pleasure's a' mine, Leddy Kerr." Rob turned on his heel and was soon lost in the crowd.

THIRTY-FOUR

My dancing days are done.
FRANCIS BEAUMONT AND JOHN FLETCHER

Elisabeth stood alone in the palace forecourt, regretting she'd not handled things better. Like his father, Rob was a caring and trustworthy friend. Had he not willingly traveled many miles bearing the saddest of tidings to her mother? In turn, she'd no doubt misread his intentions, then wounded him with her rebuff. *Badly done, Bess.* The only remedy was to apologize when their paths crossed again and hope Rob was in a forgiving mood.

Elisabeth looked toward the road leading to the Canongate, watching for her family members. Whatever had delayed them? With so many persons of rank attending the ball, perhaps the chairmen were busier than usual. Whatever the reason, she was grateful Marjory and Janet had not witnessed her painful exchange with Rob. She would tell them of her mother's marriage soon enough. But not this night.

The shifting fog penetrated her wool cape, crawled up her sleeves, and wrapped its cold tendrils round her neck. Autumn had firmly taken up residence in the capital. At least Donald was no longer required to sleep out of doors. Along with many of the Jacobite officers, he was billeted at the inn at White Horse Close, where she'd met with Simon. Her heart tightened, remembering the look on his face. *I fear I must leave ye, Bess.*

And so you did, dear brother of mine. So you did. She stared into the dark night, wishing she might see him walking toward her, knowing it would never be so.

Instead, she glimpsed Janet and their mother-in-law emerging from their hired sedan chairs. By the time she reached them, the two women were brushing the dust from their skirts and casting disparaging looks at the plain leather-and-wood conveyances, battered and worn from constant use.

"Most unsatisfactory," Marjory grumbled, paying the chairmen nonetheless. She pulled the hood of her cape closer to her chin. "Come, ladies. Lord Kerr promised to meet us at the palace entrance. He'll think we've abandoned him."

Once the dowager slipped a gloved hand round each daughter-in-law's arm, the threesome crossed the forecourt in full sail, their capes billowing from their shoulders. Gentlemen bobbed their heads in recognition, and their ladies were quick to curtsy. It seemed the Kerrs' daring support of the Jacobite cause had not gone unnoticed.

Elisabeth eyed the imposing entranceway to the palace, twice the height of a man and broad enough for four to enter abreast. Above it hung a frontispiece of the Royal Arms of Scotland. In the flickering torchlight she could pick out two enormous unicorns on either side. On the crowned cupola a clock marked the hour. She peered through the fog, struggling to see the hands. *Almost nine.* Donald would not be long in coming.

Whether from the chilly night air or from anticipation, Elisabeth shivered. Might they move a bit faster?

Her mother-in-law was quick to protest. "I declare, Lady Kerr, you will have me walking out of my shoes at this pace."

"The sooner we are inside," Elisabeth reminded her, "the sooner you may dispose of your cape and let everyone admire your beautiful new gown." Her praise was genuine. Miss Callander had outdone herself. The dowager's burgundy-colored taffeta was a paean to lace, ruffles, flounces, and bows. Janet's gown was simpler in design, the watered silk in golden maize a fitting complement to her auburn hair. Her plump forearms were encased in elbow-length ivory kid gloves, and a double strand of pearls circled her throat.

In her black mourning gown, Elisabeth felt all but invisible, though she would gladly wear a coarse linen shift if it might honor Simon's memory.

"Lady Kerr!"

When her name floated across the forecourt, she recognized the voice at once. *Donald.* All three women turned to greet the Kerr heir, a stone's throw away. He looked taller, though that was quite impossible, and more handsome than ever in his blue officer's uniform. When Elisabeth spotted the white cockade proudly displayed on his tricorne, tears clouded her eyes. *My braw Jacobite.*

"I meant to be here sooner," he explained, then bent to kiss each of their hands in turn, lingering over Elisabeth's as if they'd been apart for years rather than a fortnight.

When he stood, her skin warmed beneath his gaze. "I've missed you," she said softly so the others would not hear.

"And I've missed you, milady. Rather fervently." His eyes said the rest.

Having patiently waited her turn, the dowager addressed her son. "You look very well," she told him, her countenance shining with maternal affection. "When shall we expect your brother?"

"Andrew will be along shortly," Donald assured his mother, then offered his arm. "You'll be far more comfortable withindoors." Walking at a stately pace, Donald led

310

them through the entranceway and into the open quadrangle with its classical facades, one for each floor. "Doric, Ionic, and Corinthian," Donald said proudly as if he'd designed them himself.

"But where is the *ball?*" Janet asked, her tone shrill.

Donald hid a bemused smile. "Not to worry, Mrs. Kerr. We've only to follow the crowd."

He guided them toward the entrance to the old tower built for King James V. The young prince's admirers and supporters soon surrounded them, all making their way up a narrow turnpike stair. An occasional torch, mounted high above their heads, lit the way. Everyone spoke at once, their laughter echoing off the masonry walls.

Certain she could not be heard above the din, Elisabeth didn't attempt to converse with Donald as she slowly climbed the stair, preparing her heart for whatever the evening might hold. Naturally she could not dance while in mourning. But if she met the prince, discharged her duty to Mrs. Sinclair, and enjoyed Donald's company for a few hours, her night would be well spent.

One by one the invited guests reached the top of the stair and filed into a long candlelit space, their voices swallowed up by the sheer size of the room, with its polished wood floor and lofty ceiling. If there was a far wall at the

311

opposite end, Elisabeth could not see it for the crush of people. Perhaps when daylight poured through the many windows facing the quadrangle, one might easily grasp the dimensions. But at night, lit only by candelabras, the room was a vast universe unto itself, a world without end.

Beside them a well-laid log fire burned brightly in the hearth, although the room was already warm. Somewhere fiddlers were tuning their instruments, and the clinking of glass and silver filled the air. Hundreds of folk were milling about, exchanging greetings, bowing and scraping, hoping to impress. Elisabeth slipped her hand round the crook of Donald's elbow, grateful to have him by her side.

Donald swept his other arm across the room's expanse. "You can see why 'tis called the Great Gallery."

"No other name would do," Elisabeth agreed. Portraits lined the wood paneled walls, one after another after another. The subjects each displayed a confident stance, their gazes stern, as if daring the artist to make them look anything less than heroic.

"Scotland's kings and queens, beginning with Fergus Mór," Donald explained. "More than one hundred of them, all by the same artist."

Janet arched her brows. "Surely we've not had half that many monarchs." She examined some of the smaller paintings nearby, then shrugged. " 'Tis one portrait, painted over and over."

A familiar chuckle heralded Andrew's arrival. "Quite right, dear wife." He removed his tricorne and kissed her cheek in greeting. "I had the same opinion when first I saw them all. From painting to painting, only the attire changes."

"And so has your own costume, dear boy." The dowager motioned him closer. "Come, let me have a look at you."

Andrew obliged his mother, standing at attention while she conducted her inspection. "Do I pass muster, then?"

"Aye," the dowager said on a sigh, "much as I am reluctant to concede it."

Janet appraised her husband as well. "Sir, you are a credit to your regiment."

"As are you, Lord Kerr," Elisabeth said, pride and fear warring within her. She remembered the first sign of Donald's interest in the Jacobite cause. *I am intrigued.* Why had she not been more cautious instead of encouraging him? The dowager would never forgive her if something happened to her beloved heir.

"There you have it, lad." Donald clapped his hand on Andrew's shoulder. "Our mother and wives approve. We need look no further."

"I approve of your uniforms," the dowager clarified, "but not your politics."

"And I'd be happier with a bit more correspondence," Janet chided her husband. Shorter than the rest of them, she stood on tiptoe, trying in vain to look about the crowded room. "Lord Kerr, have you sufficient influence that you might introduce us to some of the prince's illustrious guests?"

"I confess there are many gentlemen of rank whose identities we've yet to discover. We know Secretary Murray, of course, and Lords Elcho, Ogilvie, Pitsligo, and Nairne. And the Duke of Perth."

Janet's eyes brightened. "A duke, you say?"

"So he is," Andrew boasted. "If there is someone you care to meet, Angus MacPherson is here, and he knows them all."

Janet frowned at her husband. "What business does a tailor have attending a royal ball?"

"The prince's business," Donald said firmly. "Angus MacPherson has made himself . . . ah, quite useful of late. He's present this night but not for the dancing. At the moment I'll wager he's buttonholing one Highland chief or another, seeking more clansmen for the cause."

Andrew lifted a cup of ale from a passing tray. Not his first of the night, Elisabeth suspected. "My brother is right," he said expansively. "Locate Angus MacPherson, and I promise you'll find the prince at his elbow."

"Well! I've never met a prince." Janet was the first to move, pulling the rest of them in

314

tow. "Might he dance with me, do you suppose?"

"The prince has more important matters to attend to," Andrew told her. "If you wish a dancing partner, my dear, look no further than your husband."

The Kerrs walked a few more steps, weaving past ladies fluttering their fans and gentlemen downing pints of ale, before a familiar voice called out, "Hoot! If it isna Lord Kerr and his bonny wife."

Angus MacPherson made his way round the couples assembling for the first dance of the evening. "Come, come!" the tailor cajoled them. " 'Tis time yer family met His Royal Highness." He added in a stage whisper, "The prince is in verra guid spirits. Alexandre de Boyer, the Marquis d'Éguilles, has landed in Montrose with money and arms."

Swept down the length of the room with her family, Elisabeth soon discovered that the Great Gallery did, in fact, have a far wall, where a bank of windows overlooked the gardens. But it wasn't the dark panes glistening in the candlelight that commanded her attention; it was Charles Edward Stuart.

The bonny young prince sat enthroned before them, with his high, smooth brow and his tightly curled periwig. His posture, his demeanor, even the dignified manner in which he turned to greet them bespoke his royal birth. So did the candelabras standing round him, bathing him with light, and the clan chiefs in their Highland finery, watching over him with a fierce pride.

A month ago she'd seen the prince from a distance entering the forecourt of Holyrood-house. Now he was close enough to touch, surrounded by fawning ladies and earnest young gentlemen trying to solicit his favor.

The prince smiled at her and then waved Angus forward. Whispered words were exchanged. Angus stepped to the side, his broad face beaming as he began his introductions. "May I present Lord Donald Kerr o' Selkirk, one o' yer newly enlisted men, and his wife, Leddy Elisabeth Kerr."

She sank into a low curtsy, almost touching the floor with her forehead. A moment later she nearly lost her balance when the prince himself reached down and lifted her to her feet.

His eyes met hers. "My dear Lady Kerr. I know you are in mourning for your brother." The prince's English bore a noticeable Italian accent from his years in exile, but his voice was kindness itself. "You have my utmost sympathy. And my deepest gratitude for your sacrifice."

Elisabeth swallowed the lump rising in her throat, fighting to maintain her composure. *Simon, dear Simon!* Would she ever think of him without weeping?

"I am honored," she finally managed to say,

then curtsied again. Standing once more, she remembered the small roll of beribboned poetry and held it out to him. "From the young scholars of Mrs. Euphame Sinclair, an esteemed schoolmistress."

The prince received her offering with aplomb and passed it to another for safekeeping, murmuring his thanks before resuming his seat.

When Elisabeth stepped back, Angus MacPherson quickly introduced the others. Andrew bowed with great decorum, and Janet was won to the cause the moment the prince inclined his royal head in her direction.

"And now," Angus said, "may I present the Dowager Lady Marjory Kerr, mither o' Lord Donald and widow o' Lord John Kerr o' Selkirk."

The prince regarded her mother-in-law with marked interest. "My advisors tell me your late husband did not support my father's cause. Yet you have shown me great honor, madam, entrusting me with your sons." He paused, as if inviting an explanation.

"Your Royal Highness." The dowager curtsied with the grace of a lady half her age. "I ask only that you return my sons to me, for they are all I treasure in this world."

"Ah, madam." His smile was so tender the young ladies at his feet nigh to swooned. *"Ubi enim est thesaurus tuus, ibi est et cor tuum."*

Elisabeth could almost hear Effie Sinclair whispering in her ear, translating the Latin. *For where your treasure is, there will your heart be also.* The prince was correct. Donald and Andrew were indeed a treasure, which the dowager wanted close by her side, like the gold safely hidden beneath her bedchamber floor.

But those sons belonged to Charles Edward Stuart now, and he would not easily let them go. Not with an invasion of England on the horizon.

THIRTY-FIVE

The dangers gather
as the treasures rise.

SAMUEL JOHNSON

"What think you of this one?" Janet held out her third poem of the morning, the ink still fresh.

Marjory took the paper with some reluctance. However elegant her daughter-in-law's handwriting, Janet's poetry left something to be desired. Taking care not to let her face give her away, Marjory skimmed the latest offering.

Poem by a Lady on Meeting His Royal
Highness the Prince Regent

O handsome prince! Such warmth, such
grace!
When thou looked down to see my face,
My heart did make a solemn vow,
As I beheld thy royal brow.

319

The rest was equally cloying. Marjory pursed her lips at a loss for how she might respond without hurting her feelings.

"Mr. Ruddiman will no doubt be eager to publish these," Janet said, smiling as she reached for another sheet of paper. "I believe each one is better than the last."

"Oh, aye," Marjory quickly agreed, averting her gaze. Thomas Ruddiman, publisher of the *Caledonian Mercury,* had printed many a Jacobite verse, penned by various unnamed gentlewomen. Surely he would have the good taste not to put abroad her daughter-in-law's efforts.

Janet moved her pen swiftly across the page, her hazel eyes alight, her dimples showing. The notion that Janet Kerr had formed an attachment to the prince was astonishing to say the least. Aye, she was a Highlander by birth, but she'd always turned up her nose at the Jacobites. Now she wholly embraced their cause, wearing an entire row of white silk cockades across the bodice of her gown lest anyone doubt her newfound devotion.

Was it Andrew's resolve to bear arms for the prince that convinced Janet to discard her allegiance to King George? Or had a single evening at the palace, a glittering moment in the presence of royalty, captured her heart?

Marjory fiddled with the lace trim on her sleeves, avoiding the embarrassing truth: the charming young prince had stolen her heart as well. When she'd asked His Royal Highness to send Donald and Andrew home, she'd meant at once, not when the Rising ended. But the prince's response had been so gallant, she'd pleaded with him no further, swept up in the admiration — nae, adoration — of Charles Edward Stuart.

If such behavior was daft, Marjory was not alone. Even Charlotte Ruthven was seen on the High Street displaying a white cockade on her cape. The ladies of Edinburgh were mad for Prince Charlie, prompting naysayers to decry his "petticoat patronage." But who better to support him than loyal wives and mothers when his army required brave husbands and sons?

Besides, Marjory had never heard a word from Lord Mark Kerr. Who knew what sort of turmoil the government was thrown into after Gladsmuir? She and her family had chosen the right side. Marjory was certain of it now.

Busy with her writing, Janet paused long enough to shake her feathery quill at Elisabeth, who sat quietly reading by the fire. "Will you not try your hand at poetry, Lady Kerr?"

"I am afraid I have no gift for it," Elisabeth said, closing her book. "But 'tis a fine day for sewing. I shall be in my bedchamber should anyone have need of me." She disappeared with a whisper of black silk.

In seasons past Marjory might have objected, insisting a sewing needle belonged in the hands of a servant. Of late she'd begun to see things differently. If her grieving daughter-in-law found solace in hemming a gown or stitching a seam, so be it. Elisabeth had the sense to work in private, offending no one. Nor did she bring out each finished garment, expecting others to applaud.

"Ah!" Janet said, appraising the lengthy verse before her. "I do believe this will be your favorite."

The sound of unfamiliar voices in the entrance hall provided a timely escape. " 'Twill have to wait, I'm afraid." Marjory quickly rose to investigate.

When Gibson stepped into the drawing room to announce their visitors, he bore a look of surprise. Nae, of shock. "Catherine Maxwell, Countess o' Nithsdale, and the Leddies Barbara and Margaret Stuart o' Traquair."

Marjory instinctively touched her hair, then the neckline of her very ordinary green gown, wishing she looked more presentable. She'd entertained many a lord and lady but never three daughters of the Dowager Countess of Traquair, whose grand estate stood not ten miles from Tweedsford. Whatever had brought them to her door?

"Lady Nithsdale," Marjory began, offering

a deep curtsy. "What an unexpected honor." Poetry forgotten, Janet stepped beside her to greet their guests as well, hiding her ink-stained fingers behind her back.

"The honor is ours," Lady Nithsdale said as all three women curtsied.

Impeccably dressed, the Earl of Nithsdale's wife and her unmarried twin sisters were as handsome as any portrait, with their dark hair and luminous eyes, their oval faces and full features. All three were perhaps a decade younger than she, Marjory decided. Even standing near a well-lit window, their fair complexions were as smooth as porcelain.

"We meant to call a fortnight ago, after the prince's ball," Lady Nithsdale said, her expression most sincere. "Can you forgive us, Lady Marjory?"

"Of course," she said, her mind spinning. *Forgive a countess!* "Come and have tea, won't you?" At any hour, in any situation, a pot of black tea was the best recourse. "Janet, kindly invite Lady Elisabeth to join us." Marjory looked askance at her daughter-in-law's hands, hoping she understood. *Do something about the ink.*

The six were soon seated round the drawing room table, the Traquair ladies having divested themselves of their cloaks, gloves, and hats. However warm the temperature inside, out of doors the weather was cool, rainy, and bleak. Not at all a day for visit yet here they were.

Marjory prayed their morning tea would be up to her guests' expectations. Mrs. Edgar did not disappoint. Wearing her best apron and cap, she served freshly baked treacle scones, still warm to the touch. Marjory knew the housekeeper had baked them for the afternoon, so she thought it very canny of Mrs. Edgar to serve them now. Barbara Stuart dotted her scone with butter, clearly delighted with the rich texture, while her sister, Margaret, praised their housekeeper's baking talents. Lady Nithsdale merely smiled, as if enjoying a secret known only to her.

All through tea Marjory nodded at Gibson whenever something was needed. *Hot water. Fresh linens. More scones. Clean spoons.* Each time he followed her pointed gaze, then swiftly did her bidding.

The Kerrs soon discovered Lady Nithsdale's favorite topic of conversation: her two daughters. "Mary is thirteen, and Winifred, ten," she explained. "Named after their grandmothers."

Rather famous grandmothers, as Marjory recalled. Lady Mary gave birth to seventeen children, and Lady Winifred rescued her husband from the Tower of London the night before his execution. Weighty legacies for girls of any age to bear.

"A mother is always happiest with her ildren beneath her roof," Marjory said.

Lady Nithsdale sighed expansively. "I *do* miss them, and their father as well. Still," she said, brightening, "my sisters and I have a duty to our prince while he is in Edinburgh." She leaned closer, gently easing aside her empty teacup. "You have done far more than your duty, Lady Marjory. Two sons willing to fight for the cause! Would that I had lads of an age to offer His Royal Highness."

"I did not offer them," Marjory was quick to say, wanting no credit for their decision. "Lord Kerr and his brother presented themselves at the palace on their own accord."

Lady Nithsdale lifted one elegant finger. "Ah, but you did not stand in their way. And now that you've met the prince, you understand their zeal."

"I do," Marjory said, then surprised herself by adding, "and I believe I share it."

"Well done." A satisfied look on her face, Lady Nithsdale turned to Elisabeth, who'd been unusually quiet that morning. "No one at this table has made a greater sacrifice than you, Lady Kerr."

Elisabeth's eyes remained dry and her voice steady. "My brother gave his life for a cause greater than himself. I hope my husband will not be required to do the same. Though he is willing —"

"Indeed." Marjory quickly changed the subject. "Have you news, Lady Nithsdale, of how long the prince's men will tarry in Duddingston?"

"We cannot be certain," the countess replied, exchanging glances with her sisters. "Rumor has it the prince will invade England by month's end."

Janet's eyes widened. " 'Tis but a week."

"Aye," Barbara sighed. "We'll surely soak our handkerchiefs with tears when the officers leave."

"Oh, we shall," her sister Margaret agreed. "They are ever so courageous."

Marjory knew the Traquair ladies enjoyed daily forays to the palace, making themselves at home in the Duke of Hamilton's apartments with Margaret Murray of Broughton, the beautiful Lady Kilmarnock, and the fair-haired Lady Ogilvie.

Might *she* be invited to join their illustrious circle? Was that the purpose of this visit?

Marjory took a quick sip of tea, if only to hide her excitement. Imagine! Mingling with His Royal Highness and his council, who met in the prince's drawing room each morning to discuss their plans and policies. Everyone knew their names: Gordon, Lochiel, Keppoch, and the rest. Even if 'twere only for a week, Marjory would feast on the memories for a lifetime.

When she looked up, she found Lady Nithsdale studying her closely.

"I wonder, Lady Marjory, if we might speak privately? 'Tis a matter of some urgency."

"Certainly." *This is it, then. The invitation.* Marjory stood, aware of her gestures, her posture, hoping the countess would not find her manners wanting. She asked Elisabeth to entertain their guests, then escorted Lady Nithsdale to her chamber, trying to remain calm.

Once they were seated in the best of her upholstered chairs, Marjory inclined her head in what she hoped might be a flattering pose and waited for the countess to speak first.

"Lady Marjory, what I am about to ask of you is quite confidential."

"Oh?" She tried to sound nonchalant.

Her brown eyes glowed. "I can think of only a handful of ladies in all of Edinburgh to whom I might extend such an opportunity."

"You are most kind." Marjory could no longer contain her smile. She would wear her gold damask tomorrow, her dark pink silk on Saturday, and her flowered chintz on Sunday. "Tell me what you have in mind."

Lady Nithsdale lightly touched Marjory's sleeve. "As I am sure you are aware, the prince's council meets each morning."

"Aye." Marjory beamed. "So my son has told me."

"Yesterday their discussion was of particular importance." The countess lowered her voice. "As you can imagine, mounting a military campaign is very costly."

"I'm sure it is," Marjory said, suddenly

sure of anything. Must she pay for the privilege of sipping tea at Holyroodhouse?

The countess pressed on. "You've no doubt met Lord Elcho, the prince's aide-de-camp."

"I saw him once. At the ball." Marjory paused, trying to sort out the connection. If Lord Elcho's approval was required for admission to the prince's inner chambers, Donald might be of assistance. At the moment she could speak only the truth. "We were not introduced."

"Easily remedied." Another one of her dazzling smiles. "Few people know this, but Lord Elcho met with the prince at Gray's Mill and presented His Royal Highness with a most worthy contribution."

Marjory nodded yet dared not inquire the sum. Money was hardly an appropriate topic of conversation among gentlewomen.

Then, bold as brass, Lady Nithsdale stated the amount. "Fifteen hundred pounds."

Marjory's eyes widened as a slight gasp slipped out. *Fifteen hundred?*

"Aye," the countess agreed, "a fortune to some. But to those of us with property, a wise investment." The many rings on the countess's fingers caught the light, winking at Marjory. "You have chosen well, supporting the prince. Now your gold could ensure victory for the right side. Our side."

My gold. Marjory's gaze was drawn to the corner of her woolen carpet where four hundred guineas lay beneath the floor. And there, under the mahogany washstand, another four hundred. Leather purses filled with gold were hidden all over the room. Perhaps she could spare one or two for the prince.

"You have already given your greatest treasure," Lady Nithsdale reminded her gently.

My sons. Marjory stood, then slowly walked toward the nearest loose board, as if in a trance. What was money compared to Donald and Andrew?

"When Lord Elcho shared his fifteen hundred pounds, the prince immediately made him his aide-de-camp. Think what His Royal Highness might do for your sons if you made a similar gift to the cause. *Think*, Lady Marjory!"

Marjory closed her eyes, longing to rub her temples, which were already beginning to throb.

If her gold earned the prince's favor . . .

If her gold assured her sons a place of honor . . .

If her gold might keep them safe . . .

A snippet of truth, learned long ago, flitted through her mind. *With favour wilt thou compass him as with a shield.* Could the Lord alone protect her sons? Or in time of war, was her trust better placed in gold? Something she could touch. Something of value.

Lady Nithsdale was standing beside her

now, the scent of lavender wafting from the rich folds of her gown. "When victory comes, as it surely will, the prince will repay you, Lady Marjory. 'Tis not a gift, really, but a loan. What say you, madam? For the sake of your sons?"

A loan. Marjory took her first full breath in many minutes. *A good man showeth favour, and lendeth.* Aye, that was an easier prospect. She would be investing the family's gold, not giving it away.

"Lady Nithsdale, if you will kindly repair to the drawing room, I will take a close look at my resources." Marjory opened the chamber door for her, inclining her head. "I shan't be long."

The countess laughed, a bright, musical sound. "I believe 'twill be a treasure worth waiting for."

Thirty-Six

O moon, thou climb'st the skies!
How silently, and with how wan a face!
Sir Philip Sidney

Gazing out her bedchamber window, Elisabeth heard the clock chime half past four. Already darkness was falling. On the High Street below, folk walked with their heads bent down, fighting the sharp October wind that blew hard from the west. The coffeehouses, taverns, and oyster cellars overflowed with patrons. Many were singing Jacobite ballads, their off-key voices filled with bravado and soaked in ale.

In six weeks Charlie had beguiled the capital, body and soul. Edinburgh Castle still remained in the hands of King George's men, but from its portcullis downward, the town belonged to the bonny prince.

Elisabeth looked up, searching the eastern sky. Soon the full moon would begin rising, as round and as gold as the dowager's guineas delivered into the prince's hands by Angus

MacPherson. " 'Twould be unthinkable for me to do so in person," her mother-in-law had explained on Friday last. "I trust Mr. MacPherson to see our gold safely to Holyroodhouse. He'll make certain Lord Kerr and Andrew are by his side for the . . . presentation."

Whatever Lady Nithsdale had said or done to persuade her, the dowager had been most generous, it seemed. The amount was not mentioned, but Elisabeth saw the look in Angus's eyes when he began stuffing the many leather purses inside his clothing. "His Royal Highness will be verra pleased," he'd said, a bit flustered, his waistcoat bulging. "I'll send a caddie, bidding Rob to bring my greatcoat. We'll take care o' things, Leddy Kerr. Have nae fear."

Hours later Angus had returned from the palace with a note from Secretary Murray of Broughton, expressing the prince's heartfelt gratitude. The dowager had seemed disappointed not to receive a letter in the prince's hand and even more perturbed that an invitation to morning tea never came from the Traquair ladies. "I cannot simply present myself at the palace door," she'd fretted all week long. "Who knows what sort of reception I might find?"

Her agitation was somewhat placated when she learned her sons had advanced in rank, appointed to the prince's Life Guards under

Lord Elcho. Elisabeth was grateful as well. The Life Guards were a prestigious group of gentlemen and merchants assigned to protect the prince. Not only was the position an honorable one; it was also less hazardous. When the time for battle came, they would not lead the charge.

A brief note from Donald was read aloud last evening at supper.

Your gift of Kerr gold secured us fine mounts, French uniforms, and some degree of respect. I hope you will not feel the loss of those guineas too dearly, Mother.

If the dowager missed having so many leather pouches beneath her floor, she did not say so. What she did miss were her sons, which she bemoaned on a daily basis.

Elisabeth felt quite the same. She'd not seen Donald since her visit to White Horse Close more than a week ago, and then 'twas only for an hour. To stem the growing problem of desertion among his men, the prince insisted they keep to their quarters. Hence, Jacobite officers who were billeted at the inn took turnabout, vacating their cramped sleeping quarters for an hour to accommodate visiting wives. The room was dank and dirty, the bedsheets worse, but at least in that small, windowless room Elisabeth had Donald all to herself.

Most of the females she passed on the stair weren't wives at all but tavern maids and servant girls. "The prince is anxious to leave Edinburgh," Donald told her when last they were together. "If his men remain in town much longer, he fears they'll be thoroughly debauched by women and drink." Elisabeth understood those fears. Though Donald seldom drank to excess, women were another matter.

The note she'd received from him that morning was a terse command rather than a loving request. *Tomorrow night at eight.* Not a word of endearment, not even a signature. Did her husband miss her as she missed him? Or did he think of her only occasionally, when he lay alone on his narrow bed? *If he lay alone . . .*

Nae. Elisabeth banished the thought before it took root. Tomorrow evening at eight she would sink into his embrace and count herself fortunate to be the wife of Lord Kerr of Selkirk.

Hearing footsteps approach, Elisabeth turned toward the door.

"Leddy Kerr?" Mrs. Edgar softly knocked, then entered the bedchamber, balancing a steaming cup of tea and a plate of sweet almond biscuits. She held them up with a tentative smile. "With milk and sugar, the way ye like it."

Murmuring her thanks, Elisabeth sat at her

dressing table and moved aside her sewing basket to make room for the housekeeper to serve her tea. When Elisabeth noticed her scissors gleaming in the candlelight, an idea came to mind. "Mrs. Edgar, would you kindly snip a lock of my hair?"

"Nae mair than a lock?" The housekeeper took the scissors to hand, cutting the air to test them. "I thocht whan the moon was *fu'*, a leddy cut her hair a' the way round. To make it grow, ye ken."

Elisabeth took a sip of her tea and smiled. "Aye, so I've heard. But I need just one small curl."

"Oo aye." Mrs. Edgar nodded. "For Lord Kerr."

"If you would." Elisabeth put down her teacup and bowed her head slightly. " 'Tis so thick in the back, I'll hardly miss it."

Mrs. Edgar took her time, choosing one spot, then another, until she found what she was looking for. She snipped with great care, then held out her hand, a slender curl nestled in her palm. "Will this do?"

"It will indeed." Elisabeth reached for a piece of stationery and Donald's paper knife. She quickly fashioned a small square and folded it round the lock of hair. Would he think the gesture too sentimental? Or would he keep it in a pocket close to his heart? Perhaps if she gave him something useful along with it, Donald would not find her gift too trifling.

"Mrs. Edgar, do you know the whereabouts of Lord Kerr's winter gloves? I've looked high and low and not found them." Made from sturdy lambskin and lined with rabbit fur, the handsome pair was her anniversary gift to him December last. Now that colder weather was upon them, his thin kid gloves would never do. And a Life Guard needed to look his best for the prince.

"I'll find them," the housekeeper assured her as she began searching through his clothes press. She took her time, lifting out each item of clothing, checking his coat pockets, and reaching into the far recesses of the narrow drawers. "There ye are!" Mrs. Edgar's arm disappeared inside the furniture as she strained to claim the prize. After much effort she pulled out one leather glove, then a second, and grinned as she held them up by the fingers. "A *saicret* nae mair," Mrs. Edgar said proudly, giving them a gleeful shake.

A small white card slipped out and fell soundlessly onto the carpet.

"What's this, now?" Mrs. Edgar bent down to collect it and paused only for an instant before slipping the card in her oversized apron pocket. "Och, 'tis nothing."

Elisabeth saw the color rising up the housekeeper's neck and the look of pity in her eyes. "Come, Mrs. Edgar. Is it truly nothing?"

Her lower lip began to tremble. "Nae."

"Let me see it, please." Elisabeth held out her hand.

"Och, Leddy Kerr." Mrs. Edgar slowly pulled the card from her pocket. "I wish ye wouldna read it."

Elisabeth hesitated, so sorrowful was the woman's expression. But she had to read it, had to know what troubled her housekeeper so. "Whatever words are on this card, you are not to blame, Mrs. Edgar. Not for a moment."

"Bliss ye, milady." She sniffed, her tears coming in earnest. "I wouldna hurt ye for anything."

Elisabeth took the small card, surprised to find her hands shaking.

One side was plain. No embossing, no ink. When Elisabeth turned the card over, Mrs. Edgar looked away.

The words were few, but they were enough.

May these gloves warm your hands,
as your hands warmed me.

J. M.

Neat, round letters, penned with care. The writer had weighed every word. *Your hands warmed me.* Donald, her husband, her love, had touched this woman. Nae, had warmed her.

J. M.

"Who is she?" Elisabeth whispered, pinching the card as if to make it speak. *Jean? Jessie? Jo?*

"I dinna ken," Mrs. Edgar said, wringing her apron strings, her face a picture of misery. "Half the toun has a family name beginning with *M.* Is it McDonald, mebbe? McKenzie? Mitchell? Och, milady, I canna say wha she might be." Her brow darkened. "Though I ken a wird or two would suit her verra weel."

Elisabeth lifted her head, an image dancing before her eyes. The widow at Assembly Close. A handsome woman several years older than she. *Jane Montgomerie.* When she looked down at the card, there she was.

J. M.

The letters began to swim as Donald's voice whispered inside her. *You alone have my heart.*

"Nae!" With a soft cry she threw the card into the fireplace. " 'Tis not true. I do not have your heart, Donald. I do not. *I do not!*" She fell to her knees, crushing her black gown against the carpet.

Mrs. Edgar knelt beside her. "Is there anything I can do, milady?"

Elisabeth shook her head, her face awash in tears.

They remained there, lady and maid, until every trace of light in the windows disappeared. At last Mrs. Edgar rose and helped Elisabeth to her feet and gently seated her at her dressing table before finding two clean handkerchiefs.

"Thank you," Elisabeth murmured, embarrassed to be seen in such a state.

She watched Mrs. Edgar fasten the shutters round the room, then light fresh beeswax candles, filling the air with the scent of honey. Muted sounds floated up from the street below. A man laughing. The clip-clop of a horse. A mother calling to her children. Elisabeth listened but did not truly hear so disjointed were her thoughts.

Finally Mrs. Edgar stood before her, hands folded at her waist. "Have ye niver wondered why Peg flitted like she did?"

"Peg Cargill?" Elisabeth dabbed at her eyes. "I believe she feared the Highlanders."

"Nae, milady. She feared yer husband."

Elisabeth stared at her in disbelief. *Not one of our own servants. Not Peg.*

"She didna tell a soul but me," Mrs. Edgar said grimly. "Mind ye, he didna misuse her. He leuked, but he didna touch. Still, 'twas mair than the *puir* lass could bear."

"I see." Indeed, Elisabeth saw it all quite clearly: the hunger on his face, the desire in his eyes. "You're certain Peg told no one else?"

"She promised me she wouldna. And I've not breathed a wird, not even to Gibson."

Elisabeth glanced toward the door, thinking of the household. "No one must be told, Mrs. Edgar. Especially not the Dowager Lady Kerr."

She frowned at that. "Should a mither not ken what her son is capable o' doing?"

Elisabeth sighed, shaking her head. "Naught would be gained by it. Either she would count your story as false and hold it against you. Or she would discover it to be true and suffer endlessly from the shame." She stood, taking Mrs. Edgar's chapped hands in hers. "I must apologize on Lord Kerr's behalf."

"Och, milady. I kenned what kind o' man ye married. The gossips are not aye right, but they're not aye wrong." Mrs. Edgar's voice softened. "Dinna blame yerself. Ye ken what the Buik says. 'A faithful man wha can find?' "

I thought I'd found one. Elisabeth gently released her. "I'm afraid I've kept you from your duties."

"Not at a', milady. I'll be in the kitchen if ye've need o' me." Mrs. Edgar looked at her a moment longer, compassion in her gray eyes, before she curtsied and was gone.

Alone in her chamber Elisabeth held on to the bedpost, feeling faint as the truth sank in. *The gossips were not always wrong.* Meaning Jane Montgomerie wasn't the only woman her husband had bedded. *I made the acquaintance of many women.* Aye, so he had. Not only before they married, but after the wedding as well.

Her head fell forward. *How many, Donald?* She sank onto their bed, her eyes again filling with tears. *How many times have you betrayed me?*

Nae, she would not ask him that.

But she would ask him why.

"Why, Donald?" She spoke the words aloud, her throat tight with grief. "Why is my love not enough?"

THIRTY-SEVEN

The living man who does not learn,
is dark, dark, like one walking in the night.
MING LUM PAOU KEËN

"Will ye tell yer wife, milord?"

Donald noted the spark in Rob Mac-Pherson's eye. Was it curiosity? Or mistrust? Rob had become a permanent fixture at White Horse Close, slipping among the ranks, exchanging vital information, yet never drawing attention to himself.

"Aye, I'll inform Lady Kerr when I see her this eve," Donald told the tailor's son. "Though I imagine she's received news of the council's ruling by now. They've hardly kept it a secret." Donald cast his gaze round the inn's noisy public room crowded with Jacobite officers raising their glasses with loud huzzahs. Their long-awaited orders had finally come. *Prepare to march southward. First place of rendezvous: Dalkeith.*

"Mebbe they're lifting their glasses to King

Geordie," Rob said with a wry smile. He took a long drink of ale. " 'Tis the auld Hanoverian's birthday, ye ken. Two-and-sixty."

Donald nodded. "I heard the guns saluting him from the harbor." Nearly a dozen English ships were anchored off Leith, blocking the promised help from the French. The newly arrived *Gloucester,* with its fifty guns, increased the looming threat.

The Jacobites had already tarried in Edinburgh too long, trying to raise capital, struggling to increase their numbers. They could delay no longer.

"Naught but one hour," Lord Elcho had warned his men. "Then send your ladies home and be ready to depart at a moment's notice."

Donald consulted his watch yet again. *Our last hour, Bess.*

His brother stood near the inn door, watching for their wives, an anxious look on his face. Andrew's color was poor — flushed cheeks above an ashen neck — and his wheezing more pronounced. Donald repeatedly cautioned him to rest whenever he could, but his brother insisted on becoming the equal of the other guards. To his credit, Andrew's seat on his mount had improved considerably over the last month. Instead of just polishing his French musket, he'd learned how to employ it.

His brother's determination had fueled his

own. Donald found he was a better rider for the effort and a more accurate marksman. But in the dark hours of the night, fear and apprehension gnawed at his soul. The enlistment notice had traveled home in *his* waistcoat, not Andrew's. If anything happened to his brother, Donald would wear the guilt round his neck like a noose.

He eyed his pocket watch. *Nearly eight.*

Rob elbowed him. "There's yer leddy."

Donald stood just as Elisabeth turned in his direction. As if for the first time, her beauty struck him like the flat blade of a rapier, knocking him back on his heels. Glossy hair gathered on the crown of her head. Long, graceful neck. Full, sweet mouth. And dark blue eyes looking for him.

"I've not seen her in a week," he admitted to Rob, climbing over the rough bench where he'd been sitting. " 'Twill be a short hour, I fear."

Rob looked up at him, his black eyes sharp as stones. "I hope ye ken what a lucky man ye are."

"Aye," Donald said over his shoulder, already making his way through the restless crowd, dodging uplifted tappit-hens with ale sloshing over the rims and red-headed Highlanders swaying on their feet.

Prudently, Elisabeth waited for him. Even with Gibson by her side, she might be swept into some drunken captain's lap with his stout arm round her waist, the stubble of his beard chafing her tender skin. The thought of it sent Donald crashing through a knot of soldiers. "Lady Kerr!" he called out loudly enough to stake his claim on her.

Andrew and Janet, not wasting a moment, had already started for the stair, bound for a vacant room, when Donald finally reached his wife's side. "You came," he said a bit breathless, wishing he sounded more like a royal guardsman and less like a besotted fool.

"I was summoned." Elisabeth held up his brief, scrawled note. " 'Tis eight o' the clock, aye?" Though her tone was light, her point was not lost on him.

Donald bowed and kissed her gloved hand. "I had only a moment before the caddie departed for the High Street," he explained, wishing he'd not been so brusque with his pen. "Will you forgive me, milady?"

Elisabeth looked into his eyes, any trace of amusement gone. "I shall endeavor to, milord." She lightly rested her hand on his arm rather than curling it round his elbow. "Shall we?"

Her cool demeanor puzzled him. Was Elisabeth not as eager for their hour together as he? She'd written him letters almost daily, expressing her affection in no uncertain terms. Perhaps his impending departure troubled her. "Have you heard the news from Holyroodhouse?" he asked, testing his theory.

"Over supper," she admitted, drawing closer to his side as they wove through the room, thick with peat smoke. "Gibson informed us the army might be leaving soon."

"We ride out with the prince on the morrow," Donald said as gently as he could, "though we've not been told the hour."

Elisabeth looked at him. "You'll send word? So your mother and I may see you off?"

"Depend upon it." Just as he'd suspected, Elisabeth was upset because he was leaving, nothing more.

A chorus of ribald comments followed them up the stair. Donald led her to a warren of small rooms, muffled voices behind each door. "I fear our lodgings are no better than last time," he warned her, a musty smell rolling over them when they entered the room. A mouse skittered along the far edge of the wall, and filmy traces of a cobweb hung from the ceiling. He'd done his best to straighten his belongings. Andrew hadn't been so diligent, nor had Duncan Belhaven, the Life Guard who shared their room. "At least we have the place to ourselves. Andrew made other arrangements."

"Good," she said, unfastening her wool cape, "for I prefer not to share you with anyone."

Donald heard something in her voice. Not anger or impatience. More like resignation.

Little wonder with such squalid accommodations.

As Elisabeth smoothed her hair in place, he studied her regal profile, reminding him again of how much he'd missed her. And how much he loved her. Had he not told her so on the afternoon of his departure? *I do love you. God help me, I do.* Far from idle words, they were meant as a pledge of faithfulness even though he was not certain such fidelity was possible.

The strumpets loitering about the inn at White Horse Close offered little temptation. Lucy Spence, however, was harder to resist. On two occasions the young widow had appeared at the inn door, her identity well concealed and her intentions abundantly clear. Other than their brief interludes in a hastily borrowed room, he'd been a model husband since enlisting, though he could hardly boast of such things to his dear wife.

He latched the door behind them. "We shall miss our feather bed," he confided, glancing at the narrow heather mattress tossed on a bare wooden floor. The unpainted walls, low beams, and dearth of windows made the room especially dreary. "I did manage to find candles, such as they are." He held up two stubs in plain iron holders.

"And I brought you something." Elisabeth loosened the strings of her reticule. "To keep you warm." She held up his gloves.

"Well done, Bess. I fear we have a cold winter ahead." He took the lambskin gloves from her hands. "I last wore these on Candlemas. At Lady Northesk's ball in Covenant Close."

Elisabeth nodded, not quite meeting his gaze. "We both wore dark blue that evening."

"Aye, we did." He slipped his left hand inside the glove, relishing the softness of the rabbit fur against his skin.

"I thought you might have missed them," Elisabeth said, watching him closely.

"Indeed I did." When he tried on the right glove, Donald discovered something sharp edged and stiff inside. "What have we here?" As he pulled out a square of paper, his wife's complexion turned the color of fresh snow on the Eildon Hills.

She did not speak, only gazed at the paper as he unfolded it.

"Oh, Bess." He touched the curl of dark hair resting inside. "For remembrance, is it?"

"So the auld wives say." She turned her head, blinking as if a speck of dust were trapped in her eye.

He refolded the paper and slid it back inside. "To keep it safe," he told her, then tossed the gloves on a battered corner table, wanting far more of his wife than a lock of hair. "Bess," he said softly, drawing her closer, kissing her neck. "We've not much time. Let me help you."

After a moment's hesitation she lifted her arms, giving him access to the laces and ties, the stays and hoops that held her mourning gown in place. His nimble fingers moved with practiced efficiency while he murmured endearments, hoping to put her at ease.

"You look lovely tonight," he began, lightly touching her cheek in passing. "I believe black suits you after all. Do tell Mrs. Edgar she's turned into a respectable lady's maid," he said, admiring the sweep of Elisabeth's hair. Though he longed to pull out her many hairpins and run his hands through the thick and fragrant mass, he could never hope to put it all aright when their brief tryst ended.

When only her chemise remained, Donald made short work of his clothing, and they were both left shivering in the unheated room. "Come, milady." His heather bed was neither warm nor comfortable. It mattered not. He drew his woolen plaid over them and wrapped her in his embrace.

"Donald," she said on a sigh, "we must —"

"Make haste, aye?" He kissed her thoroughly, reveling in the taste of her. "My bonny Highland Bess," he whispered, "let me warm you with my hands." He felt a slight tremor run through her body. "Chilled to the bone, are you? Well, I've a remedy for that."

He tried to be gentle, but he could not be patient. Not this night.

THIRTY-EIGHT

Shame rises in my face,
and interrupts the story of my tongue!
THOMAS OTWAY

The tallow candles were almost spent as Donald brushed a last kiss across his wife's brow. He eased onto his side and rested one hand on her slender waist. "You've been quiet this evening."

Elisabeth turned away from him, pressing her cheek against the threadbare sheet. "I have something to tell you."

"Oh?" he said, hearing the strain in her voice. Was it some unpleasantness with his mother? The dowager seldom hid her disdain for Elisabeth.

When she looked up, he was dismayed to see tears spilling down her cheeks. "Bess, what is it?" He smoothed them away, only to watch her eyes fill again as she slowly rose to a sitting position and gathered the wool plaid round her. He gave her some room, trying to steal a closer look at her in the waning candlelight. "Will you not tell me what grieves you so?"

She dabbed at her tears with a corner of the linen sheet. "I found a note. Inside one of your winter gloves."

A note? "And you read it?"

She nodded, coloring a little. "Forgive me, but 'twas neither folded nor addressed. A small white card with two lines."

Donald frowned. He did not like the sound of this. "What did the card say?"

Elisabeth's voice was low but her words sure. " 'May these gloves warm your hands, as your hands warmed me.' Signed by J. M."

He knew at once. *Jane Montgomerie.* 'Twas the sort of thing the sentimental creature would do. Never guessing where her note might land. Or whom it might hurt.

Elisabeth looked up at him, her chin trembling but her eyes dry. "Have you nothing to say?"

His mind reeled, searching for some explanation. "My love," he began haltingly, "that was some time ago —"

"Nae." Elisabeth tugged the wool blanket closer, covering her bare skin. "Your gloves were new last winter. A gift for our second anniversary."

Losh. He'd not remembered that.

"Donald, 'tis plain that you . . . that you spent time with the Widow Montgomerie long after we married."

He blanched. "How did you learn the lady's name?"

"I watched you dance with her. So did the rest of Edinburgh society. We are none of us blind, Donald."

Her words were bravely spoken, but he saw how she gripped the blanket so tightly her knuckles lost all color. What a simpleton he'd been to think his wife would never discover the truth. He had to say something, anything. "Beloved, you must understand —"

"Stop." Her eyes were dark as midnight, her brow creased with pain. "Nae more lies, for I cannot bear them."

A bitter taste rose in his throat. "Ask what you will, then."

Elisabeth's very soul shone in her eyes. "Have there been other women since we married?"

Aye. Many women. His shoulders slumped beneath the weight of his sins. "Elisabeth, I hardly know where to begin."

"Then begin with the truth." Her voice broke. "If you love me at all . . ."

"You know that I do." He reached for her, but she shrank from his touch.

"Nae." She shook her head so vehemently that hairpins scattered across the dirty floor. "You love this." She aimed a pointed gaze at the mattress beneath them. "But you do not love me. Not enough to be faithful."

Donald could no longer look at her, so

great was his shame. He heard his father's voice: *And why wilt thou, my son, be ravished with a strange woman?* Why indeed when Elisabeth Kerr was everything a man could hope for in a wife?

He loved her, aye, but he'd also deceived her. Over and over, time and again. How could he hope for mercy?

"Bess, I have deeply wronged you," he finally said, lashing himself with the truth. "You have every right to despise me."

When she did not respond, he had his answer.

After a long silence he heard her rise and quietly begin dressing, pulling on her stockings, gathering her petticoats, finding her shoes. One of the candles gave out, leaving the room darker still.

He stood behind her, longing to comfort her, knowing he was the last man on earth who could do so. "At least let me help you dress."

She did not move as he arranged her clothes, her gaze fixed on the remaining candle.

Words rushed to his lips, but he could not speak them. *I do love you, Bess. The others meant nothing to me. You alone have my heart.* She'd heard them all before. *I've failed you as a husband.* Aye, she'd heard that too. But his words were not enough.

Anxious to make amends, he gathered as many hairpins as he could and fastened the loose strands of her hair in place, without comb or mirror or any skill whatsoever. "Forgive me," he said when he finished, stepping back.

"For tonight?"

"Nae, lass." He swallowed. "For all of it."

She turned toward him. "Oh, Donald . . ."

"I am more sorry than I can ever say." He looked into her eyes, letting the scales fall away, holding nothing back. "I cannot alter the past. But I can change the days to come."

"Please." She pressed her fingertips to her mouth as if his words sickened her. "Do not make such a promise."

" 'Tis not a promise," he protested, "but a fact. When the Rising is over, when the prince's men return home, a different husband will cross your threshold. A husband who is faithful. A husband who honors his vows."

She bowed her head. In the still, shadowy room she said in a broken voice, "Donald, how I wish that might be so."

"It *will* be so." He reached for her hands, though his own were shaking. "Nae, from this moment on, it *is* so."

A loud knock at the door startled them both. "Kerr, the hour is spent." Duncan Belhaven's words were slurred, his laughter churlish. "I trust ye've finished as weel, milord."

"We have not." Donald leaned down, his forehead almost touching hers. "In truth, we have just begun."

THIRTY-NINE

Haste is needful in this desperate case.
                    WILLIAM SHAKESPEARE

Elisabeth studied the hands clasping hers. Pale skin, long fingers, slender wrists. The hands of a gentleman. The hands of a rake. *Many women.* He'd confessed as much weeks ago. Why had she not listened to the truth behind his words? *I have a weakness . . .*

" 'Tis time I took my leave." Elisabeth eyed the door, her only means of escape. "Mr. Belhaven is waiting, and Gibson is down the stair."

"Please, dear wife." Donald drew her closer. "They can tarry a moment longer."

When he gazed into her eyes, her resolve began to waver. His regret had seemed genuine, had it not? And his vow sincere?

Before she knew it, his arms were encircling her. Donald kissed her so tenderly she could not help responding, telling herself that he meant what he said, that he loved her still, that he —

"Enough," she pleaded, easing away from him, her body and soul at such odds she could barely put two words together. *Help me.* 'Twas the cry of her heart, though none could hear it. *Help me know the truth.*

Donald touched her cheek before releasing her. "If you insist, milady. But remember my vow. You alone and no other."

As he began gathering his clothes, she draped her wool cape across her shoulders, then drew the hood over her disheveled hair, her heart aching. Donald's request prodded at her. *Forgive me. For all of it.* How could she possibly do so? Yet how could she not if she loved him?

Help me. The words kept darting through her mind like birds in a gilded cage. But she dared not seek advice from Marjory or Janet, and her Highland mother was lost to her, it seemed. Elisabeth glanced at her great-grandmother's silver ring. The Nameless One was lost as well, a cold and distant moon. She would find no solace there.

Elisabeth shivered, though not from the cold. She'd never felt so alone. Was there nowhere she could turn for comfort? No one she could trust completely?

Her husband was still dressing when Duncan Belhaven knocked again, demanding the use of their shared lodgings. A woman's airy laugh slipped through the cracks in the door — a jarring counterpoint to the strained atmosphere within.

The soldier bellowed, "Surely ye've finished by now."

"Aye, aye," Donald grumbled, yanking on his coat, then jamming his feet into half-buckled shoes. Stock untied, periwig in hand, he flung open the door and scowled at his roommate. "Have you nae patience, man?"

"Nae mair than ye did, Lord Kerr." Broad-shouldered and copper-haired, his fellow Life Guard strode into the room, one of the tavern maids firmly attached to his side. "We've not the luxury of a lang hour. Jeanie must return to her labors." Mr. Belhaven winked boldly at Elisabeth. "I'll thank ye to take yer leave, milord. And yer bonny mistress with ye."

Donald's eyes narrowed. "Lady Kerr is my wife."

"Och! Begging yer pardon, mem." His exaggerated bow did not improve matters.

For a moment Elisabeth feared Donald might challenge him with steel or fist. Both were ill advised since the other man was taller, broader, and clearly stronger. Instead Donald snatched his riding boots from the corner, grabbed Elisabeth's hand, and stormed into the hall without another word.

The door shut behind them with a decided bang.

"Idiot," Donald grumbled, stamping toward the stair, though his anger seemed to dissipate with each footfall.

A single wall sconce illumined the sagging wooden floor and unpainted walls of the narrow hallway. When they reached the midway point, Donald turned to look at her, his features bathed in a bright yellow pool of light. "Pardon my temper, lass. Belhaven is a good soldier, but he sorely tries my patience."

She merely nodded, shocked by what the candles revealed. Deep furrows were carved into his chalky brow, and fear haunted his eyes. Whatever bravado her husband might show the world, the sad truth stood before her. Elisabeth took the white cambric stock from his hand. " 'Tis my turn to dress you." She tied the stiffened fabric round his neck, willing her hands to remain steady.

Donald's gaze never left hers. "We'll not be alone like this on the morrow."

"I know," she said quietly. The whole of Edinburgh would descend on Holyroodhouse to see the prince ride forth. But here in the empty hallway, no one watched or listened.

"My dear wife." He lightly rested his hand above her birthmark, hidden beneath layers of wool, silk, and linen. "I must ask you again. Can you find it in your heart to forgive me?"

She swallowed the lump rising in her throat. *You are forgiven.* Aye, she could speak the words. But would she truly mean them? The faces of all the women who'd danced with her husband, or smiled at him, or flirted with him swept through her heart like midwinter snow. "I am not certain."

"What must I do, then?" Donald caught her chin before she could turn away. "I've vowed to change my habits, and I will. Can you not trust me?"

"I . . . cannot." Tears stung her eyes. When he started to circle his arm round her waist, she stepped out of reach. "Please don't."

A look of anguish crossed his features. "Have I lost your love as well?"

"Nae." Elisabeth stepped out from the shadows so he might see her face as clearly as she saw his. "Even if I wished it so, I could not stop loving you."

Donald's voice was low. "*Do* you wish it?"

Pain pressed down on her like a millstone, grinding her will into dust. As deeply as it hurt to love him, 'twould hurt far more to lose him. "Nae," she said at last.

He kissed her brow, clearly relieved. "Then I shall work to earn your trust. And your forgiveness as well."

A door flew open at the far end of the hall. Slurred voices and muffled laughter spilled out before the door abruptly closed and silence returned. The distraction gave Elisabeth time to gather her cape round her and her courage as well.

"Lord Kerr, I must go."

He did not object, only straightened his clothes, then offered his arm as if they were any happily married couple with naught on their minds but a good night's sleep. "Milady?"

While they retraced their path down the stair and through the noisy public room of the inn, Elisabeth's mind ran ahead to their parting on the morrow. So much had yet to be said. How could they repair the torn threads of their marriage across the miles with mere pen and ink?

"No sign of my brother and his wife," Donald said above the din, "but I believe I see Gibson waiting at the door."

She peered across the room, her view impaired by too much smoke and too few candles. Or was it the fresh wash of tears in her eyes? "Aye, 'tis him."

Donald moved his arm round her waist as if expecting her to be torn from his side. Alas, the prince would accomplish that in less than a day. Weeks, even months, might pass before she welcomed her husband home. Who knew what sort of man might return to cross her threshold? Scarred and weary from battle, hardened by the cruelties of war, the Donald she knew might never return.

A different husband. That was what he'd promised her. Yet for all his faults, for all his weaknesses, Donald was the man she loved.

You are a fool, her mind said.

You are faithful, her heart responded.

When they reached the inn door, Gibson greeted his master with a deep bow. "Guid eve, milord. I trust ye are weel."

Donald delivered his riding boots into the servant's hands. "I shall look far better when you've polished these. Send them by caddie in the morn, aye?"

As Gibson juggled the boots in one hand and his lantern in the other, Janet stepped round him, her chin thrust forward at a haughty angle, her small mouth drawn into a pout.

Donald inclined his head. "Many apologies, madam."

"I have been waiting a very long time," Janet grumbled.

Elisabeth realized Andrew was nowhere to be seen. "Are you quite ready?" she asked.

"Quite." Janet spun on her heel, sweeping her hem across the rough floor.

Something was amiss. Elisabeth could hardly sort it out with her own emotions in turmoil.

"Forgive me, milady, but I must go." Donald tightened his hold on her. "I'll send a messenger the moment I've news of our departure."

She eyed him a moment longer, fixing in her memory his tall, lean frame, his cool blue eyes, the narrow line of his mouth. "Look for us in the forecourt," she said softly, curtsying before her tears began in earnest.

As Donald bowed in return, she hastened for the open door leading to White Horse

Close, forcing herself not to turn round, not to look back, not to call out his name.

FORTY

What a whirlwind is her head,
And what a whirlpool full of depth and
   danger
Is all the rest about her.
                GEORGE GORDON, LORD BYRON

Janet tarried at the top of the forestair, an impatient look on her face.

"The dowager will have worn the carpet thin, fretting over us."

Elisabeth leaned down, pretending to brush the dust from her skirts, all the while mastering her emotions. "Gibson will hire sedan chairs and have us in Milne Square well before the drum sounds," she assured her sister-in-law, grateful the two would not travel home on foot. The climb was long, the night cold, and Janet's company often less than cordial. "I trust Mr. Kerr is well?"

"Well enough," Janet snapped, then turned and started down the stair.

Her sister-in-law seemed even more *pernick-*

itie than usual. Since Janet's gown was neat and every hair in place, perhaps she and Andrew had kept their distance in the confines of their borrowed room. Elisabeth hoped the couple had not argued on their last evening together, a regrettable way to send a man off to war. Her own distressing hour with Donald was hardly better.

"This way, leddies." Holding aloft his lantern, Gibson led the way, scowling at any and all who looked in their direction. Shrouded in darkness, the courtyard teemed with soldiers and travelers, cutpurses and ne'er-do-wells. Gibson carried neither pistol nor sword on his person, but Elisabeth knew he would not hesitate to reach for the small dirk hidden beneath his livery if needed. When they reached the Canongate at the end of the vaulted pend, he quickly hailed a sedan chair for her and pressed a silver sixpence into the chairman's hand. "I'll have anither for yer sister-in-law afore lang," he promised, and sent Elisabeth westward.

With Donald's boots on the floor beside her, she gripped the seat and braced herself for the jostling ride uphill. They hurried past change house and tavern, brewery and well, tolbooth and kirk before charging through the Netherbow Port and into the town proper. She heard the chairmen shouting in Gaelic, not slowing their pace until they trotted by the entrance to Halkerston's Wynd and into Milne Square.

Disembarking at Baillie's Land, she beckoned a caddie bearing a paper lantern to tarry by her side while she waited for Janet. For a ha'penny he would lead them safely up the stair and carry Donald's heavy boots as well. "My sister-in-law will be here shortly," Elisabeth promised the lad as they stood shivering in the cold, vacant square.

Out of the corner of her eye, she watched a small figure emerge from the dark recesses of the wynd and approach her with confident steps. A woman, Elisabeth quickly realized, younger than she, small and lithe, with fair hair and light-colored eyes that gleamed in the lantern light. She'd seen her before. At market perhaps?

Boldly sauntering up to her, the lass thrust out her palm. "Have ye a coin to spare a fisherman's widow?" Her brown drugget gown was clean but worn, the sleeves patched, the lacing in her bodice frayed.

Instinctively Elisabeth touched the silk reticule hanging from her wrist. Some cut-purses were women who devised clever means of distracting their marks. But the lass didn't bear the look of a thief. She also didn't have a silver beggar's badge sewn to her clothing, permitting her to beg in the parish.

"I am sorry to hear of your loss," she told the young widow, holding out a ha'penny. "Do you live in the neighborhood?"

"Aye, not far from here." The lass tipped her head, studying Elisabeth for a moment, then took the copper coin and gave her a half curtsy in return. "Just now I'm bound for the Canongate."

Elisabeth gaped at her. "Surely you'll not travel unescorted? 'Tis nearly ten o' the clock."

"I'm quick on my feet," the widow said with a cunning smile. "And I've a gentleman waiting for me at White Horse Close." She turned to leave. "Guid morrow to ye, Leddy Kerr."

Her too-familiar manner gave Elisabeth pause. "You know my name?"

"Och! Wha in Edinburgh doesna?" the widow said over her shoulder. "Mine is Lucy Spence." With that she fairly skipped off, disappearing into the night.

The caddie made a sound of disgust. "A crafty *limmer*, that one," he grumbled. "Begging yer pardon, mem."

Elisabeth turned her head, hoping to stem the flood of gossip before it began. There were soldiers aplenty in White Horse Close waiting to greet such a woman. Whatever the Widow Spence's unfortunate situation, the details were hers to keep.

Pushing back her hood from her brow, Elisabeth looked up at the night sky and caught a glimpse of the moon. A tiny sliver of light was missing from one side. For the next fortnight cottagers would cut their peat,

367

gardeners would plant bulbs, and wise couples would delay their weddings.

By design she'd married Donald on the sixth day of the moon, a most fortuitous day. Yet all her devotion had not yielded what she'd hoped for: a contented husband at her table and children round her skirts. Instead, her husband was untrue and her womb empty.

Gazing at the bright orb, she remembered the words her grandmother had taught her and wondered if they might yet rekindle her dwindling faith.

Glory to thee forever
Thou bright moon, this night.

She waited but sensed nothing. She listened but heard not a whisper. The stillness inside her was absolute, like a well gone dry, hollow and abandoned.

The caddie held up his lantern. "Leddy, she's here."

Janet emerged from the sedan chair, her complexion as white as bleached muslin and her balance unsure. "Lady Kerr?" she said weakly, stretching out her hand for support.

Elisabeth was beside her at once, helping her toward the stair as she motioned to the caddie. "Go two steps ahead, lad. And hold the lantern as high as you can."

The turnpike stair was too narrow for them

to manage side by side. Elisabeth walked behind her sister-in-law, one hand lightly resting on the small of her back. "No need for haste," Elisabeth said calmly. "We'll cross our threshold soon enough."

But the climb took far longer than expected. Janet was unsteady on her feet and confessed to feeling nauseous. " 'Twas the sedan chair," she moaned, "or the oysters."

Since early September Elisabeth had watched her sister-in-law consume heaping plates of oysters harvested from beds in the Firth of Forth. As to Janet's unsettling journey in the sedan chair, Elisabeth had never seen such a marked reaction. Still, her discomfort seemed very real indeed.

When they neared the fifth floor, the caddie ran ahead and banged on the door, announcing them in a breathless voice. "The leddy's taken ill!"

Mrs. Edgar was on the landing in an instant, helping Janet manage the last few steps. "Whatever has happened to ye, Mistress Kerr? Come, let me see ye to yer bed."

Elisabeth paid the caddie an extra ha'penny. "Tarry on the stair," she told him quietly. "We may have need of the apothecary."

"Aye, mem." He touched the brim of his dirty wool bonnet. "Say the wird, and I'll flit to Mr. Mercer's on the High Street."

By the time Elisabeth had closed the door and shed her wool cape, Mrs. Edgar was loosening Janet's stays before she tumbled to the carpet in a faint. Elisabeth came to the housekeeper's aid first, moving Janet to her bed, then pressing a damp cloth against her sister-in-law's brow, offering what little information she had. "Her illness came on rather suddenly," Elisabeth said, omitting any mention of oysters. The rest of the household had eaten their evening meal without consequence.

Mrs. Edgar slipped off Janet's damask slippers and began rubbing her stocking feet, clucking like a mother hen. "A cauld nicht for thin shoes," she fretted. When Elisabeth asked what might be required from the apothecary, Mrs. Edgar had a swift answer. "Tincture o' fresh ginger root to settle her stomach."

Elisabeth dispatched the caddie on his errand, then found the dowager in the drawing room, pacing back and forth across the carpet.

Marjory motioned Elisabeth closer to the mantelpiece. "Tell me, Lady Kerr." Her hazel eyes were filled with concern. "What transpired at the inn?"

Elisabeth pressed her lips tightly together lest she blurt out the truth. *Your son confessed to adultery. And begged my forgiveness.* Instead, she said what she could. " 'Twas filthy, crowded, and noisy."

"I'm not surprised." Marjory glanced at

Janet's bedchamber door and added, sotto voce, "Your sister-in-law seems most distraught. How was she earlier this evening?"

"Rather out of sorts," Elisabeth admitted. "But her color was fine and her balance steady. Only when she arrived in the square did she mention feeling nauseous. I suspect the sedan chair —"

"And I suspect something else." Her mother-in-law had a knowing look in her eyes. "I have long waited for one of my sons to produce an heir."

Elisabeth's heart skipped a beat. "You believe Janet is —"

"I do," Marjory said firmly. "She's been more irritable of late and seldom breaks her fast before ten in the morning. I was the very same with both my sons." The dowager clapped her hands together like a woman about to pray. "Isn't it thrilling?"

Elisabeth managed to nod. "Aye. Thrilling."

"Andrew may give us some hint on the morrow," Marjory was saying. "In the meantime we'll keep a close eye on Janet. Women cannot hide such secrets for very long, you know." Skirts in hand, Marjory swept into Janet's bedchamber with Elisabeth dutifully following behind.

The wood-paneled room, smaller than Elisabeth's bedchamber and with half as many windows, felt snug and warm, the coals in the fireplace still glowing. With Andrew's weaponry gone, Marjory could not abide having bare walls and so had acquired a series of small oil paintings at auction. "For a song," she'd confided, "with so many folk leaving town."

Mrs. Edgar was fussing over her charge, plumping Janet's bed pillows, then pouring fresh tea in her cup. "Peppermint leaves and chamomile flowers," the housekeeper said proudly. "The verra best for whatever ails ye."

"She forced me to eat a dry oatcake too," Janet said, making a face. "Days old and no butter."

"My mither wouldna use onie ither remedy," Mrs. Edgar declared. "Plain and dry. See if ye dinna feel better afore ye sleep."

Janet exhaled, sinking deeper into her feather mattress.

Mrs. Edgar quit the room, leaving Elisabeth and Marjory to draw their chairs closer to the bed. Janet's unbound hair fanned across her pillow. A pale violet sleeping jacket framed her wan face.

The dowager spoke first, patting Janet's hand as she did. "I am glad to see you eat something. You've been absent from table the last few mornings."

Janet turned her head as if embarrassed. "Nae appetite, I'm afraid."

"Might there be some reason?"

Elisabeth winced, thinking the dowager's question too probing. A gentlewoman was not usually forthcoming with such intimacies. At least not until her condition was undeniable.

"Though I cannot be certain," Janet began, slowly turning back to look at them. "There is a chance . . . quite a *good* chance . . ."

"I thought so." Marjory beamed at her daughter-in-law as if Janet had just given birth to three sons. "Your secret is very safe with us. Isn't that so, Lady Kerr?" The dowager bricfly exchanged glances with Elisabeth, then focused all her attention on the apparent mother-to-be. "Andrew must be very proud."

Janet's face clouded. "He is more concerned with bearing arms than my bearing his child."

"Nae," Elisabeth protested gently. "Even the most zealous Jacobite would rejoice at such news."

The cloud across Janet's face turned stormy. "You are the true Jacobite among us, Lady Kerr. If 'twere not for you, our husbands would still be living in Milne Square instead of riding for England."

Elisabeth chafed beneath her accusation. "Were you not the one writing poetry in honor of the prince?"

"Ladies, that's quite enough," Marjory insisted. "My sons have chosen to support the Stuarts, and so have I." She abruptly stood, ending further discussion. "Donald and Andrew are brave and noble men, virtuous in every regard. We shall send them off with naught but praise for their courage. Are we agreed?"

"Aye," they both said, though not quite in unison.

Noble. Virtuous. Elisabeth knew Donald would ever remain so in his mother's eyes.

She rose and bid Marjory and Janet good night, then passed through the door into her empty bedchamber. The room was noticeably cooler than Janet's, the fire reduced to dying embers. At least her thick tapestries held the late autumn winds at bay and contained whatever heat remained.

Mrs. Edgar tapped on the door, then entered with a steaming cup of tea. "Ye leuk a wee bit *dwiny* yerself, milady." While helping Elisabeth out of her gown, the housekeeper said nothing about her poorly laced stays or her crooked chemise, her tousled hair or her soiled stockings. Mrs. Edgar was especially gentle with soap and cloth, toweling Elisabeth dry as if she were made of porcelain.

She murmured her thanks, certain Mrs. Edgar understood all she could not say. *He took his pleasure. Then he broke my heart.*

When she was alone once more, Elisabeth finished her tea, then blew out the last candle and slipped beneath the covers, waiting for a soft blanket of sleep to settle over her. Tears came instead.

However would she face the day ahead with

its twin heartaches? She'd never done anything so difficult before. And she would have
to do them both at once.

Forgive her husband, yet bid him farewell.
Trust him, and then let go.

FORTY-ONE

The parting of a husband and wife
is like the cleaving of a heart;
one half will flutter here, one there.
ALFRED, LORD TENNYSON

The gloaming would not linger, not on the last day of October when a biting wind blew round every corner and thick, gray clouds scuttled across the early evening sky.

Elisabeth stood in the midst of the prince's Life Guards, their uniforms crisscrossed with leather bags, their horses saddled and restless. The dowager and Janet had hurried off to find Andrew in the crowded palace forecourt, giving Lord and Lady Kerr a few moments alone. To settle accounts. To say goodbye.

Astride his chestnut gelding, Donald already had the mien of a veteran soldier. His sword hung from a broad tartan belt strapped across his chest, and Gibson had polished his master's black riding boots until they shone.

"How fine you look," Elisabeth said, gazing

up at her husband.

He touched the brim of his gold-laced tricorne, an intent expression on his clean-shaven face. "May I return the compliment, milady?"

"You may." She offered him a faint smile, though her heart was anything but light. Within the hour the prince would ride east to Musselburgh with Lord Elcho's Life Guards and Lord Pitsligo's regiment, more than four hundred men and their mounts. *And my Donald.*

Elisabeth looked down, lest he mark her distress. She'd returned home last night with her heart in tatters, seeking the strength to forgive him. *For all of it.* Whether she had the courage to do so remained to be seen.

"Lady Kerr?" Her husband dismounted with ease, the brass buttons on his coat catching the last bit of light. "I would know your thoughts." He stood before her, one hand loosely holding the reins, the other touching her cheek, his winter gloves a painful reminder of truths spoken and unspoken.

"My thoughts are scattered to the winds," she finally admitted, not ready to say more.

" 'Tis anyone's guess how far those winds might travel on Hallowmas Eve." He turned toward the Salisbury Crags, where the brilliant orange flames of a bonfire leaped upward. "On the last of October in Castleton, did you march round with torches?"

She nodded, vividly recalling her brother chasing after the lads from the neighboring glens with burning bracken, then tossing his torch inside a circle of stones. "Simon was all for building the tallest bonfire in the parish. Our mother feared her thatch might go up in smoke."

Elisabeth felt the loss of Simon keenly that evening. He should have been in Duddingston mustering with the foot soldiers, preparing to march southeast to Dalkeith. Instead, he lay beneath a cairn in a farmer's field, lost to her forever.

Donald took her gloved hand in his. "Your brother was a fine lad. And a good soldier."

"He was indeed." She looked down at her mourning clothes. Come spring, when Mrs. Edgar wrapped her black gown in wormwood, the memory of her brother would remain in her heart, closer than any silk bodice.

"Lady Kerr," her husband said firmly, "do not imagine I will share his fate."

She lifted her gaze to meet his. "I'll not even consider the possibility."

"Nor will I." He nodded toward the palace. "Six weeks in the capital, yet the prince added very few titled gentlemen to his ranks."

He added you. A thread of guilt tugged at her heart, pulled more tautly by Janet's accusation. *You are the true Jacobite among us, Lady Kerr.* Would Donald have taken such a risk without her influence? From childhood Elisabeth had longed for the Stuarts to regain the throne. Then she'd lost Simon. Now Donald was leaving.

Return to me. That's what she wanted to say to him. *Come home.*

The bells of Saint Giles began chiming the hour. At five o' the clock the sky had grown darker than Donald's midnight blue coat. When the last bell echoed through the air, he surprised her with a song.

The night is Hallowe'en, lady,
The morn is Hallowday.

Recognizing the auld ballad, Elisabeth finished the verse, while Donald listened.

Then win me, win me, and ye will,
For well I know ye may.

He inclined his head. "Shall I indeed win you back, Lady Kerr?"

Only then did she pay heed to the words she'd sung: *win me, win me.* 'Twas one thing to forgive a man, quite another to surrender to him. She lowered her gaze. *You ask too much, Donald.*

He leaned closer, his breath warm against her cheek. "I'll not break your heart again. I can promise you that."

"You've made a great many promises,

milord." Elisabeth regretted the words the moment they were spoken. But when she started to apologize, Donald lightly touched her lips.

"Nae, Bess. What you say is true. I've made too many vows and broken most of them. Save one." Then he kissed her, and in his kiss she tasted tenderness and passion and regret. "I love you, Bess. You alone and no other."

Because she loved him, she believed him. All that remained was to forgive him.

When he lifted his head, his eyes were dark with a different sort of longing. "Will you —" His horse suddenly stamped the ground, yanking him from her.

Round the forecourt, guardsmen were mounting their horses. She could delay no longer. If Donald meant to ride for England with her forgiveness in his pocket, she alone could place it there.

She glanced up, thinking to look for the waning moon. *Nae.* The strength to forgive her husband could not be found in the night sky. Nor could she hope to manage on her own. Touching her forehead to Donald's chest, she closed her eyes. *Please.* If there were words she was meant to say, she did not know them. *Help me.*

In the crowded, noisy forecourt, an answer came. *Hearken unto me.*

Elisabeth stilled. *Aye.* She'd heard this voice before, comforting her the night she learned of Simon's death. *Hear, and your soul shall live.* Every part of her listened now, as if she were taking a long drink of water or a deep breath of air, drawing it in.

Drop by drop the well of silence inside her began to fill. *My soul thirsteth for God, for the living God.* Elisabeth did not fully understand the words. Yet she sensed the truth of them. *Great is thy mercy.* If this living God offered boundless mercy, could she let it flow through her like water, like wind?

Donald lifted her head until their gazes met. "Please, Bess." He brushed a loose strand of hair from her eyes, then gently kissed her brow. "Forgive me?"

In the murky darkness she saw the sheen in his eyes. Or perhaps the tears were hers. *Donald, my sweet Donald.*

He was not always honest. He was not always good. Yet he loved her in his own way. And she loved him completely.

"You are forgiven," she whispered, then touched her mouth to his, tasting the salt in his tears.

FORTY-TWO

There exists no cure for a heart
wounded with the sword of separation.
HITOPADESA

Marjory could not take her eyes off her sons,
even though her heart was breaking. Mounted
on fine horses, their shoulders squared and
their heads held high, Donald and Andrew
were as bonny as the young prince they
served and every bit as courageous.

My sons.

Had they truly fit in her arms once, their
heads nestled in the crook of her elbow? Had
they climbed into her lap and pressed their
sticky hands against her cheeks? Marjory
could barely imagine it, looking at them now.

She sensed their father, Lord John, standing beside her, admiring the fair-haired, blue-
eyed lads they'd nurtured to manhood. *They
look like soldiers, milord. They look like you.*
Marjory valiantly fought back tears, gladly
enduring the cold and the dark for one more

minute with her precious sons.

They were hardly alone. A vast throng filled the palace grounds to witness the end of the rebel occupation. Thousands had come on foot, in carriages, on horseback to shout, to cheer, to weep.

Above the clamor rose the voice of her sons' commanding officer. Not as old as Donald and certainly not so handsome, David Wemyss, Lord Elcho, was nonetheless impressive with his large, dark eyes and smooth brow. At the moment he was directing his men into orderly lines, no doubt anticipating the prince's appearance and a swift departure for Musselburgh.

"I must go, Mother." Andrew shifted his seat on his mount. "My brother is a far better correspondent. Look to his letters for news."

"So I shall." Marjory gave him a brave smile, reaching up to touch his sleeve. "I will pray for you both," she promised. Had she not done so every night since their enlistment? Nae, since their birth. *Guard them and guide them, according to thy will.*

When Janet stepped forward to bid her husband farewell, she was dry-eyed and stoic. "See that you come home, Mr. Kerr." She lifted up her gloved hand for a parting kiss, then rested her hand on her waist in a none-too-subtle manner.

Janet styled her delicate condition "a possibility," but Marjory recognized the signs. A summer baby, she'd decided, and bound to thrive. Even though her daughter-in-law would be seven-and-twenty, Janet was in excellent health.

"Mother?" Donald nudged his horse a step closer, then touched the brim of his tricorne. "May I count on you to look after Elisabeth?"

"Aye," she quickly agreed. Anything to ease his mind. "You'll write as oft as you can?"

"I shall, though do not expect a letter soon. I've little knowledge of our route and even less of our destination," he confessed. "Some believe we'll follow the east road toward Northumberland. Others say we'll cross to the west and take Carlisle."

Marjory shuddered. *Take.* The reality of what lay ahead came into sharper focus.

"You will be cautious?" she pleaded, no longer caring if her eyes grew wet with tears. Donald's musket, his sword, his dirk were not meant for adornment. He would hold them in his hands; he would use them. "Let others engage the enemy in battle," she begged him, keeping her voice low. "Guard the prince, and you'll have done your duty."

When he looked down at her with compassion in his eyes, she realized the absurdity of her request. Did she think her sons would merely ride their horses and sleep beneath the stars? They were soldiers. They would fight.

Donald lightly touched her shoulder. "God be with you, Mother."

"And with you." She pressed her handkerchief to her trembling lips. *Make them strong. Keep them safe.*

Donald inclined his head to look past her. "If I might have a last word with Lady Kerr."

With a guilty start, Marjory stepped back to make room for Elisabeth, who'd been patiently waiting. Donald's features softened as he bent down to kiss her. Elisabeth stood on tiptoe, her graceful hands cradling his face.

Marjory tried to look away but could not. How tender they were with each other! Lady Ruthven could gossip all she wished. Donald had but one love.

Elisabeth's parting words were an ardent plea. "Promise you'll return to me, Lord Kerr."

"Nae," he said with a mock scowl. "You're to look for a different husband, remember?"

Elisabeth smiled through her tears. "Aye, so I shall."

Some private understanding, Marjory decided. Though her son *would* be a changed man when he returned. Andrew too. Her throat tightened.

Donald straightened in his saddle, never taking his eyes off his wife. "I'll not soon forget the words spoken this night."

"Nor will I," Elisabeth assured him, her

voice breaking. "Go, beloved. Your prince awaits."

"Godspeed," Marjory cried softly. She could say no more.

As Donald and Andrew eased their horses through the crowd and maneuvered into position, she strained to keep an eye on their progress until their blue uniforms were lost among the dozens like them. "Come home to me," Marjory whispered, pressing her hand to her heart, wishing she might mend it, knowing she could not.

Standing shoulder to shoulder, with Gibson not far behind them, the three Kerr women watched the Life Guards prepare to greet their prince. His carriage drew near, a splendid coach-and-four with glass windows and lanterns made of brass. Charles emerged a moment later to the deafening roar of huzzahs, his countenance more radiant than any torchlight.

Without thinking Marjory waved her handkerchief, overcome with emotion at seeing the young prince again. If only his father, James Stuart, were on hand! Surely the exiled king would be as proud of his son that night as she was of hers.

A familiar face momentarily distracted her.

"Yer lealty is weel placed, mem." Angus MacPherson bowed, then turned to join them in observing the spectacle. "And sae is yer gold."

"Mr. MacPherson," Elisabeth said, patting her cheeks dry. "I expected to find you astride a horse this eve, preparing to ride out with the army."

"Oo aye, and soon I shall be. At my age I may niver have anither chance. Ance I see the prince's men on the road to Musselburgh, I'll join the ithers marching southeast to Dalkeith." The tailor, dressed in a wool greatcoat and riding boots, rocked back on his heels, unbridled pride shining on his face. "We'll a' be gone from the toun by morn."

Marjory sighed at the sad reminder. Edinburgh society had quickly grown accustomed to the royal suppers and balls at Holyroodhouse. With the onset of winter, the capital would be a very dour place indeed.

"Look," Janet said, nodding toward the prince, who'd abandoned his carriage to lead his mounted guards on foot. "Will he walk all the way, do you suppose?"

"Aye, weel he might," Angus replied, "for His Royal Highness likes to set a guid example for his men. He'll sleep at Pinkie Hoose, whaur he spent the nicht after Gladsmuir. 'Tis but five or six miles east o' here."

Marjory remembered the old house with its massive square tower, having once ventured out with Lord John for a day of golf on the Musselburgh links. When the prince retired in warmth and comfort beneath the Marquess of Tweeddale's roof, would her sons sleep on the cold, damp ground? She shivered beneath her cape, wishing she'd sent them each with another plaid.

Elisabeth tugged her hood tighter round her neck. "Will you close your shop?" she inquired of Angus.

"Nae, Rob will carry on at the Luckenbooths. O' course, he'd rather go with me, but . . ." His smile faded. "His foot, ye ken. Rob canna ride weel nor march on rough ground."

When Elisabeth nodded, Marjory saw the sympathy in her eyes. "How disappointed he must be."

"Have nae fear," Angus said, quickly regaining his good spirits. "Rob will be serving the prince in his ain way. And there's not a finer hand with a needle in Edinburgh." He tipped his hat. "Excepting yers, Leddy Kerr."

Marjory bristled at the reference to her daughter-in-law's former labors. Better those days were long forgotten. Elisabeth was a gentlewoman now.

"I hope ye'll not mind," Angus continued, "but I've asked Rob to call at yer hoose from time to time. To see that ye're weel and give ye what news he can."

Elisabeth nodded. "We'll be glad for his company, will we not, madam?" She glanced at Marjory as if seeking her consent.

"Your son is welcome to call at Milne Square," Marjory assured him. They were tradesmen, aye, but they'd duly served the Kerr family.

"Rob kens which messengers are to be trusted with a letter," Angus said. "He'll be honored to do whatsomever ye need. The prince is grateful for yer sacrifices, Leddy Kerr."

Marjory lowered her gaze lest he see the fear in her eyes. Her gold was no real sacrifice. But she would not give up her sons.

From the distant High Street, the bells of Saint Giles marked the hour of six as the last of the prince's men turned onto the road heading east.

Forty-Three

Words are mighty,
words are living.

ADELAIDE ANNE PROCTER

Elisabeth was numb.

She hovered as close to her bedchamber fireplace as she dared, shivering from cold and exhaustion, unwilling to shrug off her wool cape until some feeling returned to her stiff fingers and toes.

The evening had ended badly. Once the prince departed Holyroodhouse and the immense crowd dispersed, an empty sedan chair could not be found, not even with a whole fistful of sixpence to offer. Poor Gibson was beside himself. The Kerr party had little choice but to trudge home, arriving in Milne Square with icy feet and chapped faces.

Elisabeth's heart and mind seemed frozen as well. Donald was truly gone. Not a half mile downhill but many miles away with no promise of when he might return. Yet she had asked for help and received it. She had said,

"You are forgiven," and meant it.

A voice had stirred inside her. No mistaking that.

Mrs. Edgar came up behind her with a cautious step. "Leddy Kerr, if I may." She gently lifted the cape from her shoulders. "I'll have Gibson add mair coals to yer grate."

"Our dear Mrs. Edgar." She smiled down at her. "However would we manage without you?"

A moment later Gibson appeared with the coal bucket. He held a handkerchief pressed to his nose, his cheeks still red from the cold night air. "Will there be anything else, milady?"

"Aye." Elisabeth noted his sagging shoulders. "A good night's rest for you."

"Bliss ye," he said with a weary smile, then bowed and took his leave.

Elisabeth closed her eyes. *Finally. Alone.*

She eased out of her mourning gown and the usual array of petticoats, glad Donald was not on hand to see her ungraceful efforts. At least her whalebone stays, laced in the front, were easily undone, as were the tapes securing her pocket hoops. When nothing remained but her linen chemise, she pulled the pins from her hair and bathed herself at the washbowl, grateful for the hot water but less so for the chilly air. Brushing her hair beside the fireplace, warmed by the rising heat, she finally stopped shivering.

As she finished the last few strokes, Elisabeth absently scanned the row of leather-bound volumes that lined the mantel before her. Scottish poets, mostly: Barbour, Dunbar, Barclay, Lindsay, Thomson. She loved hearing Donald read his favorite verses aloud, enjoying the cadence of them, the varying tempos, like music without notes.

Her brushing slowed as she considered again the words that poured into her heart in the palace forecourt earlier that evening: *Hearken unto me.* Nae, they were not merely words; they were poetry.

On impulse Elisabeth reached for the nearest book at hand, Ramsay's *Tea-Table Miscellany,* and began paging through, thinking to find something akin to what she'd heard echoing inside her. She paused at a verse Donald once read to her with a bemused expression on his face.

Altho' I be but a country lass,
Yet a lofty mind I bear — O,
And think myself as good as those
That rich apparel wear — O.

A clever appraisal but nothing at all like the words she'd heard.

As she replaced Ramsay's *Miscellany,* Elisabeth eyed the thick family Bible, which lay turned on its side, lest it tumble into the fireplace and take the others with it. Donald

392

once said his father had treasured the Scriptures and read from them nightly. Now the sacred writings were seldom touched in the Kerr household, though her mother-in-law could quote long passages when it suited her. Words she'd learned as a child, the dowager explained. Words that had mattered a great deal to her once.

Elisabeth opened the heavy book, carefully balancing it on the broad mantelpiece. She turned the leaves, the paper faded with age, the print small but still legible. Near the center were pages upon pages of poetry. Her gaze alighted on one verse among the many.

When I consider thy heavens,
the work of thy fingers,
the moon and the stars,
which thou hast ordained.

Her eyes widened. 'Twas the same voice she'd heard that evening. Different words, yet surely from the same source, infused with truth and with power. And there was her old friend, the moon. *Ordained,* the verse said, by *thou.* Meaning the Nameless One? When Elisabeth reached the last verse, she found her answer.

LORD our Lord, how excellent is thy name
in all the earth!

Thy name. She stared at the page, trying to reconcile what she'd always thought to be right with what the Bible said to be true. The One who ordained the moon was not nameless. He was the One to whom Reverend Wishart prayed by name. The Lord, the Almighty.

Elisabeth closed the book with a soft thud, though her confusion was not so easily put aside. Why would the Almighty speak to her when she'd always sought the counsel of another?

Help me. That was all she'd said. So few words.

But Someone had heard. And Someone had answered. Perhaps even now the Almighty was present in her bedchamber. Watching over her. Listening to her.

Unnerved by the thought, she quickly blew out the candles round the room, then slipped beneath the covers, and waited for the night to wrap her in its silent embrace.

Elisabeth rose later than she meant to, lulled back to sleep by the steady rain ushering in a cold, wet November day.

Her mother-in-law's light tapping at the door had awakened her. "You've been hiding from us all morning," Marjory chided her gently. "Come have tea."

Elisabeth dressed in haste and joined them at the dowager's table. Janet and Marjory were both wearing green costumes of different hues. Elisabeth eyed the gold silk edgings on Marjory's gown, the cream-colored lace on Janet's. She was content to wear her black gown, but her fingers itched to create something new with her needle. Perhaps that afternoon she would see what might be done with the blue watered silk in her clothes press.

Mrs. Edgar sailed into the chamber with her tea tray. "Ye'll not go hungry this forenoon." Cinnamon, ginger, and clove mingled in the air as she served her rich gingerbread brimming with sultanas. If Janet's appetite was any indication, her morning queasiness was well ended.

Their cake enjoyed and their teacups refilled, the three women settled back in their chairs, quietly taking stock of one another. Marjory put into words precisely what Elisabeth was thinking. "What will this new life of ours be like without Donald and Andrew close at hand?"

"I've wondered that as well," Janet said, staring at the rain-drenched windows facing the square. "I confess I very much like calling upon my friends each day and hope I might continue to do so." She turned to Marjory, her gaze skipping over Elisabeth as if she weren't there. "Unless you object, Lady Marjory."

"While your sister-in-law is in mourning, you may keep up appearances for us," Marjory told her, "until it becomes improper for you to do so."

Janet frowned. "Whenever would it be . . . oh!" Her cheeks turned crimson. "Of course." She looked down at her lap as if to hide her embarrassment, but the color continued creeping round her face until it reached her hairline.

How odd, Elisabeth thought, to see her sister-in-law so flustered. Janet was not one to shy away from delicate subjects. Quite the opposite.

Gibson paused in the open doorway. "Leddy Kerr?" When Marjory waved him in, he pulled the *Caledonian Mercury* from his coat, taking care not to drag the Jacobite broadsheet across his wet sleeve before placing it on the table. "Will ye be wanting the *Evening Courant* this afternoon?"

"I see no need," Marjory told him, patting the broadsheet. "Mr. Ruddiman's paper will keep us informed of the prince's whereabouts. 'Tis all the news we require in this household."

"I've a report from the toun as weel," Gibson said, a note of pride in his voice. "Mair than five thousand o' the prince's men have assembled at Dalkeith on foot and five hundred on horse."

"A respectable number," Marjory agreed. All three women instinctively turned toward the south-facing windows as though by some miracle they might catch a glimpse of the army five miles away.

No sooner had Gibson quit the room than he reappeared with a visitor. "Mr. Mac-Pherson for Leddy Kerr."

When Elisabeth looked to the door, Rob MacPherson's dark eyes were aimed in one direction: hers. She held out her hand in greeting. "Your father said you might call on us. And here you are."

"Milady." He seemed to fill the room with his broad frame and thick head of hair.

"Will you join us for tea?" She signaled Mrs. Edgar, who was standing nearby, looking a bit anxious, as she always did when visitors arrived.

"I canna tarry," he said. "Minding the shop, ye ken."

"So you are." Elisabeth did not quite meet his gaze. The awkwardness of their last encounter before the prince's ball still stretched between them like a spider's web.

He cleared his throat. "Leddy Kerr, if ye'll not mind, I'd like a wird with ye. Alone."

The seriousness of his expression brought her to her feet. More ill news from Braemar, she feared. Or was it from the prince? "This way, Mr. MacPherson."

Inviting guests into one's bedchamber was a common practice in the crowded rooms of Edinburgh, but Elisabeth seldom did so. Without a tea table like Marjory's or a long, silk-covered couch like Janet's, her room was not arranged for visitors. Instead she had Rob move two of her upholstered armchairs beside one of the long windows overlooking the High Street.

"Now at least we may sit," she said, "though our prospect has little to recommend it, Mr. MacPherson. Naught but gray sky and gray rain."

His eyes narrowed. "Will ye still not call me Rob? We've kenned each ither for nigh unto twenty years."

"Another Jacobite reminding me of my age," she scolded him lightly, thinking of Simon. *Four-and-twenty. Like blackbirds in a pie.* "I mean only to show you the utmost respect, Mr. MacPherson."

Rob frowned but did not argue. When he lowered himself onto one of her upholstered chairs, he eased his impaired foot aside without comment.

Elisabeth knew that John Elder, the shoemaker from Marlin's Wynd, had fashioned a special shoe to hide Rob's club foot and improve his gait. But she would never draw attention to it. Instead, she met his gaze and smiled. "Tell me what brings you to Milne Square."

"Ye do, Bess." He leaned forward, his elbows propped on his knees, his dark gaze sincere. " 'Tis certain I've niver found a warm walcome from onie ither in this hoose."

"Surely the dowager —"

"She tolerates me, aye, but she doesna think me worthy of yer acquaintance."

Elisabeth opened her mouth to differ and then remembered the Sabbath morn in Milne Square when the dowager made her feel very small indeed. "I must apologize for my mother-in-law," she finally said, keeping her voice low. "She is not intentionally unkind. 'Tis just her way to be . . ." *Haughty? Condescending?*

"Rude," he finished for her.

"Oh now, Mr. —"

"Nae. We both ken 'tis true. The leddy has guid manners, but she doesna aye bear them about."

Elisabeth knew the proverb well and could not argue. The dowager's behavior was proper but not always kind. Hoping to put an end to the matter, Elisabeth reminded him, "You've still not told me why you've come."

Rob reached inside his brown wool coat. "I've brought something for ye."

As he withdrew his hand, Elisabeth wondered at the cost of a silver thimble large enough to fit on his sizable thumb. "Your father boasted that none in Edinburgh had a finer hand with a needle than you."

Rob shook his head. "My faither is an auld man with a soft heart and puir eyesight." He held out what he'd drawn from his coat. "Yer husband bid me deliver this, Bess. Said I was to hand it to nae one but yerself."

FORTY-FOUR

In a man's letters you know, Madam,
his soul lies naked.

SAMUEL JOHNSON

Elisabeth took the letter, still warm from
Rob's waistcoat.

"When did my husband give you this?"

"*Yestermorn* at the inn." His gaze was even,
revealing nothing. "Lord Kerr said ye were
not to read it 'til he was gone."

She studied the neatly folded paper sealed
with a dollop of candle wax and a thumbprint. What might Donald put in writing that
he could not tell her in person?

"I dinna ken what his lordship has written,
but I pray 'tis the truth." Rob abruptly stood
and held her gaze until he turned to go.
"Guid day to ye, Bess."

He quit the room before she could answer
him, leaving by way of Janet's empty bedchamber, then the drawing room, as if he
meant to avoid the others. The stair door
opened and closed a moment later, and he

was gone.

The truth. Elisabeth examined the outside of the letter, which bore no name or address. *Odd.* Even privately delivered letters, which did not travel through the Post Office, were usually addressed in the event they were lost en route.

She edged closer to the window and its meager gray light, then broke the seal and unfolded the single paper, her apprehension growing. Not only was her name not on the outside; it was not on the inside either, though the letter was clearly from Donald. She recognized his hand at once.

Thursday morning, 31 October 1745

Lord willing, we will see each other this evening in the palace forecourt before I depart. Whatever you can or cannot manage to say or do, I am determined to give you a complete accounting — for my sake as a means of confession, but most of all for your sake.

When she saw what followed, Elisabeth sank deeper into her chair. *Why, Donald? Why must you tell me this?* In his bold, almost careless handwriting he'd scrawled the names of all his conquests. *Many women.* Stunned, Elisabeth whispered their names aloud.

Susan McGill of Warriston's Close
Maggie Hunter of Brown's Land
Barbara Inglis of Libberton's Wynd
May Robertson of Dickson's Close
Jane Montgomerie of Geddes Close
Betty Jameson of Boswell's Court
Lucy Spence of Halkerston's Wynd

A blur of faces rose before her. Fair hair, brown hair, red hair, black hair. Some younger, most older than she. They were not among the gentry. She did not know them well. Yet she had stood beside them at the Luckenbooths, eying the gold jewelry at Mr. Low's. Sat across from them at the Tron Kirk on a Sabbath Day. Reached for the same ribbon at Mrs. Auchenleck's millinery.

Nae! How could she see these women in the High Street without weeping, without crying out, without calling them what they were? *Hizzies. Limmers. Howres.*

Her stomach in knots, she stared down at the letter, desperate for an end to the pain. But Donald had not finished unburdening his conscience.

I am sorry to report there were also a handful of maidservants about the city, whose names I do not recall. And Anna Hart, as you no doubt surmised.

I have a weakness . . .

403

More than a weakness. A sickness.

Tears stung her eyes. Not because of the scandalous number, but because of the appalling manner in which Donald Kerr used women and cast them aside. Her hands gripped the letter so tightly her nails dented the paper. *You are not the man I married. You are not the man I loved. My Donald was caring and thoughtful and true . . .*

Nae. She was deluding herself still. Her husband was none of those things. With her eyes swimming, she could barely make out the rest.

I would never burden you with this if I did not believe, with all my heart, you would rather know the worst and be done with it.

Did he think this knowledge would somehow put her mind at rest? That knowing the truth would make it easier to bear? *Oh, Donald. I do not know which of us is the greater fool.*

There are no others. In the months to come, if you hear my name whispered about, you will know what is true and what is false.

You are the false one, Lord Kerr. Angry with herself, angrier with him, Elisabeth yanked the handkerchief from her sleeve and pressed it to her wet cheek. *False to me, false to your family.*

> Please destroy this and do not bind these names to your heart. I have promised to change, and so I shall.

She huffed at his letter as if Donald himself were standing before her. How could he change his ways while riding through English villages full of maidservants who might gladly welcome a handsome Scotsman into their beds? Elisabeth wanted to believe him — what faithful wife would not? — but she had no evidence of change and far too much proof of wrongdoing.

She read the last paragraph, the letters growing smaller as he neared the bottom of the paper.

> If you forgave me before I left, now you know the full extent of your mercy. If you have not forgiven me, then we are of the same mind, for I cannot forgive myself.

There was no signature. Any man might have written it. Had the letter fallen into the wrong hands, only the women listed would be at risk of public scandal. *Donald, how could you be so heartless?* She squeezed her damp handkerchief until her fingers hurt. *And how could I have been so blind?* Hadn't she ignored

405

the evidence? Dismissed the gossips? Pretended his flirting meant nothing instead of facing the truth unfolding before her eyes? Aye, a hundred times, aye.

You are forgiven.

She'd said the words last night, drawing upon a power not her own, knowing only that Donald had been unfaithful yet ignorant of all the shocking details. But she could not unsay what had been said nor undo what had been done. And what of his conquests, this litany of women? Was she expected to forgive them as well?

Elisabeth leaned back against the upholstery, letting her anger and disappointment and heartache wash over her, too exhausted to wrestle with her feelings any longer. As if from miles away, sounds floated through the house. Marjory and Janet chatting softly in the next room. Mrs. Edgar preparing dinner in the kitchen. Gibson setting their places at the drawing room table.

Unbidden, one of the names from Donald's letter pricked her memory like a needle. *Lucy Spence of Halkerston's Wynd.* Elisabeth sat up, her mind clearing. Hadn't she met Lucy on Wednesday eve in Milne Square? The young widow without the beggar's badge, who'd held out her hand for a coin.

Lucy's voice taunted her. *I've a gentleman waiting for me at White Horse Close.*

406

Was Donald that gentleman? If so, then he'd not changed at all, breaking his vow within an hour of making it. Unless Lucy Spence meant someone else, some other gentleman . . .

Elisabeth rose to her feet, weary of knowing too little, even wearier of knowing too much. Studying the letter once more, she committed each of their names to memory. *Do not bind them to your heart.* Donald knew nothing about the workings of a woman's mind. Elisabeth would see these names and imagine their faces for the rest of her life.

But she would indeed destroy the letter. No hiding place was dark enough, no secret drawer secure enough to conceal such a brutal record of betrayal. She leaned over the fireplace and touched a corner of the letter to a glowing hot coal.

When the flame began to lick the edges, Elisabeth let his unsigned letter slip from her hands into the grate and watched Donald's sins turn to ash.

FORTY-FIVE

For who, alas! has lived,
Nor in the watches of the night recalled
Words he has wished unsaid
and deeds undone.

SAMUEL ROGERS

"I shall return no later than eight o' the clock," Marjory informed her daughters-in-law, who were both settled close by the fire, books in hand. Since the abrupt departure of the tailor's son that morning, Elisabeth had grown strangely quiet and had spent most of the day in seclusion, sewing. Janet, on the other hand, had not stopped talking and had followed Marjory about the house, filling the air with lively, meaningless chatter.

"Well, *I* shall reappear far later than eight," Janet was saying now, looking rather like a cat with its paw on a mouse's tail. "Lord and Lady Dalziel are famous for their supper parties. And the guestlist promises to be even more delicious." A glittering young couple in Edinburgh society, the Dalziels shed their radiance on any they drew into their circle, Janet and Andrew included.

Marjory smiled at her older daughter-in-law, thinking of next summer. A nursemaid would be required. Mrs. Gullane of nearby Carruber's Close might suffice. And they'd need a wee cradle fashioned from oak to match Andrew's bedchamber furnishings. Mr. Blyth in Chamber's Close could manage that. Marjory knew she was getting ahead of herself, but she couldn't help imagining her sons back home and a grandson newly arrived.

At present she was not entirely pleased with the fit of her velvet gown. She consulted her looking glass yet again and shook her head. Too snug in the bodice, too short in the waist. Had Miss Callander erred? Or had Mrs. Edgar's biscuits taken their toll? Marjory lifted her chin and pulled back her shoulders, drawing in her stomach. If she stood just so, Lady Falconer's guests might not notice the poor fit. Most of them would be dear friends who'd seen her wearing this gown before and would hardly notice.

Marjory glanced at the elegant card once more. Swirls of black ink covered the crisp white stock with gilding round the edges. *A musical evening at the home of Lady Joanna Falconer in Pearson's Close. On the first of November at five o' the clock.* The invitation had arrived the week Donald and Andrew enlisted and so was promptly mislaid. Had Elisabeth not found it by accident that forenoon, propped on the drawing room mantelpiece behind a neglected stack of books, Marjory would not be eying the clock now, dressed and eager to be off.

Of late she'd begun to miss her tea-table companions and her whist-playing friends, all of whom were sure to be in attendance: Lady Woodhall, Lord Dun, Lady Glassie, Mrs. Forbes, Lady Northesk, and, alas, Lady Ruthven. Marjory would avoid Charlotte as gracefully as she could, knowing the others would make her welcome.

" 'Tis a shame Lady Falconer did not include you in her invitation," she told Elisabeth, who would spend the evening alone. "Unfortunately, her drawing room is small and her list of acquaintances rather long." At nearly seventy years of age, Lady Joanna Falconer was one of Marjory's wisest and kindest of friends. Joanna would never exclude someone for the sheer pleasure of doing so. Not even a friend's Jacobite daughter-in-law.

"Had she invited me, I could not attend," Elisabeth reminded her, touching her black gown. "I shall be quite content to sew."

"Use all the candles you need," Marjory told her, feeling generous. "Shall we go, Gibson?"

The walk to Pearson's Close was not far enough to require a sedan chair, but it was very much uphill. Marjory kept a firm grip on Gibson's arm, minding her footing on the slippery plainstanes. Though the rain had ended, the air was still damp. Fog creeping up from the Firth of Forth swirled round her cape.

"How empty the High Street is," she said with a shiver. Doors were closed and shutters were fastened as if 'twere midnight, not a half hour past sunset. Highlanders, with their tartan trews and noisy bagpipes, no longer pervaded the scene. An eerie silence remained in their wake.

"I wonder who our musicians might be this evening," Marjory said, if only to keep her spirits up. Like the gray and chilling atmosphere, a sense of grimness, of sobering consequences, hung about the town.

"Here we are, mem." Gibson turned right into Pearson's Close, holding his lantern high as the narrow walls swallowed up what little light remained.

Marjory stepped over the gutter that ran down the center of the close, holding up her skirts and wishing she might hold her nose as well. Winter was an improvement over summer, but only a little. When they reached the forestair leading up to Lady Falconer's door, Marjory heard familiar voices and saw the shimmer of candles in the windows. Her heart lifting, she hastened up the stair like a child come home for Yuletide.

Instead of a bell or knocker, the entrance sported an iron ring, which Gibson dragged up and down a notched rod. Though Marjory winced at the grating noise, many an Edinburgh residence had its *risp.*

She held her breath in anticipation, already picturing Lady Falconer's snowy hair and bright eyes. When the door opened, Gibson stepped forward to announce her to Chisholm, the butler, whose stern visage made a poor showing for his mistress.

"Leddy Kerr o' Milne Square," Gibson said proudly.

But his counterpart frowned. "I dinna believe Leddy Falconer was expecting ye, mem."

"Not expecting me?" Marjory blinked at him. "But I received an invitation." She touched her velvet reticule and realized the card was not inside. "It seems I've left it at home, but surely the invitation itself is not needed." Marjory tried to see round him. "Perhaps if I might speak to Lady Falconer in person."

Chisholm's frown deepened. "The leddy is presently with her guests."

"But I am meant to be one of them!" Marjory insisted, her voice rising. "If you please, sir, let me enter."

Behind him a dozen conversations faded into silence. "Chisholm?" Lady Falconer's voice floated toward the door. "Have Lady

Kerr step into the entrance hall."

Marjory crossed the threshold, her feet leaden, her heart lodged in her throat. "Lady Falconer, whatever is the matter?"

Her elderly friend approached, pewter-colored taffeta rustling with each step. "I am surprised to see you here, Lady Kerr." The jewels in her white hair sparkled in the candlelit hall. But her gaze was not welcoming and her voice cooler still.

"Was an invitation sent to me by mistake?" Marjory was determined to find some explanation. "I received it several weeks ago."

"Much has happened since then," Lady Falconer said evenly. "In particular, your family's loyalty to the crown has taken a most unfortunate turn."

Indignation rose inside Marjory like chimney smoke. "You would banish me from your door for supporting the prince?" When she had no immediate answer, Marjory sputtered, "What of Charlotte Ruthven? She was seen wearing a white cockade in the High Street. Did you turn her away as well?"

Lady Falconer paused as if measuring her words. "Many a titled royalist danced at Holyroodhouse. But they did not send their sons off to fight King George's army."

"Who's to say who'll be our king?" Marjory replied more sharply than she intended. "The Jacobites were victorious at Gladsmuir."

Lady Falconer drew herself up. "Indeed,

413

with their scythes and their broadswords, they cut down hundreds of brave young soldiers, who died for the right cause and the right king."

Marjory's righteous anger swiftly turned to dust. *The right cause. The right king.* If every person in Lady Falconer's drawing room shared the same sentiments, the Kerrs had no friends left in Edinburgh and no standing whatsoever in society.

A most unfortunate turn. Lady Falconer had all but spoken the word that hung in the air like a rope dangling from the black gallows in the Grassmarket: *traitor.*

The older woman stepped closer and in a low voice confessed, "I do not envy you, Lady Kerr, for you have chosen a difficult path. You will find the city much changed come the morrow when the castle opens its gates, and the wrath of King George is loosed on Edinburgh."

Marjory cringed. *And my wrath shall wax hot.* She'd not fully weighed the consequences of supporting the Jacobite cause. None of them had.

"All is not lost, madam." Lady Falconer reached for the *Edinburgh Evening Courant* on her hall table and pressed the broadsheet into Marjory's hands. "Read the notice from George Wade. There is hope for your sons, though they must not delay."

Dazed, Marjory clasped the folded newspaper. What recourse might a British field marshal offer her Jacobite sons? Nothing they would be willing to consider, she feared.

Hearing the clink of sterling against china and the strings of a fiddle being tuned, Marjory lifted her gaze to peer over her friend's shoulder. Her heart yearned to be among her friends and peers as if nothing had happened. As if she and her sons were still faithful to the crown and no one in her household was an enemy of their sovereign king. Marjory could not stop herself from asking, "Might I still join you this evening? You can be sure the prince will never be mentioned."

Lady Falconer looked genuinely distraught. "For the sake of my guests . . . for your own sake, Lady Kerr . . . I bid you good night." With the slightest of bows, she withdrew into the shadows as Chisholm slowly closed the door.

Forty-Six

He's turn'd their heads, the lad,
And ruin will bring on us a'.
                    CAROLINA OLIPHANT, LADY NAIRNE

Marjory slumped into Gibson's arms.

He righted her at once. "Now, now, mem. Dinna take what the leddy said to heart. In a week 'twill a' be richt again."

Marjory heard the doubt behind his words. Society would not quickly forget her family's loyalty to the prince, and they both knew it very well. "Take me home," she begged him.

Gibson escorted her down the forestair, handling her with such care that tears sprang to her eyes. At least her household remained faithful even if her friends did not. Mrs. Edgar would be waiting with supper. Elisabeth and Janet would offer their sympathy. And her sons, when they learned of it, would fight all the more valiantly, defending a mother sent away in shame.

Overcome, Marjory nearly lost her balance on the stair. She'd supported her sons, had she not? And their prince? "I did what I could," she said under her breath, gripping the stair rail for support. "I did what seemed right."

Gibson patted her arm. "I ken ye did, mem."

Home beckoned like a sanctuary. None would judge her there. None would call her traitor.

As they retraced their steps through Pearson's Close, the bells of Saint Giles chimed the half hour. The evening air had grown colder and the fog thicker, as the muted sound of the bells proved.

The broadsheet Lady Falconer had given her in parting was still clutched in Marjory's hand. *There is hope for your sons.* Could it be true? Marjory let that hope grow inside her like a seedling after the rain. If something could be done to rescue their reputation. If her sons' lives and fortunes might both be spared. If it was not too late.

When they reached the High Street and started past the mercat cross, she pulled at Gibson's sleeve, making his lantern bob about. "This cannot wait until we're home."

He did not protest, merely held the lantern aloft while she unfolded the *Evening Courant* with trembling hands. The notice was quickly found — dated the thirtieth of October — but the small print was not so easily read in the murk. She held the page a handbreadth

417

away from her eyes and squinted at the lines of ink, urging Gibson to bring the lantern closer.

It seemed Field Marshal George Wade had posted the notice on behalf of King George. A few words were hard to sort out in the meager light, but those she read pierced her heart like a sharpened dirk.

. . . his subjects inhabiting the Highlands of Scotland and others who've been seduced . . .

"That's the truth of it," Marjory breathed. "My sons were seduced by the prince and his cause. We all were."

. . . to take arms and enter into a most unnatural rebellion . . .

"Aye, aye," she said, nodding at the broadsheet as if Wade himself were present. However persuasive the Stuart claims, opposing the sovereign who held their title and lands was not only unnatural; it was patently unwise. Why were these things so difficult to see in the midst and so easy to see from a distance?

. . . all such who shall return to their habitations on or before the twelfth day of November next and become available to his Majesty and his government shall be objects of

"My sons will be forgiven!" In her excitement and relief, she clamped her hand on Gibson's arm, nearly knocking his lantern to the ground. "We have only to bring them home, and the king's clemency is assured."

"Is that a', mem?" He frowned at the paper. Unlike Mrs. Edgar, he could not read more than a few rudimentary phrases.

Marjory skimmed the words again and realized that was not all the king required. "Ah, I see. Donald and Andrew would fight for the government rather than for the prince." A simple exchange of uniforms. Aye, and of loyalties, but they would not be the first men to do so. She'd heard stories of Scotsmen who'd fought for the British at Gladsmuir and then deserted to join the prince's army. And Lowlanders who had come out for the prince, then changed their minds and enlisted in support of the king.

Would her sons be willing to make such a sacrifice if it meant saving their title and lands and securing their safety? Surely there was still time.

Lady Falconer's words grew louder inside her. *They must not delay.*

"What if the lads willna agree?" Gibson prompted her. "What does Wade say to that?"

. . . if they shall continue in their rebellion,

they will be proceeded against with rigor suitable to the nature of their crime.

"They will be charged with treason," Marjory said in a low voice. Marshal Wade did not elaborate on the punishment. He did not need to. The penalty for treason was death. Donald, as a titled peer, would be beheaded, which was considered a merciful sentence. Andrew, as a second son, would be hanged, drawn, and quartered.

"Nae, it cannot be!" Marjory stared at the paper in horror. Why had she let them enlist? Why had she let them go? "Take me home," she whimpered, fearing she might be sick and add to her shame. "Home, I must get home."

A gnarled hand clutched hers as Gibson hurried her along the street, aided by the downward slope. "Dinna *fash* yerself, Leddy Kerr. Yer sons are canny enough to see what must be done."

I hope so. Oh, I pray so. Marjory pressed her handkerchief to her mouth, afraid to speak.

When they reached Baillie's Land, the turnpike stair made her feel even more nauseous. She nearly fell through the door into the arms of Mrs. Edgar, who helped her to her bedchamber, then made her presentable again when the worst was over. Marjory had never been so sick to her stomach nor had a better reason. *My sons, my dear sons.*

Elisabeth was waiting for her in the drawing room, her expression filled with concern. "I'm so sorry you were taken ill. Was it something you ate at Lady Falconer's?"

Before Marjory could respond, Janet hurried in from her bedchamber. She was dressed for an evening with Lord and Lady Dalziel, though her hair was not yet styled nor her face powdered. "Whatever has happened, madam? You look a sight."

Marjory sank into a chair, her head throbbing and her stomach still queasy. "I've much to tell you, none of it good." Both young women joined her by the fire, their faces anxious, their mood sober.

Marjory was too drained to paint a gentle picture. "Lady Falconer did not receive me."

"Surely not!" Janet gaped at her in disbelief. "Why would she be so uncivil?"

"Because we have turned our backs on the king." Marjory's voice was flat, pressed down with grief. "Because it is an act of treason. Edinburgh society will have nothing to do with us now."

Her daughters-in-law were shocked into silence.

When she found the strength to do so, Marjory continued. "We should have . . . Nae, *I* should have known better. One does not oppose a king without consequence."

"Is there any remedy?" Elisabeth asked.

"Aye, but 'twill be a difficult pill for my

sons to swallow." She held out the broadsheet, folded open to Marshal Wade's notice. They read it in turn while Marjory watched their expressions. Irritation wrinkled Janet's brow. Elisabeth's eyes bore a hint of despair.

"What is to be done?" Janet wanted to know. "Shall we write to them, beg them to come home?"

Elisabeth slowly shook her head. "As Life Guards, Donald and Andrew would never desert the prince, for there is no honor in that. And Lord Elcho would have them shot for desertion. We cannot ask them to return home. We cannot even wish it."

Marjory sank against the back of her chair, barely conscious. *I have lost my sons.* For an instant it seemed there were no candles in the room, no fire in the grate. Only shadows swirling round her.

She heard Janet conversing with Elisabeth, their voices low. Heard a coach pass by on the High Street, harnesses jingling in the hollow night air. Heard the clock chime the hour of six.

And then Marjory heard a phrase from long ago echo in her heart.

Return unto me.

She well remembered the words and who'd spoken them.

"Help me," she whispered so softly no one could hear but the Almighty. Was he listening? Did he still watch over her as he once had?

Marjory closed her eyes and opened her heart ever so slightly. *My sons are all I have, Lord. Please.*

FORTY-SEVEN

Morning fair
Came forth with pilgrim steps in amice
   gray.

JOHN MILTON

Elisabeth emerged from the murky interior of her sedan chair into the pale morning light. "You'll return for me at noontide, Mr. Fenwick?"

"Aye," the chairman assured her, pocketing his sixpence. "Leuk for me whan Saint Giles plays her last tune." He headed back whence he came, toward the town proper. With the prince's men gone from Duddingston and Holyroodhouse deserted, few travelers would be found at the foot of the Canongate.

The sun had been up for less than an hour. Elisabeth drank in the fresh, cold air as she eyed the crowstepped gables and wooden dormers of the Canongate. The homes were altogether grander and not nearly so tall as the dizzying lands of the High Street. Beneath her feet oblong paving stones were meant to give a horse purchase on the sloping street, and above her stretched a colorless sky without a hint of sun or a threat of rain.

By employing the dependable Mr. Fenwick as her chairman, Elisabeth had overcome her mother-in-law's halfhearted protest. "Visiting injured soldiers? Are you certain 'tis wise?" Marjory had fretted. "A charitable deed, to be sure, but . . ."

Neither Marjory nor Janet understood why Elisabeth had ventured out that morn. She could hardly explain it herself. "I need to do something useful," she'd told them. That was the truth, so far as it went. Elisabeth also longed to be on her own. Away from Milne Square with its confining walls of wood and stone. Away from the Kerrs, if only for a few hours.

Marjory had been inconsolable last evening despite Elisabeth's attempts to lift her spirits. "If the prince and his men are as victorious in England as they were at Gladsmuir, your worries will be for naught," she'd assured her mother-in-law, though it did not seem to help.

Janet, who'd gone to sup with the Dalziels at Marjory's urging, had returned home less than an hour later in tears, having found an equally cold reception. "Whatever has happened to our city?" Janet had wailed, throwing herself across her bed, crushing the gown Mrs. Edgar had spent two hours ironing. "When the prince resided at the palace, we were all Jacobites!"

Were we? Elisabeth had held her tongue but not without effort.

Gazing down the street toward Holyroodhouse, she remembered Janet's heated words from three days past. *You are the true Jacobite among us.* Would there be many supporters left in Edinburgh now that Prince Charlie and his five thousand Highlanders were gone?

Elisabeth sensed a tidal change coming, a swift and thorough shift of opinion and practice. The capital would be all for King George now. Ministers would return to their pulpits, magistrates would resume their duties, and the town guard would bang their ten o' the clock drums once more. Edinburgh Castle, no longer under siege, would open its portcullis, and the royalist troops would reclaim the town for King George.

Life would return to normal for most. But for loyal Jacobites, things might never be the same. Marjory and Janet had experienced that firsthand last evening. Elisabeth had little doubt her turn was coming. This morning's mission would leave no doubt of her allegiance to the prince.

Taking in another draught of fresh air, she resolutely walked toward the entrance of Queensberry House, a temporary hospital for Jacobite officers and soldiers injured at Gladsmuir. These were the men who'd fought beside Simon, the ones who'd survived but could not march out with the prince.

She'd passed by the makeshift infirmary each time she visited White Horse Close and wished she might stop for a visit. This morning upon waking she'd thought again of these men — strangers, yet true to the cause — who might be feeling rather abandoned just now. For Simon's sake, for their sakes, she would offer what comfort she could.

The residence of a duke, Queensberry House had a suitably impressive exterior. Harled walls, stretched three floors high, were lined with windows and topped with a mansard roof. Two large wings pointed toward the street, creating the open courtyard she was now crossing. Her footsteps echoed between the walls on either side of her. Since she was not expected, Elisabeth had worn her white cockade prominently displayed on her cape, hoping she would not be rebuffed at the door.

A man of forty-odd years in waistcoat and shirt sleeves answered her knock. He'd not shaved in days, by the look of him, and wore a flesher's apron streaked with blood. Surgeon or meat dresser, his broad smile boded well as did his hearty welcome.

"What a Jacobite rose is this!" His bow was as ebullient as his speech. "I am Martin Eccles, madam. One of the surgeons, at your service."

"Lady Donald Kerr," she responded, curtsying with a quiet sigh of relief. Now that she was through the door, how best to proceed? "I thought I might be of some use caring for the men. My brother, Simon Ferguson, fought at Gladsmuir —"

"He did indeed." Mr. Eccles escorted her into the entrance hall, with its marble floors, Corinthian pillars, and a rich cornice outlining the high ceiling. Candles flickered in all four corners, illuminating the statuary on the stair. "When the prince called for surgeons, I was the one who dressed your brother's wounds. Fine young man, with the zeal of ten." He shook his head, a sorrowful expression on his weathered face. "I did all that I could for him, Lady Kerr. But . . ."

" 'Twas not your fault." She paused to clear her throat lest the strain in her voice add to his guilt. "My brother died as he lived."

"Courageously," he assured her, nodding. "Well, madam, you've not come for my benefit but for the lads', aye?" He smoothed a hand over his bare, freckled crown, then pointed her to an open doorway. "This way, if you please."

Elisabeth followed him into a square room with paneled walls, a fine molded chimney piece, and sufficient windows to usher in the much needed light of day. She counted eight beds, such as they were: wooden planks on stout legs with the thinnest of mattresses. Nonetheless, the soldiers appeared well cared for. Their dressings looked cleaner than she'd feared, and their limbs were set with sturdy planks.

To a man, they were smiling at her. Nae, grinning.

One lad with wavy black hair and crooked teeth called out, "Is this what the apothecary sent to make us weel?"

Another soldier cried, "I'll take my medicine without complaint."

"Gentlemen," the surgeon cautioned them, "this is Lady Kerr, come to . . . eh, change your bandages . . ." He looked at her to be sure, then continued. "And to offer a word of encouragement, nae doubt. Her brother, Simon Ferguson, fought bravely at Gladsmuir. Aye, and died bravely as well."

At this the men pounded on their bedframes with their fists and shouted as one, "Huzzah! Huzzah!"

Their obvious respect for Simon brought tears to her eyes. Why had she not visited his fellow soldiers weeks ago? "Forgive me for not coming sooner," Elisabeth began, slipping off her cape. The men quieted at once, sobered perhaps by the sight of her black gown. She told them, "My husband, Lord Donald, and his brother, Andrew, rode out with His Royal Highness on Thursday eve. Let us see what can be done to heal your wounds and send you off to join them."

The same young lad piped up. "But if ye'll

be coming round to see us, milady, we'll none of us want to go." The others laughed, and a roll of bandages was pitched in his direction, along with a few good-natured insults. He protested, "I didna say I wouldna fight!"

Elisabeth plucked the bandages from amid his sheets. "Then I'll be sure to start with you."

Mr. Eccles pointed out the few supplies available: alum for cuts, camphor for itching, ginger for nausea, oil of turpentine and yarrow to staunch the bleeding, comfrey and figwort for healing compresses. Several of the soldiers had broken bones that time alone would mend, but those with ugly gashes and musket wounds would benefit from the physic herbs.

"I'll be in the next room, should you have need of me." Mr. Eccles finished with a cheerful bob of his head, then disappeared through the door.

"Now then, gentlemen." Elisabeth quickly detached the black ruffles lining her sleeves and laid them aside with her cape, then borrowed a few pins from her hair to fasten her gown's full cuffs out of the way. "I trust you'll not mind smelling of heather," she said, reaching into her hanging pocket for a bar of Donald's favorite soap.

The lad nearest her blushed profusely. "Onie smell will be an improvement, milady."

More laughter ensued as she filled a basin

with steaming hot water from the room's crackling hearth. She'd borrowed one of Mrs. Edgar's aprons, hoping to spare her gown, and had stuffed the pockets full of clean linen squares. The simple act of bathing the young man's face and hands, then attending to the wound on his leg gave Elisabeth a deep sense of satisfaction. When she finished, her hands would be chapped and her sleeves soaked, despite her efforts to keep them dry. But it was a worthy cause.

She learned each of their names in turn. Grant Findlay, her first patient, was the youngest and bearded Will McWade, the stoutest. Every visible inch of Thomas MacPadden was covered in red hair, and Alex Baird served as their unofficial leader by virtue of his daunting height and strength. Robert Glendinning hailed from Aberdeen, and David Grassie, despite his two broken legs, had a hearty laugh. Alasdair Campbell, who spoke only Gaelic, was elated when Elisabeth responded in kind. But it was green-eyed John Hardy she was most glad to meet. He'd marched from Perth with Simon and knew her brother well.

"A stubborn lad," John said, then looked at her as if prepared to apologize.

"I've never known his equal," she agreed, remembering the brother who'd clambered up trees he was told not to climb, forded rivers he was ordered not to cross, and eaten berries he was warned would make him sick, which they did. Elisabeth's smile was bittersweet. "Simon did not bend, nor did he break." *Not even beneath the hand of Ben Cromar.* The thought strengthened her spine and put her to work serving her brother's comrades.

Beginning with soap and water, she spent perhaps a quarter hour with each patient. They were a brave lot, not once flinching when she cleaned their wounds or tightened the rags holding their splints in place. In her youth she'd cared for Simon's gashes and sprains, so nothing she saw that morning made her feel faint. While she went about her work, the men plied her with questions concerning the prince's departure. Had Secretary Murray arranged a formal ceremony? Did His Royal Highness look well? Was the elderly Lord Pitsligo fit to ride?

Elisabeth was in the midst of describing the prince's grand carriage when a loud commotion on the street cut her short. Angry shouts and cries of alarm could be heard, and the clatter of hoofs filled the courtyard. Elisabeth hastened to the nearest window, the hair on the back of her neck prickling. Was there trouble in Dalkeith? Had some of the prince's men returned?

She swept open the curtains, then froze. *Not the prince's men. The king's.* As she watched, more than a dozen British soldiers stormed the entrance to Queensberry House, teeth bared, swords drawn, vengeance in their eyes.

FORTY-EIGHT

Ay me! What perils do environ
The man that meddles with cold iron!
SAMUEL BUTLER

"Dragoons!" Elisabeth cried, backing away from the window. She looked to her patients and found they were nearly as horrified as she, with no weapons at hand and their limbs wrapped in bandages and splints.

But they did not give in to fear.

Those who were able to stand, even on one leg, got up from their beds at once and grabbed whatever they could find to defend themselves: water pitchers, chamber pots, wooden crutches, or a sharp iron poker still hot from the fire. Men too injured to move from their beds braced themselves, faces like flint, daring whoever came through the door to meddle with them.

"Behind me, Leddy Kerr!" Alex Baird ordered, his broad chest and thick arms more menacing than the sharpest blade.

Elisabeth did as she was told, grasping the

bandage scissors like a dagger and raising them just above her head. She would not be taken without a fight. Nae, none of them would.

She could hear the dragoons in the entrance hall cursing at the surgeon, who valiantly stood his ground. "We have naught but injured soldiers here!" Martin Eccles shouted. "Where is your sense of honor, gentlemen?"

"Honor?" an English voice roared. "Highlanders have no honor." A sharp cry was followed by an awful thud.

Elisabeth fought down a wave of nausea. She could not succumb to weakness or fear. Not now. She drew strength from the men round her as they silently closed ranks.

"The Jacobites showed no mercy," shouted another voice in the hall, louder than the first. "Nor will we. Not this day."

The sound of boot heels striking the marble floor grew closer. Elisabeth's heart was in her throat as her small contingent prepared for the onslaught. They did not have to wait long.

Splintered wood flew like sparks from a fire as the door exploded off its hinges. Four dragoons burst into the room, their polished rapiers matched by the lethal gleam in their eyes. Others in their company continued down the hall, blistering the air with their words.

Elisabeth did not flinch beneath their fierce gazes, though she gritted her teeth to keep from crying out. *Help us. Someone.*

"I see no honorable men, do you?" growled their leader, a thick-necked brute.

"Nae, Mr. Morgan," one of the dragoons behind him said. "But I do see a woman."

Alex Baird ground out, "Nae, ye see a leddy."

Standing behind him, Elisabeth watched the muscles in Alex's shoulders swell, while his arms seemed to turn to solid oak. In his hands a three-legged stool and a heavy pewter plate were formidable weapons. Though his left calf was wrapped in a splint, knee to foot, the dragoons would have to get past the rest of him first.

"Leddy Kerr is in mourning for her brither," Alex told them, his voice low, like distant thunder. "He was killed by one o' yer muskets."

"A well aimed one, apparently," Morgan said, making the others laugh. All four moved closer, sizing up the Jacobites as if choosing their first victims.

Elisabeth tightened the grip on her scissors. "My brother died a hero. But your men fled from the field."

It was true, and they all knew it. The dragoons had run for their lives at Gladsmuir, abandoning their horses, red coats tucked between their legs.

"Are the four o' ye cowards as weel?" Alex taunted them. "Threatening wounded soldiers wha bear nae weapons?"

Morgan suddenly thrust his sword into Will McWade's round belly. "This man has a weapon."

With a cry of pain, Will dropped the clay pitcher in his hand. It shattered into jagged pieces on the hardwood floor.

"See that?" Morgan withdrew his sword with a swift jerk. "You could hurt someone with those pottery shards."

A stunned expression on his face, Will pressed his linen shirt against the wound. The spot of blood quickly bloomed into a dark, red circle. He stumbled back, his face growing ashen as the stain spread.

Elisabeth longed to help him but dared not move.

David Grassie shouted from his bed, "This is an infirmary, not a field o' battle. By yer ain law, ye canna wound us further."

"No need to inflict new wounds, really." Morgan glanced over his shoulder at the others, a murderous look in his eye. "The ones you have now will suffice."

As if on signal, the four swept through the room like a whirlwind, unleashing their fury, snapping and twisting the soldiers' recently set bones with their bare hands, using their daggers to slice open wounds not yet healed. The Highlanders fought back however they could, tearing at the men's coats, clawing at their faces, pulling out their hair in fistfuls.

But the dragoons were determined to exact their revenge.

"Stop!" Elisabeth cried, lunging at the smallest of the four men. She'd no more than torn his sleeve before he wrested the scissors from her hands and cast them into the fire, then grabbed her round the neck.

"No one tells Gilbert Elliot whan to stop." He pushed her to the floor with a vile oath, then bent over her and began fumbling with the buttons on his breeches, leering at her, his breath reeking of brandy. She screamed for help, struggling against her skirts and hoops.

Alex and John responded at once, throwing themselves at the Englishman with a Highland battle cry. The dragoon crumpled to the floor beneath their weight and did not rise when her two rescuers hauled each other to their feet, then kicked the man's ribs for good measure.

"Are ye hurt, Leddy Kerr?" When Alex turned to assist her, Elisabeth flinched at the sight of his lower leg, newly broken, the bone protruding from his flesh. His hand was cold when he reached down to help her stand, and his face was drenched in sweat. "Milady," he said hoarsely, then promptly collapsed.

As swiftly as it began, the rampage ended. The three dragoons who could walk dragged out the fourth and summoned the others. Snarling epithets as they departed, the men soon rode off — some downhill toward Holyroodhouse, some uphill toward the Castle — leaving a battered and bloody mess in their wake.

A collective groan rose from every corner of Queensberry House. Through a veil of angry tears, Elisabeth eyed her Jacobite brothers strewn about the room. She would attend to their needs first. Surely there were nurses elsewhere who'd been spared and could help the others. These eight men were her primary concern.

Elisabeth retied her apron strings and got to work cleansing fresh wounds and applying compresses. Will McWade worried her the most, especially when neither yarrow nor turpentine staunched his bleeding. She could not press hard enough nor tie a bandage tight enough round his soft middle, and Will was too weak to apply sufficient pressure himself.

Since John Hardy lay nearby, she asked for his help, then winced when she saw how much it cost him to move even a few inches. "Can you use your good hand, John, to hold his compress in place?"

"Aye, Leddy Kerr," he said with a faint smile.

While John helped her, she examined his wound. A heartless dragoon had pierced the skin along freshly formed scar tissue, cutting open John's thigh nearly to the bone. She was grateful Janet was not with her that morning. Skittish as her sister-in-law was in the presence of blood, and expecting a child besides, Janet would have quickly become her ninth patient.

Elisabeth lost all track of time as she kept busy kneeling, bending, washing, bandaging, and offering whatever words of comfort came to mind. Black-haired young Grant, in somewhat better shape than the others, hobbled about as her assistant, emptying and refilling the basin with hot water. Donald's heather soap was soon depleted and replaced with a serviceable bar made from lye.

It wasn't until she heard voices in the hall that Elisabeth remembered the splintered wood hanging from the door hinges. "Have a care!" she called out as Mr. Eccles stumbled through the open doorway, supporting another man in worse condition.

"Lady Kerr," the surgeon said weakly. "This is Mr. Cunningham. He, too, is a surgeon, though he'll not be of much help at the moment."

Nor, she realized, would Mr. Eccles. One eye swollen, his face and hands badly beaten, the surgeon was in no condition to hold a needle. What was to be done when she had a roomful of men requiring stitches? Thomas MacPadden had an especially bad gash on his forearm, and John Hardy's thigh was oozing blood.

Then there was the matter of resetting Alex

Baird's lower leg. He'd passed out on the floor — a blessing, if only to spare him the pain — but the Highlander was too large for her to move on her own. It seemed the surgeons themselves needed attending first.

"Come and sit, both of you." Elisabeth guided them to the only chairs that had survived the assault, then bathed their wounds with the last of the heated water. She eyed the long, narrow-necked stoup hanging by the fireplace. The Canongate wellhead was not far from the mansion's door. Did she dare send Grant Findlay beyond the safety of these walls with the dragoons still abroad?

The lad followed her gaze and guessed her thoughts. "Ye'll be needing me to fetch mair water." He lifted the stoup from its peg. "I'll not be lang."

Mr. Eccles grimaced as she dabbed his head wounds with powdered alum diluted with water. "I am sorry as any man can be, Lady Kerr. You came as an angel of mercy, only to be burdened with the lowest of duties."

"I came so I might be useful," she told him. In truth, she had never felt so alive, as if a glowing branch from the hearth were burning inside her.

"On behalf of the prince's men, we are most grateful, madam." Mr. Eccles closed his eyes while she held a warm cloth to his cheek. " 'Tis certain the Almighty sent you."

The surgeon's comment did not go unnoticed. Did God send people about, like caddies in the street, running errands and delivering messages? If so, she had a request. "We'll be needing surgeons," she told Mr. Eccles gently, not wanting to offend him. "Whom might I call upon?"

Mr. Cunningham, silent until now, came to life, lifting his blood-caked head. "You'll not find a Jacobite surgeon in Edinburgh. The prince took them all to Dalkeith, save us."

Her busy hands stilled. No surgeons? Whatever was to be done? These men would die without proper care. Yet 'twas against the law for anyone to practice medicine who'd not been approved by his fellow surgeons.

Martin Eccles had little interest in legalities, it seemed. He was studying her hands with marked interest. "Have you any skill with a needle? 'Twill be some time before I can be trusted with anything sharp." The surgeon held up his badly mangled hands. "One of the dragoons thought it sport to use the butt of his pistol like a hammer."

She lightly touched his fingers. "I am no surgeon, Mr. Eccles. But I am a seamstress."

He looked up, mouth agape. "Surely not by trade?"

"Not presently," she said, thinking of the years she'd sewn for Angus's customers. Then her heart skipped a beat. *Rob MacPherson.* Aye, he could stitch the men's wounds. And within the law if Mr. Eccles remained at the patient's bedside while Rob worked. "Do you know the tailor Angus MacPherson?"

Mr. Eccles nodded. "A loyal Jacobite. Rode out with the prince."

"His son is here in Edinburgh. I'm sure he would come at once and serve you well."

"We'd be glad for his help," Mr. Cunningham admitted. "Might you call upon him, Lady Kerr? We're neither of us fit for the High Street."

Mr. Eccles frowned at him. "You ask too much of the lady, sir."

"Not at all." Elisabeth untied her apron, casting a wistful gaze round the room. Much as she wanted to nurse each of them to health, they needed a strong man with capable hands, someone who could move them onto their beds and stitch their gaping wounds. If he was willing, Rob was the man for the task. "I shall take a chair to the Luckenbooths," she told the surgeons, uncertain how that might be managed. Mr. Fenwick had no doubt come and gone by now.

"Take great care in the street," Mr. Eccles cautioned her. "The dragoons know which families support the prince. And some of them have seen your courage. Even now they may be waiting for you, Lady Kerr."

FORTY-NINE

Idle rumors were also added
to well-founded apprehensions.

LUCAN

A shiver ran down Elisabeth's spine as if the cold point of a knife were being dragged from the nape of her neck to the curve of her waist. "I shall hide beneath my hooded cape," she promised the surgeon, "and not emerge from the chair until I reach Mr. MacPherson's shop."

Her answer seemed to satisfy him, though she'd not entirely convinced herself. Janet's words rang more true by the hour. *Whatever has happened to our city?*

"Here's young Findlay with our water." Mr. Eccles gestured toward the splintered remains of the doorway. "Have you brought a report for us as well?"

"Aye." The lad emptied the water into an iron pot and swung it over the fire, then hung the stoup on its peg. "Half the toun is

444

blethering on their stairs."

Elisabeth knew where the other half could be found: hiding behind their doors, Marjory and Janet among them.

"What news, then?" Mr. Cunningham prompted him.

The curtain of black hair across his face did not hide the lad's discouragement. "The dragoons found Cameron o' Lochiel's wife at hame and abused her harshly. Spat in the guid leddy's face and called her wirds I darena say." The lad shot a furtive glance in Elisabeth's direction.

She'd seen the sort of men they were. Their cruel words were not hard to imagine.

"They've been to Holyroodhouse as weel," Grant continued. "Tore doon the silk whaur the prince laid his head, broke all the fine gilded glasses, and took whatsomever they liked from the Duke o' Hamilton's rooms. In the Great Gallery they slashed the paintings." His countenance darkened. "Queen Mary's worst o' a'."

The surgeons exchanged glances, then Mr. Eccles said, "We've another errand for you, lad. Hail a sedan chair for our Lady Kerr, if you please. 'Tis not safe to have her tarrying in the street."

"Aye, sir." Grant hastened to the door, trying to disguise his limp with a jaunty gait.

A moment ago Elisabeth had been loath to depart. Now she was clearly needed elsewhere. No home was safe from these marauders, not even her own.

She slipped off her bloodstained apron, intending to leave it behind. Mrs. Edgar would understand. Scooping a bowlful of lukewarm water from the pot, she bathed her hands and face, then unpinned her sleeves, drenched as expected. Once she reattached the ruffles, at least her forearms were spared the feel of damp fabric.

When she fastened her wool cape, the white cockade caught her eye.

Mr. Cunningham grunted. "You'll want your rose well hidden, much as it grieves me to say it."

Elisabeth turned away from the men and pinned the cockade safely inside her bodice, where no dragoon would find it. Then with a heavy heart she made her rounds, bidding each soldier farewell, wishing she had a healing salve or soothing tincture to put things aright.

Alex Baird was last, still stretched across the hardwood floor with a bundle of clean rags for a pillow. As she bent down to speak to him, she begged the surgeons to set his injured leg before she left. "I cannot bear to think of you suffering a moment longer," she told the braw Highlander, using one of the rags to wipe his damp brow. "On behalf of my husband, thank you for guarding my virtue."

"Lord Kerr is a fortunate man," Alex said, his eyes unfocused from the pain. "And Gilbert Elliot got what he deserved. Now, whisky, if ye please. And dinna watch, milady, for 'twill not be a bonny sight."

Mr. Cunningham produced a silver flask, then gave Alex a leather strap to clamp between his teeth. With some difficulty the two surgeons knelt beside him. Their battered fingers could not stitch a man back together that day, but using palms, forearms, and elbows, they managed to wrest Alex's leg into place. Elisabeth gave them room to work but did not turn away, standing beside Alex in his travail. Had he not stood by her?

"Leddy Kerr!" Grant Findlay called from the door, startling her. "I've a chair waiting for ye."

Mr. Eccles slowly rose, his manners never forgotten, even in a sick room. "I wish you well, milady. Kindly send the tailor's son if he'll come. And when the government's temper is spent, I hope you'll return." He nodded at the men round him struggling to lift themselves onto their elbows so they might see her off. "You've made many friends here."

"Indeed I have." Elisabeth lifted her hand to each one, not trusting herself to speak.

Soon she was retracing her steps through the front entrance. How strange it felt to be out of doors after many hours in that small, square room. Had she even heard the bells at noontide? Elisabeth crossed the courtyard, grateful to breathe in air that did not smell of camphor or turpentine. She was nearly at the street before she realized the chairman waiting for her was her own Mr. Fenwick.

"What a surprise to find you here!" she said. One concern put to rest, at least.

But Mr. Fenwick was not so sanguine. "I came leuking for ye ilka hour." He pulled open the door and motioned her inside, all the while glancing up and down the street. "There's an ill wind blowing o'er the toun."

Elisabeth shivered, his words more chilling than the brisk November day. "Take me to the Luckenbooths on an errand first," she told him, "and then deliver me home. I'll not mind paying you twice."

He shook his head. " 'Tis nae yer *siller* I'm after but yer welfare." He banged the door closed, then bent to lift the chair, calling out to his partner in the rear. The two men hastened up the Canongate as though Auld Nick was on their heels.

Elisabeth held on as if her life depended upon it, believing it well might. Having pulled her hood forward, she could not see out the side windows without turning her head. The front window, close enough to touch with her outstretched hand, afforded a sufficient view and an alarming one.

Royalist soldiers, on foot and on horseback,

could be seen coming and going from the closes and wynds — climbing up forestairs, knocking on doors, and accosting citizens in the street. Though these soldiers did not appear so fearsome as the ones who'd called at Queensberry House, not a one bore a smile, and all carried weapons.

She longed to ask Mr. Fenwick what he'd heard and seen since they parted that morn. Perhaps when he delivered her to Milne Square, with its quieter courtyard, they might have a brief conversation.

At the Netherbow Port, the sedan chair came to a halt. A week ago a Highlander would have waved them through with nary a second look. But this was a royalist porter returned to his post. He scowled at Mr. Fenwick's black sedan chair as if it contained a French spy with seditious papers beneath her cloak.

She held her breath, hoping Mr. Fenwick's spate of words would drown the fellow's suspicions. After a very long pause, they took off again, and the Tron Kirk steeple and its clock came into view. *Nearly three.* Elisabeth moved her hood long enough to eye Milne Square in passing. She noticed a few soldiers gathered in a knot and stabbing at the air with their bayonets. Arguing, she wondered, or pointing? *This house. Nae, that house.*

Her heart began to thud in her chest. Had these men knocked on her family's door? Or

449

kicked it down, as they had at Queensberry House? Nae, the stair door was too thick for that. Would Mrs. Edgar admit them? Loyal as she was to the family, their housekeeper was not a Jacobite. Nor was Gibson. But surely they would protect the dowager. Surely they would guard Janet, even not knowing she was with child. Surely.

Please, please, please.

Near tears, Elisabeth leaned forward, prepared to leap from the chair the moment Mr. Fenwick stopped at the MacPhersons' door. She would not entertain the very real possibility of Rob not being there. He had to be home, had to be willing to help the surgeons at Queensberry House. She could not abandon Will and Alex and John and the others. If it came to it, she'd return and stitch their wounds herself.

Yet she was also needed at home. *Hurry, hurry, hurry.*

The sedan chair stopped so quickly she tumbled to the floor, then nearly into the street when Mr. Fenwick flung open the door.

"Och, milady!" He helped her stand, then brushed the dust from her cape. "Begging yer pardon."

She waved away his concerns. "You're to wait for me," she reminded him, then picked up her skirts and hurried toward the door of Angus's ground-floor shop.

But the door was closed. And locked, she

soon discovered. The windows showed a dark interior with not one candle lit on that gray afternoon. She pressed her nose to the glass, feeling like an intruder. As her eyes adjusted, she could make out the familiar shapes of Angus's cutting table and his beloved sewing cabinet.

What she could not see was any sign of life. The MacPhersons had their lodgings behind the shop, yet those windows were dark as well. They had no risp at the entrance, and the tinkling bells that signaled a customer only rang when the door opened.

She had no choice but to knock. Still there was no answer.

" 'Twould seem he isna here," Mr. Fenwick said, peering over her shoulder. "We'd best take ye hame, Leddy Kerr."

"Aye, aye," she said, turning away from the door in frustration. Naught to be done but send a caddie with a message for Martin Eccles, begging his forgiveness.

They reached Milne Square in minutes. Mr. Fenwick gave the knot of soldiers a wide berth and deposited her at the door in such a manner they would not see her alight from the chair. She paid him, thanked him, then took the stair at a run, holding her skirts higher than truly proper. And to think she'd planned to tarry and speak with the chairman in the square! She had little interest in town gossip now. Not when her family might be in jeopardy.

Just as young Findlay had said, the stair was filled with folk. Servants, mostly. They leaped up to make room for Elisabeth as she tried to get past them without being rude. To a person, they looked at her with wide, curious gazes. Milne Square was home to few Jacobites. No doubt they thought her a novelty to be inspected and then discussed out of earshot.

When Elisabeth reached the door, she was relieved to find it still solid and well locked. At least this knock would be answered.

And it was, but not by Marjory or Janet or Gibson or Mrs. Edgar.

"Leddy Kerr!" Rob MacPherson pulled her within, then shut the door with a forceful bang. The hand on her arm was not gentle, and a muddle of emotions crossed his face: fear, joy, anger, and relief.

Elisabeth felt quite the same. "Mr. Mac-Pherson, I was just —"

"Wheesht!" Rob nearly shook her, so abrupt was his release. "Wherever have ye been? D'ye not ken what's happened?"

Taken aback, she stared at him in the shadowy entrance hall. "I was in the Canongate. And at your shop. Please, tell me —"

"Nae." His expression grim, he stepped aside. "Leuk for yerself."

FIFTY

My loss is such as cannot be repair'd.
JOHN DRYDEN

Marjory heard Elisabeth's voice in the distance. Only two rooms separated them. And several lost hours. *Before.* That's how Marjory would think of this day. *Before. And after.*

She called out, thinking she was shouting. "Lady Kerr?" But her throat was too raw and her voice too thin. She was not shouting at all. She was whimpering.

Speak up, madam. Where is your gold?

Marjory shifted, her knees beginning to ache, despite the wool carpet beneath them. She sank back on her heels, then slowly leaned forward, until her brow almost touched the carpet. *I am bowed down greatly.* Aye, she was kneeling but to no avail. All her prayers had gone unanswered.

Footsteps drew near. Then a cry of dismay. "Oh, my dear lady!"

Hearing her daughter-in-law's voice, Marjory slowly lifted her head.

"Come." Elisabeth gently pulled Marjory to her feet and then into her arms. "I am sorry," she whispered in her ear. "So very sorry."

Marjory sank into her daughter-in-law's embrace, too exhausted to resist.

The others stood round, bereft of words. Janet was still weeping, though an hour had passed, while Mrs. Edgar had wrung her apron to rags. Gibson, who blamed himself, could not meet her gaze. And Rob MacPherson had come too late.

When Marjory eased away from Elisabeth, she was struck by the anguish in her daughter-in-law's eyes. She'd seen the drawing room, then. Feeling lightheaded, Marjory sat rather quickly on the edge of her bed. "Lost," she said mostly to herself. "All is lost."

Elisabeth drew a chair beside her and took her hand. "I should have been here. I might have helped . . ." Her words faded into silence.

Marjory shook her head. "There were so many. Six soldiers. Eight. No one could have stopped them." She turned toward the window, surprised to see rain falling. When had that begun? "Daylight will be gone soon. Have we any candles left?"

"None, mem." Mrs. Edgar looked down at the toes of her worn leather shoes as if it were her fault the candles had been taken.

Rob MacPherson produced a purse full of

coins. "John Herriot will have what's needed."

"We cannot allow you to pay for them," Elisabeth protested, but the money was already in Gibson's hands, bound for the candle maker in Carruber's Close. "Tallow will do very well," Elisabeth called after him.

Marjory swallowed the bile rising in her throat. Never in all her privileged life had she known the oppressive odor of tallow candles. The thought of mutton and bullock fat instead of fragrant beeswax on her mantelpiece was beyond bearing.

But she would bear it. Aye, and much worse.

A brief silence fell over the room. The stair door opened and closed.

"The candles in their hands were what I noticed first," Marjory said to no one in particular. "When Gibson answered their knock, the soldiers each held a burning candle. So nothing would be missed, they said."

Elisabeth touched her arm. "Do not torture yourself, madam. Mr. MacPherson can inform me of the details."

"Aye, he can tell you what he found when he arrived." Marjory waved her hand listlessly at the silk upholstery cut to shreds and the table lace in tatters. "But he cannot tell you what happened."

"*I* can." Janet dried her cheeks with her handkerchief. "They poked their candles into every nook of this house on the pretense of searching for arms."

Elisabeth turned to look at her. "But your husband gave —"

"I *told* them that. Still, they'd heard about the weapons Mr. Kerr displayed on our bedchamber wall. And they were determined to find them." Janet began to weep again. "Have you seen what's left of our new oil paintings?"

"Nae," Elisabeth said softly, "not yet."

Rob MacPherson spoke up. "I wasna here, but their *wickit* deeds speak loudly enough. Whan the only weapons they found were Lord John's rusty dagger and Gibson's dirk, they took what they liked and destroyed what they pleased."

"Can nothing be done?" Elisabeth asked.

"Aye, but not within the law." Rob's expression darkened. "The government has marked yer family as traitors to the king. They may do whatsomever they like with yer goods, even with yer lives."

Marjory stared at her dressing table. One glass bottle remained. Her powders and perfumes had been emptied onto the floor, ruining the carpet. Her jewelry now lined a dragoon's pockets.

How long had it taken? Twenty minutes, a half hour? She'd staggered from room to room, watching them fling open chests and yank out drawers and scatter the contents, using their swords rather than their hands to sort through her belongings. Piercing, cutting, tearing as they went. Without compassion and without apology.

Cursed be their anger, for it was fierce; and their wrath, for it was cruel. Aye, just so.

At least they'd not found her gold. Not even when they stomped across the floor of her bedchamber with their heavy boots. They'd asked repeatedly where her guineas were hidden. As if they suspected. Nae, as if they *knew.* She'd lied to their faces. Told them her money resided at Edinburgh Castle, that she'd sent it there in September when the Royal Bank had moved their effects. She'd held her head high, daring them to doubt her story. "Does that not prove I am loyal to our king?"

They were unconvinced and settled for Lord John's prized bottle of Ferintosh whisky and all the claret and brandy they could carry off. As to the Bordeaux she'd been saving for Yuletide, the soldiers passed the bottle round, pouring it down their greedy throats while they ravaged her house. Marjory had never felt so violated.

She was very grateful Janet was not harmed, nor the babe in her womb. Relieved that she and Mrs. Edgar were not put to shame. And very thankful Elisabeth was absent when the king's men came, for she would have been a plum too sweet for their filthy hands to resist.

When Marjory looked up, Mrs. Edgar had

returned to the room with two of Elisabeth's embroidered pillows, the ones Effie Sinclair had praised. Tears filled the housekeeper's eyes as she held them out. "Leuk," she moaned, "yer bonny pillows."

Elisabeth touched the torn fabric, inspecting the damage. "Put them in my bedchamber. I'll see what can be done to repair them."

"But, milady," Mrs. Edgar said, "ye've not seen yer room."

Marjory glanced at the closed door, wishing she might spare her daughter-in-law. "You should not face this alone. Perhaps Mr. Mac-Pherson —"

"Aye, mem." The tailor's son stepped forward at once. "Come, Leddy Kerr." He took Elisabeth's left hand in his, then slipped his right arm behind her waist, as if they were preparing to dance the allemande. Marjory knew better. He was anticipating Elisabeth's reaction when she opened the door.

As the two crossed the room, Marjory dispatched Mrs. Edgar to begin setting the kitchen to rights, though Marjory had no appetite for supper and suspected no one in their household did. She also urged Janet to rest for a bit in her bedchamber. " 'Twill do you good to have your feet up." Janet offered no protest and followed Mrs. Edgar through the drawing room door.

Gibson had put the table and chairs back in place, but there was no hope for the shattered drinking glasses or the broken china. Most of her silver had been carted off in Lord John's leather trunk.

Marjory remained seated, too weary to stand, too heartbroken to think about all that must be done. Much as she longed to lie down for a moment, the soldiers had carved up her bedding with their swords, then sullied her pillows with ashes from the coal grate.

She'd chosen the one clean spot on her bed. There would she wait while Elisabeth discovered what their loyalty to the prince had cost them.

FIFTY-ONE

I can see nothing
but ruin and destruction.
CHARLES EDWARD STUART

Elisabeth stared at her bedchamber. "What have they done?"

"What the English do best," Rob said bitterly, tightening his hold round her waist. "Ance they kenned this was Lord Kerr's room, they showed nae mercy."

Elisabeth could not take it all in, so thorough was the devastation. She made herself look at one corner, then another as the memory of her elegant bedchamber faded into a cold reality.

Her silk bed curtains hung like battered streamers. Feathers, torn from the mattress, littered the entire room. No shutters remained on any of the windows, having been brutally ripped off their hinges and discarded in a pile. Her writing table was in pieces, her fine stationery everywhere, and the toppled inkpot had drained onto the carpet, leaving an ugly black stain.

"Why?" she cried softly, bending to retrieve an ivory comb at her feet.

Rob remained by her side, a solid anchor amid the storm. "Wha kens why men destroy a' that is bonny and guid? Vengeance for their loss at Gladsmuir, I'll wager. And a warning to yer husband. Ye'll see what they've done with his papers."

When her gaze landed on Donald's mahogany secretary, her stomach lurched. The shelves and pigeonholes were completely bare. Not a map, not a ledger, not an atlas. "Oh, Rob," she moaned as she picked her way across the room, lifting her skirts, watching where she stepped. "Donald's fine maps. He gave some to the prince, but there were many others."

Rob followed close behind her, then took her hand when they reached her husband's desk. "Thank ye," he said in a low voice.

Confused, she turned to look at him. "Should I not be thanking you for coming to our rescue? I've done nothing for you, I'm afraid."

His dark eyes glowed. "Ye called me Rob. I thocht I might not niver hear ye speak my name."

Only now did she notice the warmth of his hand clasping hers. Embarrassed, she said, "I should not have spoken so freely."

"Nae, but ye should." Rob tugged her one

step closer. "We're *freens,* are we not?"

Broad as he was, he blocked her view of the room. For a moment there was no destruction; there was only Rob, standing too close in the fading afternoon light.

"Aye, we are friends." Elisabeth squeezed his hand, then gently pulled hers free. "As it happens, I came home by way of your shop."

"Hame from whaur?" he asked. "Yer mither-in-law wasna sure whaur ye went this morn, or I'd have come for ye."

Elisabeth wrinkled her brow. "Did I not say Queensberry House?"

"A' she told me was the Canongate. But she was in quite a state whan I arrived. Mebbe she didna remember."

"I cannot blame her." Elisabeth glanced at the adjoining door. *Poor Marjory.* These were her furnishings, her valuables that were broken or stolen and all for a cause she'd only recently embraced.

Rob tipped his head. "Why were ye leuking for me, Bess?"

All at once her heart was lifted from the ruins at her feet and reminded of the wounded soldiers who needed their care. "Your services with a needle are required at Queensberry House this very hour. The dragoons wreaked a different sort of havoc there."

When she described how they'd treated the injured soldiers, Rob was furious, as she knew

462

he would be. "I'll do my best to help oor men," he assured her, "but God help those wha hurt thcm. If they cross my path, they'll not take anither step."

Angry as Rob was, Elisabeth was glad she'd not mentioned her would-be assailant, lest Rob insist on avenging her honor. She'd seen enough blood this day. "Martin Eccles is expecting you. A good man."

Rob nodded thoughtfully as though sorting things out in his mind. "I'll leavc whan Gibson returns." The room was bathed in shadows now without a single candle to dispel the gloom. Rain still pelted the windows and all the louder without her wooden shutters to muffle the sound.

"I ken verra weel the dragoons will not spare oor shop or lodgings. 'Tis only a matter o' time." He glanced toward the far corner of the room. "I wish I didna have to say this, Bess, but ye've yet to see the worst." He lightly placed his hands on her shoulders, then turned her toward the mantelpiece and stepped aside.

Her eyes widened. "They didn't . . ."

"Aye, Bess. They did."

She stumbled toward the hearth, still faintly glowing. Even in the dim light, she could see the fuel they'd burned instead of coal.

Books.

Donald's entire collection.

His beloved Thomson. Barbour with its

fine, thick binding. Thomas Boston with the ribbon still marking the page where they'd last read. *The Pilgrim's Progress* with young Donald's own sketches in the margins. All the plays of Shakespeare bound in morocco leather. Poetry. History. Theology. Her husband's precious books torn asunder, then tossed onto the grate until they spilled over in a massive heap. Set on fire, then left to burn.

How would she ever tell him?

Elisabeth bent down, not caring if her skirts dragged through the soot. *"The Gentle Shepherd,"* she said in a broken voice, picking up the charred remains of Ramsay's play. The pages, still warm, fell apart in her hands. "Donald and I often read this aloud together." Her eyes filled with tears. "He would be Patie, and I would be Peggy."

Rob crouched beside her, resting a hand on her shoulder. In a voice low and tender, he quoted the much-loved pastoral. "I *greet* for joy, to hear thy wirds sae kind."

"Aye," she whispered. "How could anyone be this cruel?"

"I dinna ken, Bess. Men do what is richt in their own e'es." He slowly rose, bringing her up with him. "I see the Buik was spared."

She followed his gaze to the mantelpiece, where the Bible lay on its side, untouched.

Picking it up with one hand, Rob hefted the thick volume with a look of satisfaction.

"Even men with evil in their hearts canna destroy this."

Elisabeth had a strong urge to take the book in her arms and hold it close — whether to protect it or to draw strength from it, she could not say. But her hands were covered with soot, and she dared not soil its sacred pages.

"Leddy Kerr?" Gibson stood in the doorway. "I bought candles but not sae monie as I'd hoped." He held them up. "Mr. Herriot sold me only a pound, and his scolding tongue came with it."

Rob frowned. " 'Tis begun, then. Royalists turning their backs on onie folk with a whiff o' Jacobite air about them."

Gibson fished out a handful of coins from his pocket and deposited them in Rob's free hand. "Yer siller, Mr. MacPherson. Now I must see if there's a candlestick left in the hoose." He departed the way he'd come, through Marjory's room, leaving Elisabeth alone with Rob once more.

A lengthy silence settled between them as Rob placed the Bible on the mantelpiece. "I should go," he said at last, though he sounded reluctant to do so.

"You must," she agreed. "The men at Queensberry House are counting on us both."

Rob offered her a wry smile. "They'll not be blithe to see me walk through the door instead of ye." His features, lit only by the glow of the smoldering fire, were more striking than she'd realized. Not handsome, like her husband's, but strong.

"Once you stitch their wounds, they shall call you blessed," she assured him. "In truth, I wish I were going with you —"

"Then come, Bess." His eyes shone. "Come with me. 'Twould gladden their hearts."

"And sadden my family's, I'm afraid." She looked about the room, wondering where she would sleep, how she would bathe, or what the morrow might bring. "I must stay and be useful here," she told him, "though part of my heart will travel to the Canongate with you."

His dark gaze searched hers. "Will it, Bess?"

She looked down, lest he see something that was not there. "Mr. MacPherson —"

"Nae," he said gruffly, lifting her chin, forcing her to look at him. " 'Tis Rob now. We'll not go back."

"All right. Rob, then. But only when we're alone."

"Verra weel." Desire, like the morning sun, rose in his eyes.

She took a small step backward, unsure of her footing in the cluttered room. "Thank you for caring for my family on such a dreadful day."

Rob quickly closed the gap between them. " 'Tis not yer family I care for." He spoke so

466

softly she had to incline her ear. " 'Tis ye, Bess. I'll not pretend otherwise."

She turned her head. "Rob, I am a married woman."

"Aye. Married to a man wha has niver been leal to ye."

Elisabeth's heart sank. Had Donald confessed his infidelity to Rob? Or had her friend merely heard the blether in the street? She faced him once more. "What have you learned?"

"The truth." His voice was steady and so was his gaze. "I've nae doubt Lord Kerr loves ye. But he doesna care how oft he hurts ye. And I care verra much."

"Please, Rob. Do not say such things." She lifted her hand near his mouth, meaning to silence him even as she felt the warmth of his breath on her fingertips. "I am Lady Donald Kerr. Whatever my husband has done, I shall always be faithful to him. Always."

"And I shall aye be leal to ye." Rob boldly kissed the palm of her hand. "Guid eve, milady."

FIFTY-TWO

Reason bears disgrace,
courage combats it,
patience surmounts it.

MARIE DE RABUTIN-CHANTAL,
MARQUISE DE SÉVIGNÉ

The Tron Kirk was as cold as a tomb. Dank, bone-chilling air seeped through Marjory's cape and gloves, leaving her shivering in the pew even with her daughters-in-law seated on either side to keep her warm.

They'd slept the same way last night, crowded onto a single mattress like poor women in a garret hovel. Janet's bed was the only one the dragoons had not demolished, perhaps because she'd been weeping beneath the bedcovers when they burst into her chamber. Instead of dragging her to the floor, they'd slashed her many gowns into ribbons and her oil paintings as well — paintings Marjory had yet to pay for, having only just received the bill from the auction room in

Writer's Court.

Other debts would come to roost on Martinmas, a day of feasting and of reckoning, when bills were settled and servants paid their wages. For the first time in her life, Marjory feared she might reach for the leather purses beneath her floor and come up wanting. With the prince's army on the move and the countryside plagued with highwaymen and thieves, she could not safely send for the quarterly rents from her Tweedsford factor, Mr. Laidlaw. Her only recourse was to count her gold and pray the tally was sufficient.

The three Kerr women stood as Reverend Wishart began his opening prayer. Odd to be in church without her sons. Odd to be in church at all after six idle weeks while the prince held court at Holyroodhouse. Mrs. Edgar had managed to feed the Kerr women a cold breakfast that morn and dress them in whatever gowns had survived. Nothing could be done about their house. Not on the Sabbath. The morrow was soon enough to begin such an onerous task.

Before the congregation resumed their seats, several neighbors turned round to look at the Kerrs, the daggers in their eyes sharpened to a fine point. The entire southeast parish knew of their disgrace. Perhaps all of Edinburgh knew by now. Marjory did not lower her gaze. She was Sir Eldon's daughter and Lord John's widow. Let them stare. She would not cower in shame.

"I believe James Hogg is gloating," Janet whispered, nodding at the Tron Kirk's lecturer.

The staunch royalist ascended the pulpit bearing a smug expression, then firmly closed the pulpit door. He barely glanced at the Scriptures before reciting his memorized text. "I have counsel and strength for the war. Now on whom dost thou trust, that thou rebellest against me?"

Marjory knew this was not her imagination: Mr. Hogg was speaking directly to her. His long, pointed nose was aimed at their pew like an arrow tautly drawn, and his narrow gaze even more so. For the next half hour, Marjory chafed beneath his stern instruction. Aye, her sons were rebelling against King George, however unwisely. But they were not rebelling against the Almighty.

Sitting on a wooden pew on a cold November morning, suffering the unspoken judgment and condemnation of her neighbors, Marjory longed to take Mr. Hogg's place, stand before the congregation, and recite a cherished verse of her own, learned long ago. She sat up straighter, remembering every word. *I will not be afraid of ten thousands of people, that have set themselves against me round about.*

Nae, she would not be afraid, certainly not for herself. Nor would she mourn for her belongings, which her gold could easily restore. As to her place in society, she numbered a countess among her friends now. Still, her sons mattered most.

The warmth of her daughters-in-law by her side brought to mind Donald's request before he rode off with the prince. *Look after Elisabeth.* Marjory dutifully glanced at the Highland lass in her austere gown. A beauty, to be sure, but clearly barren. Though Andrew had not made the same request, Marjory would take care of Janet and her babe. The young woman seemed to be feeling better, having eaten more oatcakes and gooseberry jam than usual that morn.

Before the minister's prayer a psalm was sung, one of Marjory's favorites. When the precentor lined out the words, she offered each line back to him with such fervor that heads turned once again. Her voice was not as musical as Elisabeth's, but she sang boldly and with conviction.

> LORD, how are they increased that trouble
>   me!
> many are they that rise up against me.

Marjory's voice faltered. *Many indeed.* Lady Woodhall, Lady Falconer, and Lady Ruthven, her tea-table companions, had turned their backs on her. So had Lady Glassie, Lady Northesk, and Lady Boghall, her most esteemed peers.

And her new friends were gone. Lady Nithsdale and her sisters had flitted to Traquair, while Margaret Murray and young Lady Ogilvie had accompanied their husbands on the prince's campaign. Marjory had not spied a single white cockade in the kirk that morn or a swatch of Highland tartan in the streets.

The madness was over. A sober-minded season had come.

Marjory blinked away tears as she sang.

But thou, O LORD, art a shield for me;
my glory, and the lifter up of mine head.

The Almighty had not preserved her household goods. But he'd spared her family. Unlike the soldiers at Queensberry House, not a bone was broken in their house at Milne Square. And the Lord did lift her head, and her heart as well, beyond the century-old oak roof and the bells in the Tron steeple. With the last note echoing round her, she whispered deep within. *Are you yet my shield, Lord? Do you love me still?*

Though she heard no words, she sensed his presence. Some assurance, that.

The morning sermon proved gentler than the lecture. Reverend Wishart did not rail against the Jacobites or praise King George. Instead, he spoke of the Almighty. "In his days shall the righteous flourish," he promised, "and abundance of peace so long as the moon endureth."

Elisabeth's gasp was so soft no one else seemed to notice. But Marjory did and glanced over at her. Perhaps the mention of peace had touched her daughter-in-law. Or was it the enduring moon?

The moment worship ended, the Kerrs hastened down the aisle and through the arched door into the quiet High Street. Unlike the Sabbath morn when the surging crowd had nearly trampled them, on this noontide the pedestrians lingered in the street and carriages passed at a stately pace.

"Lady Kerr!" a high voice sang.

Hearing their shared title, Marjory and Elisabeth both turned to find Effie Sinclair coming toward them. Though she was slowed by her diminutive steps, her eyes sparkled, and her smile was most welcoming.

After the usual courtesies Mrs. Sinclair said in a conspiratorial tone, "How courageous of you three to come this morning." She waved them closer like a tiny wren gathering her chicks beneath her wings. "Many who wore the cockade have left the city or remain behind their doors. Others quietly slip round the town, hoping not to be noticed." She turned back the sleeve of her gown long enough to expose a corner of white silk. "If what I heard is true, you three endured a terrible hardship last night. Still you did your Sabbath duty this morn."

"As you say, 'tis our duty." Marjory tried to sound humble but could not hide her pleasure. Effie Sinclair was frugal with her compliments.

"You shall always have my friendship and support," Effie said, then tipped her small head to look up at Elisabeth. "My dear, bring your family next time you come for tea."

Elisabeth smiled down at her schoolmistress with fond affection. "Indeed I shall." The two were soon engaged in conversation about former classmates from Elisabeth's school days in Blackfriars Wynd, while Marjory and Janet were left to nod and feign interest.

A caddie appeared at Marjory's elbow. Eight or ten years of age, he had a mop of brown hair and a pair of startling blue eyes. "Are ye Leddy Kerr?" he asked in a low voice, looking round as if afraid of being seen in her company. When Marjory nodded, he shoved a sealed letter into her hands. "From the tailor's son, mem."

She produced a ha'penny from her reticule. "Did he ask you to wait for a reply?"

"Nae!" The boy snatched the coin from her hand and darted toward Niddry's Wynd without looking back over his shoulder.

FIFTY-THREE

A letter does not blush.

CICERO

Marjory noticed the mediocre paper quality and inferior sealing wax. From Mr. Mac-Pherson, she imagined. What other tailor's son would take the liberty of writing her? She slipped the letter into her reticule and pulled the drawstrings shut, intending to read it when they returned home.

Once Mrs. Sinclair started for Blackfriars Wynd, the Kerr women were free to cross the High Street, dodging round sedan chairs, carriages, and men on horseback. No one approached them, though Marjory heard their names whispered in passing, often with "rebel" or "traitor" or "Jacobite" in the same breath and sometimes with all three.

Mrs. Edgar and Gibson had gone ahead of them after service and so were waiting with dinner when they arrived. Gibson relieved them of their capes and hurried them to table, perhaps to keep them from despairing over the wretched state of their drawing room.

A moment later Mrs. Edgar served hot bowls of Scotch barley broth, even though it was not quite one o' the clock. " 'Tis too cauld to stand on ceremony," the housekeeper said, and Marjory agreed.

After cooking on a low fire all night, the soup, made with sheep's head, a bundle of sweet herbs, and a generous measure of barley, was thick and flavorful. The dish was served with crusty bread pulled from the oven well before midnight lest Mrs. Edgar be found baking on the Sabbath.

Marjory made no objection to their simple, two-course meal. They had no company, no one to impress. Rich, hot broth suited the frigid day, especially when followed by cold almond custard baked in little china cups that had escaped yesterday's debacle.

"We're reduced to two candles at table," Marjory admitted. Janet had been squinting as she buttered her bread, making rather a show of trying to see.

"With winter upon us, economy should be our rule." Elisabeth's gaze traveled from broken figurines to shattered teacups. "Shall we begin in this room on the morrow?"

Marjory refused to look at her surroundings, savoring her last spoonful of custard, sweetened with rosewater. "Aye," she finally said. "I'll ask Gibson to hire two maidservants. We'll see what can be salvaged and have them sweep up the rest."

Janet and Elisabeth exchanged glances. "What if no one is willing to work for us?" Janet asked.

Marjory bristled at the suggestion. "Our gold is not tainted," she told them. "Mrs. Sinclair shares our sympathies. Perhaps she can suggest someone."

Elisabeth nodded thoughtfully. "Or she may let us borrow one of her maids for the afternoon. I could ask Mr. MacPherson as well."

At the mention of his name, Marjory reached for her reticule. "I'd almost forgotten. Mr. MacPherson wrote me." A very short letter, Marjory discovered. Just two lines and rather nonsensical, she thought, reading them aloud.

Two for larder this day. One for my foot.

Marjory frowned at the paper. "If these words are not misspelled, what can they possibly mean?"

Elisabeth asked her to read them more slowly, then said, "I believe he's sharing information best kept secret and so has written them in a sort of code. 'Two' might mean our two husbands. And 'one' would be his father." Elisabeth sounded out the words several times, then nodded. " 'Twould appear

Donald and Andrew rode for Lauder. A village in the Borderland, aye?"

Marjory studied the paper. "So it is, en route to Kelso." Clever of Mr. MacPherson to provide such timely news. "But where is 'my foot'?"

Elisabeth smiled. "I believe he means 'Moffat.' It seems the prince has divided his troops to confound the enemy."

"Let us hope he is successful." Marjory drew one of the candles closer to read the second line. Just as there had been no salutation at the top, there was no signature at the bottom. Only a few words, which she read aloud.

I meant what I said. Loyal. Always.

Marjory sighed, irritated by his cryptic prose. "Another mystery you must solve for us, Elisabeth."

Her pale skin bloomed like a rose. "Perhaps the letter was misdelivered."

"The caddie said it was for Lady Kerr," Marjory said, then realized her mistake. "Ah. He meant you." When she looked at the line again, the words took on a different shade of meaning. "To whom is Mr. MacPherson loyal?"

"He is loyal to . . . ah, the prince," Elisabeth said. "The MacPhersons have always supported the Stuarts."

"Then why bother to mention their fidelity?" Marjory held out the letter, wishing to be rid of it and all that it implied. The tone was too secretive, too personal. An unmarried tradesman had no business writing to a married gentlewoman. "All the years you've known this young man, he's been a Jacobite?"

"Oh, aye." Elisabeth quickly folded the letter. "Rob has ever been faithful."

Marjory narrowed her gaze. "Is it 'Rob' now?"

Elisabeth's pink cheeks darkened. "A habit from childhood, nothing more."

Marjory remembered another letter Mac-Pherson had brought to their door the morning after Donald's departure. And the private meeting that followed in Elisabeth's bedchamber. "I've not heard you use his Christian name before."

Janet surprised Marjory by coming to Elisabeth's defense. "An honest mistake."

"Then an honest answer is called for." Marjory stood, casting aside her linen napkin. "Pardon us, Janet. I must speak with your sister-in-law alone."

Marjory led the way, her emotions churning. Elisabeth had known the tailor's son far longer than she'd known her Donald. Was there something illicit between them? Elisabeth had once disappeared in the wee hours of a September morn and, upon returning, said she'd had business with Mr. MacPherson. What sort of business?

By the time Marjory reached the far corner of her bedchamber, she could no longer rein in her temper or her tongue. "Lady Kerr, have you been unfaithful to my son?"

"Nae!" Elisabeth cried, her shock apparent. "I would never . . . not for a moment!"

Marjory wanted to believe her, if only for Donald's sake. But Elisabeth was far too flustered for an innocent wife. "What is this tailor's son to you that he insists on speaking with you privately?"

Elisabeth's color remained high. "Mr. MacPherson is simply an old friend."

"A friend to your family?" Marjory asked pointedly. "Or to you?" When her daughter-in-law did not answer quickly enough to suit her, Marjory pressed the issue. "I must ask you again, have you honored your wedding vows? I sometimes wonder. Lord Donald has certainly honored *his,* yet you've still not presented him with an heir."

Elisabeth did not shrink beneath her accusations. In fact, she seemed taller than ever. "From the first hour we met, I have been faithful to your son."

Marjory saw the tears in her eyes. Not of shame, she decided, but of conviction. "Lady Elisabeth, I am relieved —"

"Mr. MacPherson is my friend, and Lord Kerr is my husband. You can be very sure I do not confuse them." With that, Elisabeth quit the room with a sweep of her skirts and a firmly closed door.

Fifty-Four

The only faith that wears well . . .
is that which is woven of conviction.
JAMES RUSSELL LOWELL

Elisabeth stood alone in her bedchamber, arms folded across her bodice, her cheeks still warm. To be falsely accused of adultery when Donald was the guilty one! How she longed to fling open the door and recite a list of names for his mother's edification. "Susan McGill. Maggie Hunter. And let us not forget Lucy Spence . . ."

Stop, Bess. Stop punishing yourself.

Aye, she'd reviewed the list quite enough. And telling Marjory the truth about her profligate son would only sharpen the pain for all of them.

Elisabeth took a long, slow breath. When her face had cooled and her temper with it, she started across the room, stepping over chapters of literature and history torn from their bindings. Last evening she'd been too exhausted, and the room too dark, to do

482

more than make a path through the disarray. Now she had sufficient light, but was reluctant to disregard the Sabbath. *The LORD blessed the sabbath day, and hallowed it.* Aye, even she knew that one. If she had any intention of embracing this God, honoring his day might be the place to begin.

How to spend the few remaining hours of daylight, then?

She stood in the middle of her bedchamber, looking at two closed doors, feeling rather trapped. One door led to Janet's room, though her sister-in-law would never let her walk through without an explanation. *What is all this about Rob MacPherson? What did the dowager ask you?* The other door led to Marjory's room. If Elisabeth went that direction, her mother-in-law would assume she'd returned to make a confession and so probe more deeply. *Were you innocent when you married? Does Donald know of your relationship with the tailor's son?*

Nae, she would remain in her bedchamber, at least for the moment.

Reading a book would engage her well enough, but the only volume left untouched by fire or steel was the family Bible. Elisabeth claimed the thick book from the mantelpiece, surprised again at the weight of it. She gathered a handful of pillows closer to the windows, arranged her hoops and skirts about her, and settled down with the Scriptures in her lap.

Reverend Wishart often chose something in the middle, so she did too, letting the Bible fall open where it would. After decades of use the paper had turned the color of weak tea spilled on linen. Each page felt like a well-worn shirt ironed by a firm hand. But the type was still quite black, marching along in neat lines.

Elisabeth was not surprised to find the Bible had opened to Psalms. In the Lowlands children were fed psalms more regularly than porridge. Bending closer, she began to read.

O LORD, thou hast searched me, and
   known me.

She was struck at once by the intimacy of the words. The author was speaking to the Almighty as if he knew him and clearly was known by him. But first he was *searched*. She shuddered at the image. Who could bear such a close inspection, having nowhere to hide?

With certain trepidation, she chose another verse.

Thou hast beset me behind and before,
and laid thine hand upon me.

Wasn't that precisely how she felt at the moment, trapped in her ruined bedchamber?

484

She couldn't move forward to Monday and put things back in order, yet she couldn't step backward to Friday, when her room was still her own tidy refuge. Instead, she could only sit in the mess and the muck, pressed down by a sense of loss.

Nae, Bess. She swallowed hard. *'Tis guilt that weighs on you.*

Guilt about many things but especially about her husband. If she'd not urged Donald to support the prince, he would still be by her side, and none of this would have happened.

Suddenly uncomfortable, she shifted the Buik on her lap, knowing her guilt went far deeper. If she'd voiced her fears instead of running away from home, her mother might never have married Ben Cromar. And if she'd returned to Braemar rather than abandoning her brother, she might have spared him years of ill treatment.

Donald. Mother. Simon.

Elisabeth stared at the page, undone.

She could do nothing to make amends. Nothing. She could not even beg their forgiveness. Donald had marched off to war. Her mother had tossed her letter into the fire. And Simon was gone forever.

"I'm sorry," she whispered into the chilly, empty room. Her voice was thin, like a child's. And her heart was breaking.

Tears blurred her vision, dropping onto the

page as she bent forward. "Forgive me. Please, forgive me." She feared her pleas were spoken in vain and heard by no one, but she had to say them. Had to.

Forgive me. Forgive me.

It was some time before her tears began to ease. Only then did she realize, looking down at the verse, that nothing was said about being burdened by loss or by guilt.

Nae, the weight was something else entirely.

. . . thine hand upon me.

She dried her tears, staring at the words. The Almighty's *hand* was upon the one who wrote them? Instinctively she looked up, trying to imagine what that might feel like. The idea of being hemmed in by the Almighty, of having his hand laid upon her, was both comforting and terrifying.

The moon at least kept its distance.

But this Holy One drew very close indeed.

She quietly shut the book and eased it from her lap. What might Donald say if he knew the sort of questions she was asking? She'd never told him about the Nameless One. Could she bring herself to speak of the Almighty?

Perhaps in a letter she might broach the subject without feeling so awkward.

Elisabeth collected her scattered stationery, her ink pot, and a quill pen from the floor, then mixed a bit of dry ink powder with water from her pitcher. In lieu of her damaged writing desk, she sat at Donald's secretary, then took up her pen and began.

Sunday, 3 November 1745

My dearest husband,

Our weather has turned colder. The November wind is biting and carries the scent of the sea.

She shook her head. Donald hardly needed such a report when he faced the elements round the clock. Something more personal was needed.

You are greatly missed here — by your wife most of all. The days are long and the nights longer still. I trust you have enough blankets to warm you since I cannot.

She would not entertain fears of another woman warming his bed. She would *not*. Her husband had given his word. In turn, could she not give him her trust?

Elisabeth dipped and blotted her pen, then paused, wondering if she should tell Donald about the damage wrought by the dragoons. One could never be sure where a letter might land. She'd need to choose her words with care.

In the city the king's authority is upheld once more. Those who opposed it have been reminded of their duties, some more severely than others.

Rob would see that his father delivered her letter. Angus could tell Donald in person what she dared not put in writing. As to her husband's damaged books, she would make no mention of them and try her best to replace his favorites. Books were dear, however, and of late her mother-in-law seemed hesitant to share her guineas.

Elisabeth described their renewed services at the Tron Kirk, as well as her Saturday morning spent caring for the wounded soldiers. She did not mention whether they were royalist or Jacobite. Infirmaries for both could be found, and Donald would know which patients she'd gladly served.

She had just enough room at the bottom of the page to put forth an idea she hoped he might consider.

You have told me how your father led your family in a time of worship after supper each evening. When you return, might you be willing to do the same for our household? I think you may find a receptive audience at your table.

Your loving and faithful wife

Elisabeth lifted her pen, having second

thoughts about including the word *faithful*. Would he frown and think it a barbed reminder of his own unfaithfulness? She could not simply draw a line through the word nor cut it out with scissors, as some did. Nae, she would leave it and hope the word *loving* outweighed the sting of *faithful*.

Whatever his weaknesses, she loved her husband. And missed him more than pen and ink could ever capture.

FIFTY-FIVE

But all's to no end, for the time will not
  mend
Till the King enjoys his own again.
MARTYN PARKER

Marjory stared at the worn leather purses heaped on her bed. She'd lifted each loose board and searched between every dusty floor joist, but there were no more to be found. Before the prince's arrival in September, she'd counted twenty-two purses, each one bulging with guineas. Now only three remained.

How can there be only three, Lord? She well knew the answer to that.

When she rose from the edge of the bed, the coins shifted with a faint jingle, as if taunting her. Marjory thought of her cashbook in the top drawer of Lord John's desk and the growing stack of bills beside it. She owed money to everyone in town, or so it seemed. Mr. Geddes for their poultry, Mr. Porteous for Janet's winter gloves, Mr. Elder for her new kid leather shoes, Mr. Mercer for a supply of Stoughton's Elixir. Without the rental income from their Tweedsford estate in hand and with Martinmas looming, however would she manage?

Marjory began to pace. The rich plum cakes she'd enjoyed that afternoon — full of butter, sugar, cream, and all those lovely currants — now lined her stomach like cobblestones. In the future she would instruct Mrs. Edgar to serve plain oatcakes with their tea. Even butter and jam were becoming too dear.

How long might her three hundred pounds need to last? Until the prince's campaign ended. Until her sons returned home. Until the road from Selkirk to Edinburgh was safe for her factor to travel. Until a time no one could name, not even Charles Edward Stuart.

The latest *Evening Courant*, folded on her dressing table, included very little about the army's recent movements, though one report from Edinburgh caught her eye. *We are now happily delivered from the Highland Host so that the citizens begin to peep out of their lurking places.*

"Happily delivered?" Marjory had scoffed, having spent the day overseeing two hired maidservants, who'd cleaned and swept and discarded until the six rooms of their house were more or less in order. Still, the torn upholstery required mending, the glassware and dishes needed replacing, the paintings were little more than strips of canvas, and Janet was reduced to one gown. Her daughter-in-law would have to borrow some of her own costumes from last season. The blue green satin, perhaps, or the burgundy damask, though they'd need to be altered when Janet's waist began expanding.

Marjory tarried at one of the windows overlooking Milne Square, watching a caddie with his paper lantern dart across the plain-stanes. How early darkness came in November! With Martinmas one week hence, numbers swirled through her head. Twenty-five pounds for half a year's rent. Ten pounds for their seats at the Tron Kirk. Gibson and Mrs. Edgar were owed half their annual wages — forty shillings for Gibson, thirty for Mrs. Edgar.

At least the family coffers were spared ten shillings for Peg Cargill. They'd not heard a word from the lass since she flitted to Coldingham. Marjory had been slow to replace her since Mrs. Edgar had not complained about the additional work. But what a frightful expense for two maids this day. A sixpence each!

Marjory gathered the remaining purses and hid them beneath the loose flooring nearest her bed, taking care not to sully her gown nor catch a splinter in her hand. She smoothed the carpet back in place, lest anyone think to look there. A useless measure, she realized. Why fret about her household carelessly spending her gold when she'd already done so herself?

Most of the purses had traveled through her door last month, concealed inside Angus MacPherson's greatcoat. Fifteen hundred gold sovereigns bound for Holyroodhouse. *Fifteen hundred.* A princely sum, Marjory had thought at the time, amused by her pun and basking in the glow of the prince's gratitude. Now she saw her too-generous behavior for what it was: pride. *The pride of thine heart hath deceived thee.* Aye, hadn't it just?

Some might point to Lady Nithsdale's talent for persuasion, but Marjory blamed no one but herself. Hearing that Lord Elcho had parted with such a fortune, she'd risen to the challenge and matched his astounding gift. Or rather his *loan,* as Lady Nithsdale had insisted. In any case, her guineas were gone, with no promise of their return.

Marjory had not confessed her imprudence to a soul. Only Mr. MacPherson and his son knew the amount, and they were sworn to secrecy. She'd convinced herself it was an investment in her family's future. That it would guarantee her sons' safety and, when the prince claimed the throne for James, would assure them a place of honor in his kingdom.

But if she was wrong, if they were all wrong,

and the prince was not victorious —

The knock at her bedchamber door was a welcome interruption. "Come," Marjory called, in urgent need of good news.

Gibson entered, gray hair damp from the evening air, a letter in his hand. "From the Post Office, mem. Addressed to ye."

She noted at once the neatness of the handwriting, the formal sweep of each letter, and the fine quality of the paper. But when she saw King George's royal seal embedded in the wax, Marjory nearly sank to the floor.

My sons, my sons!

"I have ye, mem." Gibson supported her arm long enough to steady her. " 'Tis only a letter, Leddy Kerr. Ye faced far worse on Saturday whan the dragoons came."

The thick red wax had stained the paper. *Like blood.* Marjory couldn't bring herself to touch it. "Will you, Gibson?"

He broke the seal and pressed open the creases in the paper, his fingers bent and wrinkled but strong as ever. "I pray it willna be ill news, mem."

Marjory looked at the signature first, and her fears eased a bit. " 'Tis from Lord Mark Kerr, a distant relation of Lord John's." Answering her letter at last, it seemed. "I'll read it to everyone at supper, aye?"

"Verra weel, mem." Gibson bowed and quit the room as quietly as a cat while Marjory began reading. She was struck at once by the coldness of Lord Mark's tone.

To the Dowager Lady Marjory Kerr
Milne Square, Edinburgh
Wednesday, 30 October 1745

Lady Marjory:

Your letter of 3 October was most trouble-some. One cannot imagine what compelled the sons of Lord John Kerr to take up arms against their Sovereign.

Marjory knew precisely what had compelled them: a bonny young prince with a hero's bearing and a rightful claim to the throne. Her sons' desire to test their mettle had spurred them on as well. She understood that now.

If these sons of yours will not heed their own mother, they will hardly take the advice of a stranger.

His language was patently dismissive. Did he care so little for her sons and for her? Miffed by his words, she had to force herself to keep reading.

I must tell you, madam, your entire house-hold is in grave danger because of their treason.

Her skin, already chilled, turned to ice. Her entire household had already faced grave danger, had already suffered . . .

A terrible possibility rose before her like a specter.

What if Lord Mark had ordered the soldiers to pillage her house, prompted by her letter? What if she had brought this destruction to her own doorstep?

Nae!

Marjory stared at the letter, barely able to breathe. *Every wise woman buildeth her house: but the foolish plucketh it down with her hands.* She had not been wise. She'd indeed been foolish. Without meaning to, she'd betrayed her family and sacrificed their belongings.

She'd meant to save them. But she had not.

There, in Lord Mark's hand, was the word that would condemn her sons to death. *Treason.* She pressed on, though she had to read each sentence twice to make sense of it, so addled were her thoughts.

You will be aware by now of His Majesty's offer of clemency to any rebels who return home on or before the twelfth of November.

Aye, she was aware. Had she not kept the *Evening Courant* that Lady Falconer had presented to her on Friday eve? *There is hope for your sons.* No mother would discard even a scrap of hope.

If your sons ignore the king's mercy, madam, I cannot offer any promise for their future. I trust the twelfth of November will find them at home in Edinburgh or Selkirk, prepared to defend their King.

Loyal Servant to
His Royal Highness, George II
General Lord Mark Kerr

Come home. Marjory held on to the letter, saying the words over and over in her mind. *Come home, come home.* She could not speak them aloud, dared not commit them to paper. She remembered Elisabeth's comments, hard as they were to hear. *We cannot ask them to return home. We cannot even wish it.*

A niggling thought jabbed at Marjory. Perhaps Elisabeth did not want her husband to return. Perhaps . . .

Nae. 'Twas not possible.

As she refolded the letter, Marjory heard voices in the entrance hall, one in particular. *Rob MacPherson.* She laid the letter on her bare dressing table and moved toward the door, a sense of urgency hastening her steps.

The tailor's son was standing in the drawing room, hat in hand. Broad and brooding, dark haired and dark eyed, Rob MacPherson was nothing like her Donald. Marjory could not imagine Elisabeth finding such a man attractive.

She inclined her head, a sparse acknowledgment. "What brings you here, Mr. Mac-Pherson?"

"Guid eve, mem." He bowed when he saw her, though he did not smile. "I dinna mean to intrude. I only wanted to be certain Leddy Kerr received my note yestermorn. And to see how ye were faring."

Marjory had never heard him speak so many words at once. "Lady Kerr did indeed receive your note. And, as you see, we are well."

"Aye." His gaze traveled the room. " 'Tis meikle improved syne last I was here, though I'm sorry for yer losses."

Elisabeth joined them a moment later. "How fortunate that you've come, Mr. Mac-Pherson." She produced a letter. "Might you see this delivered to my husband, Lord Kerr?"

Marjory couldn't help noticing Elisabeth's emphasis on Donald's role and title. As if reminding this tailor's son of his place. And of hers. *Well done, lass.*

He took the letter with some reluctance. "I canna say how lang 'twill take, milady. But I'll see yer letter on its way."

"You are most kind," Elisabeth said, though she did not look at him when she spoke, nor did she invite him to sit.

Heartened as she was to see her daughter-in-law's reticence, Marjory wanted to be very sure there was nothing between them. "Mr. MacPherson, have you plans for Martinmas?"

498

'Twas hard to say who looked more surprised, Elisabeth or Rob.

"Nae plans, mem," he finally said. "O' course, the shop will be closed for the day . . ."

Marjory smiled. "Then you'll be free to join us for our Martinmas dinner?"

Rob glanced at Elisabeth. " 'Twould be a pleasure, mem."

"We'll expect you at one o' the clock." Marjory nodded, a polite dismissal.

He bowed and took his leave. Though Elisabeth followed him to the entrance hall, she kept her distance and did not linger at the door.

Marjory clasped her hands together, strengthening her resolve. If Elisabeth was innocent, 'twould be most unfair to suspect her. But if there was something between them, Marjory would do whatever was necessary to protect Donald's good name. She'd failed him in so many ways as a mother. She would not fail him in this.

FIFTY-SIX

It fell about the Martinmas
When nights are lang and mirk.
SEVENTEENTH-CENTURY SCOTTISH VERSE

Elisabeth lifted the spoon to her mouth, enjoying the rich soup even before she tasted it. Peppercorn, thyme, and bay leaf created a heady aroma, but the pungent oxtail made the dish Donald's favorite on Martinmas.

He was in England now. Whatever his plans for Martinmas, they would not include a meal like this. Elisabeth slowly put down her spoon, the broth having lost its flavor.

Mrs. Edgar was by her side at once. "Is the oxtail not to yer liking, milady?"

" 'Tis delicious," Elisabeth assured her, retrieving her spoon. Mrs. Edgar had labored all morning on their meal, even though the Scottish term day was meant to be free from work. Elisabeth's father never touched his loom on Martinmas, and no wheels spun in the cottages round the hills and glens of Braemar.

500

"A fine soup," Rob MacPherson announced, his plate already empty.

Elisabeth saw him eying the wheaten bread. Perhaps if Rob were alone at home, he would wipe a thick slice round his plate to soak up the last drop. Simon had often done the same. Donald, with his fine manners, would never have stooped to such behavior at table, though he'd proven to be less than a gentleman in other ways. She could not imagine Simon ever being unfaithful had he married. As for Rob, she could not say.

Aye, she could. *I meant what I said. Loyal. Always.*

Rob's contribution to their Martinmas feast was a bottle of claret: a welcome gift since the dragoons had depleted their store. Donald's seat remained vacant, a constant reminder of his absence. Elisabeth suspected that Rob was invited solely because her mother-in-law wanted to see them together, side by side, as a test of her fidelity. Rob had yet to say or do anything untoward, for which Elisabeth was grateful.

Marjory motioned Mrs. Edgar to bring the next course. "I hope you'll not mind, Mr. MacPherson, but we'll not be serving haggis."

Elisabeth knew her mother-in-law could not bear the traditional Martinmas dish of chopped meat and oatmeal boiled in a sheep's stomach. A common dish in every Highland cottage but not at all common at the Kerr table.

"I've had monie a plate o' haggis this season," Rob assured her. "My faither and I have a woman wha cooks for us. Not a week goes by without sheep pluck on oor table."

" 'Tis good that you enjoy it, then." Marjory's smile was forced. "We'll be having the usual fish, flesh, and fowl."

"And apple tart," Janet added, anticipation shining in her eyes. If Janet had her way, every meal would begin with something sweet. And end with it too.

Elisabeth, sitting with her back to the windows, had to glance over her shoulder to see if the day remained dry. Not for long, judging by the thickening clouds. The Firth of Forth brought cold air and brisk winds blowing in from the North Sea, vastly changing the weather from one hour to the next. The air was dry for now at least and not so bitterly cold as yesterday morning at the Tron Kirk, where they'd huddled under their wool capes and moved their feet to keep them from growing stiff.

"Haddies," Rob said with a broad smile when Mrs. Edgar served him fish with a brown sauce. As a dinner guest he was easy to please. Few things appeared more often on Edinburgh tables than haddocks. Roasted leg of lamb with oysters came next and then oven-browned pullets with potatoes. Elisa-

beth ate enough of each course to keep Mrs. Edgar from frowning, while Rob enjoyed two servings of every dish.

Once the tarts were served, their guest was well sated. "I canna remember a finer Martinmas meal than this one, Leddy Kerr," Rob told her.

"Mrs. Edgar will be glad to hear it." Marjory stood, bringing him quickly to his feet. "Will you have coffee by the fire, Mr. Mac-Pherson?"

"Aye," he said, "if ye'll allow me to repay yer hospitality with three gifts."

"The claret was present enough," Elisabeth assured him, but it seemed he had more in mind.

Gathered in a half circle were four upholstered chairs, each one draped with a plaid to cover its scars. While the women took their seats, Rob remained standing, his elbow propped on the mantelpiece. "Gifts, you said?" the dowager prompted him.

"The first is a verra auld song, meant for the day."

When he cleared his throat and began to sing, his small audience was pleasantly surprised as a rich baritone poured forth, the notes full and the words tender.

Martinmas wind, when wilt thou blaw,
And shake the green leaves aff the tree?
O gentle Death, when wilt thou come?

For of my life I am wearie.

"Oh!" Janet exclaimed. "Please sing it again. From the beginning, if you know it."

"I ken a' the verses, milady." Rob proved it, sharing in song the sad tale of a broken-hearted maid. Mrs. Edgar and Gibson quietly cleared the table and trimmed the candles, taking in the rare treat, for none in the Kerr household sang except at kirk.

When he finished, Janet said with a melodramatic sigh, "Too tragic. Have you no good news for us?"

"My second gift this term day," Rob said, folding his hands behind his back. "News from England."

Marjory sat up, clearly interested. "Do tell us what you've learned."

"Aye, do," Elisabeth urged him, thinking only of Donald.

"The reports are a day auld or mair," he cautioned, "but I'll give ye whatsomever news I can. The prince leads his men on foot, they say, as strong and as brave as ilka soldier on the field. Whan they crossed the Tweed, the leddies o' Jedburgh flocked into the street to kiss the prince's hand. But none o' their men joined oor army." Rob shook his head. "Would that they had, for I've heard as monie as a thousand Hielanders have deserted the prince."

Though Marjory gasped at the number,

Elisabeth was not surprised. " 'Tis too far south," she said. "Too close to the English."

"Aye. Whan the prince heard some were lagging behind, planning to desert, he mounted a horse and rode to the rear, spurring them forward." His countenance darkened. "But ithers crept o'er the hills in the gloom o' nicht, headed for hame."

Marjory eyed Elisabeth. "Are men not shot for this?"

"Some have been severely punished," he admitted. "For ithers, 'tis enough to threaten them with burning their hooses and crops."

Elisabeth watched Marjory's expression change, as if envisioning Tweedsford in flames. A wave of sympathy washed over her. Her mother-in-law had two sons bearing arms and two properties to manage. A worthy reminder, Elisabeth decided, for the days when Marjory's complaints grew tiresome.

"On Friday last," Rob was saying, "the prince and his men crossed the border to England. Alas, whan the Hielanders unsheathed their broadswords to shout their huzzahs, Cameron o' Lochiel cut his hand on his blade."

Elisabeth saw the problem at once. " 'Tis a bad omen."

Rob nodded grimly. "Ye can be sure his men thocht sae."

"Did you say you had a third gift, Mr. MacPherson?" Her mother-in-law sounded impatient. Or simply tired.

"Indeed I do." Rob reached inside his waistcoat and produced a letter. "For Leddy Kerr." His dark gaze met hers. "From Lord Kerr."

"Oh!" Elisabeth could not hide her excitement, nearly tearing the paper as she broke the seal. "I feel quite certain he means us all to hear it."

Marjory brightened at once.

"Ye'll not want to trust your letters to the Post Office," Rob cautioned them. "They've taken to reading the letters o' Jacobites, scrawling *Treason* or *Rebel* across the page, then delaying the letters a fortnight or mair."

"How perfectly dreadful," Janet said, making a face.

"You alone are to see our letters delivered," Marjory told him.

"As ye say, mem."

Elisabeth thought of the letter she'd given Rob on Monday last, even as she skimmed through the one in her hands. "Now, then. Let us see what Lord Kerr has for us."

To My Beloved Family
Wednesday, 6 November 1745

I trust this letter finds its way to you and finds you in good health.

"Rather formal," Janet remarked, though

506

Elisabeth thought she detected a faint note of envy in her sister-in-law's voice since there was no letter from Andrew.

Marjory quickly came to Donald's defense. "His writing must be circumspect, for all our sakes. Continue, Lady Kerr."

We have this day arrived in Jedburgh. It is difficult to be so close to home and yet not have the opportunity to call upon our factor.

"When the throne is won and peace returns, we should all visit Tweedsford," Marjory said emphatically. "In the spring, perhaps. 'Tis quite pleasant."

Elisabeth tried to cover her astonishment. Since her marriage to Donald, his mother had never made such a suggestion. "I would very much like to see it," Elisabeth told her before returning to his letter.

The weather is tolerable, the food and accommodations are adequate, and the company well shod.

"At least their horses have shoes," Elisabeth mused.

Rob remained standing at the mantelpiece, arms folded across his broad chest. "Yer husband does a fine job of saying what needs to be said with none the wiser. 'Tis a guid skill for a Life Guard."

Elisabeth was surprised to hear Rob speak well of her husband, knowing what he thought of Donald. And what he thought of her. When she read the next line, her heart tightened.

We have heard of an offer being made regarding the twelfth of this month, but no parties here are interested.

Marjory spoke first, her tone flat. "He knows, then."

Rob grunted in response. "King Geordie's printed notices found their way to the prince's camp. My faither said they used the paper to start their fires." He shifted his stance. "D'ye ken a proclamation was read from the mercat cross this day? All able-bodied men are invited to enter into his Majesty's service. Such men are assured a discharge at the end o' six months or whan the rebellion is" — he looked ready to spit — "*extinguished.* That was the wird they used."

Elisabeth was only half listening, reading back through Donald's brief letter. She wished it were longer but was grateful to hold in her hands solid proof that five days ago her husband was alive and well.

"Has he written anything else?" Marjory asked, leaning closer to look for herself.

"No more words and no signature." Elisabeth held out the letter. "Only a few numbers."

"Ah." Marjory left at once and returned a moment later with the family Bible in her arms. " 'Twill be one of the psalms. When my sons were wee lads, I taught them to memorize verses by writing the numbers on one side of a card and the words on the other."

Elisabeth could not imagine her mother-in-law doing such a thing. Had Marjory's years in Edinburgh changed her that much?

Marjory nimbly turned to the passage as if she knew well the landscape of the Scriptures, then read the verse aloud. "For thou hast girded me with strength unto the battle." She looked up, her eyes glassy. "Aye, I taught Lord Kerr that one. And very long ago it was too."

Janet sniffed. "Well, I have never heard my brother-in-law speak so devoutly."

"If not, he'll do sae now." Rob unfolded his arms and reached for the Bible, which was growing noticeably heavy in Marjory's hands. "Few men on the field o' battle dinna cry oot to God."

FIFTY-SEVEN

Through the hush'd air
the whitening shower descends.

JAMES THOMSON

" 'Tis snowing." Marjory peered through Effie Sinclair's window, certain her eyes were deceiving her. Snow was uncommon in the capital, especially in the middle of November. The sky, the air, and the tall lands across the wynd were all washed in a pale, frosty gray.

The boarding school mistress joined her guests at the window, the top of her carefully piled hair only reaching Marjory's shoulder. "We've seen many winters without so much as a flurry." Effie's warm breath left a circle of steam on the icy pane.

Elisabeth, too, had abandoned their tea table, leaving behind their empty plates and tea-stained saucers. "Mr. MacPherson told me the prince and his men are soon expected to march south from Carlisle. I do hope the weather is a bit warmer there."

The concern in Elisabeth's voice and her

poignant expression were further assurance of her fidelity. Marjory felt almost guilty for doubting her daughter-in-law's devotion. She need not have worried. A man like Rob Mac-Pherson, with his poor table manners and rough way of speaking, would hardly turn a lady's head. Especially one married to a gentleman of Donald's caliber.

Still, with his many Jacobite ties, the tailor's son had kept them informed of the army's activities, for which Marjory was grateful. He often relayed news the *Evening Courant* might not report for another week — or not at all if the account favored the prince. The most recent news from Mr. MacPherson was heartening. On Friday last the Duke of Perth took Carlisle, by Saturday the castle was won, and on the Sabbath their bonny prince made his triumphant entry into Carlisle, striking terror in the heart of many an Englishman.

Marjory turned away from the window to glance at the mantel clock. "Mrs. Sinclair, I fear we are keeping you from your scholars."

"Not at all," Effie assured her. "I have three young ladies in my charge this season. They are having tea at the moment, followed by a writing lesson at four o' the clock." She turned to Elisabeth, smiling with her whole face. "Unless I might presume upon my most accomplished seamstress to offer them instruction in sewing."

Elisabeth glanced at the darkening sky. "I

would enjoy nothing more, Mrs. Sinclair, but . . ."

" 'Tis not the hour for it," Effie was quick to agree. "Some forenoon, perhaps, when the light is more amenable to threading a needle. For the moment I must bid you farewell." Capes and gloves were quickly donned, then thanks and curtsies offered round.

No sooner did Effie's door close than a fierce, biting cold sank its teeth into Marjory's neck. Shivering, she followed Janet and Elisabeth down the stair until they reached the paving stones of Blackfriars Wynd. A thick veil of snow hung over the dark lane, falling steadily. The occasional candle near a window, diffused by the snow into a faint, shimmering cloud of light, provided the only relief from the blackness before them.

"This is my fault," Marjory said, pulling them closer to her sides. "We should have taken our leave the moment I saw the first flurry."

Janet withdrew inside the hood of her cape. "At the very least while it was still light."

"We've not far to walk," Elisabeth encouraged them. "And we need not worry about dragoons on the High Street. No one will be out on such a night."

"As we should not be," Marjory said with a heavy sigh. Why had she not made some arrangement with Gibson to collect them at four o' the clock? Elisabeth was right — they did not have far to walk — but the street was uphill and slippery, and the snow fell harder by the minute.

They locked arms and began the slow trek up the wynd, knowing the High Street was ahead though they could not see farther than their outstretched hands. Marjory prayed Elisabeth was right about the dragoons remaining withindoors. Not only had Edinburgh Castle belched red-coated men like a sickness over the town, but on Thursday last two thousand more foot soldiers and dragoons had entered through the Netherbow Port.

Clinging to her daughters-in-law, Marjory put one hesitant foot in front of the other. "Our shoes will be ruined," she said, accepting the blame for that as well.

"You've no need to apologize for the weather," Elisabeth said. " 'Tis not something within your control. 'For he saith to the snow, Be thou on the earth,' aye?" She'd surprised them several times of late with a verse of Scripture. Perhaps that was to be expected, living in a house with only one book. "Here is the High Street." Elisabeth helped them navigate the icy plainstanes as they turned left. "We're halfway home."

Their voices sounded oddly muffled, as if the snow were swallowing their words. In all her years Marjory could not remember a storm this early in the season. When she spied the familiar arcades of Milne Square, she nearly wept with joy.

The turnpike stair in Baillie's Land was colder still, and the stone steps treacherous. As soon as they reached their fifth-floor landing, Marjory fell against the door, praying Gibson would hear their knock and unlock the door at once.

Instead, Rob MacPherson ushered the Kerr women into their house. "We'd hoped ye might remain at Mrs. Sinclair's for the nicht," he said, "though 'tis guid yer a' hame."

Marjory pushed back the hood of her cape, staring at him in confusion. "Where is Gibson that you are pressed into service as a footman?"

Rob quickly closed the door, about to answer her, when Mrs. Edgar came at a run.

"Leddy Kerr!" Her face was flushed, and her words tumbled over themselves. "Gibson has given us a wee fright. First his head was verra het and now his chest. He's begun to cough as weel." She glanced toward the drawing room. "I dared not put him in one o' yer beds, but his ain was too cauld here by the door."

Marjory threw off her cape, the word *cough* sufficient to capture her attention. "Well done, Mrs. Edgar. Now, licorice and tartar, if you please." Helen Edgar had helped tend her ailing sons a decade earlier. Between them, they would see the man well cared for.

Gibson was stretched out on a thick plaid before the fire, his face and neck the color of fresh beetroot. He lifted up a shaky hand. "Och, mem, I'm sorry ye found me sae dwiny."

"We'll have none of that," Marjory told him, drawing the footstool near so she might sit beside him. "When did this begin?"

"Yestermorn, though I paid it nae mind." He shrugged. "I didna want to worry ye."

"Too late," Marjory chided him gently, placing her hand on his brow and cheek and then his chest. Worse than she'd feared: almost as hot as the coals in the grate. She turned to Rob, standing behind her. "Will the apothecary come out in such weather?" she asked. "Perhaps if you simply describe Gibson's symptoms, Mr. Mercer will know what to send."

"I'll bring the man *and* his medicines," Rob promised and was gone.

Mrs. Edgar appeared a moment later, cup and spoon in hand. "Spanish licorice and salt o' tartar in boiled water, just as ye asked. 'Tis bluid warm. Two spoonfuls, if ye please, sir."

Gibson lifted his head enough to take his medicine, then fell back on the plaid with a groan.

Janet bent over him. "My, he's quite red."

"Careful!" Marjory shot to her feet, nearly knocking her daughter-in-law over in her haste. "You cannot risk getting so close, dear.

515

Not in your . . . condition."

Janet frowned. "My . . . oh! Nae, I cannot." Without another word she fled for her bedchamber. "Do not expect me at supper."

Elisabeth and Mrs. Edgar remained, looking as helpless as Marjory felt. Neil Gibson's sixty years were showing, his skin drawn taut against his bones, his bald crown dotted with brown spots. Though his breathing was even, his color worried her, and his fever more so. She would know better once she heard his cough.

By the time Rob MacPherson returned with the apothecary, Marjory had heard Gibson cough several times. When she apologized to Mr. Mercer for requiring his services on such a stormy night, the stout man pushed his spectacles in place, then brushed away her concerns.

"I am only across the High Street. And I could not be sure of what to send until I examined Mr. Gibson for myself. If I might trade places with you, madam?"

Marjory joined the others gathered behind him while the apothecary poked and prodded in an efficient fashion, making small grunting sounds under his breath as he worked. Gibson gazed up at him through bleary, half-opened eyes.

Mr. Mercer stood at last, yanking his waistcoat over his round belly with little success. " 'Tis not consumption," he said with some authority.

Marjory and Mrs. Edgar exchanged relieved glances.

"For the fever," Mr. Mercer continued, "make use of the snow and pack it round his neck. You'll also be wanting Dr. Hardwick's fever powder." He produced a brown paper packet. "For the cough, peel and slice a turnip, cover the pieces with coarse sugar, let them stand in a dish until the liquid drains, and give him a spoonful whenever he coughs." The apothecary was already in his coat and eying the door. "Unless you have further need of me, I bid you good night."

Mrs. Edgar escorted him through the entrance hall, reviewing his instructions, while Rob MacPherson started down the stair ahead of him, wooden pail in hand, intending to bring back a supply of new-fallen snow.

Only when all of Mr. Mercer's instructions had been followed and Gibson was sleeping by the fire, his fever beginning to abate, did Marjory think to ask what had brought Rob MacPherson to their door in the first place. "Did Mrs. Edgar send for you?" she asked as the three of them sat on the long sofa.

"Nae, mem." Unlike at Martinmas, he'd not been in a talkative mood this evening. "I thocht . . . that is, I came to tell ye I had visitors this afternoon. The dragoons . . . ah, searched oor shop."

Marjory understood at once. "They did not

merely search it. They sacked it, didn't they?"

"Aye, sae they did." He rubbed his hand over his jaw. "Tore the bolts o' fabric to shreds. Shattered oor lang leuking glass. Chopped the sewing cabinet into kindling—"

"Oh, Rob," Elisabeth moaned, "not the cabinet your father cherished."

He looked at her. "Aye, Bess. The verra one."

A cold chill moved along Marjory's forearms. They'd addressed each other by their Christian names. Had she not been sitting between them, Rob might have taken Elisabeth's hand, so warm was his gaze. If 'twas not longing Marjory saw in those dark depths, it was uncomfortably close to it.

She stood at once, breaking the spell. "Lady Kerr? 'Tis eight o' the clock."

But Elisabeth mistook her cue. She did not ask the tailor's son to leave. She invited him to stay. "Mr. MacPherson, will you share our supper?" Elisabeth asked. "The hour is late, and your lodgings are . . . not what they once were. We'll not have as elaborate a meal as Martinmas, but you are welcome to sup with us."

He dipped his chin, accepting her invitation. " 'Twould be a pleasure, milady."

Once offered, hospitality could hardly be revoked. Marjory was torn as well, for Rob MacPherson had proven to be a good friend

518

to their family. They'd come to count on him for news. Aye, and for protection. Nothing to be done but watch the man and pray her suspicions were unfounded.

No sooner had they taken their seats at table than Elisabeth offered to stand in Gibson's place, helping Mrs. Edgar serve the meal.

"Lady Kerr!" Marjory scolded her, but her daughter-in-law was already out of her seat and moving toward the kitchen.

"We can hardly ask our guest to serve himself," Elisabeth reminded her, knowing Marjory could pose no argument.

"It seems we shall be served by a lady," Marjory said.

Mr. MacPherson smiled, a rare occurrence. "She is indeed that, mem."

Elisabeth returned bearing plates of mussel brose, though Mrs. Edgar was adamant she would serve the rest. "There are but three of ye," she said firmly, "and I'm meant to do it." She soon brought minced collops, flavored with nutmeg. Then roasted onions, hot from the oven. Finally a plate of macaroons and coffee, though Marjory did not suggest moving to sit by the fire, lest they disturb Gibson from his sleep.

From first bite to last Marjory watched Mr. MacPherson court her daughter-in-law. No other word could describe his behavior. He studied Elisabeth's eyes, her mouth, her hands. When her linen cloth slipped from her lap, he retrieved it almost before it touched the floor. If she said something mildly amusing, his low, rumbling laugh was sure to follow. And if she grew quiet or pensive, he matched his mood to hers.

Marjory took consolation in this: Elisabeth did nothing to encourage him. In fact, she seemed completely unaware of his slavish devotion. Perhaps in time Rob would lose interest, realizing how much Lady Kerr loved her husband. Short of confronting him, Marjory knew there was little she could do.

She was beginning to realize how few things were hers to manage. Not the weather, certainly. Not the furnishings beneath her roof. Not the health of those round her. Not the fate of her sons in battle. And not the faithfulness of the wives they left in Edinburgh.

Marjory looked down, lest anyone see the fear in her eyes. *Come home, Donald. Soon.*

FIFTY-EIGHT

They that know the winters of that country
know them to be sharp and violent,
and subject to cruel and fierce storms.
            WILLIAM BRADFORD

Elisabeth awakened the next morning to find
the High Street blanketed with snow. She'd
expected the storm to end while the household slept. But the snow kept falling, and the
wind blew hard from the west.

Days passed in a white blur. Rumors crept
into town from the neighboring villages. *A
foot of snow. Two foot. Six.* "The severest
known," the *Evening Courant* reported, "the
snow in some parts being upwards of twelve
foot. Two men perished in the snow near
Peebles. They were going home from the mill,
and though they knew the road perfectly well,
the snow was so deep that they were suffocated."

The tragic story weighed on Elisabeth's
heart even as her fears for Donald and

Andrew grew. Was the weather to the south as severe? Were the brothers strong enough to ride o'er the cold, snowy hills? Or had they succumbed . . .

Nae, nae, nae. Elisabeth could not let her imagination wander down such murky paths.

Instead she reminded herself daily of the rebel victories on English soil. The Jacobite army had taken Carlisle, then pushed on to Lancaster and Preston, with the prince's gaze fixed on London. That much they knew. But the farther from home the army marched, the harder it became for Rob to gather any news that could be trusted, so conflicting were the reports from the south. And mail was unbearably slow, sometimes weeks in coming. Her three letters from Donald were hidden beneath her carpet like the dowager's gold lest a dragoon come looking for them.

Elisabeth could do nothing but wait, keeping her needle busy and her mind occupied as the days grew shorter and the nights colder.

On the first Saturday in December, when the temperature hovered below freezing and the windows were covered with frost on both sides of the glass, Rob MacPherson came knocking on their door.

"The prince has reached Derby," he announced, pulling off his gloves and hat in the entrance hall and stamping the ice from his boots. Gibson, his health restored except for a lingering cough, ushered Rob into the drawing room. The Kerr women were seated round a card table by the fire, whiling away the frigid afternoon playing omber, a card game designed for three.

Rob cocked his brow at the pile of buttons in the center of the table.

Janet shrugged. "Our mother-in-law insists we cannot afford to gamble even ha'pence."

Elisabeth discarded her handful of playing cards, the number of tricks she'd taken all but forgotten. "Please, Mr. MacPherson, tell us the latest news."

He joined them at the small table. "On Wednesday last the army reached Derby, not much mair than a hundred miles from London. The bells were ringing as the vanguard rode into the mercat place followed by Lord Elcho and his Life Guards."

Elisabeth pictured her braw husband astride his mount. "Did the rest of the army enter the town?"

"Aye. With the skirl o' the pipes and their standards flying, they made a bonny show of it. The next morn the clansmen went in search o' cutlers to sharpen their swords, with the Duke o' Cumberland close on their heels."

Elisabeth's breath caught. Cumberland, the king's second son, was the same age as Prince Charlie but more experienced as a soldier —

and more ruthless.

"I dinna ken what happened next," Rob confessed.

Janet tossed her cards onto the table in obvious frustration. "Were they victorious over Cumberland or not? Have they marched on to London?"

Rob wagged his head. "We've men riding up and doon the countryside leuking to find oot. There are rumors traveling round ilka tavern from London to Inverness. Some true, some not. We'll ken afore lang."

The truth came in a letter from Donald almost a fortnight later. By then Elisabeth had heard the grim news whispered in the pews at kirk and shouted on the street by pamphleteers. But seeing it written in her husband's hand made it far more real. And far more troubling.

Rob brought Donald's letter to her door on a bleak Tuesday at noontide. "I'm bound for Queensberry Hoose," he said, "to bid the last o' the soldiers farewell."

She closed the door against the wind that howled up the stair. "You've done Martin Eccles a great service," she told him.

Rob held out the letter from Donald. "I'm obliged to help whaur I can."

His gaze was so intense she nearly closed her eyes. *Please don't, Rob.*

"If ye'll not mind," he said in a low voice,

"I'd like to stay while the letter's read. For onie news, ye ken."

She could not refuse him. Donald's letters were meant for the whole household. And wasn't Rob the one who made sure she received them? Though he never used the word, Elisabeth was quite certain Rob served as a spy for the Jacobites, gathering intelligence and disseminating vital information. The tailoring shop was ransacked because of Angus's service on the field. The British never suspected the dark, taciturn son with a marked limp, who remained behind, quietly going about the prince's business.

Marjory was the first to see the letter in her hand. "Gibson, call the others." She waited, hazel eyes shining, until Janet and Mrs. Edgar quickly joined them. "Now then, Lady Kerr."

Elisabeth unfolded the bulky letter, surprised to find another one nestled inside, addressed to her alone. Five pairs of eyes watched the second letter disappear into her hanging pocket. " 'Tis some private-matter," she said offhandedly. Had Donald expressed his feelings for her? Or had he penned another sordid confession unburdening further guilt, all the while adding to her shame?

She would know soon enough. First she read aloud his letter for the household.

To My Beloved Family
Friday, 13 December 1745

By necessity I must be brief. I only wish to assure you I am alive and unharmed. So is my brother.

"Thanks be to God!" Marjory dropped into an upholstered chair. "They are safe. 'Tis the only news that matters."

"Aye," everyone agreed, nodding at their mistress. Elisabeth dared not point out that the letter was several days old. She read on, knowing Donald could not reveal more than was prudent, though his carefully edited words said enough.

We did not engage the enemy in Derby or proceed to London, but are instead returning to Scotland on a familiar route.

"They're not returning." Rob's voice was low, but sharp as steel. "They're retreating."

"Why?" Elisabeth studied the letter, seeking an answer between the hurried lines of ink. "They've had naught but victories."

"Aye." His expression was as black as Greyfriars Kirkyard at midnight. "The prince was a' for London. But with three English armies afoot, his commanders called for retreat."

Marjory looked at him, the hope in her eyes waning. "Will my sons be coming home, then?"

"We canna be certain," Rob replied and said no more.

Elisabeth continued reading, though the news was not good.

When we marched south in November, the villagers rang their kirk bells and watched in wonder. Now, marching north, we are met with hostility and anger.

She'd overheard grisly stories of Jacobite soldiers being abused, even killed, by violent English mobs. Such tales did not bear repeating, though they bore the sting of truth. *Come home, Donald. Soon.*

"Is there nothing more?" Marjory asked her.

Elisabeth finished the letter, already thinking of the one in her pocket.

I cannot say where we shall spend Yuletide. Our thoughts and prayers are with each of you, this day and always.

Once again Donald had not signed his letter except with chapter and verse. "Gibson, if you might collect the Scriptures from my chamber. 'Tis Psalm 18:3 we're needing."

He returned shortly and balanced the book for Elisabeth while she found the verse.

"I will call upon the LORD, who is worthy to be praised," Elisabeth read. "So shall I be saved from mine enemies."

"May it be so . . ." Marjory's voice broke. "Please, may it be so . . ." She pressed her handkerchief to her mouth and squeezed shut her eyes, moaning to herself, "My sons, my sons . . ."

FIFTY-NINE

The holiest of all holidays are those
Kept by ourselves in silence and apart;
The secret anniversaries of the heart.
    HENRY WADSWORTH LONGFELLOW

"Your sons will return," Elisabeth said softly, knowing it was an empty promise. But she couldn't watch her mother-in-law suffer and not comfort her in some way. When she took Marjory's hand, it felt surprisingly small and limp.

Her mother-in-law opened her eyes. Both hope and doubt shone in her tears. "How can you be certain they'll come home?"

Elisabeth hesitated, not wanting to speak amiss.

Rob MacPherson came to her rescue. "The army is nearing Carlisle, mem. Within the week yer sons may cross the border." His low voice thrummed with conviction, but Elisabeth heard the word *may* and knew he was treading with care. The dowager did not forget or forgive easily, especially not broken promises.

" 'Tis some consolation," Marjory agreed, "to think of them in Scotland." She sniffed, drying her eyes. "As always, Mr. MacPherson, we appreciate your loyal service to our family."

It was a gentle but firm dismissal, which Rob did not miss. "I bid ye guid day, mem."

Elisabeth walked him to the door, keeping a slight distance between them, though she could still sense the heat of his body, as if he'd lined his waistcoat with live coals.

"Will ye fast on the morrow?" Rob asked, though surely he knew how she would respond.

King George had proclaimed a public fast to quell the unnatural rebellion, as the English loved to call it. The fast was not a request but a royal command, set to commence on the eighteenth of December. Not everyone in his kingdom was required to fast that day. Only his subjects in Scotland.

"King David humbled his soul afore God with fasting," Rob said as if testing her.

"I might fast for Almighty God," Elisabeth said firmly, "but not for King George."

Rob nodded at that. "Weel said, Leddy Kerr." His gaze fell to her pocket. "I imagine ye're eager to read the letter from yer husband."

"I am," she admitted. "Monday will be the third anniversary of our wedding."

530

The moment the words were spoken Rob's features darkened. " 'Tis unfortunate ye must spend the day alone."

"Since my husband will do the same, we will be joined in that way if no other."

Rob frowned but did not comment.

Voices in the drawing room reminded Elisabeth they'd tarried at the door long enough. "I must go," she said, taking a step back and dropping a curtsy. "If I do not see you before year's end —"

"Nae, Bess. Ye'll see me. 'Tis a lang fortnight 'til Hogmanay." His bow was curt and his exit more so. The door closed before she could bid him good-bye.

Elisabeth waited for the heat in her face to cool and the tension in her body to ease. She touched the letter in her pocket like a talisman. *This is the man I love. And the one who loves me.*

Mrs. Edgar approached from the kitchen. "Did ye not invite Mr. MacPherson to stay for dinner? 'Tis not but crawfish soup and mutton chops, but I've plenty to spare."

Elisabeth heard the faintly scolding note in her voice. "We'll invite him to sup with us over Yuletide," she promised. "At the moment I've a letter to read before dinner."

Seeing the others round the fireplace, Elisabeth slipped through the kitchen and then Janet's bedchamber to reach her own, avoiding the drawing room. She unfolded the let-

531

ter, not surprised to find it began without
date or address.

My Darling Wife,

I miss you every waking hour and pray that
you are content. I would give all I own in
this world to hold you in my arms.

Oh, my love. Elisabeth not only heard Donald's voice; she felt his touch and almost
tasted his kiss. *Content?* Not until he was
home. Not until she was in his embrace.

I trust you received a letter shortly after I
left and have destroyed it.

The paper was gone but the names remained. *Susan McGill, Jane Montgomerie,
Lucy Spence.* Guilt pierced her heart at the
much-rehearsed litany. *He did not ask you to
remember them, Bess. He asked you to forget.*
She looked down at the letter through a
veil of tears.

If you have chosen to withdraw your forgiveness, none would fault you, least of all your
husband. Until then, I cling to the three
words you spoke in the forecourt and pray I
may someday deserve them.

You are forgiven. Words she could not take

back even if she wanted to. And she no longer wanted to.

Was mercy deserved? Earned? Or simply received? She only knew it was never ending. *His mercy lasteth ever.* On the Sabbath at the Tron Kirk, the precentor had sung those words over and over. Each time she'd sung them in response, the truth sank in a wee bit deeper. *His mercy faileth never.*

Only two more lines of Donald's letter remained. How she wished he might have written page after page! That he wrote to her at all in the midst of an army encampment was a gift that would suffice for many an anniversary to come.

Elisabeth read the last of it, letting each word do the work of ten.

The anniversary of our marriage approaches. I will spend the day giving thanks for my bonny wife, who was faithful when I was not.

Yours.

"You *are* mine, beloved," she whispered, smiling through her tears. "And I am yours."

When all of Scotland fasted on Wednesday for King George, Elisabeth fasted and prayed for her husband. When royalist troops began to pour into Edinburgh from the west, she strengthened her resolve with a verse from Scripture: *Ye shall not fear them: for the LORD your God he shall fight for you.* And in late December, when the broadsheets reported the Duke of Cumberland was pursuing the rebel army into Scotland, Elisabeth drew comfort in this assurance: Donald was drawing near.

SIXTY

Enter upon thy paths, O year!
Thy paths, which all who breathe must
   tread.

BARRY CORNWALL

The new year began in silence and in darkness. Marjory shivered in bed, the covers pulled round her neck. She could not tell the time since the dragoons had stolen her mantel clock, but daylight was surely hours away.

Before retiring for the night, Marjory had snuffed all the candles in her bedchamber and instructed the household to do the same. Hogmanay revelers spying even a flicker of light in their windows would have climbed the turnpike stair and come banging on their door, certain they'd be welcomed and served a dram of whisky no matter how late the hour. As it was, the cacophony from the High Street below had kept Marjory awake long past midnight. The skirl of the bagpipes, the ringing of the Tron Kirk bells, and the sounding of ship horns in Leith's harbor ushered in the year 1746 with the usual uproar.

On her first Hogmanay in Edinburgh, Marjory had leaned out their High Street window, intoxicated with the sheer excitement of it all — Donald on one side of her, Andrew on the other, and a bemused Lord John half asleep in his favorite chair. Two weeks later her sons lay in their beds, struggling to breathe. Two years later Lord John lay in this bed, drawing his last breath.

Marjory had learned to dread January. 'Twas the longest month of the year, with its short days and its endless, frigid nights. The sun seldom shone, the clouds never moved except to spill copious amount of rain or snow or both, and the cold winter fog, called *haar,* crawled in from the sea and lingered all day. The household burned coal and candles as if they cost nothing to replenish, and a decent cut of fresh beef could not be found in the Fleshmarket, not for all the guineas beneath her floor.

There were precious few coins now. Fewer every day. She could not bear to think what Lord John would say if he knew she'd gambled their fortune on an exiled prince.

Marjory sighed into the pitch-black room. *I miss you, John. So very much.* She quickly blinked to stem her tears. Ill luck came to those who wept on New Year's Day. Instead she touched the empty pillow beside her, remembering the many tears she'd cried in seasons past.

She was forty when he died, past her child-bearing years. When her time of mourning ended, Marjory discovered that any man who looked at her twice — Lord Drummond among them — was counting her money, not courting her favor. Within a few years she decided she did not need a husband. She had her sons, and they had their wives. Come summer, a grandchild would be placed in her arms. Janet had yet to reveal any details. Perhaps her babe would arrive sooner. If so, 'twould be quite small, since Janet's waist had yet to expand so much as an inch.

Marjory had not been that fortunate. With each of her lads, she'd grown to the size of a sedan chair and moved about with the same lack of grace. Her confinement kept her from public disgrace, but she'd been embarrassed to have Lord John see her in such an ungainly state. With Andrew serving the prince, Janet and he both might be spared those awkward months. Then Andrew could return to find his child born and his wife as he remembered her.

But if Donald and Andrew came home sooner, no one would be happier than Marjory. Nae, not even their wives. As their mother, she'd known them from their very first breaths, with their mouths open wide and their plaintive cries piercing her heart.

My bonny wee lads.

Marjory threw back the covers, cold air putting a swift stop to the renewed threat of tears. But oh, they were dear boys, grown into fine men. The prince and his army were in Glasgow now, less than fifty miles west. To think of her sons so close! She was glad they were in Scotland to greet the new year. If Almighty God still took notice of her, she prayed he might bring her sons home before month's end.

Marjory located her slippers by feel, not by sight, and exchanged her sleeping jacket for a simple gown that laced up the front. She imagined the time near six o' the clock, the hour when Lord John died. Wasn't she the one who'd stopped the pendulum and draped the looking glass and opened the window? Every New Year's Day since, she'd awakened at the same time as if prompted by some inner voice. She found the annual ritual comforting. It was a quiet, solitary way to honor the father of her sons.

As she tiptoed across her bedchamber, Marjory noticed again how clean everything smelled. Last evening Mrs. Edgar and Gibson worked tirelessly at their Hogmanay tasks: scrubbing every corner of the house, sweeping the coal grates, and carrying out the ashes, making the house ready for the new year.

Marjory found a candle stub at last and

bent over her coal fire to light the wick. She wrinkled her nose at the offensive smell of tallow, a constant reminder of their reduced circumstances. When the Rising was over, she would purchase beeswax candles by the pound.

Holding her taper aloft, Marjory walked into the empty drawing room, taking care not to stub her toe on the chair legs. She squinted at the clock. *Quarter after six.* The table was set for breakfast, though she cringed when she saw wooden plates instead of fine china and horn spoons rather than sterling silver. She had good dishes and silver at Tweedsford, of course, but did not dare bring them to Edinburgh with more royalist soldiers marching into town almost daily. The High Street was thick with them.

Marjory started toward one of the windows overlooking Milne Square when a sharp knock at the stair door made her nearly jump out of her skin. "Gibson!" she cried, her candle shaking as she hastened for the entrance hall, fearing the worst. *Not the dragoons. Not again.*

Gibson tottered to the door, his fringe of hair mussed, his livery wrinkled from sleep. He pulled open the door, then announced in a gravelly voice, "Mr. MacPherson."

Marjory glared at the man who filled her doorway, her alarm quickly turning to vexation. "Sir, whatever are you doing calling at this hour?"

Rob bowed, a solemn look on his face. "Meikle guid luck to this hoose," he said, "and meikle guid luck to this family."

She recognized the blessing at once, a Hogmanay tradition.

Gibson nodded approvingly. "He makes a verra guid first foot, mem."

Marjory could not argue the point. Since the ideal "first foot" — the person who first crossed one's threshold on New Year's Day — was a dark-haired bachelor, Rob MacPherson more than qualified.

"I waited yestreen," Rob explained, "thinking to come at midnight, but I didna see a candle in the window, so I couldna knock. Until this morn."

Had he watched their windows all night? Marjory could not decide if the idea was disconcerting or comforting. "And have you brought the proper gifts?" she asked, guessing the answer.

"Aye." From inside his greatcoat Rob withdrew a piece of coal, a silver sixpence, a crumbling piece of cake, and a fine bottle of Bordeaux.

She stared at him in amazement. "The streets are run amuck with the king's soldiers. However did you manage to land such a prize?"

Rob shrugged. "I ken a free trader or two."

Marjory had no doubt of that. Jacobites

delighted in supporting smugglers, who cheated the king of his excise taxes. " 'Tis only right we make you welcome, however early the hour. Gibson, will you take Mr. MacPherson's coat and see if Mrs. Edgar is stirring?"

"Weel stirred," the housekeeper assured her, sailing into the entrance hall from the kitchen, patting her white cap in place. "Het pints and black bun will be on the table in nae time, mem."

Rob's sober countenance lightened at the mention of the Yuletide staples. "Will your daughters-in-law be joining us?" he asked, following Marjory into the drawing room.

"Lady Kerr often rises before the rest of the household," Marjory told him, "but I cannot speak for Mrs. Kerr."

Within the hour all were present, tucking stray hairs in place and rubbing the sleep from their eyes. For good or for ill, the tailor's son was almost a member of the family now and did not seem to mind if the Kerrs appeared at table a bit disheveled.

Elisabeth was quiet that morning. When het pints were served — spiced ale mixed with eggs, cream, and sugar — she held the warm drink in her hand but barely tasted it. And when black bun was brought forth from the oven — a fragrant cake stuffed with currants and nuts — Elisabeth pinched off a small bite and left the rest.

Rob eyed her closely, but then, he always did. "Too early for such rich fare, Lady Kerr?"

"Perhaps." She offered a wan smile. "I did not sleep well. Too much commotion in the street."

"There'll be meikle mair o' that," Rob said grimly, his pint drained and his plate covered with crumbs. He looked round the room as if to be sure all were listening. "I've come this morn to give ye news ye'll not be glad to hear."

SIXTY-ONE

I feel my sinews slackened with the fright,
and a cold sweat trills down all over my
 limbs,
as if I were dissolving into water.
JOHN DRYDEN

"News?" Marjory stared at the tailor's son,
her hands quickly turning to ice. "I
thought . . . that is, I was certain Lord Kerr
and his brother were safely in Glasgow. Did
you not tell me so yourself, Mr. MacPherson?"

"I did," he was quick to say, "and they are
in Glasgow, for the moment. But 'tis yer ain
safety that worries me. On the morrow
General Hawley's men will begin arriving in
Edinburgh. And ye must be ready, leddies,
for this man's reputation is worse than the
Duke o' Cumberland's."

Marjory looked at her daughters-in-law and
saw her own apprehension reflected in their
young faces. Royal or not, Cumberland was
known to be cruel in his dealings. If Hawley

was more contemptuous than his master, Rob was right to be concerned.

"The man's a bully," Rob continued. "Henry Hawley fought the Jacobites at Sheriffmuir in the last Rising. He's carried the stink of it in his nostrils ever since. They say his quarters are decorated with the bones of a deid soldier. And that he's not above hanging his ain men after a defeat. Mark my wirds, he'll build a gallows in the toun whan he arrives."

Marjory sank against the back of her chair, stunned. "If he kills his own men, what must he do to his enemies?"

Rob merely nodded, his silence more frightening than his words.

"You said we must be ready," Janet prompted him.

He leaned forward. "Come the morrow ye must *licht* candles in a' yer windows to show yer lealty to King Geordie. If ye dinna do sae, the approaching troops will break a' the glass."

Elisabeth gaped at him. "In the dead of winter?"

"Aye. The windows o' empty houses will be broken as weel. 'Tis why monie folk round the toun are offering the king's troops a glass o' spirits, a pound o' bread — whatsomever it takes to appease them."

"Surely we are not expected to do the same?" Marjory huffed at the very thought.

"I will not be hospitable to any man bent on killing my sons! Furthermore, I have a house-ful of women to protect and one of them with child . . ." Marjory froze. To confess such a thing to a neighbor, and a bachelor at that! Janet appeared about to swoon, and Elisabeth turned the color of ripe strawberries.

Marjory quickly tried to make amends. "I beg your pardon, Mr. MacPherson. I should never have mentioned so . . . ah, private a matter."

But Rob was not looking at her. He was looking at Elisabeth with an expression of pure agony.

Marjory saw the truth in his eyes. *He thinks Elisabeth is carrying Donald's child.* She saw another truth there as well. *He is desperately in love with her.*

"I didna ken . . . about the bairn," he said, his voice so low she strained to hear him.

"And that is entirely my fault," Marjory said, this time aiming her words at Janet, whom she'd wronged terribly. But Janet would not meet her gaze.

Marjory tried again to recover from her faux pas. "What I meant to say, Mr. Mac-Pherson, was that we have four women in the house and not a weapon among us."

Without taking his eyes off Elisabeth, Rob slowly pulled a dirk from his boot and placed it on the table, the lethal blade gleaming amid the crockery. "Now ye do, mem."

Marjory eyed it for a moment, then gingerly picked it up, surprised by the heft of it. "Are you certain you can spare this?"

Rob's voice was flat. "I've anither at hame."

Marjory laid the dirk on the table with care as if it might bite, like a serpent. "Once again, sir, you've come to our rescue."

"Indeed you have," Elisabeth told him.

Marjory studied them both. Was Elisabeth aware of the depth of Rob's feelings? Only a feebleminded woman could look at the man and not read his heart. And her daughter-in-law was anything but feebleminded. Something would have to be done. If Lord Kerr returned and learned of Rob's betrayal of their friendship, he would run his sword through the man's heart.

Nae. Marjory would not let herself dwell on such possibilities. Did she not have enough worries in the here and now without dwelling on events that might never happen?

Janet, at least, had recovered from her embarrassment. "Perhaps residing on the fifth floor will keep us from harm," she said.

"It didna spare yer hoose the last time," Rob reminded them. "Soldiers can also break yer windows from the inside oot."

Marjory refused even to consider it. "We must be ready on the morrow."

"Aye, for the troops. As to General Hawley himself, leuk for him to arrive in toun on *Up-*

halieday or thereabouts."

Epiphany, the English called it. Only yesterday morning Marjory had entertained a fleeting hope that her sons might return in time for the last day of Yule. Perhaps *she* was the one with a feeble mind. Donald and Andrew were coming east, aye, but they were not coming home. A battle larger than Gladsmuir was on the horizon. The prince and his men had faced brief skirmishes in England, but this was something else. She heard it in the angry voices that crept up the stair and saw it on people's faces at the Tron Kirk on the Sabbath last.

Wars and rumours of wars. Aye, just so.

When she looked up, Rob was on his feet. "If ye'll forgive me, leddies, I'll take my leave. The blether on the High Street is thicker than cauld porridge. Mebbe I can learn mair of what's to come." While Gibson helped him into his greatcoat, Rob gave the manservant clear instructions. "Licht yer candles, bolt yer door, and open it to none but me."

"Whatsomever ye say, sir," Gibson told him, nodding vigorously.

Gibson was no doubt relieved to have a younger, stronger man watching out for their safety. Marjory was grateful for Rob's help as well. But the tailor's son could not stake any claim on Elisabeth. Nae, not even in his imagination. When Gibson escorted him out, Marjory noted with satisfaction that Elisabeth did not follow Rob with her gaze.

As soon as the door was bolted shut, Janet touched her sleeve. "I wonder, Lady Marjory, if I might have a word with you."

"Of course." Marjory began composing her thoughts as the two walked into her bed-chamber. She would begin with a heartfelt apology and see where it led. Perhaps she might be given some hint of when the child could be expected or a sense of how Janet was feeling. In the midst of fear and pain and war, the promise of a wee child was a balm to Marjory's soul, as it surely would be to the whole household when they learned the happy news.

The two women sat together by the fire, perched on upholstered chairs that had seen better days. Marjory spoke first. "I must apologize once more —"

"Nae." Janet grabbed her hand rather firmly. "Things are not as they seem."

Marjory saw the shadow fall across Janet's face. *She has miscarried.* "My poor girl —"

"Nae, you do not understand." Janet looked down. "I am not expecting."

"I am so very sorry," Marjory said gently. "When did you lose the child?"

Janet cleared her throat. "You cannot lose what you never had."

Marjory's heart skipped a beat. "Whatever do you mean, Janet?"

"Only this." Janet lifted her head. Her eyes

548

were dry. "The last night my husband and I were . . . together, I told him I was carrying his child. And I *might* have been. That is . . . it was not entirely a fabrication . . ."

Marjory stared at her, speechless.

"I thought if I were expecting it might change his mind about going off with the prince." Janet sighed, letting go of Marjory's hand. "Obviously my little ploy didn't work."

"You lied . . . to Andrew? To all of us?"

"Well . . ." Janet flapped her hand about. "Don't women sometimes *think* they are with child and then realize they are not?"

"Aye, but . . ." Tears stung her eyes. *There will not be a child. I will not be a grandmother.* "Why did you not tell us when you realized . . . when you knew?"

Janet had the decency to blush. "I confess I rather liked playing the expectant mother. Everyone fusses over you and brings you wee treats. You can nap whenever you please and have breakfast at noontide. I kept meaning to tell everyone . . . well, at least to tell *you* . . . but the time never seemed right. Until today, when something *had* to be said."

"I see." Marjory was undone. That such a woman lived under her roof and ate at her table and shared her son's bed was beyond comprehension. A year ago she'd thought her a fine prize for Andrew. Now she knew Janet Murray had been no prize at all.

Her daughter-in-law stood, sighing as if a

great burden had been lifted. "I'm afraid you'll have to straighten out Rob Mac-Pherson before he tells someone. It won't do to have the neighborhood minding my waist-line."

Marjory watched her quit the room without a backward glance. Only then did she quietly grieve for the grandchild she'd lost yet never had. She dabbed at her eyes, grateful no one came looking for her. They might think her daft or weak, and she could not afford to be either. Not when she needed to be wise in her husband's stead and strong for her sons.

The first day of this dreaded month and already fear and disappointment had been heaped at her door. None but the Almighty knew what else January might hold.

Sixty-Two

'Tis winter, yet there is no sound
Along the air
Of winds along their battle-ground.
RALPH HOYT

A storm was brewing to the south. At three o' the clock on Friday the seventeenth, the sky was gunmetal gray tinged with purple. It was not cold enough to snow but cold enough, with a stiff wind rattling the panes. Elisabeth gazed down at the High Street, emptier than she'd seen it in days. Townsfolk scurried across the plainstanes, looking over their shoulders, not stopping to chat with neighbors. Frightened.

Elisabeth now had a faint idea of what imprisonment felt like. Although their house at Milne Square bore no resemblance to a squalid tolbooth, she'd spent the last fortnight behind a locked stair door, neither coming nor going, while Edinburgh played host to their enemy.

After menacing the town for a week, General Hawley and his royalist troops had departed through the West Port earlier that week, bound for Linlithgow. Farther west, outside of Falkirk, the prince and his Highland army lay in wait. "Mair than eight thousand strong," Rob had said with pride, their numbers having grown since their return to Scotland. Elisabeth hoped they were very strong indeed since a new wooden gallows stood in the Grassmarket, compliments of Hangman Hawley, the name his own men whispered behind his back.

Voices drew Elisabeth's attention to the entrance hall, where her mother-in-law was upset about something. Janet, seated by the fire, looked up as well.

"You *must* find us more candles." Marjory was pleading with Gibson as if he were hoarding them beneath his thin mattress.

"Mr. Herriot willna sell them to me." Gibson sounded forlorn. "Nor will Mr. Watson o' Libberton's Wynd."

Barbara Inglis lives there.

Elisabeth tried to brush away such thoughts as quickly as they surfaced, but they soon returned. Knowing the names and addresses of all Donald's conquests had begun to color her view of Edinburgh. The closes and wynds she'd traveled for many seasons had a different feeling about them. Warriston's Close was no longer the home of her favorite baker, Mr. Orr, with his buttery caraway buns; now Warriston's Close was where Susan McGill lived.

Marjory asked, "Have you tried Mr. Sprott of Blackfriars Wynd?"

Janet was across the room and standing by Gibson's side in a trice. "I have oft given Mr. Sprott my custom," she said with a confident toss of her hair. "If I go with you, we'll come home with candles."

Marjory frowned. "I'm not sure that's wise. Mr. MacPherson cautioned us against leaving the house."

"Oh, but most of Hawley's men are gone," Janet said with a careless shrug. "Anyway, 'tis not far to Mr. Sprott's. And with Gibson by my side, you've no need for concern."

Elisabeth moved toward them, a knot of fear tightening inside her. She knew Janet was weary of being withindoors, just as she was. But the king's soldiers were still patrolling the High Street. Furthermore, they'd identified every Jacobite household and were ruthless in their search for spies and informants. Janet was neither, of course, but suspicion alone could land her in the tolbooth.

'Twas too great a risk.

Seeing Janet reach for her cape, Elisabeth acted quickly. "What if you sent a note with Gibson instead? Your words alone might prompt Mr. Sprott to accept our shillings."

"A woman can be far more persuasive in person." Janet's mind was clearly made up.

Her cape was already settled round her shoulders. "If you've shillings in your pocket, Gibson, I am ready."

Elisabeth tried again. "Could we not wait and ask Mr. MacPherson to help us?"

"We have but two candles left," Marjory explained, "and Mr. MacPherson has not been to see us in days. He may very well have joined his father at Falkirk. I'm afraid we must do what we can, Lady Kerr." She placed two shillings in Gibson's weathered hand. "Bring back four pounds of tallow candles. And take good care of my son's wife."

Janet, looking pleased with herself, led the way across the threshold. She and Gibson soon disappeared round the curve in the stair.

Marjory bolted the door behind them, then turned to Elisabeth. "You are unhappy with me for letting her go."

"Nae," Elisabeth assured her. "Janet was determined to leave no matter what anyone said."

"Perhaps you are right." Marjory sighed, tightening the strings of her leather purse. "As you often are, my dear."

After nearly four months without Donald and Andrew beneath their roof, Elisabeth had watched each woman's distinct personality emerge. Marjory gave in to Janet too easily, and Janet never gave in at all. The role of peacemaker had fallen to Elisabeth just as it had when she lived at Mrs. Sinclair's boarding school.

Seeing her mother-in-law's troubled expression, Elisabeth asked, "Might I read to you?" On Monday last Marjory had pressed some of her precious shillings into Gibson's hand and sent him to Mr. Creech, the bookseller, to purchase a replacement for Donald's ruined copy of *The Seasons.*

She handed Elisabeth the book from the mantelpiece. "When my son returns home, he will be heartbroken to find his library gone."

Nae, he will be furious. "Which of the seasons shall I read?" Elisabeth asked.

"Not *Winter,*" Marjory said firmly. "Give me a taste of *Spring,* and let me pretend it is not the middle of January."

They sat together on the sofa, which was drawn close to the fire. Elisabeth positioned the candle stand so she might read the tiny print. Marjory could not afford the larger copy with its fine leather binding and settled instead for a clothbound edition hardly bigger than a deck of playing cards.

Elisabeth gazed at the opening page. Aye, here was the needed respite.

Come, gentle Spring, ethereal mildness, come,
And from the bosom of yon dropping cloud,
While music wakes around, veil'd in a shower

555

Of shadowing roses, on our plains
    descend.

When Elisabeth paused, Marjory said, "Did I tell you James Thomson was schooled in nearby Jedburgh? His mother, Beatrix, once told me her son spent each New Year's Day burning most of his writing from the year past." A ghost of a smile flitted across Marjory's features. "I don't suppose we could convince our Janet to do the same with her poetry?"

An unexpected knock sounded on the stair door. Three sharp raps, then two: Rob MacPherson's signal.

Elisabeth put aside *The Seasons* and hastened to greet him. When she reached the entrance hall, Mrs. Edgar was already pulling open the door to usher him within.

"Leddy Kerr." His countenance matched the darkening clouds beyond their windows. "News from Falkirk." He strode into the drawing room, his greatcoat flapping about his boots. "Mrs. Kerr will want to hear this as weel."

"She's not here," Elisabeth told him. When she explained where Janet had gone and why, Rob's sullen mood did not improve.

"Have I not made clear the danger ye're in whan ye leave this hoose?"

"Aye," Marjory assured him, "but we're in need of candles, and Janet thought . . .

well . . ."

"I'll see that ye have a stone o' candles come the morn."

"Bless you," Marjory said. If accepting a tradesman's help chafed at her sensibilities, she kept it well hidden.

"The news, then." Rob did not take off his hat or gloves nor take an offered chair. "General Hawley is at Callendar Hoose near Falkirk, whaur the guid Lady Kilmarnock is busy keeping the man from his duties for King Geordie. Meanwhile, the Jacobites had a council o' war and determined to fight Hawley's troops. And the toun folk have filled the streets o' Falkirk as if 'twere a mercat day, thinking to watch the battle."

Elisabeth's heart pounded, imagining the scene. "Are they fighting even as we speak?"

Rob's gaze was even. "I canna say, leddies. The news is cauld lang afore it reaches Edinburgh. But, aye, 'twould seem this is the day, mebbe even the hour. Ye can be certain the prince and his men are ready. The last I heard from my faither, yer lads were in guid health and prepared to fight."

Without thinking, Elisabeth reached for Marjory's hand. Her mother-in-law returned her tight clasp. "Promise you will come at once when you know the outcome?"

"Depend upon it, guid news or ill." Rob glanced at the windows facing the square. "At the moment I'm bound for Blackfriars

Wynd to see Mrs. Kerr safely home." With that, he was gone as abruptly as he'd come.

Standing in the quiet house, listening to the blustery wind, Elisabeth released Marjory's hand with a light squeeze and asked, "Would a cup of tea help?"

"It might." Her mother-in-law met her gaze as if truly seeing her rather than looking past her. "At least 'twill keep our hands warm and our minds occupied."

Mrs. Edgar brought them a proper tea, including cream and saffron cakes, served on mismatched china cups and plates rescued from a wooden kist. With fewer plenishings and no bed curtains, Marjory's bedchamber sounded almost hollow. The clink of cup and saucer, the stirring spoon, the fork against the china, all were more noticeable. Neither woman had much to say, and their eyes were repeatedly drawn to the threatening sky.

When the clock struck half past four, Marjory jumped at the sound and dropped her fork on the plate with a terrible clatter. With a soft cry, she leaned back, one hand on her heart. "However will I keep my wits about me through the evening?"

"I imagine 'twill be the morn before we hear any news," Elisabeth said, wishing it were not so. The battle at Gladsmuir had lasted a mere quarter hour. But twice as many men were gathered at Falkirk. The conflict might last for hours, even days.

Darkness was upon them. The first drops of rain had just begun splattering against the window when they heard Gibson's voice at the door. Both women hurried to the entrance hall and found the manservant distraught and Rob grim and silent.

Janet was the color of fine sifted flour.

"Whatever has happened?" Elisabeth asked her as gently as she could.

"A dragoon . . . pulled me . . . against a wall. But he . . . Mr. MacPherson . . ." With a moan Janet collapsed into Elisabeth's arms.

"Oh, my dear!" Elisabeth tried to support her, but her sister-in-law's limp body was too heavy for her. "Mr. MacPherson, if you will . . ."

"I have her." Rob lifted Janet with ease and carried her to her bedchamber, with the household on his heels.

Mrs. Edgar took charge at once, tucking extra pillows beneath Janet's head and slipping off her shoes. The housekeeper soon had a cool, damp cloth on Janet's forehead and a cup of water pressed to her lips. "She'll be needing air," Mrs. Edgar said pointedly.

Rob inclined his head toward the kitchen. " 'Tis best if we speak elsewhere."

A moment later Marjory and Elisabeth were standing with him in the warmest corner of the house. Rob addressed their concerns at once. "She wasna harmed, merely frightened, and I canna blame her. Whan I found them, a dragoon had pushed Gibson to the ground, and Mrs. Kerr . . . weel, she told ye herself." A tremor moved across his broad shoulders. " 'Twas guid I arrived whan I did. Onie later . . ."

Marjory did not look down quickly enough to hide her dismay. "However can we thank you?"

"I ken 'tis difficult, but if ye'll stay within-doors —"

"We will," Elisabeth pledged. "After all, we cannot expect you to watch over us every hour."

Rob's gaze was steady. "I'd gladly do sae, Leddy Kerr."

Marjory lifted her head, like a roe deer sensing danger in the wood. "Mr. Mac-Pherson, how is your father?"

Rob's shoulders sagged a bit. "He's not sae young as he ance was, and the cauld is hard on his joints. The prince has given him leave to come hame after Falkirk. I leuk for him at oor shop in a day or two."

Mrs. Edgar opened the kitchen door enough to peek round it. "Mem, yer daughter-in-law is asking for ye."

Marjory excused herself, though not without a pointed glance at Elisabeth. "I'll not be a minute."

Left alone in the kitchen with Rob, Elisabeth cast about for a safe topic of conversation.

"Tell me, Bess." His voice was low, warm. "What's on yer mind this nicht?"

SIXTY-THREE

Wha drew the guid claymore for Charlie?
An' claw'd their backs at Falkirk fairly?
JACOBITE BALLAD

Elisabeth ran her finger along the edge of the dresser, scrubbed clean by Mrs. Edgar's diligent hands. "My thoughts, as always, are with my husband. And with your father." She looked up to find Rob listening intently. "Angus was very kind to me when I moved to Edinburgh."

Rob shifted his stance, moving a bit closer. "Onie time ye came by the shop, ye brightened his day. And mine as weel."

"You barely spoke to me," she reminded him.

He shrugged. "What could a tradesman's son say to a Hieland beauty?"

"Oh, Rob. You think too little of yourself," Elisabeth scolded him, "and far too much of me."

He sobered at that. "Mair than ye ken, Bess."

The door to the kitchen quietly opened. "Your sister-in-law is resting," Marjory said. "Mr. MacPherson, will you join us for supper?"

Rob glanced at Elisabeth, then took a step toward the stair door, putting some distance between them. "Thank ye, mem, but I must be hame when my faither returns."

They both walked Rob to the door, sending him on his way with a pocketful of Mrs. Edgar's saffron cakes and a thick slice of cold mutton. He paused on the stair. "Ye'll not leave the hoose 'til ye hear from me, aye?"

Elisabeth heard his words for what they were: a warning. "We shall look for you and your father on the morrow," she said, matching her confidence to his. She watched him descend the stair, then bolted the door, a dead, metallic sound meant to make her feel safe. Instead, she felt cut off from the world, isolated, and closed in. An uncomfortable sensation for a woman raised in the Highlands with its endless expanse of sky and mountain. How did Rob bear living in the city? How, for that matter, did she?

"Shall we return to *The Seasons*?" Marjory held up the small book.

Elisabeth needed more than poetry on such a night. "Might we read from the Scriptures instead?"

Her mother-in-law lifted her eyebrows but did not object.

They sat at the dining table, the large Bible open, a single candle lighting the page. Elisabeth turned to the psalms and began reading aloud. The simple exercise both calmed and invigorated her, perhaps because the phrases themselves held such power. *Be thou my strong rock. Thou art my rock and my fortress.* The Nameless One had never given her such words to speak.

Janet joined them at eight for a quiet supper: steaming plates of chestnut soup flavored with bacon and rich with pigeon. A fitting meal for a cold, wet, miserable night. With each spoonful Elisabeth thought of Donald, wondering when he'd last enjoyed something hot and nourishing. *Come home, my love. Let me care for you.*

When the clock struck nine, Elisabeth bid the household good night and prepared for bed. Even after Mrs. Edgar skimmed the warming pan round her sheets, Elisabeth could not stop trembling from the cold. Then she remembered the Braemar plaid hidden in her clothes press. She slipped out of bed and pulled out the wool, as broad as her father's loom and four ells long. After unfolding the plaid over her bedcovers, she crawled beneath them both. 'Twas not the same as having Donald by her side, but at least she was finally warm. She blew out her candle, closed her eyes, and sought the refuge of sleep.

■ ■ ■ ■

Elisabeth barely heard the frantic pounding on the stair door. Was she dreaming? Or was the sound coming from another house a floor above or below them?

"Leddy Kerr!" Mrs. Edgar burst into her room. " 'Tis Mr. Baillie, come with news!"

Elisabeth flung off the bedcovers, then wrapped herself in her father's plaid and darted through two bedchambers. She found the household standing in the drawing room, their hair and clothes disheveled from sleep, and their landlord, Mr. Baillie, holding a lantern and breathing hard.

"I'm visiting each hoose," he said between gasps, "starting with Mr. Hill in the garret. And now I've come to yer door, certain ye'd want to be told." He drew himself up. "The Jacobites were victorious at Falkirk."

A moment of stunned silence. Then a burst of joy.

"God be praised!" Marjory sang out, clasping Elisabeth's hand, squeezing hard. "They are safe. My sons are safe."

My beloved husband. Elisabeth smiled through her tears. "And Angus MacPherson too."

Even Janet, who seldom wept, dabbed at her eyes.

Mrs. Edgar threw her apron over her head,

weeping, while Gibson patted her shoulder. "A' is weel, Mrs. Edgar. A' is weel."

"Ye're the only ones glad to hear the news," Mr. Baillie grumbled. "Though I dinna think meikle o' that Hangman Hawley."

"Is he deid?" Gibson looked hopeful.

"He's returned to Edinburgh this verra nicht," the landlord reported. "Messengers are shouting the news up and doon the High Street. Several hundred o' Hawley's men are deid and hundreds mair taken prisoner."

Several hundred. Elisabeth's joy was quickly tempered by the thought of so many lives sacrificed. "How long did the men fight?"

Mr. Baillie shook his head. "I dinna ken, Leddy Kerr. The weather was frichtsome. They say a vile rain, blowing hard from the south, hit the dragoons square in the face."

"Serves them richt," Gibson said under his breath.

Elisabeth remembered the autumn afternoon when they'd stood at the window and watched the young dragoons march by with their polished brass buttons. How many of them lay on the bloody ground at Falkirk, run through by a Highland claymore? She did not blame her Jacobite brothers for doing what they must. But hundreds of mothers, Scottish and English both, would soon learn their sons were no more.

Mr. Baillie pulled off his hat long enough to smooth back his gray hair, then reclaimed his lantern. "I've mair folk to visit who've not heard the report. After a', 'tis the middle o' the nicht." He lumbered out, leaving the Kerr household wide awake.

"This calls for a pot o' chocolate," Mrs. Edgar said, then hurried off to the kitchen, taking Gibson with her.

Janet was the first to speak. "Might the prince return to Edinburgh? And our husbands with him?"

"Take care you do not hope too much," Marjory cautioned her. "We'll know more when we see Mr. MacPherson."

"Aye," Elisabeth said, gazing at the black, rain-soaked windows. "We will."

After such an eventful night, the household slept later than usual the next morn. Mrs. Edgar did not rise until eight o' the clock, when the first gray light illumined her kitchen windows. Elisabeth slept until almost ten, the other women an hour later still.

A steady rain had rendered the city gray and lifeless. Elisabeth sat at table with a dish of porridge, noticing the frayed and thinning places in her black gown. Mrs. Edgar did what she could to keep it clean, using the juice of an orange for ink stains and removing candle wax with a hot coal wrapped in linen. But daily wear had taken its toll. Just two more months and she would quietly retire her mourning clothes, never forgetting the brother in whose honor she wore them.

When Mrs. Edgar brought her toast and orange marmalade, Elisabeth invited their housekeeper to join her. "Keep me company?"

"Och, Leddy Kerr." Mrs. Edgar glanced at the dowager's closed door. "It wouldna be richt."

"Please?" Elisabeth patted the empty place beside her. "I cannot possibly eat all this toast, and your mistress would not have us waste a single piece."

Mrs. Edgar perched on the edge of the chair, ready to leap up at the slightest footfall, though she managed to eat two pieces of toast nicely browned at her own hearth. Only a skim of butter, Elisabeth noticed, and none of her mother-in-law's favorite marmalade, made from expensive oranges imported from Seville. When Janet's door opened, Mrs. Edgar curtsied and ran for the kitchen, leaving behind a plate full of crumbs.

Not long after their late breakfast, it was time for a pot of tea, and then an hour later, dinner. The afternoon dragged on, the rain never stopping. Rob had promised to supply them with candles, but in the meantime they carried one from room to room rather than leave any unattended. Elisabeth rather liked the practicality of it, but she could tell Marjory was grieved at having such economy forced upon her.

Friday eve's jubilation was all but forgotten when the gray afternoon faded into evening. By five o' the clock the windows were black once more, and the rooms were filled with shadows. Elisabeth tried to embroider but could not hold her needle steady enough. She tried to read but could not concentrate.

When she offered her services in the kitchen, she was turned away by Mrs. Edgar, who gently reminded her of her place.

"D'ye see, Leddy Kerr?" The housekeeper held out her hands, red and chapped from years of labor. "Now hold oot yer hands." Reluctantly Elisabeth complied, embarrassed by the comparison. "Dinna say ye're sorry," Mrs. Edgar told her, "for this is the work the Lord has given me."

Elisabeth could do naught but praise the woman for her faithful efforts, though she was still left with empty hands and empty hours, waiting for the MacPhersons to appear. "A day or two," Rob had said. When Saturday drew to a close without a word, the Kerrs were left anxious and weary, too tired to stay awake and too nervous to sleep.

"If you'll not mind, I'll stay up and read a bit," Elisabeth told her mother-in-law.

"Suit yourself, my dear. Mrs. Edgar will see that you're warm enough."

Curled up on the sofa in the drawing room with her plaid wrapped round her and fresh coals added to the grate, Elisabeth felt like a tall child being tucked into bed. "Ye've only to call oot, Leddy Kerr, and I'll hear ye weel enough from the kitchen."

Bidding her good night, Elisabeth held *The Seasons* in one hand and propped her head in the other as she began to read about Summer, the child of the sun. Engaged at first, she found by the fourth page that her attention was waning and the pull of sleep was harder to resist. When the book slipped from her hand, she stirred just slightly, then drifted back to sleep, the heat from the coals warming her face.

This time Elisabeth was the first to hear someone knocking at their door.

Three sharp raps, then two.

She almost threw her plaid across the hot coals, so quickly did she rise. *They're here!* She hastened to the door, not caring that her hair was mussed and her dress wrinkled. Rob would not mind. Nor would his dear father.

Her hands shook as she undid the bolt, then yanked the door open, holding her breath until she saw him, until she was sure. "Angus!"

Father and son stood on the landing, Angus slumped against Rob's shoulder, both of them bleary eyed and soaked from the rain.

"Please, come inside." Elisabeth pulled them into the house, surprised at how slowly Angus was moving. He looked older, the lines in his face carved with the sharp blade of hunger. When a startled Mrs. Edgar popped her head round the kitchen door, Elisabeth ordered claret and meat for the men, then led them to the nearest comfortable chairs, sending Gibson off to hang up their wet coats and fetch more coal.

Only when the MacPhersons were seated did Elisabeth notice how unkempt Angus was: his shirt filthy, his kilted plaid matted with blood, as if he'd not paused once on his long journey home. "Surely you've not come straight from the field at Falkirk?"

Angus hung his head. "I had to, Bess."

She pulled her chair closer, her heart thudding in her chest. "Angus, what has happened?"

He looked up, his red-rimmed eyes filled with tears. "I have verra bad news."

Elisabeth stared at him. *He cannot mean. He cannot . . .*

"Nae . . ." The word came out on a sob. "Please . . ."

Rob reached for her hand, but she leaped up, desperate to escape the truth she saw in their eyes. "Not . . . my husband . . ."

Angus stood. "I am sorry, Leddy Kerr."

"Nae!" she cried and sank to the floor.

SIXTY-FOUR

O weep, O weep, ye Scottish dames!
Weep till ye blind a mither's e'e!
ALLAN CUNNINGHAM

Marjory sat up in bed, her heart in her throat. An anguished cry echoed through the house. *Elisabeth?* Aye, and male voices too.

Marjory tossed aside the bedcovers, trying not to imagine the worst. She heard her daughter-in-law weeping, the mournful sound bringing tears to her own eyes. *Why, Elisabeth? Why are you crying?*

Yanking a robe over her shoulders, Marjory ran barefoot across the carpet, praying, praying. When she flung open the drawing room door, she found her daughter-in-law collapsed on the floor.

"Lady Elisabeth!" Marjory knelt beside her at once, barely noticing Rob MacPherson and his father, who stood back to make room for her. "My dear girl, what is it?"

Elisabeth looked up. Her face, contorted

with pain, was almost unrecognizable. "Lord Kerr . . ."

A jolt went through Marjory. *Nae.* She pressed her hands tightly to her mouth. *Not Donald. Not my son.*

Rob crouched down next to her. "My faither and I are verra sorry —"

"Nae!" Marjory turned away from him, feeling faint. " 'Tis not possible . . ."

Rob caught her at once. "Let me help ye, mem." He stood, lifting her up with him.

A moment later Marjory was on the upholstered sofa, not certain how she got there. "Elisabeth," she moaned, stretching out her hand. Rob brought her daughter-in-law to her side. They sat leaning against each other, hands tightly clasped, while Mrs. Edgar spread the abandoned plaid across their legs, quietly weeping as she tucked the wool in place.

"Mrs. Edgar," Rob asked, "will ye bring Mrs. Kerr to us as weel?"

A moment later Janet entered the room, wrapped in a gray shawl, a wary expression on her face. Gibson stood nearby, his eyes dry but his face ashen.

"Tell us," Marjory pleaded. "Tell us . . . what happened." She did not want to know, but she had to know. *Oh, my Donald. Oh, my son.*

The men were seated before her, elbows on

knees, expressions grim. Angus spoke first, his voice ragged. "I dinna ken whaur to begin . . ."

"Describe the scene," Rob urged him, "just as ye did for me."

Angus stared into the fire as he spoke. " 'Twas late in the afternoon beneath a murky sky. The prince's army held the high ground on Falkirk Muir. Whan our enemy charged o'er the crest, *heiven* unleashed a tempest, with driving rain and a cauld wind. We dragged the Englishmen aff their mounts by their coattails, then stabbed them with oor dirks."

Marjory felt Elisabeth shudder.

Rob saw it as well. "Mind the leddies," he told his father.

"Aye, aye." Angus sighed, shaking his head. " 'Twas anither Gladsmuir. The fury o' the Hieland clans was mair than the English could bear, on horse or on foot. Their gunpowder was wet, their licht was gone, and their courage was flagging. But one wing o' the English army, led by Hawley's aide-de-camp, held their ground and kept firing."

Angus paused and looked up, fixing his gaze on Elisabeth. "Lord Kerr and his brother rode into the fray, swords drawn. They fought like Hielanders. Ye woulda been sae proud." His voice faltered as tears filled his eyes. "But then young Andrew lost his seat . . ."

Janet gasped. "My husband?"

"Aye. Whan he started to fall, Lord Donald reached for him. A dragoon with a bayonet . . ." Angus hung his head. "Och, the Englishman was sae close he stabbed them both."

Marjory's mouth went slack. *Not Andrew too. Not both my sons.*

"Angus . . ." Elisabeth's voice was barely above a whisper. "You do not mean Lord Donald and his brother were *both* killed?"

He looked at Janet before he spoke. "I'm afraid I do, leddies. We lost but forty o' the prince's men at Falkirk. Two o' the best were yers."

Janet gave a strangled cry, then crumpled in her chair.

Marjory stared at Angus blankly. "I cannot . . . You must be . . . mistaken . . ."

The sorrow in his face was answer enough. "We took them to the parish kirk, thinking to tend their wounds. But they were gone, mem. We buried them in the kirkyard, along with Robert Munro, Colonel Whitney, and two Stewarts of Appin."

The Highland names meant nothing to Marjory. Only two names mattered. *Donald. Andrew.*

Numb, she watched Angus draw a small bundle from inside his shirt. He unfolded the soiled cloth, then held up two pairs of gloves. "I thocht these might be a comfort to ye."

575

He laid the lambskin gloves in her lap. "Yer sons will have nae need o' them in heiven."

Marjory stared at the gloves for a moment, then bent forward, trying to contain her anguish. No words came, only a deep groaning. *My sons. My sons.* Pain cut through to the marrow of her bones.

Her prayers had not saved them. Her gold had not spared them.

The Englishman stabbed them both.

Marjory covered her head with her arms, rocking back and forth, her heart so ravaged she could not reason, nor could she speak. Tears streamed from her eyes. *Take me too. Take me too.*

Voices ebbed and flowed round her. None of the words made sense. Any notion of time or place was gone. Only her grief was real and inescapable.

"Help me," she moaned. But no one could. No one could help her. She alone was to blame. She should never have let them go.

With her eyes squeezed shut, she pictured her sons as she had last seen them in the forecourt of the palace. Shoulders squared, heads held high. Smiling down at her.

God be with you, Mother.

"Nae," she whimpered. *He is not with me, Donald. He is not.*

Many minutes passed before Marjory noticed Elisabeth's hand resting on her back, a gentle, soothing touch. Then she opened her eyes and saw Mrs. Edgar laying a damp cloth across Janet's brow, murmuring condolences.

I should be comforting them. That was the thought that broke through her pain.

Marjory made herself sit up, ignoring her throbbing head and her churning stomach. She shifted in her seat to face Elisabeth, shocked at what she found.

Elisabeth's skin was as pale as milk, and her cheeks were wet with tears. But her vacant eyes were what truly frightened Marjory, as if her daughter-in-law had faced death and could not look away.

"This is my fault," Elisabeth whispered.

"Nae . . ." Marjory's voice broke. " 'Tis mine."

Sixty-Five

The day breaks not,
it is my heart.

JOHN DONNE

Elisabeth slowly lifted the window sash. Sometime after midnight the rain had moved out to sea, leaving the morning sky clear and cold.

"My sweet Donald," she whispered, her breath visible in the frosty air. She listened in vain for his tender response. *My bonny Bess.*

A fresh spate of tears spilled down her cheeks. How could he be lost to her forever? The only husband she'd ever known, the only man she'd ever loved? Such a thing was not possible. He was too young to die. Too handsome, too brave, just as Simon was.

Elisabeth pressed her forehead against the glass, unsteady on her feet, utterly exhausted. She'd slept alone for some months, but never had her bed felt so empty as it had last night. Instead of sleeping, she'd soaked her pillow by the hour, hoping her sorrow and guilt might ease. They had not.

Simon had chosen to fight for the prince. But Donald had fought for her. Had he not said as much? *I thought 'twould please you.* Because she was a Highlander. Because she was a Jacobite. Because she'd praised her bonny prince.

Forgive me, Donald. Please, please, forgive me.

Too late for apologies now.

Chilled by the morning air, she closed the sash and moved toward the washstand, reaching for a towel to dry her tears. Her cheeks felt chapped and raw, and the skin round her eyes, bruised and swollen. She splashed her face with care, then bathed and dressed. Barely glancing in the looking glass, she gathered her hair in a simple knot. Strange to go through her daily routine as if life were unchanged and this Sabbath day were like any other.

Carrying her lone candle into the drawing room, she avoided the chair where she'd heard the news and the place on the floor where she'd collapsed in despair. Those first terrible minutes would be etched in her mind forever. Poor Angus had left their house barely able to stand.

Elisabeth found her seat at the vacant table laden with a cold Sabbath breakfast. Only the tea was hot.

Mrs. Edgar quietly entered the room, coming to fill Elisabeth's cup. "Ye've not slept," the housekeeper said gently.

Elisabeth shook her head, wondering if she might find the energy to speak again. Or eat. Or walk about the room. She wanted only to shutter the windows and hide beneath her bedcovers and weep until she could weep no more.

"The ithers havena slept either," Mrs. Edgar told her. "And wha can blame ye? I'm sorry as can be, milady. Sorry as can be."

Elisabeth nodded, staring at her tea, waiting for the strength to pick up the cup.

When Janet and Marjory joined her at table, they, too, looked unkempt and ill rested. They nodded at one another, then broke their fast in silence. The food tasted like sand, but Elisabeth made herself eat a bite of everything. She would need her strength. They all would.

When her mother-in-law wasn't looking, Elisabeth studied Marjory's downcast expression. They had comforted each other well into the night. Would they do so again this day?

You, Lady Kerr, have corrupted both my sons.

So Marjory had said on the day Donald and Andrew enlisted. Elisabeth had never forgotten the dowager's sharp gaze and sharper words. Marjory had made no such charge last evening. Had, in fact, been more tenderhearted than Elisabeth had ever seen her. But she feared the day when Marjory's grief gave way to anger and the slender tie between them was severed for good.

Elisabeth bowed her head and prayed in silence. Not to the Nameless One but to the One whose name was Holy. *Give me hope. Please, give me hope.*

Her bannock untouched, her tea cold, Marjory finally broke the silence. "We'll not be expected at the Tron Kirk this morn."

Elisabeth looked up. *Not expected? Or not welcome?* When her mother-in-law did not elaborate, Elisabeth made a tentative suggestion. "Perhaps we could read from the Scriptures after breakfast?"

Marjory sighed. "Very well."

Half an hour later the breakfast dishes were cleared and the thick Bible lay open on the table between them. Janet had excused herself, murmuring of a headache. Elisabeth did not fault her sister-in-law. Her own brow was tight with pain.

"Shall I read?" Elisabeth smoothed her hands across the pages, hoping she had chosen a proper psalm for the morning. "In the Kirk, they pray before reading. Might you do so?"

Her mother-in-law said nothing, only bowed her head. Elisabeth did the same and waited.

A long silence passed, then Marjory spoke, her voice weak and unsteady. "Almighty God,

581

bless the reading of thy Word." She paused as if she might have more to add, then abruptly said, "Amen."

They lifted their heads in unison. Marjory sat, stiff and silent, as Elisabeth began to read.

"Unto thee, O LORD, do I lift up my soul." She nodded at the familiar picture the words drew, thinking of altars built on hillsides in the Highland fastness. But how could a soul be placed on an altar?

She pressed on. "O my God, I trust in thee." *Trust.* That was indeed a sacrifice. To trust in a God she could not see. To trust, though her heart was shattered. She read aloud the next line. "Let me not be ashamed, let not mine enemies triumph over me."

Marjory spoke up, her chin trembling. "But we *have* been shamed. And our enemy has triumphed."

Elisabeth was at a loss how to respond. Marjory's complaint rang so true. She hoped some answer would follow. "Yea, let none that wait on thee be ashamed . . ." Elisabeth paused. "I am not certain what this means, except we're to wait on the Almighty. Perhaps he banishes our shame?"

When Marjory nodded dully, Elisabeth did not press her but moved on, hoping she'd not chosen the passage amiss. She read through the next few verses until she reached one that almost leaped from the page. "Turn thee unto me, and have mercy upon me; for I am desolate and afflicted."

She lightly touched the words, stunned to find her feelings so clearly expressed. Desolate, afflicted, aye, and in great need of mercy. "But I thought we turned to God," she said softly. "Does he also turn and look upon us?"

When she lifted her gaze, Elisabeth found Marjory had fresh tears in her eyes. "He looked upon me once," her mother-in-law admitted. "Aye, he did." She ducked her head but not before her features crumpled and a faint sob escaped from her lips.

Elisabeth waited for a moment, then slipped a clean handkerchief into Marjory's open hand. "This day will be the hardest," she said, her throat tightening. "Surely the morrow will be better."

SIXTY-SIX

Why wilt thou add to all the griefs I suffer?
                                    JOSEPH ADDISON

Monday, alas, was harder still.

The weather was dry, yet bitterly cold, with no sun to lift their spirits. Another restless night with little sleep set the household on edge. Their emotions were brittle, and their conversation bore a note of impatience.

Elisabeth reminded herself of the phrases she'd read yesterday morning — *wait on thee, trust in thee* — and tried not to make things worse.

Janet was especially pernickitie. "What am I to do for a mourning gown?" She glared at the two dresses borrowed from Marjory's clothes press some time ago, neither of them black. "I'll not have our visitors thinking less of me."

"We cannot afford new gowns," Marjory said. "My dark gray one will suit you for the moment." She sent Mrs. Edgar to fetch it, then turned to study her reflection in Janet's looking glass. "I had hoped never to wear this again."

Elisabeth could not help noticing the black gown smelled of wormwood and fit too snugly in some places, though it was in all ways proper, unadorned and somber.

When Mrs. Edgar appeared with the gray gown, Marjory and Elisabeth repaired to the drawing room so Janet might dress. It was only nine o' the clock. No callers would knock on their door before eleven. Caddies or menservants might deliver notes of sympathy at any hour, though none had arrived yet.

Marjory was too agitated to sit, pacing the room instead, her taffeta skirts rustling as she walked. "My sons belong with their father in Greyfriars Kirkyard, not miles away in Falkirk."

Elisabeth nodded. Had she not felt the same when Simon was buried in a farmer's field? "Angus would've brought them home to us if he could have," she said gently.

She would never tell Marjory what Rob had confided to her. Other than the handful of officers buried in the kirkyard with Donald and Andrew, the dead from both armies were buried by the townsfolk in a common trench dug into the hill where the men fell. Elisabeth would silently thank Angus every day of her life for seeing Donald laid to rest in hallowed ground.

When Janet joined them in the drawing room, her displeasure with the dowager's gray gown was evident. She yanked at the tight sleeves and moaned about the unflattering style until Elisabeth offered a solution.

"I will gladly sew a mourning gown for you if we can afford the fabric." Elisabeth looked to Marjory for her consent and was surprised when it was quickly offered.

"I can spare one guinea," Marjory said. Janet did not roll her eyes, but Elisabeth sensed her disapproval. She would let her work speak for her and hope Janet might soften toward her in the process.

The hour for callers approached. Their house was in good order, the claret was ready to pour, and Mrs. Edgar had a seedcake, fresh from the oven, cooling on the table. When eleven chimes rang out from the tall case clock, the women sat up straighter in their circle of chairs by the fire and waited for their friends and neighbors to pay their respects to the dead.

No one came.

Not in the first hour nor in the second. Not while the women ate a hasty dinner at one o' the clock nor in the afternoon. No notes were delivered, no messages received at the door. No one in Edinburgh, it seemed, mourned the loss of two young men guilty of treason.

"We are cursed," Marjory moaned when the last light of day faded from the windows.

The uncut seedcake, the pristine wine glasses, and the empty chairs stood witness to her charge.

Elisabeth stayed by Marjory's side, providing sips of claret and fresh handkerchiefs, until her tears subsided and a new kind of grief settled in.

Anguish gave way to a lifeless melancholy as Marjory slumped in her chair, absently fingering the plain trim on her sleeve. " 'Tis no use," her mother-in-law said, her words devoid of emotion. "We've no friends left."

"Aye, we do," Elisabeth reminded her. "The MacPhersons have been more than friends to us."

"Tradesmen," Marjory said dismissively, though Elisabeth saw a hint of regret in her eyes. "It must be said, they did tell us about . . . That is, we might not have known for days, even weeks . . ." She sighed heavily. "I mean only that I miss my old friends, Lady Woodhall and Lady Falconer especially."

No mention of Lady Ruthven, Elisabeth noticed.

Marjory dabbed her eyes. "This eve you'll want to write your mothers."

"Aye, so I shall," Elisabeth said, disheartened at the prospect. Though she'd written her mother several times, Elisabeth had not received a letter from home since before her mother's wedding. The letter Simon had brought to her was the last. As to her own letters, Rob had watched her mother tear one in two and toss it into the fire. Perhaps she did that with all of them.

"The Post Office cannot object to delivering our correspondence now," Marjory said, her tone petulant. "Our sad reports are of no use to King George."

A light tapping at the stair door instantly transformed Marjory. She sat up, dried her tears, and in all ways resumed the role of Dowager Lady Kerr as she looked toward the entrance hall, chin held high, anticipating their first visitor at last.

"Mrs. Effie Sinclair," Gibson announced.

Elisabeth heard the relief in his voice and saw it on Mrs. Edgar's face as the housekeeper stood by the table, ready to be of service. Janet followed their mother-in-law's example — head up, shoulders back, face composed — as Elisabeth welcomed their faithful friend. "We are so grateful you are here."

"Had it not been for my students," she assured them, "I would have come sooner." Effie's expression was so tender that Elisabeth fought back tears yet again. "May the Almighty comfort you in your affliction."

Mrs. Edgar quietly served her a slice of seedcake while Effie spoke to each woman in turn, offering a specific word of encouragement. "It has been many years since Mr. Sinclair passed away, but I remember the heartache well," she finally said, then took Elisabeth's hand in hers. "Lady Kerr, you and Mrs. Kerr will honor your husbands best by remaining widows and caring for your mother-in-law. She is your family now."

Elisabeth nodded, not knowing what to say. She'd been too racked with pain to consider the future. Was that what Donald would expect of her? That she care for his mother the rest of her days? Or should she return to Castleton, to her own mother, and see if some reconciliation might be made? Where did a daughter's loyalty belong?

Elisabeth glanced at Janet. Her eyes gave away nothing, but the set of her jaw suggested her feelings on the subject.

Mrs. Sinclair remained as long as propriety allowed, then stood to take her leave. "You will be in my prayers," she said in parting, squeezing each hand.

Elisabeth accompanied her to the door, thanking her for coming. "You are the only caller we've had," she admitted.

Mrs. Sinclair looked up at her in dismay. "Can this be true?"

"I'm afraid so. Had Lord Kerr and his brother fallen in the defense of King George, the mourners might have filled the house and trailed down the stair. Instead, our men bravely died for our prince."

"They did so willingly," Effie reminded her, "and most honorably." She patted her hand.

"I'll call again if I may."

"Aye, please come." Elisabeth gazed down at the tiny woman who'd been like a mother to her when she'd first arrived in Edinburgh, just as Angus had ably filled the shoes of her father. "And do pray for us."

"So I shall." Effie's small eyes glistened. "Unless I am mistaken, you are seeking the Almighty with more . . . confidence, aye?"

"I am." Elisabeth looked down. After a lifetime of worshiping the Nameless One in secret, she was unaccustomed to discussing matters of faith.

" 'Tis not a thing that can be taught, Lady Kerr, though I tried my best when you were under my tutelage." Effie smiled, her cheeks like round red apples. "He preserveth the faithful. And I believe you are among them." She donned her dark blue wool cape and was gone, leaving Elisabeth standing at the door.

Sixty-Seven

The mother heart within me
Is almost starved for heaven.
MARGARET ELIZABETH SANGSTER

"Why can I not visit Lord John's grave?" Marjory looked at Janet, seated across from her at breakfast. " 'Tis perfectly acceptable for a grieving widow, and I would not be out in society."

Marjory waited for her objections, certain they would come.

"To begin with, the weather is ghastly," Janet replied matter-of-factly. With Andrew gone, her older daughter-in-law had cast aside any pretense of being charming. "Winter has returned, madam, dressed in ice and snow and bitterly cold winds. And it is a long walk to Greyfriars Kirkyard."

"Or a sixpence ride in a sedan chair," Marjory reminded her stiffly, though her words had no bite. Janet knew very well she could not afford such a luxury. And it *was* a bit of a walk down Peeble's Wynd to the Cowgate.

Marjory had traveled there on foot only once. And on a fair spring afternoon, not a frozen Wednesday in January.

But she wanted to go, very much *needed* to go. To remind herself that she once had a husband, that she once was loved, that her life had some purpose, some greater meaning. She was neither wife nor mother now and would never be a grandmother. What was a mother-in-law without sons? Useless. Or worse, a burden.

Marjory shuddered at the realization.

"You see?" Janet said. "You're chilled even in the house." She punctuated her words by brandishing a well-buttered triangle of toast. "Furthermore, you cannot venture anywhere near the Grassmarket. That horrible General Hawley is keeping his hangman busy, punishing his troops who showed cowardice at Falkirk or tried to desert. Nae, madam." Janet bit the corner of her toast with her small, sharp teeth and took her time chewing and swallowing. "Your place is here, safe within our walls."

Marjory did not give Janet the satisfaction of seeing her quit the table in a pique. But once Janet finished her breakfast, Marjory abandoned her cold tea, seeking Elisabeth's company. At least her younger daughter-in-law respected her.

She found Elisabeth in her bedchamber with yards of black fabric unrolled across the carpet: Janet's mourning gown in progress. Marjory eyed the muslin pattern pinned to a dress form borrowed from the MacPhersons and noted the chalk lines drawn on the silk at her feet. "Already hard at work, I see."

Elisabeth held up her scissors. "I'll need Gibson to sharpen the blades on Donald's whetstone before I dare take them to this silk." Her cheeks, so pale of late, grew slightly pink. "I confess I tried to stab a dragoon with a pair of scissors at Queensberry House."

"Well done," Marjory said. "And I'm grateful you assisted the surgeons at the infirmary. Had my sons been given such care . . ." She closed her eyes as a wave of grief washed over her.

After a moment she felt Elisabeth's cool fingers on hers. "Angus did everything he could for them."

"That is my only consolation." Marjory lifted her head. Her daughter-in-law's eyes mirrored her own sorrow; her bonny face hid nothing. "You loved my son very much."

"Aye." Elisabeth's voice fell to a whisper. "I still do."

Marjory thought of their tender parting on the last day of October. And her son's heart-felt request: *May I count on you to look after Elisabeth?* And the look on Donald's face when Elisabeth stood on tiptoe to kiss him good-bye. It seemed only right to assure her. "My son loved you as well."

593

Elisabeth's eyes grew glassy. "I hope 'tis true."

"I feel certain you are the only woman he ever loved," Marjory continued, "though I imagine many loved *him*. Such a handsome man, our Donald."

Her daughter-in-law merely nodded.

Thinking it best to change the subject, Marjory said, "Will you show me your plans for Janet's gown?"

They spent a pleasant half hour together with Elisabeth describing in detail the various pleats and folds, buttons and tabs she intended to use. "No lace," she hastened to add, "for I know 'tis costly. But the wee ruffle round the neckline will serve, and the pin tucks on the bodice may provide a bit of interest."

Until now Marjory had paid scant attention to Elisabeth's sewing skills. She was rightly impressed. "I will be eager to see the finished gown and so will your sister-in-law." Though she would never confess it, Marjory wished she'd given Janet her old mourning gown so this new creation might be hers. An entirely selfish thought, of course. But honest.

Elisabeth was showing Marjory how her present gown might be altered for a better fit when Mrs. Edgar came looking for them.

"Ye've a visitor, leddies. Mr. MacPherson."

Marjory glanced at her mantel, still looking

for the clock she would never see again. By now it was sitting above a cozy hearth in Lancashire or Yorkshire, marking the hours for some infernal Englishwoman.

Rob was waiting for them in the drawing room, his hat and greatcoat removed, a glass of claret and a plate of seedcake on a small table by the fire. "Leddies," he said with a proper bow, "I'm here to offer my sympathy. And to see how ye're faring."

"We're glad you've come." Elisabeth spoke for all of them since Janet had not bothered to make an appearance. "Kindly sit with us."

"I wanted to call at the first hour on Monday," he explained, "but waited 'til today, thinking ye might not want a tailor walking through the door with a' yer gentry friends here."

"Very thoughtful of you," Marjory told him, "though you need not have worried. Had you visited us on Monday morn, you'd have been the only one."

His dark countenance took on a ruddy tint. "Ye mean to tell me Edinburgh's fine lords and leddies didna see fit to walk up yer stair? Whan ye've lost two guid men in the prime o' their young lives?" Rob sat back, fists on his knees, a marked scowl on his face. "What sort o' freens are those?"

"No friends at all," Elisabeth admitted.

Marjory could hardly argue. When Lady Falconer closed the door on her, the rest of society quickly followed suit. Rather than dwell on that depressing fact, Marjory broached another topic. "Your father is not with you. I trust he is well?"

Rob exhaled. "He is not, mem. Not weel at a'. I've had the apothecary come twice this week. Mr. Mercer says 'tis his heart. I thocht my faither had the heart o' ten men, but —"

"Foxglove tea," Marjory said at once, not wanting to hear the details lest they awaken too many memories. "Lord John drank a cup nightly to ease his chest pains."

"I thank ye, mem. We'll try it this verra nicht." Rob shifted in his chair. "Enough of oor woes, for 'tis ye I'm meant to comfort." He was looking at Elisabeth now. Clearly the offer of sympathy was meant for her.

"We have each other," Elisabeth answered him, inclining her head toward Marjory, "and so we do not suffer alone."

"I am glad to hear it, Leddy Kerr."

Marjory saw the yearning in his eyes and the way he leaned toward her, his hands open. *If I were not here, he would take her in his arms.* Elisabeth would not allow it, of course. But his longing was as palpable as the scent of nutmeg wafting from Mrs. Edgar's kitchen.

Would Elisabeth follow Effie Sinclair's advice? Remain a widow and stay by her side? At four-and-twenty, Elisabeth was young enough to marry again and bear children.

Should she be forced to care for a woman twice her age with no prospects, no hope? Marjory could never ask Elisabeth or Janet to make such a sacrifice. But if she did not, who would care for her as she grew older, in the same way Rob watched over Angus?

She had no husband or sons, no parents or siblings, and no friends. No one in the world cared whether she lived or died.

No one.

Marjory abruptly stood, prompting Rob to his feet.

"Mem?" he asked.

"You are welcome to stay, Mr. MacPherson. But I . . . forgive me." Marjory fled the room for her quiet bedchamber to mourn in private. And to pray.

Hands trembling, she closed the door behind her and locked it, then the door to Elisabeth's room too. Marjory hastened to her bedside and sank to her knees, folding her hands as a child might.

"Please . . ." One word and her heart broke open. "Please . . . help me." She pressed her forehead against her hands, afraid to ask for what she needed, afraid the Almighty no longer cared. "I knew you once," she whispered. "Might I turn to you again?"

Desperate, she clung to the words she'd learned long ago. "Look upon mine affliction and my pain . . ." She drew a ragged breath. "And forgive all my sins." *Too many, too many.*

"My husband," she moaned, "my precious John. And my sons, my dear sons. All dead because of me. If I'd learned to be content at Tweedsford. If I'd honored my husband's wishes. If I'd protected our children . . ."

Weary and spent, she crawled onto her bed, crushing her gown, dislodging the pins from her hair. "Forgive me," she pleaded. How could that be sufficient? "O God, in the multitude of thy mercy hear me. Please, please, hear me."

SIXTY-EIGHT

Patience is sorrow's salve.
                    CHARLES CHURCHILL

Change was coming. Elisabeth felt it in her
bones. Prince Charlie and his army had
retreated farther north into the Highlands,
and Marjory's guineas were reduced to shillings and pennies. Only winter remained,
bleak and unending. Though the days were a
bit longer in February, the temperature
struggled to get above freezing.

Elisabeth gazed down at the icy puddles
scattered across the High Street. She was
determined to brave the cold and visit Angus
MacPherson now that his weak heart bound
him withindoors. If Marjory did not object,
Elisabeth would ask Gibson to escort her to
the Luckenbooths that very morning.

She had stepped out of doors only twice
since Donald's death. Once to visit Mr.
Mercer's shop across the High Street when
Gibson's troublesome cough made a sudden
reappearance, and once to the Post Office to

send a letter to her mother. Both were acceptable errands for a widow. The dragoons patrolling the street were the greater worry. General Hawley and the Duke of Cumberland had both come and gone from Edinburgh, heading north in pursuit of Prince Charlie and his army. But while the gallows still stood in the Grassmarket, the town's Jacobites laid very low indeed.

She donned her clothing, then styled her hair as if she'd never had a lady's maid to slip gowns over her head or lace her stays. Mrs. Edgar still dressed Marjory each morning, and Janet as well, but Elisabeth thought to spare their housekeeper a few duties at least. A brief pause at her mirror and she was off to seek her mother-in-law's blessing.

She found her sitting by a window, trying to thread a needle, nearly in tears from the effort. "May I help?" Elisabeth made quick work of it, then kept the needle in hand. "If it's your button that needs sewing, Lady Marjory, I'll gladly do so."

Marjory handed over the green gown and its matching silk button with a sigh. "I'd hoped to master *one* simple task. Shouldn't a woman know how to repair her own clothing?"

Elisabeth was thrown off balance, hearing the discouragement in her mother-in-law's voice. If the Dowager Lady Kerr of Selkirk felt obliged to do her own sewing, their financial position was even worse than she'd realized.

"Let me show you." Elisabeth sat beside her and pretended Marjory was one of Mrs. Sinclair's students, teaching her step by step. Her mother-in-law was a quick study and tied the finishing knot herself. "You see?" Elisabeth said proudly. "You'll not be daunted by a button again."

" 'Tis my mother's fault," Marjory said, examining her work. "Lady Nesbitt made it clear that a gentlewoman might embroider, but she was never to do common sewing. You've convinced me otherwise."

Elisabeth tried not to let her amazement show. When she asked if she might visit Angus, Marjory surprised her a second time by agreeing at once, though her mother-in-law gave her a list of precautions.

"Cover your face with the hood of your cape, and stay close by Gibson's side. You'll need a ready answer if a dragoon stops you. Tell him you are bound for James Stirling's in the Luckenbooths to fetch a quarter pound of tea."

"Shall I carry two shillings to prove it?"

Marjory eyed her. "You *are* a canny girl." She pulled two silver coins from her hanging pocket and lent them to Elisabeth. "On your way, then."

Elisabeth followed Gibson down the turnpike stair, her teeth chattering. She'd sent ahead a caddie with a note so Rob would expect her. How odd it felt to step into the square after looking down on it for so many weeks! She followed Marjory's advice to the letter and withdrew inside the folds of her hood, resisting the urge to study every passerby, wondering if they were friend or foe.

They started up the High Street, facing into the icy wind blowing down from Castle Hill. Elisabeth pretended not to notice the lanes they passed along the way: Geddes Close, home to Jane Montgomerie, and Warriston's Close, where Susan McGill lodged. Did they know of Donald's death? The thought of other women mourning the loss of her husband made her ill. Nae, it made her angry. How dare they grieve her beloved Donald! She reached for Marjory's words like a healing balm. *You are the only woman he ever loved.*

"Almost there, Leddy Kerr." Gibson kept a firm grip on her hand, circled round his elbow. They quickened their steps past the mercat cross, where the latest news regarding the unnatural rebellion in the Highlands was being proclaimed.

Elisabeth still longed to see the Stuarts restored to the British throne. But the farther the prince and his men withdrew from the London road, the less likely victory seemed. The glorious cause had already cost far too much.

When they reached the door to Angus's tailoring shop, her heart sank. The glass window was newly repaired, but peering inside, she could see the damage wrought by the dragoons' November visit. The long looking glass was gone, along with Angus's sewing cabinet, and the shelves of fabric seemed vastly depleted.

Here came Rob, answering their knock. "Leddy Kerr," he said, his pleasure at seeing her unabashed. "Gibson, if ye'll not mind, I'll see the leddy hame. I'm sure ye're needed at Milne Square."

His words were not a dismissal, though Gibson's lowered brow suggested otherwise. "Are ye certain, Leddy Kerr? I'll not mind to stay, however lang ye'll be."

Rob was right. Gibson's time would be better spent at home. And her friend could easily walk her down the hill that afternoon. "I'll be home by four," she told Gibson, sending him gently on his way. " 'Til then, I'm well cared for here."

The manservant took his leave, the bell tinkling as the door shut behind him.

"Ye'll be warm enough by the fire," Rob promised, guiding her through to their lodgings behind the shop. "My faither is eager to visit with ye, Bess. 'Twill do him some guid, I've nae doubt."

Their single room was very tidy, especially for two men. The small beds were covered in beautifully woven plaids, the oak furnishings were simple in design yet solidly built — rather like the MacPhersons themselves — and the tallow candles on the hearth and table gave the room a warm glow.

The man seated by the fire was the one she'd come to see. To her dismay he'd aged ten years since they last spoke. "Angus!" she cried softly, hurrying to his side. His skin had a gray pallor, and his hair was now more silver than black.

Angus came to life at her greeting. "Och, my bonny Bess!" He kissed her hand, then hung on tight. "Ye've come to see yer auld freen."

"Not so very old," she chided him. "And I must apologize —"

"Nae, ye must not," he said gruffly. "Ye've been mourning yer husband, and sae ye should. How's yer mither-in-law? This canna be easy for her."

Elisabeth perched on a three-legged stool beside his chair and filled his ear with all the news from Milne Square even as she took careful note of the changes his illness had wrought over the last month. Angus was definitely weaker. His movements were slower and his breathing more strained. She was pleased to find his sense of humor had not diminished. And when Rob served them a dinner of hearty Scotch broth and fresh bannocks, Angus's appetite was as healthy as ever.

"Ye must dine with us mair often," Rob told her at table. "I've not seen my faither eat a second plate o' broth in some time."

Angus waved his horn spoon at Rob. "Ye'll not be speaking o' me as if I wasna present," he scolded his son good-naturedly. "But the lad is richt. Having ye here has done my puir heart guid."

"Then I shall come every week," she promised.

Rob eyed her with a steady gaze. "I hope ye will, Bess."

"Come sit by the fire," Angus said, "and I'll tell ye what I ken o' the prince." His scowl was prodigious. "Ye're thinking an auld man locked in his lodgings wouldna ken onie news from afar, aye? Weel, I have my ways, lass, and monie a Jacobite kens whaur I live."

Rob's smile greatly altered his face, softening his hard features and smoothing his brow. "Aye, they come knocking at a' hours o' the day and nicht, bearing tales from the north." He brought a chair from their table. "Dinna sit on the *creepie,* lass. Ye'll be mair comfortable on this."

She took the offered seat, then inched closer to the fire, wishing she'd chosen warmer stockings and stouter shoes.

"His Royal Highness split the army in two at Crieff," Angus told her. "Last I heard, the prince was at Dalwhinnie, but that was three days syne."

Elisabeth asked him gently, "Is there hope yet for the cause?"

He grabbed her hands and squeezed them hard, pressing her rings into her fingers. "Och, lass! There's aye hope."

SIXTY-NINE

I will indulge my sorrow, and give way
To all the pangs and fury of despair.
JOSEPH ADDISON

Still warm from their afternoon spent by the fire, Elisabeth and Rob started downhill toward Milne Square. Though the bitter wind kept most folk withindoors, the plainstanes were free of ice and snow, and the sky hinted at neither.

"Will ye come ilka week, like ye said?" Rob asked.

"I'll do my best." She could see that was not good enough. "Truly, I will, Rob. If my mother-in-law will not mind —"

"Why should she mind?" he grumbled. "Ye've nae need to answer to the leddy for yer time."

"But I do," Elisabeth told him. "I owe her a great deal. She accepted me into her family —"

"Accepted?" Rob moved in front of her, halting their progress. "D'ye hear yerself,

607

Bess? Making excuses for a woman wha calls herself a leddy whan 'tis neither birth nor siller that makes a person guid." Elisabeth started to object, but he pressed his point. "Leddy Kerr hasna treated ye as weel as ye deserve. Nor did her son." His dark countenance said the rest.

"Rob, I'll not have you speak ill of my husband. Or my family."

His tone changed at once. "I'm sorry, Bess. I had nae richt."

She sighed, regretting she'd spoken so directly. "I know you mean only to protect me, Rob."

"Aye, aye," he was quick to say, turning so she might take his arm once more. "That was a' I meant to do." He drew her close as they started walking again. " 'Tis my nature to watch o'er folk I care about."

She merely nodded rather than pursue the subject. She knew Rob cared for her a great deal more than he should.

They were nearing Writer's Court when a stranger called out, "Leddy Kerr?"

They turned toward the door of a merchant who was beckoning them into his shop. "Milady, might I have a wee bit o' yer time?"

Elisabeth glanced at the sign painted above the lintel — *Patrick Cowie, Merchant, Jewelry and Silver Bought and Sold* — then followed Rob within, more than a little curious. She'd never given the jeweler her custom. Whatever could he want with her?

Mr. Cowie's ground-floor shop was as small and poorly lit as the others in the Luckenbooths, but his merchandise appeared of a higher quality than most. A large, glass-topped case full of beautiful pins, rings, earrings, and necklaces was positioned to catch a woman's eye, her own included.

He was beaming at her now, this red-headed merchant whose thick eyebrows and bushy mustache were engaged in a heated competition. " 'Tis fortunate ye came along, Leddy Kerr. Your brooch just arrived from Paris. I meant to send a caddie aff with a note —"

"My *brooch?*"

"Aye. Lord Kerr ordered the piece September last. He was verra specific about the style and color." Mr. Cowie reached beneath the counter and pulled out a small wooden box. "I think ye'll be pleased with the likeness, mem." His hands, covered in fine red hair, deftly opened the lid. "Made o' queen conch shell from the West Indies."

Elisabeth stared at the oval pin exquisitely carved in a creamy peach and ivory shell and encased in sterling silver. *I shall have a cameo engraved in Paris.* A promise made by her husband on a bright September morn.

The cameo was a woman's face. Her face. *Oh, Donald.*

Elisabeth gingerly lifted the brooch from its

velvet lining, marveling at the intricate swirls and tiny details. "It's lovely," she finally said, placing it back in the box with care, then brushing away her tears. "I shall look forward to wearing it."

"I've nae doubt," the merchant agreed. Then he added, "I'm sorry for yer loss, Leddy Kerr. Mebbe this will add a sweetness to yer sorrow, aye?" He replaced the lid on the box and proceeded to tie it up with a silk ribbon, making rather a show of it. "Ye'll be wanting to take this with ye?"

"Please." She glanced at Rob, having almost forgotten he was with her, so taken was she with Donald's final gift to her. Rob stood in the corner, sullen and brooding. "We'll leave in a moment," she promised.

The merchant placed the neatly wrapped box in her hands. "Will ye take the bill with ye, or shall I send it round at month's end?"

Her hands grew cold. "The . . . bill? Did Lord Kerr not already pay for this?"

"Hoot!" he said with a laugh. " 'Tis not how it's done, milady. I often order special pieces for my guid customers. Whan they arrive, if they like them, they pay me, and if they dinna, I sell them to anither." He waved his hand at the display case. "Some o' these came into the shop that way. Ithers I buy from leddies whan they tire o' wearing them. Like this jade brooch. Mebbe ye'd like it as weel?"

When he started to lift the glass, Elisabeth stayed his hand. "Not today." She swallowed. "How much is my cameo?"

The merchant consulted his ledger, then blithely told her the amount.

'Twas enough to feed the Kerr household for a month, if not two. "Oh, Mr. Cowie, I cannot possibly keep it."

His countenance fell. "But yer husband, mem . . . he meant for ye to have it."

"I know he did." She clutched the box to her breast. *My generous Donald! I am so sorry. So very sorry.*

Rob stood close behind her, boldly resting one hand on her waist. "Mr. Cowie, if Leddy Kerr and I might have a moment."

"Oo aye." The merchant rubbed his hands together expectantly, then moved toward the door leading to the back of his shop. "I'll not be far," he assured them.

Elisabeth put down the box. "We do not have . . . Rob, my family cannot begin to afford this."

He drew closer. She felt the warmth of his body along the length of her back, and his breath against her ear. "I can, Bess."

"Nae, Rob." She turned round and was almost in his embrace. " 'Twould not be right. This was my husband's gift to me. And you are . . . you are . . ."

"Yer freen." He looked down at her, slipping off his glove to smooth away her tears,

611

his fingers warm and scented with leather. "Yer guid freen, if ye will. And I'll not see yer heart broken again. Not when I can help."

"Rob, please —"

He touched her mouth with his fingertips, stilling her words. "And I *can* help, Bess. I've had a lang time to save my siller. I've mair than enough to buy yer wee pin."

" 'Tis a most charitable offer." She bent her head, undone by the love she saw in his eyes.

"Please leuk at me, Bess."

"I am a widow, Rob. I am in mourning . . ."

He lifted her chin, not letting her escape his gaze. "I ken what ye are, Bess. And I ken what I feel for ye. Will ye not let me do this one kindness?"

"Nae," she whispered, "I cannot." *Cannot, must not, will not.* Stepping free of his touch, she fled for the door.

"Leddy Kerr!"

She held up her hand, not looking back. *Please, Rob. Let me go.*

She slowed her steps only a little when she reached the plainstanes, not wanting to draw the attention of the Town Guard or, worse, a dragoon. But she had to get away from Rob MacPherson. He knew her too well. And he loved her too much. She aimed straight for Milne Square, dodging sedan chairs and wheeled carts and men on horseback and women in fur capes, never once looking over her shoulder to see if Rob was following.

All at once a young woman darted into her path, nearly knocking her off her feet. "I beg your pardon," Elisabeth murmured, though it was not her fault.

The young woman pushed back the hood of her threadbare cape. "Ye dinna remember me, Leddy Kerr?"

Elisabeth stared at the fair-haired lass with the light-colored eyes. *A crafty limmer, that one.* "You are . . ." She wet her lips, suddenly gone dry. "You are Lucy Spence of Halkerston's Wynd." *The last name on Donald's list.*

The young widow smiled. "Aye, ye *do* remember. And weel ye should, milady." Lucy winked at her. "I took yer coin that eve we met and ran aff to White Horse Close to be with yer husband."

Elisabeth wanted to slap her. Wanted to scream at her.

He did not love you. You were not the only one.

Instead Elisabeth stood her ground and begged for a strength she did not possess. *O God, be not far from me: O my God, make haste for my help.*

But the Widow Spence was not finished with her yet. "Whan I saw ye just now, Leddy Kerr, I wanted to tell ye I was sorry for yer loss." She ducked her head, her blond hair unkempt, her neck raw from the wind. "I lost my husband too. And I ken how ye must feel."

Elisabeth bit down on her lip so hard she tasted blood.

Lucy looked up, her expression almost sincere. "I thocht it might comfort ye to hear that whan I went to White Horse Close on that last nicht, yer husband turned me awa."

I can change the days to come. Donald had kept his word after all.

"Aye, he turned me awa," Lucy continued, "twice, afore he finally took me to his room."

Elisabeth stared at her, all hope ebbing away. "He . . . took you . . ."

"Aye. Whan we finished, he had tears in his e'es. I ken they were not for me." She turned to go, then said as an afterthought, "Lord Kerr luved ye, and that's a fact."

Elisabeth watched the widow stroll off, while her own feet seemed frozen to the ground. "Aye," she whispered into the wind, "he loved me."

But not enough.

SEVENTY

While shame keeps its watch
virtue is not wholly extinguished from the
    heart.

EDMUND BURKE

"Forgive me, mem. Oor bill was presented to ye in January. And again in February." Mr. Chapman, the meal seller, tapped his finger on the bill in question. "Now 'tis March."

In all her eight-and-forty years, Marjory had never had a tradesman come to her door to collect payment. Gibson had always paid her bills in person — with trustworthy coins, not paper bank notes — and always on time. From the day the Kerrs arrived in Edinburgh, they'd been favored customers of every merchant in town.

But no more.

The shame of it left her speechless. "Mr. . . . ah, Chapman," she began, then splayed her very empty hands. "I don't quite . . . I am not in a position to . . . pay you."

His eyebrows, the color of the oats he'd sold

her, were arched in a look of surprise. "Whan might we expect yer bill to be settled, mem?"

Marjory tried to sound confident. "Whitsuntide. I realize that is several weeks . . . I mean to say, several months hence. I do hope you'll forgive the delay, Mr. Chapman." Fearing his reprisal, she added in a low voice that begged for sympathy, "We've had two deaths in our family this winter."

"And ye have my condolences, ye surely do. The month o' May, then." He bowed and departed in haste, his coattails flapping as he bolted down the stair.

Marjory closed the door, feeling nauseated. She'd used the loss of her sons to bargain with a tradesman. No wonder he'd fled, embarrassed for her.

Janet appeared in the entrance hall. "Who was at the door, Lady Marjory?"

"Mr. Chapman, the meal seller."

"How very odd," Janet said. "He usually has one of his lads make deliveries."

Marjory turned to her, needing to be truthful with the family at least. "He came hoping to take something with him: payment in full. I had to send him away with naught in his pockets."

Her daughter-in-law looked properly shocked. "Is it so bad as that?"

"Worse." Marjory started for Elisabeth's bedchamber. "The time has come for both of you to be informed of our situation."

"Oh?" Janet walked beside Marjory, her mouth opening and closing like a fish.

They found Elisabeth seated close to the window, sewing a man's shirt.

Before Marjory could ask for an explanation, Elisabeth held up the bleached muslin, expertly stitched. "A birthday present for Angus."

"The man is a tailor," Marjory reminded her. "Can he not sew his own shirts?"

Her daughter-in-law tipped her head, appraising her work. "Aye, but it's a welcome change to have someone do it for you."

Perhaps her gift was not so scandalous, Marjory decided. Certainly nothing compared to what she'd just told Mr. Chapman. "At the moment we must speak candidly, the three of us."

Marjory sat by the fire in the least damaged of the upholstered chairs, while Janet chose the second best one, pulling it so close to the fire she risked singeing her new mourning gown. Elisabeth took a chair with most of the brocade torn loose and placed her single candle on the mantelpiece, dispelling a bit of the gloom. In Scotland early March was far from spring.

Marjory struggled with where to begin. "As you know, I've managed Donald's inheritance since the death of his father. The rent from our tenants has provided a steady income. Lord John's own resources were sizable, and

I brought a goodly sum of money into our marriage as well." She paused, mustering her courage. "Alas, Mr. Laidlaw could not forward the rents at Martinmas because of the Rising. And I invested most of our guineas in the prince's cause. All of which leaves us in rather dire straits."

Janet frowned. "Is there nothing hidden beneath the floors at Tweedsford that you might send for later?"

"Nae, I regret to say. We brought all our gold to Edinburgh once it became clear . . . once we decided to stay." *When you decided, Marjory. When you all but demanded.*

"Surely the Rising will be resolved by Whitsuntide," Elisabeth said, ever the optimist concerning the prince. "Then your income from Tweedsford can safely travel north."

"Aye, but . . ." Marjory watched their faces. "At the moment we have almost nothing to live on." She pulled out the last leather purse full of coins. Her gold had turned into mere silver and copper. Not by magic — no indeed — but by her own indiscretion. A simple proverb nagged at her. *How much better is it to get wisdom than gold!* She always learned these things too late.

"Our rent is paid through Whitsuntide," she told them, "so we'll not lose the roof over our heads. Mrs. Edgar and Gibson have their wages through May as well. Still, we must

618

look for ways to be frugal. I'm afraid our black gowns will have to do for some time, perhaps a year —"

"A *year?*" Janet moaned. "I cannot be seen wearing the same gown for a twelvemonth!"

"A widow isn't meant to be seen," Elisabeth reminded her, not unkindly.

"*You* visit the MacPhersons," Janet shot back.

"Aye, but my friends don't care what gown I'm wearing."

"Well, *I* care very much! It tarnishes our good name to be —"

"Ladies, if you please." Marjory offered a silent prayer of thanks that she'd borne sons. "There are graver concerns. Food, for example. I cannot ask Mr. Chapman to give us more meal, so porridge and oatcakes will soon disappear from our table."

Janet rolled her eyes but said nothing. "Cottagers food" she'd often called such mainstays of the Scottish diet.

"The flesher and the fishmonger will also become strangers at our door," Marjory warned them, "unless we are very prudent with our pennies and make do with potatoes and turnips on occasion."

Janet started to raise another protest, but Elisabeth quickly intervened. "Mrs. Edgar's *tatties* and *neeps* are quite nourishing. What else might we do, Lady Marjory?"

"We've another two months before the days

lengthen and the weather warms. Until then, we must be especially mindful of our candles and coal, or they'll claim much of what's left of our money." Marjory slowly emptied the leather purse into her lap, the coins speaking more loudly than her words. She heard Elisabeth's sharp intake of air and saw Janet's rounded eyes. "Aye. This is all we have."

Elisabeth stood and blew out her candle at once. "Something must be done. Let me ply my needle on our behalf. Angus might have a bit of work for me, or I could see if Miss Callander has need of my services."

"Do you mean to sew for *money?*" Janet cried, her disgust apparent. "Won't we be the talk of Edinburgh? Lady Elisabeth Kerr . . . a *seamstress!*"

Elisabeth looked down at her with a cool gaze. "You seemed well pleased with the gown I stitched for you."

"But that was for *family.*" Janet sniffed. "A different matter altogether."

Marjory was torn, rather liking the idea but not wanting to expose Elisabeth to ridicule. "Perhaps you might teach sewing at Effie Sinclair's school," she proposed. "Nothing unladylike there."

Elisabeth shook her head. "I couldn't ask her to take me on when she has so few students. Now that the streets are overrun with British soldiers, Edinburgh is not the proper place to board a young lady scholar."

620

She sat once more, her expression earnest. "I'm not afraid of work, Lady Marjory. Do at least consider letting me sew."

Janet folded her arms across her bodice. "And what would you have me do? Paint china cups and sell them in the Luckenbooths?"

Marjory tried to smooth her ruffled feathers. "Come, Janet —"

"I'm not *meant* to work," she said, almost in tears. "I am a gentlewoman!"

"We all are." Marjory reached forward and took both their hands. Elisabeth's skin was warm and dry to the touch, Janet's cool and clammy. "This situation is entirely my fault. Had I not given so much money to the prince —"

"Why *did* you do such a thing?" Janet demanded, pulling her hand free.

"To protect my sons," Marjory told her. "And because I sincerely believed Charles Edward Stuart capable of regaining the throne for his father."

"But you don't believe it now," Elisabeth said. It was not a question.

Marjory squeezed her hand. "I know the prince's cause has been near to your heart all your life. But those of us who came later to his support are . . . less certain of the outcome." She could not say more. Not when her sons had died for their beliefs.

Janet stood, her face stark against her black

gown, the light from the coal fire throwing her shadow against the wall. Her hands were clenched and her voice low and strained. "You threw away your gold, Lady Marjory. *Our* gold. You did not protect our husbands. You killed them."

"Janet!" Elisabeth was clearly horrified. "You cannot say such things."

"I thought we were supposed to be honest with one another," Janet retorted and stormed out of the room.

Undone by her cruel words, Marjory stared at the fire, shame crowding out every other emotion. "Your sister-in-law is right."

"Nae, she is not," Elisabeth said firmly. "Lord Donald assured us it was his decision alone. Do you remember?"

Marjory nodded pensively. "He was always truthful, my Donald. I cannot think of a promise he did not keep. Can you, dear?" When Elisabeth didn't respond, Marjory looked up. Even in the darkened room, she saw the tears in her daughter-in-law's eyes.

SEVENTY-ONE

Necessity urges desperate measures.
MIGUEL DE CERVANTES

"Here's the last o' them, Leddy Kerr." Mrs. Edgar shook out Elisabeth's rose-colored gown and spread the voluminous skirts across her bed. "Eleven gowns in a'."

Elisabeth smoothed her hand over the fine silks and polished satins, the elaborate brocades and soft velvets. A few costumes were her own designs. Miss Callander had stitched the others. "I cannot wear them for another year," Elisabeth said, convincing herself she would not miss them, that the money her gowns might earn was worth more than the pleasure of keeping them in her clothes press. "Perhaps, when my time of mourning ends, we'll be in a position to order a new dress or two."

"Aye, milady." Mrs. Edgar did not sound convinced. Neither was Elisabeth.

The dowager's coin purse was empty. Potatoes and turnips had replaced beef and mutton, and their thick morning porridge was reduced to a thin, colorless broth. Tea leaves were carefully strained and reused until the flavor was faint and the inside of the cup was easily seen through the tea. When Elisabeth suggested using coffee, which was less expensive, she was quickly overruled. "Ladies of quality drink black tea," Marjory had insisted. Biscuits were served with their watery tea only if the miller offered a reasonable price for his flour. Wheaten bread at dinner was a luxury now.

"Have ye told yer mither-in-law about selling yer gowns?" Mrs. Edgar asked her.

Elisabeth heard no judgment in the housekeeper's voice, only a thread of concern. "She agreed Gibson and I might carry them to Miss Callander's in Lady Stair's Close and see what the seamstress will offer for them. I feel certain Lady Marjory will be glad for the money. Perhaps she may decide to sell her gowns too."

Mrs. Edgar did not make a sound, but Elisabeth read the expression on her face. *Not likely, milady.*

Elisabeth's eye was drawn to one gown in particular: the lavender satin, with its Brussels lace, silk gauze, and gold-dipped sequins. Could she truly sell Donald's gift, worn but twice? When she touched the sleeve, the words from Donald's letter stirred inside her. *Now you know the full extent of your mercy.*

She'd forgiven him that October eve, not realizing what true mercy required: forgiving her husband again and again, each time his sin came to mind, each time the pain surfaced, each time she was tempted to take back her words. *You are forgiven.*

"Are ye having second thochts, milady?"

Elisabeth began tugging on the shoulders of her lavender gown, slowly pulling it free from Mrs. Edgar's tidy pile. With a cool whisper, the satin pooled at her feet. She picked it up, then held it against her body and turned toward the looking glass, hearing Donald's words. *A rare beauty. Like you, my love.*

She confessed, "I cannot part with this one."

Mrs. Edgar took the gown from her without a word and stored the satin folds inside the empty clothes press, her efficient movements almost soundless.

"Do you think me a fool, Mrs. Edgar?"

The housekeeper's guileless gray eyes met hers. "Not for a moment, milady."

Within the hour Mrs. Edgar had wrapped the remaining gowns in a sheet, preparing them for the journey up the High Street to Miss Callander's shop in the Lawnmarket. "Gibson canna manage them alone," she said. "Might Mr. MacPherson help carry yer gowns?"

Elisabeth glanced out the window toward

the Luckenbooths. Since their abrupt parting outside the jeweler's shop a month ago, Rob had sent her several notes filled with remorse. *I did not mean to offend. My intentions are wholly honorable. I hope you can forgive me, Bess. My father misses you very much.* The last note had worn down her resistance. When she'd visited the MacPhersons with Angus's finished shirt, Rob had been on his best behavior. They were back on steadier footing now, friends again.

But she was careful not to be alone with him.

"Aye," she agreed, "have Gibson ask Mr. MacPherson. Perhaps he'll not mind helping us this forenoon."

Rob shifted the knotted sheet from one hand to the other. "Ye're certain this is but ten gowns?"

"I know they're heavy," Elisabeth admitted, keeping pace with him as they climbed the bustling High Street. "Miss Callander expects us at eleven o' the clock."

Would it be awkward, this meeting? Elisabeth knew the value of her gowns but not what the seamstress might be willing to pay. If it meant the Kerrs could settle their bills and have meat on their table again, she would gladly accept almost any amount. But since Marjory's gold had paid for the gowns and the fabric to make them, the final decision was hers. "No less than five pounds for the best gowns, four for the others," the dowager had cautioned her.

The March air was damp and cold, though no wind stung their cheeks. Gibson, the shorter of the two men, led the way uphill, bearing his end of the bundle without complaint as they passed the mercat cross, then the tolbooth. When they ducked into Lady Stair's Close and started up the turnpike stair to the third floor, Elisabeth discovered how canny their housekeeper was. A large trunk would have been impossible to navigate up the narrow stair, but their long bundle, however cumbersome, took the constant turning without mishap.

Miss Callander answered at their first knock, her eyes brightening at the sight of Rob coming through her door. "What a surprise, Mr. MacPherson!" Her cheeks soon matched her strawberry hair. Though she was rushing the season wearing spring green, the color was very flattering and the style of her fashionable gown no doubt Parisian. In her late twenties, Meg Callander still had a youthful lilt to her voice. "Come in, Lady Kerr. A pleasure to have you here."

The room was small but well lit, with no shutters or curtains to block the light. An abundance of beeswax candles shone in the gilt-framed looking glass. Elisabeth noted the painted folding screen, the papier-mâché dress form, and the cherry sewing cabinet with its ivory drawer pulls. But it was the vibrantly hued seamstress who commanded the room, despite her diminutive size. Miss Callander had been most sympathetic when she learned of Elisabeth's loss. "Bring your gowns to me, and let us see what can be done," she'd said the last time they spoke.

Now that they were here, Elisabeth found herself reticent to ask for help. But it had to be done, for her family's sake. "Miss Callander," she began, "you will recognize some of your gowns from seasons past. Others here are my own."

"Ah! Those I wish to see first," she insisted. "Mr. MacPherson, if you might unroll the sheet for us?" In a moment the dresses were spread before them like a peacock's colorful feathers.

"I made this one two Januarys ago." Elisabeth lifted a dark blue gown with delicate silver braiding on the bodice. She remembered the long wintry hours seated beside her bedchamber window, needle in hand, the lustrous blue silk draped across her lap.

"Lovely," Miss Callander declared. "Now if I might see the yellow taffeta."

Rob and Gibson stood quietly to the side as the women examined each gown in turn with Elisabeth holding them up, then Miss Callander nodding her approval.

"I shall add some fresh trim," the seamstress decided. "Perhaps remake the sleeves. Whatever is required so none will be the wiser." She lowered her voice. "I hardly need tell you a terrible cloud has settled over your household, Lady Kerr. I must alter your gowns such that my customers will not recognize them as yours. Do forgive me."

"I understand," Elisabeth said, all too aware of the Kerrs' diminished place in society. She did not mind for herself, but Marjory's shame and disappointment were painful to watch. "Might you take some of my gowns?"

"Oh, every one. Your designs are quite impressive." Miss Callander touched the embroidered neckline of an emerald green silk draped across a chair. "Were you not a lady, I'd encourage you to enter the trade."

Elisabeth's heart lifted. "Would you have some use for me, perhaps? In your employ?"

"Oh, Lady Kerr." Miss Callander's small features tightened. " 'Twould not be proper. Nae, nae, I cannot consider it, however fine your skill with a needle."

Heat rose from her neck. "Forgive me," Elisabeth murmured.

"Nae, I am the one who is sorry," she assured her. "We are all trapped by society, *n'est-ce pas?* As to my offer . . ." The seamstress counted prettily on her fingers, then announced, "Three pounds each."

"So little?" Elisabeth couldn't contain her disappointment. *Only thirty pounds in all.* She didn't know the extent of their debts but feared they would quickly swallow the meager earnings. "Might you consider five pounds for the pale green silk with the ruching? Or four pounds for the pink taffeta with the tulle quilling?"

"Exquisitely made," Miss Callander agreed, "but they are hardly new. My resources are such . . ." She gave a ladylike shrug. " 'Tis the best I can offer you, Lady Kerr. Aye or nae?"

SEVENTY-TWO

When all is said and done,
He's but a tailor's son.
SCOTTISH FOLK SONG

Elisabeth rubbed her forehead in distress. Would thirty pounds suit her mother-in-law? Or would Marjory be furious that she'd sold the gowns for so little?

When she turned to Rob, seeking his opinion as a tradesman, he nodded. So did she, albeit reluctantly. "Very well, Miss Callander. I accept."

"Ah." The seamstress smiled coyly. "I thought you might."

A small purse was quickly produced — heavy with coins, yet not nearly the weight of ten gowns. Elisabeth tried not to think of seeing her beautiful dresses on the High Street that spring, worn by other gentlewomen who could afford them.

She looked down at the purse in her hands. *Let me not be ashamed.*

"Will you have tea before you go?" Miss

Callander asked, all the while smiling at Rob. "You are invited to stay as well, Mr. Mac-Pherson."

Before Elisabeth could decline, Rob did so for both of them. "We'll not keep ye from yer labors," he said rather brusquely. "Shall we go, Leddy Kerr?"

Moments later the three of them were descending the stair. Rob led the way, with Gibson bearing the sheet under his arm, the gold safely nestled in its folds. When they reached the street, Rob wrapped her hand round the crook of his elbow. "To keep ye safe," he said as they started down the hill.

"That hardly seemed a fair bargain," Elisabeth confessed, matching her gait to his.

" 'Twas not," he grumbled. "Meg Callander will double the price whan she sells them and make a tidy profit."

Elisabeth's spirits sank. "Should I have insisted on more?"

"Nae, for I ken the lass, and she'd not have paid it. Besides, ye dinna want to seem desperate, Leddy Kerr."

"But we *are* desperate," she said in a low voice, hoping no one would hear. "I'm only sorry I have no jewelry I might sell to Mr. Cowie. November last the dragoons took the few pieces I owned, including my seed pearl earrings and choker." Her favorites, worn with Donald's gown, were now tucked in some Englishwoman's jewelry box.

Rob frowned. "Ye own nae jewelry at a'?"

"Only my two silver rings." She released his arm long enough to hold out her gloved hands, satisfied to see the slight bump on each ring finger.

Rob eyed them both. "How lang will ye wear yer wedding band?"

"As long as I live. Longer still, if it's not yanked from my cold fingers."

Rob hastily wrapped her hand round his arm once more. "And what o' the ither ring?"

"A gift from my mother." She did not elaborate, silently counting the days since the new moon. 'Twas the sixth day, meant for hailing the moon. How little that mattered to her now when she could pray every day, at any hour. *Evening, and morning, and at noon, will I pray.* Even more remarkable was the promise that followed. *And he shall hear my voice.*

She glanced at the ring beneath her right glove. If she no longer trusted the Nameless One, could she slide the silver band off her finger? A ring passed down by her great-grandmother? Nae, if only for sentiment's sake. Nor could she remove Donald's ring. However unfaithful he was to her, she would not be unfaithful to him.

"Lord Kerr fell at Falkirk two months ago this day," she said.

Rob stiffened. "D'ye think on him ilka hour?"

"I do, aye." She could see that did not please him.

The small party continued in silence until they reached the door of Rob's tailoring shop. "Will ye come and see my faither?" he asked, unlocking the door.

Elisabeth gazed through the window, knowing she could never refuse. "Aye, but we must let Gibson hurry home. 'Tis almost the dinner hour, and he'll be needed."

With a bob of his head, the manservant took off for Milne Square.

"Come, Bess." The bell jingled as Rob shut the door, leaving his Closed sign in place. "I've little custom on a Monday," he explained, guiding her through the dimly lit shop. Though it was the middle of the day, they found Angus fast asleep, the bedcovers drawn round his neck.

Rob extinguished the candle by his father's bed. "He's not weel, Bess." Indeed, the older man's skin was waxy and pale, and his breathing was ragged.

She looked down at him, her heart aching. "I am very sorry to hear it."

Rob was quiet for a long time, then said, "My mither died whan I was a wee lad. 'Twas my faither wha raised me."

Elisabeth heard the gruff affection in his voice. "I was too young to remember your mother, but I heard many a story about Mrs. MacPherson and her venison gravy."

"Oo aye," Rob said. "Dinna tell a soul, but she flavored it with green walnut pickle." He stepped closer and spoke more softly, lest they wake Angus. "She threatened to pour a bottle doon my throat onie time I misbehaved."

"Daily, then," Elisabeth chided him.

Her gaze was fixed on Angus, but her other senses were attuned to Rob, now standing directly behind her. Nae, not standing. Looming, as dark and as silent as Creag Choinnich, rising behind her mother's Highland cottage.

Though his presence unnerved her at times, Rob understood her in ways the Kerrs never could. She and Rob had grown up in the same mountain fastness. Saw the world through the same lens. Knew the same people and shared the same history. Though she was a lady now and he was a tailor's son, they were not so very different.

"I miss home," she said simply.

Rob's breath was warm against her hair. "I feared ye'd forgotten the Hielands."

"Never." She swallowed the lump in her throat. "Perhaps when the Rising is over . . . perhaps I'll return for a visit. If my mother . . ." Elisabeth bowed her head. "If she'll have me."

"Ye ken she will, my bonny Bess." His arm slipped loosely round her waist. "I'll gladly escort ye hame to Braemar parish whan the time comes."

She shook her head. "I'm a widow, Rob. You know very well I cannot travel so far with an unmarried man."

"Aye the proper leddy." His voice was low and musical, each phrase beginning on a higher note and ending farther down the scale. "What if the man were married?"

"Rob!" She spun round in surprise, barely noticing that his arms now encircled her completely. "Do you plan to wed?"

"I do," he said, the line of his jaw firm. "January next, whan the leddy is free to marry."

Elisabeth felt strangely discomfited by his news. "Is the lass from Castleton? Or from Edinburgh?"

His steady gaze met hers. "Both."

"Oh, Rob . . ." Elisabeth turned her head, hiding her dismay. Had she not known this day would come? "I do not . . . I cannot . . ."

"Aye, ye can." He slowly tightened his embrace. "I've waited for ye a' my life, Bess Ferguson. And I'll not be denied. Not without a verra guid reason."

My heart still belongs to Donald. Was that not reason enough?

"Rob, please. What if your father woke and found us like this?" Her question gave him pause, long enough for her to ease out of his embrace.

But he did not let go entirely. His hand still

636

firmly grasped hers. "My faither kens my feelings for ye, Bess. And ye do as weel." He tugged her toward their table near the fire. "Ye've not had yer dinner. Come, let me serve ye broth and bread and tell ye what I have in mind. If yer answer is nae, then I must accept it. But hear me oot afore ye answer, aye?"

Elisabeth already knew her answer. But how could she refuse to listen when he'd served her family so faithfully? Still wrapped in her cape, she found a seat at the plain wooden table. Rob ladled two servings of cock-a-leekie soup from the fragrant pot simmering on the fire and placed them on the table with butter and a loaf of crusty bread.

She tried not to tear into her food, but she was hungry. The flavorful chicken and leeks, cooked in veal stock, filled an empty place inside her. And she needed time to think, time to sort through the best way to refuse his well-intentioned offer of marriage. *It is too soon, Rob.* Nae, that was not the whole of it. *Your love borders on obsession.* That was closer to the truth. In Rob's presence she felt both safe *and* in danger, if such a thing was possible.

When she put aside her horn spoon, sated at last, she looked up to find Rob's dark eyes measuring her. "Have ye nae food at Milne Square?" he asked.

Embarrassed, she averted her gaze. "Aye, we do, though 'tis not quite so hearty."

He reached across the table and easily circled her wrist with his thumb and forefinger. "Ye've lost weight."

"Maybe a little."

He was beside her at once, pulling off her cape, frowning at what he saw. "Why did ye not tell me, Bess? I thocht ye sold yer gowns because ye didna need them or didna want them. Not because yer table was bare." He stood and paced the floor, his voice a low rumble. "Had I kenned the truth, I'd have forced Meg Callander to pay ye mair for yer gowns. Why did ye not tell me?" he asked again.

Elisabeth drew her cape round her shoulders, feeling exposed. "I did not want to trouble you with family business —"

"Ye *are* my family," he said, "or, at any rate, ye will be. I canna save them a', Bess, but I can surely save ye." He sat down again, his chair pulled close to hers, one arm propped on the table. "I promised to tell ye my plan, and sae I will. Come the first o' May, whan the weather breaks, I'll escort ye hame to Castleton o' Braemar. And whan yer twelve-month o' mourning has passed, we'll marry."

"But . . ."

"I dinna need yer answer now," he protested. "Not until ye've given it meikle thocht." He pulled a letter from his waistcoat and placed it before her. "I've written it a' doon, Bess. Read it whan ye're alone. On

638

Monday next I'll come to Milne Square and expect yer answer, aye or nae."

Elisabeth gazed at the folded letter, knowing it contained all his hopes for the future. "You've honored me greatly, Rob."

He touched her cheek. "I want to do mair than honor ye, lass. I want to marry ye."

She looked into his dark eyes. He was not wealthy, but he would never be poor. He was not cultured, but he knew much of the world and how it worked. He was not a gentleman, but he was an honest man.

Aye, he was a tailor's son, but wasn't she a weaver's daughter?

And Rob loved her. Would love only her, the whole of his life. If he doted on her endlessly, besetting her at every turn, was that not better than a man whose affections she could never fully trust?

Rob brushed his lips across her brow. "Come, I'll walk ye hame, Bess. In a week, whan I knock on yer door, I hope to hear guid news."

SEVENTY-THREE

I know not how to tell thee!

THOMAS OTWAY

Elisabeth woke at dawn, the sky outside her window a pale blue wash of color. As she bathed and dressed herself, the air in her bedchamber was cool but not freezing. Rob's letter, unfolded and read many times, lay on her dressing table.

A week ago she was sure of her answer. Now she was less certain.

Was it Rob MacPherson who wooed her? Or was it the hills and glens of Braemar? She could not separate the two in her mind.

This much she knew: Edinburgh was no longer her true home. Tall lands and narrow wynds, which once quickened her pulse, now made her feel hemmed in. The crowded High Street with all its diversions held little appeal for a penniless widow. And everywhere she turned, she saw Donald. Or thought she did, then realized it was someone else with a slender build and a fair periwig.

Having her hopes raised, then dashed again and again was numbing. Would marrying Rob MacPherson next January put an end to her pain?

Elisabeth stood facing the window, absently dragging a brush through her hair, rather than look at the bed she'd shared with her husband for nearly three years. To consider marrying another seemed a sacrilege. She'd not informed anyone of Rob's proposal for that very reason. Why upset the household — her mother-in-law in particular — if the answer was going to be nae?

Elisabeth glanced at Rob's letter, wisely written in Gaelic. She put down her brush and opened the letter once more, scanning the lines she almost knew by heart. His words were written in a bold, unpolished hand. The ink was the very color of his eyes.

My dear Bess,

I have loved you as long as I have known you.

She did not doubt Rob for a moment. Whenever they were together, his gaze was riveted on her as if no one else existed. Such complete attention was unnerving. But at least she never questioned his loyalty.

From the adjoining rooms came the sounds of her family stirring from their sleep. Determined to make up her mind before breakfast, Elisabeth read on.

This spring I would be honored to escort you to Castleton of Braemar and deliver you into your mother's arms.

Elisabeth's heart tightened. Would her mother swing open their cottage door and gather her in a fierce embrace, whispering, "All is forgiven, all is forgotten"? Or would the new Mrs. Cromar close that same door in her daughter's face, shutting her out forever?

If you accept my proposal of marriage, Bess, I will do everything in my power to make you happy.

A bewitching notion, having a husband dedicated to her happiness. Could she do the same? Put his pleasure above hers? Though Rob had yet to ask that of her, surely he had the right to expect she would return his boundless affection.

My heart and my hands are yours, and everything I own in this world, if you will have me as your husband come January.

No man could offer more. Donald had given her a title and a fine home, aye. But his heart and his hands were never hers entirely. *May these gloves warm your hands, as your hands warmed me.* She could not fathom Rob being unfaithful to her, nor had she ever heard a whisper of gossip about him.

But were devotion and provision enough to win her heart?

Elisabeth stared at the words on the page, tracing the ink with her fingertips. She would marry for no other reason but love. Never mind that society laughed at such conventions. Before she could wed Rob MacPherson, she had to love him.

And she did not.

There was her answer.

Forgive me, Rob. Elisabeth slowly folded his letter and slipped it inside her hanging pocket. He'd not told her what hour to expect his call. Whenever he came, she knew what must be said. But *how* to say it without crushing his hopes and breaking his heart? She knew the wise proverb: *A soft answer turneth away wrath.* But she did not fear his wrath; she feared his silence.

Not long after the clock chimed the hour of four, there was a knock at the stair door. Three sharp raps, then two.

Marjory nodded at Mrs. Edgar to pour their tea. "And bring a cup for Mr. MacPherson. He'll be most disappointed when he learns we've no sweet biscuits."

643

Elisabeth heard the tension in her voice. More than once in the last week her mother-in-law had found some way to remind her that the thirty pounds she'd brought home from Miss Callander's could have — nae, should have — been much more. After settling their many accounts, Marjory had earmarked the remaining balance for meal and meat.

"I do not think Rob MacPherson comes to call because of the biscuits," Janet said pointedly, looking at her.

Elisabeth started to rise, planning to greet him at the door, knowing what she would tell him. *Let us wait until we are alone to speak.*

But Marjory snagged her hand and gently pulled her back into her seat. "Gibson will see to our guest. One should never appear too eager for company, my dear."

Put in her place in every sense, Elisabeth could only look toward the door and hope she might express her concern in some other way. *Say nothing, Rob. Not in front of the household.*

He entered the drawing room bearing a small market basket covered with a linen cloth. "I've been to Mr. Orr's," he said, handing the basket to Gibson.

Elisabeth recognized the yeasty aroma at once. "Caraway buns. How very thoughtful."

He shrugged, though she could see her words pleased him. "Warriston's Close isna far from my shop."

When Mrs. Edgar returned with a plate bearing his bakery gift, stuffed with sweet caraway comfits, Rob asked the housekeeper, "Ye saved a bun for yerself, I hope? And one for Mr. Gibson?"

She shook her head, placing his offering on the table. "I didna think it richt."

He nicked two buns from the plate. "They'll fit nicely in yer apron pocket." Mrs. Edgar thanked him profusely and hastened to the kitchen to enjoy her tea.

None of this was lost on Marjory, Elisabeth noticed. Her mother-in-law watched Rob join them at table as if it were his own. Then Marjory listened without comment as he described the latest activities of the prince's army at Blair Atholl, where they'd besieged the castle.

"Lord Mark Kerr's dragoons have headed north as weel," Rob told them. "Ye're a relative o' his, aye?"

"A very distant relative," Marjory said, "on my husband's side."

Elisabeth saw some emotion flicker across her mother-in-law's face but could not define it. Pride, perhaps. Or regret. The Jacobite Rising was no longer a welcome topic of conversation at Milne Square, having cost them everything.

When their teacups were empty and their plates bare, Rob folded his hands in his lap and leaned forward. "I've come today with a proposal."

Elisabeth shot him a look of dismay. *Please, Rob!*

Marjory did not even blink. "And what is it you propose?"

"That I escort Leddy Kerr to her Hieland hame sae she might comfort her grieving mither."

Marjory took her time answering him. "Mr. MacPherson, you are an unmarried man and in no position to escort my daughter-in-law any farther than the Luckenbooths." She dabbed the corners of her mouth, then folded her linen napkin, dismissing his suggestion just as neatly. "I am certain Lady Kerr would say quite the same."

"She already did, mem."

Marjory narrowed her gaze. "Then why have you broached the topic again?"

"Because I intend to marry —"

"Mr. MacPherson." Elisabeth rose, forcing him to stand. "Perhaps this is not the time and place —"

"Indeed." Marjory was on her feet and gesturing toward the fireplace. "Shall we move our conversation to a more comfortable setting?"

Janet found a chair at once, her features alight with expectation. "Do tell, Mr. MacPherson. Who will be your lucky bride?"

Elisabeth's feet were leaden as she crossed

the room and sat by the low fire. However difficult it might have been to refuse his proposal in private, it would be far worse now with an audience.

Rob stood by the mantelpiece, his clean-shaven face slightly tinged with red. "The leddy has not agreed to my suit," he confessed. "However, I hope to have an answer this verra day."

"This day?" Marjory looked at Janet and Elisabeth in turn. "Then should you not seek out her company rather than drink tea with three widows?"

"Her answer will not take lang, mem." Rob leveled his gaze on Elisabeth, any trace of humor gone from his voice. "She need only say 'aye' or 'nae.' "

Oh, Rob. I cannot hurt you like this.

" 'Tis easy enough." Janet pounced on the idea as if they were playing a game. " 'Aye.' That is my guess."

Marjory lifted one eyebrow. "I, too, believe the lass will say 'aye.' What do you think, Lady Elisabeth?"

Can you not see it in my eyes, Rob? Must I say the word aloud?

After a moment Rob prompted her in a low voice, "Come, Leddy Kerr. What will my future bride say to me?"

In agony Elisabeth stared at the floor. "I imagine she would want to tell you in private, Mr. MacPherson."

"Because she is ashamed?"

"Nae." She looked up at once. "Because she cannot reduce her feelings to a single word."

His voice was as even as his gaze. "Take a' the wirds ye like, Leddy Kerr. But I'll have my answer now."

Silence fell across the room.

Marjory looked at both of them, her eyes narrowing. "Just as I thought. You mean to marry my daughter-in-law. *You!* A trades-man."

"Aye." Rob straightened, his chest expanding. " 'Tis honorable work, dressing gentlemen like Lord Kerr."

Marjory was on her feet at once. "How dare you mention my son's name while you plot to steal his wife?"

"I offered to take her hame to the Hielands. And marry her whan her twelvemonth o' mourning ends. Nae mair, nae less. The choice is entirely hers."

Marjory stared down at her. "Is this true?"

Elisabeth stood, using her height to bolster her courage. "Aye, that was Mr. MacPherson's proposal."

Marjory bristled. "You were married to a peer of the realm. Why would you demean yourself —"

"*Demean,* is it?" Rob growled, his brow as dark as a storm. "Yer son demeaned her weel enough. With Jane Montgomerie and Susan

McGill and —"

"Rob!" Elisabeth cried out. "Please don't do this!"

He looked at her darkly. " 'Tis the truth, Leddy Kerr, as ye verra weel ken."

"Nae." Marjory fell back a step. "These . . . accusations. They cannot be true. My son was . . . faithful."

"Nae, he was not." Rob's voice softened only a little. "A young widow by the name o' Lucy Spence came to visit Lord Kerr while he lodged at White Horse Close. Thrice I saw them thegither —"

"Stop!" Marjory sank onto her chair, her hands over her ears. "Do not say such things about my son. Please, Lady Elisabeth . . . please tell me this slander is not true."

Elisabeth knelt beside her. "Lord Kerr was a loving husband and a good son. That is all that matters now."

"He was, he was." Marjory moaned into her handkerchief.

"Rather *too* loving," Janet scoffed. "I'd heard the rumors and hoped they were idle gossip. Now I understand what sort of family I married into." She stood and turned on her heel, retreating to her bedchamber.

Elisabeth watched her go, almost relieved. Marjory needed her full attention.

She rested her hand on her mother-in-law's shoulder, which shook with her quiet sobs. "Try not to dwell on this," Elisabeth said gently. Donald's own words came to mind: *Do not bind these names to your heart.*

Rob stood above her now, offering his hand. "Leddy Kerr, if I might have a wird."

She looked up at him, seeing him with new eyes. Clearly Rob had taken no small pleasure in ruining Marjory's good opinion of her son. And to what end? Soothing his trampled pride.

Elisabeth stood without taking his hand. "Step into the entrance hall, Mr. Mac-Pherson, and speak your piece." She led the way, not looking over her shoulder, any doubt of her decision banished.

When they reached the stair door, she turned to look at him, keeping her distance. "Rob, how could you be so thoughtless?"

His expression was contrite, but his tone was not. "I am sorry, Bess. It needed to be said."

"Nae, it did not." Elisabeth spoke with equal conviction. "Her son is dead. His memory is sacred to her. In truth, 'tis all she has. What you've done is unconscionable."

Rob suddenly gripped her shoulders, his temper flaring. "Why d'ye defend these people? They dinna love ye as I do. Ye're a Hielander, Bess, and aye will be to them."

"They are my family now —"

"Nae!" He shook her soundly. "Yer family lives in Braemar."

"My mother lives there, aye." She twisted

free of his grasp. "But I left my father and my mother and cleaved unto my husband."

"Aye, a profligate," Rob muttered.

Elisabeth slapped him. Not hard, but hard enough. "Do not speak ill of my husband." Tears stung her eyes. "Do not speak of him at all."

He covered his cheek, his words low, almost menacing. "Ye were meant to be mine, Bess."

"I was never yours." She flung open the stair door. "I belonged to Lord Kerr. And now I belong to God. I bid you farewell."

SEVENTY-FOUR

Who has not felt how sadly sweet
The dream of home, the dream of home.
THOMAS MOORE

Marjory stood at the door to Elisabeth's bed-chamber, her ear almost touching the wood. Was she mistaken? Or was her daughter-in-law crying herself to sleep again this night? She could not fault the lass. Had she not wept through many a midnight hour? But this was unusual for Elisabeth.

Marjory eased away, honoring her daughter-in-law's privacy. Now that Rob MacPherson had not darkened their door in a fortnight, Elisabeth seemed more at peace. But what were these tears at night? Certainly they weren't shed for the tailor's son. Mrs. Edgar, who'd been listening from behind the kitchen door, said Elisabeth practically threw the man down the stair.

Marjory was only sorry she'd not seen it for herself.

Elisabeth had been right to refuse his

proposal. Aye, and to turn him out. The withdrawal of Rob's support was no loss to Marjory, yet she hoped her daughter-in-law was not suffering because of it. He was her childhood friend, and his father was gravely ill.

Still, the terrible accusations Rob had made, the women's names he had spoken with such certainty taunted her by the hour.

A loving husband and a good son. So Elisabeth had assured her. But what the lass didn't say was more troubling. *Donald was faithful.* Nae, she'd not said that.

Charlotte Ruthven had been right after all, then. *I saw Lord Kerr with Susan McGill.* One of the names Rob had spat out. *A widow of dubious repute.*

Marjory moved to the window, staring into the darkness, sick with the thought of it. Was that why Elisabeth wept at night? Because of Donald's sordid affairs? Her daughter-in-law had apparently known for some time, all the while remaining faithful, guarding his secrets, bearing her pain in silence.

Marjory carried her lighted taper to her bedside, her heart heavy with sorrow and with shame. An adulterer for a son. How could she live with that burden? She had taken him to kirk each Sabbath, read him the psalms, taught him the commandments. *How did I fail you, Donald? Was I not a good mother?*

653

When she knelt to pray, Marjory pressed her forehead against the edge of her bed, desperate for answers. "Almighty God, you know how much I loved my sons." She squeezed her eyes, trying to shut out the pain but could not. Her tears landed soundlessly on the carpet. "Forgive me . . . forgive me . . ." No more words came.

She had failed everyone she loved.

Everyone.

She remained there for some time, simply weeping.

When at last she could take a full breath, Marjory stood and dried her eyes on the sleeve of her nightgown. She'd spoken few words. And yet she knew the Almighty was listening. *The Lord seeth. The Lord heareth. The Lord knoweth.* He always spoke so clearly. Why did she find it difficult to trust him?

She stepped out of her brocade slippers and climbed into bed, utterly spent. A soft April rain was falling. She drew the bedcovers round her neck and burrowed deep into her pillow, already feeling drowsy.

Unbidden, thoughts of home crept through her mind like a gray cat slipping down a lane, soundless and barely noticed, yet beckoning her to follow.

Home, home, home.

Lambing season had begun in the Borderland. The rolling hills were covered with bright green grass by now, and wildflowers dotted the meadows. Winter's heavy snowfall would mean abundant crops come summer. There was no place lovelier than home in the spring.

Marjory sighed into the empty room, having found her answer. Come Whitsuntide she would return to Tweedsford with her daughters-in-law.

To leave behind a litany of mistakes. To make amends. To start anew.

As if from a distance, Marjory heard a soft tapping on her door.

And then Mrs. Edgar with a plaintive entreaty.

"Come," Marjory called out to her, struggling to sit up.

Mrs. Edgar popped her head round the door, then quietly entered, full of apologies. "I'd hoped to find ye still awake, mem."

"No matter. I only just now fell asleep," Marjory said, tucking her bedcovers round her, then brushing aside her tousled hair.

Mrs. Edgar stood before her, twisting her apron in her hands. "I'm sorry to trouble you, but . . ."

Marjory studied the housekeeper more closely. The lines creasing her brow had deepened, and a worried look clouded her gray eyes. "What is it?" Marjory asked, genuinely concerned.

"I've had a letter from my mither in Lasswade. Ye ken she's a' alone."

Marjory felt a knot tighten inside her. "Is she . . . unwell?" *Is she dead?*

"Nae, but she is auld and verra frail."

When the housekeeper fell silent, Marjory prompted her. "And?"

"Ye see, mem . . ." Mrs. Edgar hung her head. "My mither has begged me to come hame and care for her."

Marjory sat up straighter, hoping she'd misunderstood her. "Do you mean to return home . . . for good?"

"Aye." She dabbed her eyes with her apron strings. "I would niver do such a thing if 'tweren't my mither asking."

"I'm sure of it," Marjory said, her heart sinking. She tried to picture her household without Helen Edgar and could not.

"Mebbe this wee bit will help." Digging in her pocket, the housekeeper withdrew six shillings, which she carefully counted out. "I ken siller is hard to come by, mem. These are my wages 'til Whitsuntide."

"Oh! I wouldn't think of taking it," Marjory protested. "That money is yours."

Mrs. Edgar would not be persuaded. "Take it, mem. If Gibson makes a canny bargain in Fishmarket Close, ye'll have smoked haddies for a fortnight."

Marjory touched the housekeeper's hand, chapped and red from her labors. "I'd rather have you for a twelvemonth."

"I'm sorry, mem. Truly, I am."

"But I'm the one who must apologize. You were due a new gown in January. No wonder you're keen to leave us."

"Nae!" The housekeeper looked up, clearly appalled at the suggestion. "I wouldna leave ye o'er a silly gown. But, mem, 'tis a' we can do to feed the five of us. If I'm not here, there'll be only four mouths to feed."

And no one to cook. Marjory did not wish to heap any guilt on Mrs. Edgar's shoulders. "If your mother needs you, then certainly you must go."

The housekeeper merely bobbed her head, her cheeks wet, her nose running.

Marjory offered her lace handkerchief, her own emotions reeling. She depended upon Helen's faithful service. Trusted her completely. When she'd thought of returning home to Tweedsford, she'd imagined Helen Edgar coming with her. "We'll speak more of this in the morn," Marjory told her.

"I hope to leave this Friday," the housekeeper confessed. "I'll be sure to finish a' my tasks afore I go. I'm sure we can find someone to cook yer meals and a lass to clean ilka week."

"But we'll not find another Mrs. Edgar," Marjory said with a heavy sigh, turning her head so her disappointment would not show.

"I'm verra sorry, mem. I'll bid ye guid nicht for now." The door closed softly behind her.

Marjory did not sleep well, nor did she dream. Instead she stared at the ceiling and whispered the words she knew to be true: *The Lord seeth. The Lord heareth. The Lord knoweth.*

Friday came too soon.

"The hoose is scrubbed clean from one end to the ither," Mrs. Edgar promised, already wearing her wool bonnet and a thin plaid cape. A small leather bag with her few personal belongings sat by the stair door.

"You've worked very hard this week." Marjory clasped her housekeeper's hands as if she might keep her a bit longer. Elisabeth and Janet stood on either side of her, one with a tender expression and the other with an air of impatience.

"Gibson kens whaur ilka thing can be found," Mrs. Edgar said, nodding at him in the doorway. "He'll do a' the marketing and keep yer coal grates fu' and yer water pitchers too."

Marjory was somewhat comforted by Gibson's fervent nodding. But it was a great deal to ask of one servant. And if Gibson became ill again . . . Well, she simply could not think of it. Not this day.

"Mrs. Sinclair's maidservant, Betty, will clean ilka Thursday," Mrs. Edgar promised. "But as to wha will cook . . ." She bit her lip.

"Do not trouble yourself," Marjory told

her. "We've made arrangements. Haven't we, Elisabeth?" She looked to her daughter-in-law, hoping she'd not changed her mind.

"We have," Elisabeth said firmly. "None will starve in this house."

"Guid, guid." Mrs. Edgar smiled even as her eyes began to fill. "Weel, then, I must be going." She busied herself with the strings of her cape, already well tied. " 'Twill not take me lang to reach Lasswade. Naught but seven miles. I'll be at my mither's door by three."

Marjory sighed. "I wish I could afford a carriage for you . . ."

"Hoot!" She laughed, making her tears spill over. "A hoosekeeper in a coach-and-four? Nae, mem. I'll find a wee family or some dairymaids to walk beside. Dinna fash yerself."

"Promise you will write to us," Elisabeth said, tugging Mrs. Edgar's bonnet in place. "I've put a few leaves of paper in your bag. We'll not mind the pence for your post."

"I read better than I write," the housekeeper admitted, "but, aye, I'll send ye news."

Nothing remained but to say farewell and bid Mrs. Edgar a safe journey. Janet was perfunctory, Elisabeth was warm, and Gibson was too overcome to speak.

Marjory followed her into the entrance hall. "Gibson will walk you to the end of the Canongate." They paused by the door. "Our prayers will go with you to Lasswade."

Mrs. Edgar bowed her head. "I've been honored to serve ye, Leddy Kerr. To leuk after Lord John . . . and to care for yer sons . . ." She broke down, sobbing into her new handkerchief. "I will sorely miss ye, mem."

Marjory placed her hands on the housekeeper's rounded shoulders, her eyes beginning to swim. "And I will miss you. So much." She tried to say more but could not. For one moment Marjory forgot that she was the Dowager Lady Kerr and pulled her beloved housekeeper into her arms. "Godspeed, dear Helen. Godspeed."

Seventy-Five

But dearest friends, alas! must part.

JOHN GAY

Elisabeth stood in the kitchen, a white apron tied over her mourning gown. At her elbow Scotch collops were stewing in a pan, filling the air with the scent of onions and sweet herbs. Janet pretended not to know who was preparing their meals, while Marjory expressed her gratitude each time they sat at table. "We cannot afford even the most inexperienced scullery maid," she'd said earlier at dinner, "and yet the Almighty has provided us with the best of cooks."

Elisabeth had smiled at that. As if a Highland lass had a choice about learning her way round a kitchen! She had caught and cleaned eel, had perfected the art of smoked venison and salmon, and could fix milled oats in a dozen different ways. For this evening's supper she'd chosen a simple dish, making do with a single serving of veal for all four of them.

In the end Marjory had not accepted Mrs. Edgar's six shillings, even though the housekeeper hadn't earned them, having departed before the end of her term. "She will need those coins," Marjory had insisted, "for her mother and for herself."

Elisabeth was taken aback. Something was happening to her mother-in-law. Whether it was the loss of her sons or the loss of her fortune, the Dowager Lady Kerr she'd once known seemed to be disappearing, and a real woman — with flesh and bone and heart — was slowly taking her place.

When a visitor came knocking on the stair, Elisabeth was glad she'd closed the door to her kitchen. Janet was right about this: if their neighbors discovered Lady Kerr in the kitchen, the gossip would never cease. She heard Mr. Baillie in the entrance hall, talking with Gibson. Delivering something, apparently.

Their landlord departed after a bit, and Gibson appeared in the kitchen, bearing a letter addressed to her. "Mr. Baillie meant to bring this up on Friday. Said he forgot."

Much as she longed to read it, the collops were ready to take off the fire and would not improve by stewing a minute longer. She slipped the letter inside her apron pocket and attended to her cooking. The last few minutes of daylight filled the drawing room windows as they sat down to supper at eight o' the clock. Gibson brought their plates to table, and Elisabeth sat with the others, her apron left in the kitchen.

"Delicious," her mother-in-law said after two bites. "Will you soon run out of dishes to prepare? Shall we borrow a copy of *The Compleat Housewife* for you? Perhaps Mr. Ramsay has the book in his circulating library."

"I'll be fine for a month or two," Elisabeth assured her. But if Mr. Laidlaw, the Kerrs' factor, did not bring the quarterly rents from Tweedsford soon, she would resort to her many recipes featuring oats.

Marjory seldom spoke of money now. There simply was none. Yesterday morning Marjory, too, had sold her gowns to Miss Callander, who'd offered only two pounds each. Gibson carried the gowns there himself, two at a time. When Marjory returned with her meager profit, Elisabeth reminded her she had a seamstress for a daughter-in-law. "When we can afford silk again," she'd told Marjory, "I'll dress us all in style."

Elisabeth produced a treat for dessert. "A fresh orange from Lisbon. Mr. Strachan of New Bank Close was anxious to sell them and gave me a very fair price." She split open the orange, sending a fragrant mist into the air, then handed each of them a quarter, Gibson included.

Janet eyed her fruit. "But I thought you had no coins left in your purse."

"His daughter fancied my enameled hair comb." Elisabeth savored one juicy slice of orange, then admitted, "An easy exchange was made."

"Has it come to that, then?" Janet savagely tore her quarter into slices, spraying juice everywhere. "Selling all we own or wear?"

"Aye, it has come to that," Marjory said simply. "I sent a letter to Mrs. Pitcairn, inquiring of her possible interest in our furniture."

"The *rouping wife?*" Elisabeth was relieved to hear it. The female auctioneer had a reputation for clever dealing and would treat Marjory more fairly than their miserly seamstress had. She looked about the room, wondering how much anyone might be willing to pay for chairs with mended upholstery and missing cushions. She'd done the best she could with her embroidery needle. But held up for auction, piece by piece, their plenishings would make a sad lot indeed.

Marjory followed her gaze. "I know we'll not earn a large sum. But I cannot afford the repairs, and we truly don't need all this." She waved her hand about. "I sent the letter this morn. We'll see what she says."

The letter. Elisabeth only now remembered Mr. Baillie's delivery, left in her apron pocket. She hurried to the kitchen rather than ring for Gibson, who was running his feet off trying to care for three women. She found him

664

heating water brought up from the Netherbow wellhead. In months past they would
have paid a caddie to haul water up the stair;
now the job fell to Gibson.

Elisabeth quickly found the letter and was
about to invite Gibson to join them in the
drawing room to hear it read when she looked
more closely at the handwriting. Plain, bold
strokes of black ink. *Rob MacPherson.*

Not trusting her legs to hold her, she
perched on Mrs. Edgar's old stool. She did
not regret turning down Rob's proposal or
sending him away, but she did wish she'd
done so with more grace. Would his letter be
an apology? Or a reproach?

She unfolded the thick paper and smoothed
out the creases, then leaned toward the
firelight. A longer letter than she'd expected,
dated the day Mrs. Edgar quit Milne Square,
bound for home.

Friday, 11 April 1746

Lady Kerr —

She was no longer *Bess* to him. Just as well.
It meant Rob understood such days were
over. Elisabeth read on.

I have very sad news. My father died this
morn.

665

"Nae!" She pressed the letter to her heart. *Not my dear Angus.*

Gibson abandoned his water pitchers and hastened to her side. "What is it, milady?"

"Mr. MacPherson . . ." Elisabeth leaned against the dressing table. "He cannot be . . ."

"The tailor's son, ye mean?"

"Not Rob but dear Angus." She squeezed out the words. "He's . . . gone."

"Och, can it be so?"

"Tell the others," she begged him. Gibson did her bidding at once, leaving her alone with Rob's letter. She dried her eyes with her apron, trying to read the words, trying to grasp the truth.

He had a restless night. I thought to come for you but did not want to offend. I sent this letter by way of Mr. Baillie, trusting him to deliver it.

But he did not. Elisabeth gripped the paper, guilt washing over her. Rob thought she knew last Friday. Now it was Tuesday.

I will bury my father at Greyfriars at ten o' the clock on Saturday. Meet me in the kirkyard, if you will.

"Oh, Rob." Her heart broke in two. *I would have come. I did not know.*

To think of Angus waiting for a bedside visit

that never came. And Rob standing by his father's grave, hoping she might join him and share his grief. *Please, please forgive me!*

"Lady Elisabeth?" Marjory stood in the doorway. "I am very sorry to hear this news." She drew closer, her face lined with sympathy. "I know how much Angus MacPherson meant to you."

"Aye, he did." Elisabeth buried her head in the crook of her arm and wept.

SEVENTY-SIX

Unthread the rude eye of rebellion,
And welcome home again discarded faith.
WILLIAM SHAKESPEARE

The ten o' the clock drum was echoing down
the empty High Street when Elisabeth retired
to her bedchamber, her body exhausted and
her heart weary. If she'd not sent Rob away
so rudely, perhaps he might have come to her
or taken her to see Angus and let her pour
out her gratitude for all the years he'd
watched over her.

But Rob had not come nor had his letter —
not until any hope of seeing Angus was lost.

The delayed letter was not her fault. She
knew that. But she should have realized Angus was dying. She should have made an effort. She should have ignored her feelings
toward Rob and visited his father . . .

Enough, Bess. She sagged against the pillows. Her list of regrets grew by the hour.
With a deep sigh she drew her bedside candle
closer, then unfolded Rob's letter. 'Twas the

last line that now weighed on her heart.

> I leave on the Sabbath for Inverness to join the prince's men and finish the work my father began.

Rob had never mentioned such plans to her. Maybe this was a promise he'd made to Angus in his final hours. Or perhaps, when she refused him, Rob chose to devote himself to his prince. The result was the same. Two days ago he'd departed for the Highlands, thinking Elisabeth Kerr did not care whether he lived or died.

I do care, Rob. Not as a future wife but certainly as an old friend.

Given the chance, she would have begged him to stay in Edinburgh rather than head north into the gathering storm. Monday's broadsheets reported the Duke of Cumberland and his royalist army marching to Inverness, where Prince Charlie and his Jacobites were assembling. After two months of skirmishes here and there, a battle was looming, far larger than Gladsmuir or Falkirk.

The end was coming. Elisabeth felt it in her bones. The prince's men were dwindling in number, and the duke's were growing by the hundreds. Rob was no doubt prepared for what awaited him in Inverness, but still she feared for his life. *God be with you, Rob.*

On the bed beside her lay the Buik, the

cover stained and tattered from all the hands that had touched it. She pulled it onto her lap, as she did every night of late, and turned to the psalms. Sometimes the words comforted her; other times they challenged her. Often they left her in tears. She could not always explain why.

Elisabeth spread her fingers across the pages, her silver rings gleaming in the candlelight. She touched them in turn, remembering all they'd once meant to her. Strength, provision, comfort, security. She tugged on her wedding band to see if it would move. *Nae.* Perhaps because her hands were warm, the other ring was firmly in place too. Both were remnants of another life.

She moved her hands aside, revealing her chosen verse for the evening.

"Our soul waiteth for the LORD." Aye, she knew something about waiting. Waiting for a husband, now lost to her. Waiting for a child that never came. Waiting to be embraced by a society that shunned her. But how did one *wait* for the Lord? Perhaps the waiting itself was an act of obedience.

"He is our help and our shield." She pictured the Highlanders on the field of battle with their round, leather targes held close to their chests, shielding them from the enemy's blows. Might the Almighty protect her in the same way, unseen yet invincible?

The truth was, she had no one to protect

her now. Not Donald, not Angus, not Rob. She closed her eyes but could not shut out the words that pressed on her heart. *Wait for him. Seek his help.*

"Elisabeth?" Her mother-in-law entered her room with tentative steps. "Pardon me for intruding."

"Nae, nae, come in," Elisabeth said, waving her closer.

Marjory pulled a chair beside her bed. "Now then, Lady Elisabeth —"

"Bess," she said, surprising them both. "My brother always addressed me by that name. Donald preferred it as well." So did Rob, for that matter. " 'Twould please me, if you're willing —"

"I am," her mother-in-law quickly assured her. "And you may call me Marjory in private." A brave step for a woman who'd always been so proud of her title.

Elisabeth smoothed her hand across the open book in her lap. "I've been reading the Scriptures. The words are . . . quite moving."

Marjory lowered her gaze. "I felt that way once, as a young woman. The Almighty was very real to me then."

"Is he not real now?"

"Aye, but . . ." Marjory's voice faded into silence.

Thinking to put her at ease, Elisabeth said, "The Almighty has so many names. What do you call him?"

"I call him . . ." Marjory pressed her hand to her mouth. "I . . ."

Elisabeth watched her mother-in-law struggle, fighting tears. "If you'd rather not . . ."

"Nae, nae." Marjory's voice was strained, her expression more so. "I call him Lord. But there was a time . . . oh, Bess, there was a time I called him my friend."

Stunned by her confession, Elisabeth hurried to comfort her. "The Buik says he is the same yesterday and today and forever. So he must still be your friend."

Marjory shook her head. "I have changed —"

"But he has not," Elisabeth said firmly, then paused. It was as if she knew something she'd not known a moment before. Like lighting a candle in a darkened room and instantly being able to see every corner. "If you trusted him once, you can do so again. Perhaps we might learn together?"

Marjory lifted her head with a weary sigh. "I wouldn't know where to begin."

Elisabeth knew at once. "The same way you taught your sons when they were lads." She dared to touch Marjory's wet cheek. "Might you think of me as your daughter?"

"Oh, Bess, I would be honored to have you as my daughter." Marjory tried to smile, though Elisabeth could see it was an effort. "As it happens, I am considering returning home at Whitsuntide. I assumed you and Janet would accompany me to Tweedsford, unless your mothers might prefer —"

"Nae!" Elisabeth quickly said. " 'Tis best if I go with you." She could not tell her mother-in-law the ugly truth of it. *I am not wanted at home.* She'd written her mother a dozen times since her marriage to Mr. Cromar. Not one letter was answered.

"Whitsuntide is but a month hence." Marjory stood, releasing a long sigh. "You needn't fear, Bess. I'll not abandon you."

Elisabeth watched her move toward the door. "Nor I you, Marjory."

SEVENTY-SEVEN

What various scenes,
and O! what scenes of Woe.
SIR WALTER SCOTT

On Thursday next Elisabeth woke before dawn. She moved soundlessly through Janet's bedchamber and into the kitchen, shivering in her nightgown. A cold, steady rain from the north beat upon the windows as she filled her porcelain pitcher with hot water from the kettle, sparing Gibson at least one task.

That she'd slept at all was surprising with both Mrs. Edgar in Lasswade and Rob Mac-Pherson in faraway Inverness weighing on her heart. She prayed for them each night and committed them to the Almighty's care. Trust was not coming easily to her, but it was coming.

She quietly carried the water pitcher to her bedchamber, then bathed and dressed, glad to have steaming hot water on such a dreary morn. When her hands were soapy, her rings almost slid off her fingers.

At breakfast Janet smeared her bannock with the last dab of marmalade in the house. "Something is afoot this morn. You can hear it in the voices floating up from the square now that the rain has stopped."

Elisabeth had heard them too. "I plan to visit Rob MacPherson's shop. Though his letter said he was leaving for Inverness, perhaps he changed his mind." A slender hope, to be sure, but Elisabeth was clinging to every thread in reach. And Rob would never come looking for her. "Gibson will escort me. I'll be in no danger."

"You are certain?" Marjory asked her across the table.

"Aye." Elisabeth was already slipping on her cape. The mid-April morning was not only wet but also chilly. "I'll be home by one o' the clock to prepare dinner. You'll not mind eating later?"

Marjory offered a sad smile. " 'Tis fashionable now to dine at two."

Fashionable? Elisabeth looked at the remains of their sparse breakfast and thought of the meager dinner that would follow: a single plump pigeon Gibson had snared from an abandoned *doocot,* a handful of very old carrots, and four small potatoes she'd received in trade for a length of green silk ribbon. She had no broth or pudding to offer, though they did have two oranges left to share. As for supper, she would surely pass a fishwife on the High Street anxious to sell her husband's morning catch or a pie seller willing to make a bargain. Elisabeth had a few ha'pence in her pocket. A very few. If Marjory was ready to part with her furniture, it was none too soon.

" 'Til one, then." Elisabeth followed Gibson through the house and down the stair, accustomed to people looking the other way as she walked by. The Highland widow of a Lowland traitor was a woman with no country to call her own.

The street was crowded with folk, many standing in tightly knit groups, all talking and gesturing at once, their faces dark with fear. The same words kept striking Elisabeth's ears as she hastened uphill toward the Luckenbooths. *Inverness. Cumberland. Nairn. Culloden House.* No bits of gossip she heard in passing were alike. Numbers of troops and conditions of armies changed with every step. No one was singing Jacobite ballads, as they had October last. Not a soul spoke fondly of their bonny Prince Charlie. Only the word *Jacobite* was used, and seldom kindly.

Ten steps away from Rob MacPherson's shop, Elisabeth knew her friend was gone. The Closed sign hung askew on the door, and one of the small windowpanes was broken. The rest of the glass would soon follow, too tempting for a wee lad with a stone in his hand. She peered inside and saw no

676

signs of life. Nothing that suggested a tailor and his son had ever lived and worked there.

"Perhaps he is staying in town with friends," Elisabeth ventured. "Or he might have traveled home to Braemar."

"Mebbe sae, milady," Gibson agreed, though she suspected he meant only to be polite.

Discouraged, she started back downhill, grateful not to see as many red-coated dragoons patrolling the High Street that morning. Whether they were sequestered in nearby Edinburgh Castle or fighting for King George in the Highland capital of Inverness, she could only guess.

When the gill bells of Saint Giles began ringing, Elisabeth took Gibson's arm, pulling him closer so he might hear her above the clamor. "I've not spoken to Mrs. Sinclair in a week. Suppose we see if she's safe and sound."

He bobbed his head. "Whatsomever ye like, milady."

With a steady wind at their backs and gray, scuttling clouds pushing east toward the Firth of Forth in the distance, the two walked down to Blackfriars Wynd. When they passed Mr. Sprott's, Elisabeth was glad they were no longer in need of candles since they could ill afford them. Now that the sun rose long before they did, candles were only required at supper and into the night. Soon they might manage without them entirely if they went to bed with the setting sun.

They climbed Effie's stair and were surprised to find her door slightly ajar. "Mrs. Sinclair?" Elisabeth sang out, peering into the entrance hall. Several wooden kists were stationed at the door. A moment later Effie's maidservant, Betty, came round the corner toting another.

"Och, Leddy Kerr!" She nearly dropped the chest in surprise. "I'll fetch my mistress. She'll be glad to see ye afore we leave."

"Leave? But . . ." Betty was gone before Elisabeth could ask the question.

Mrs. Sinclair appeared an instant later. "My dear Lady Kerr." She pulled her into the house with both hands, thoughtfully nodding at Gibson as well. "I cannot think what brought you to my door this morning, but I am very glad to see you."

"And I you." Elisabeth looked about the school's furnishings, draped in sheets. "Betty said you are leaving?"

"*Fleeing* is closer to the mark," Effie confided. "An old friend of my grandfather's sent a message by courier, urging me to quit the city at once. He has some inkling of Cumberland's plans. I've arranged to take a carriage leaving for Berwickshire at twelve o' the clock." She closed the door, then leaned against it, catching her breath. "Your family must not remain in Edinburgh, Lady Kerr.

678

'Tis not safe for anyone, especially not those of our persuasion."

Elisabeth nodded, understanding. "We were planning on traveling south at Whitsuntide. But I'm afraid a carriage is out of the question."

"Are things so bad as that?" Effie asked, concern filling her small brown eyes.

"Don't worry about us for a moment," Elisabeth said, unhappy with herself for hinting at their money woes. "Once we reach Tweedsford, all will be resolved."

"I am glad to hear it," Effie said, patting her hand. "Now, I must beg your forgiveness, but . . ."

"We shall leave you to your packing." Elisabeth kissed each round cheek, then departed, her heart aching as they descended the turnpike stair. Would she ever see her beloved schoolmistress again? "Too many farewells," she confessed to Gibson when they reached the wynd. As they walked home, Elisabeth remembered a wintry evening when the Kerr women had struggled along the same path through the falling snow, only to find Gibson ill when they reached Milne Square. "Your health seems quite restored," she said.

"Aye, milady. Just as weel, for we'll not have Betty's help ilka Thursday."

"Oh!" Elisabeth stopped in her tracks, having completely forgotten. "Betty was to clean for us this afternoon." In truth, they could no longer afford a sixpence each week for her services. "We'll manage somehow, Gibson." She briefly considered putting a dusting cloth in Janet's hand, then discarded the idea. Better to do the work herself than endure her sister-in-law's complaining.

The two were soon home, sharing all they'd heard in the street.

"I've told Janet of my decision to return home to Tweedsford," Marjory said as Elisabeth drew closer to the fire, warming her hands. "If Sir Robert's friend is rightly informed, perhaps we should leave sooner than May."

"We should," she urged her, greatly relieved. "Effie Sinclair would never abandon her school in haste unless she was very sure."

Marjory nodded. "I expect Mrs. Pitcairn on Saturday. If she purchases all we own, Bess, we'll be free to leave for Selkirk at once. If indeed you are ready?"

Elisabeth eyed the few coals in the grate, the single candle on the mantel, and nodded. "More than ready."

Seventy-Eight

Much dearer be the things
which come through hard distress.
HERBERT SPENCER

Marjory clasped her hands, hoping her anxiety did not show. "What say you, Mrs. Pitcairn? Will you buy our plenishings to sell at auction?"

The rouping wife, a tall, angular woman full of years, regarded the drawing room sofa with a practiced eye, her spectacles hanging precipitously near the end of her long nose. She nodded for a bit, then made several notations. "I'll take them a', mem. But ye'll not like the price."

Marjory's hopes plummeted. Everything depended on how many pounds and shillings the rouping wife offered. With the clear April light pouring through the window, Marjory saw her furniture through Mrs. Pitcairn's eyes, and the view was unimpressive.

The auctioneer touched the silk upholstery, slashed by the dragoons. "Someone with a deft hand mended this."

"My daughter-in-law," Marjory admitted. Over the winter months Elisabeth had employed her needle wherever possible, adding clever bits of embroidery to cover her repair work. "She is very skilled."

"Mmm." Mrs. Pitcairn spent a few more minutes taking inventory, then scratched a number in her notebook and held it out for her approval. " 'Tis my best offer."

Marjory abruptly sat in the nearest chair. "Is that all?" Lord John had paid ten times that amount.

"I'll remind ye every piece is used and most are damaged." Towering over her, Mrs. Pitcairn tapped on the notebook. "Aye or nae, mem?"

Marjory closed her eyes rather than stare at the disheartening sum. "Aye."

"Sold, then." Mrs. Pitcairn closed her notebook with a snap. "I'll auction them on Friday next at the Golden Fan below Blackfriars Wynd. My men will come round on Thursday at noontide to collect everything. Will that suit?"

Marjory nodded, the decision made for her. They would depart in five days, leaving behind an empty house.

The woman withdrew from her skirt pocket a large leather purse heavy with coins. She counted out the agreed-upon sum, deposited it in Marjory's hand, then yanked her purse shut. " 'Til Thursday, then. Shall we wet oor bargain?"

Heat flew up Marjory's neck. "I'm afraid the dragoons took all our whisky."

Mrs. Pitcairn clucked her tongue. "Ye'll shake the dust aff o' yer feet whan ye leave this toun."

"So I shall," Marjory agreed, suddenly very weary of living in the capital. Who could have envisioned such a day? She saw Mrs. Pitcairn to the door, then sat down at Lord John's mahogany desk in the entrance hall and released a lengthy sigh.

The house was quiet. She'd sent Elisabeth and Janet to Mr. Ramsay's circulating library for an hour, thinking the whole unseemly process might be more bearable without her daughters-in-law on hand to share her humiliation.

Gibson emerged from the kitchen, steaming cup in hand. "I thocht ye might be needing yer tea, mem."

The aroma alone revived her. Stirring in a half lump of sugar, she told Gibson, "I'll tally up the last of our debts and have you settle them for me on Monday."

Something flickered across his face. Disappointment? Fear?

Marjory reconsidered. There was no reason to wait. "Would you rather call on our creditors this afternoon?"

"Aye," he said, the relief evident on his face.

She knew he took the brunt of any complaints from merchants and would be as glad as she to see their obligations met.

Marjory pulled out her cashbook and the burgeoning stack of unpaid bills, then took a long drink of tea to fortify her. The glistening pile of pounds and shillings would not be hers for long. She began her bookkeeping, praying she would not come up short. She had nothing else to sell. And nowhere else to turn.

> Mrs. McIntosh, for washing: one pound, two shillings.
> Mr. Stonehouse, for coal: three pounds, one shilling.
> Mrs. Dunsmuir, for tea and loaf sugar: one pound, four shillings.

Marjory eyed her teacup. Having given up almost every other indulgence, she refused to feel guilty for maintaining one small habit.

She made a careful list for Gibson, indicating who was to be paid by using simple drawings. He would be making more than a dozen stops that afternoon, including one at White Horse Close to arrange a carriage for Thursday morn. After their bills were accounted for, only a dozen or so shillings remained. Marjory held the coins cupped in her palm, thinking how in days gone by she would easily lose this much at cards and think nothing of it. Now each coin was precious and not to be wasted.

With some reluctance she pressed one more shilling into Gibson's hand. "Bring us a dozen potatoes," she told him. "If you find a good price on trout in the Fishmarket, buy that as well. Let the color of the gills and the look of the eyes be your guide. And bacon from Mr. Gilchrist in Fleshmarket Close, if you will."

"Aye, mem." He'd hidden all her coins in various pockets. "I'll return as soon as ever I can."

Marjory leaned forward, but she could not see the hands on the clock in the next room. He would be home by six o' the clock, she guessed, in time to assist Elisabeth with their supper.

Shortly after Gibson departed down the stair, her daughters-in-law returned, their faces sober. "Still no news from Inverness," Elisabeth said, tugging off her cape, "though an official report cannot be long in coming. The rumors all point to a battle, but precisely where and when . . ." She shook her head.

"I have already lost my sons," Marjory reminded them, slipping the remaining shillings in her pocket. "Whatever the outcome, King George can take nothing else away from me. He cannot charge the dead with treason nor take lives already given."

"But we supported the prince as well,"

Elisabeth said softly. "With our coins and our poems and our hearts."

Janet frowned. "Are you saying we are in danger?"

"I am saying it is not King George who concerns me but his son, the Duke of Cumberland. His reputation marks him as heartless and cruel. He is the reason Mrs. Sinclair left in haste."

"We'll not be long behind her," Marjory promised.

"What of Mrs. Pitcairn?" Janet wanted to know. "Was the woman generous?"

"She was . . . honest," Marjory admitted. "At least we'll not depart Edinburgh in debt. I've asked Gibson to arrange for a morning coach on Thursday."

"Five days," Janet breathed, as if trying to take it in.

"We should start packing at once." Elisabeth ducked into the kitchen, then reappeared with three linen aprons. "I've a small kist in my room that should hold my few belongings."

Janet took the apron with obvious disdain. "I cannot believe I must pack my own trunks."

Marjory snapped back, "And *I* cannot believe you would expect either of us to do it for you." When Janet's mouth dropped open, Marjory felt only a little guilty.

"We'll all help each other," Elisabeth suggested. "Suppose we begin in your bedchamber."

Within the hour two large trunks were filled with Janet's petticoats, hats, gloves, and shoes. Though the dragoons had spared none of her gowns, Janet did have several pieces of jewelry the men hadn't found, including an expensive pair of gold and emerald earrings. When no one was looking, Marjory plucked them from Janet's dressing table and held them to her ears, admiring how the dark green jewels sparkled in the looking glass.

"My father gave me those," Janet said from the doorway.

Marjory quickly put the earrings back where she'd found them. "Lovely," she murmured, then returned to folding handkerchiefs. Janet easily owned a dozen, all edged in delicate lace. "We'll pack my trunk next," Marjory said. " 'Twill not take long."

While she and Elisabeth labored, lining a small trunk with her nightgowns and stockings, Janet mostly watched. Marjory could not remember what it was about her older daughter-in-law that had once appealed to her. Had Janet changed? Or had she?

Marjory glanced at the window as the clock chimed six. Two more hours of daylight remained for Gibson's errands, though most shops would have closed by now. When he hadn't returned by seven o' the clock, Marjory lost interest in packing and simply stood by the window, looking down at the High Street. And when Elisabeth placed their supper on the table at eight, as the last rays of the sun were fading behind the rooftops, Marjory could barely taste her broth, however highly seasoned.

"He'll not be much longer." Elisabeth meant to comfort her, but her words carried little weight. Who knew what might have happened? Gibson was not a young man. He'd left the house with his pockets stuffed with coins. And Edinburgh was rife with strangers.

Marjory put down her spoon. "Should the three of us look for him? Perhaps together . . ." Her voice trailed off at the sound of footsteps on the landing. When the door opened, she flew to the entrance hall.

"Och, mem!" Startled, Gibson nearly stumbled back onto the landing.

Marjory gave him room, waving him inside. "Forgive me, but . . ."

"Aye, nae wonder ye're worried, late as I am." He hung his coat on the hook by his bed, then turned to her. "It took a lang time to find a' the folk. Some were at the mercat cross, ithers at the Star and Garter, and some were having supper behind their shops and couldna hear my knock." He patted his many pockets, satisfied they were empty. " 'Tis done, mem. Yer carriage hame is arranged. And a' yer debts are paid."

Marjory almost kissed his brow she was so relieved. "Come, have some broth with us at table."

His bushy eyebrows drew together. "I should eat in the kitchen . . ."

"Not this night." Marjory led him into the drawing room, where Elisabeth had taken her cue and had a place waiting for him.

He sat, then fished something out of his waistcoat. "I stopped by the Post Office." He held out a letter. "For ye, mem."

Marjory recognized the hand. *Helen Edgar.* "From Lasswade," she announced, opening it at once.

To Lady Marjory Kerr of Milne Square
Saturday, 12 April 1746

I arrived home after a pleasant walk.

Janet rolled her eyes. "Only Mrs. Edgar would consider walking seven miles pleasant."

"Do keep reading," Elisabeth urged, giving Janet a withering look.

My mother is frailer than I had hoped. But she is eating better now that I am cooking for her.

"No surprise, that," Elisabeth said. "My cooking doesn't hold a candle to hers."

"Ye've made a fine broth," Gibson insisted, then downed another spoonful.

I had forgotten the size of our garden and the quietness of village life. We have chestnut and sycamore trees beyond our door. A barn owl hoots at night.

Marjory paused her reading, thinking of Tweedsford with its native woods and abundance of birds. Aye, she was ready for home. More than ready, as Elisabeth said.

I miss each of you and wish you well.
Yours always,
Helen Edgar

Marjory folded the letter, a faint mist clouding her vision. "I am glad she is safely home. Lord willing, we shall say the same of ourselves one week hence. Gibson, while you were out, did you learn any news from the north?"

"The usual blether," he said with a shrug. "Wha can say whan we'll hear? Inverness is sae far awa."

With the sun well set and their last two candles barely dispelling the darkness, the household retired earlier than usual. Marjory was beneath the covers and drifting to sleep within minutes.

At first she thought the booming noise she heard was thunder. But the sound was too loud and too close, rolling down the High Street from Edinburgh Castle, rattling her windowpanes.

Marjory sat up at once. *The cannons.*

Horrified, she leaped from bed and ran into Elisabeth's bedchamber. "The king's men!" Marjory cried. "They're firing the great guns from the batteries. I fear 'tis a victory salute."

Elisabeth flung back her covers. "Nae, it cannot be!"

Marjory lifted the sash, and they both leaned out. Below them, people were streaming into the High Street, many in their nightclothes with plaids thrown about their shoulders. All were waving, cheering, shouting as another round of discharges echoed the dreaded news.

SEVENTY-NINE

Here burns my candle out;
ay, here it dies.

WILLIAM SHAKESPEARE

"The prince's men were defeated in half an hour." Gibson stood in the doorway, still breathing hard from his hasty trip down the stair and back. "Nae quarter was given. A thousand Hielanders lay deid on Drummossie Muir."

"Nae!" Elisabeth moaned. "Not a *thousand* . . ."

Marjory closed her eyes, feeling sick. She could not fathom such bloodshed.

Gibson mopped his brow. "The Duke o' Cumberland's aide-de-camp arrived at the castle with a dispatch at midnight."

Abandoning any hope of sleep, Marjory moved to the fireplace to light a candle. " 'Tis past two o' the clock now."

Gibson followed her, keeping his voice low. "There's mair, Leddy Kerr. Cumberland's men were ordered to put to death a' the wounded with pistol, club, or bayonet. Them that escaped the field o' battle are being hunted doon and killed. Aye, and their luved ones as weel."

Marjory bent down, touching the wick to the live coal, her hand trembling. "Is there no mercy in Cumberland's heart?"

"Nae, mem. Not for them wha supported the Jacobite cause."

As we did. The truth struck a hard blow, knocking the wind from her. Had the king not taken enough? Would his son inflict further punishment still? *Pistol, club, or bayonet.*

Elisabeth was walking toward them now, her cheeks wet with tears. "Is there news of Rob MacPherson?"

Gibson shook his head. "Nae, milady."

"What's to become of us?" Elisabeth said, her voice like broken glass.

Without a moment's hesitation, Marjory slipped her arm round her daughter-in-law's waist. "We'll soon be bound for Tweedsford." The farther removed from the Highlands, the better, though she would not confess as much to her daughters-in-law.

Janet's door opened. She yawned and entered the room, rubbing her eyes. "Whatever is the commotion in the street?"

When Marjory told her, Janet's face paled. "Must we wait 'til Thursday to leave?"

Gibson answered her. "Whan I arranged for yer carriage, I was told there were none to be had afore then."

Marjory held out her arm to encircle Janet as well. "It seems we are not alone in quitting the capital." When Janet did not step closer, Marjory pretended to brush a fleck of lint from her nightgown, stung by her daughter-in-law's rejection. "We've much to accomplish in the days ahead," she reminded them. "For now, 'tis the Sabbath. I suggest we spend it in prayer."

Though the noise in the street eventually subsided, none in the Kerr household could think of returning to bed. Elisabeth took Marjory's words to heart and read aloud from the Buik through the few remaining hours before dawn, the three of them gathered round Marjory's tea table. "Oh that I were as in months past, as in the days when God preserved me," Elisabeth read. "When his candle shined upon my head, and when by his light I walked through darkness."

Marjory bowed her head, listening. *I remember such days.* She had lived without fear, ever aware of God's presence in her life, shining brighter than any beeswax taper. When she looked up and saw Elisabeth leaning across the Buik, her eyes glowing and her voice fervent, Marjory fought a twinge of envy. To have that passion again! To burn for all that was holy.

Perhaps when she returned to Tweedsford, when she knelt beside her old bed, perhaps then the Almighty would banish the darkness inside her for good.

The Sabbath morning passed quietly. The women broke their fast, prayed at length, then gathered at the window when the Tron Kirk rang its bell.

Marjory watched the throng pouring through the kirk doors across the High Street, wishing she might join her Edinburgh friends once more and worship the Lord. But the Kerrs were anathema. None would welcome them now.

"Shall we attend services when we live in Selkirk?" Elisabeth asked.

"Every Sunday," Marjory said firmly. The kirk session, charged with keeping a close eye on the morals of their parishioners, would forgive her brief dalliance with the Jacobite cause. She was, after all, the Dowager Lady Kerr.

As the morning wore on, the three women drank watery tea with thin gingersnaps. Elisabeth apologized for their hard texture. "I'm trying to make our butter last until breakfast on Thursday."

Marjory bit into her biscuit and did not let Elisabeth see her wince. The lass was doing the best she could. None could fault her. Except Janet, who buttered the top of her gingersnap as if it were toast and then fussed, "Why even bake them if you intend to scrimp on the recipe?"

"So you might have something to complain about," Elisabeth gently said, putting Janet very neatly in her place.

At noontide the bell rang again, and the doors of the kirk opened, releasing the parishioners into the street. Women were dressed in brighter colors than Marjory had seen in some time. A celebration of spring, she imagined; and of victory for King George.

She peered down at two people approaching Milne Square. They reached the open arcade leading into the square before Marjory recognized her old tea-table friend, Lady Woodhall, and her manservant, with his shock of red hair.

Elisabeth saw them too. "Shall I have Gibson prepare fresh tea?"

"Aye." Marjory quickly began gathering dishes. "As strong as he can make it." Her heart was pounding. What would bring Lady Woodhall to her door? 'Twas not a social call. Not on the Sabbath.

Even Janet helped her clear the table and straighten the house. By the time the expected knock came, all three Kerrs were seated in the drawing room, hands folded, as if they had nothing to do but wait upon callers.

When she was announced, Lady Woodhall entered the room with purpose, a silver-capped walking stick in her hand and a steely look in her eye. She did not take the offered seat but stood before them. The Kerrs rose as well, honoring her advanced age and exalted station.

"Lady Marjory," she began, "I shall not mince words. You must leave Edinburgh at once. What I heard this morn after services was enough to freeze my blood."

Marjory felt a chill of her own. "Wh-what did you hear?"

"You, and all who supported the Stuarts, are in mortal danger." Lady Woodhall cast her sharp gaze round the room. "I see you have already been subjected to the army's cruelty. Soon their punishment will grow more severe. There are rumors of firing squads, of homes being burned, of women . . ." She shuddered. "How soon can you leave the city?"

"We've a carriage for Thursday morn."

"Ah. I am glad you have planned your escape, but I do wish . . ." Lady Woodhall cleared her throat. "If you need shelter this week, for you and your household, I hope you will come to my door. We are neighbors, after all. And friends."

"Aye." Marjory offered her hand, wishing it did not tremble so. "We are."

Lady Woodhall slipped off her glove and clasped Marjory's hand in return, her firm grip belying her years. "I wish you Godspeed.

You and your daughters-in-law." She nodded at Elisabeth and Janet as if only now noticing them, then stepped closer, her silver hair catching the firelight. "I was very sorry to hear of your loss, Lady Marjory. No mother should have to bury her children."

"Nae." She pressed her lips together and swallowed.

Lady Woodhall squeezed her hand. "I meant what I said, Lady Marjory. Come at any hour."

Monday dawned cool, gray, and damp. Marjory did not have enough coal to warm the whole house, so she closed the bedchambers and had Gibson fill only the drawing room grate. With a second layer of stockings and wool plaids draped round their shoulders, the women were warm enough. Still, they shivered, and not only from the weather.

The High Street overflowed with British soldiers. An endless river of red streamed from castle above to palace below. The same citizens who'd cheered the bonny prince and his Highland army six months ago now stood in their doorways and leaned out their windows to greet the victors with their brass buttons and their proud chins.

But in the oyster cellars and taverns of Edinburgh, the mood was darker. Rumors from the field of battle traveled about like wisps of chimney smoke. *Men were slaughtered. Left naked on the hills. Burned in their cottages. Starved in prison.* When Gibson returned from Fishmarket Close with the grim report, Marjory quickly lost her appetite for dinner. "We shall save your haddocks for supper," she told him, "and pack the contents of Lord John's desk instead."

Anything to take their minds off the atrocities.

Anything to hasten Thursday morn.

Still, the afternoon dragged on. All four of them were in the entrance hall, surrounded by papers and covered in dust, when a loud knock at the stair door startled them out of their wits.

"Who can it be?" Janet whispered, her hand on her throat.

Marjory stared at the door. It was not a fist she heard but something harder. *The butt of a pistol.* Then came a voice shouting her name. "Marjory Kerr. Open in the name of His Royal Highness, King George."

She couldn't move, could barely breathe. Had they come for her? Would her household be harmed? *Please, Lord. Please help us!*

When a second knock came, louder than the first, Gibson unbolted the door, his whole body shaking.

Before a word was spoken, two uniformed British soldiers crossed the threshold, their boot heels striking the wooden floor. Marjory nearly wept at the sight of them. Tall and slender, with fair complexions, they might have been Donald and Andrew.

But they were not.

Their gazes were hard, and the lines of their mouths were drawn with a scornful hand. One of them produced a letter. "For you, madam."

Marjory recognized the elegant handwriting of Lord Mark Kerr. His Royal Highness's seal was pressed into the thick red wax.

The young dragoon spoke again. " 'Twas delivered to the castle yesterday morning by Viscount Bury, aide-de-camp to the Duke of Cumberland. Will you not take it, Mrs. Kerr?"

Mrs. Kerr. Marjory had never been so addressed in her life. She nodded toward the desk. "There, if you please." She did not want to touch the letter. Not unless she had to. "Have you been commanded to wait for a reply?"

"Nae, madam," the other answered. "Only to see it delivered into your hands."

Elisabeth stepped beside her, their shoulders touching. "Then your duty has been discharged," her daughter-in-law told them in a clear, calm voice. "Good day to you, gentlemen."

They raked her with their gazes but said nothing more. When they retreated to the stair landing, Elisabeth quietly closed the door and bolted it. "They're gone, madam."

Marjory collapsed onto Lord John's chair

and threw herself across his desk. "I cannot," she whispered against the sleeves of her gown. "I cannot open it."

The others circled round her. "Would it help if I read it to you?" Elisabeth asked.

Marjory lifted her head long enough to look at the letter. That it contained ill news was certain. "Aye," she finally said. "Let us gather by the fire where it is warm, at least."

When the three women were seated, so closely their knees nearly touched, Marjory nodded at Elisabeth, who held the letter in her hands. Gibson stood at attention in silent support.

The seal did not break easily when Elisabeth opened the letter, as if defying them from the outset. She leaned toward the single candle on a stand by her elbow and began to read aloud.

To Marjory Kerr
Milne Square, Edinburgh
Thursday, 17 April 1746

Mrs. Kerr:

Janet fumed, "Why does he insist on calling you 'Mrs. Kerr' when 'tis *my* name?"

Marjory did not answer, fearing the reason. *My dear Lord John, can ever you forgive me?* She held her breath as Elisabeth read on.

It is most unfortunate that your sons gave
their lives on Falkirk Muir, in particular for
so vile and despicable a cause.

"Our husbands were neither of those
things," Janet protested.

"But their deaths *were* most unfortunate,"
Marjory said, not wanting to argue with her.
Not now.

Elisabeth must have skimmed ahead. Her
face was the color of milk-washed linen.
When she began reading again, her voice was
noticeably thinner.

I regret to inform you of the consequences
of their treason and yours.

Elisabeth looked up. "Oh, my dear lady." A
tear slipped from the corner of her eye. "I am
so sorry."

As her daughter-in-law continued reading,
Marjory sank deeper into her chair with each
terrible revelation.

Lord Donald Kerr of Selkirk is declared attainted, having been found guilty without
benefit of a trial.

Attainted. The worst of charges, reserved for
the worst of crimes against the Crown. *My
poor sons.* To be so disgraced and not live to
defend their actions.

702

His Lordship's title is revoked and has reverted to the Crown.

Elisabeth paused. "Then I am . . . no longer Lady Kerr."

"Nae, nor I." Marjory stared at the glowing coals, knowing what would come next. *Please, please. May it not be so, Lord.* Surely a grieving widow could not lose everything. Not all she owned. *Not everything.*

Elisabeth read the words aloud before the letter slipped from her hands onto the carpet.

Tweedsford, his former Lordship's estate in Selkirkshire, is now forfeit to the Crown, and its contents seized for payment of fines.

"Forfeit?" Janet cried. "Meaning it is no longer ours? Whatever shall we do?"

With great effort Marjory lifted her head. "We shall go home."

EIGHTY

The good widow's sorrow
is no storm, but a still rain.
THOMAS FULLER

Marjory bent down to retrieve the letter so
slowly 'twas like reaching through deep water.
She glanced at the final line, then was sorry
she'd read it.

You and your sons were duly warned,
madam. It is regrettable that none of you
took notice.

*I did not need your warning, milord. I needed
your help.* She folded the letter, covering the
bold signature of Lord Mark Kerr.

Elisabeth rested her hand on Marjory's
arm. A warm, comforting touch. No one
spoke. Muted cries from the street and passing footsteps on the stair were the only
sounds.

Finally, when she could hold the truth
inside no longer, Marjory said in a low voice,

"I feared this day might come."

"Yet you said nothing." Janet sniffed.

Feeling the sting of her disapproval, Marjory confessed, "It was easier to avoid the subject. To hope it would never happen."

"But it *has* happened." Janet's retort bore a sharp edge. "We depended upon your sons to provide for us. And then we depended upon you."

Silently pleading for wisdom, Marjory looked at both of her daughters-in-law, at Elisabeth's trusting expression and Janet's doubting one. "We will still leave on Thursday morn," she assured them, though she was not at all sure. "We will still make our home in Selkirk. I have . . . acquaintances there from years past." *Many years past. Perhaps too many.* Marjory had not written to a single one of them since leaving home. Would they even remember her?

Janet frowned. "These friends of yours. They will provide lodging?"

"I could not ask that of them," Marjory admitted. "But they might know of a prospect . . ." Even saying the words, she realized the futility of such an expectation. Who would offer lodging to three penniless women?

Janet's voice rose with her ire. "You expect us to travel forty miles with no hope of a bed or a meal waiting for us?"

"We do have relatives there, however distant," Marjory told her. That, at least, was not a fabrication. Anne Kerr, one of Lord John's cousins, still resided in Selkirk.

"Perhaps we could write to these relatives?" Elisabeth had such hope in her eyes that Marjory found her own spirits lifting. No wonder Donald had loved this young woman.

"I will pen a letter at once," Marjory agreed, already composing one in her mind even as she prayed. *Please let Anne be willing, Lord. Please.*

"In the meantime I'll attend to our supper." Elisabeth stood, gazing down at her. "You'll find stationery and sharpened quills on Donald's secretary."

Donald. A twinge of pain. *Not Lord Donald. Not ever again.* Marjory waited, letting the sadness move through her. She had already lost her husband and sons. The loss of their title was trifling in comparison.

Moments later she was seated at her tea table with paper, pen, and ink at hand. A soft rain had begun to fall, washing the window-panes. Gazing at the pale gray sky, she considered how best to begin. *I am coming home to Selkirk with my two daughters-in-law . . .*

Marjory held the quill but could not put pen to paper. Tears stung her eyes. Did she think this was so easily managed? A few lines on a page and all would be settled? One woman might be absorbed into a household, but not three.

Still, her daughters-in-law were counting on her to provide for them. *How can I, Lord, when I have nothing?* She stared at the blank page, her heart aching. Janet and Elisabeth had been willing enough to accompany her to a fine estate. But Cousin Anne's humble lodgings in Selkirk were another matter. And what if Anne turned them away the moment they arrived?

I am coming home to Selkirk with my two daughters-in-law . . .

Nae. The prospect was too risky and far too uncertain. Marjory pressed against her brow, holding back the pain. *Must I let go of them as well?* Tears dropped onto the paper as the answer became clear. *Aye.* She would send Janet and Elisabeth home to the Highlands. To the houses they knew and the families who loved them. However unexpected their return, a warm greeting was certain.

But not for her.

Marjory reached for a fresh piece of stationery, then bowed her head, drying her tears. *Please make a way for me, Lord. Lead me and guide me.*

Her memories of Anne Kerr were faint. She was perhaps six-and-thirty now, a *stayed lass,* unless she'd finally married. Thoughtful and soft-spoken, Anne was a fair-haired woman with a gentle smile. Marjory imagined her husband's cousin standing before her as she began to write.

To Miss Anne Kerr
Halliwell's Close, Selkirk
Monday, 21 April 1746

Dear Cousin Anne:

I pray this letter finds you, and finds you well.

How much to tell Anne? All of Selkirk would learn of the forfeiture when a new owner appeared at Tweedsford, if not sooner. Would her cousin be sympathetic? Or suspicious?

Alas, I have buried my husband, John Kerr, and my sons, Donald and Andrew. I am coming home to Selkirk.

There it was in ink. She would travel alone. Marjory had weathered so many difficult good-byes of late, but she could not imagine parting with both her daughters-in-law at once. Janet might be glad to be rid of her, but Elisabeth . . .

Marjory looked toward the kitchen. *My dear Bess.* The weaver's daughter from Braemar, who'd quietly won her heart. *You chose well, Donald.* She swallowed the lump rising in her throat and returned to her letter, praying Anne might be half so generous as Elisabeth.

Of my late husband's relatives, you are the only one I know who still resides in Selkirk. I expect to arrive on Saturday next. Might you kindly accommodate me until I find lodgings of my own?

She hoped her cousin's eyes would gloss over the word *until*. It might be a long time before Marjory found somewhere else to abide. She remembered Halliwell's Close as a quaint and cozy place in the heart of town. If Anne still lived there and if she had sufficient room, might she make a home for her? For good? *Please may it be so, Lord.*

Marjory suddenly realized Gibson would also need somewhere to lay his head. Dare she ask for that as well?

This letter comes to you by way of our manservant of many years, Neil Gibson. I would be forever in your debt if you directed Mr. Gibson to an appropriate lodging place until I arrive.

> Eagerly anticipating the renewal
> of our acquaintance,
> Your cousin,
> Marjory Kerr

She had no title nor property to mention.

Two names, nothing more. Hardly impressive. But she did not need her cousin's respect or admiration. She needed her help.

And she needed Gibson's assistance as well. Marjory found him at table, dutifully polishing the family's last three silver spoons. A more loyal servant did not exist in Christendom. "Come," she murmured, glad neither daughter-in-law was within earshot.

"What is it, mem?" he asked as she led him to the farthest corner of her chamber.

She kept her eye on the door and her voice low. "On Thursday I will take the carriage to Selkirk, just as you've arranged. But I am sending my daughters-in-law to their Highland families by way of Perth."

"Have ye not told them?"

"Nae, nor will I. Not until that morn." She sighed. " 'Twill be hard enough to bid one another farewell. Better to surprise them and send them on their way."

Gibson nodded, though he did not look convinced.

"On the morrow kindly stop at White Horse Close and make the necessary changes in our arrangements."

"Aye, mem. But I'll need mair shillings to do sae."

She dug several coins out of her pocket, for once not begrudging the expense. These were the widows of her sons. They deserved a chance at happiness, not a lifetime of caring for an aging mother-in-law.

"As for my own journey," she told him, "I cannot afford to send a letter ahead by messenger. Nor would I dare prevail upon a distant relation to pay for my post when it arrives. But if you might travel ahead of me, Gibson, and deliver my letter to Anne Kerr . . ."

He bowed. "Whatsomever ye need, mem."

Only then did Marjory realize what she was asking of him. Gibson would have no position waiting for him in Selkirk. She could not employ him nor expect strangers to readily bring another manservant into their household. "Gibson, I am afraid . . ."

"I ken, mem. Ye'll have nae need o' me whan ye arrive."

"Oh, I shall always need you," she was quick to say. "But I cannot pay your wages nor offer you food or lodging."

He nodded as if prepared for this news. How could he not be in a household where plenishings were ravaged, then sold at auction, and a title and property were lost in a single afternoon?

"I'll provide a written character," she promised him, "with so glowing a commendation of your services that any of the grand houses in Selkirkshire would welcome you through their door. Perhaps even the new owner of Tweedsford . . ." Her voice faltered.

"Nae," he said firmly. "I canna serve at

Tweedsford unless the Kerrs are resident."

Lord Mark's disastrous letter had not brought tears to her eyes. But Gibson's few words did. "God bless you," she whispered, blinking lest she embarrass them both.

Tuesday morning the women had breakfast earlier than usual, with Gibson standing at the end of the table, ever waiting to be of service.

Marjory had finished her letters, praying they might be well received. She was asking a great deal of a woman she did not know and was more than a little nervous about traveling alone. Reaching for a word of solace, Marjory quickly found it and held it close to her heart. *Hide me under the shadow of thy wings.*

Elisabeth emerged from the kitchen with Gibson's rough leather bag, ready to be strapped to his back. "I've packed several meals for you," she told him, placing his bag on the table. "Hard cheese, fresh bannocks, and boiled eggs. I trust you'll find a wee burn when you're thirsty."

"Aye, aye." Gibson thanked her profusely, bobbing his head.

Marjory joined them at the foot of the table. "You'll no doubt remember the journey takes four days if you keep a reasonable pace over the Moorfoot Hills." She hesitated, then said what was pressing on her heart. "I am sorry we cannot afford . . ."

"Nae, mem," he said gruffly. "I nae mair belong in a carriage than Mrs. Edgar." He waved his hand toward the window. " 'Tis a fine spring day for a walk. I've a plaid for my bed and a feast for my stomach. Nae doubt a farmer will let me ride in his oxcart. I'll reach Selkirk lang afore ye do."

She nodded. "At least by a day or two." *If all goes well. If God is kind.* "You'll not forget to stop by White Horse Close?" Marjory sought his gaze. "To be sure our carriage seats are . . . properly arranged?"

"I'll not forget, mem."

Nothing remained but to bid Gibson farewell.

All three of them followed him into the entrance hall. Even Janet looked sad to see him leave.

"Ye'll a' be safe?" he asked them.

"We will." Marjory tucked a shilling into the palm of his hand and folded his fingers round it. Her eyes grew moist. "I wish I had more to give you."

He ducked his head, working hard to keep his emotions at bay. "Ye've been sae guid to me, mem. Sae verra guid."

"You are the one who's been good to the Kerr family all these years." Marjory blew her nose into her handkerchief, then laughed a little. "We've no need for tears, have we? Not when we'll see each other again soon. By

713

week's end, Lord willing."

"Aye." He wiped his eyes with the back of his hand.

Marjory patted his waistcoat pocket. "You have both letters? For Cousin Anne and for your future employer?"

"I do, Leddy Kerr."

"I'm no longer to be addressed as lady," Marjory reminded him.

His chin jutted out. "Niver mind what the king says. Ye'll aye be Leddy Kerr to me."

My dear Gibson. She kissed his ruddy cheek before he turned toward the door.

EIGHTY-ONE

On these small cares of daughter, wife, or
    friend,
The almost sacred joys of Home depend.
HANNAH MORE

Thursday dawned with a moist wind from
the west and a dark sky full of low clouds.
Not an auspicious day for a journey.

Marjory was bathed and dressed and pacing through the house by five o' the clock,
making very sure naught had been forgotten.
Mr. Baillie would oversee the noontide
removal of her plenishings by Mrs. Pitcairn's
men. Better not to be on hand, Marjory had
decided. Seeing her home of ten years dis-
mantled was more than she could bear.

Their coaches would depart four hours
hence — hers to the south, Janet and Elisabeth's to the north. She'd almost told them
of their different destinations, then reminded
herself it was wiser to wait. If they'd insisted
on going with her, she might have relented,
and that would never do. Now the hour was

upon them, and the arrangements were made. She could send her daughters-in-law on their way, knowing she'd done her best by them.

For your sake, my beloved Donald. And for yours, dear Andrew.

And for her own sake as well — she could not deny it. If she tried to make a home for her daughters-in-law in Selkirk and failed to do so, she would never recover from the guilt.

Marjory paused by the coal grate, empty since Monday, and pressed one hand to her stomach, wincing. Too little food and even less sleep. Last eve the city had flung open its doors and celebrated the British victory at Culloden with skyrockets exploding from the castle in a vivid array of colors. Kirk bells were rung up and down the High Street, and a bonfire was lit on the Salisbury Crags. Decorative illuminations filled the windows, with *W.D.C.* for William, Duke of Cumberland, and *Deliverer of Great Britain,* and scenes with *Justice* trampling *Rebellion,* her sword thrust in its heart.

The three of them had watched the festivities with an odd sense of detachment. This was not their victory; this was no longer their home.

Marjory stood in the midst of her bedchamber now, struggling to remember what the room had once looked like. Empty shelves and faded places where paintings once hung spoke of a life that was no more.

I will look unto the LORD. She had nowhere else to turn. He had closed every door; he had fenced every path. *Though he slay me, yet will I trust in him.* Aye, it had come to that. He had taken everyone and everything she loved. If he took her as well, so be it.

Her eyes were dry but only for the moment. When she looked into Elisabeth's lovely face, when she sent her daughter-in-law on her way . . .

Nae. Not yet, not yet.

Marjory heard her stirring in the next room. Might she speak with her alone before Janet awoke? Marjory tapped on the door and waited for a response before entering.

"Good morn," Elisabeth said, then bent to splash her face with the remaining contents of her water pitcher. She dried her cheeks, eying Marjory round her linen towel, a faint twinkle in her eye. "Will they have hot water in Selkirk, do you suppose?"

"I believe they will," Marjory answered, already regretting this visit. She did not wish her last words with Elisabeth to be evasive. "The lads will be here for our trunks at seven."

"Breakfast will not take long. We have one orange to share and a rather hard bannock." Elisabeth leaned forward to brush her dark hair with long, even strokes, then quickly swept it all into a smooth knot atop her head and pinned it in place with little effort.

"Do you do everything so efficiently?" Marjory asked.

Elisabeth smiled. "You know better."

"I'm not sure I do," Marjory said. "You sew and embroider beautifully, you're a fine cook, and this household would have fallen to pieces without you, especially the last fortnight."

Her daughter-in-law shrugged slightly. "I'm honored you think so."

"Surely your mother would feel the same way." Marjory watched her expression closely. "She'd be very proud to see the woman you've become, Bess."

Her smile faded. " 'Tis hard to say. I've not seen her in so very long."

Marjory circled the room lest she blurt out her plans and ruin everything.

Elisabeth began lacing her stays. "Will we be in danger, do you think, traveling by coach?"

This, Marjory could answer. "Our surname should keep us safe. There are many Kerrs in the British army. They'll not suspect us."

Elisabeth sighed. "Maybe 'tis just as well our titled days are behind us."

"For traveling, aye." Marjory stopped at the window. "Though I confess I've been glad to be Lady Kerr for thirty years."

Elisabeth hurried to her side. "Forgive me.

'Twas not well done to remind you of your losses."

Marjory turned to her. "But they are your losses too. You and Donald should have moved to Tweedsford long ago. When I think of all you might have been spared . . ."

"Nae." Elisabeth met her gaze. "If the Almighty directs our steps, we've no need to look back over our shoulders."

When did you become so wise, Bess? Marjory knew the answer: when her daughter-in-law started reading the Buik and taking it to heart. *Aye, and beckoning me to do the same.* Could she truly bid this young woman good-bye?

"I will miss my husband every day of my life," Elisabeth confessed. "Yet I am grateful that God is my refuge. He is enough, Marjory. Truly, he is."

Across the bedchamber Janet's door opened. "I am ready," she announced, waltzing into the room.

Though Janet was dressed for the day, her hair and gown both needed brushing. Marjory dared not suggest it. But Elisabeth did.

"Come, let me be your lady's maid," she said smoothly, "and you may do the same for me." She styled Janet's auburn hair with a minimum of fuss and brushed the lint and dirt from her black gown while Janet expounded on the gloomy weather.

By the time Elisabeth offered her sister-in-law the brush in turn, Janet had forgotten their exchange of duties and hurried to the looking glass to admire the view. Elisabeth followed her across the room and stood behind her, gazing into the glass. A full head taller than Janet, Elisabeth pressed the brush firmly into her hands. "This won't take you a moment."

Janet spun on her heel and began dragging the brush over Elisabeth's gown, spending more time grumbling than brushing, while Elisabeth praised every stroke.

When at last Janet finished, Marjory led the way into the drawing room, though it was nothing of the sort. All that remained was a collection of furniture, lined against the wall, waiting for the auction room. "Suppose we eat in the kitchen."

They stood round the dressing table and shared withered orange slices and crumbling pieces of bannock. The water from the pot over the dying coal fire was lukewarm, and so was their weak tea. But it was sustenance. Marjory would give them both two shillings, enough for food and lodging on their trip north, and keep very little for herself since she did not have as far to travel.

Odd to think of Gibson well on his way to Selkirk. Following the winding course of the Gala Water, he might have reached Middleton by now, even Stow, with Galashiels to come and Selkirk not far beyond it. *Home.* Just picturing it made her orange taste sweeter and her tea stronger.

When the clock chimed seven, all was in readiness. Mrs. Edgar would be unhappy to know her cooking pots and iron pans were being left for the next tenant, along with an assortment of dishes and glassware. Every bit of linen in the house was packed in their bulging trunks, though, and each woman carried a knife and spoon. Inns and coaching halts expected travelers to provide their own utensils.

Marjory looked at the tall case clock, the hardest of all her possessions to leave behind.

Elisabeth assured her, "The sun will tell us the time of day."

"When it's shining." Janet frowned at the window. It had started to rain.

The half-dozen lads Marjory had hired to carry their trunks came banging at the door. Sturdy boys, perhaps ten or twelve years old, with grimy faces and mischievous smiles, they carted away Janet's two large trunks, plus three smaller ones filled with Marjory's and Elisabeth's few belongings and household goods. Lord John's papers and the family Bible made the smallest trunk the heaviest. A lad with stout arms and plenty of bravado insisted on carrying that one himself.

Marjory closed the door for the final time, hearing the bang ring through the empty rooms. Though her throat was tight, she did not weep. 'Twas only a house, not a home. For all the joys she'd known in those six rooms, there'd also been sorrow in abundance.

"Are you quite all right?" Elisabeth asked her, waiting on the stair.

Marjory turned round. "I am fine." And she was, for the moment. *But not when I bid you good-bye, dear Bess. Not then.*

EIGHTY-TWO

It is only persons of firmness
that can have real gentleness.
FRANCOIS, DUC DE LA ROCHEFOUCAULD

Janet walked ten steps ahead of them on the stair, apparently afraid her trunks might take off down the High Street. But Marjory trusted the lads carrying their valuables. They knew they would not be paid until all convened at White Horse Close.

When she reached Milne Square, Marjory paused for a final look at the ten stories of Baillie's Land. Few pedestrians were out at that early, rainy hour. Just as well, for the Kerrs did not have time to linger. They turned left and started down the High Street, the lads cavorting round the plainstanes with their heavy leather trunks as if they weighed nothing. Marjory did not bother to scold them.

"Our coach driver will toss them about as well," Elisabeth said, reading her mind.

When they walked by Halkerston's Wynd,

Elisabeth gazed down the narrow lane but said nothing. Marjory did not ask why.

The rain, no more than a nuisance at first, began coming down harder, and the wind pressing on their backs was more insistent. "If we had a sail, we might be at the foot of the Canongate by now," Janet said, raising her voice above the elements.

They were indeed moving quickly, already passing Dickson's Close. Marjory's heart began to thump at a faster pace. She'd imagined a leisurely stroll through town while she told her daughters-in-law their true destinations. Instead, time was slipping through her hands.

When they reached Blackfriars Wynd and paused for a last look at Effie Sinclair's fine boardinghouse, Marjory knew she could delay their discussion no longer. She stepped between her daughters-in-law, hooking her arms with theirs so they might all walk together.

"My, this is cozy," Janet said as they started out, their progress disjointed until they matched their gaits.

Marjory swallowed. *Help me say what I must. Help them understand.* "I have . . . something to tell you both."

When they turned toward her, Marjory met each woman's gaze in turn: Janet, with her wide-set hazel eyes, and Elisabeth, with her luminous blue ones. "I have given this a great deal of thought," she continued, wishing she did not have to lift her voice to be heard above the rain and wind. "As much as I long to have you with me in Selkirk, your mothers are the ones who deserve your company."

Elisabeth's downcast expression took her by surprise. "Now that my mother has remarried . . . well, I am not at all sure she would take me back into her home."

Marjory's breath caught. "Oh, of course she would. Even now she may be writing to you, pleading with you to come home to Castleton. No doubt Lady Murray feels quite the same."

Janet pulled them to an abrupt stop. "What are you saying, madam? Is our company abhorrent to you? Would you prefer we not join you in Selkirk?"

Marjory looked from one to the other. Already she'd made a terrible mess of things.

She started again. "What I would prefer is that we be honest with one another." Marjory eased them forward, drawing them closer. "Although I've sent Gibson ahead with a letter for Cousin Anne, I'm not certain she has room for three of us. And if she does not, where else would we stay?" She exhaled, overwhelmed again by the thought of it. "I cannot take that risk."

"Nor can we abandon you." Elisabeth's voice was strained. "Our husbands would surely expect us to care for their mother."

"But you *have*," Marjory insisted. "You've loved my sons and mourned them honorably." She squeezed their arms with genuine affection. "God bless you, my daughters. You've shown nothing but kindness to me."

Janet's gaze narrowed. "I thought 'twas honesty you were after."

"But you're still here, Janet," Marjory reminded her. "You did not quit Edinburgh after your husband joined the prince nor after our sad news from Falkirk. All through the autumn and winter, and now through the spring, you've remained faithful to me."

For a fleeting instant Marjory saw a hint of warmth in her daughter-in-law's eyes. *Janet heard me, Lord. 'Tis a start.*

The rain had eased a bit. All three of them lifted their heads to gaze at the Netherbow Port soaring above them with its round turrets and square clock tower. They were truly leaving the city now, passing through the narrow gate for the last time.

Once they reached the Canongate, Marjory tried a new approach. "It is time you both thought of the future. You're still young enough to marry again and bear children. And well you should."

"But we're in mourning." Janet's whining tone had returned.

"Aye," Marjory agreed. "Come January next, though, you'll leave your black gowns behind."

726

Janet frowned. "And choose a new husband?"

"He might do the choosing," Marjory reminded her, "or his mother might." *As I chose you, Janet.*

She looked up to be sure their young porters were still in sight. It seemed the rain had put a damper on their spirits. They were trudging along now, single file, yet keeping the trunks out of the puddles.

Elisabeth spoke, her tone thoughtful. "Effie Sinclair told us we would honor our husbands best by remaining widows and caring for you."

"So she did." Marjory wished the venerable lady had said otherwise. "You'll not be putting aside your vows to my sons. Their deaths release you to marry again. And I release you from any obligation as well." Her words no doubt sounded cold, yet she was setting them free for their own good. Surely they could see that.

Elisabeth stopped and turned toward her. "I do not wish to be released. My place is with you, Marjory. *You* are the one who knows the Almighty."

For a moment she was speechless. "You would risk everything and come with me . . . because of my *faith?*"

"Aye." Elisabeth's sincerity only made things worse.

Marjory turned to her other daughter-in-law, hoping for the answer she wanted. "And you, Janet. Is it your intention to join me in Selkirk as well?"

Janet nodded, though with perhaps less conviction. " 'Tis my duty, mem."

Marjory stepped back, nearly throwing her hands in the air in frustration. She'd already paid for their travel on the northbound coach. They couldn't come with her now even if she wanted them to. And she truly did not. Not with her future so uncertain.

She looked at their dear faces and was undone.

Please, please do not make me hurt your feelings.

Marjory prayed for wisdom and began anew. "What do you think you'll find in Selkirk?" she asked them. "A royal burgh, aye, but with few prospects for marriage. I'm certain *I* will not marry again. And if I did, would you wait for me to have two more fine sons for you to wed?"

Elisabeth touched her arm. "Marjory, we are not looking for husbands —"

"Not now, perhaps. But when your time of mourning ends, what then? Selkirk has cobblers, weavers, tanners, coopers, and an alehouse keeper. None of them are titled. None will keep you in velvet and silk, as my sons did."

"But I am the daughter of a weaver," Elisabeth said. "I would be going home to a rustic

728

cottage in a Highland clachan far smaller than Selkirk." She leaned down to meet her gaze. "Do you not want to take us with you, Marjory?"

Of course I do. Very much. And yet I do not. For your sakes.

" 'Tis God's will," Marjory said as firmly as she could. "He has seen fit to humble me. But I cannot do the same to you." She started downhill toward White Horse Close at a loss for what else to tell them, except the inescapable truth.

They were traveling north. They were going home.

And so was she.

EIGHTY-THREE

Faith is the flame that lifts
the sacrifice to heaven.
JAMES MONTGOMERY

Elisabeth followed close behind her mother-in-law, desperate to convince her. "Being poor doesn't frighten me. Nor does widowhood. But returning to a home where the Almighty is not worshiped, where the Buik is not read . . . truly, that is my greatest fear."

Not my only fear, dear Marjory. But the only one that matters.

Marjory slowed her steps. "Are you saying your mother doesn't believe as we do?"

Elisabeth hesitated, weighing her words. "My mother serves . . . a different god." *Say it, Bess. Speak the truth.* "I once did the same. 'Twas a nameless one and powerless as well."

There. A secret no more.

She held her breath. *Please, Marjory. Please understand.*

Beneath her woolen hood a troubled look

fell across her mother-in-law's brow. "Did Donald know of this . . . different god of yours?"

"He did not," she hastened to explain. "No one in Edinburgh knew. But I've abandoned the auld ways. In truth, I should have done so long ago. You can be certain 'tis finished." Her courage nearly spent, Elisabeth bowed her head, her eyes fixed on the plainstanes. One thing remained. "Can you possibly forgive me?"

After a lengthy silence, she felt the touch of Marjory's gloved hand on her cheek, lifting her face until their gazes met.

" 'Tis not my forgiveness you need, Bess." Even so, mercy shone in her mother-in-law's hazel eyes. Sorrow was there as well, like a thin layer of gauze. And a tender regard she'd never hoped to find.

"I'm grateful for the Lord's mercy," Elisabeth said softly. "And for yours. Promise you will take me with you? For I cannot go home. Truly, I cannot."

The assurance she longed for did not come. Instead her mother-in-law abruptly turned toward White Horse Close. "Ladies, we must not tarry a moment longer. Coachmen favor a prompt departure, Mr. Dewar in particular."

Elisabeth hurried after her with Janet on her heels. Did her sister-in-law wish to return to the Highlands? Or was her heart set on

731

Selkirk too? If only they'd found a moment to speak in private! 'Twas too late now. Too late for many things.

But never too late to pray. *Strengthen thou me according unto thy word.*

No sooner did her heart lift up her request, than the answer resounded inside her. *I will strengthen thee; yea, I will help thee.*

As they neared White Horse Close, Elisabeth saw the lads with their leather trunks stationed at the pend, shifting from one foot to the other. The rain had stopped but only to catch its breath. Solid gray clouds promised a thorough soaking along their journey. Elisabeth had worn her light wool cape and packed her heavier one, thinking the air might grow warmer as they headed south.

Now she was going north.

Elisabeth shivered, only in part from the wind. Something had to be done. Might she yet persuade her?

"Come, lads." Marjory's voice echoed off the vaulted walls of the pend. "Carry our trunks to their proper coaches." She walked ahead of them, weaving her way through the crowded courtyard.

Elisabeth and Janet followed her, holding their black skirts above the muck. Porters and stablers, farriers and horse hirers were busy about their work, sending folk on their way to London or Glasgow or Carlisle. The smell of horseflesh and human sweat, of mud and dung and hay and oats was almost overpowering.

Janet looked to the inn door at the far end, her expression pensive. "Nae soldiers on the stair."

As Elisabeth gazed at the second-floor windows, memories assailed her. Of her last night with Donald in a small, dank room lit by two guttering candles. Of his bold touch, his warm kiss, his lean body next to hers. Of the promises he'd made but had not kept. Of the mercy he'd asked for and received.

"Six months ago . . ." Janet sighed.

Elisabeth looked round at the jumble of peaked roofs and stone forestairs of White Horse Close. " 'Tis difficult to be here and to remember."

"Harder still to leave Edinburgh." Janet sniffed. "When I think of the balls at Assembly Close, of the friends Andrew and I made . . ."

Elisabeth turned and reached for her hand, grateful when her sister-in-law did not pull back. "Janet, I am sorry you and I were not closer."

"How could we be?" Janet asked, a wounded look in her eyes. "You were titled, and I was not. You were always the bonniest lass in the room, and I . . ." She started to pull away.

Elisabeth squeezed Janet's hand before she

slipped from her grasp. "Those things no longer matter. If indeed they ever did."

"Perhaps," was all Janet said.

Marjory hurried up, rather flustered. "We've little time left," she told them, the hood of her cape pushed back. The rain had turned her auburn hair into a halo of curls and wisps. "Mr. Rannie is your coachman. He will drive you as far as Perth, then hire another carriage for each of you. All has been paid in advance."

Janet's frown deepened. "When did you decide this? And why did you not consult us?"

Marjory sighed. "When Lord Mark's letter arrived and I knew Tweedsford was lost to us." She looked at Janet with compassion in her eyes. "I did not ask your opinion, because I feared you might object —"

"But we *do* object," Janet insisted. "You cannot simply cast us aside."

"By no means," Marjory said firmly. "I am sending you home to your mothers because I care for you. And because they can provide for you." She leaned forward and kissed Janet's cheek. "I want only the best for you, my dear. Andrew was fortunate to have you for his wife."

Janet did not respond, merely kissed her cheek in return, then sighed. " 'Twould seem I am bound for Dunkeld since you've made all the arrangements."

"So I have." When Marjory pressed two

shillings into her hands, Janet's scowl eased.

Elisabeth kept her hands by her side. *I don't want your shillings, Marjory. Please don't make me take them.*

"Come and meet Mr. Rannie," their mother-in-law was saying. "I've asked him to take special care of both of you." Marjory guided them across the paved courtyard to a well-used black coach pulled by two horses, harnessed and ready for their day's work. "Here they are, sir. My daughters-in-law, Mrs. Donald Kerr and Mrs. Andrew Kerr."

"Leddies." Mr. Rannie doffed his hat, then swung open the narrow door. "If ye will." Not much taller than Marjory, the sturdy coachman had ginger hair, a close-clipped beard, and years of travel carved into his face. "Nae time to waste."

Her heart pounding, Elisabeth eyed their trunks being hoisted to the top of the carriage, then watched her sister-in-law climb through the narrow door, managing her hoops and skirts with ease.

I am next. Elisabeth could barely breathe. *Please, Lord. What am I to do?*

"Good-bye, then," Janet said, leaning through the door.

Marjory reached up to touch her cheek. "Godspeed, dear girl. Kindly give my best regards to Lady Murray."

While Janet settled back on the upholstered seat, Marjory turned, looking up at her expectantly. "Now then, 'tis your turn, Elisabeth."

She waited, not moving, not breathing. *Help me, help me.*

"Elisabeth?" Marjory said again.

"Bess," she whispered at last. "You promised to call me Bess."

"So I did." Marjory pressed her lips together, her chin trembling. "My precious Bess."

Elisabeth clasped her mother-in-law's hands, imploring her with her eyes, with her voice, and with her heart. "Please, Marjory. You must believe me. I cannot go home to Castleton. I cannot."

"But you *must*," Marjory said, clearly agitated. "Your sister-in-law is going home to Dunkeld —"

"And I am going home with you." Her voice broke. "Please . . . please do not turn me away. Don't you see? My father and brother are dead, and my mother will not have me. You are my only family now, Marjory. You are all that I have."

"Oh, Bess —"

"Please! 'Tis my duty to go with you. And my calling. Aye, and my joy." Tears spilled down her cheeks. "When I married your son, I left my name and my family behind. I am a Kerr now and always will be."

"But —"

"Nae!" Elisabeth tightened her grip. "I am

going with you to Selkirk. Just as you said, 'tis God's will. Don't you see, dear Marjory? You belong to him. And so do I."

EIGHTY-FOUR

Hope, like the gleaming taper's light,
Adorns and cheers our way.
OLIVER GOLDSMITH

"My dear Bess." Marjory could not see her sweet face for the tears clouding her eyes. " 'Tis too great a sacrifice."

"Nae, 'tis no sacrifice at all." Elisabeth squeezed her hands. "Not when you love someone."

Marjory could not speak. Could barely swallow. *How can she love me, Lord? How can you love me?*

"Will the leddy be taking the coach or not, mem?" Mr. Rannie held the door open, his patience wearing thin.

Elisabeth answered for her. "Not this coach." She released Marjory's hands, then pointed to the top, where the luggage was stored. "If you might retrieve my trunk. That small brown one there."

Janet was on her feet at once, sticking her

head out the door. "Are you not coming with me?"

Elisabeth shook her head. "You'll be in good hands with Mr. Rannie. He'll see you home to Dunkeld."

Janet glared at him. "You are quite certain I will be safe, sir?"

"Only if you remain seated," Mr. Rannie told her firmly.

With an exaggerated groan, Janet settled back into her seat, making a show of smoothing her skirts. "I suppose Lady Murray will not mind so very much. I *am,* after all, her only daughter."

"Godspeed," Elisabeth told her, stepping away as other travelers prepared to board the coach.

At Mr. Rannie's curt nod, a lad pulled down Elisabeth's trunk, then stood with it on his shoulder. "Whaur does it go, milady?"

"With my mother-in-law's." Elisabeth pointed to another black carriage with two passengers already waiting inside. "See her leather trunk on top? There's just enough room to fit mine next to it."

As her trunk bobbed across the courtyard, Mr. Rannie eyed them both, his expression darkening. "Ye'll not be expecting to have yer shillings returned to ye? The ither seat on the northbound coach is paid for, whether it has a leddy sitting on it or not."

Marjory's heart sank. *Oh, Lord, now what's*

to be done?

But her daughter-in-law wasn't ruffled in the least. " 'Tis only fair, Mr. Rannie. You may keep your shillings. I wish you well on your journey."

His brief scowl having vanished, he doffed his hat once more. "Guid day to ye, then, leddies."

"Come." Elisabeth tugged on Marjory's sleeve. "Let's see what can be done. What is our coachman's name?"

"Mr. Dewar," the man said, marching up to them. "And ye, mem, have delayed oor departure." Short and round, stuffed into a broadcloth coat, Mr. Dewar nodded his bald head toward his coach. "I've folk bound for Galashiels wha are anxious to be aff."

"Have you room for another passenger?" Elisabeth asked him, looking over his shoulder. "I have decided to join my mother-in-law."

"Aye," he said, rubbing his thick hands together. "I have the room if ye have the siller."

Marjory felt her purse, woefully light. She could spare most of it. But it would not be enough. Might he be merciful to two widows? She pulled out her last four shillings, leaving naught but pennies behind.

" 'Tis six shillings to Selkirk," Mr. Dewar reminded her. "That's what yer man paid me for yer seat, mem, and what I'll ask for the

740

young leddy's seat as weel."

Marjory looked back at Janet's coach, already turning in the courtyard, heading for the pend and the street beyond. Too late to send Elisabeth north now. *Lord, can you not help us?*

"Mr. Dewar." Elisabeth was tugging off her gloves. "You say 'tis silver you need?"

"Aye, mem." He shook the four shillings in his hand. "Two shillings mair and ye'll be bound for Selkirk. Aff for a visit, aye?"

"Nae, off for good," Elisabeth said confidently. "I'm told Selkirk has a fine auld kirkyard. I expect I'll be buried there someday."

The stout coachman blanched. "Not onie time soon, I hope."

"Nae. Lord willing, I will have many years with my mother-in-law." Elisabeth smiled down at her, then stretched out her graceful hands. "As you see, Mr. Dewar, I have two silver rings. And very fine rings they are. Broader and thicker than most and made of the finest sterling."

He eyed them with interest. "So they are. Were ye thinking o' paying for yer seat with yer rings? Even with the shillings, they'll not be quite enough."

Marjory watched, aghast, as Elisabeth calmly slipped both rings off her hands. *Is there nothing else that can be done, Lord?*

Elisabeth studied each silver band carefully,

reading the inscriptions inside. "I have already left this one behind." She placed among his shillings the intricately carved ring Marjory had often admired. "But *this* love will live in my heart forever."

When Elisabeth added her silver wedding band to the coachman's coins, Marjory could bear it no more. If her daughter-in-law could make such a sacrifice, could she not do the same? With trembling hands she removed Lord John's ring and quietly laid it on top.

"Oh, Marjory." Elisabeth touched the slender indentation on her ring finger that had taken thirty years to form. "Are you certain?"

She nodded, overcome. *Very certain.*

Mr. Dewar cupped his hands round his silver, grinning broadly. "Now I'm satisfied and will be mair sae whan we're aff. Leddies?"

Elisabeth stepped back so Marjory might board the carriage first.

Marjory's knees barely supported her as she climbed inside. *Help me deserve her, Lord. Help me be worthy of her affection.* To have such a daughter-in-law caring for her needs was a gift only the Almighty could have provided. Surely he would see to both their needs. Aye, surely he would.

Marjory sat facing the front of the carriage, grateful the other two passengers had chosen to sit facing the back. She always felt queasy watching the scenery pass in the wrong direction. And she wanted to look forward now. Toward Selkirk. Toward home.

A moment later Elisabeth was seated beside her, arranging her skirts. "Aren't we a pair, traveling in our black gowns?" she said gently.

The two gentlemen seated across from them both lifted their hats. A father and son, Marjory decided.

"You have our deepest sympathy, ladies," the older of the two men said. He was perhaps fifty and the other man a few years older than Bess. "Since Mr. Dewar has not introduced us, please permit me to do so. I am Mr. Thomas Hedderwick of Galashiels, and this is my son, William."

Marjory nodded. *Father and son. Just as I thought.*

"We're both pleased to meet you," Elisabeth responded. "I am Mrs. Donald Kerr, and this is my mother-in-law, Mrs. John Kerr."

Marjory's smile tightened at the sound of her new name. *Mrs. John Kerr.* She was still a lady, she reminded herself. Still a gentlewoman. There were some things even King George could not take away.

The carriage jolted forward, tossing them about like so much luggage.

Marjory righted herself, sitting up a bit straighter, all at once feeling rather constrained by her whalebone stays. She would

743

not lace them so tightly on the morrow. Nae, nor the day after that.

When she took a full breath, a strange and not unpleasant sensation came over her.

It wasn't fear. Not this time. It was freedom.

White Horse Close

AUTHOR NOTES

Farewell, Edina! pleasing name,
Congenial to my heart!
A joyous guest to thee I came,
And mournful I depart.

THOMAS CAMPBELL

Oh, Edinburgh. If you only knew how often I think about your narrow, crooked streets and your misty-moisty air and your splendid craggy castle, so close to the sky it's like something from a fairy tale.

The Kerr women are eager to leave Edinburgh and rightly so, but I cannot wait to return to this fun, funky, and altogether fascinating city. Though a great deal has changed since Prince Charlie's arrival in September 1745, it's astonishing how much of the Old Town remains. All the main thoroughfares are in place: Grassmarket, Lawnmarket, High Street, and Canongate. On opposite ends of the Royal Mile, Edinburgh Castle and the Palace of Holyroodhouse continue to welcome visitors, both royal and common. And on any given afternoon you may hear the skirl of the pipes or spy a braw lad in a tartan kilt and know without a doubt you're not in Kansas anymore — or in Kentucky, for that matter.

Alas, Milne Square was swept away when construction on the North Bridge began in 1763. And though the Tron Kirk still stands, it's no longer a place of worship. But you can blithely stroll through the pend into White Horse Close or sit on a wooden pew inside Saint Giles or climb atop the Salisbury Crags and imagine Elisabeth Kerr by your side, taking in the fine view.

For character names I usually turn to kirkyards and census records, but for this novel I had a gem of a resource: *A Directory of Edinburgh in 1752,* compiled by J. Gilhooley. Since these are fictional folk, I played mix and match with most of the names, but you'll find a number of historical characters waltzing through the pages of *Here Burns My Candle,* including Margaret Murray of Broughton with her white cockades; Thomas Ruddiman, the publisher of the *Caledonian Mercury;* and Mrs. Effie Sinclair, who taught the mother of Sir Walter Scott. Allan Ramsay, whose circulating library is mentioned, doesn't have a speaking role, but here's the juicy bit: he was secretly a Jacobite.

By the by, the Sassenachs — that is, the

English — called the first battle Prestonpans because of the location, but the Highlanders called it Gladsmuir because of Thomas the Rhymer's prophecy. In the same way, what the Highlanders called the Jacobite Rising, the English called the Jacobite Rebellion. As with all history, much depends on where you're standing. Today most folk refer to the last Rising simply as "the '45."

Lord Mark Kerr — pronounced "care" with a wee roll to the *r* — played an interesting role in the '45. After Sir John Cope and his troops were humiliated at Gladsmuir, Sir John supposedly fled to Berwick, the northernmost town in England. Lord Mark greeted him with the wry observation that Sir John was the first general in Europe to bring news of his own defeat. Whether the tale is true or simply a Jacobite fable meant to discredit Sir John, the story has stuck to this day, thanks to one verse of the popular Jacobite song "Hey Johnnie Cope":

Says Lord Mark Car, "Ye are na blate;
To bring us the news o' your ain defeat;
I think you deserve the back o' the gate,
Get out o' my sight this morning."

The ministers mentioned in *Here Burns My Candle* were also living and breathing folk. Rev. Dr. George Wishart and James Hogg both served at the Tron Kirk in 1745. Thomas

Boston, a parish minister in Selkirkshire, was so devoted to his flock that, when his health was in steep decline, he delivered his last sermon from the manse window. His book *Human Nature in its Fourfold State,* which Elisabeth reads aloud one Sabbath, held a place of honor on many a Scot's bookshelf. James Thomson, the author of *The Seasons,* also hailed from the Borderland. When James was sixteen, his minister father died while performing an exorcism. Goodness.

Of course, the most famous historic figure in the novel is Charles Edward Stuart. He was first dubbed "bonny" in a letter written by eighteen-year-old Magdalen Pringle. Her eyewitness account of the prince's grand entry into Edinburgh is singularly charming: "The windows were full of Ladys who threw up their handkerchiefs and clap'd their hands and show'd great loyalty to the Bonny Prince."

Some readers have informed me that my novels make them hungry. (Ah, but they're calorie free, at least!) I'm not much of a cook, but I do adore old cookbooks. My latest fave is *The Art of Cookery Made Plain and Easy* by Hannah Glasse. Though the book was originally published in 1747, facsimile editions continue to roll off the press. The recipe names are a hoot: "To dress a pig the French way" and "A second sort of fine pancakes." Then there's this one: "To keep Venison or

Hares sweet, or to make them fresh when they stink." Aye, please do.

The Art of Cookery was one of many resources strewn about my feet as I wrote. Of the eight hundred Scottish volumes on my shelves, here are my top ten books about this grand time and place in history:

Hugo Arnot, *The History of Edinburgh* (1799)

Walter Biggar Blaikie, *Edinburgh at the Time of the Occupation of Prince Charles* (1910)

Rev. D. Butler, M.A., *The Tron Kirk of Edinburgh* (1906)

Robert Chambers, *Traditions of Edinburgh* (1929)

John Sibbald Gibson, *Edinburgh in the '45* (1995)

Henry Grey Graham, *The Social Life of Scotland in the Eighteenth Century* (1906)

Michael Hook and Walter Ross, *The 'Forty-Five* (1995)

Sir Herbert Maxwell, *Edinburgh: A Historical Study* (1916)

Stuart Reid, *1745: A Military History of the Last Jacobite Rising* (1966)

David Wemyss, Lord Elcho, *A Short Account of the Affairs of Scotland* (1907)

As lovely as books about Scotland can be, friendly Scots are an even better resource when it comes to sorting out what's what. At

Caddon View Country Guest House in Innerleithen, Joyce Lees and Molly Robertson served as my dialect coaches, while Steve and Lisa Davies fed me the tastiest dish of salmon on the planet.

At nearby Traquair House, the oldest inhabited house in Scotland, I had an audience with Catherine Maxwell Stuart, the twenty-first Lady of Traquair and a descendant of our Catherine Maxwell, Lady Nithsdale. "Audience" may be overstating things; we sat and chatted in her office with dogs running about and pictures of her darling children scattered round! Imagine my delight when one of her guides took me to the lower drawing room to see portraits of Lady Nithsdale's sisters, Barbara and Margaret Stuart, looking exactly as I'd described them in chapter 35. I may be the first American tourist who got teary-eyed gazing at those paintings.

A late October visit to Braemar, Elisabeth's childhood home, found us tramping about Braemar Castle on a private guided tour, courtesy of Andy and Sheila Anderson, who offered a warm welcome on a cold afternoon. Blessings to Doreen Wood, who put us in touch with them and provided a fine phrase for our story: "the eerie mating call of the red deer echoing round the frosty hills." Later that evening my husband and I heard that full-throated sound just as snow was beginning to fall. Still gives me shivers to think of it.

Closer to the village center, Kindrochaide Castle is reduced to rubble now, albeit very *nice* rubble, while the Victorian cottage where Robert Louis Stevenson began writing *Treasure Island* is as cozy as ever.

If you're curious about the origin of Elisabeth's pagan rites, worshiping the moon has a long and sordid history. The Bible clearly states that any man or woman who "served other gods, and worshipped them, either the sun, or moon, or any of the host of heaven" would be stoned to death (see Deuteronomy 17:2–5). No wonder Elisabeth was worried about the kirk session discovering her secret! Alexander Carmichael's *Carmina Gadelica,* a collection of Gaelic blessings, hymns, and poems from the Highlands and Islands, features many incantations dedicated to the moon; five of them were included here.

As to Andrew's malady, you'll find no better description of consumption than this passage from *Nicholas Nickleby* by Charles Dickens: "A dread disease, in which the struggle between soul and body is so gradual, quiet, and solemn, and the result so sure, that day by day, and grain by grain, the mortal part wastes and withers away." Known by its modern name — tuberculosis or TB — the disease is still common round the world and still deadly.

On a happier note, my editorial team remains in excellent health, with well-sharpened pencils and keen eyes. Deep and abiding thanks to Laura Barker, Carol Bartley, Danelle McCafferty, and Sara Fortenberry for your incredible patience and prodigious gifts. Benny Gillies — a fine Scottish bookseller, proofreader, mapmaker, and friend — provided his services again, for which I am most grateful, and artist Simon Dawdry captured White Horse Close perfectly. Extra-special hugs go to my in-house editors, whom I cherish: Bill Higgs, who has a special gift for grammar, spelling, and word usage; Matt Higgs, who watches for accuracy, continuity, and character development; and Lilly Higgs, a storyteller in her own right, who gleefully brainstorms with me at all hours of the night. To each and to all, many blessings and many thanks.

I've reserved my most heartfelt gratitude for *you,* dear reader, and am ever thankful for your support and encouragement. If you'd enjoy receiving my free newsletter, *O Gentle Reader!* e-mailed just twice a year, kindly pop on my Web site: www.LizCurtisHiggs.com.

And if you'd like free autographed bookplates for any of my novels, simply contact me by mail:

Liz Curtis Higgs
P.O. Box 43577

Louisville, KY 40253-0577

I hope you'll also join my Facebook Fan Page or follow me on Twitter. Not very eighteenth century but a fun way to stay in touch!

Finally, if you've not read my previous Scottish historical novels, then *Thorn in My Heart, Fair Is the Rose, Whence Came a Prince,* and *Grace in Thine Eyes* await you. Meanwhile I'm busy exploring the Borderland for our next journey with Marjory and Elisabeth. No doubt you recognized the source material for this Scottish tale: the beloved book of Ruth. Check out the Readers Guide for more about the fictional-biblical parallels. We covered the first eighteen verses of Ruth in *Here Burns My Candle.* Look for the balance of the story to unfold in *Mine Is the Night.* Two books should tell the tale. No, really. I promise.

Until we meet again, you are a *blissin!*

Liz Curtiz Higgs

READERS GUIDE

History is a mighty drama,
enacted upon the theatre of time,
with suns for lamps and
eternity for a background.

THOMAS CARLYLE

1. History plays a major role in *Here Burns My Candle*. Not only Scottish history, but also ancient history steps onto the stage since our two main characters, Marjory and Elisabeth Kerr, are drawn from the biblical story of Naomi and Ruth. How did your familiarity with the original story shape your reading experience? What surprises did you find along the way? In what ways were the characters different than you expected? What are the benefits of taking a fictionalized look at a well-known story?

2. Although Elisabeth Kerr is featured on the cover, the novel opens by introducing us to her mother-in-law, Marjory Kerr. How

would you describe Marjory in the first chapter? And in the final chapter? What changes did you notice in her attitude toward the Almighty One over the course of the novel? And how did your feelings toward Marjory change, if at all, from first page to last? In your own experience, is growth more often borne of joy or of pain? Why might that be the case?

3. Ruth is celebrated as one of the "good girls" of the Bible, yet we often forget she began life as a pagan Moabitess, captured here in Elisabeth's worship of the Nameless One. Why do you think Elisabeth continued the auld ways even after marrying into a churchgoing family? In what ways does the power of tradition shape our attitudes and actions? In chapter 4 Elisabeth poses many questions about the Almighty One. If you were sitting across from her right now, how would you answer her?

4. Donald and Andrew have their biblical counterparts too. Donald is based on Mahlon, whose name means "weakling" or "infertility." How does that description fit Donald? What other words might you use to characterize him? What, if anything, did you like about Elisabeth's husband? Andrew is patterned after Chilion, whose name means "pining" or "consumptive." Again,

how do those words suit Andrew? Would Lord John have been proud of his sons, as Marjory was on that October eve in the forecourt of the palace, described in chapter 42? Why or why not?

5. Faithfulness and forgiveness are two themes interwoven throughout the story. In what ways are Marjory, Elisabeth, and Donald faithful? And unfaithful? For what does each need forgiveness and from whom? If you were in Elisabeth's place, faced with a loved one's request to "Forgive me . . . for all of it," how might you respond? In what ways do these characters' struggles with faithfulness and forgiveness reflect our desire to connect with others on a more meaningful level?

6. The epigraphs that open each chapter are meant to capture the heart of the action to come. How does the quote from George Herbert — "Words are women, deeds are men" — suit chapter 32? To what extent does his statement reflect your assessment of female-male differences? Choose an epigraph you especially like from the novel. Why does it appeal to you, and how does the quote match the chapter it introduces?

7. Marjory calls Elisabeth "a keeper of secrets." In truth, all the major characters

in this story have something to hide. When Simon reveals his painful past, how does that impact Elisabeth's heart? When Donald confesses his litany of sins on paper, how does that affect the lives of those around him? And what secrets do Marjory and Elisabeth each harbor? In life, as in fiction, how might keeping secrets cause more harm than sharing the truth with those we love and trust?

8. Though Rob MacPherson has no biblical counterpart, he plays an important role in this story. What do his interactions with Elisabeth reveal about her character? And what does his relationship with Marjory tell us about her? How does Rob compare with Donald? Do you find Rob appealing or disturbing, and why? In what ways does Rob fall short of true hero status? What sort of future would you choose for him?

9. Loss is one of the central themes of the novel, summarized in Marjory's own fears: "Surely a grieving widow could not lose everything. Not all she owned. *Not everything.*" Name all the things, big and small, that are taken from Marjory. Which of these losses struck you as most unexpected? If you've experienced one or more of these losses, how was your life affected? How would you cope if you truly lost everything?

To what or whom would you look for strength and help, whatever the extent of your loss?

10. When Elisabeth chooses which direction her future will take, do you think she is running *away* from something or *toward* something, and why? Does Elisabeth fit the definition of a true heroine: a woman who loves sacrificially? If so, how? If not, what is she lacking? Her newfound faith will surely be tested in the sequel, *Mine Is the Night.* What indications do you have about how Elisabeth might respond to future trials and tribulations? What about Marjory? What course do you imagine their relationship will take in the months ahead?

11. Now that you've read this eighteenth-century interpretation, read the real story in Ruth 1:1–18. As you consider the passage verse by verse, what parallels do you find between the Scottish novel and the biblical original? What "famine" might Lord John and Lady Marjory have experienced that sends them packing for Edinburgh? Why do you suppose Orpah turns back, just as Janet does? In Ruth 1:18 Naomi falls silent; Marjory does the same in the final chapter. Why, in each story, might that be the case?

12. Our Readers Guide opens with a quote from Thomas Carlyle, a nineteenth-century Scottish historian and essayist. In what ways does the historical reality of the Jacobite Rising of 1745 serve as a fitting backdrop for this story? What more recent historical event might also provide an interesting setting for this story and its themes? What eternal truths did you find illuminated in the hearts and lives of these characters? Finally, what do you love most about historical fiction, and what did you enjoy about *Here Burns My Candle* in particular?

For more about the author, visit
www.LizCurtisHiggs.com.

SCOTTISH GLOSSARY

a' — all
aff — off
ain — own
ance — once
anither — another
auld — old
awa — away, distant
aye — yes, always
bairn — child
blate — shy, bashful
blaw — blow
blether — jabber, gossip
bliss — bless
blissin — blessing
bluid — blood
boll — a dry measure
braw — fine, handsome
bricht — bright
brither — brother
Buik — the Bible
burn — brook, stream

cauld — cold
clachan — hamlet
close — passageway, courtyard
creepie — low chair, footstool
deid — dead
doocot — dovecote
doon — down
dreich — bleak, dismal
dwiny — sickly, pining
e'e — eye
faither — father
fash — worry, trouble, vex
forestair — an outside staircase
freen — friend
frichtsome — frightening
fu' — full
greet — cry, weep
guid — good
haar — cold mist or fog
haddies — haddocks
hame — home
heiven — heaven
het — hot
Hielander — Highlander
hizzie — hussy
hoose — house
hoot! — pshaw!
howre — whore
ilka — each, every
ither — other

jalouse — imagine, presume
ken — to know, recognize
kenned — known
kist — chest
land — a tenement house
lang — long
lawfu' — lawful
leal — loyal
lealty — loyalty
leddy — lady
leuk — look
licht — light
limmer — disreputable woman
linn — waterfall
loosome — lovely
losh! — lord!
Luckenbooths — locked stalls
luve — love
mair — more
mebbe — maybe, perhaps
meikle — great, much
mem — madam
mercat — market
meridian — social midday drink
mirk — dark, black, gloomy
mither — mother
monie — many
muir — moor
neeps — turnips
nicht — night

niver — never

och! — oh!

onie — any

oo aye — yes (from French *oui*)

oor — our

oot — out

pend — a vaulted passageway

pernickitie — cantankerous, touchy

plainstanes — flat paving stones

plenishings — goods, provisions

plumpshower — heavy downpour

pu'd — pulled

puir — poor

reiver — robber

richt — right

rightfu' — rightful

risp — coarse rasp, used at doors

rouping wife — female auctioneer

sae — so

saicret — secret

siller — silver

smeddum — courage

stayed lass — an old maid

syne — since, ago, thereafter

tatties — potatoes

thankrif — grateful

thegither — together

thocht — thought, believed

tolbooth — town prison

toun — town

unchancie — dangerous, unlucky
Uphalieday — Twelfth Night
verra — very
wa' — wall
walcome — welcome
wappen — weapon
wauken — awaken
weel — well
wha — who
whan — when
whatsomever — whatever
whaur — where
wheesht! — hush!
wickit — wicked
wird — word
wynd — narrow, winding lane
yestermorn — yesterday morning
yestreen — yesterday evening